Advanced Practice
for the
2015 MCAT™

Developed by Medical School Professors

Med–
PATHWAY

Printed in the United States of America

www.med-pathway.com
1-844-MED-MCAT (633-6228)

First Edition
ISBN# 978-0-9864332-0-7

Printed by: Bang Printing
               Valencia, CA, USA

Written by: **Phillip B. Carpenter Ph.D.,
Scott D. Lane Ph.D., Jin H. Yoon Ph.D.,
Richard Baker Ph.D., Kevin A. Morano Ph.D.,
David MacLean Ph.D.,** and **Eric J. Wagner Ph.D.**

Edited by: **Michelle Steiger Ph.D., Melissa Singh Ph.D.,
Priya Baraniak Ph.D., Joshua Gowin, Ph.D.,** and
Alana Ronnquist, Ph.D.

Key Contributor: **Todd Albrecht**

Production Editor: **Leisa McCord**

Cover Designers: **Jin H. Yoon** and **Eric J. Wagner**

Table of Contents

Table of Contents

The MCAT has changed...

Welcome to Med-Pathway, the home of the 2015 MCAT experts. The MCAT is the single greatest barrier to acceptance into medical school, and Med-Pathway is here to help you navigate through this obstacle and succeed on this important test. We are comprised of medical school professors with active research laboratories. We teach medical, graduate, and pre-med students (just like you). Collectively, we have published > 170 peer reviewed, scientific research papers in both the biomedical and behavioral sciences. Moreover, we have more than 20 years of medical school teaching experience and in excess of 20 years of MCAT test preparation experience. Our company is called Med-Pathway because we have extensive experience at both ends of the medical training process.

Most of the currently available MCAT test preparation publications commonly reteach basic, foundational material. This is the material that you should have learned in college, particularly as it formulates the prerequisite knowledge tested on the MCAT. Unfortunately, these books typically amount to encyclopedias providing basic information, which does not effectively prepare you to apply this foundational knowledge to experimental or clinical settings. This skill is critical for success on the new MCAT.

The new MCAT has been reformatted to emphasize the application of the foundational knowledge gained from undergraduate courses. Students are expected to apply this knowledge in the context of experimental science and medicine. Thus, memorizing long lists of facts and pathways is a very inefficient model for MCAT preparation. Rather, students are expected to have acquired the general knowledge outlined by the AAMC in the content categories from college courses and to be able to apply this foundational knowledge to experimental and clinical science. As this is how research is performed, a major goal of pre-medical and medical education is to train doctors that think like scientists. Therefore, understanding experimental design and execution is paramount for success as it correlates with the future ability to read and interpret patient lab results during diagnosis. This doctrine has been specifically decreed by the AAMC: "The new exam will ask test takers to show that they can think and learn like scientists.... Future physicians will need to know where to find credible information and how to translate new discoveries into high-quality care.... [therefore], the new exam will place greater emphasis on scientific reasoning and analysis skills." (aamc.org/mcat2015; AAMC (2012), *Preview Guide to the MCAT^{2015} Exam*)

Our mission at Med-Pathway is to provide advanced passages and testing materials that stress scientific scenarios from the three major science-driven sections of the new MCAT exam, as well as to provide thought-provoking passages to increase your critical reasoning skills. These passages are accompanied by extensive annotations (including numerous graphics) and are meant to emulate the style of the "flipped classroom format" where our teaching is done after you experience the passage. After you master these passages, you will be on your way to success on the MCAT. This book is designed to guide you through a process in which you will learn how the AAMC wants medical students to think (i.e. like physician-scientists). This is why the newly revised MCAT will challenge not only your knowledge of content, but also will demand that you integrate information, interpret data, and reason about content in the biomedical sciences. By creating challenging passages in all key content areas, and by making those passages relevant to current biomedical science, Med-Pathway is designed to shape the way students assimilate test content, and integrate that content using critical reasoning skills. This is what you need to rise to the challenge of the MCAT. But before you dive in to the passages, we recommend that you read the following pages. We will discuss the new format of the MCAT, how you should study, and why this book will be highly beneficial to your preparation.

What was the rationale for changing the MCAT?

The AAMC will periodically review and model the current MCAT to reflect the dynamic nature of medicine, particularly with respect to how basic science and research impact the development of new therapeutics and treatments in the clinic. The 2015 MCAT represents the fifth time the exam has been changed since its initial inception over 80 years ago. The design for the 2015 MCAT started in 2008, when the AAMC commissioned the Medical Review Committee #5 (MR5) to examine the MCAT and recommend changes that would make the MCAT more relevant to those challenges faced by medical doctors today. Composed of individuals ranging from medical school deans and professors to residents and students, the MR5 committee sought input from numerous organizations. In particular, the committee was influenced by two expert panel reports: *Future Physicians* (2009) and *The Behavioral and Social Sciences Foundations for Future Physicians* (2011). The consensus of the committee was that the current MCAT should, in addition to testing critical reasoning, query academic competencies by examining a student's ability to apply their fundamental knowledge in the biological, physical, and behavioral sciences in the context of solving scientific problems, particularly as they impact human health and disease.

Who writes the new MCAT?

The AAMC commissions various behavioral scientists, medical professors (like us in Med-Pathway!) and clinicians to write the different sections of the MCAT exam. They write passages and free standing questions on the exam that cover biochemistry, biology, general and organic chemistry, physics, and a new section covering the behavioral sciences. The current MCAT emphasizes biochemistry, so students should focus on evaluating their knowledge of key content categories in the biological and physical sciences through the prism of biochemistry. Our passages also reflect this.

How is the new MCAT structured?

The new MCAT will take 6 hours and 15 minutes of actual test time. It is composed of four sections that each carry equal numerical weights when scaling the overall score. The titles of the sections are: I. Chemical and Physical Foundations of Biological Systems; II. Critical Analysis and Reasoning Skills; III. Biological and Biochemical Foundations of Living Systems; IV. Psychological, Social, and Biological Foundations of Behavior. This is also the order in which the passages will appear on the exam. With the exception of the Critical Analysis and Reasoning Section, each science-orientated section will consist of 59 questions and will last 95 minutes. Additionally, each of these sections will consist of 10 passages that contain between 5-7 questions each. In addition, clusters of 15 questions that are not associated with a passage (the so-called Free Standing Questions) will be on each section. The Critical Reasoning section is slightly shorter and will consist of 53 questions that are associated with 9 passages and you will be given 90 minutes to complete the section.

I. Chemical and Physical Foundations of Biological Systems	II. Critical Analysis and Reasoning Skills
59 Qs / 95 mins 10 Passages 15 Free Standing Qs	53 Qs / 90 mins 9 Passages
III. Biological and Biochemical Foundations of Living Systems	IV. Psychological, Social, and Biological Foundations of Behavior
59 Qs / 95 mins 10 Passages 15 Free Standing Qs	59 Qs / 95 mins 10 Passages 15 Free Standing Qs

How is the new MCAT scored?

The previous MCAT was composed of three sections (Physics/General Chemistry, Biological Sciences, and Verbal) where each section was scored on a 1-15 scale. This meant that the maximum obtainable score was the sum of the three sections, or 45. In addition, a written score ranging from J-T was added as a suffix to the numerical score.

The new 2015 MCAT does not have a written exam, but will add the scores from the four sections (Chemical/Physical, Critical Reasoning, Biological, and Behavioral) to arrive at the total score. However, in contrast to the previous exam, individual section scores will be reported in a range from 118-132 (both the mean and median are expected be ~125). This translates to a total range of achievable scores ranging from 472-528 with the mean centered near 500. Thus, a 500 on the new MCAT will represent a score at the 50th percentile. This means that students scoring a total of 500 will have performed better than ½ of the students taking the test. The score scales for the revised exam, with the new distributions centered near 500, will minimize clustering of scores towards the higher levels of the scale. In contrast to the previous MCAT, the new exam will provide a percentile rank as part of the score report. As with nearly all standardized tests, scores are expected to follow a normal distribution. The AAMC estimates that approximately 85,000 people will take the MCAT in 2015. Approximately 70% of test takers are expected to score between 493 and 507. Students will receive score reports that include total MCAT scores, percentile ranks, confidence intervals, as well as score profiles. This information will be provided for the total score and for the individual section tests (Chemical/Physical, Critical Reasoning, Biological, and Behavioral).

The expected distribution of raw and scaled scores by number, percentile, and standard deviation units are shown in the tables and figures in the following pages, for both the section test scores and the overall MCAT score. These projected values are based on data obtained from the AAMC regarding the new number of questions, scoring range and expected mean, previously published test standard deviations, and the approximate number of students who take the test annually. When applying to medical schools, you may have access to information about the percentile scores of the median applicant to a particular school. The tables and figures below will help you determine the new MCAT score that you need to be competitive for consideration at a particular medical school.

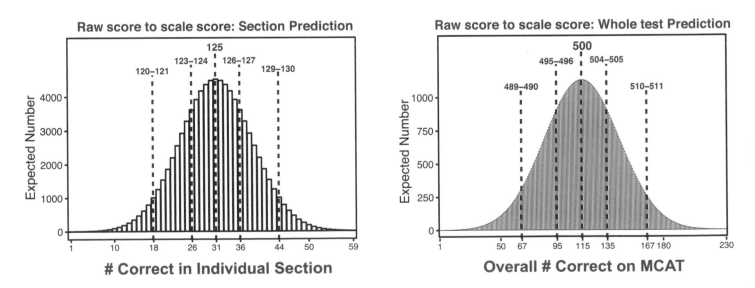

Histogram of Expected Overall Test Score Distributions: 2015 MCAT. Each bar represents the projected number of test takers (out of 85,000 total) who will achieve that raw score (number correct). Red dashed lines represent scores at the projected 5th, 25th, 50th, 75th, and 95th percentiles. Blue numbers above red dashed lines represent the anticipated MCAT scaled score equivalent.

Table 1 represents a more detailed view of what we anticipate the scaling of raw scores (number correct) to MCAT scaled scores will look like. This table is a highly reasonable estimation of how the AAMC will score the real exams and is based upon the statistical descriptions provided in their website (aamc.org/mcat/2015). In other words, this is a pretty good estimate. The distribution presented here assumes that there will be 85,000 students taking the test. For example, if you were to get 28 questions correct for a given science section, then your predicted MCAT score would be a 124. This is a 34.46% and we would predict that 4,173 other students also got 28 questions correct. It is probably not pragmatic to shoot for getting all 59 questions correct, as only 4 individuals out of 85,000 should do this!! If you are shooting high, then breaking 40 correct (which is a 128 or higher) would put you near the 90th percentile. Our goal at Med-Pathway is to help you achieve a highly competitive score and gain entrance to medical school.

Table 1. Score predictions of a 59-question Science Section.

Number Correct	MCAT Scaled Score	Expected Percentile Score	Expected Number
1	118	0.01	2
2		0.01	3
3		0.01	4
4		0.02	7
5		0.03	11
6		0.04	17
7		0.07	27
8		0.11	41
9		0.17	61
10		0.26	90
11		0.38	129
12		0.56	183
13	119	0.82	254
14		1.17	346
15		1.64	465
16	120	2.28	612
17		3.10	792
18		4.15	1007
19	121	5.48	1257
20		7.12	1542
21		9.12	1859
22	122	11.51	2201
23		14.31	2560
24		17.53	2925
25	123	21.19	3284
26		25.25	3621
27		29.69	3922
28	124	34.46	4174
29		39.49	4364
30		44.70	4482
31	125	50.00	4522
32		55.30	4482
33		60.51	4364
34	126	65.54	4174
35		70.31	3922
36		74.75	3621
37	127	78.81	3284
38		82.47	2925
39		85.69	2560
40	128	88.49	2201
41		90.88	1859
42		92.88	1542
43	129	94.52	1257
44		95.85	1007
45		96.90	792
46	130	97.72	612
47		98.36	465
48		98.83	346
49	131	99.18	254
50		99.44	183
51		99.62	129
52	132	99.74	90
53		99.83	61
54		99.89	41
55		99.93	27
56		99.96	17
57		99.97	11
58		99.98	7
59		99.99	4

Table 2. Score predictions for the 53-question Critical Reasoning Section.

Number Correct	MCAT Scaled Score	Expected Percentile Score	Expected Number
1	118	0.01	3
2		0.01	5
3		0.02	9
4		0.03	15
5		0.06	25
6		0.09	40
7		0.15	62
8		0.24	96
9	119	0.38	144
10		0.59	211
11		0.89	303
12	120	1.31	425
13		1.90	585
14		2.71	786
15	121	3.77	1035
16		5.16	1332
17		6.92	1677
18	122	9.12	2065
19		11.80	2489
20		14.99	2934
21	123	18.70	3384
22		22.94	3818
23		27.67	4215
24	124	32.84	4551
25		38.35	4808
26		44.11	4969
27	125	50.00	5024
28		55.89	4969
29		61.65	4808
30	126	67.16	4551
31		72.33	4215
32		77.06	3818
33	127	81.30	3384
34		85.01	2934
35		88.20	2489
36	128	90.88	2065
37		93.08	1677
38		94.84	1332
39	129	96.23	1035
40		97.29	786
41		98.10	585
42	130	98.69	425
43		99.11	303
44		99.41	211
45	131	99.62	144
46		99.76	96
47		99.85	62
48	132	99.91	40
49		99.94	25
50		99.97	15
51		99.98	9
52		99.99	5
53		99.99	3

Table 2 represents a more detailed view of what we anticipate that the scaling of raw scores (number correct) to MCAT scaled scores will look like on the Critical Reasoning Section. This table uses all of the statistical assumptions applied for the Chemical/Physical Foundations, Biological Foundations, and Behavioral Foundations sections. The key exception is, of course, that the Critical Reasoning Section has only 53 questions.

Putting it all together, Table 3 shows the total number correct on all four sections of the new MCAT and how this value is translated to a scaled score, percentile, and the number of individuals predicted to achieve those scores. Note that our statistical prediction models are in accordance with the AAMC defined values in that a 500 will be the midpoint and is set to be the 50%. Our goal of Med-Pathway is to help you achieve a highly competitive overall score that will facilitate your acceptance into medical school.

Despite what many think, the MCAT is not scored on a curve. With the exception of the first 2015 MCAT offered, the MCAT "equates" scores. Imagine two students that took the exam months apart and received identical scores of 500. On the surface, you might think that each student answered the same number of questions correctly, but this will not necessarily be the case. As each student took a different MCAT covering different topics (no single MCAT exam covers equivalent or all competencies), one test may have been more "difficult" than the other. Keep in mind that there are numerous "MCAT isoforms" and the test that you take is like a random draw. Because of this, it is very challenging to construct various MCAT isoforms of equivalent difficulty. To adjust for these differences, the administrators of the exam modulate the scoring scales to compensate for this.

Table 3. Relationship between Number correct and MCAT scores.

Est. # Correct Range	MCAT Scaled Score	Expected Percentile Score	Expected Number
1–4	472	0.01	1
5–8	473	0.01	1
9–12	474	0.02	2
9–12	475	0.02	4
13–16	476	0.03	7
13–16	477	0.03	12
17–24	478	0.05	20
25–30	479	0.08	33
31–33	480	0.50	52
34–36	481	0.50	82
37–39	482	0.50	125
40–42	483	0.66	186
43–46	484	0.77	272
47–51	485	1.15	388
52–55	486	1.70	542
56–59	487	2.44	738
60–64	488	3.45	984
65–69	489	4.78	1281
72–78	490	6.49	1630
70–74	491	8.63	2028
75–79	492	11.27	2465
80–87	493	14.44	2928
88–92	494	18.17	3399
93–96	495	22.11	3856
97–100	496	27.22	4276
101–106	497	32.47	4634
107–109	498	38.09	4907
110–112	499	43.98	5079
113–119	500	50.00	5138
120–123	501	56.02	5079
124–128	502	61.91	4907
129–132	503	67.53	4634
133–137	504	72.78	4276
138–141	505	77.56	3856
142–146	506	81.83	3399
147–150	507	85.56	2928
151–155	508	88.73	2465
156–159	509	91.37	2028
160–164	510	93.51	1630
165–168	511	95.22	1281
169–173	512	96.55	984
174–178	513	97.56	738
179–182	514	98.30	542
183–186	515	98.85	388
187–192	516	99.23	272
193–196	517	99.54	186
197–200	518	99.77	125
201–203	519	99.83	82
204–206	520	99.89	52
207–209	521	99.91	33
210–212	522	99.95	20
213–215	523	99.99	12
216–218	524	99.99	7
219–221	525	99.99	4
222–224	526	99.99	2
225–227	527	99.99	1
228–230	528	99.99	1

What happens the day of the MCAT?

The rules for test day are designed to foster security and are described in detail by the AAMC (aamc.org/mcat/2015). We shall summarize here. After filling out a sign-up sheet and presenting valid ID, your fingerprints and photograph are taken. Then you pass through a metal detector into the testing room. Sounds like you just got arrested! Valid forms of identification include a driver's license or passport, but student or employee IDs are not. Your picture ID must remain visible to the exam proctors for the duration of the exam.

No personal items are permissible in the testing room, unless you have prior approval (30 days or more before the exam date) from the Office of Accommodated Testing Services. Some personal items to be approved include medical aids such as prosthetic devices, casts, crutches and medications including insulin pumps, inhalers and food. Hats and clothing with hoods are not permissible. Scarves are also not allowed with the exception of religious scarves such as hijabs. Footwear may not be removed during the exam. The test center provides scratch paper, earplugs, pencils, and a locker with a key to all test takers. As no watches, phones, or clocks are allowed in the testing center, the time is readily accessible to the examinee on the computer screen.

Once the exam has started, there will be a ten-minute period by which the examinee signs a non-disclosure agreement that appears on the computer screen. The MCAT exam is proprietary intellectual property and for security reasons, all examinees must agree not to disclose any information regarding the exam. Examinees are forbidden to share, discuss, or post exam questions. They are also not allowed to discuss any exam topics presented or to outline any steps taken to arrive at an answer or to discuss any content they may have felt was experimental. MCAT officials will investigate any suspicious conduct that arises during the course of the examination. Individuals found guilty of violating any of the MCAT policies can be sanctioned in a number of ways that range from the voiding of scores to the filing of civil lawsuits.

Once started, the exam will not stop, although there are scheduled breaks. Optional breaks lasting 10 minutes have been built to fall between the first two and last two sections. An optional 30-minute lunch break is available between the second and third sections. We highly recommend taking these breaks. During the breaks, you cannot leave the testing center. Further, it should be obvious that you cannot access cell phones or study material during this time as well.

Voiding scores. At the end of the MCAT exam, the computer will give the examinees the option of scoring or voiding their results. So, if you had a really bad day on the MCAT, you will have one and only one opportunity to void your score. In the past, some students who clearly didn't care about spending extra money on MCAT registration, have gone into the MCAT with the purposeful intention of voiding their score just to see what a "real" MCAT looks like. We call this the "Devil you know versus the devil you don't know" strategy. After the decision to score or void has been made, the examinee will fill out a satisfaction survey. After the exam, students can submit test center concerns in writing to the AAMC. Students can access their MCAT scores by consulting the AAMC MCAT website, usually about four weeks after they have taken the exam. By virtue of registering, you have consented to submitting your scores to the AAMC for their research purposes.

What content does the MCAT cover?

Section I. Chemical and Physical Foundations of Living Systems. As outlined by the AAMC, this section will test material presented in the following undergraduate courses: Biochemistry (25%), Introductory Biology (5%), General Chemistry (30%), Organic Chemistry (15%) and Introductory Physics (25%). The materials in these courses will be organized based upon a "Foundation Concept" classification, which is further broken down into Content Categories. The table below provides the specific details of this section. It is important to note the added emphasis on biochemistry and the relative dilution of physics (only 25%!!). The passages in this book largely reflect these numbers. The following tables are all adapted from various AAMC sources, including *The Preview Guide to the MCAT²⁰¹⁵ Exam (2012), The Official Guide to the MCAT²⁰¹⁵ Exam, AAMC 2014).*

Foundational Concept	% of Section	Content Categories	Primary Discipline	Sub-domains	Other Disciplines
4 - Physical principles of how living organisms perform functions	40	4A	physics	kinematics mechanics, energy periodic motion	biology
		4B	physics	fluids, circulation gases, respiration	biochemistry general chem.
		4C	general chemistry	electrostatics, circuits magnetism,electrochemistry nervous system	biology physics
		4D	physics	sound, light molecular structure, optics	biology organic chem.
		4E	general chemistry	atomic theory, stoichiometry, periodic table.	organic chem. biochemistry
5 - Chemical interactions and molecular dynamics of living systems	60	5A	general chemistry	acids/bases ions, solubility titration	biochemistry
		5B	general chemistry	bonding, stereochemistry liquids	organic chem.
		5C	organic chemistry	separations and purifications,	biochemistry
		5D	biochemistry	nucleic acids, proteins, lipids, carbohydrates	biology organic chem.
		5E	general chemistry	enzymes, kinetics, equilibrium, thermodynamics	biochemistry biology

Section II. Critical Analysis and Reasoning. This section will not explicitly test your background knowledge in any specific undergraduate courses. Rather, you will be required to read thought-provoking passages and utilize your reasoning skills to answer a series of questions that are associated with the passage. These questions will fall into three general categories: comprehension of material presented, ability to reason and analyze from the material presented within (and between) the text, and finally your ability to reason and analyze beyond what is provided in the text. The passages will cover a wide array of material within the humanities and social sciences that will be written using a combination of dense vocabulary and complex language. The flow chart below provides an overview of how the Critical Analysis and Reasoning Section will be broken down (adapted from AAMC (2012), *Preview Guide to the MCAT2015 Exam, The Official Guide to the MCAT2015 Exam, AAMC 2014*).

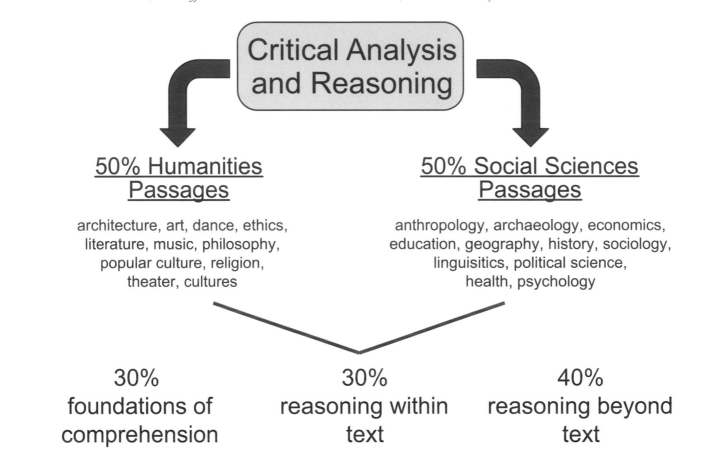

Critical Analysis and Reasoning

50% Humanities Passages

architecture, art, dance, ethics, literature, music, philosophy, popular culture, religion, theater, cultures

50% Social Sciences Passages

anthropology, archaeology, economics, education, geography, history, sociology, linguisitics, political science, health, psychology

30%
foundations of comprehension

30%
reasoning within text

40%
reasoning beyond text

Section III. Biological and Biochemical Foundations of Living Systems. This section will feature four undergraduate courses: Biochemistry (25%), Introductory Biology (65%), General Chemistry (5%), and Organic Chemistry (5%). The materials in these courses will be organized based upon a "Foundation Concept" classification, which is further broken down into Content Categories. The table below provides the specific details of how this section is broken down. It is important to note the added emphasis on biochemistry throughout the material as well as the level of integration between the topics. A major emphasis of this book is to feature biochemistry and how it is connected to virtually all aspects of biology. Adapted from AAMC (2012), *Preview Guide to the MCAT[2015] Exam, The Official Guide to the MCAT[2015] Exam, AAMC 2014*).

Foundational Concept	% of Section	Content Categories	Primary Discipline	Sub-domains	Other Disciplines
1 - Structure and function of proteins and their amino acid components	55	1A	biochemistry	amino acids, proteins and enzymes, enzyme kinetics	biology organic chem.
		1B	biology	genes, DNA repair transcription, genomes, recombinant DNA	biochemistry
		1C	biology	genetics, meiosis, evolution	-
		1D	biochemistry	metabolism, metabolic reguation	biology, organic chem.
2 - Cell biology and cell physiology	20	2A	biology	membranes, organelles, tissues	biochemistry
		2B	biology	prokaryotes, virology	
		2C	biology	mitosis, development tumorigenesis	biochemistry
3 - Anatomy and physiology	25	3A	biology	nervous system, endocrine system, electrochemistry	biochemistry, general chem.
		3B	biology	respiratory, circulatory, immune, digestive, excretory, reproductive, muscle & skeletal systems	-

Section IV. Psychological, Social, and Biological Foundations of Behavior. This section will feature four undergraduate courses: Introductory Psychology (65%), Introductory Sociology (30%), Introductory Biology (5%). The materials in these courses will be organized based upon a "Foundation Concept" classification, which is further broken down into Content Categories. The table below provides the specific details of how this section is broken down. This section will cover a broad range of content from a number of disciplines, including psychology, sociology, neuroscience, and public health. It is noteworthy that the majority of the content will be from the field of psychology, including its many subdomains (adapted from AAMC (2012), *Preview Guide to the MCAT²⁰¹⁵ Exam, The Official Guide to the MCAT²⁰¹⁵ Exam, AAMC 2014*).

If you have taken undergraduate coursework in psychology, sociology, and neuroscience, some of the material shown in the diagram may be familiar to you. However, your prep work should also include familiarizing yourself with course material in these fields, including both introductory and perhaps mid-level textbooks and online summary materials covering the topics shown below. Introductory-level courses in psychology will touch upon much of this material, but the MCAT may have additional detail that requires further study. Additionally, you should be familiar with basic principles in statistics, the primary theories that guide much of sociology, and more specialized areas in sociology related to medicine and healthcare (e.g. medical and health sociology, public health and demographics, racial, and social inequality, and criminal justice).

Foundational Concept	% of Section	Content Categories	Primary Discipline	Sub-domains	Other Disciplines
6 - sensing perceiving learning	25	6A	psychology	experimental psych sensation & perception physiological psych	biology neuroscience
		6B	psychology	learning & memory cognitive psych developmental psych language	biology linguistics neuroscience
		6C	psychology	physiological psych sensation & perception	biology neuroscience
7 - cognition social interaction	35	7A	psychology	physiological psych personality psych abnormal psych developmental psych	biology neuroscience
		7B	psychology	social psych	sociology
		7C	psychology	learning & memory cognitive psych clinical psych / health psych	neuroscience
8 - self identity development social interactions	20	8A	psychology	personality psych developmental psych social psych	sociology
		8B	psychology	social psych	sociology
9 - cultural influences social structures	15	9A	sociology	theories of sociology medical / health sociology sociology of culture	social psych health psych public health
		9B	sociology	epidemiology/demographics	social psych
10 - social stratification social inequality public health	5	10A	sociology	medical / health sociology criminal justice	public health

What skills will the MCAT require?

When fundamental knowledge is combined with specific skill sets, then physicians will be better equipped to make important decisions regarding the course and methodology of treatment for their patients. That's the rationale of the AAMC. Therefore, the MCAT science passages will consist of questions derived from four different categories. Table 4 shows the four categories and their expected distributions by percent across the exam. Note the heavy emphasis that is placed on higher order learning domains that focus on problem solving and reasoning: the point where clinical medicine and science intersect. In addition to detailed explanations and numerous diagrams, the passages presented here are equipped with annotations that designate the skill categories that each question is derived from.

In working through the passages throughout this book, you will be challenged with questions in each of the identified key skills (Concepts, Reasoning, Research, and Data). If you find you are doing well on Research and Data but struggling on Concepts and Reasoning, this may indicate that you need to spend more time becoming familiar with the content material in that particular Scientific Foundation Section (I, III, or IV). On the other hand, if your recall of the Concepts is strong, but you are struggling with Research and Data questions, you should invest extra time and attention to the annotations. Med-Pathway annotations are designed to teach you how to tackle these kinds of questions and develop the skills of data application that will be a major focus of the revised MCAT.

Table 4. Distribution of MCAT science exam questions into four basic categories.

	Concepts and Principles	Reasoning and Problem Solving	Research Design and Execution	Data-Based and Statistical Reasoning
% of Questions per section	35%	45%	10%	10%
	- identify, recall, and define basic concepts - recognize relationships between ideas	- apply conceptual ideas to solve problems - interpret observations and make predictions	- use scientific inquiry to assess methodology - understand conrols and hypotheses	- interpret and make conclusions from data - identify statistical patterns within results

How should I prepare for the MCAT?

Our vast MCAT experience has revealed that approximately **350** hours of studying is required to prepare even the best students for the challenge of the MCAT. Study guides that focus on re-teaching the sciences that you <u>already</u> paid your tuition dollars to learn in class only represent a surface coating on mastering the MCAT. As the total testing time for the new MCAT is over 6 hours, students must realize that they will need to acquire test-taking stamina and that this can only be achieved through practicing. Med-Pathway is the exercise you need for your brain in order to acquire the endurance necessary to succeed on the MCAT. Such study skills will be required not only for success on the MCAT, but also for success in medical school. This is particularly true with respect to the USMLE Step I exam currently taken at the end of the second year in medical school. Students must pass Step I in order to receive an MD degree. So put down your cell phone and ignore your distracting friends and start dating Med-Pathway. Take the MCAT, get a rock star score, and break up. It's ok, we understand.

There is no substitute for knowledge and the ability to apply it to novel situations such as those presented in this book. So for those test prep guys out there emphasizing the art of "gaming" the multiple choice MCAT exam: your number is up. Often times, inexperienced teachers write multiple-choice exams that can be "gamed" due to the intrinsic nature of eliminating answer choices on multiple-choice exams. The MCAT is far more sophisticated and rarely, if at all, makes mistakes in multiple choice questioning.

Taking the prerequisite courses required for medical school is, in itself, preparing for the MCAT. Depending on your major, elective courses in topics such as immunology, physiology, and genetics as well as the humanities are encouraged. A great way to prepare for the critical reasoning test ("verbal") is to read a lot. Newspapers such as *The Wall Street Journal* and magazines like *The Economist* are great examples to improve reading comprehension. Further, engaging in research and participating in journal clubs also serve to buttress your knowledge and skill sets for the MCAT. These courses and learning experiences should provide the foundational knowledge required for success on the MCAT; Med-Pathway helps with the application of this knowledge and the solidification of your critical thinking skills. In addition to having a command of the prerequisite information needed for the MCAT, the "real" studying for the MCAT <u>must</u> come in the form of doing practice test passages and exams that force the students to apply their knowledge. This is the driving force behind Med-Pathway. It is now time to engage with advanced practice materials to get you into MCAT shape. This book has been created for this important part of the journey. That's because the emphasis of the current MCAT on problem solving and the dissuasion from memorizing facts and pathways requires a resource such as Med-Pathway. So we would recommend that instead of memorizing the steps of the Krebs cycle (everybody picks on the Krebs cycle), that you understand conceptually what the Krebs cycle is doing. Understand that the Krebs cycle oxidizes the two carbon equivalents of acetyl CoA and generates a lot of reducing power in the mitochondria. Realize how this is linked to the conversion of pyruvate into lactate and therefore appreciate the clinical significance of lactic acidosis. Of course you should be able to <u>recognize</u> a reaction that occurs in the TCA cycle, but we would dissuade you from memorizing it for the exam, particularly as the MCAT is likely to give you an image of the Krebs cycle reactions.

The AAMC states that students should demonstrate the level of knowledge on the MCAT comparable to what is taught at undergraduate institutions. This is an interesting statement because instruction and areas of emphasis vary from institution to institution as well as from teacher to teacher within the same institution. For example, some classes may focus on research methodologies (i.e. laboratory work and journal clubs) and some may just simply consist of lectures derived from a textbook. Regardless, students should grasp the fundamental principles from each discipline as outlined by the AAMC and recapitulated here, yet also be able to apply this knowledge to various clinical and experimental scenarios. Therefore, the MCAT will query examinees about the significance of published experimental findings from academic journals, some of the very journals in which the founders of Med-Pathway have authored articles. Clearly, a thorough knowledge of the scientific literature is beyond the scope of the MCAT, but interpreting the meaning of selected experimental data as it pertains to the various disciplines and topics outlined by the AAMC is not. That is, students should acquire a "depth of knowledge" (i.e. competency) on how to read and interpret scientific data, a skill often overlooked in undergraduate courses. Med-Pathway will help you master this critical scientific skill. The passages presented in this book present scientific data in various forms (i.e. log plots, scatter plots, bar graphs) that are commonly seen in the scientific literature. Therefore, understanding how to interpret scientific data as well as to appreciate how research is conducted with respect to experimental design and the development of hypotheses is far more important than in depth knowledge on a given topic, such as autoimmune diseases. Therefore, facts are necessary but not sufficient for the types of problem solving required for success on the MCAT.

As an example, we will further analyze the MCAT topic of autoimmune disease, as it is part of the MCAT content "Recognition of self vs. non-self, autoimmune diseases." This appears in Foundation 3A (see diagram for Section III). In this sense, the AAMC has determined that a general understanding of autoimmunity represents a "competency." But, what exactly does this mean, particularly as there are more than 80 autoimmune diseases? Certainly the AAMC and the people who write passages for the MCAT do not expect test takers to know every autoimmune disease. That would be excessive and too difficult, especially as immunologists don't even know all of this information.

So what should you know? Remember that the passage is likely going to have some representative questions that incorporate a view of immunity through the prism of biochemistry. Take the Med-Pathway passage on autoimmunity as an example of what you could expect to see. Like Med-Pathway, any passage on the topic of immunity will likely query your understanding of the structure and function of immunoglobulins. Indeed, these important proteins are widely used in research and clinical medicine. Physicians routinely measure the levels of various antibodies in the serum of patients. For example, an allergist might measure serum IgE levels. Further, various laboratory techniques that use antibodies such as Western blotting and affinity chromatography are also likely testing angles. Lastly, with respect to the structure of antibodies, students should apply their foundational knowledge of amino acids and appreciate that the heavy and light chains are covalently linked through cystine linkages and how this can be influenced through the use of reducing agents such as dithiothreitol.

What about biology? Students should also know fundamental biological principles behind the immunology of autoimmunity. In the context of autoimmunity, we describe two prevailing models for how autoimmune disorders develop: molecular mimicry and sequestration. These two concepts are probably applicable to most autoimmune disorders. The autoimmunity biological sciences passage in Med-Pathway focuses on thyroid disorders, but could have easily focused on any of the dozens of other autoimmune disease such as lupus. The passage could have also asked questions that focused on T and B cells as well as the major histocompatibility complex (MHC). No MCAT book or test for that matter will be able to cover **ALL** autoimmune diseases and the underlying immunology behind them. However, through combining your knowledge of the basic principles of immunology with the ability to interpret and apply scientific data, virtually any passage encountered in autoimmunity, or in immunology in general, should be encountered with confidence.

The discussion of autoimmunity in the context of the thyroid (Grave's and Hashimoto's diseases) provides the opportunity to integrate immunology with endocrinology. Additionally, in the physical sciences passages, we come back to the thyroid and Grave's disease and show you how the topic of autoimmunity can be applied to the physical sciences. As such, this passage focuses on clinical treatment, the physics of radioactive iodine treatment, the chemistry of iodide and the endocrinology of T3 and T4 hormones. Therefore, several important fundamental topics are tested, both in the biological and physical sciences in the context of autoimmunity. What should be appreciated is how basic and clinical sciences are woven together to address disease. The passages show how fundamental knowledge through multiple disciplines is integrated together. This is the spirit behind deriving passages for the MCAT.

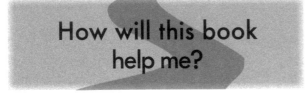

Med-Pathway provides passage content as well as online exams that challenge students at a level equal to or greater than the MCAT. After mastering Med-Pathway passages and online exams, you will have honed the critical thinking skills required for success on the MCAT. Although the passages within this book cover all of the Foundational Content Development Scheme areas listed by the AAMC, it is impossible to produce a book that covers every single possible topic in passage format. It is important to also note that the order of the passages in this book follow the Foundational Content Scheme rather than the order of how they will appear on the MCAT. Indeed, because of the expansive list of topics and the numerous possible combinations (i.e. 80 autoimmune disorders), no MCAT study resource could possibly provide passages addressing all permutations. That is not the point of Med-Pathway, and neither should be it be the point of your MCAT preparation. Rather, the point is to develop and sharpen your critical thinking skills, particularly with respect to how they are used in the application of scientific knowledge in experimental and clinical settings. This is important because you will need to learn to critically analyze data derived from unfamiliar scientific scenarios during the MCAT. This book presents some of these scenarios and links the basic sciences to the diseased state in multiple passages. This includes familial breast cancer, gallstones, atherosclerosis, multiple sclerosis, and various behavioral disorders likely to be observed in the clinic. Thus, Med-Pathway presents a robust sampling of science and reasoning puzzles designed to give you the edge in critical thinking for the MCAT. It's time to take another step forward in the path.

Sincerely,
Med-Pathway

Biological and Biochemical Foundations of Living Systems

Enzyme Kinetics

Circulating blood glucose is distributed to peripheral tissues where muscle hexokinase (or hexokinase I) rapidly phosphorylates glucose. Hexokinase I has a high affinity for substrate and any free, excess glucose leaves the muscle and circulates to the liver where it is converted into G-6P via glucokinase. This isozyme has a lower affinity for glucose than hexokinase and is not regulated by feedback inhibition. Such differential properties between glucokinase and hexokinase I reflect the individual roles that the liver and skeletal tissue each play in glucose metabolism.

Researchers engineered pHEXO bacterial plasmids expressing wild-type (WT) or two mutant human hexokinase I enzymes. Each mutation changes a glutamate required for enzyme activity. Each plasmid construct was designed to encode an N-terminal "6-histidine epitope tag" (His_6) by introducing both CAT and CAC codons into the DNA (**Fig. 1**). The histidine residues facilitate affinity purification from cell extracts by coordinating a nickel ion that also coordinates to groups attached to sepharose beads.

After purification, the concentration of each enzyme was equalized by dilution to 1.0 μg/μl in a reaction buffer with Mg^{+2} and ATP. Reaction velocity was measured as a function of substrate concentration. This allowed for a determination of the k_{cat} and the K_m as hexokinase I obeys Michaelis-Menten kinetics. The k_{cat} measures the catalytic efficiency of an enzyme under saturating conditions and is referred to as the turnover number. (**Fig. 2A**). The k_{cat} and K_m values were determined and compared to known values of other enzymes (**Fig. 2B**). Enzymes with large k_{cat}/K_m values are highly efficient through the combination of a high velocity with high substrate affinity.

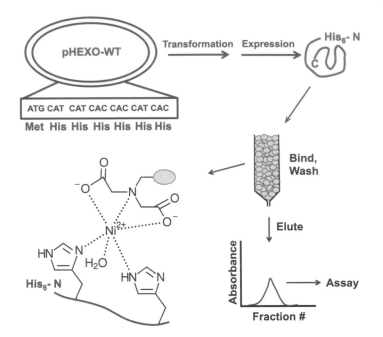

Figure 1. Expression and purification of hexokinase I.

A.

$$I \quad E + S \underset{k_{off}}{\overset{k_{on}}{\rightleftharpoons}} ES \overset{k_{cat}}{\longrightarrow} E + P$$

$$II \quad V = \frac{V_{max}[S]}{K_m + [S]}$$

B.

ENZYME	K_{cat} s^{-1}	K_m (nM)
CARBONIC ANHYDRASE	10^6	800
HEXOKINASE I	200	0.15
HEXOKINASE I MUTANT #1	7.2	0.14
HEXOKINASE I MUTANT #2	91.1	0.15
LYSOZYME	0.94	6.0
GLUCOKINASE	60.0	1.7

Figure 2. A. I. Michaelis-Menten kinetic scheme. II. Relationship between kinetic parameters. V = initial velocity. **B.** A comparison of kinetic values for His_6-tagged Hexokinase I enzymes and others.

18

1) pH can be used to elute His$_6$-tagged proteins from nickel affinity columns. Which of the following conditions would be ideal for this?

A. pH = 3.0 as histidine has a charge of +1.

B. pH = 3.0 as histidine has no net charge.

C. pH = 10.0 as histidine has a charge of +1.

D. pH = 10.0 as histidine has no net charge.

2) The dissociation binding constant (K$_D$) of the ES complex is equal to:

A. $k_{on/off}$ and has units of concentration.

B. $k_{on/off}$ and has units of concentration^{-1}.

C. $k_{off/on}$ and has units of concentration.

D. $k_{off/on}$ and has units of concentration^{-1}.

3) An inhibitor of hexokinase I was active only when bound to the enzyme-substrate (ES) complex. This would:

A. decrease the K_m by uncompetitive inhibition.

B. increase the K_m by uncompetitive inhibition.

C. decrease the K_m by competitive inhibition.

D. increase the K_m by competitive inhibition.

4) How would the increased expression of hexokinase I in response to insulin change the V_{max} for the enzyme?

A. increase.

B. decrease.

C. no change.

D. cannot be determined.

5) Which of the following correctly represents the enzymology of glucokinase and hexokinase?

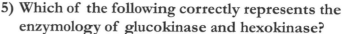
■ Glucokinase   ■ Hexokinase

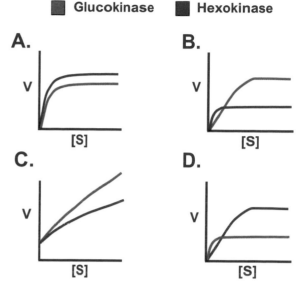

6) Researchers discovered a small molecule that inhibited glucokinase. Its mode of action was determined using the double reciprocal plot shown below. The mechanism of action of this inhibitor most likely proceeds through binding:

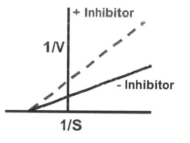

A. at the active site and decreasing the K_m.

B. outside of the active site and altering the K_m.

C. at the active site and increasing the K_m.

D. outside of the active site and altering the V_{max}.

7) Which of the following is most consistent with the mutants in the glutamate codon in hexokinase?

A. #1 is mutated to lysine and affects substrate binding.

B. #2 is mutated to an aspartate at the active site.

C. #1 is mutated to aspartate at the active site.

D. #2 is mutated to lysine and affects substrate binding.

Enzyme Kinetics

Annotations.
1) A 2) C 3) A 4) A 5) B 6) D 7) B

	Foundation 1: Biochemistry-A			Foundation 5: Water-A		
	A			**A**		
Concepts	3					
Reasoning	2,4,7					
Research				1		
Data	5,6					

Big Picture. This passage takes a "simple" enzyme, hexokinase I, and examines its role in metabolism, and its relationship to glucokinase. The questions did not emphasize the gene expression system used to express hexokinase I (i.e. genetic code and translation), but rather, some fundamental properties on amino acids and the biology of the enzymes are queried. We made some assumptions about your prior knowledge of enzymes and acid/base chemistry, which is always emphasized on the MCAT and will be throughout this book. Understanding how biomolecules behave at various pH values is highly relevant to clinical medicine, particularly as many drugs can only cross the membrane in the stomach (pH = 1.5) or intestines (pH = 8.0) when uncharged.

The first paragraph sets up the fact that the isozymes hexokinase and glucokinase, despite catalyzing identical reactions, have different kinetic properties. Why? It's important to know the role of the two isozymes in glucose control and you will see this in medical school too: the liver provides glucose to the muscle after glycogen is depleted. This is key and understanding how enzymes work is critical, particularly as numerous drugs act as enzyme inhibitors.

Enzyme kinetics is a common topic on the MCAT. The kinetic discussion in this passage largely focuses on how to apply the meaning of K_m. Remember: low K_m values indicate that a lower concentration of substrate [S] is required for the enzyme to reach ½ V_{max}.

1) A. pH = 3.0 as histidine has a charge of +1. In Figure 1, it can be seen that the histidine side chains (imidazole) must have no charge in order to coordinate with nickel. This is because the lone electron pairs on the histidine side chains form the coordinated covalent bond with the metal. Once the nitrogens obtain a formal charge, binding cannot occur as the electrons have been lost for bonding. Therefore, a charge of +1 will facilitate elution from the column. **This eliminates choices B and D.** What about choices A and C? How do you determine what the charge of histidine will be at a given pH? You need to know the pK_a of the side chain. Although it is not given to you, we expect you to recall from biochemistry class that histidine is the amino acid that has a pK_a closest to physiological pH, which is 7.4. Although pK_a values can vary as a function of the environment that the amino acid lies in, the pK_a of histidine is usually given as ~6.0, meaning that at physiological pH, over 90% of the histidine residues will be uncharged. This can be calculated from the Henderson-Hasselbalch equation: $pH = pK_a + \log [A^-]/[HA]$. You might also see it written as $pH = pK_a - \log[HA][A^-]$. Both are correct and it doesn't matter which one you use as long as you know how to manipulate the equation. Note that because pH and pK_a are both defined in terms of logarithms, there is a 10-fold difference in the concentration of species per pH unit.

The ratio of acid (HA) to conjugate base (A^-), or their relative abundance (**Fig. 3**), can be calculated at any pH provided that the pK_a value is known. Therefore, for histidine at pH = 3.0 ($pK_a > pH$), the proton will not be titrated and the histidine will be charged (mostly HA). At pH = 10, ($pK_a < pH$), the proton will be titrated off and the charge will be neutral (the conjugate base is uncharged). Note that when positively charged, the imidazole ring will share the charge over both nitrogen atoms through resonance (**Fig. 3**). **Choice C is wrong** because there will be no charge.

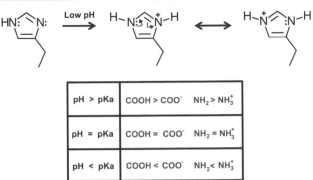

pH > pKa	COOH > COO⁻	NH₂ > NH₃⁺
pH = pKa	COOH = COO⁻	NH₂ = NH₃⁺
pH < pKa	COOH < COO⁻	NH₂ < NH₃⁺

Figure 3. Top, structure of histidine side chain at pH 7.4 and lower. **Bottom**, table showing relationship between pH, pK_a, and charge due to titration and prominent forms of carboxyl and amino groups at various pH.

2) C. $k_{off/on}$ and has units of concentration. The dissociation equilibrium constant describes the reaction ES → E + S. The equilibrium constant can be written as [E][S]/[ES] which is the same as $k_{off/on}$ and the units will be concentration.

3) A. decrease the K_m by uncompetitive inhibition. The first thing to recognize is that an uncompetitive inhibitor can only bind to an enzyme when the enzyme is bound to its substrate, otherwise the binding site for the inhibitor will not be formed (**Fig. 4**). This **eliminates choices C and D** as this is not competitive inhibition. So what about the K_m? How does it change? If you didn't memorize that the K_m decreases with an uncompetitive inhibitor, then you can solve this starting with equation I from Figure 2 (that is part of the reason why it is presented). After taking into account the new equilibrium (**Fig. 4**), it can be seen that the ES complexes are depleted due to the formation of ESI complexes.

In order to preserve the original equilibrium between substrate [S] and enzyme [E], more substrate [S] will bind to enzyme, driving the formation of new ES complexes via Le Chatelier's principle. As a result, a lower concentration of substrate is required to reach $V_{max}/2$. This is the definition of a lower K_m, making **choice B incorrect**. As an aside, it should be clear that the V_{max} would be reduced because the ESI complexes cannot form product.

1. **Start with equation given in Fig. 2.**

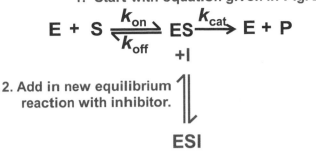

2. **Add in new equilibrium reaction with inhibitor.**

ESI

3. **Deplete ES complexes, driving E + S reaction forward.**

Figure 4. Uncompetitive inhibition depletes ES complexes.

4) A. increase. Increasing the enzyme concentration increases the V_{max} for a reaction because you will form more product as a function of time with the additional enzyme.

5) B. Hexokinase I saturates before glucokinase (**Fig. 5**) and this occurs so that excess glucose can be used by the liver to make glycogen and/or fat. The passage states that, "Hexokinase I has a high affinity for substrate and any free, excess glucose leaves the muscle and circulates to the liver where it is converted into G-6P via glucokinase." From this, it can be deduced that hexokinase saturates faster, or has a lower V_{max}, than glucokinase. **Choice B is the correct answer** and this also **eliminates choice D** as it is the opposite of choice B. A second clue from the passage concerns the K_m values that can be found in the Table. Recall that K_m values are inversely proportional to the affinity between enzyme and substrate. Thus, a low K_m means a high affinity and vice versa. This is suggested, albeit subtly, in the last sentence in the passage: "Enzymes with large k_{cat}/K_m values are highly efficient through the combination of a high velocity with high substrate affinity." Since we already know that k_{cat} refers to reaction velocity, the K_m must refer to substrate affinity. A high k_{cat}/K_m value reflects a high k_{cat} value and a low K_m (or higher affinity).

Choice A is wrong because an enzyme would not exhibit any reaction velocity at a zero substrate concentration. **Choice C is also wrong** as the graph shows two curves, but neither reach saturating levels.

Therefore, you cannot make any conclusions about which enzyme saturates first and, further, there is no way to tell what the K_m values are because V_{max} is not on the graph!

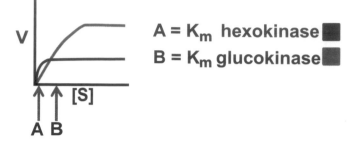

A = K_m hexokinase ■
B = K_m glucokinase ■

Figure 5. Hexokinase and glucokinase have different affinities for glucose.

6) **D. outside of the active site and altering the V_{max}.** This is otherwise known as noncompetitive inhibition. This form of inhibition proceeds through the inhibitor binding outside of the active site. The key is to decipher how the V_{max} and/or K_m values change in the presence of inhibitor in a double reciprocal, or Lineweaver Burk, plot. You should commit this to memory (**Fig. 6**). The first thing to look for is how the two lines (+ and − inhibitor) in the plot behave at the X intercept. Note that either with or without the inhibitor, the X intercept values are equal in question 6. This means that the K_m is not changed as the X intercept represents $-1/K_m$. **Choice B is therefore wrong**.

Recall that in noncompetitive inhibition the inhibitor can bind to the enzyme whether or not the substrate is present. Noncompetitive inhibition reduces the V_{max} of the reaction, but not the K_m (**Fig. 7**). This is because the substrate can still bind to the enzyme (same K_m), but the presence of the inhibitor binding outside of the active site precludes the formation of product (reduces V_{max}). Therefore, **choices A and C are wrong** because they discuss inhibition at the active site, which is competitive.

One hallmark feature of competitive inhibition is that the process is reversible, meaning that the inhibitor can be titrated away from the active site by substrate. Therefore, at some higher concentration of substrate, the V_{max} will be restored, but the K_m values are different.

There are three major forms of inhibition (**Fig. 7**): competitive, noncompetitive, and uncompetitive. A fourth form of inhibition is termed mixed inhibition. You should know the types of inhibitors, their consequences on enzyme function, and how to distinguish between different types. Note how the V_{max} and the K_m values change as a function of inhibitor type. In the presence of the inhibitor, this value is often called K_i.

$$V = \frac{V_{max}\,[S]}{K_m + [S]}$$ ← Take the reciprocal

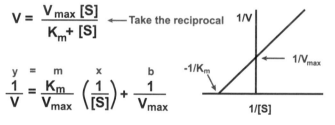

$$\underset{\substack{y}}{\frac{1}{V}} = \underset{\substack{m}}{\frac{K_m}{V_{max}}} \underset{\substack{x}}{\left(\frac{1}{[S]}\right)} + \underset{\substack{b}}{\frac{1}{V_{max}}}$$

Figure 6. Double reciprocal plot.

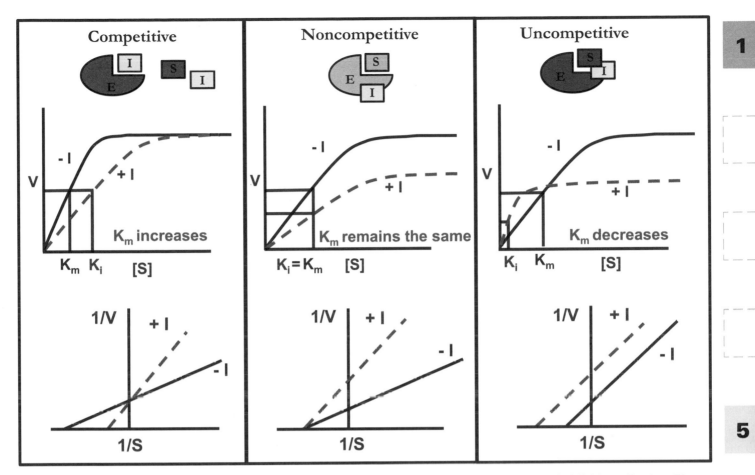

Competitive	Noncompetitive	Uncompetitive

K_m increases K_m remains the same K_m decreases

7) **B. #2 is mutated to an aspartate at the active site.** Focus on the differences between mutants #1 and #2. Note that the K_m is basically the same, meaning that the affinity for the substrate will be the same. We saw in question 5 that in case you did not recall the relationship between K_m and substrate affinity that the passage provides information to figure this out. **Choices A and D are eliminated** as substrate binding will not be affected. The k_{cat} values are significant different with mutant #1 exhibiting a ~30 fold decrease relative to the wild-type enzyme. The passage states that glutamate was mutated to another amino acid. As glutamate is acidic, a mutagenic substitution with an acidic amino acid like aspartate would be expected to have far less of a deleterious impact on enzyme activity than a substitution with a basic amino acid such as lysine. **Choice B is the best answer** because mutant #2 retains nearly 50% of its activity with aspartate. This same logic effectively **rules out choice C** because mutant #1 has almost lost all activity (see Table 1). We assume that you know which amino acids are basic and which are acidic, <u>without necessarily having to memorize their structures</u>.

Figure 7. A, B: Competitive inhibition: E + I → EI; EI + S → E + P. Noncompetitive inhibition: E + I → EI; EI + S → ESI; E + I + S → E + P. Uncompetitive inhibition: ES + I → (ES)I.

23

Farnesylation

Terpene derivatives such as farnesyl pyrophosphate (FPP) can be used to farnesylate proteins, a posttranslational modification that covalently attaches to cysteine (C) residues residing in "CaaX" motifs. In this motif, "a" represents an aliphatic amino acid and "X" can be any of several residues including serine. Farnesylation usually occurs near the C terminus of substrate proteins and introduces a hydrophobic region.

Two distinct mechanisms, each using the sulfhydryl cysteine side chain as a nucleophile, have been proposed for the farnesylation of proteins (**Fig. 1**). Farnesyltransferases utilize zinc as a co-factor and this stabilizes the active site cysteine thiolate in the CaaX motif (**Fig. 2A**). Mutagenesis studies have shown that the coordinating zinc ligands "optimize" the charge to achieve a net charge of -1 at the zinc center, which is defined as the zinc ion and its coordinating residues. This balances thiolate stability with its strong, intrinsic reactivity (**Fig. 2A**). To test which mechanism farnesylation proceeds through, a series of reactions were performed with a purified yeast protein farnesyltransferase and the substrate FPP or various modified, unnatural derivatives (**Fig. 2B**). The enzymatic transfer of farnesyl groups was measured with a peptide substrate labeled with a fluor whose concentration does not affect reaction rates. The generation of data on two key parameters, the catalytic rate constant k_{cat} and the Michaelis constant, is presented (**Fig. 2C**).

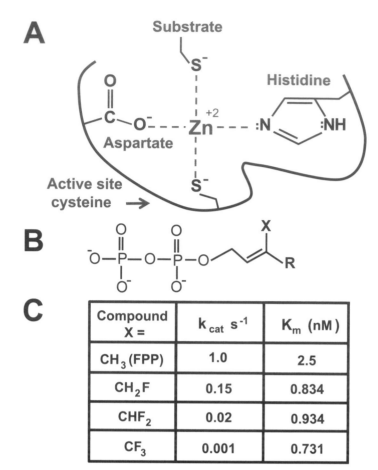

A

B

C

Compound X =	k_{cat} s^{-1}	K_m (nM)
CH_3 (FPP)	1.0	2.5
CH_2F	0.15	0.834
CHF_2	0.02	0.934
CF_3	0.001	0.731

Figure 2. A. Coordination at zinc center stabilizes thiolate nucleophile. **B, C.** Determining the mechanism of farnesylation with test substrates.

Figure 1. Two distinct mechanisms for protein farnesylation on cysteine.

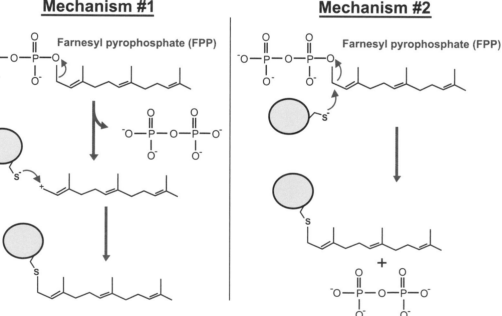

1) In an electrophilic mechanism, a carbocation intermediate is formed as shown.

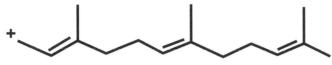

This <u>primary</u> carbocation can best be described as:

A. aryllic.

B. alkylic.

C. vinylic.

D. allylic.

2) The following kinetic rate law best describes the farnesylation reaction:

A. rate = k [electrophile].

B. rate = k [electrophile][nucleophile].

C. rate = k [nucleophile].

D. rate = k[electrophile]^2.

3) The alkylation between cysteine and the isoprenoid FPP occurs through a:

A. sulfhydryl linkage.

B. thioether bond.

C. cystine linkage.

D. thioester bond.

4) Which of the following would be the most critical physical parameter for using the FPP analogs as an accurate assessment tool in determining the mechanism of farnesyl transfer?

A. The FPP analogs should display competitive inhibition with FPP.

B. The FPP analogs should display noncompetitive inhibition with FPP.

C. The FPP analogs should be required to target the farnesylated protein to the membrane.

D. The FPP analogs should bind to the enzyme with the same affinity as FPP.

5) Mutations at amino acid residues that coordinate the zinc co-factor in a yeast farnesyltransferase can maintain zinc binding, yet change the overall charge at the zinc center from -1 to 0. This can be performed with a substitution of:

A. aspartate with lysine that would increase enzyme activity.

B. aspartate with histidine that would decrease enzyme activity.

C. histidine with lysine that would increase enzyme activity.

D. histidine with aspartate that would decrease enzyme activity.

6) The pK$_a$ of the cysteine side chain in a free amino acid is approximately 9.0, but when bound as a substrate to a farnesyltransferase in a CaaX motif, the pK$_a$ drops to about 5.0. Assuming that the pH of the reaction is 7.0 during catalysis, the ratio of [SH]/[S$^-$] =

A. 10^4.

B. 10^2.

C. 10^{-2}.

D. 10^{-4}.

Farnesylation

Annotations.
1) D 2) A 3) B 4) A 5) B 6) C

	Foundation 1: Biochemistry-A		Foundation 5: Thermo/Kinetics-E	
	A		E		
Concepts	1				
Reasoning	3,6				
Research	4				
Data	5		2		

Big Picture. Enzyme mechanisms are important (and frequent) MCAT topics, particularly the SN1 and SN2 reactions. You should be able to distinguish between those conditions that favor SN1 versus SN2 reactions and when they occur. This requires the basic understanding that the SN1 mechanism proceeds through a carbocation intermediate, whereas the SN2 reaction does not. Most students encounter SN1 and SN2 reactions in Organic Chemistry and are taught the stereochemical consequences of these reactions. For example, SN1 reactions can generate racemic mixtures through new chiral centers and SN2 reactions invert the electrophilic carbon configuration. As the reaction in this passage is governed enzymatically, multiple products will not be formed. Further, students are often given tables with reaction rates, allowing them to be able to distinguish between the two mechanisms. This particular passage was challenging in that the concentrations of the electrophile were NOT varied; instead, the nature of the substituent groups on FPP was varied.

Additional questions probed your understanding of zinc cofactors as well as amino acid properties and how they can affect activity. In particular, it focused on the sulfhydryl group of cysteine, which is present in both the enzyme <u>and</u> <u>substrate</u>.

1) **D. allylic.** Although the structure looks like a simple primary carbocation, it is actually a primary allylic carbocation and is stabilized through resonance. This is because the empty p orbital of the carbocation can be occupied by π electrons present within the double bond, generating a resonance structure (**Fig. 3**).

Figure 3. Resonance stabilization of an allylic carbocation.

You should also be able to immediately recall what the other answer choices look like and to recognize them as being incorrect (**Fig. 4**). Allylic carbons are sp^3 hybridized and are adjacent to an sp^2 carbon that is known as a vinyl carbon. Alkyl groups are formed when a parental alkane molecule loses a hydrogen atom as is shown for methane and the formation of a methyl group. Further, just as an alkyl group is formed from an alkane, an aryl group is formed from a phenyl group.

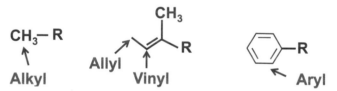

Figure 4. Important nomenclature.

2) **A. rate = k [electrophile].** The trick to the correct answer is to recognize that the compounds tested in the table yield lower reaction rates as more electron withdrawing groups are added. This is an inductive effect and is consistent with an SN1 mechanism (**Fig. 1**). In this case, the addition of fluorine destabilizes a carbocation intermediate. As per choice A, the rate law of an SN1 reaction depends only on the electrophile (farnesyl substrate), and not the nucleophile (protein to be farnesylated). The passage also states: "The enzymatic transfer of farnesyl groups was measured with a peptide substrate labeled with a fluor whose concentration does not affect reaction rates." Remember that the peptide substrate is tantamount to the protein substrate with the CaaX motif, and is therefore the nucleophile for the reaction. This rules out an SN2 mechanism, which depends on the concentration of nucleophile. All other answer choices are therefore eliminated.

Let's examine the mechanism of the reaction further and the chemical principles behind it. The passage shows two distinct possible mechanisms for farnesylation. You should readily distinguish these as nucleophilic substitution reactions, one of which is a first order reaction (SN1; mechanism #1) and the second of which is a second order reaction (SN2; mechanism #2). Therefore, mechanism #1 proceeds through a carbocation intermediate, and #2 does not. In consideration of the carbocation mechanism, you must recall your fundamental knowledge of carbocation stability. As carbon is electroneutral, anything that alters this is potentially destabilizing. Recall that methyl (alkyl) groups <u>donate</u> electrons and stabilize carbocations. In other words, the more methyl groups attached to a carbocation, the more stable it is. That is why the order of carbocation stability is often written as: 3° > 2° > 1°.

In an SN1 mechanism, fluorine destabilizes the carbocation intermediate via induction (**Fig. 5**). Induction refers to the distribution of electrons in sigma bonds and is significantly influenced via the intrinsic electronegativity of atoms. Therefore, the reaction proceeds through an SN1 mechanism and has a rate law that is dependent on the concentration of the electrophile.

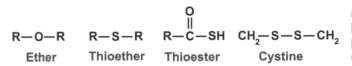

Figure 5. Increasing the fluorine content of FPP derivatives destabilizes the allylic carbocation through induction and reduces the rate of formation of product. The arrows show magnitude and the direction of electron induction.

One important last point to note is that despite the evidence supporting the existence of a carbocation intermediate for farnesylation (i.e. SN1), the sulfur still bonds to the primary carbon of FPP. Why doesn't it react with the other, tertiary carbocation in the resonance structure (**Fig. 3**)? This is most likely due to the fact that the enzyme governing the reaction favors this position due to steric and other effects.

3) **B. thioether bond.** The ROR linkage represents an ether bond and the RSR linkage, which is how cysteine is farnesylated, is called a thioether (depicted in **Fig. 1**). You should be familiar with all of the structures shown in Figure 6. The sulfhydryl linkage, as seen for the side chain of cysteine, is R-SH. As an aside, thioesters, unlike esters, represent high-energy bonds (e.g. acetyl CoA) and the cysteine linkage should be familiar to you from disulfide linkages that form parts of various protein tertiary structures.

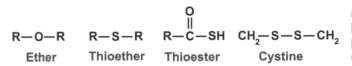

Figure 6. Structure of important sulfur linkages.

4) **A. The FPP analogs should display competitive inhibition with FPP.** The analogs must be able to bind to the active site in order to generate a product whose kinetics can be compared to the behavior with the normal FPP substrate. That is, FPP analogs should be able to compete for active site binding with FPP itself. This is competitive inhibition; **choice A is correct.** Although not absolutely required to answer this question, you should know that competitive inhibition is reversible as an increase in substrate concentration will restore the V_{max} of the reaction (**Fig. 7**).

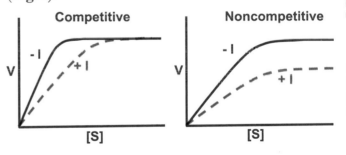

Figure 7. Competitive vs. noncompetitive inhibitors.

That the FPP analogs bind to the active site is clearly seen from the K_m values listed in Figure 2. As K_m is inversely proportional to binding affinity, the analogs actually <u>bind</u> better than FPP itself. Thus, the reduced catalytic rate for the analogs, as observed via the k_{cat} values, is not a consequence of reduced affinity between the modified substrates and the enzyme. The reduced catalytic rate is a consequence of a destabilized carbocation as described above. **Choice B is wrong** because noncompetitive inhibitors do not bind at the active site and this would mean that the FPP analog would not be able to make a product. **This also eliminates choice D** because the analogs clearly do not bind to the enzyme with equal affinity, nor do they need to as discussed. **Choice C is wrong** because the passage states that the substrate utilized is a peptide fluor, indicating that the mechanism of the reaction was used with an unnatural substrate. There is no a priori reason why this substrate should be targeted to the membrane. Moreover, it does not matter because the goal is to understand the mechanism of farnesylation, not how farnesylation is recognized as a target for membrane localization.

5) **B. aspartate with histidine that would decrease enzyme activity.** Figure 2A shows all of the amino acid side chains mentioned in this problem except for lysine. Recall that the side chain of lysine consists of a primary amine functional group that has a +1 charge at physiological pH. This is because the pK_a for lysine is ~10. **Choices A and D are wrong** because the amino acid substitutions generate charges at the zinc center of +1 and -2, respectively. Both choices B and C have net charges of zero at the zinc center after mutagenesis. So how will the activity of the enzyme be affected? The passage is subtle on this, but recall that the net charge of -1 at the zinc center balances thiolate stability with its strong, intrinsic reactivity. In order for the thiolate to function as a nucleophile, it must be released from its coordination to zinc. If the positive charge on the zinc atom is increased by raising the net charge from -1 to 0, the charge on zinc becomes too strong and this sequesters the thiolate nucleophile. The thiolate

is unavailable for farnesylation, and the activity of the enzyme is lowered. Thus, the zinc atom is coordinated with amino acids that "fine tune" its charge so that the nucleophile is stabilized (i.e. its activity is controlled) and can also be released upon substrate binding.

6) **C. 10^{-2}.** This question applies the Henderson-Hasselbalch equation that you will frequently see. Now might be a good time to tattoo this on your arm next to your significant other's name:

$$pH = pK_a + \log [A^-]/[HA].$$

In this case, A^- represents the conjugate base, or S^-, and HA is the conjugate acid, or SH, which is the unionized sulfhydryl side chain of cysteine. Solve for the ratio of $[A^-]/[HA]$ given that the pH = 7.0 and the pK_a = 5.0 (during catalysis, not free cysteine). You know that pK_a is on a log scale, so that a difference of one represents a 10-fold change. By plugging and chugging, you will arrive at $\log [A^-]/[HA]$ = 2. The antilog of 2 is 100, meaning that $[A^-]/[HA]$ = 100/1, or $[HA]/[A^-]$ = .01 There is 100 times more ionized cysteine at this pH than unionized.

As additional information, recall that a deprotonated cysteine side chain acts as a nucleophile in the depicted farnesylation reaction (**Fig. 2**). Why does a cysteine side chain of a free amino acid have a different pK_a than a cysteine residue in a protein? Recall that the environment is what determines the strength of acidity. In this case, the zinc co-factor is driving the reduced pK_a value. By having the active site pK_a much lower, a stronger, charged nucleophile is generated.

PATHWAY

Muscular Dystrophy

Facioscapulohumeral Muscular Dystrophy (FSHD) is unique among repetitive element genetic diseases as it involves the reduction of a subtelomeric region of chromosome four. This repeat region, termed D4Z4, is normally present in 11-100 copies in healthy individuals, but is reduced to <10 in FSHD patients. An individual repeat is 3.2 kb in length and contains a single gene encoding the double homeobox 4 (Dux4) protein, which is normally not expressed in somatic cells. Symptoms manifest typically in the second decade of life and are usually more severe in males.

Recent research has determined that, in addition to reduction in D4Z4 repeats, FSHD is only observed in a genetic background that includes unique sequences flanking the D4Z4 repeat. The specific haplotype, or stable collection of single nucleotide polymorphisms, contains a sequence that functions as a cleavage and polyadenylation signal (PAS) for the terminal Dux4 gene unit. Thus, in individuals with FSHD, both the reduction in D4Z4 repeats and the existence of the permissive haplotype (termed "A") allows for the pathological accumulation of the toxic Dux4 protein in muscle cells (**Fig. 1**).

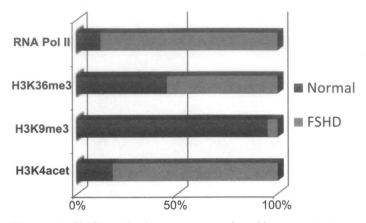

Figure 2. ChIP analysis represented as % present at D4Z4 repeat region.

Investigators hypothesized that a reduction in D4Z4 repeats leads to a local loss in histone H3 lysine (K) modifications that normally cause a transcriptionally silenced state. To test this hypothesis, chromatin immunoprecipitation (ChIP) assays were conducted with antibodies against various modified (trimethylated, me3 or acetylated, acet) lysine side chains of histone H3 to detect changes in their occupancy of the D4Z4 repeats. ChIP assays involve: 1) the treatment of cells with formaldehyde to allow protein-DNA crosslinking; 2) sonication of the cells to fragment DNA; 3) immunoprecipitation of the protein-DNA fragments using antibodies; 4) PCR using specific primers to quantify the associated DNA. The results of ChIP analysis of healthy versus FSHD patient cells are shown in Figure 2.

Figure 1. Model of FSHD molecular pathogenesis. A reduction to <10 repeats in conjunction with haplotype A is required for FSHD.

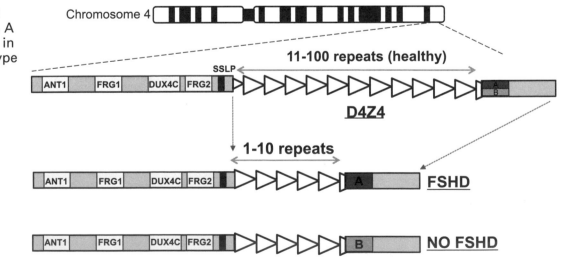

1) **Formaldehyde crosslinking is important in ChIP analysis. Which of the following is true concerning this reaction?**

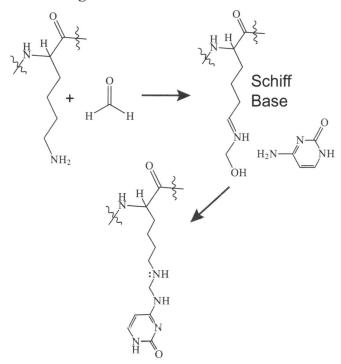

A. Net formal charge is unchanged on the lysine nitrogen and the cytosine is a nucleophile.

B. Net formal charge is unchanged on the cytosine nitrogen and the lysine is a nucleophile.

C. Net formal charge changes by +1 in the lysine nitrogen and the cytosine is a nucleophile.

D. Net formal charge changes by +1 in the cytosine nitrogen and the lysine is a nucleophile.

2) **The best interpretation of the ChIP experimental results is that they:**

A. do not support the hypothesis and suggest that decreased H3K9me3 may mediate transcriptional upregulation.

B. support the hypothesis and suggest that H3K36me3 may mediate transcriptional upregulation.

C. support the hypothesis and suggest decreased H3K9me3 may mediate transcriptional upregulation.

D. do not support the hypothesis and suggest that H3K36me3 may mediate transcriptional upregulation.

3) **Dux4 is a double homeobox protein that is thought to activate transcription initiation. All of the following represent alternative pathways to increase gene expression except the:**

A. stabilization of mRNA by RNA binding proteins.

B. increased efficiency of RNA polymerase elongation.

C. decrease in activity of repressive RNA polymerase elongation factors.

D. increased rate of mRNA decay.

4) **To interpret data in a ChIP assay, all of the following experimental variables must be satisfied except:**

A. equal fragmentation of DNA following sonication.

B. equal levels of isolated DNA/protein crosslinks.

C. antibodies specific for targeted antigens.

D. PCR primers that are the same length.

5) **Can the Southern blot technique using a D4Z4 probe definitively distinguish between healthy and diseased FSHD individuals?**

A. No, because Southern blotting is not specific for DNA.

B. Yes, because the blot will be able to distinguish D4Z4 repeat number.

C. No, because Southern blotting will not determine which haplotype is present.

D. Yes, because the flanking haplotype A will be identified.

6) **Based upon information in the passage, the genetic mode of inheritance of FSHD can be best described as:**

A. sex-linked recessive.

B. autosomal dominant.

C. autosomal recessive.

D. maternal inheritance.

Muscular Dystrophy

Annotations.
1) A 2) C 3) D 4) D 5) C 6) B

	Foundation 1: Gene Expression-B Genetics-C		Foundation 5: Water-A		
	B	**C**		**A**		
Concepts	3					
Reasoning	4	6		1		
Research	5					
Data	2					

Big Picture. This passage is meant to scare you and, let's face it, it is SCARY! Chances are very high that when you read this passage you spent a lot of time just trying to pronounce the disease (FSHD) and obsessing over the diagram. It is not important that you pronounce the name, but what is important is that you get the basic points of the passage. This passage can be broken down into three main parts: 1) the molecular details of FSHD; 2) the hypothesis and the experiment that tested it and; 3) the details of the experimental approach (ChIP).

All of the questions in this passage addressed each of these main points, so it was important to have a basic understanding of them. With respect to point 1, you should have understood that to develop FSHD, an individual requires both the reduction in the D4Z4 repeats AND a poly(A) site flanking the terminal repeat. A second fact was interwoven into the passage and was the idea of a haplotype, which was defined in the passage as a stable collection of SNPs. Point 2 was significantly more camouflaged behind the dense language commonly used by biologists. Specifically, the hypothesis is written as cryptically as possible, but it really is just saying that when the repeats are below 10, there is more transcription at the D4Z4 locus. This increase in transcription is due to a loss in histone H3 post-translational modifications at the lysine position. Finally, point 3 was the ChIP assay and experimental details. This was directly tested in question 4.

1) **A. Net formal charge is unchanged on the lysine nitrogen and the cytosine is a nucleophile.** There is no net change in formal charge of the nitrogen atom in the lysine side chain. Further, the cytosine nitrogen undergoes nucleophilic attack of the Schiff base as per the question. The words "Schiff base" (also known as imide) within the question stem are meant to intimidate you and is not important for answering the question. However, you needed to realize which structure is the lysine and which is the cytosine and then be able to calculate formal charge. The MCAT requires that you have basic familiarity with common and biologically relevant structures. This means for sure you need to know the differences between an amino acid side chain (in proteins) versus a nitrogenous base (in DNA). Note in the labeled diagram below that the formal charge of nitrogen within the lysine (circled in red) goes from 0 to +1 and then back to 0. Thus, there is no net change in charge. Moreover, in the second step of the reaction the amino nitrogen present in cytosine (green) undergoes a nucleophilic attack of the terminal carbon of lysine. The lone pair of electrons in the amino group of cytosine attacks an electrophilic carbon bound to OH. This group leaves as water and generates the cross linked product.

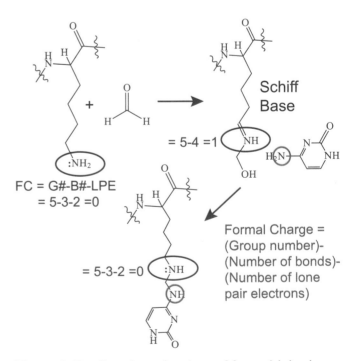

Figure 3. Predicted mechanism of formaldehyde crosslinking.

2) **C. support the hypothesis and suggest decreased H3K9me3 may mediate transcriptional upregulation.** The hypothesis predicts that upon D4Z4 repeat reduction in FSHD patients, there is a local loss in negative histone H3 lysine (K) modifications that normally lead to a transcriptionally silenced state. It is evident from the graph that RNA polymerase II (RNAPII) density is increased in FSHD patients, demonstrating an increase in transcription. This is also supported by the increase in acetylation, a well-described marker for gene activation. Moreover, it is clear from the graph that there is a large reduction in the H3K9me3 modification in the FSHD patient, suggesting that this is the negative H3 lysine modification that normally causes transcriptional repression. Identifying the inverse relationship between RNA polymerase and H3K9me3 was key to the question (**Fig. 4**) Note that H3K36me3 is not appreciably changed between the two states (**Fig. 4**). This fact **ruled out choices B and D**. The data is only supportive of **choice C** as this is the only one that adheres to the details of the experimental findings.

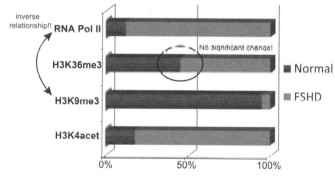

Figure 4. Analysis of ChIP data.

3) **D. increased the rate of mRNA decay.** The stem states that Dux4 is a double homeobox protein, but this is not important for solving the question. For your enrichment, a double homeobox protein contains two homeobox domains (surprising), which are domains that bind to elements within or near the promoters of Hox genes. Hox genes are typically activated during embryogenesis and are known for being involved in limb and body pattern development. Again, this was not important, but we felt we had to say it anyway. What mattered is that you realized that the question was only asking for you to identify a way to DECREASE gene expression. **Choice A**, stabilizing mRNA is a common way to increase gene expression as is **choice B**, which is to make RNAPII more efficient at elongation. **Choice**

C is the double negative of choice B and is therefore synonymous. **Choice D is correct** because increasing the rate of mRNA decay would cause a global reduction in mRNA levels, thereby reducing gene expression.

4) **D. PCR primers that are the same length.** To really get an understanding of this question, it is worth reviewing the basics of ChIP. This technique is no longer considered obscure and it becoming a mainstay in the epigenetics field. The passage did give some basics on the technique, but just enough to give you a general sense. Follow the diagram (**Fig. 5**). Living cells are first treated with formaldehyde to crosslink proteins to DNA. This "freezes" whatever proteins are associated with DNA at the time of chemical addition. The cells are then lysed and subjected to sonication with high-energy sound waves that shear the DNA. An important consideration of this step is to generate a relatively uniform distribution of protein/DNA fragments so that regions of DNA can be isolated that are of equal relative concentration between the two states that will be compared. This eliminates **choices A and B**. A specific antibody is then added to the DNA/protein fragments (**choice C is incorrect**) and is then used for immunoprecipitation (IP). Following the IP step, proteins are digested before DNA purification. The DNA is then subjected to PCR using gene-specific primers. The length of the two primers used in the PCR does not have to be identical, only that they are specific (**choice D is correct**).

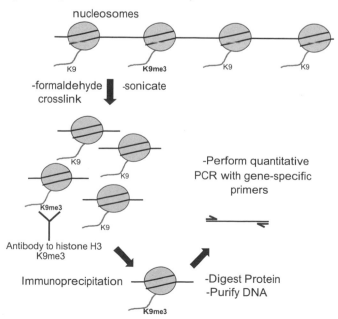

Figure 5. ChIP flow chart.

5) **C. No, because Southern blotting will not determine which haplotype is present.** This question is deceptive and meant to trick you, but it is very fair. Below is a schematic of how a Southern blot would be set up in this case (**Fig. 6**). Genomic DNA that is subjected to restriction digestion is resolved in an agarose gel. This separates DNA fragments based upon their charge-to-mass ratio (i.e. size). Typically, a positive control DNA sequence known to hybridize via complementarity is used as the probe. A negative control will not hybridize to the target sequence. The resolved DNA is transferred to a nitrocellulose membrane and then probed with a radiolabeled probe (typically a smaller piece of DNA). The question stem states that the D4Z4 repeat is used as a probe, so the Southern blot will be able to determine the number of D4Z4 repeats present. However, the use of this probe will not provide any information regarding the <u>haplotype</u> of the individual. Only DNA sequencing will yield that information. Therefore, this technique cannot distinguish between healthy or diseased patients.

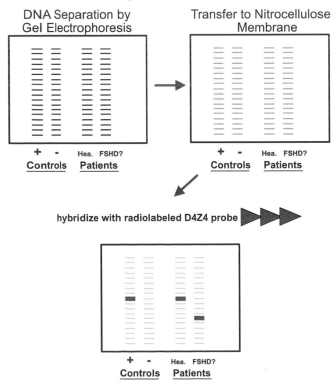

Figure 6. Southern blot technique. Used to test for the presence of a specific DNA sequence (and its size) using a radiolabeled probe. Note that "Hea." refers to a healthy individual and "FSHD?" refers to a candidate patient that may have FSHD.

6) **B. autosomal dominant.** This is a classic example of MCAT misdirection. Note that the passage states that the symptoms of FSHD are usually more severe in males than females. This is an idiosyncratic function of the disease itself and does reflect the genetic inheritance pattern of FSHD. Figure 1 clearly shows that the D4Z4 repeat is located on chromosome 4, as opposed to the X or the Y chromosome. Therefore, it <u>must</u> be autosomal linked. This immediately **rules out choice A**. Given that maternal inheritance is primarily passed on through mitochondrial genomes and that FSHD occurs through changes in chromosome four, **choice D is also incorrect**. This leads to either autosomal dominant or autosomal recessive. There are no further clues in the passage to directly implicate either inheritance pattern. You must therefore use reasoning skills to deduce the more likely form of transmission. Traditionally, autosomal recessive genetic diseases manifest a phenotype when both alleles are deficient in function. Autosomal dominant genetic disorders are most commonly associated with one of the alleles GAINING function. In the case of FSHD, the two molecular genetic changes described in the passage result in the <u>gain in Dux4 expression</u>. This is most consistent with an autosomal dominant pattern and is indeed the case. Therefore, **choice B is the correct answer**.

PATHWAY

Breast Cancer

Replication forks often encounter a "nick" in one DNA strand that represents a single stranded break (SSB). If left unrepaired, DNA replication is terminated at a DNA double-stranded break (DSB). This causes a cell cycle arrest and renders cells sensitive to agents like ionizing radiation.

The PARP enzyme is instrumental in facilitating SSB repair, yet cells lacking PARP are largely normal. Unrepaired SSBs evading PARP regulation are converted into DSBs that are usually repaired by homologous recombination (HR), a process that requires an intact sister chromatid as a template to synthesize new DNA. HR is initiated by Rad51 and completed with the aid of the downstream mediators BRCA1 and BRCA2 (BRCA).

The model in Figure 1 has been proposed. Upon formation of a DSB during S phase, exonuclease activity generates single stranded DNA through re-sectioning of the broken ends and this forms a filamentous complex with the Rad51 protein. This single-stranded DNA structure invades homologous DNA duplexes through the formation of "D loops" whose resolution allows DNA replication re-initiation. Cells defective in HR generate translocations and other potentially lethal structures like dicentric chromosomes.

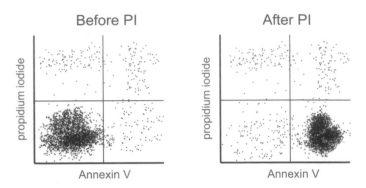

Figure 2. Flow cytometry of BRCA1$^{-/-}$ cells before and after addition of PARP inhibitors (PI). Each pixel represents a cell stained with either propidium iodide and/or Annexin V.

Mutations in the BRCA genes are linked to familial breast cancer. Research into the mechanism of HR has led to the hypothesis that PARP enzyme inhibitors could be used as therapeutic treatment for familial breast cancer. To test this, BRCA1$^{-/-}$ cells were treated with PARP inhibitors (PI) for 72 hours. As a control, BRCA1$^{-/-}$ cells were also collected before treatment. Both samples were prepared for flow cytometry, a technique that identifies DNA content and other markers of interest with antibodies. Both treated and untreated cells were incubated with a fluorescent dye that stained DNA (propidium iodide) and annexin V, an antibody used to detect the lipid phosphatidylserine (PS). Because PS localizes to the cell surface from the inner membrane during apoptosis, it has served as a reliable marker for this process. The data is presented in Figure 2.

Figure 1. Role of DNA repair proteins in DNA repair at a replication fork. Cells evading PARP regulation generate DSBs in S phase that are repaired through homologous recombination. Sister chromatids in red and green. Hatched arrow = aberrant HR.

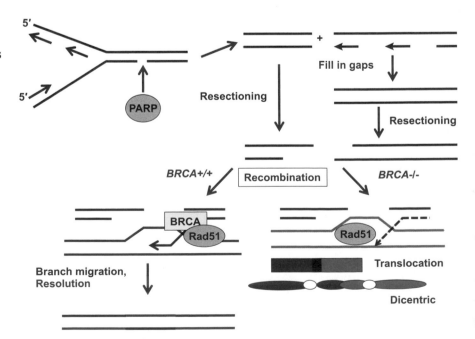

1) **Rad51 is most accurately designated as a:**

   A. tumor suppressor.

   B. oncogene.

   C. pro-apoptotic factor.

   D. DNA replication factor.

2) **In the case of BRCA-mediated repair, DNA resectioning generates a:**

   A. 3′ hydroxyl group by a 5′ to 3′ nuclease.

   B. 5′ phosphate group by a 3′ to 5′ nuclease.

   C. 3′ hydroxyl group by a 3′ to 5′ nuclease.

   D. 5′ hydroxyl group by a 5′ to 3′ nuclease.

3) **In response to the treatment of the cells in Figure 2, which of the following is most likely true?**

   A. Chromosome number increases.

   B. Levels of phosphatidylserine increase.

   C. Levels of translocations increase.

   D. HR frequency increases in BRCA1$^{+/+}$ cells.

4) **In what phase of the cell cycle would HR be most active?**

       I. Mitosis
       II. G1
       III. G2
       IV. S phase

   A. I, II

   B. I, III

   C. II, IV

   D. III, IV

5) **Which of the following is true with respect to the hypothesis concerning PARP inhibitors?**

   A. It is correct because the inhibitors decrease cytotoxic effects of DNA damaging agents.

   B. It is correct because the inhibitors increase cytotoxic effects of DNA damaging agents.

   C. It is incorrect because the inhibitors decrease the efficiency of DSB repair.

   D. It is incorrect because the inhibitors increase the frequency of HR.

6) **Two cell lines lacking p220 or p116 or a control line were treated with ionizing radiation. Based upon the graph below, which of the following is true?**

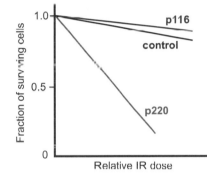

   A. p116 is IR sensitive and DSB repair-deficient.

   B. p220 is IR resistant and DSB repair-deficient.

   C. p116 is IR resistant and BRCA1-deficient.

   D. p220 is IR sensitive and BRCA1-deficient.

Breast Cancer

Annotations.
1) A 2) A 3) C 4) D 5) B 6) D

			Foundation 1: Gene Expression-B Genetics-C		Foundation 2: Cell Physiology-C		
		B	**C**		**C**		
Concepts			4				
Reasoning		3			1		
Research		5,7					
Data		2,6					

Big Picture. Understanding BRCA proteins is an important topic in clinical medicine as well as the MCAT as it involves the fundamental processes of DNA repair and DNA replication. In the presence of PARP inhibitors, the single stranded DNA breaks turn into double stranded DNA breaks (DSBs). These breaks are normally fixed through the process of HR. However, in the absence of BRCA function, the cells perform aberrant DNA repair and generate translocations and dicentric chromosomes. This triggers apoptosis and cell death and is measured in Figure 2. PARP inhibition is not a lethal event, but in the context of BRCA deficiency, it artificially becomes so (**Fig. 3**). In genetics, this phenomenon is called synthetic lethality. In other words, synthetic lethality describes a loss of function that normally isn't lethal to cells that are otherwise normal but when there is a secondary deficiency in a redundant pathway, the genetic loss of function becomes lethal.

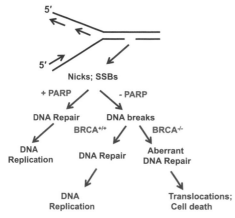

Figure 3. Synthetic lethality with PARP inhibition and aberrant DNA repair in BRCA1$^{-/-}$ cells.

1) **A. tumor suppressor.** Tumor suppressors regulate cell growth division cycles and proliferation and act like "brakes" for the cell cycle. The passage notes that during DSB repair the cell cycle is arrested. As Rad51 is clearly involved in HR, a form of DSB repair, we expect you to deduce that Rad51 is a tumor suppressor. **Choice B is wrong** because oncogenes promote cell growth and can be thought of as the opposite of a tumor suppressive function such as HR.

Rad51 is not a DNA replication factor, but rather functions in HR, a process that is invoked in S phase as a consequence of replication failure due to factors such as DSBs. This **eliminates choice D**. Lastly, **choice C is wrong** because Rad51 is directly engaged in a DNA repair event whose purpose is propagate cells after correction of the DNA damage. Pro-apoptotic factors would be expected to promote cell death.

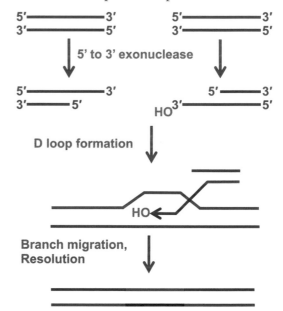

Figure 4. Resectioning to generate a 3' OH group.

2) **A. 3' hydroxyl group by a 5' to 3' nuclease.** From the passage and Figure 1, it is clear that re-sectioning in this case generates a 3' hydroxyl group as this process is designed to facilitate DNA replication during homology-directed repair. Recall that DNA replication must use a 3' OH that is nucleophilic. The only way to generate this structure is through a 5' to 3' exonuclease (**Fig. 4**).

Note that in Figure 1, the 5′ and 3′ ends are labeled only in the initial figure. After the replication fork forms the DSB at the nick, the fragmented DNA is not assigned 5′ and 3′ positions. However, you should know what they are as is diagrammed in Figure 4. Further, if you ever see unlabeled 5′ and 3′ DNA, the convention is to label the top strand with a 5′ on the left and a 3′ on the right.

3) **C. Levels of translocations increase.** The data in the scatter plot of Figure 2 shows two things: 1) the amount of DNA as measured by the propidium iodide signal remains the same after treatment and; 2) the amount of Annexin V staining increases after treatment. The latter is a marker for apoptosis and the passage states that this process increases with translocations. We can infer that the increase in apoptosis after treatment is a consequence of translocations formed during aberrant DNA repair in BRCA$^{-/-}$ cells, making **choice C correct.** As the DNA amount stays the same, there appears to be no increase in chromosome number via treatment; therefore, **choice A is wrong. Choice B is wrong** because the levels of phosphatidylserine (PS) do not change upon treatment, but rather, the location of PS on the outer surface of the cell membrane occurs in response to apoptosis that is induced via treatment with PARP inhibitors. When localized to the inside of the cell, PS cannot be detected with an antibody due to steric effects, but once on the outside of the cell, the PS can be detected. **Choice D is a wrong answer** because the experiment in Figure 2 was performed with BRCA1$^{-/-}$ cells and this tells us nothing about BRCA1$^{+/+}$ cells. The statement, however, is true because PARP inhibition generates DSBs that are repaired via HR (**Figs. 1, 3**).

4) **D. III, IV.** The passage states that HR is "a process that requires an intact sister chromatid as a template to synthesize new DNA." From this it should be clear that this could only occur during DNA replication in S phase and during G2 phase, the point at which the chromosome have been duplicated but not yet segregated in mitosis. **Choice D is the only correct answer.**

HR is a DNA repair process that occurs under an arrested (or "checkpoint induced") cell cycle, primarily in S phase, but also in G2. These are points in the cell cycle where sister chromatid templates are present and HR is active. Since HR uses the sister template, Rad51 is most active during the S/G2 phases of the cell cycle.

5) **B. It is correct because inhibitors increase cytotoxic effects of DNA damaging agents.** The passage states: "Research into the mechanism of HR has led to the hypothesis that PARP enzyme inhibitors could be used as therapeutic treatment for familial breast cancer." In order for the hypothesis to be correct, the inhibitors should kill breast cancer cells. As more apoptosis is observed with Annexin V staining of treated BRCA1$^{-/-}$ cells, this is exactly what is observed through the flow cytometry experiment in Figure 2. This **eliminates choices C and D.** To arrive at the correct answer choice B, think of the PARP inhibitors as a DNA damaging agent because they create DNA damage, namely DNA double stranded breaks (DSBs). When such damage is generated in a BRCA1$^{-/-}$ background, the inhibitors increase cell death, and are therefore cytotoxic. **Choice A is therefore wrong.**

6) **D. p220 is IR sensitive and BRCA1-deficient.** As stated in the passage, defects in proteins involved in DSB repair and HR are often sensitive to agents that damage DNA, including IR. This includes Rad51 and BRCA proteins. As shown in the figure, cells defective in p116 have a very similar IR sensitivity profile to the control cells. That is, they are largely resistant except at higher levels of IR. Thus, p116 cannot be deficient in DSB repair or BRCA1, **eliminating choices A and C. B is eliminated** because BRCA1-deficient cells are IR sensitive, not resistant.

Androgen Receptor

To orchestrate gene transcription with RNA polymerase II function, the termini of the histone tails of histone H3 are methylated at specific lysine (K) residues, including H3K4, H3K27, and H3K36. Methylation of H3K4 is often found near promoters, but methylation at H3K36 is often enriched at the 3′ end of transcribed genes. Thus, H3K36 methylation has been associated with gene activity, and this is in contrast to H3K27. Changes in H3 methylation have been shown to occur in response to hormones such as estrogen and testosterone.

Whsc1 is a methyltransferase thought to link androgen signaling to histone methylation of the androgen target gene XP3A. The protein product of Whsc1 is a histone methyltransferase specific for H3K36. In order to determine the role Whsc1 plays in histone methylation and its relationship to androgen signaling, cell lines defective in Whsc1 function were generated. For this,

the Whsc1 gene was "knocked down" in the LnCaP cell line using the technique of RNA interference. Both control and knockdown LnCaP cells were treated with the synthetic androgen R1881. The effect on gene expression was measured using a quantitative PCR reaction (or real time PCR) and is presented in Figure 1. In qPCR, mRNA is isolated for the generation of complementary DNA (cDNA), which serves as a template for measuring the levels of various genes. In one type of qPCR reaction format, a fluorescent probe hybridizes to the target sequence and emits a signal, that when separated from its quenching agent, is linearly related to the amount of DNA present. The probe is released from the quenching agent due to nucleotide degradation by the elongating DNA polymerase. In each PCR cycle, DNA is exponentially amplified as a function of the PCR amplification efficiency, which can vary significantly for each gene due to a number of experimental factors.

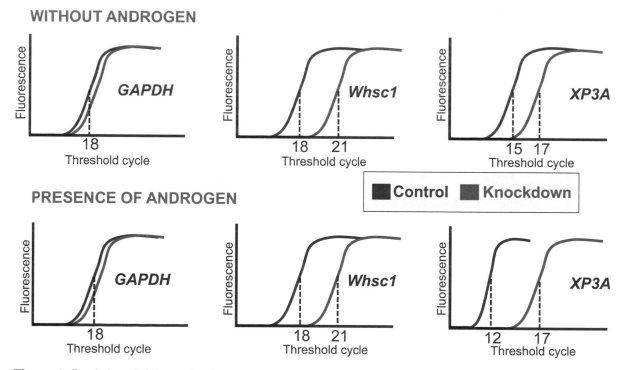

Figure 1. Real time PCR results from three genes for control and knockdown Whsc1 cells in the presence and absence of androgen. GAPDH is a housekeeping gene used as a control. Threshold cycle refers to the cycle of PCR where the probe fluorescence is above threshold and is dependent on the amount of input DNA.

1) Methylation at which of following lysine residues would contribute most to the heterochromatic state?

A. H3K36

B. H3K4

C. H3K27

D. H3K20

2) The enzyme used for qPCR with fluorescent probes as described must possess which type(s) of activity?

      I. 5′ to 3′ exonuclease
     II. 3′ to 5′ exonuclease
    III. 5′ to 3′ polymerase
    IV. 3′ to 5′ primase

A. II, IV

B. III

C. I, III

D. IV

3) In order to directly compare the amount of GAPDH and XP3A qPCR signal fluorescence, which of the following cycling parameters must be equivalent?

A. Relative amplification efficiencies.

B. RNA polymerase used in the reactions.

C. Length of respective primer sequences.

D. % GC content of each primer.

4) From the data presented, it can be inferred that the role of Whsc1 in transcription is to function as a:

A. co-activator of the androgen receptor.

B. co-activator of XP3A.

C. co-repressor of the androgen receptor.

D. co-repressor of XP3A.

5) Which of the following is true with respect to the relative message levels of GAPDH and Whsc1 in control cells?

A. GAPDH > Whsc1.

B. Whsc1 > GAPDH

C. GAPDH = Whsc1

D. Cannot be determined

6) With respect to the data presented, it can be concluded that the amount of Whsc1 transcript left after knockdown is approximately:

A. 3%.

B. 12%.

C. 33%.

D. 50%.

7) LnCaP cells are most likely derived from:

A. liver hepatocytes.

B. prostate epithelium.

C. a kidney adenocarcinoma.

D. pancreatic acinar cells.

Androgen Receptor

Annotations.

1) C 2) C 3) A 4) A 5) D 6) B 7) B

	Foundation 1: Gene Expression-B			Foundation 3: Other Systems-B		
	B			B		
Concepts				7		
Reasoning	1,2					
Research	3					
Data	4,5,6					

Big Picture. This passage portrays an experimental scheme that is very representative of current protocols in molecular biology used for understanding gene function: the combined use of RNA interference (RNAi) and quantitative PCR (qPCR). Fundamental to this passage is an intrinsic understanding of the technique of PCR. Traditional PCR is non-quantitative. However, in this case "real-time," or qPCR is introduced. Questions 2-5 tested your ability to both interpret the data from the experiment and to understand fundamental details of the qPCR technique. To facilitate your understanding, and as a platform for the explanations to follow, we have generated a schematic (**Fig. 2**) outlining the design of qPCR. During the polymerization step of PCR, the polymerase will destroy the probe hybridized to the target DNA, thereby liberating the fluorophore from the quenching agent. The amount of released fluorophore is proportionally related to the amount of input DNA and is measured in qPCR.

1) **C. H3K27.** As fundamental knowledge, you should know that heterochromatin represents transcriptionally silent regions of the genome. Euchromatin is therefore transcriptionally active. This is also referred to at the end of the first paragraph of the passage: "H3K36 methylation has been associated with gene activity, and this in contrast to H3K27." By this logic you can **eliminate choice A**. This reasoning also allows you to identify that H3K27 methylation is reflective of a heterochromatic state, making **choice C the correct answer**. Note that H4K20 is not even mentioned in the passage and that although H3K4 methylation is mentioned, there is no information on its function in transcriptional regulation of chromatin structure (only its presence near promoters).

2) **C. I, III.** All DNA and RNA polymerases synthesize DNA/RNA in a 5' to 3' fashion. This is fundamental knowledge. Therefore, the answer must have statement III in it, **eliminating choices A and D**. This was a particularly important point to realize because the difference between the remaining answer choices B and C is whether or not statement I is valid. To get credit for this question, you no longer had to consider statement II. The validity of statement I can be inferred from the passage: "The probe is released from the quenching agent due to nucleotide degradation by the elongating DNA polymerase." The only way for this to happen is through a 5' to 3' exonuclease activity of the polymerase.

3) **A. Relative amplification efficiencies.** First, realize that DNA polymerases carry out PCR and not RNA polymerases; therefore **choice B is incorrect**. Moreover, the specific properties (e.g. % GC content

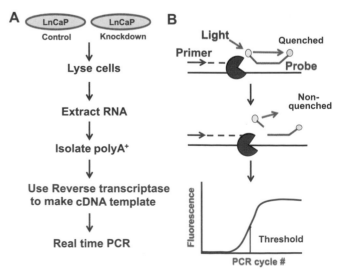

Figure 2. A. RNA interference in LnCaP cells. **B.** Fluorescence-based real time PCR. Only one PCR amplification primer is shown.

42

or their respective lengths) of the two primer sets used to amplify GAPDH and XP3A do not have to be the same. However, they must function the same. Importantly, the GAPDH and XP3A qPCR products, commonly referred to as "amplicons," must be amplified with equal efficiency to make direct comparisons.

Imagine the scenario where starting levels of DNA "X" and "Y" are identical. If amplicon X is amplified twice as efficiently as amplicon Y, then the measured levels of DNA product will always be overestimated by 2-fold. Amplification efficiency is a function of the behavior of PCR reactions that can only be determined experimentally. That is, they cannot be simply predicted from primer properties. Thus, two distinct PCR amplicons (in this case X and Y) could have different amplification efficiencies even though their respective primer pairs have identical lengths and %GC content.

4) **A. co-activator of the androgen receptor.** The passage states that, "Whsc1 is a methyltransferase thought to link androgen signaling to histone methylation of the androgen target gene XP3A." Based upon this statement, **choices B and D can be ruled out** because XP3A is a target gene and therefore highly unlikely to be a co-activator or co-repressor.

Below, Figure 3 encapsulates the important data to answer this question. Notice that the addition of androgen lowers the threshold cycle number for

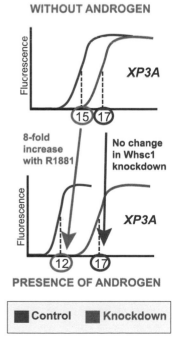

WITHOUT ANDROGEN

PRESENCE OF ANDROGEN

Control ■ Knockdown

Figure 3. Whsc1 regulates the inducible expression of XP3A in response to androgen.

XP3A. Therefore, its expression is induced by androgen 2^3, or 8-fold. These results demonstrate that XP3A is an androgen-inducible gene. Also, notice that this induction fails to occur when Whsc1 is depleted via knockdown. This counterintuitive relationship between threshold cycle number and input DNA levels is fundamental in qPCR. In conclusion, the most parsimonious interpretation is that Whsc1 regulates the androgen-inducible expression of XP3A. Note that this is the definition of a transcriptional co-activator. Therefore, **choice A is the correct answer.**

5) **D. Cannot be determined.** This question tested similar logic to question 3 but was pitched in a different way. As explained for question 3, a direct comparison between two different amplicons is only possible if their amplification efficiencies are identical. What makes this question exceedingly challenging is the data leads you to believe that GAPDH and Whsc1 have identical expression levels because they have the same threshold cycle. This point is further bolstered by the passage statement: "In each PCR cycle, DNA is exponentially amplified as a function of the PCR amplification efficiency, which can vary significantly for each gene due to a number of experimental factors." Therefore, although both GAPDH and Whsc1 amplicons reached threshold at cycle 18, this does not mean that their expression levels are equivalent.

6) **B. 12%.** The levels of Whsc1 mRNA are lower in the knockdown by three cycles (**Fig. 1**). As stated in the passage, "In each PCR cycle, DNA is exponentially amplified...", therefore, a difference of three cycles represents a $2^3 - 8$ fold decrease in Whsc1 mRNA levels. An 8-fold reduction is tantamount to 12.5% remaining, thus, **choice B is the credited answer.**

7) **B. prostate epithelium.** Recall that the prostate is a walnut-sized organ that lies below the bladder and next to the urethra and contributes to the formation of sperm. The LnCaP cells respond to androgen as the XP3A gene is induced by R1881 (a synthetic form of testosterone). You should know that androgens (such as testosterone) are male hormones and are active in the male urogenital tract. Therefore, LnCaP cells must be derived from tissue that actively expresses the androgen receptor. Thus, **choice B is the correct answer** as the other choices are not male-specific.

Yeast Secretory Genetics

Scientists used yeast genetics to identify a collection of temperature sensitive mutants deficient in the process of secretion. Analyses of the individual mutant genes, described below, collectively delineated the secretion pathway and ultimately won the Nobel Prize in medicine for Schekman and colleagues.

Table 1. To identify genes involved in secretion, a genetic screen was conducted to isolate yeast with loss of function mutations. Following clonal isolation of individual haploid mutants, pairwise crossing was conducted to determine the number of individually affected genes, also known as complementation groups. The resultant diploids were screened for invertase activity, which is a secreted enzyme that hydrolyzes sucrose.

Table 2. Once the secretion complementation groups (Sec) were established, microscopic assessment of organelle morphology was undertaken to characterize the nature of the defect for each mutant. Morphologies were classified based upon the most pronounced, abnormal phenotypes: exaggerated endoplasmic reticulum (ER), so-called Berkeley bodies (BB), and small vesicles (Ves).

Table 3. Finally, a series of double mutant diploids was constructed and the morphological phenotypes were analyzed to determine the order of events in yeast secretion based upon genetic epistatic relationships. The phenotypes of the double mutants were then recorded with respect to their morphological defect.

	#1	#2	#3	#4	#5	#6
#1	-	+	+	+	+	-
#2	+	-	-	+	+	+
#3	+	-	-	+	+	+
#4	+	+	+	-	+	+
#5	+	+	+	+	-	+
#6	-	+	+	+	+	-

Table 1. Invertase secretion of diploids generated from single mutant crosses. + and – refer to ability to secrete or not secrete invertase.

Allele	Structure
Sec1-1	Ves
Sec12-4	ER
Sec20-1	ER
Sec14-3	BB
Sec13-1	ER
Sec4-2	Ves
Sec9-3	Ves
Sec7-1	BB

Table 2. Sec mutant phenotypes.

	Sec1-1	Sec12-4	Sec20-1	Sec14-3	Sec13-1	Sec4-2	Sec9-3	Sec7-1
Sec1-1	X	ER	ER	BB	ER	Ves	Ves	BB
Sec12-4	ER	X	ER	ER	ER	ER	ER	ER
Sec20-1	ER	ER	X	ER	ER	ER	ER	ER
Sec14-3	BB	ER	ER	X	ER	BB	BB	BB
Sec13-1	ER	ER	ER	ER	X	ER	ER	ER
Sec4-2	Ves	ER	ER	BB	ER	X	Ves	BB
Sec9-3	Ves	ER	ER	BB	ER	Ves	X	BB
Sec7-1	BB	ER	ER	BB	ER	BB	BB	X

Table 3. Crosses and resulting phenotypes from yeast secretion mutants.

1) The process of yeast meiosis generates four haploid progeny from a:

A. diploid cell via reductive division.

B. haploid cell via non-reductive division.

C. diploid cell via non-reductive division.

D. haploid cell via reductive division.

2) The number of individual genetic loci represented by the clones in Table 1 is:

A. 2

B. 4

C. 8

D. 10

3) Invertase activity can be assayed from cell culture media after centrifugation. When assayed at the non-permissive temperature, sporulation of a cross between the Sec4-2 mutant and a wild type strain would be expected to yield:

A. 0 spores with high supernatant glucose.

B. 4 spores with low supernatant glucose.

C. 2 spores with high supernatant glucose.

D. 0 spores with low supernatant glucose.

4) Why did Schekman identify temperature sensitive mutations in the secretory pathway?

A. Secretion is only required at high temperature.

B. Secretory mutants are temperature sensitive.

C. Secretion is sensitive to temperature.

D. Secretory genes are essential.

5) The epistasis experiments are most consistent with the following directional flow of proteins through the secretory pathway:

A. ER → vesicles → Berkeley bodies → cell surface

B. Vesicles → ER → Berkeley bodies → cell surface

C. ER → Berkeley bodies → vesicles → cell surface

D. Berkeley bodies → ER → vesicles → cell surface

6) Which statement best describes the phenotype of secretory mutant Sec13-1?

A. ER-derived vesicles are not fusing with the cell surface.

B. Invertase is trapped at an early stage of the secretion process.

C. Invertase is trapped in the Golgi due to lack of sucrose modification.

D. The ER is failing to re-absorb membrane and proteins.

7) As the Benedict's test measures the presence of reducing sugars, it can be used to measure invertase activity. Samples proficient in invertase activity would produce the reducing sugar glucose and the:

A. reducing sugar galactose.

B. non-reducing sugar galactose.

C. reducing sugar fructose.

D. non-reducing sugar fructose.

Yeast Secretory Genetics

Annotations.

1) A 2) B 3) C 4) D 5) C 6) B 7) C

	Foundation 1: Genetics-C Metabolism-D			Foundation 5: Biomolecules-D		
	C	**D**		**D**		
Concepts	1					
Reasoning	5	6		7		
Research	4					
Data	2,3					

Big Picture. This passage focuses on how the budding yeast, Saccharomyces cerevisiae, can be used as a genetic tool for studying protein secretion. The use of this model organism has been exploited in numerous genome-wide settings to catalog relevant protein contributions to cellular processes, many of which are very similar to human biology.

You should be familiar with the fundamentals of the secretory pathway (**Fig. 1**), from the recognition of signal sequences by signal recognition particle (SRP) to the vectorial processing of secretory proteins from the ER and Golgi into secretory vesicles poised for membrane exocytosis. This passage tests this by presenting genetic data, the type that was used to experimentally determine the mechanism of protein secretion. One wrinkle is the "Berkeley body," a term you have probably not heard of. If you just follow the data, you can estimate its position within the secretory pathway.

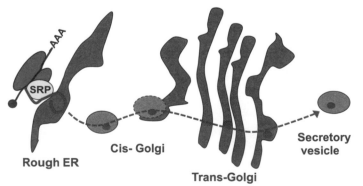

Figure 1. Directional flow of proteins in the secretory pathway.

1) **A. diploid cell via reductive division.** This question requires an understanding of genetic terminology. It was not essential that you had a specific, prior understanding of yeast meiosis, but rather, general knowledge of human meiosis was enough. In humans, meiosis initiates from a diploid cell and concludes with four haploid gametes. This fact could have been readily applied to yeast. In addition, the concept of reductive vs. non-reductive cell division is an important factor distinguishing mitosis (non-reductive) from meiosis (reductive) and was not discussed in the passage. This is fundamental material and is shown below (**Fig. 2**).

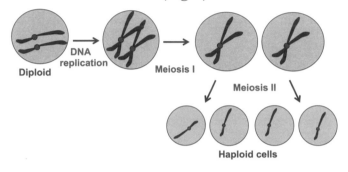

Figure 2. Generation of four haploid progeny from a diploid cell via reductive meiotic division.

2) **B. 4.** This question dealt with Table 1 and tested your ability to interpret complementation crossing. While the concept of complementation is a staple in most undergraduate genetics courses, it is a commonly misunderstood principle. Before tackling this problem, consider a simpler scenario: two genes encoding proteins involved in secretion (gene A and gene B). Suppose that a yeast strain has a temperature-sensitive mutation in gene A (and hence is annotated as "a" for that gene), but is otherwise wild-type for gene B. The genotype of this haploid yeast is therefore: aB. Further suppose that a second yeast strain has the reverse genotype and is: Ab. If the two haploids are mated to form a diploid, then the resultant diploid genotype would be: AaBb. In this case, the diploid would not exhibit a temperature-sensitive secretion defect. This is because the two strains of yeast are said to complement each other's mutations (**Fig. 3, left panel**).

Now, consider the alternative situation where there are two haploid mutant yeast strains, each having a mutation in gene A but otherwise wild-type for gene B. The haploid genotypes would therefore both be aB and a mating between these two haploids results in a diploid with the genotype: aaBB. Given its homozygous recessive state, this diploid yeast strain would exhibit a temperature-sensitive secretion defect. Thus, these two haploid strains would FAIL to complement each other (**Fig. 3, right panel**).

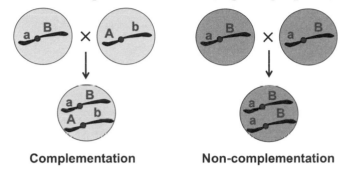

Complementation   **Non-complementation**

Figure 3. Yeast Complementation.

From the data in Table 1, we can see that crosses between Clones 1 and 6 as well as 2 and 3 (note reciprocal behavior) are non-complementing, resulting in 4 independent groups. This makes **choice B correct**. Note that the total number of minus signs in the table (10) is not a correct answer, making **choice D incorrect**. This is because a cross between haploids with the same mutation will never complement thereby removing all "self-crossing" haploids from consideration.

Experimentally, the reason that these types of analyses are conducted is to determine the number of different (and distinct) genes involved in a common pathway. In this question, mutations that are in separate secretory genetic loci will complement each other and exhibit wild-type behavior (phenotype) due to being heterozygous (**Fig. 3**).

3) **C. 2 spores with high supernatant glucose.** Keeping in mind that spores are haploid gametes, this question requires an understanding of the test cross between the Sec4-2 and wild-type strains combined with inferring the activity of invertase from the glucose levels. A recessive phenotype crossed to a wild-type strain is a classic example of a "test cross." The concept of a test-cross is a fundamental genetic concept; two haploids (wild-type = "Sec$^+$" and Sec mutant = "Sec$^-$") mate to form a (Sec$^+$/Sec$^-$)

diploid undergoing meiosis (**Fig. 2**). Given Mendelian inheritance, this will result in two Sec$^+$ and two Sec$^-$ spores. This logic could have already **ruled out choices A, B, and D**. The two Sec- spores will have low amounts of secreted invertase and therefore low glucose levels in the medium supernatant. This further **rules out choices B and D**.

4) **D. Secretory genes are essential.** The idea of temperature sensitive mutations represents a key breakthrough in the study of gene function. This is because it allows the researcher to explore the implications of a loss of function mutation in a gene that is essential for viability. If a gene encodes an essential function (i.e. required for life), then, by definition, any loss of function mutation in that gene will kill the organism, disallowing the researcher to study anything at all! Dead yeast tell no tales. However, if a mutation can be isolated that only exhibits a loss of function at non-physiological temperatures – but does not affect gene function at normal temperatures – then the scientist can use the temperature change as a way to keep the organism alive. This discussion justifies why **choice D is the credited answer**. Some of the other answer choices are representative of a challenging MCAT question architecture: non-credited answers can be true statements that do not actually answer the question. These can be very hard to avoid. For example, secretion is likely to be temperature sensitive but this does not explain why isolating temperature-sensitive mutations was a necessity, making **choice C a non-credited answer**. Further, the secretory mutants isolated are temperature sensitive (by definition), but this fails to explain why they were isolated in this fashion to begin with. This means that **choice B is also not credited**. Finally, **choice A is wrong** because secretion is not restricted to occur only at high temperatures.

5) **C. ER → Berkeley bodies → vesicles → cell surface.** The question tests your ability to discern patterns in results. The concept of epistasis is a fundamental principle of genetics that even the most seasoned geneticist can screw up! Although there are eight alleles to consider, there are only three different phenotypes as shown in Table 2. The key is to consider all of the pairwise combinations and to identify which phenotypes "win" a biological version of rock, scissors, and paper. This can be played with the

crosses in Table 3. In this case: ER always "wins out" over BB and vesicles, BB only beats vesicles, and vesicles beat nothing. For example, observe from Table 3 that a cross between Sec1-1 (phenotype ER) and Sec14-3 (phenotype BB) gives a phenotype of ER. This is because the events in the ER precede those that use the BB (derived from Golgi) in protein secretion.

There are two ways to arrive at the correct in this problem: (1) use the above rules or (2) rank the most prevalent phenotypes. For example, notice that the "ER" phenotype appears the most often. This is because a defect in secretion that manifests as an exaggerated ER phenotype (e.g. Sec 12-4, both across and down in Table 3) will be "upstream" of all other possible phenotypes. This is the very definition of the term epistatic. Using either of these strategies supports **choice C as being correct**.

6) **B. Invertase is trapped at an early stage of the secretion process.** From Table 2, we can see that Sec13-1 mutants have an "exaggerated ER." None of the answer choices referenced this term directly so you had to infer its meaning, and then apply that inferred meaning to the answer choices. This is a common theme on the MCAT and is challenging because you had to generate your own interpretation and run with it. Let's just say that "exaggerated ER" translates to an enlarged ER that is very easy to see using microscopy. You now have to determine how well the answer choices supported this inference. **Choice A is not credited** because if ER-derived vesicles were being produced and not fusing with the membrane, then this would be expected to result in the accumulation of vesicles, not an "exaggerated ER." **Choice C is not credited** because the passage associated invertase with sucrose as its substrate and not as a modification. Finally, **choice D is not credited** because if the ER were failing to reabsorb membrane and proteins, the resultant ER phenotype would be "diminished" and not "exaggerated." Conversely, an enlarged ER phenotype would predict a buildup in ER-mediated secreted proteins (e.g. invertase), making **choice B the credited answer**.

7) **C. reducing sugar fructose.** From the passage, invertase hydrolyzes sucrose, which is a disaccharide composed of glucose and fructose. This **eliminates choices A and B**. Recall that galactose is a reducing sugar as it is an epimer of glucose. Epimers are diastereomers (molecules with 2 or more chiral centers) that differ in configuration at only one chiral carbon; carbon 4 in the case of glucose and galactose (**Fig. 4**).

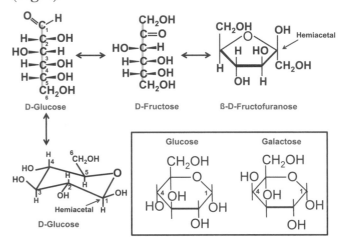

Figure 4. Interconversion of glucose into fructose and difference between glucose and galactose.

Ok, so now what are reducing sugars? Short answer: they contain free aldehydes that can be oxidized into carboxylic acids. Fructose is a reducing sugar because it can be converted into glucose, which contains an aldehyde. **Choice C is correct**. While the conversion of fructose into glucose can occur spontaneously, recall that in glycolysis, glucose-6 phosphate is enzymatically converted into fructose 6-phosphate.

As the Benedict's reaction is specific to aldehydes (shown below) it will detect not only reducing sugars, but also other aldehyde-containing molecules. Beware: if a non-reducing sugar is dissolved in an aldehyde-containing solvent, a false positive result will occur.

$CuSO_4$ + aldehyde → Cu_2O + carboxylic acid

In the reaction, the soluble blue copper (II) is reduced into a red, insoluble Cu2O precipitate that is readily detected.

Fat Synthesis

Insulin expedites the oxidation of glucose into acetyl CoA (AcCoA). If AcCoA is incapable of being oxidized in the TCA cycle, then carbon skeletons accumulate as citrate, a carbon precursor transported into the cytosol for fatty acid synthesis (**Fig. 1**). Increased levels of fats and triglycerides positively correlate with obesity and are believed to be causal for insulin resistance, a condition linked to type II diabetes. Insulin activates tyrosine kinase signaling and insulin resistance occurs when more insulin is required to achieve the same biological response relative to normal conditions. This is assessed through glycogen synthase activity in muscle.

In addition to glucose, fructose exerts its lipogenic functions through its role in glycolysis and its ability to influence gene expression. Fructose stimulates feeding behavior, possibly through increased resistance to leptin.

To examine the relationship between fructose and insulin resistance, researchers posited that LIP23, a fructose-induced gene, regulates the synthesis of key metabolites in a fructose-dependent manner. Cohorts of normal or LIP23-deficient (LIP23$^{-/-}$) mice were examined for muscle glycogen synthase activity in a high fructose diet. In parallel, other groups of mice were fed normal diets or ones enriched in fructose in the presence of ^{14}C–acetate for 16 weeks prior to determining the serum levels of various metabolites (**Fig. 2**).

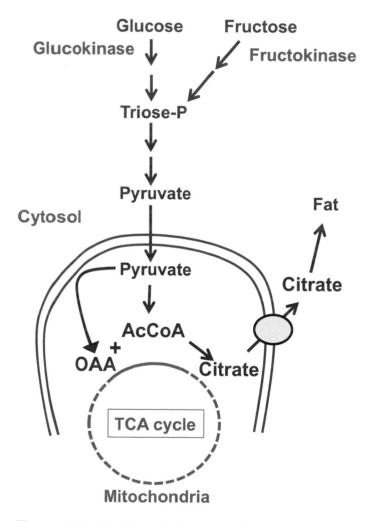

Figure 1. Metabolism of glucose and fructose and their role in fat synthesis. Citrate transporter is shown in yellow.

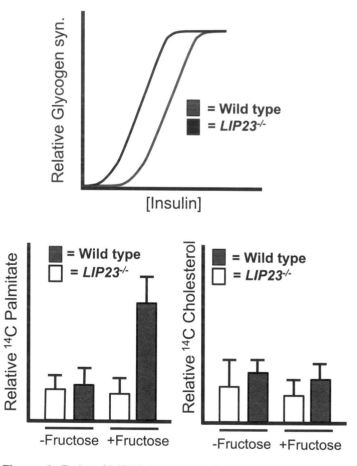

Figure 2. Role of LIP23 in metabolism. Top, Glycogen synthase activity in LIP23$^{+/+}$ and LIP23$^{-/-}$ samples on high fructose diet. Bottom: Relative palmitate and cholesterol levels in LIP23$^{+/+}$ and LIP23$^{-/-}$ samples. Experiments repeated three times and plotted. Standard deviations are shown.

1) **Which of the following would contribute the most towards fatty acid synthesis?**

A. Increased rate of OAA reduction to malate.

B. Decreased rate of isocitrate oxidation.

C. Increased rate of lactate formation.

D. Decreased rate of pyruvate oxidation.

2) **In wild-type mice, in the absence of fructose:**

A. glucose inhibits tyrosine kinase signaling.

B. cholesterol synthesis decreases.

C. LIP23 levels decrease.

D. mitochondrial citrate transport increases.

3) **In response to fructose, LIP23 promotes insulin:**

A. resistance and hypotriglyceridemia.

B. resistance and hypertriglyceridemia.

C. sensitivity and hypotriglyceridemia.

D. sensitivity and hypertriglyceridemia.

4) **A loss of function mutation in a gene encoding which of the following could shift the activity profile of glycogen synthase as shown below?**

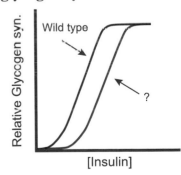

A. fatty acid synthase

B. fructokinase

C. citrate synthase

D. insulin receptor

5) **A reduction in the levels of which of the following could best contribute to obesity in LIP23-deficient mice?**

A. neuropeptide Y

B. leptin

C. cortisol

D. glucagon

6) **DNA sequencing would reveal that the LIP23 gene encodes a protein that is most likely:**

A. isocitrate dehydrogenase.

B. glycogen synthase.

C. fatty acyl dehydrogenase.

D. a citrate transporter.

7) **The most direct precursor to cholesterol in its biosynthetic pathway is:**

A. pyruvate.

B. citrate.

C. acetyl CoA.

D. glucose.

8) **Which of the following comparisons between wild-type and LIP23-deficient mice is the least important in the design and interpretation of the experiment?**

A. Equivalent production of chylomicrons.

B. Equivalent serum leptin levels.

C. Equivalent ingestion of fructose.

D. Equivalent levels of succinate dehydrogenase.

Fat Synthesis

Annotations.
1) B 2) C 3) B 4) D 5) B 6) D 7) C 8) A

	Foundation 1: Metabolism-D			Foundation 3: Neurobiology-A		
	D			**A**		
Concepts	1,7			5		
Reasoning	2,3,6					
Research	8					
Data				4		

Big Picture. This passage introduces the notion of "insulin resistance" and tests your ability to apply it to basic metabolic concepts in introductory biochemistry. As fundamental knowledge, you know that insulin promotes anabolic pathways such as the synthesis of fatty acids, triglycerides, glycogen and cholesterol. Further, it was important to have foundational understanding of how glucose and fructose oxidation impacts other processes, notably fatty acid synthesis.

A key element of the passage is to understand how to interpret the sigmoidal curve. Note that as the curve shifts to the right, <u>more</u> insulin is required to achieve the <u>same</u> level of glycogen synthase activity (**Fig. 3**). This is insulin resistance.

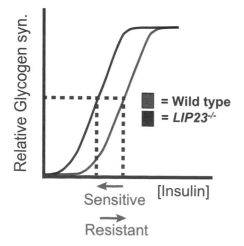

Figure 3. Insulin resistance and sensitivity as a function of LIP23. A shift to the right increases the levels of insulin required to achieve the same biological end point (i.e. 50% glycogen synthase activity) as wild-type conditions. A shift to the left causes the opposite effect: insulin sensitivity.

1) B. Decreased rate of isocitrate oxidation. When mitochondrial citrate levels are high, citrate is transported into the cytosol where it serves as a substrate in fatty acid synthesis. An increase in citrate is driven by several possible factors including excessive AcCoA (**Fig. 4**). Decreasing isocitrate dehydrogenase activity would elevate mitochondrial citrate levels by preventing the oxidation of isocitrate in the Krebs cycle. This block in TCA oxidation allows for citrate to be transported into the cytoplasm where it is utilized for the de novo synthesis of fatty acids. By slowing down the TCA cycle, citrate is shunted through Le Chatelier's principle to the cytoplasm and then used as substrate in fatty acid synthesis. This makes **choice B correct**.

In Figure 1, citrate has two fates: A) conversion into fat and; B) oxidation in the TCA cycle. Citrate is isomerized to isocitrate and this is subsequently oxidized to α-ketoglutarate. This is not explicitly shown in Figure 1, but you should recall this basic TCA knowledge. **Choice A is wrong** because the conversion of OAA into malate will produce less citrate. This "reverse" step in the TCA cycle occurs during gluconeogenesis. **Choice C is wrong** because increasing lactate production reduces pyruvate. Pyruvate forms the carbon backbone for conversion into AcCoA and then citrate. Finally, **choice D is wrong** (and should be viewed as being really the same as choice C): decreasing pyruvate oxidation provides less carbon for the generation of AcCoA and citrate.

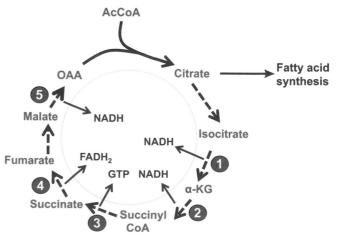

Figure 4. TCA cycle showing the five steps that generate reducing power and GTP.

2) C. LIP23 levels decrease. From the passage, "…researchers posited that LIP23, a fructose-induced gene, regulates the synthesis of key metabolites…" Therefore, in the absence of fructose, there would be less LIP23 expressed, corresponding to lower protein levels. This makes **choice C correct**.

Glucose would activate tyrosine kinase signaling indirectly through insulin, thereby **impeaching choice A**. From the data shown in Figure 2 (and below in Figure 5), the levels of cholesterol were equivalent (after taking into consideration the error bars) between both groups of mice. Therefore **choice B is incorrect. Choice D is incorrect** because, in the absence of fructose, there is less fatty acid synthesis as measured by ^{14}C palmitate. This is indicative of less citrate being exported from the mitochondria into the cytosol (**Fig. 5**).

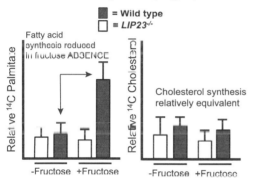

Figure 5. Fructose induces fatty acid synthesis but has no affect on cholesterol synthesis.

3) B. resistance and hypertriglyceridemia. Figure 2 shows a dose response curve between levels of secreted insulin and their corresponding influence on the activity of muscle glycogen synthase. Recall that insulin promotes glycogen synthesis in the muscle and liver, making glycogen synthase testing an effective diagnostic. Note that a rightward shift in the curve represents an increase in "insulin resistance," the biological phenomenon where more insulin is required to achieve the same response. The opposite, a left shift, is therefore indicative of the increased insulin sensitivity (**Fig. 3**). As shown in the Big Picture, LIP23-deficient mice exhibit a leftward shift and are therefore insulin sensitive. This is interpreted to mean that LIP23 normally functions in a process that contributes to insulin resistance in a high fructose diet. Therefore, **choices C and D are eliminated**.

The bottom panels of Figure 2 also show that LIP23-deficient mice generate less palmitate than wild-type mice in the presence of fructose. As palmitate is incorporated into triglycerides, the data suggests that LIP23 also promotes hypertriglyceridemia. Therefore, **choice B is correct**.

4) D. insulin receptor. Notice that the mutation in the gene (marked by "?" in figure in question stem) causes a rightward shift, or, as shown in Figure 3, generates insulin resistance. This can be readily explained by a mutation in the insulin receptor (**choice D is correct**). For example, imagine that a point mutation in the receptor caused a reduction in its binding affinity for insulin. The lower affinity for ligand would require that, in order to reach the "normal" signaling output, a higher insulin concentration would be necessary for appropriate receptor-ligand signaling to occur. **Choice B is wrong** because the inability to phosphorylate and activate fructose through a fructokinase mutation would neutralize the lipogenic potential of fructose because no substrate for fat synthesis would be available from fructose metabolism. Further, note that the question does not involve the use of a high fructose diet (in contrast to what is presented in the passage). If either the genes encoding citrate synthase or fatty acid synthase are mutated, then there will also be no substrate available to make fat. As the passage discusses the positive correlation between fat and insulin resistance, this makes **choices A and C incorrect**.

Although not required to answer the question, you should be able to recall the basic mechanism of how insulin receptor signaling occurs through tyrosine phosphorylation. This is because tyrosine kinases are important signaling molecules that are often mutated and function as oncogenes. Although each one activates a different pathway, there are some common features to this mode of signaling. The insulin receptor is a classical tyrosine kinase-signaling molecule (**Fig. 6**).

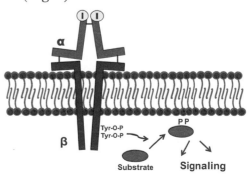

Figure 6. Insulin (I) receptor signaling.

Fat Synthesis

Arranged as two heterodimers held together by disulfide bridges, the α subunit binds to insulin, causing a conformational change in the β subunit. This change allows for the insulin receptor to autophosphorylate on tyrosine residues, a common theme in tyrosine kinase signaling. The phosphorylated insulin receptor can then act as a tyrosine kinase to phosphorylate other substrates that are involved in insulin regulation.

5) B. leptin. The passage mentions that fructose stimulates feeding behavior, possibly through increased resistance to leptin. Leptin therefore inhibits feeding behavior, meaning that reduced levels of leptin will increase the duration of hunger in animals (**Fig. 7**). A decrease in leptin will increase the amount of food consumed and would be expected to increase body weight leading to obesity.

Leptin is a small protein hormone secreted by adipose tissue and is important for regulating body mass. Leptin-deficient mice are famously obese and have very strong appetites, meaning that leptin inhibits feeding behavior. One way this is thought to occur is by inhibiting Neuropeptide Y (NPY), a factor that promotes feeding (**Fig. 7**). Therefore, **choice A is wrong** as reducing NPY levels would not promote feeding, and would be expected to reduce body mass. **Choice C is wrong** because cortisol is a stress hormone and low blood sugar is a form of stress. As low blood sugar triggers hunger and promotes feeding behavior, low cortisol levels would attenuate this. Therefore, cortisol promotes feeding behavior and a lack of cortisol would reduce body mass. **Choice D is wrong** because glucagon, in a manner analogous to cortisol, is released in response to low blood sugar. Always think of glucagon as acting in the liver and doing the opposite of insulin.

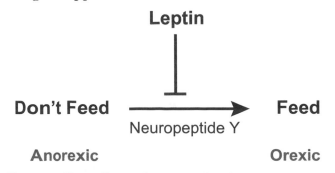

Leptin

Don't Feed ⟶ Feed

Neuropeptide Y

Anorexic   Orexic

Figure 7. The adipose hormone leptin suppresses neuropeptide Y (NPY) and reduces appetite.

6) D. a citrate transporter. We know that LIP23 promotes insulin resistance (**Fig. 2**) and this correlates with obesity. Additionally, the data in the passage shows that in the presence of fructose, LIP23 promotes fat synthesis as measured by ^{14}C incorporation into palmitic acid (**Fig. 8**). Be careful interpreting the graph as the deduction that LIP23 promotes fat synthesis is based upon the graph showing that <u>in the absence</u> of LIP23 there is <u>reduced levels</u> of ^{14}C-palmitic acid! This observation is consistent with LIP23 encoding a citrate transporter as is shown in yellow in Figure 1. One additional clue comes from the passage: citrate is "a carbon precursor transported into the cytosol for fatty acid synthesis." **Choice A is wrong** because isocitrate dehydrogenase would oxidize citrate, making less carbon available for fatty acid synthesis. Glycogen synthase, the answer in **choice B, is wrong** because the conversion of glucose-6 phosphate into glycogen will reduce the carbon available for conversion into pyruvate and then AcCoA. **Choice C is wrong** because fatty acyl dehydrogenases function in the oxidation of fats, not their synthesis. You should recall that the term "dehydrogenase" means taking away hydrogen atoms and their electrons, another name for oxidation.

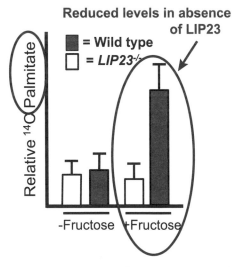

Figure 8. LIP23 promotes fat synthesis in the presence of fructose.

7) C. acetyl CoA. Acetyl CoA (or AcCoA in this passage) is the most direct precursor to cholesterol as shown in Figure 9. One clue comes from the passage in the experimental description. Recall that radiolabeled acetate was used, yet both ^{14}C-palmitate and ^{14}C-cholesterol were measured. This implies that acetate is converted into cholesterol. Of course acetate is converted into AcCoA, making **choice C the correct answer**.

AcCoA is turned into "isoprene" units known as isopentyl-pyrophosphate (PP) and dimethylallyl pyrophosphate. These fundamental building blocks are used in condensation reactions to generate geranyl-PP and farnseyl-PP. Although we do not elaborate further here, isoprene units are known as terpenes and their biochemistry is important as inhibitors in this pathway (called statins) are commonly used to lower cholesterol in at risk patients. We have also discussed isoprenoid units in the context of cysteine farnesylation.

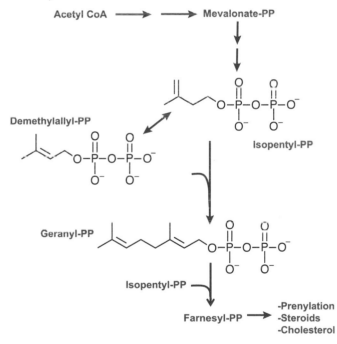

Figure 9. Synthesis of cholesterol and steroids from AcCoA and terpene intermediates.

8) A. Equivalent production of chylomicrons. Recall that chylomicrons are protein-lipid particles that are synthesized in the intestine from dietary lipids. They also contain cholesterol. The production of chylomicrons in this case is not germane to the analysis because they are <u>downstream</u> of cholesterol synthesis. Because the study involves insulin and fructose and discusses the role of fructose in feeding behavior, it is important to control feeding behavior to interpret any results properly. Therefore, one important factor is to assess the serum leptin levels in wild-type and LIP23-deficient mice. We have already discussed the role of leptin in feeding (**Fig. 7**). By extension, the levels of fructose ingestion are also important to control. Therefore, **choices B and C are incorrect**. Equivalent levels of succinate dehydrogenase, a TCA cycle enzyme (**Fig. 4**) are an important factor to consider as failure to oxidize carbon in the TCA cycle would hinder carbon flux through TCA and promote fat synthesis through the accumulation of citrate. This makes **choice D incorrect**.

Glycogen Metabolism

In a coordinated fashion, pancreatic hormones regulate glycogen synthesis and degradation. For example, insulin stimulates glycogen synthase, whereas glucagon (and epinephrine) stimulates the activity of glycogen phosphorylase. In contrast to insulin, glucagon or epinephrine activate protein kinase A to regulate downstream targets (**Fig. 1**).

To study the hormonal regulation of glycogen, Salbutamol, a drug specific for the ß-adrenergic receptor, was given to rodents. All mice were initially given Salbutamol at t = 0, but one-half was also treated with Acebutolol at t = 30 mins. Muscle glycogen levels were measured in conjunction with the activities of glycogen synthase and phosphorylase (**Fig. 2**). Glycogen synthase activity was determined by measuring the levels of UDP–[^{14}C]Glucose incorporation into purified glycogen isolated from muscle extracts. Phosphorylase activity was determined by measuring the amount of ribulose-5P formed from the direct oxidation of glucose 6-phosphate.

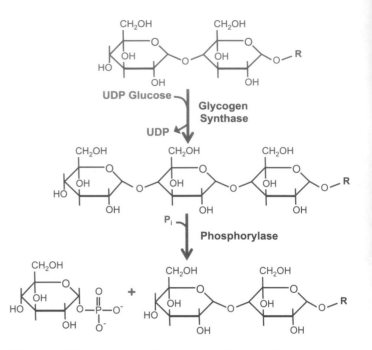

Figure 1. Glycogen synthesis and degradation.

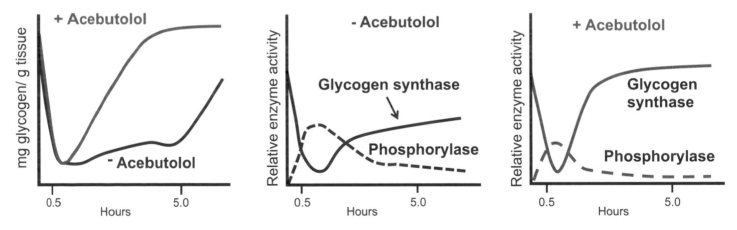

Figure 2. Left, glycogen levels after treatment. Middle, enzyme activity in response to Salbutamol. Right, enzyme activity in response to both Salbutamol and Acebutolol.

1) Which of the following is true with respect to the mechanism of action of the drugs used in the study?

    A. Both Acebutolol and Salbutamol are agonists.

    B. Accbutolol is an agonist and Salbutamol is an antagonist.

    C. Both Acebutolol and Salbutamol are antagonists.

    D. Acebutolol is an antagonist and Salbutamol is an agonist.

2) Glycogen levels are regulated through cAMP signaling. At t = 5 hrs (-Acebutolol), cAMP levels would be most affected by the activity of which class of enzyme?

    A. phosphatase

    B. phosphodiesterase

    C. kinase

    D. cyclase

3) In addition to hormonal control, muscle phosphorylase is allosterically regulated by various metabolites. Which of the following would be expected to directly stimulate muscle phosphorylase activity?

    A. ATP

    B. Glucose 6-P

    C. AMP

    D. cAMP

4) α-D glucose 1-phosphate can be converted into β-D glucose 1-phosphate. These two molecules are related to each other as:

    A. enantiomers.

    B. diastereomers.

    C. meso compounds.

    D. conformational isomers.

5) Mutations in muscle phosphorylase are causal in McCardle's disease. The resulting defect in glycogenolysis leads to:

    A. muscle fiber cross-bridge dissociation.

    B. myosin being maintained in the rigor state.

    C. increased binding of tropomyosin to myosin.

    D. a decreased release of calcium from sarcomeres.

6) Based upon the passage, phosphorylase is:

    A. active when phosphorylated, and produces an α-D glucose product.

    B. inactive when phosphorylated, and produces an α-D glucose product.

    C. active when phosphorylatcd, and produces a β-D glucose product.

    D. inactive when phosphorylated, and produces a β-D glucose product.

7) The absolute configuration around carbon #2 in glucose 1-phosphate is:

    A. R and rotates the plane of polarized light to the right.

    B. S and rotates the plane of polarized light to the left.

    C. S, but direction of rotation in plane of polarized light cannot be determined.

    D. R, but direction of rotation in plane of polarized light cannot be determined.

1

3

Glycogen Metabolism

Annotations.

1) D   2) B   3) C   4) B   5) B   6) A   7) D

	Foundation 1: Metabolism-D			Foundation 3: Neurobiology-A Other Systems-B		
	D			**A**	**B**	
Concepts	4,6,7					
Reasoning	3				5	
Research						
Data	2			1		

Big Picture. This passage uses data to describe how β-adrenergic receptor agonists and antagonists influence glycogen levels. How glycogen levels are regulated is important in medicine, particularly as the liver uses glycogen in conjunction with gluconeogenesis to regulate blood sugar levels. Glucagon is primarily specific for the liver and uses the glucagon receptor, yet, epinephrine can target the liver as well as muscle through the structurally similar β-adrenergic receptor. Figure 3 shows the canonical hormonal signaling pathway that should be foundational knowledge from undergraduate classes. Note that heterotrimeric G proteins are intimately involved in adenylyl cyclase activation and that protein kinase A (PKA) indirectly activates phosphorylase via phosphorylase kinase. These points were not tested in this passage, but you could easily see them on the MCAT.

Figure 3. Signaling through 7TM receptors activates a cAMP-dependent phosphorylation cascade that promotes glycogenolysis. Note that the liver is the principle tissue that releases free glucose into circulation.

1) **D. Acebutolol is an antagonist and Salbutamol is an agonist.** From Figure 2 it is clear that the addition of Salbutamol and Acebutolol has differential affects (one goes up and one goes down) on β-adrenergic receptor function as indirectly measured through glycogen levels. This immediately **eliminates choices A and C**. A β-adrenergic receptor agonist would stimulate the activation of adenylyl cyclase and PKA (**Fig. 3**). Consistently, the addition of Salbutamol rapidly increases phosphorylase activity as inferred through the measurement of rapidly declining glycogen levels (**Fig. 4**). Therefore, any treatment that decreases glycogen levels (i.e. through increased phosphorylase and reduced glycogen synthase activities) will act as an agonist; **choice D is correct**. Since Acebutolol has the opposite effect of Salbutamol, it must be an antagonist.

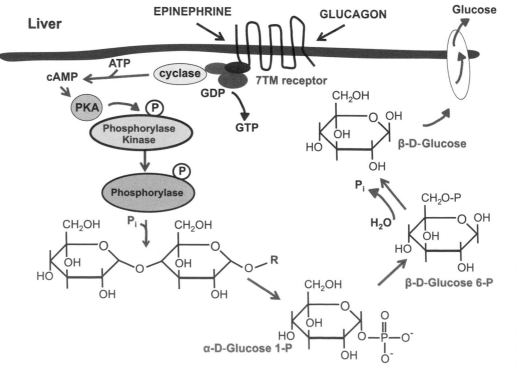

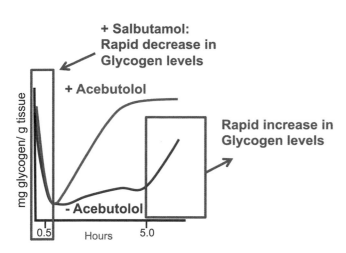

Figure 4. Salbutamol is an agonist.

2) B. phosphodiesterase. This question refers to data presented in the left panel in Figure 2 (and re-represented in **Fig. 4**). At the 5.0-hour time point, in the absence of Acebutolol (red line), the rate of glycogen increase occurs most rapidly. For this to occur, the rate of synthesis must be greater than the rate of breakdown, the latter of which is no longer occurring. The primary mechanism for down-regulating glycogenolysis is to reduce cAMP signaling. This is done by a phosphodiesterase that converts cAMP to AMP (**Fig. 5**).

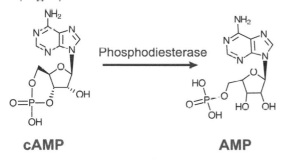

Figure 5. Conversion of cAMP to AMP by Phosphodiesterase.

At the 5.0-hour time point, the drug is no longer effective and glycogen repletion is occurring through the down-regulation of signaling through cAMP (**Fig. 4**). Paragraph 1 discusses the activation of protein kinase A in response to epinephrine/glucagon. From biochemistry you should be able to link cAMP formation to protein kinase activation during glycogen breakdown (i.e. epinephrine/glucagon secretion).

As an aside, it is assumed that you are familiar with the role of hormones, G protein coupled receptors (also called 7 trans-membrane receptors or 7TM), and subsequent signaling cascades. These are important as numerous drugs elicit their therapeutic action through these types of receptors. We will also examine them again in the context of retrograde neurotransmission. Although other modes of signaling exist (i.e. diacylglycerol), this passage focuses on cAMP-dependent signaling.

3) C. AMP. ATP hydrolysis is intimately connected to muscle contraction (as seen in question 5). Energetically depleted muscle tissue has exhausted its ATP stores and largely consists of AMP, a molecule that has no high-energy phosphoanhydride bonds (**Fig. 5**). Thus, AMP represents "low energy charge," or a low energy state. This is exactly the type of signal that would be expected to activate phosphorylase, an enzyme that regulates the breakdown and availability of glucose. Such allosteric regulation coordinates energy mobilization with supply. **Choices A and B are wrong** because these molecules would be expected to inhibit phosphorylase. Why mobilize glycogen for glucose oxidation if there is already ATP and glucose-6 phosphate available? **Choice D is wrong** because cAMP binds to PKA prior to it activating phosphorylase via phosphorylation.

4) B. diastereomers. Diastereomers possess at least two chiral carbon centers, yet are molecules that differ in absolute chiral configuration in at least a single carbon. Those diasteroemers that differ in configuration around only one chiral center are termed epimers. If the epimeric carbon is also the anomeric carbon, as is the case of the α and β forms of D-glucose 1-phosphate, then the molecules are called anomers (⁺ in top left panel of **Fig. 6**). You should recognize these points and also appreciate that carbon #1 is just one of four chiral carbons in glucose. Chirality will be discussed in more detail below.

The α and β forms of D-glucose 1-phosphate (and D-glucose) exist in an equilibrium in solution. The conversion of glucose between these two forms occurs through mutarotation, a process that involves the opening and closing of the ring structure. As mutarotation is freely reversible with glucose and glucose 1-phosphate, an equilibrium is established between the α and β forms. In most cases, the β form predominates. The difference between the two molecules is that they have opposite chiral configurations at carbon position #1 (**Fig. 6**, upper left), yet all other chiral centers are of the same configuration (i.e. diastereomers/epimers/anomers). Note that epimers and anomers are not answer choices.

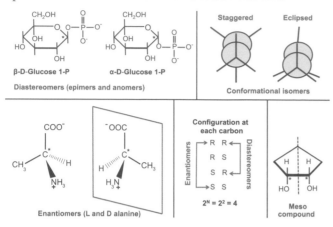

Figure 6. Various types of isomers. Note that in general the number of stereoisomers for a compound is 2^N where N = the number of chiral centers. For meso compounds, the formula is 2^N -1. Asterisks denote chiral carbon centers.

Appreciate that the α and β forms of D-glucose 1-phosphate (and D-glucose) are anomers and know how these sugar isomers are related to diastereomers and epimers as shown in Figure 7.

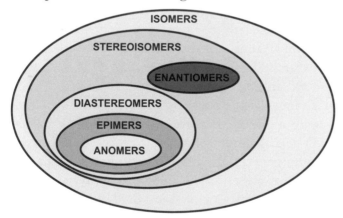

Figure 7. Relationship between isomers.

You should be very familiar with chirality and the various types of molecules that exhibit optical activity. This has been a notoriously challenging topic on the MCAT. In order to arrive at the answer of diastereomers, we will go over the essentials of chirality. Chirality, is a word derived from Greek, and refers to "handedness." Like the left and right hands, chiral molecules are non-superimposable mirror images of each other. Figure 6 shows the amino acid alanine.

Note that alanine has one chiral carbon, represented by the asterisk. The chiral carbon of alanine is sp^3 hybridized and has four <u>different</u> substituents bound to it. As this carbon is asymmetric (i.e., chiral), it cannot be superimposed on its mirror image, meaning that the two stereoisomers of alanine (D and L) possess optical activity. The D and L stereoisomers of alanine are called enantiomers. Therefore, the D and L isomers would be expected to rotate plane-polarized light in equal but opposite manners.

In general, the number of stereoisomers for a compound is represented by 2^N, where N is the number of chiral centers. For alanine, N = 1, and this refers to the D and L enantiomers (**Fig. 6**).

For most amino acids, the D form is usually called "R" and the L form generally represents "S." But what about a molecule like glucose 1-phosphate (G 1-P) that has multiple chiral centers? Glucose 1-phosphate has four chiral centers, and this includes carbon #1, the anomeric carbon (**Fig. 6**, asterisks in top left panel). Molecules with >1 chiral center can exist as diastereomers. These are molecules that have opposite chiral configurations in <u>at least</u> one chiral center. Figure 6 pictorially displays these points.

Although glucose 1-phosphate has 16 possible stereoisomers, α–D glucose 1-phosphate and β–D glucose 1-phosphate only differ in absolute configuration at carbon #1. Therefore, as per above they are related as diastereomers, yet are also epimers and anomers. **Choice A is incorrect** (enantiomers) because these stereoisomers differ in configuration at each chiral center (e.g., L and D alanine). Note that alanine has one chiral center and therefore two stereoisomers that form non-superimposable mirror images (left and right hands) (**Fig. 6**). Meso compounds are special as they contain an <u>even</u> number of chiral centers <u>and</u> possess an internal plane of symmetry as shown in Figure 6. Unlike other stereoisomers, they do not exhibit net optical activity. **Choice C is incorrect** as D-glucose 1-phosphate is not a meso compound because it lacks an internal plane of symmetry. Conformational isomers have an identical number of chiral centers, if any, and possess the same bonding pattern between atoms. They only differ in the way that the bonds rotate with respect to each other. Therefore, **choice D is wrong**. A classic example of conformational isomers is the staggered and eclipsed conformations of molecules such as ethane as shown in Figure 6.

5) B. myosin being maintained in the rigor state. To understand this question, you must know how ATP regulates muscle contraction in the context of the sarcomere (**Fig. 8A**). This is the classic cross bridge cycle between myosin and actin (or the sliding filament theory of muscle contraction). Note that ATP is required for the dissociation between myosin and actin, making **choice A incorrect**. This explains the phenomenon of rigor mortis: lack of ATP locks the sarcomeres in a cross bridge. **Choice B is correct** as the myosin head is in a high-energy conformation (the rigor state) when bound to ADP and Pi. Therefore, **choice A is wrong**, again! **Choice C is wrong** because the myosin head binds to actin, not tropomyosin. **Choice D is wrong** because ATP levels do not regulate calcium release; it is regulated by neuronal stimulation and depolarization of the membrane.

You should be familiar with the muscle cross bridge cycle. Lets examine this process in more detail. Sarcomeres, the contractile units of striated muscle, are contained within Z lines and are composed of thick (myosin) and thin (actin) filaments (**Fig. 8A**). Wrapped around actin is tropomyosin, a protein decorated with troponin. In the absence of calcium (at rest), troponin prevents the cross bridge binding between myosin and actin. Calcium release from the sarcoplasmic reticulum in response to stimulation by a motor neuron relieves this inhibition and allows for actin and myosin to bind in a manner regulated by ATP (**Fig. 8B**).

ATP hydrolysis causes myosin to change to a high energy conformation. Both ADP and phosphate is still bound to myosin. As the myosin head binds to actin in the thin filament, the cross bridge pulls the filament towards the center of the sarcomere (sliding). This power stroke causes a contraction that brings the Z bands closer together without changing the lengths of the thin and thick filaments.

6) A. active when phosphorylated, and produces an α-D glucose product. First, determine from the passage that phosphorylase is active when phosphorylated, thereby **eliminating choices C and D**. The passage states that glycogen phosphorylase is activated by epinephrine and glucagon and that these hormones also activate protein kinase A. The most

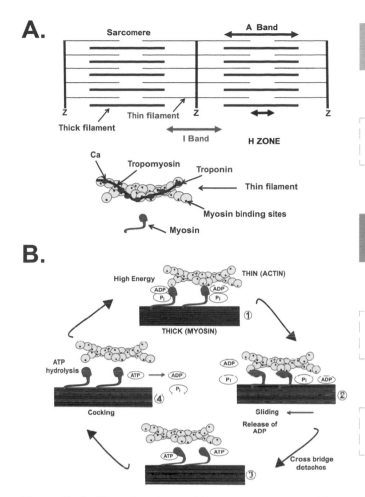

Figure 8. A. The structure of the sarcomere and its constituents. **B.** The cross-bridge cycle.

parsimonious interpretation of this is that in response to hormone, protein kinase A phosphorylates and activates glycogen phosphorylase. This is true, with the caveat that PKA <u>indirectly</u> activates phosphorylase through phosphorylase kinase.

Ok, so what about the glucose part? Figure 1 shows that glucose is phosphorylated on carbon #1. You should readily be able to recall the basic nomenclature for labeling the carbon atoms in a pyranose ring like glucose. What about the α or the β position? Note that carbon #1 from Figure 1 has the phosphate group pointing <u>down</u>. This is the α position. If the group were pointing <u>up</u>, then it would be labeled the β position. Therefore, **choice A is correct**.

The mechanism of mutarotation and the formation of the α or the β diastereomers (anomers and epimers too!) is fundamental and likely to appear on the MCAT. During the circularization of D-glucose, the OH group attached to carbon #5 acts as a nucleophile and attacks the anomeric carbon, or carbon #1 (**Fig. 9**, left). (The D isomer of glucose has the OH group at carbon #5 on the right hand side in a Fischer projection; the OH is on the left for the L configuration. Carbon #5 is the last chiral center). As this carbon lies within an sp^2 planar configuration, the nucleophile attacks the electrophilic carbon #1 from above or below the plane, generating two unique products, α and β (**Fig. 9**). Because the newly formed linkage in D-glucose is a hemiacetal at carbon #1, the formation of the circular structure is freely reversible. This is also true for D-glucose 1-phosphate, despite the fact that it has a phosphoester linkage at carbon #1. (This is not true for acetal linkages as they are irreversibly formed.)

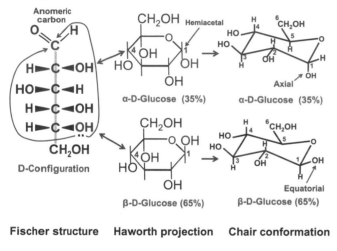

Fischer structure   Haworth projection   Chair conformation

Figure 9. Formation of α and ß anomers from D-glucose. D sugars are most common in nature.

The closing of the ring structure forms a new sp^3 chiral center at carbon #1. Recall that chiral carbon centers are sp^3 hybridized and are bound to four different substituent groups (asymmetric). In the open chain form, carbon #1 is in an sp^2 configuration. As the carbon can be converted from sp^2 to sp^3 via mutarotation, it is also referred to as the anomeric carbon. In the case of D-glucose, the β anomer is more stable than the α anomer because of steric considerations. That is, it occupies the equatorial position as seen in the chair structure.

7) D. R, but direction of rotation in plane of polarized light cannot be determined. Chiral molecules have the intrinsic property of rotating the plane of polarized light. This means that the D and L isomers of a given compound each rotate the plane of light either to the right or to the left, respectively. Consistently, an equal, racemic mixture of both enantiomers will generate a net optical activity of zero in a polarizer. For historical reasons, this nomenclature is linked to the structure of glyceraldehyde 3-phosphate and thus represents a "relative" assignment in configuration. To assign an absolute configuration to a given chiral center, the R and S system is used. For this, we use the Cahn-Ingold-Prelog rules. However, the assignment of the absolute configuration as R or S <u>will not</u> reveal any information about how the isomer rotates the plane of polarized light. You have to experimentally determine this. This **eliminates choices A and B.** Now, which is it: R or S? After you find carbon #2 in Figure 10, let's go over the rules:

1. Assign priorities (1-4) to the atoms attached to the chiral carbon such that the lowest atomic number is 4 and the highest is 1. (For isotopes, the heaviest one receives the highest priority).

2. Draw an arrow from 1 to 3. If the arrow points counterclockwise, tentatively assign the configuration as R; if the arrow points clockwise right, give it an S assignment.

3. If the priority #4 is in the back, then the absolute configuration is R. If priority #4 is in the front, then take the reverse and assign it an absolute configuration of S.

How do these rules apply to carbon #2 in glucose 1-phosphate? Well, assigning the priorities for 1 and 4 were straightforward (**Fig. 10**). The glitch occurs when deciding which carbon is assigned the number 3 priority as the #2 carbon is bonded to two additional carbon atoms. In this case, you have to go into "overtime" to determine the higher priority carbon. This is done through a comparison of the groups bound to each of the two carbons. Arrange in decreasing order of atomic size to (O, O, H) vs. (O, C, H). As the oxygen atoms are equivalent, compare the next atoms: O > C. Carbon #1 therefore has a priority rating of 2. Draw the arrow from 1-3 and then examine the position of priority group 4. In the Haworth projection, the convention is that the hydrogen is in the front, arriving at the final assignment of carbon #2 having an R configuration.

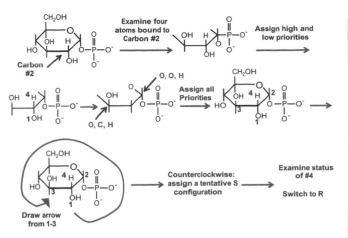

Figure 10. Assignment of absolute configuration to carbon #2.

Lysosomal Storage Disorders

Inclusion (I) cell disease is a lysosomal disorder presenting with severe psychomotor defects. I-cell patients have numerous lysosomal inclusions due to a failure to degrade molecules marked for destruction. Consequently, excess levels of lysosomal enzymes accumulate in the blood and urine. Two hypotheses were initially put forward to explain this. The first posited that I-cell membranes were "leaky" and allowed enzymes to escape. The second hypothesis stated that lysosomal enzymes failed to reach the lysosome due to an unknown defect in lysosomal targeting in I cells. To study lysosomes in I-cell disease, two experiments were performed (**Fig. 1**).

Experiment 1. The observation that normal fibroblasts could take up enzymes from the extracellular medium was exploited. Here, cell surface receptors form pinocytotic vesicles that take up enzymes. The newly formed endosomes merge with lysosomes. Incubation of fibroblasts from normal and I-cell patients in the presence of the active, purified lysosomal enzyme β-Glucuronidase was performed. This was followed by a washing step and then a further incubation period in media containing no enzyme. Afterwards, β-Glucuronidase activity was measured (**Fig. 1, Top**).

Experiment 2. This examined the ability of fibroblasts to take up the lysosomal enzyme N-acetyl β-glucosaminidase as produced from either I cells or normal cells. (**Fig. 1, Bottom**). Protein preparations from the two cell cultures were dialyzed in parallel in an acetate buffer ($pK_a = 4.75$). Various amounts of active enzyme from each line, as measured with the substrate, para-nitrophenyl N-acetyl β-glucosaminide, were incubated with fibroblasts containing low endogenous levels of N-acetyl β-glucosaminidase. After 72 hours, the levels of N-acetyl β-glucosaminidase recovered from cell extracts were determined and plotted as shown (**Fig. 1, Bottom**).

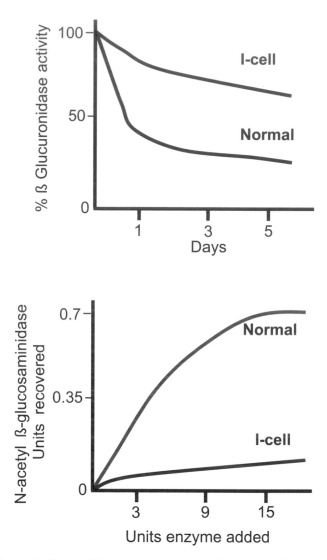

Figure 1. Role of I cells in lysosomal function. Top: Stability of β-Glucuronidase activity after uptake in two cell types. % activity measured as % of zero time. Bottom: Uptake into normal fibroblasts of N-acetyl β-glucosaminidase derived from either normal or I cells. 1 unit = 1.0 µmole per hour per mg protein.

1) Enzymes destined for lysosomes require:

      I. endosome formation.
      II. specific targeting sequences.
      III. exocytosis.
      IV. Signal Recognition Particle (SRP).

A. I, II

B. II, III

C. II, IV

D. I, IV

2) Which of the following statements is the least accurate with respect to I cells?

A. I cells lack cell surface receptors for β-Glucuronidase.

B. I-cell lysosomes have reduced levels of β-Glucuronidase.

C. I-cell derived lysosomal enzymes are poorly targeted in normal cells.

D. I cells are proficient in uptake of normal lysosomal enzymes.

3) The model that I-cell disease is caused by "leaky" membranes is:

A. correct because the levels of β-Glucuronidase in I cells are greater than the levels in normal cells after treatment.

B. incorrect because the levels of β-Glucuronidase in I cells are greater than the levels in normal cells after treatment.

C. correct because the levels of N-acetyl β-glucosaminidase taken up in normal cells exceeds that in I cells.

D. incorrect because the levels of N-acetyl β-glucosaminidase taken up in normal cells exceeds that in I cells.

4) I-cell patients do not uniformly display inclusion bodies as hepatocytes appear normal, but neurons do not. The most accurate interpretation of this is that:

A. hepatocytes do not contain lysosomes.

B. the ER and Golgi apparatuses are different in hepatocytes and neurons.

C. multiple targeting mechanisms exist for lysosomes.

D. endocytosis in the liver is different than that in the neuron.

5) Which of the following activity vs. pH profiles would be most expected for N-acetyl β-glucosaminidase?

A. 1

B. 2

C. 3

D. 4

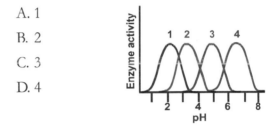

6) DNA sequencing from the genome of a patient with I-cell disease would reveal that the molecular defect in the disease is most likely a recessive mutation in a gene encoding a:

A. protein that functions in endocytosis.

B. negative regulator of lysosomal function.

C. positive regulator of secretion.

D. receptor for formation of pinocytotic vesicles.

Lysosomal Storage Disorders

	Foundation 1: Biochemistry-A			Foundation 2: Cell Biology-A		
	A			**A**		
Concepts				1		
Reasoning	5			4,6		
Research				3		
Data				2		

Big Picture. The passage presents experimental data underlying the discovery of the mannose 6-phosphate (M6-P) targeting system for lysosomes (**Fig. 2**). Note that the passage doesn't even mention M6-P and you don't need to know it either. In fact, the reported data only suggested the existence of the targeting system; the M6-P signal was discovered later.

The critical observations are: 1) I cells are capable of taking up exogenously added enzyme (**Fig. 1, Top**); 2) Enzymes derived from I cells cannot be taken up by normal cells, but enzymes derived from normal cells can be taken up in I cells (**Fig. 1, Bottom**). These results was interpreted to mean that lysosomes require a special "signal" for targeting and that this signal was absent in I cells. However, the ability to respond to the signal (i.e. receptor) was intact. This seminal observation proved true and was followed by the discovery of the M6-P recognition system. I cells have now been shown to be defective in a phosphotransferase enzyme that phosphorylates the mannose sugar in the ER.

1) C. II, IV. This question tests your basic understanding of the fundamentals of the secretory pathway as it is asking about what happens to proteins destined for lysosomes. To enter the secretory pathway, a protein usually needs to have an N-terminal signal sequence that is recognized during translation. This means that statement II is correct. **Choice D is therefore eliminated.** How do proteins enter the secretory pathway from ribosomal translation? Most, if not all, secreted proteins use the signal recognition particle (SRP); this is fundamental knowledge and recognizing this will lead to the realization that **choice C is correct**.

SRP is a ribonucleoprotein complex that recognizes signal sequences during translation, causes an arrest in the process, and brings the protein/ribosome complex to the ER where it uses the energy derived from GTP hydrolysis to deliver the protein to the ER.

Statement I is wrong (**eliminating choices A and D**, the latter for the second time) because endosomes are derived from endocytosis. This is the process of bringing things into cells and delivering them into lysosomes. This is the opposite direction of trafficking proteins from the ER to the Golgi and then to the lysosome. Statement III is wrong (exocytosis) because targeting to the lysosome does not require this terminal part of the secretory apparatus. **Choice B is wrong**.

As conceptual information, you should know the basics of secretion and endocytosis (outlined in **Fig. 2**). Step 1: SRP arrests translation and brings secretory proteins to the ER where they are glycosylated on asparagine (N-linked) residues. Step 2: vesicles with cargo bud from the ER and fuse to the cis-Golgi. Step 3: proteins destined for the lysosome are phosphorylated on mannose in the Golgi. Step 4: vesicle-containing proteins with M6-P bud off as primary lysosomes. Step 5: endosomes fuse with primary lysosomes to form secondary lysosomes. Steps 6-8: Receptor mediated endocytosis. Note that endosomes fuse with primary lysosomes and that the clathrin molecules (green rectangles) are recycled back to the membrane.

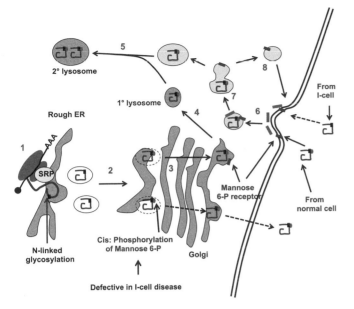

Figure 2. Key events in protein secretion and receptor mediated endocytosis. Hatched arrows represent exocytosis.

2) **A. I cells lack cell surface receptors for β-Glucuronidase.** Experiment I shows that I cells take up more enzyme than normal cells (**Fig. 3**). Thus, I cells possess the receptors to take up lysosomal enzymes via receptor-mediated endocytosis. The statement in choice A is therefore false, making **choice A the correct answer.** Further, as I cells do not properly target proteins to the lysosomes, these organelles will have reduced levels of residential lysosomal enzymes such as β-Glucuronidase. This **impeaches choice B.** The second experiment (**Fig. 3, Bottom**) shows that a lysosomal enzyme purified from I cells is inefficiently taken up by normal cells, indicating that **choice C is incorrect** because it is a true statement. Because I cells must possess receptors to mediate the endocytosis of the added β-Glucuronidase enzyme, **choice D can be discarded.**

3) **B. incorrect because the levels of β-Glucuronidase in I-cells are greater than the levels in normal cells after treatment.** Think about it this way: if I cells possessed "leaky" membranes, then they would not be able to take up and retain β-Glucuronidase <u>better</u> than normal cells (**Fig. 3**).

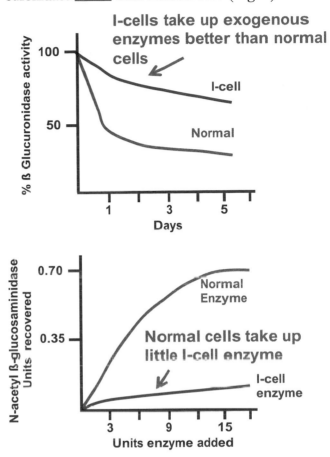

Figure 3. Interpretation of I-cell experimental data.

4) **C. multiple targeting mechanisms exist for lysosomes. Choice C is correct,** but to arrive at this, you have to rely on your intuition as there is nothing in the passage that directly discusses this topic. Take choice A for example, "Hepatocytes do not contain lysosomes." Really? The liver? The liver is a major site for chemical breakdown and lysosomes are the place where much of this occurs. Intuitively, you know that the liver contains lysosomes making **choice A wrong. Choices B and D are not credited answers** because the <u>overall</u> structures of the Golgi and ER are largely conserved in each cell. Yes, there are some differences from cell type to cell type. You might be thinking about the sarcoplasmic reticulum and the role of calcium in muscle cells, but this is an outlier. Moreover, endocytosis is mechanistically similar in each cell, although different cells will have different receptors to mediate this process.

Lysosomal Storage Disorders

5) C. 3. The passage mentions acetate buffer, and adds in the fact that the pK_a of this is 4.75. Given that the most effective pH of a buffer is at its pK_a (the point where the amount of acid is equal to the amount of conjugate base), the peak enzymatic activity closest to pH = 4.75 is the correct answer. This is enzyme activity profile #3, or choice C.

6) C. a positive regulator of secretion. A recessive mutation in a positive regulator of secretion would generate a secretion defect, which is exactly what is observed in I-cell disease. This makes the question actually very straightforward, but potentially easy to overthink. The molecular defect in I-cell disease has been established to be due to mutations in a mannose-phosphotranferase enzyme. Phosphorylation of mannose in the ER creates a lysosomal targeting signal. **Choice A is wrong** because if a protein that functions in endocytosis was the causal genetic defect in I-cell disease, then I cells would not be able to take up exogenous protein more efficiently compared to normal cells as shown in Figure 1, top panel. Likewise, if I cells were defective in the formation of pinocytotic vesicles, then they would fail to take up exogenous proteins more effectively than wild-type cells making **choice D incorrect. Choice B is wrong** because, although a negative regulator of lysosomal function is potentially a nebulous term, you should reason that a defect in a negative regulator of lysosomal function would not be expected to be deleterious to organelle function, which is a hallmark of I-cell disease.

1

2

PATHWAY

Polio

The polio virus contains a + strand RNA genome that is unusual in that it possesses a long 5′ untranslated region and a 3′ poly A tail. Scientists hypothesized that the genome-linked polio RNA binding protein VPg, a factor packaged in the capsid, is covalently linked via tyrosine and a uracil residue. In this model, a terminal transferase polymerase adds multiple uracil residues to the initial VPg-Tyr-pU moiety and this covalent modification is required for the function of the polio polymerase during replication (**Figs. 1, 2**). As an alternative possibility, VPg could bind non-covalently to cellular polymerases to facilitate viral replication.

To address the hypothesis, researchers grew poliovirus in HeLa cells radiolabeled with inorganic phosphate (^{32}P) that is metabolically incorporated into uracil nucleotides. 1.5 hours after infection, [^{3}H]-tyrosine was added. 1.5 hours later, the cells were isolated by centrifugation and lysed. Cell extracts were prepared for sucrose gradient purification and the virus was recovered by acetone precipitation. After resuspension in phosphate-buffered saline (pH = 8.0), the virions were extracted with a chloroform/isoamyl alcohol solution in order to separate protein from nucleic acid. Both the aqueous and non aqueous-containing fractions were saved, and the water-soluble portion was treated with a cocktail of RNAses that generate nucleoside monophosphates. As VPg is negatively charged at pH = 8.0, the resulting reaction was applied to an anion exchange column that employed an increasing (0-0.5M) NaCl salt gradient for elution (**Fig. 3**). After analysis of the chromatogram, the researchers concluded that the covalent model was correct.

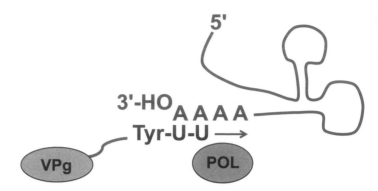

Figure 1. Covalent attachment model for VPg and polio.

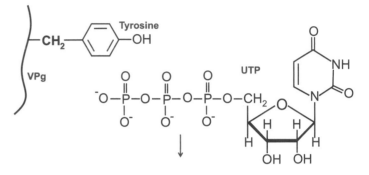

Figure 2. Role of tyrosine in covalent attachment model.

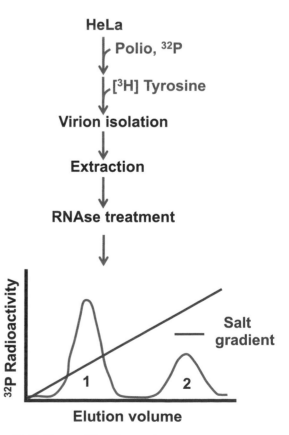

Figure 3. Polio purification scheme.

70

1) The purpose of the ion exchange column is to separate:

A. all of the ^{32}P from VPg-Tyr-pU.

B. viral coat proteins from VPg-Tyr-pU.

C. uracil nucleotides from VPg-Tyr-pU.

D. [^{3}H] tyrosine from VPg-Tyr-pU.

2) In the covalent model, the radiolabeled tritium would be predicted to be recovered in:

    I. peak 1 of the ion exchange column.
    II. peak 2 of the ion exchange column.
    III. the aqueous fraction after extraction.
    IV. the non-aqueous fraction after extraction.

A. I, IV

B. II, III

C. I, III

D. II, IV

3) Which of the following enzymes would be the most effective in cleaving the protein-RNA linkage formed between polio RNA and VPg?

A. nuclease

B. phosphatase

C. esterase

D. dehydrogenase

4) Which of the following chemical linkages most accurately describes the bonding pattern observed between the tyrosine in VPg and uracil?

A. O^4(5′ uridylyl) tyrosine

B. O^4(3′ uridylyl) tyrosine

C. O^1(5′ uridylyl) tyrosine

D. O^1(3′ uridylyl) tyrosine

5) Which of the following is true with respect to polio virus?

A. Polioviral DNA polymerase requires a priming function.

B. Polioviral RNA polymerase requires a priming function.

C. Both polioviral DNA and RNA polymerases require a priming function.

D. Neither polioviral DNA nor RNA polymerases require a priming function.

6) Which of the following ^{32}P labeled nucleotides was used as a substrate in the covalent mechanism?

A. α[^{32}P] dUTP

B. α[^{32}P] UTP

C. γ[^{32}P] dUTP

D. γ[^{32}P] UTP

7) Measles is a minus strand RNA virus that replicates in the cytoplasm. Which of the following is true with respect to measles?

A. The virus encodes for and packages its own DNA-dependent DNA polymerase.

B. The virus encodes for its own RNA-dependent RNA polymerase, but fails to package it.

C. The virus contains intron sequences.

D. The virus encodes for and packages its own RNA-dependent RNA polymerase.

Polio

Annotations.
1) C 2) B 3) C 4) A 5) B 6) B 7) D

	Foundation 1: Biochemistry-A Gene Expression-B			Foundation 2: Microbiology-B		
	A	**B**		**B**		
Concepts				5,7		
Reasoning	3,4	6				
Research		1				
Data	2					

Big Picture. Nucleophiles and electrophiles, all displayed in the context of nucleic acid chemistry, drive the poliovirus life cycle. Although you have always been taught about DNA replication and 3' OH priming, the poliovirus has taken it to a new level; it doesn't have a DNA polymerase but its RNA polymerase requires a primer! And an unconventional primer at that: the 3' OH group on a uracil bound to a tyrosine residue of the VPg-Tyr-pU protein (**Fig. 1**). Polio uses a protein-nucleic acid primer and this is very unusual. Note that the 3' end of the virus has a poly A tail for base pairing with the VPg-UU primer. Ok, so what if you didn't know the ins and outs of polio? That is fine. Although the biology is unusual, notice that the chemistry is still the same: a nucleophilic oxygen on tyrosine attacks an electrophilic phosphate. This is a classic substitution/elimination reaction that operates through a tetrahedral intermediate. There is also the conventional 3' OH group being used for polymerase elongation. So poliovirus represents a new application to chemistry that you are already familiar with.

1) **C. uracil nucleotides from VPg-Tyr-pU.** As the passage states that the ^{32}P added is incorporated into uracil nucleotides, the mechanism described will therefore generate a covalent bond between VPg-Tyr and radiolabeled uracil to make VPg-Tyr-pU (**Fig. 4**). However, as terminal transferase adds more labeled uracil residues to VPg-Tyr-pU (to make VPg-Tyr-pU$_N$), numerous radiolabeled uracil residues will ultimately be linked to VPg-Tyr-pU. After RNAse treatment, labeled UMP will be liberated, leaving behind VPg-Tyr-P-U (**Fig. 5**). Identifying this labeled uracil in VPg-Tyr-pU is key. In order to unequivocally prove the covalent model (i.e. the tyrosine residue on VPg-Tyr-pU is linked to uracil), the labeled uracil nucleotides added by terminal transferase must be separated from the ^{32}P incorporated into VPg-Tyr-pU. This separation is performed by ion exchange chromatography. **Choice C is correct.** Because, as discussed above, part of the analysis needed to prove the covalent model requires an examination of the ^{32}P incorporated into VPg-Tyr-pU. (It is the ^{32}P incorporated into the UMP that needs to be removed.) This **eliminates choice A. Choice B is incorrect** because the viral coat proteins are removed during the extraction step. Recall that viral coat proteins will encase the RNA genome of polio. To isolate VPg-Tyr-p-U, a protein associated with the RNA genome, the chloroform/isoamyl alcohol treatment will separate the nucleic acids (with VPg-Tyr-pU) from protein. As stated in the passage, the nucleic acids are extracted into the aqueous phase and, by implication, the protein coat is extracted into the organic layer. **Choice D is incorrect** because [^{3}H] tyrosine will be incorporated into translating VPg in the covalent model, obviating the desire to separate the two from each other.

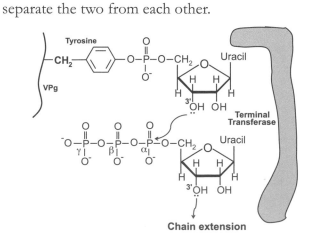

Figure 4. Terminal transferase adds uracil to the VPg-U covalent linkage.

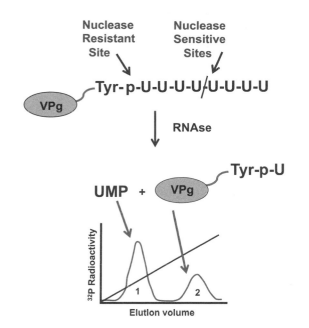

Figure 5. Use of ion exchange to separate free nucleotides from uridylylated VPg protein.

2) **B. II, III.** Immediately associate tritium with the tyrosine residue in VPg-Tyr-pU. As we know that VPg-Tyr-pU is associated with RNA, it would have been extracted in the aqueous layer. As statement III is correct, this **eliminates choices A and D.** So which peak does VPg-Tyr-pU (or the tritium) lie in? The answer is peak #2 (**eliminating choice C**), but how can you tell? The answer lies in understanding how anion exchange works (**Fig. 6**). We learned in the passage that VPg-Tyr-pU was negatively charged and we also knew that UMP is negatively charged because of its ionized phosphates. Therefore, both species will bind to a positively charged ion exchange matrix. However, as VPg-Tyr-pU is much larger and has many more negatively charged groups than UMP, it would be expected to interact more strongly with the anion exchange matrix. Therefore, as salt disrupts the ionic interactions between matrix and binding factor, it would be expected that MORE salt is required to elute VPg-Tyr-pU than it would be for UMP. UMP must elute first, meaning that it is in peak #1.

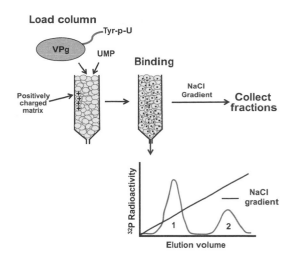

Figure 6. Anion exchange chromatography separates VPg-Tyr-p-U from UMP.

3) **C. esterase.** An esterase will hydrolyze this bond (**Fig. 7**). Technically it is a phosphoesterase, but esterase is the best answer. The tyrosine in VPg acts as a nucleophile and attacks the electrophilic α phosphate in UTP (residing in a phosphoanhydride bond), liberating PPi and generating a new phosphoester bond. Therefore, an alcohol combined with a (phospho)anhydride generates a (phospho)ester Thus, **choice B is the correct answer. Choice D is wrong** as there is no redox occurring in this reaction. There is no dephosphorylation (**choice B is wrong**), and there is no nuclease activity occurring in the reaction (**choice A is wrong**).

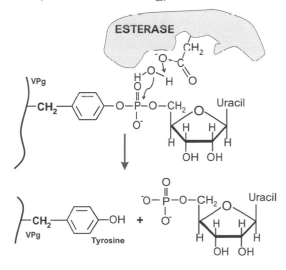

Figure 7. Hydrolysis of phosphoester bond between VPg and uracil. Typical hydrolysis reaction using general base catalysis. Active site aspartic acid generates an HO^- nucleophile from water. HO^- is a stronger nucleophile than water as it is a stronger base. HO^- attacks the electrophilic phosphate, forming a tetrahedral intermediate (not shown) that collapses, forming tyrosine and UMP.

Polio

4) A. O⁴(5′ uridylyl) tyrosine. This is a nomenclature question. Because of the nature of the nucleophilic attack from tyrosine it should be clear that the oxygen from its OH group forms part of the covalent bond. This oxygen is bound to the 4th carbon in the ring, meaning that the linkage must be O⁴. **Choices C and D are therefore eliminated.** Look at the numbering system for tyrosine and the ribose in uracil in Figure 8. This is something that you should keep in mind, especially when you consider the 5′ to 3′ polarity in nucleic acid chains.

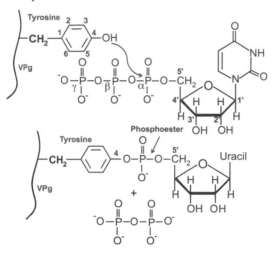

Figure 8. Nucleophilic tyrosine attack an electrophilic phosphate in a phosphoanhydride bond to generate a phosphoester linking VPg to uracil.

5) B. Polioviral RNA polymerase requires a priming function. As shown in Figure 1, VPg-Tyr-p-U can be seen as a primer for the polio virus RNA-dependent RNA polymerase. Consistently, the passage describes the requirement for VPg-Tyr-pU (and terminal transferase) in polio virus replication. **Eliminate choices A and C** because poliovirus is an RNA virus and does not have a DNA polymerase.

6) B. α[³²P] UTP. Passage Figure 2 shows UTP, a ribose sugar, as serving as an electrophile with the nucleophilic tyrosine. Immediately **eliminate choices A and C** as they are deoxyribose sugars. Next, observe that as shown in Figure 8 that the electrophilic center is the alpha position, making **choice B correct**. Recall that during DNA replication and RNA synthesis, new nucleotides are added to the growing chain through attack of the α phosphate of the nucleotide triphosphate that gets incorporated into the polymer. This releases inorganic pyrophosphate, that when hydrolyzed, further drives the reaction forward.

7) D. The virus encodes for and packages its own RNA-dependent RNA polymerase. RNA viruses are classified by the nature of their nucleic acid genomes and exist in three major forms: single stranded viruses (polio and influenza), double stranded RNA viruses (rotavirus), and retroviruses such as HIV. Single stranded RNA viruses exist in the + or − form. The genomes of + strand viruses are equivalent to that of the sense strand of an mRNA. Upon translation via host ribosomes, + strand viruses express an RNA-dependent RNA polymerase that can be used to propagate its genome. On the other hand, − strand viruses, such as measles can be thought of as antisense messages. Thus, in order for them to express any of their genes, they must first be converted into a + strand. As the host DNA-dependent RNA polymerase is disqualified from performing this reaction, − strand viruses must package (and encode) their own polymerase. **Choice D is the correct choice.** Recall that intron splicing occurs in the nucleus, meaning that viruses that replicate in the cytoplasm would not have introns as they are only in the nucleus. Therefore, **choice C is wrong**.

1

2

PATHWAY

Development

Animal oocytes arrest during meiotic prophase I, the G2 phase of the cell cycle. After hormonal induction by progesterone, these immature oocytes enter the meiotic cycle where they arrest again at metaphase of meiosis II to yield a mature, fertilizable oocyte (**Fig. 1**). After completing fertilization, haploid pro-nuclei form a diploid zygote.

To examine the role of progesterone-mediated signaling in oocyte maturation, cytoplasm from progesterone-treated oocytes (unfertilized eggs) was microinjected into untreated, immature oocytes. Over time, nearly all of the treated primary oocytes entered mitosis and arrested (**Fig. 2**). Similar results were achieved when the experiment was conducted in the presence of actinomycin D, a transcriptional inhibitor. However, in the presence of cycloheximide, a ribosomal translocase inhibitor, entry into mitosis was not observed. Further, the primary oocytes entered mitosis when the cytoplasm from enucleated cells was injected into the oocytes. Enucleated cells have had their nuclei surgically removed during G2, prior to the addition of progesterone.

A second microinjection experiment was performed with the transfer of cytoplasm from unfertilized eggs into one of the two blastomeres derived from the zygote (**Fig. 2**). Enucleated cells were used as a control. The blastomere injection experiment yielded similar results in the presence of either actinomycin D or cycloheximide. However, the microinjection of cytoplasm derived from primary oocytes or fertilized eggs failed to arrest zygote cleavage.

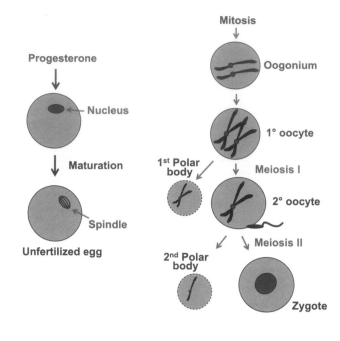

Figure 1. Oocyte development and fertilization. Note the diploid nature of the oogonium.

Figure 2. Microinjection of cytoplasm from progesterone-treated oocytes with and without nuclei. Left, injection into untreated, immature oocytes. Right, injection into the left blastomere of a 2 cell embryo.

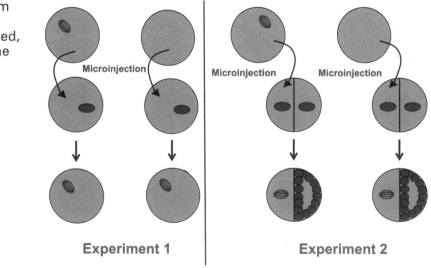

1) Which of the following is true with respect to oocyte maturation?

    I. Nuclear activities involved with oocyte maturation are under cytoplasmic control.

    II. Nuclear activities involved with oocyte maturation are under translational control.

    III. Nuclear activities involved with oocyte maturation are under transcriptional control.

A. I

B. I, II

C. II, III

D. II

2) When cytoplasm from a mature frog oocyte is injected into the left blastomere of a two-cell frog embryo, which of the following would represent the most expected outcome?

A.   B.   C.   D.

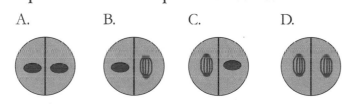

3) Which hormone controls the release of secondary oocytes from the ovaries during ovulation?

A. estrogen

B. follicle stimulating hormone

C. luteinizing hormone

D. progesterone

4) Which of the following hypotheses concerning progesterone-mediated oocyte maturation is most consistent with the experiments?

A. A cytoplasmic factor produced in mature oocytes between metaphases I and II is degraded after fertilization.

B. A nuclear factor produced in mature oocytes between metaphases I and II is degraded after fertilization.

C. A cytoplasmic factor present in prophase I of meiosis must be degraded for cleavage and development.

D. A nuclear factor present in prophase I of meiosis must be degraded for cleavage and development.

5) In humans, a secondary oocyte is:

A. diploid and has 46 chromatids.

B. haploid and has 23 chromatids.

C. diploid and has 23 chromatids.

D. haploid and has 46 chromatids.

6) Cells formed immediately after zygotic cleavage compose the:

A. morula.

B. blastula.

C. gastrula.

D. neurula.

Development

	Foundation 2: Cell Physiology-C			Foundation 3: Other Systems-B		
	C			**B**		
Concepts	6			3		
Reasoning	5					
Research				4		
Data	1,2					

Big Picture. This passage examines oocyte maturation presented in the context of the cell cycle and development. Oocyte development links diverse topics (i.e. cell cycle and hormonal control) and is highly relevant to clinical medicine. However, the terminology is potentially tricky as concepts like primary, secondary, haploid, diploid, and metaphase arrest can be hard to keep track in the context of oocyte development and the various hormones. You should know these for the test.

Historically, oocyte development has provided key insight into how cells grow and divide, a key aspect of cancer research and therapy. Those key experiments are shown in Figure 2. The data shows that cytoplasmic factors regulate the entry into mitosis. In experiment 1, the discovery that immature oocytes could be induced to enter the cell cycle and arrest at metaphase II of meiosis led to the identification of maturation promoting factor (MPF). MPF regulates mitotic entry and is composed of a heterodimeric complex consisting of Cyclin B and a protein kinase (Cdk1). The second experiment shows that a cytoplasmic factor, now called cytostatic factor (CSF), inhibits early embryonic cleavage after fertilization. It must therefore be degraded upon fertilization in order for development to proceed.

1) **B. I, II.** The data in the passage support the hypothesis that the nuclear activities involved with oocyte maturation are under cytoplasmic control. The nuclear activities referred to those processes that facilitate mitosis. This includes nuclear envelope breakdown and spindle formation as shown in the microinjection experiments. **Statement I is therefore correct.** In contrast to the transcription inhibitor actinomycin D, the translational inhibitor cycloheximide abrogates oocyte maturation through mitotic inhibition (**statement III is incorrect**). This is described in the passage and indicates that **statement II is correct** as translation of mRNA is required for oocyte maturation.

The cytoplasmic control is particularly evident as, in enucleated cells, transfer of cytoplasm into the recipient, immature oocytes induces mitosis as observed through spindle formation (**Fig. 2**). This occurs in the absence of nuclear function. Enucleated cells are those that have no nuclei as they were surgically removed from the G2 arrested primary oocytes. They serve as an important control in demonstrating that a cytoplasmic factor induces mitosis. Therefore, the data suggests that progesterone-treated primary oocytes activate a cytoplasmic factor that regulates nuclear envelope breakdown and spindle formation.

Although not mentioned in the passage, this factor exists and is known to be MPF, or maturation promoting factor (or even mitosis promoting factor). MPF is composed of a cyclin molecule and a cyclin-dependent kinase. During oocyte maturation translation of cyclin from maternal stores of mRNA is required during each cell cycle.

2) **A.** Observe that the microinjection of cytoplasm from a mature egg (arrested in metaphase of meiosis II) induces a mitotic state in the injected blastomere (**Fig. 3**). This can be assayed by the formation of the spindle. This causes the blastomere to arrest in mitosis where it fails to undergo further cleavage into a morula, unlike the second, untreated cell. Therefore, the injected cytoplasm contained a cytoplasmic factor that promotes mitosis. As this factor is derived from cytoplasm found in <u>mature</u>, unfertilized eggs, it must be generated in metaphase of meiosis II.

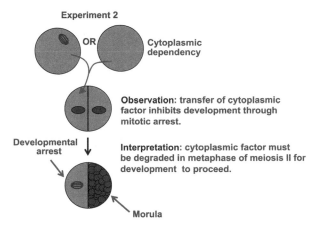

Figure 3. Effect of microinjection of cytoplasm from a mature egg that is arrested on a blastomere.

3) C. luteinizing hormone. Understanding ovulation is essential for the MCAT. The key thing to remember is the relative level of hormones at each stage of the 28 day menstrual cycle as shown in Figure 4A. Here, luteinizing hormone (LH) controls the release of the secondary oocyte into the fallopian tube on the 14th day of ovulation, the ovulatory phase. Notice that before this, in the follicular phase, the rising levels of estrogen stimulate the release of LH. However, sustained levels of elevated estrogen, as seen in the luteal phase, inhibit estrogen release. During the follicular phase, the follicle develops. A follicle is not an isolated oocyte, but rather is surrounded by a protective layer of thecal cells that proliferate during the follicular phase. Both thecal and granulosa cells produce estrogen. In conjunction with the formation of a layer of mucopolysaccharides termed the zona pellucida, the oocyte is well insulated during its development.

After release of the oocyte (**Fig. 4B**), the cycle enters the luteal phase, where estrogen and progesterone negatively regulate LH levels. In this phase, the corpus luteum, composed of the cells surrounding the mature follicle lacking the oocyte, degenerates by day 28. This causes the levels of estrogen and progesterone to decrease. The ovarian cycle affects the 28 day uterine cycle, which consists of shedding and re-building of the endometrium, the lining of the uterus that will ultimately be the site of zygote implantation and development of the fetus (**Fig. 4C**).

Keeping the levels of estrogen and progesterone artificially high during the luteal phase will inhibit the release of LH. This is because the sustained, high levels of estrogen inhibit LH release from the anterior pituitary. This is how the birth control pill works.

Most protocols, however, include a 6-day sugar pill, designed to provide for a reduction in estrogen/progesterone to allow for shedding of the endometrial lining during menstruation. After menstruation, the endometrium builds back up in response to the increasing levels of estrogen.

It is very important to understand the regulation of hormone production. As shown in Figure 5, in response to various stimuli, the hypothalamus secretes gonadotropin-releasing hormone (GnRH). This stimulates the pituitary to release follicle stimulating hormone (FSH) and LH. FSH causes the granulosa cells to release estrogen while LH is involved with the formation of the corpus luteum and progesterone secretion in the luteal phase of the ovarian cycle. These hormones also trigger meiosis (**Fig. 1**), growth and the production of the protein inhibin. In males, an analogous event occurs for spermatogenesis. Male interstitial cells, the counterpart of female thecal cells, is stimulated by LH and produces testosterone. Male sustenacular cells, the counterpart to female granulosa cells, is stimulated by FSH

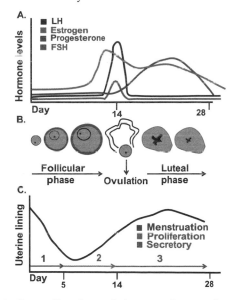

Figure 4. Coordination of the ovarian and uterine cycle.

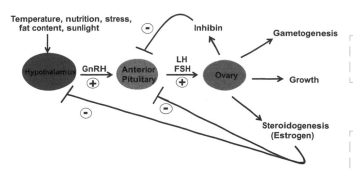

Figure 5. Hormonal regulation of ovary function.

4) **A. A cytoplasmic factor produced in mature oocytes between metaphases I and II is degraded after fertilization.** Figure 3 shows that a factor from the cytoplasm drives the left blastomere into an arrested mitotic state, preventing development into morula as seen for the untreated blastomere. The enucleation experiment rules out a function for the nucleus in arresting mitosis. As the factor arrests the cell cycle, it must be <u>degraded</u> (or inactivated) in order for development to proceed. **Eliminate choices B and D** as they both hypothesize that a nuclear factor is controlling this process.

When is this factor produced? The passage states, "...the microinjection of cytoplasm derived from primary oocytes or fertilized eggs failed to arrest zygote cleavage." As primary oocytes are arrested in the G2 phase of the cell cycle (i.e. prophase I) and fertilized eggs complete meiosis II, this factor would be present in mature oocytes between metaphases I and II and degraded after fertilization. **Choice C is eliminated**, making **choice A correct**.

5) **D. haploid and has 46 chromatids.** As seen in Figure 1, the secondary oocyte has one duplicated chromosome. This is haploid or 1N. Each chromatid is held together through a centromere and there are therefore two chromatids $\times$ 23 chromosomes = 46 chromatids in human secondary oocytes. Once the chromatids detach from the centromere, then they are called chromosomes. As an aside, it is easy to confuse ploidy with chromosome number. Ploidy is designated with an N and chromosome number is designated with DNA content (C). Thus, a haploid (1N) secondary oocyte has a DNA content of 2C.

6) **A. morula.** A morula is a solid ball of cells consisting of blastomeres, and contains at least 16 cells (**Fig. 3**). This is the structure in Figure 2. After formation of the blastocoele, the resulting body of cells is called the blastula. This is preceded by gastrulation where the three primary germ layers form: endoderm, mesoderm, and ectoderm. These layers will give rise to the organs. As flash card knowledge, you should be aware of which organs are derived from which germ layers. <u>Ectoderm</u>: forms nervous system and outer skin layer. <u>Mesoderm</u>: most organs including kidney, heart, red blood cells, and bone. <u>Endoderm</u>: alimentary canal, liver, pancreas. During neurulation, the nervous system develops from the notochord formed form the ectoderm. This is clearly not seen in Figure 2, **making choice D incorrect**.

Notes:

2

3

PATHWAY

Yeast Cell Cycle

The yeasts Saccharomyces cerevisiae and Schizosaccharomyces pombe have provided the foundation for understanding cell cycle progression. Most notably, S. cerevisiae and S. pombe divide through budding and fission, respectively. Consequently, unlike fission yeast, S. cerevisiae primarily regulates its cell cycle during the G1 phase, but S. pombe does this at the G2/M stage. However, in both organisms, a point in G1 called START regulates the moment of commitment to proceeding through the cell cycle. Further, cyclin-dependent kinase complexes control cell cycle progression in both yeasts. For example, CDC2 positively regulates both entry into S phase and mitosis and mutations in this gene can influence the timing of cell cycle progression.

Early studies with both yeast strains identified multiple classes of mutations affecting the cell cycle. The initial cell division cycle (Cdc) mutants blocked cell cycle progression, but did not block macromolecular synthesis, allowing for continual growth (**Table 1**). In S. cerevisiae, bud emergence and DNA synthesis occur simultaneously and the nucleus migrates to the neck of the bud during S phase. This allows the formation of mitotic structures (i.e. spindle) to occur earlier in budding yeast.

Isolated Cdc mutants were found to fall into three major classes. First, recessive, loss of function mutants were mostly observed to be temperature sensitive (TS). These mutants proceeded normally through the cell cycle at the permissive temperature, but arrested at their terminal point at the restrictive temperature. Secondly, dominant, gain of function mutants were found to be alleles encoding for more active proteins. The third class of mutants consisted of dominant negative mutants that encoded for proteins that bind and "titrate" out a binding partner.

Mutant	DNA Replication	Bud Emergence
CDC28	NO	NO
CDC4	NO	YES
CDC7	NO	YES
CDC24	YES	NO

Table 1. Isolation of budding yeast cell cycle mutants.

1) **Which of the following is least consistent with the data presented in Table 1?**

A. CDC28 performs a distinct function from both CDC4 and CDC7.

B. Bud emergence and DNA replication are controlled by a common upstream regulator.

C. Bud emergence and DNA replication are dependent on each other.

D. CDC28 is required for both bud emergence and progression into S phase.

2) **At the restrictive temperature, which of the following would be true of TS mutations that affect formation of the spindle?**

    I. S. cerevisiae mutants are in mitotic arrest.
    II. S. pombe mutants are in mitotic arrest.
    III. S. pombe mutants are in G2 arrest.
    IV. S. cerevisiae mutants are in G2 arrest.

A. I, II

B. I, III

C. II, IV

D. III, IV

3) **In a screen for Cdc mutations, which of the following should be observed for a Cdc mutation?**

A. Growth of mutant colonies at both restrictive and permissive temperatures.

B. Growth of colonies at only the permissive temperature.

C. Growth of colonies at only the restrictive temperature.

D. Growth of colonies at either the permissive or the restrictive temperature.

4) **The relative time spent in each cell cycle phase was documented for a fission yeast Cdc mutation grown at the permissive (Low) and restrictive (High) temperatures. This strain most likely contains a:**

A. dominant mutation in CDC2.

B. loss of function mutation in START.

C. dominant negative mutation in an S phase gene.

D. gain of function mutation in a negative regulator of mitosis.

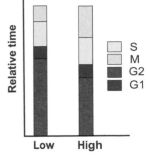

5) **Analysis of an asynchronous culture of diploid fission yeast cells using flow cytometry is shown below. What is the number of cells in mitosis?**

A. 20,000

B. 40,000

C. 60,000

D. Cannot be determined

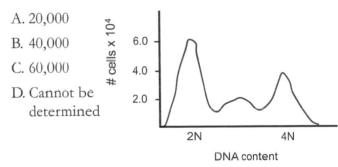

6) **Single allele inactivating mutations in the catalytic sites in the following genes could be considered dominant negative except:**

A. heterodimeric cyclin-dependent kinase.

B. monomeric glycolytic enzyme.

C. multisubunit RNA polymerase II.

D. U1 small nuclear ribonucleoprotein particle.

Yeast Cell Cycle

Annotations.
1) C   2) C   3) B   4) A   5) D   6) B

	Foundation 1: Genetics-C			Foundation 2: Cell Physiology-C		
	C			**C**		
Concepts	6			5		
Reasoning				2		
Research				3		
Data				1,4		

Big Picture. The yeast cell cycle has formulated the foundation for our understanding of cell growth and division. This passage emphasizes interpretation of data as applied to the cell cycle of two different yeasts and also requires an understanding of the differences between the two yeasts. Despite being yeasts, S. pombe and S. cerevisiae are related to each other as much as they are related to humans!

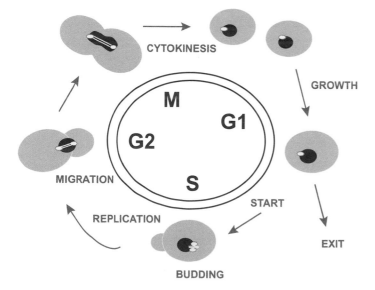

Figure 1. Budding yeast cell cycle. Spindle pole bodies and spindle formation are shown in yellow.

1) **C. Bud emergence and DNA replication are dependent on each other.** Note that correct answer statements are wrong choices because the question stem asks for the statement <u>least consistent</u> with the data. Note that the passage states, "Bud emergence and DNA synthesis occur simultaneously and the nucleus migrates to the neck of the bud during S phase." Despite this, both processes can still be regulated in a separate manner, and this is what the data in Table 1 indicate. Note that in both the CDC4 and CDC7 mutants, the cells generate a bud, but each fail to synthesize DNA. In contrast, CDC24 mutants can synthesize DNA yet they fail to bud. Therefore, both processes occur independently of each other, **making choice C correct. Choice A is wrong** because CDC28 performs a distinct function from both CDC4 and CDC7 as they do not have the same phenotype with respect to DNA synthesis and bud formation as CDC28 does. **Choice B is wrong** because CDC28 regulates both bud emergence and DNA replication as shown in Table 1. In CDC28 mutants both bud emergence and DNA synthesis are abrogated, indicating that it operates upstream, or before, both events. Indeed, CDC28 executes START and this point in the budding yeast cell cycle precedes both bud emergence and DNA replication. **Choice D is wrong** because CDC28 is required for bud emergence as in its absence no bud formation is observed. Further, CDC28 is required for START, a G1 specific event that is necessary to pass through prior to entering S phase.

2) **C. II, IV.** From the passage, "In S. cerevisiae, bud emergence and DNA synthesis occur simultaneously and the nucleus migrates to the neck of the bud during S phase. This allows the formation of mitotic structures (i.e. spindle) to occur earlier in budding yeast."

Figure 1 shows that spindle formation in budding yeast occurs in G2; therefore, statement IV is correct and statement I is wrong. This **eliminates choices A and B.** Because S. pombe undergoes fission, which is analogous to what occurs in human cells during cell division, the spindle in fission yeast would be expected to occur later, during mitosis (**Fig. 2**). Thus, mutations in spindle formation would

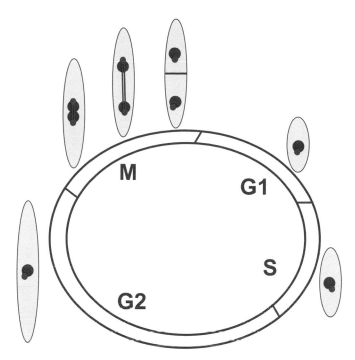

Figure 2. Fission yeast cell cycle. Note that spindle formation occurs in M phase. Spindle pole bodies are shown in red.

give a mitotic arrest in S. pombe. Statement II is correct, making **choice C the correct answer**. Statement III is incorrect because S. pombe mutants defective in spindle formation would be arrested in mitosis.

As an aside, the cell cycle events that lead to the formation of the mitotic spindle and segregation of chromosomes during mitosis is an important topic on the MCAT. Furthermore, many drugs cause cell cycle arrest at various stages. Although the passage focused on the two yeast model systems, it is important to understand their relationship to human cells. Although there are many similarities, there are some important differences that are outlined in Table 2.

Process/ structure	Budding yeast	Fission yeast	Animal cells
Spindle; spindle pole bodies	Pre-mitotic; Embedded in nuclear envelope	Mitotic; Embedded in nuclear envelope	Mitotic; Cytoplasmic (Centrosomes)
Nuclear Membrane	Intact during mitosis (closed)	Intact during mitosis (closed)	Breakdown during mitosis
Chromosome condensation	None	Condensation	Condensation
Chromosome number	16	3	22 + X and Y

Table 2. Comparison of chromosome dynamics between yeasts and animal cells. Animal cell chromosome number refers to humans.

Note that both spindle pole bodies and centrosomes are microtubule organizing centers in the yeasts and animal cells, respectively. Thus, the spindle is composed of microtubules which are rod-like structures consisting of α and β tubulin. In animal cells, centrosomes are duplicated during S phase and contain a pair of centrioles that are composed of nine triplet sets of microtubules arranged in a circular structure. The centrioles are located within a protein network. The spindle pole bodies in yeast do not contain centrioles. During prophase the duplicated centrosomes migrate to opposite poles in preparation for the formation of the mitotic spindle (**Fig. 3**).

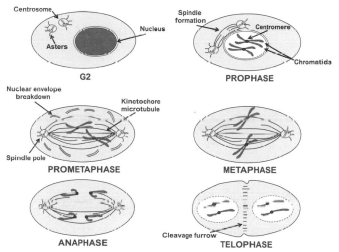

Figure 3. Nuclear dynamics during interphase and mitosis in animal cells. Note that during G2 the chromosomes are not condensed (green). Nuclear breakdown occurs in prometaphase and re-assembles during telophase.

3) **B. Growth of colonies at only the permissive temperature.** Cdc genes are essential for cell cycle progression and thus are required for viability. Therefore, Cdc mutants are conditional alleles and that, in fact, is what most temperature sensitive mutants are. Most of the time they are point mutations and the encoded protein's tertiary structure is sensitive such that, at the restrictive temperature, the protein fails to fold properly, thus reducing its function.

Yeast Cell Cycle

By treating cells with DNA damaging agents (i.e. EMS) that introduce point mutations throughout the genome, individual yeast colonies can be plated out and grown at a permissive temperature (**Fig. 4**). Through replica plating, those colonies that grow at one temperature (permissive) can be tested for their ability to grow at the restrictive temperature (which is usually higher). Thus, in order to determine from the screen which colonies are temperature sensitive, Cdc mutants must grow only at the permissive temperature.

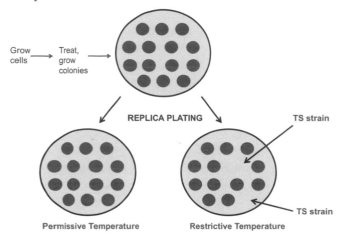

Figure 4. Generation of TS mutants.

4) **A. dominant mutation in CDC2.** The key thing to observe in the data is that at the restrictive temperature the cells spend less time in G2 and more time in mitosis (**Fig. 5**). This means that they are entering mitosis earlier than normal, especially because the G1 and S phases are the same duration under each condition. Such precocious entry into mitosis has been observed for dominant mutations in CDC2. If choice A is correct, then **choice D must be wrong** as a gain of function mutation in a negative regulator of mitosis would prolong G2 phase, the opposite of what is observed. Choice A and D are basically opposites. **Choice B is wrong** because a loss of function mutation in START would yield varying times spent in G1 at the low and high temperatures. A gain of function mutation in an S phase gene would change the duration of S phase between the low and high temperatures. However, there is no change in the length of S phase as a function of temperature, meaning that **choice C is wrong**.

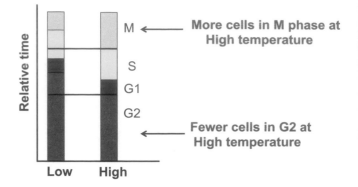

Figure 5. Precocious entry into mitosis.

5) **D. Cannot be determined.** 4N refers to diploid cells that have duplicated their genome in S phase. Therefore, the G2 peak (4N peak) is a mixture of cells in G2 as well as M phase. This is because they both have a 4N content of DNA. The G1 cells represent the 2N DNA content and S phase cells are those cells that have a DNA content between 2N and 4N. This **eliminates choices A, B, and C.** Thus, one cannot precisely tell the number of cells in mitosis using DNA content alone. To determine the % of cells in mitosis, various additional methods would have to be employed. This includes determining the % of cells with a specific phosphorylated residue of histone H3, a known mitotic marker.

6) **B. monomeric glycolytic enzyme.** Note from the passage that dominant negative mutants are described as being able to encode for proteins that, "Bind and 'titrate' out a binding partner." In this context, mutations in those factors known to form complexes could readily yield dominant negative phenotypes. This includes the heterodimeric cyclin-dependent kinases, **eliminating choice A**. Imagine that a mutant cyclin protein binds to a kinase partner, but renders the entire heterodimer inactive. In this regard, the dominant negative allele titrates out the functional kinase, generating a dysfunctional complex. Through similar logic, both the multi-subunit RNA polymerase II and the U1 ribonuclear protein particle are protein complexes that can be rendered dysfunctional by a dominant negative member of the complex. This **eliminates choices C and D**. In contrast, a monomeric enzyme, such as one functioning in glycolysis, has no binding partners to titrate away, making it more difficult to imagine that a mutation in this gene could give rise to a dominant negative phenotype. **Choice A is correct.**

Notes:

Insulin Secretion

Understanding how insulin is synthesized, processed, and released is important in developing therapeutics for the treatment of diabetes mellitus, a disease characterized by insufficient insulin function. Type I diabetics fail to produce insulin, but in type II diabetes insulin can be produced, but for various reasons, some tissues are "resistant" to its action.

Initially synthesized as the preproinsulin prohormone, insulin is secreted in response to elevated blood glucose levels. After processing by signal peptidase, proinsulin is formed and transferred to the Golgi. Further processing of proinsulin releases the 31-amino acid C-peptide to generate mature insulin, a small protein composed of two covalently linked chains (**Fig. 1**). Insulin is packaged into secretory vesicles and is released in response to stimulation by rising glucose levels in pancreatic beta cells. A major function of insulin is to repress the release of glucagon from pancreatic alpha cells. In a cell culture study of insulin secretion, several key parameters were measured in insulin-secreting beta cells in response to stimulation with glucose. The results are shown in Table 1.

Regulating the release of insulin from secretory vesicles is an important therapeutic target in type II diabetes. For this, sulfonylurea drugs are often prescribed. Their mode of action has been determined to operate through the binding of inward rectifying K^+ channels (K_{IR}) that are inhibited by the high ATP levels generated from pancreatic glucose oxidation. ATP-sensitive K_{IR} channels are potassium-selective and, when open, provide a net flux of K^+ into the cell.

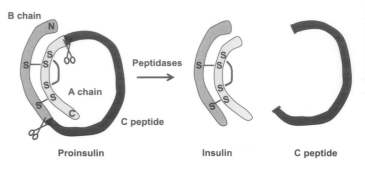

Figure 1. Proinsulin processing into insulin causes the release of C peptide.

Beta cells	ATP/ADP	Membrane Potential	$\dfrac{Ca^{+2} \text{ (in)}}{Ca^{+2} \text{ (ex)}}$
Unstimulated	.025	- 0.65 mV	.001
Stimulated	0.65	+ 0.25 mV	.012

Table 1. Measurement of key physiological parameters in both unstimulated and stimulated pancreatic beta cells. ATP/ADP represents intracellular ratio. In, ex = intracellular and extracellular calcium levels, respectively.

1) Which of the following statements are true with respect to K_{IR} channels?

  I. Open in the stimulated state.
  II. Promote Ca^{+2}-mediated insulin exocytosis in the stimulated state.
  III. Inhibited by ATP.
  IV. Promote membrane repolarization in the stimulated state.

A. I, II

B. II, III

C. I, IV

D. III, IV

2) The neurotransmitter somatostatin can inhibit insulin secretion through:

A. reducing membrane hyperpolarization and increasing K^+ conductance.

B. reducing membrane depolarization and increasing K^+ conductance.

C. increasing membrane hyperpolarization by decreasing K^+ conductance.

D. increasing membrane repolarization by decreasing K^+ conductance.

3) Excessive treatment with sulfonylureas causes:

A. hypoglycemia and membrane depolarization.

B. hyperglycemia and membrane depolarization.

C. hypoglycemia and membrane hyperpolarization.

D. hyperglycemia and membrane hyperpolarization.

4) Which of the following would least be expected in a type I diabetic patient?

A. elevated serum glucose

B. reduced adipose triglycerides

C. elevated serum fatty acids

D. elevated hepatic glycogen

5) Preproinsulin (Pre), proinsulin (Pro), and mature insulin (I) were examined by Western blotting using SDS PAGE and reducing conditions. Which electrophoretic profile correctly matches the β chains when loaded in the order: Lane 1, Pre; Lane 2, Pro; Lane 3, I?

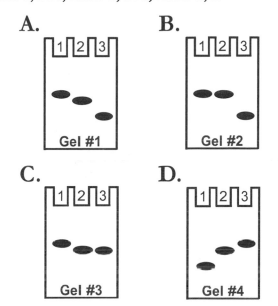

6) To study potential C peptide receptors, researchers performed binding assays by incubating renal membranes with ^3H radiolabeled C-peptides in either the L or D configurations. This was followed by treatment with unlabeled (cold) D or L competitor C-peptides as shown below. Which of the following conclusions can be drawn about renal cell expression of C-peptide receptors?

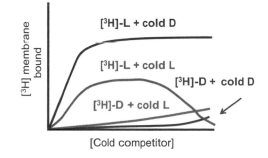

A. Renal cells express the receptor because both the D and L peptides bind to it.

B. Renal cells express the receptor because only the D peptide binds to it.

C. Renal cells express the receptor and only the L peptide binds to it.

D. Renal cells do not express the receptor because neither the D nor L peptides bind to it.

Insulin Secretion

Annotations.
1) B 2) B 3) A 4) D 5) A 6) C

	Foundation 1: Biochemistry-A Gene Expression-B Metabolism-D			Foundation 3: Neurobiology-A		
	A	**B**	**D**	**A**		
Concepts						
Reasoning				1,3		
Research		5				
Data	6		4	2		

Big Picture. This passage combines cell physiology with biochemistry in the context of insulin secretion, an important clinical topic given its link to diabetes. You should be able to recall the fundamentals of diabetes mellitus, including distinguishing between types I and II.

Membrane polarization is important for releasing insulin in response to a glucose stimulus. You should know the basics of this and to be able to differentiate between the terms depolarize, repolarize, and hyperpolarize. This is discussed below. In this vein, the passage describes K$^+$ inward channels and these are distinct from the more familiar Na$^+$/K$^+$ ATPases. K$_{IR}$ channels are inhibited by ATP and have a net effect of bringing K$^+$ into the cell. This is key for figuring out the relationship between glucose stimulation and the release of insulin. The conclusion that should be drawn from Table 1 is that glucose increases ATP levels and this inhibits K$_{IR}$ channels, keeping K$^+$ levels high outside the cell. This depolarizes the cell and opens voltage-gated calcium channels that facilitate insulin release. The model is presented in Figure 2.

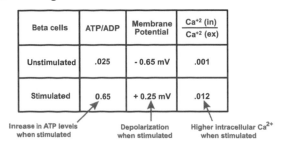

Beta cells	ATP/ADP	Membrane Potential	$\frac{Ca^{+2} (in)}{Ca^{+2} (ex)}$
Unstimulated	.025	- 0.65 mV	.001
Stimulated	0.65	+ 0.25 mV	.012

Increase in ATP levels when stimulated   Depolarization when stimulated   Higher intracellular Ca^{2+} when stimulated

Table 2. Interpretation of data from Table 1.

1) **B. II, III.** Glucose acts as a stimulant and its oxidation in pancreatic beta cells leads to increased levels of intracellular ATP. High levels of ATP inhibit K$_{IR}$ channels, meaning that they will be closed in the stimulated state. **Statement III is correct**, meaning that **choices A and C are incorrect.** Note from Table 1 that increased levels of ATP are accompanied by membrane depolarization and an increase in the intracellular levels of calcium. This calcium is required for exocytosis of insulin-containing vesicles. **Statement II is therefore correct**, meaning that you can now bypass examining the validity of statement IV and immediately mark **choice B as being correct.** But try to double check things, particularly if you have extra time on the exam. **Statement IV is wrong** because going from a negative to a positive membrane potential is depolarization. Repolarization is the opposite: going from a positive to negative membrane potential (**Fig. 3**). You should recognize that inhibition of an inward potassium channel keeps the positively charged K$^+$ ions outside of the cell. This will change the membrane potential to make it more positive, consistent with depolarization.

2) **B. reducing membrane depolarization and increasing K$^+$ conductance.** From the data in Table 1, you should have concluded that high ATP (from high glucose) is accompanied by membrane depolarization (negative to positive potential). This causes insulin to be released in the stimulated state (**Fig. 2**). Therefore, somatostatin-dependent <u>inhibition</u> of insulin release must occur (directly or indirectly) through its affect in inhibiting (or reducing) membrane depolarization. This immediately **rules out choices A and C.**

Because the membrane is depolarized through inhibition of K$_{IR}$ channels during the normal release of insulin, somatostatin enforces the opposite effect: increasing K$^+$ conductance and repolarizing the cell. This is tantamount to the unstimulated state (**Fig. 2**). **Choice B is correct.** Note that you do not need to know anything about somatostatin per se to answer the question (although it is a hormone secreted from the GI tract and the delta cells of the pancreas).

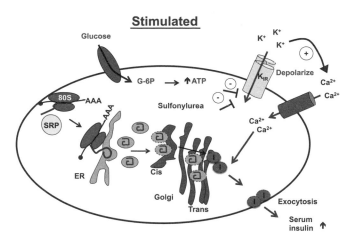

Stimulated

Figure 2. Model for release of insulin.

3) A. hypoglycemia and membrane depolarization.
Recall that membrane depolarization refers to an increase in membrane potential and this occurs in response to glucose oxidation as shown in Table 1. As discussed in the passage, sulfonylurea drugs are used to treat type II diabetics. Recall that type II diabetics are insulin resistant. This means that more insulin secretion is required in a diabetic to achieve a normal biological response. The desired action of sulfonylureas is therefore to promote insulin secretion and we know from the passage that this occurs through membrane depolarization. Sulfonylureas mimic the glucose-stimulated state. This occurs through inhibition of K_{IR} channels that keeps positively charged potassium cations on the outside of the cell membrane (**Fig. 2**). **Choices C and D are eliminated**. As insulin reduces blood sugar levels, excessive levels of sulfonylureas would cause hypoglycemia through increased levels of insulin. This **eliminates choice B (and D again)**. Note that hypoglycemia is one of the biggest problems associated with therapies such as insulin injections or those that promote insulin release.

    <u>Additional information:</u> Questions 1-3 all have answer choices requiring prior knowledge regarding membrane depolarization, hyperpolarization, and repolarization. These are potentially confusing terms because students commonly encounter them for the first time in the context of the neuronal action potential. However, pancreatic beta cells are <u>non-neuronal</u>! Keep in mind that while all cell membranes exhibit polarization; only neuronal cells generate action potentials (**Fig. 3**).

Cell membranes are polarized because they are marked by a higher negative charge inside the cell relative to outside. This is largely because Na^+/K^+ ATPases pump 3 Na^+ outside and 2 K^+ inside the membrane. However, other channels can be active and change the dynamics of charge across the membrane. Both repolarization and hyperpolarization are opposites of depolarization. They both mark a change in membrane potential that makes it more negative. Repolarization re-sets the resting potential and hyperpolarization "overshoots" the resting potential and makes it more negative. In Figure 3, the neuronal action potential is shown. In this context, repolarization refers to open voltage gated K^+ channels with closed Na^+ channels. In the case of insulin release in beta cells, the K_{IR} channels do not use sodium, yet can alter the membrane potential through regulating extracellular K^+ levels.

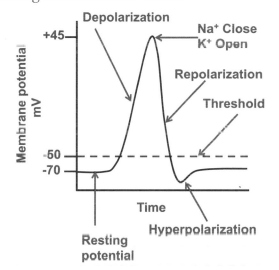

Figure 3. Key elements in neuronal action potential. Voltage gated Na^+ channels open (depolarization), increasing the charge inside of the cell. During repolarization, K^+ influx reduces the membrane potential. After reaching resting potential, the K^+ channels remain open and overshoot the resting potential.

4) D. Elevated hepatic glycogen. A hallmark feature of type I diabetes is the inability to produce insulin through an autoimmune disorder. In this condition, there is no ability to deliver glucose to tissues for utilization as energy. This is why diabetics have high blood glucose levels (**eliminating choice A**). As delivery of glucose to tissues drops in diabetics, the body "thinks that it is starving." As an adaptive measure, hepatic glycogen stores will be mobilized to provide glucose, <u>reducing</u> the amount of stored liver glycogen. Therefore, **choice D is correct**. Further, as the body thinks it is "starving," fats are mobilized through triglyceride breakdown. These circulate and are used for energy utilization by peripheral tissues, increasing the serum levels of fatty acids. **Choice C is wrong**. Mobilization of fatty acids would necessarily come from adipose triglycerides, which would also be expected to drop. This makes **choice B wrong**, and helps to explain why type I diabetics are often very thin.

5) A. Gel #1. First, you have to know how SDS polyacrylamide electrophoresis (SDS-PAGE) works. This technique separates molecules on the basis of their size. SDS is an anionic detergent (lipid) that binds to the peptide chain backbone, generating a linear structure with an equal charge to unit mass. When placed in an electrophoretic field, the negatively charged proteins (by virtue of their association with SDS) will migrate towards the cathode according to their molecular weights. The larger molecular weight species migrate slower, or are said to have a retarded mobility. Note that reducing conditions obviate any concern about the role of the disulfides bridges in the electrophoresis pattern. The cysteine residues would be fully reduced under these conditions, as is normal for SDS polyacrylamide electrophoresis.

Now recall from the passage that signal peptidase cleaves preproinsulin to form proinsulin. Therefore, the size of preproinsulin > proinsulin and this **eliminates choices B and D** as these gel patterns do not show a decrease in size from lanes 1 to 2. Lane 1 should have the most retarded electrophilic mobility as preproinsulin is the largest protein as it has yet to be cleaved.

Cleavage of preproinsulin occurs in the ER during translocation. Recall that translocation of most proteins, including preproinsulin, is mediated by the signal recognition particle (SRP) (**Fig. 2**). SRP recognizes N-terminal signal sequences on proteins destined for the secretory pathway. Since SRP is involved in insulin secretion, it recognizes the signal sequence at the N-terminus of preproinsulin. This is in the B chain and is the site of cleavage. Once at the endoplasmic reticulum, the signal sequence is cut off by signal peptidase.

Choice C is wrong because this gel pattern displays no size distinction between proinsulin and mature insulin when, in fact, we know from the passage that the 31 amino acid, C peptide has been processed out of the mature protein. The correct gel pattern reflects this as lane 3 has a smaller sized band than lane 2.

<u>Additional information:</u> Western blotting, or immunoblotting, is a widely used laboratory technique designed to detect the presence of proteins based upon their reactivity to specific antibodies. This should be considered a basic topic and is summarized below (**Fig. 4**). After running denaturing SDS gels, the protein content in the gel is transferred via an applied electric field to a solid support matrix (i.e. PVDF membrane) that becomes "the blot". The blot is coated with protein on one side of the membrane. It is then blocked with a protein solution that binds to the filter at all possible binding spots. Afterwards, the primary (1°) antibody directed against the antigen β chain of insulin is applied. Only the presence and position of the β chain will be identified in the experiment. After a sufficient amount of time has elapsed, the primary (anti-1° β chain) antibody will bind to β chains on the filter, regardless of what type of insulin molecule it resides in. After washing off unbound antibody, a 2° antibody is applied. This antibody is species specific and recognizes the constant region of the species that the 1° antibody is derived from (i.e. rabbit or mouse). The 2° antibody has a fluor covalently conjugated to its Fc region, and the β chain is indirectly detected through light emission.

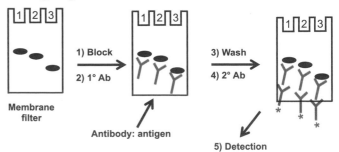

Figure 4. Overview of Western blotting.

6) C. Renal cells express the receptor and only the L peptide binds to it. Recall that in humans, only the L chiral configuration is used. Therefore, any specific membrane receptor for the C-peptide would necessarily have a stereospecific interaction for the L configured ligand. This fact would be observed experimentally by the lack of significant binding between a membrane receptor and peptides composed of D amino acids. This is most clear in the experiment using [^{3}H]-L + cold D as a competitor. The term "cold" is informal for unlabeled. Note the saturation curve, consistent with the presence of a receptor. The failure of increasing levels of cold D competitor peptide to reduce the amount of tritium detected through binding of [^{3}H]-L peptide is consistent with L-configuration binding. Moreover, this is confirmed through observing that increased levels of cold L peptide compete off the [^{3}H]-L peptide signal. Note the minimal binding of [^{3}H]-D peptide to the membranes, suggesting that this is background association with the membrane.

As basic information, you should recall that all amino acids found in proteins are chiral except for glycine; glycine has two hydrogen atoms around a central carbon. Chiral carbons are sp^3 hybridized and have four <u>different</u> groups attached to them. Alanine has one chiral center. For example, L and D alanine (**Fig. 5**) are enantiomers; they are non-superimposable mirror images of each other and rotate the plane of polarized light in opposite directions. An equal mixture of enantiomers constitutes a racemic mixture and has no net rotation of the plane of polarized light. The D and L nomenclature has its origins in Fischer' study of D-glyceraldehyde and how it rotates the plane of polarized light. D amino acids rotate the plane of polarized light to the right and are often, <u>but not always</u>, in the "R" configuration. The same is true for L amino acids and the "S" configuration.

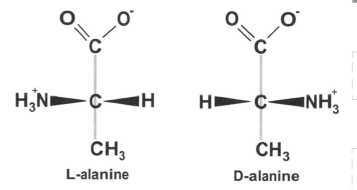

Figure 5. Fischer projections for the enantiomers L and D-alanine. Note that the most oxidized carbon is usually at the top.

Retrograde Synaptic Transmission

Inhibition of neurons is primarily driven by the neurotransmitter γ-amino butyric acid (GABA). There are multiple ways of modulating GABA inhibition, including depolarization-induced suppression of inhibition (DSI). In DSI, the postsynaptic neuron is briefly depolarized either by excitatory transmission from other neurons or, in the case of an experimental setting, through the patch clamp recording pipette. Following depolarization, the inhibitory postsynaptic potentials (IPSPs) impinging on the postsynaptic cell are reduced in both amplitude and frequency. Therefore, in DSI, depolarizing the postsynaptic neuron influences the probability of neurotransmitter release at the presynaptic cell. This reverse, or retrograde neurotransmission, is carried out by endocannabinoids.

Depolarization of the postsynaptic neuron triggers the release of endocannabinoid neurotransmitters from the postsynaptic cell, which diffuse to adjacent neurons and activate cannabinoid (CB) receptors. One such target is cannabinoid receptor 1 (CB$_1$), a pre-synaptic, heterotrimeric G-protein coupled receptor (GPCR), which can inhibit voltage-gated Ca^{+2} channels and thereby reduce the probability of neurotransmitter release.

In an effort to investigate DSI, scientists isolated pyramidal neurons from the hippocampus and prepared them for a patch clamp experiment (**Fig. 1**). These experiments allow scientists to measure the current through open channels or the membrane potential of the neuron through the patch clamp recording pipette. In this experiment, control buffer is applied to the cells, a patch clamp recording is made and after several seconds of baseline recording of GABA-dependent IPSPs, the neurons were then depolarized by a current injection through the patch-clamp recording pipette. Subsequently, IPSPs were recorded following application of two experimental drugs, compounds A or B (**Fig. 2**).

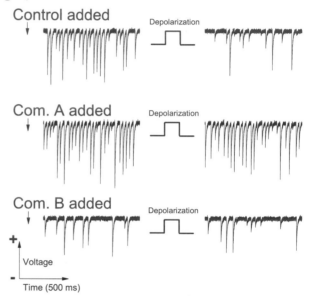

Figure 2. Recordings of IPSPs from a postsynaptic neuron following application of control buffer or buffer with either Compound A or B. IPSPs are measured before (left column) and after (right column) a depolarizing pulse.

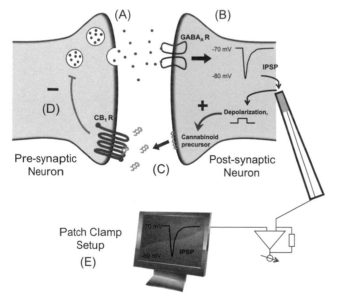

Figure 1. Pre-synaptic GABA release (A) activates GABA receptors to hyperpolarize neurons (B). Depolarization trips a negative feedback loop, where retrograde endocannabinoids (C) signal to presynaptic neurons to reduce inhibitory neurotransmitter release (D). The IPSPs are measured via a patch clamp recording setup (E).

1) **In the brain, GABA activated ion channels would cause the:**

   A. influx of Cl^- ions causing a rapid and transient membrane depolarization.

   B. efflux of Cl^- ions shifting the membrane potential from -70 mV to -80mV.

   C. influx of Cl^- ions shifting the membrane potential from -70 mV to -80mV.

   D. efflux of Cl^- ions activating K^+ channels that hyperpolarize the neuronal membrane.

2) **Which of the following is true with respect to the effects that compounds A and B have on the CB_1 receptor relative to the control?**

   A. Compound A is an antagonist because the frequency and amplitude of IPSPs are unaffected following depolarization.

   B. Compound A is an agonist because the frequency and amplitude of IPSPs are unaffected following depolarization.

   C. Compound B is an antagonist because the frequency and amplitude of IPSPs are unaffected prior to and following depolarization.

   D. Compound B is an agonist because the frequency and amplitude of IPSPs are increased prior to and following depolarization.

3) **GTPγS is a non-hydrolyzable analog of GTP and is often used to study heterotrimeric G proteins. In the presence of GTPγS, the recordings from postsynaptic neurons would now show that:**

   A. depolarization triggers an increase in IPSPs.

   B. depolarization triggers suppression of IPSPs.

   C. hyperpolarization triggers an increase is IPSPs.

   D. depolarization does not change IPSPs.

4) **To support the conclusion that the effects of compounds A and B are due to their actions at CB_1 receptors, which of the following would be the least useful experimental control?**

   A. Measuring IPSPs before and after depolarization from CB_1 receptor deficient mice.

   B. Measuring action potential thresholds from postsynaptic neurons.

   C. Measuring the effect of compound A or B in the presence of a known non-competitive antagonist for CB_1 receptors.

   D. Measuring the effect of compound A or B while introducing a general inhibitor for GPCR signaling inside the postsynaptic neuron.

5) **Which of the following experiments would unambiguously determine if the antagonistic compound works as a competitive or noncompetitive antagonist?**

   A. Measuring IPSPs in the presence of both compounds A and B.

   B. Determining if the antagonistic compound is outcompeted by the agonistic compound.

   C. Determining if a known non-competitive antagonist blocks the effects of the antagonistic compound.

   D. Measuring IPSPs in increasing concentrations of the antagonistic compound.

6) **A researcher hypothesized that ionic radius is inversely proportional to the kinetics of membrane crossing through a non-selective ion channel. If true, rank the following ions according to their relative speeds of influx.**

   A. $Na^+ > K^+ > Rb^+$

   B. $K^+ > Na^+ > Rb^+$

   C. $Rb^+ > K^+ > Na^+$

   D. $K^+ > Rb^+ > Na^+$

3

4

Retrograde Synaptic Transmission

Annotations.
1) C 2) A 3) D 4) B 5) B 6) A

	Foundation 3: Neurobiology-A			Foundation 4: Atoms-E		
	A			**E**		
Concepts				6		
Reasoning	1,3					
Research	4,5					
Data	2					

Big Picture. The passage focuses on DSI, which is an example of retrograde neurotransmission. This is distinct from classical transmission in that chemical signals flow from postsynaptic cells backwards to presynaptic cells. DSI is triggered in the postsynaptic neuron by short depolarizations, i.e. changes from the resting membrane potential of -70 mV to -50 mV. These depolarizations can be caused by a barrage of excitatory postsynaptic potentials (i.e. from many glutamate synapses activated in a short time), or triggered artificially by a scientist during a patch clamp recording, as is the case in the above example. The depolarization in the postsynaptic neuron causes cannabinoid neurotransmitter precursors to be converted into active cannabinoid transmitter molecules. These cannabinoids diffuse across the synaptic cleft from the postsynaptic neuron where they bind to and activate Cannabinoid Type-1 Receptors (CB$_1$R) on the presynaptic neuron. CB$_1$R is a G-protein coupled receptor, which can inhibit neurotransmitter release. Thus, the depolarization at the postsynaptic cell can 'work its way backwards' to the presynaptic cell to prevent GABA release. Depolarization trips a negative feedback loop, where retrograde endocannabinoids signal to presynaptic neurons to reduce inhibitory neurotransmitter release.

1) **C. influx of Cl$^-$ ions shifting the membrane potential from -70 mV to -80mV.** GABA causes inhibition of neurons. You should be familiar with common neurotransmitters and their functions in ion conductance (**Table 1**). As fundamental knowledge, you should also recall that the release of GABA from pre-synaptic neurons leads to the activation of ionotropic GABA$_A$ receptors causing a flux of chloride ions that generates a more negative membrane potential. However, the word "flux" is vague because there is no distinction between influx and efflux. Recall that an action potential, or other forms of depolarization, occurs when positively charged ions like Na$^+$ flow into a neuron. This shifts the membrane potential from its resting potential of -70 mV to a more positive potential such as -50 mV or -40 mV. Therefore, an ion of negative charge like Cl$^-$ flowing into (influx) a neuron will cause the opposite effect, hyperpolarization. Thus, the **correct answer is choice C.** This question uses the word 'ionotropic' which may cause some confusion. Ionotropic simply refers to receptors whose activation leads to the opening of an ion channel. This is in contrast to metabotropic receptors, whose activation triggers signaling through G-proteins or kinases (e.g. adrenergic receptors).

Table 1. Common ionotropic receptors

Neurotransmitter	Receptor Name	Permeant Ions	Functions
GABA	**GABA$_A$**	Cl$^-$	Neuronal inhibition
Glycine	GlyR	Cl$^-$	Spinal cord inhibition
Glutamate	GluR	Na$^+$, K$^+$, Ca^{2+}	Neuronal excitation
Acetylcholine	nAChR	Na$^+$, K$^+$, Ca^{2+}	Neuronal excitation, muscular contraction

2) A. Compound A is an antagonist because the frequency and amplitude of IPSPs are unaffected following depolarization. Shown in Figure 3 is a sample patch clamp recording of the membrane potential of the postsynaptic neuron that normally sits at -70 mV. However, every now and then a presynaptic neuron contacting the neuron being recorded releases a burst of GABA. This causes the short, sharp downward deflections that indicate that the membrane potential has decreased (becoming more negative), causing inhibition. Electrophysiologists often report two parameters in these types of experiments: amplitude and frequency. Amplitude is the size of the change in membrane potential (the size of the downward deflection) and frequency is the number of individual synaptic events in a given amount of time. Both are indices of how much inhibition the postsynaptic neuron receives.

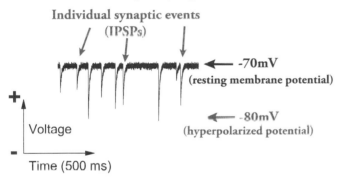

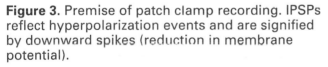

Figure 3. Premise of patch clamp recording. IPSPs reflect hyperpolarization events and are signified by downward spikes (reduction in membrane potential).

In the "control added" panel presented in Figure 2, you should recognize that the number of IPSPs (i.e. hyperpolarization events) is dramatically reduced after the patch clamp device depolarizes the neuron. This observed reduction in IPSPs after depolarization is the very definition of DSI. Further, you should consider this panel while looking at Figure 1 and conclude that the postsynaptic neuron is releasing endocannabinoids in response to the depolarization induced by the patch clamp. The other two panels show the results of adding two compounds to the experimental setup and it is evident that each has a different effect when compared to the control. One of these compounds is an

agonist of CB_1 receptors while the other is an antagonist. How can the two be distinguished? The key is thinking about what would happen to the activity of the CB_1 receptor and how this would impact GABA transmission as soon as the compound is given. If an antagonist is given, it will block all CB_1 receptors, preventing DSI. Thus, inhibition at the beginning of the experiment will be as strong (or stronger) as control and will be unaffected by a depolarization event. This effect is seen by the incubation with compound A (**Fig. 4**).

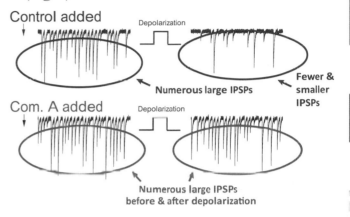

Figure 4. Compound A is an antagonist of the CB_1 Receptor.

However if an agonist is given, it will activate all CB_1 receptors. This will suppress IPSPs even <u>before</u> the depolarization is given and will continue to suppress inhibition after the depolarization. So at the very beginning of the patch clamp recording, the IPSPs will start out small and will remain so after depolarization because the CB_1 receptors are already maximally activated. Compound B has this effect (**Fig.5**).

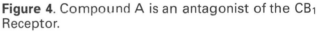

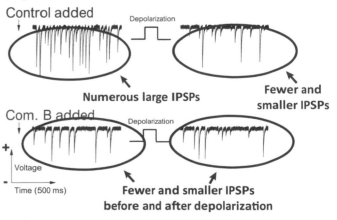

Figure 5. Compound B is a agonist of the CB_1 Receptor.

Therefore, the **correct answer is choice A**. Compound A is the antagonist because the IPSPs are unaffected relative to control (as stated in the question) after depolarization. **Choice B is incorrect** because an agonist would be expected to reduce IPSPs before depolarization. **Choice C is incorrect** since the IPSPs observed with compound B are affected relative to control and are reduced in amplitude and frequency. **Choice D is incorrect** due to its flawed logic. Although compound B is an agonist, it is not an agonist because the IPSPs are increased as stated by answer D. Rather, compound B is an agonist because the IPSPs are decreased.

3) **D. depolarization does not change IPSPs.** As discussed in the passage, the CB1 receptor is coupled to a heterotrimeric G protein whose activation, according to the passage, "...can inhibit voltage-gated Ca^{2+} channels and thereby reduce the probability of neurotransmitter release." In this scenario, the neurotransmitter is GABA (**Fig. 1**). Recall that heterotrimeric G proteins are inactive in the GDP bound form, but active as signaling molecules in the GTP bound form. Ligand binding to the G protein coupled receptor (GPCR) activates an exchange of GDP for GTP. Upon binding to GTP, the G_α subunit dissociates from the $\beta\gamma$ subunits and signals until the bound GTP is hydrolyzed back to GDP. Once bound to the non-hydrolyzable GTP analog (GTPγS), the G_α will be constitutively active which, in this case, will inhibit GABA release through the inhibition of neurotransmitter release. This is because the active G_α subunit inhibits voltage-gated Ca^{2+} channels. As calcium is required for the release of neurotransmitter through exocytosis, this process will be inhibited in the presence of GTPγS. As a consequence, there will be no additional modulation of $GABA_A$ receptors or changes in IPSPs in the presence of GTPγS. As with the previous question, the effect of GTPγS is to maximally suppress inhibition prior to the depolarization event. **Choice D is therefore the correct answer**.

4) **B. Measuring action potential thresholds from postsynaptic neurons.** This question focused on an element of research design and required that you identified an experiment that would provide no benefit to support conclusions drawn from the experiments presented in the passage. If CB$_1$ receptors underlie DSI, then genetically removing them should eliminate DSI. Therefore measuring IPSPs before and after depolarization in such mice is a very useful control making **choice A incorrect**.

The threshold for the firing of an action potential is the membrane voltage at which the voltage gated Na^+ channels activate. This triggers the all-or-none firing of an action potential. There are multiple genes encoding Na^+ channels, each of which can have different activation voltages (for example -50 mV versus -45 mV) and measuring such thresholds can inform the experimentalist if the composition of the Na^+ population has changed. However, the Na^+ channel population is not relevant at all in this experiment, because those are downstream of where DSI takes place making this uninformative and therefore **choice B is correct**.

A non-competitive antagonist will prevent any effect of the agonist, for example compound B, provided that they are both acting through CB$_1$ receptors. Therefore conducting an experiment involving a non-competitive antagonist could support the conclusion that compound B works via CB$_1$ receptors, making it a useful control. This effectively **rules out choice C**. Similar to the logic for answer choice C, if compound A works through the G-protein coupled CB$_1$ receptor, then a general inhibitor of GPCR signaling will prevent the effect of the agonist compound. Therefore, the experiment described in choice D is a useful control making **choice D incorrect**.

5) B. Determining if the antagonistic compound is outcompeted by the agonistic compound. This question was similar to question 4 in that it focused on research design, but in contrast to question 4, you were asked to find an experiment that would definitely support a conclusion. **Choice B is correct** because the key word in this solution is "outcompeted." A competitive antagonist is defined by its ability to be outcompeted. That is, if you add enough competitive antagonist to block your response by 100%, you will be able to completely recover that response by increasing agonist concentration to some level. However, if your antagonist is noncompetitive you might recover some or none of the response by increasing agonist concentration. **Choice A is incorrect**, although it initially appears reasonable. By combining the agonist and competitive antagonist you might find that the agonist effect on IPSPs with antagonist is not as strong as the agonist alone. But, strictly speaking, this would not determine if the antagonist is competitive. **Choice C is not useful** and somewhat nonsensical. A competitive antagonist blocks or inhibits receptors; it reduces the response from 100% to 0%, for example. To speak of the effect of an antagonist being blocked means that the antagonist doesn't work, that the receptors remain ready to function and provide a response. In other words, you recover your response to 50% for example. There is no way the addition of a non-competitive antagonist, another blocker, will recover such a response. You cannot get back from 0% to 100% by adding another inhibitor, regardless of competitive or not. **Choice D is incorrect** because this experiment cannot distinguish competitive from non-competitive mechanisms. By adding more of the compound in question, all you determine is that in can block at a range of concentrations and the concentration producing half-maximal inhibition. You cannot distinguish a competitive from non-competitive antagonist.

6) A. $Na^+ > K^+ > Rb^+$. Recall from periodic trends that ionic radius increases as you go down within a group or to the left within a period. As you will be provided a periodic table on the MCAT, you must identify that the element Na^+ is just above K^+. This key rule, that Na^+ has a smaller radius then K^+, means that all that is needed to answer the question is that Na^+ has a smaller radius than K^+, meaning it must go through the channel the fastest if the hypothesis is correct. Only **choice A contains this relationship**. As an aside, note that although rubidium is not a physiologically relevant molecule, scientists can use it to study channel behavior in in vitro systems.

3

4

99

Hemoglobin

Various allosteric effectors, including 2,3 diphosphoglycerate (2,3 DPG, also known as 2,3 biphosphoglycerate), bind to hemoglobin and promote oxygen dissociation. The α and β subunits lie in a cluster created through gene duplication and are differentially transcribed during development (**Fig. 1**). Tetrameric hemoglobin molecules composed of varying subunits have distinct biochemical properties. For example, fetal hemoglobin (Hb-F) consists of two α and two γ chains and binds to 2,3 DPG with lower affinity than the adult form (Hb-A) that consists of two α and two β chains.

Hemoglobinopathies represent an array of disorders that result in reduced oxygen binding characteristics. One example is sickle-cell disease (SCD), which is caused by a single amino acid change in the β chain. Studies have emerged to devise methods to "reactivate" fetal globin expression in SCD patients to alleviate symptoms. Three compounds were tested on erythrocytes isolated from healthy adult subjects. Two of the compounds were synthesized in a lab, while the third was 2,3 DPG. Measurements of hemoglobin oxygen affinity were then taken (**Fig. 2**).

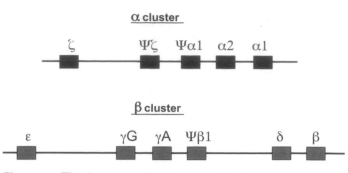

Figure 1. The human globin gene cluster.

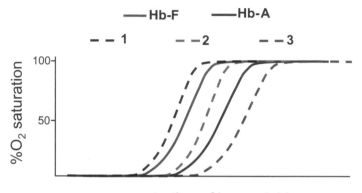

Figure 2. Binding affinities for Hb-A hemoglobin tetramers after treatment with three compounds. The binding affinities for Hb-A and Hb-F are plotted as reference.

1) Incorporation of iron into adult hemoglobin pre-treated with an oxidizing agent would be expected to mimic which of the compounds described in the passage?

   A. Compound 2 because ferrous iron increases affinity to O_2.

   B. Compound 3 because ferrous iron increases affinity to O_2.

   C. Compound 2 because ferric iron decreases affinity to O_2.

   D. Compound 3 because ferric iron decreases affinity to O_2.

2) Extended exposure at high altitude (14,000 ft) would primarily increase the levels of 2,3 DPG in which cell type?

   A. erythrocytes

   B. active muscles

   C. inactive muscles

   D. lung

3) Which compound is most likely 2,3 DPG?

   A. compound 1

   B. compound 2

   C. compound 3

   D. cannot be determined

4) High levels of local carbon dioxide in tissues undergoing extensive respiration have what effect on hemoglobin?

   A. Increased O_2 affinity due to an increase in protons.

   B. Decreased O_2 affinity due to an increase in protons.

   C. Increased O_2 affinity due to a decrease in protons.

   D. Decrease O_2 affinity due to a decrease in protons.

5) When administered to adult test subjects with SCD, a drug increases the expression of the gamma globin gene. The drug would be expected to mimic the behavior of which compound?

   A. compound 1

   B. compound 2

   C. compound 3

   D. cannot be determined

6) SCD is an autosomal recessive mutation. In a large and isolated population it is found that 9% of the inhabitants suffer from the disease. Calculate the percentage of the population heterozygous for the mutant allele.

   A. 3%

   B. 42%

   C. 49%

   D. 32%

7) After birth, histone deacetylases located at the γ-globin promoter would most likely be:

   A. active because removing acetyl groups from histones is transcriptionally repressive.

   B. inactive because removing acetyl groups from histones is transcriptionally repressive.

   C. active because removing acetyl groups from histones is transcriptionally activating.

   D. inactive because removing acetyl groups from histones is transcriptionally activating.

Hemoglobin

Annotations.
1) D   2) A   3) C   4) B   5) B   6) B   7) A

	Foundation 1: Biochemistry-A Gene Expression-B Genetics-C			Foundation 3: Other Systems-B		
	A	**B**	**C**	**B**		
Concepts		7	6	4		
Reasoning						
Research						
Data	1,3,5			2		

Big Picture. This passage discusses a classic hemoglobin problem through use of experimental analysis and data interpretation. There was a general emphasis on basic gene expression and circulatory system properties. Four of the seven questions relied solely on your ability to understand the experiment. Thus, it was critical to understand the graph that was presented. The important point to gather from the graph is that lines shifted to the left have higher affinity for oxygen because it takes less hemoglobin to reach 100% saturation (**Fig. 3**).

The second key point to gather from this passage was that adult hemoglobin (Hb-A) has less affinity for oxygen than fetal hemoglobin (HB-F). This is because it binds to 2,3 DPG with <u>higher</u> affinity. This is fertile ground for the MCAT because it is a built-in counterintuitive principle. Moreover, reducing the affinity between hemoglobin and oxygen is not always a bad thing. Tissues rely on this property so hemoglobin will actually release oxygen to them. We would not want hemoglobin to hold onto it forever! Think of the Bohr shift as toggling hemoglobin's greed for oxygen: you want him to be greedy for O_2 in the lungs yet generous in dispensing O_2 in actively respiring tissues.

1) D. Compound 3 because ferric iron decreases affinity to O_2. This question combined a concept derived from your outside knowledge with your ability to interpret information presented in the graph. Beginning with the graph, the answer choices only dealt with Compound 2 and 3 relative to adult hemoglobin alone (**Fig. 3**). You should have realized that Compound 2 increases hemoglobin affinity for O_2 while Compound 3 decreases it. This **ruled out choices B and C.**

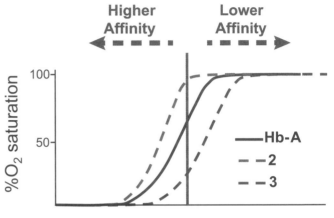

Figure 3. Comparison of Compound 2 versus 3 on hemoglobin binding affinity.

The question stem states that iron was pretreated with an oxidation agent, which would cause it to be converted to the Fe^{3+} state. The challenge to this component of the remaining two answer choices was that you needed to appreciate which suffix goes with which oxidized form of iron. This nomenclature detail may seem annoying, but is certainly within reason to be asked on the MCAT. Use this memory aid: if you were out on a date with someone, you would say it's just the <u>two</u> of <u>us</u> (ferr<u>ous</u>). However, if your less than pleasant friend were to join the two of you, their negative effect as a <u>third</u>-wheel would probably make you <u>sick</u> (hence fer<u>ric</u>). So to translate directly, ferric ion is Fe^{3+} while ferrous is Fe^{2+}. Based upon this logic, only **choice D is correct**.

2) A. erythrocytes. The concentration of oxygen in the atmosphere decreases as a function of altitude. This significantly challenges the circulatory system's ability to deliver oxygen to the tissues. Over time, erythrocytes will produce more 2,3 DPG in order to shift hemoglobin into a more tensed conformation, allowing it to better release oxygen to tissues. The misleading aspect to this question is that several of the answer choices rely on the consequence of this action, particularly actively respiring muscles. However, the cell that produces the majority of the 2,3 DPG at high altitudes is the erythrocyte where all of the hemoglobin is stored and therefore **choice A is correct**.

3) **C. compound 3.** Following the discussion in question two, 2,3 DPG reduces the affinity of hemoglobin for oxygen by stabilizing the tensed configuration. This would predictably shift the curve to the right. As is shown below, only compound #3 behaves in this manner (**Fig. 4**); therefore **choice is C is correct**.

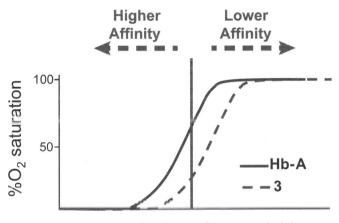
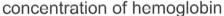

Figure 4. Compound #3 behaves like 2,3 DPG and shifts the oxygen affinity curve to the right.

There could have been some confusion had you considered the question to refer to fetal hemoglobin being treated with 2,3 DPG. This incorrect scenario would have implicated both Compound 2 or 3 as possible answers. The passage (and the legend for Figure 2) explicitly stated that adult subjects were used as a source for the hemoglobin.

4) **B. Decreased O₂ affinity due to an increase in protons.** Think of it logically to start out with: what do active tissues need? More or less oxygen? Of course they need more, so hemoglobin would have to have a decreased affinity for oxygen in order to deliver the goods to the active tissues. This **rules out choices A and C**. High levels of CO_2 result in high levels of carbonic acid thereby reducing the pH of the environment. This is because high levels of carbonic acid results in increased levels of protons through dissociation into bicarbonate, making **choice B correct**.

5) **B. compound 2.** At first this question seems relatively straightforward as turning on fetal globin expression should increase the affinity for oxygen and shift the curves to the left. However, the problem was determining which Compound, 1 or 2, was the best answer choice as each shifts the oxygen affinity curve of Hb-A to the left by increasing the affinity for O_2 (**Fig. 5**).

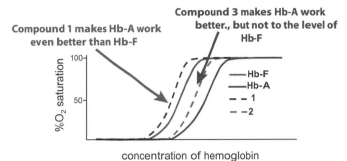

Figure 5. Compounds 1 and 2 both increase Hb-A oxygen affinity, but Compound 1 makes it exceed Hb-F. This would not be possible as the question stem states that the compound is working through activating Hb-F transcription.

The critical concept in the question stem was that adults were treated with a compound are already expressing the adult form (β) of globin. The question did not state that the compound inactivated the expression of the adult form or switched expression from one to the other. Rather, it just stated that the compound activated transcription of the fetal form. Therefore, the population of hemoglobin will be a mixture of both the adult and the fetal subunits (Hb-A, or $\alpha_2\beta_2$ and Hb-F, or $\alpha_2\gamma_2$). The average of these would therefore be compound #2. You should be familiar with the general pattern of expression of the various globin genes as a function of development as shown in Figure 6.

6) **B. 42%.** This question tests your background knowledge of Hardy-Weinberg Equilibrium. Recall the equation: $p^2 + 2pq + q^2 = 1$ (or $p + q = 1$), where p is the allele frequency of the dominant allele and q is the allele frequency of the recessive allele. Moreover, p^2 refers to the percentage of the population that are homozygous for the dominant alleles, q^2 represent the percentage of the population that are homozygous for the recessive alleles, and 2pq is the percentage of the population that is heterozygous. Notice the question stem refers to a large and isolated population, which are two of the tenets of Hardy and Weinberg. Recall that the other three criteria required

to achieve Hardy-Weinberg equilibrium are: (1) no natural selection, (2) random mating, (3) no mutations. These are needed in order to apply their formula. This is a classical way to ask the question because the question stem provides the frequency of the population with the recessive phenotype, or q^2. If $q^2 = .09$ the $q = 0.3$, meaning then that $p = 0.7$. Now you know the allele frequencies of both the dominant allele ($p = 0.7$) and the recessive allele ($q = 0.3$). The question asks for the percentage of the population with the heterozygous phenotype, which is equal to $2pq$. In this case it is equal to $(2)(0.7)(0.3) = 0.42$.

7) **A. active because removing acetyl groups from histones is transcriptionally repressive.** The combination of the data presented in Figure 2 and in the passage should have sent the message that fetal γ-globin is expressed during gestation and then turned off at birth. The full pattern of expression for the hemoglobin subunits is shown in Figure 6. While essential, this knowledge is insufficient to answer this particular question. Rather, you need additional information on what a histone deacetylase (HDAC) would do to a promoter. This is fundamental in gene expression and is desired knowledge for the MCAT. By acetylating histones at lysines, histone acetyltransfereases (HAT) can selectively neutralize the positive charge on histones. This interferes with their natural affinity for the negatively charged DNA. This has an activating effect on transcription by "loosening up" chromatin. HDACs, on the other hand, reverse this process and generally have the negative effect of inhibiting transcription. You would therefore expect the HDAC to be active at the γ-globin promoter to inhibit its transcription at birth, therefore **choice A is correct**.

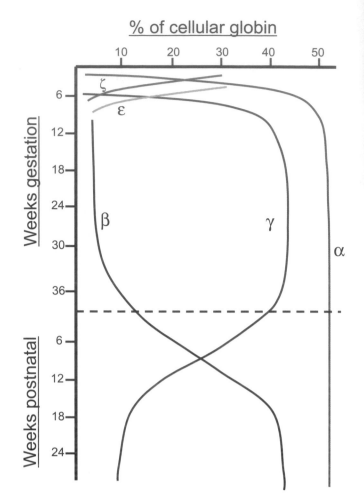

Figure 6. Expression pattern of human globin subunits during development (above dotted line) and shortly after birth (below dotted line).

Notes:

Autoimmunity

Multiple mechanisms have been posited for the development of autoimmunity: 1) The sequestration of antigens during development in places such as the eye lens and central nervous system shields these tissues and their epitopes from pre-existing auto-reactive antibodies. Upon injury or infection and consequent release of an antigen from sequestration, a self immune response is triggered; 2) "Molecular mimicry" suggests that when foreign peptides from exogenous antigens with sufficient similarities to a host peptide are recognized as self, a cross-reactive B and T cell response is observed.

Grave's and Hashimoto's disease are two thyroid autoimmune disorders. Normally, the pituitary-hypothalamus axis regulates secretion of the thyroid-stimulating hormone (TSH) through thyroid releasing hormone (TRH) (**Fig. 1**). Circulating auto-antibodies in Grave's disease stimulate thyroid function through activating the TSH receptor. These antibodies cause increased production of the thyroid pro-hormone thyroxine (T4) and the more active hormone T3 triiodothyronine. Hashimoto's patients possess large numbers of lymphocytes that infiltrate the thyroid and cause chronic inflammation. In some cases of Hashimoto's, patients generate auto-antibodies against the TSH receptor that block its function.

In a diagnostic thyroid test, two patients were subjected to intravenously administered TRH. After ~30 minutes, TSH levels normally rise and then fall to baseline after one hour. However, in two patient samples, the levels of TSH as measured through an ELISA assay were markedly different, indicating thyroid dysfunction (**Fig. 2**).

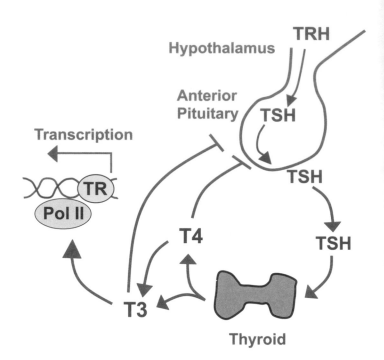

Figure 1. The hypothalamus-pituitary axis regulates the production of thyroid stimulating hormone (TSH). TR = thyroid hormone nuclear receptor; Pol II = RNA polymerase II.

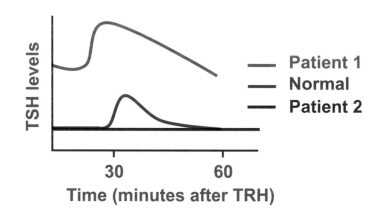

Figure 2. TRH stimulation test. TSH levels were measured in two patients and compared to a normal control sample after treatment with TRH.

1) Which of the following is the most consistent diagnosis regarding the patients who underwent TRH treatment?

A. Patient 1 has hypothyroidism, consistent with Grave's.

B. Patient 1 has hyperthyroidism, consistent with Hashimoto's.

C. Patient 2 has hyperthyroidism, consistent with Grave's.

D. Patient 2 has hypothyroidism, consistent with Hashimoto's.

2) Thyroid disorders can be caused by defects in the thyroid (primary) or in the pituitary (secondary). Which of the following diagnoses is most consistent regarding the patients who underwent TRH treatment?

A. Patient 1 has primary hypothyroidism.

B. Patient 2 has secondary hypothyroidism.

C. Patient 2 has primary hyperthyroidism.

D. Patient 1 has secondary hyperthyroidism.

3) Multiple sclerosis can be explained by both genetic and viral-mediated mechanisms. Which of the following models of autoimmune disease development are consistent with this?

A. The sequestration model is consistent with genetic, but not viral-mediated mechanisms.

B. The mimicry model is consistent with viral- but not genetic-mediated mechanisms.

C. Both mechanisms are consistent with sequestration and the mimicry models.

D. Neither mechanism is consistent with the sequestration and mimicry models.

4) In some autoimmune diseases, multiple antibody classes recognizing the same epitopes are affected. To generate various antibody classes, the isotype IgM switches to another isotype structure that has equivalent:

A. constant regions.

B. variable regions.

C. variable and constant regions.

D. primary structure.

5) Reducing agents such as dithiothreitol (DTT) can alter antibody structure. Extensive treatment of purified IgG with DTT would generate which of the following SDS electrophoresis patterns?

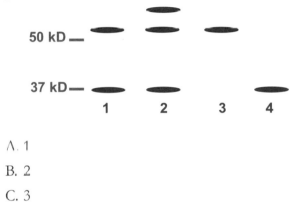

A. 1

B. 2

C. 3

D. 4

6) Which of the following observations would be most consistent with sequestration-driven autoimmune disease?

A. Detection of antibodies directed against red cell surface proteins in a patient with hemolytic anemia.

B. Failure to negatively select autoantibodies that cause autoimmune hyperthyroidism.

C. Development of autoimmune myocarditis in a patient with a history of cardiac ischemic attacks.

D. Detection of anti-nuclear antibodies in the estrogen-driven development of lupus.

Autoimmunity

Annotations.
1) C 2) A 3) C 4) B 5) A 6) C

	Foundation 1: Biochemistry-A			Foundation 3: Other Systems-B	
	A			**B**	
Concepts					
Reasoning				3,6	
Research					
Data	5			1,2	

Big Picture. Clearly, immunology is an important subject in medicine. However, immunology is a vast and complicated topic. What should you know and at what depth should you know it for the MCAT? Just know the fundamentals, including the basic knowledge of B and T cells in adaptive (humoral) immunity, antibody structure and diversity, and autoimmune disorders. This passage focuses on autoimmunity in the thyroid, yet has questions that also probe your comprehension of antibody structure. The passage did not test an understanding of adaptive immunity and its distinction from innate immunity.

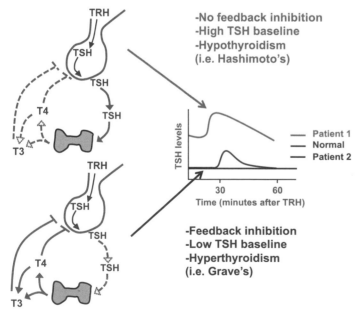

-No feedback inhibition
-High TSH baseline
-Hypothyroidism
(i.e. Hashimoto's)

-Feedback inhibition
-Low TSH baseline
-Hyperthyroidism
(i.e. Grave's)

Figure 3. TSH levels in both hyper- and hypothyroidism.

1) **C. Patient 2 has hyperthyroidism, consistent with Grave's.** Deduce that Grave's disease results in <u>hyperthyroidism</u> as the passage states: "In Grave's, circulating auto-antibodies stimulate thyroid function through activating the TSH receptor." **This eliminates choices A and D** (hypothyroidism).

Now, how to distinguish between Grave's and Hashimoto's? In Grave's, stimulation of TSH would generate T3 and T4 as shown in Figure 3. Recall from the passage that the thyroid hormones limit their own synthesis through feedback (negative) regulation. This is also shown in the Figure 1. Increased T3 and T4 levels would suppress the release of pituitary TSH. In terms of the TRH test discussed in the passage, patients with Grave's would be expected to respond poorly to administration of TRH as TSH release is abrogated through high levels of T3 and T4 that result from Grave's. This is consistent with Patient 2. **Choice C is the correct answer.**

2) **A. Patient 1 has primary hypothyroidism.** As per above, Patient 2 has hyperthyroidism, **eliminating choice B**. Deduce that Patient 1 has hypothyroidism as would be seen in Hashimoto's. Recall from the passage that, "Hashimoto's patients possess large numbers of lymphocytes that infiltrate the thyroid and cause chronic inflammation." The resulting thyroid impairment causes hypothyroidism through lack of T3 and T4. **This eliminates choice D.**

Ok, so what about the distinction between primary and secondary thyroid disease? The question stem defines the terms for you: "Thyroid disorders can be caused by defects in the thyroid (primary) or in the pituitary (secondary)." In Hashimoto's disease, the thyroid hormones (T3 and T4) are not made in the thyroid. Therefore, Hashimoto's (patient 1) is a primary thyroid disease. This **makes choice A correct.** To make sure, lets examine choice C: "Patient 2 has secondary hypothyroidism." The data represented in Figure 3 shows that Patient 2 fails to respond to TRH treatment, meaning that the thyroid is active and shutting down T3 and T4 hormone synthesis via feedback regulation. This, as discussed above, is hyperthyroidism. However, the pituitary is failing to secrete TSH under these circumstances, indicating that Patient 2 has a secondary thyroid condition.

3) C. Both mechanisms are consistent with sequestration and the mimicry models. Multiple sclerosis is an autoimmune disorder where self-directed antibodies attack the myelin sheath. By its very nature, molecular mimicry models rely upon homologous sequences as mimicry is derived from structure/function. It should readily be seen that a viral protein possessing sequence similarities to self-antigens could be mistaken as self by the immune system. In fact, differences of just a few amino acid sequences can trigger an autoimmune response in hosts. (Because of this, genetic mutations could also generate mimicry.) With respect to sequestration, anything that can break down the barriers that generate the separation of potential self-antigens from the immune system could be causal for disease. Both genetic and viral mechanisms could eliminate barriers (i.e. tissue inflammation, bleeding, etc.), causing autoimmunity from a sequestration mechanism.

4) B. variable regions. Isotype switching (also called class switch recombination) changes the constant region of immunoglobulin M (IgM) to one with any of several other isotypes (for example IgG, IgA, IgE). Isotype switching generates a new type of antibody effector. These two antibody classes recognize the same epitope due to possessing equivalent variable regions (**Fig. 4**), but have different cellular locations. **Choice B is the correct answer.**

You should understand the basic aspects of antibody diversity, including how isotypes are created. Both V(D)J and class (or isotype) switch recombination is required to generate the immunoglobulin heavy chain. In contrast, the light chain (as well as the T cell receptor) is made only via V(D)J recombination. The basics of this are shown in Figure 4. Let's go through this. First, notice that both V(D)J and isotype switching proceed through the generation of DNA breaks. Specifically, during immune cell development, DNA double stranded breaks (DSBs) are generated by RAG enzymes for V(D)J or the enzyme AID for isotype switching. By deleting various portions of DNA, there are numerous combinations of V, D, and J segments that can generate many different structures that recognize antigen. Therefore, V(D)J recombination creates immunological diversity.

You should know that the variable region recognizes epitopes and that the constant region determines the class of antibody. Further, antibodies "start out" as IgM and then can have their constant regions replaced with various effector classes, including IgM, IgA, IgG, IgD, and IgE. The class of antibody largely dictates location within the body. For example, IgA is largely found in saliva, tears, and mucosal membranes. What drives switching? In response to various cytokines, heavy chains can replace the IgM constant portion with another isotype class (**Fig. 4**). Therefore, IgM antibodies that switch to IgA have identical variable regions, but differential constant regions. **Choices B and C are wrong.** As the constant regions are formed exclusively from the heavy chain, the primary structures of IgM and IgA are different, **eliminating choice D.** The question stem uses the word "epitopes," but this word is not mentioned in the passage. Epitope is a fundamental term that you should already be familiar with. If not, then what is an epitope? The variable region of an antibody recognizes its antigen by binding to an epitope. Epitopes can be sugars, lipids, nucleic acids, or proteins and peptides. In the context of proteins, which is most relevant for this passage, an epitope can be as little as five contiguous amino acids. As proteins fold in three dimensions (tertiary or 3° structure), two amino acids that are not adjacent to each other in the primary sequence can lie juxtaposed in 3D space. These two residues might contribute to a "conformational" epitope.

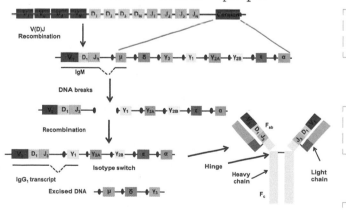

Figure 4. V(D)J recombination and isotype switching are two DNA repair pathways used in production of heavy chains. Fab = variable region; Fc = constant region.

5) A. 1. Recall that antibodies are heterodimers composed of two heavy and two light chains linked together by disulfide bonds. (**Fig. 5**). Intramolecular disulfide bonds are also present and contribute to the formation of immunoglobulin folds. These structural motifs are also observed in MHC and T cell receptor molecules.

DTT treatment of an immunoglobulin would reduce the disulfide bonds in the heterodimer, releasing a heavy chain and a light chain (**Fig. 6**). Two different protein bands would be expected during electrophoresis. **Choice A is correct.** Extensive treatment with reducing agents such as DTT will cause the oxidized cysteine residues in the disulfide bonds to be reduced back to the thiols present in the cysteine side chain. Note that the heavy chain migrates near 50 kD and the light chain migrates near 35 kD. **Choice B is wrong** because there are three bands. Although one could argue that the high molecular weight band is derived from a heavy-light chain covalently linked structure, this would be unlikely as the stem describes "extensive treatment with DTT". **C and D are wrong choices** as there is either a heavy or a light chain only.

6) C. Development of autoimmune myocarditis in a patient with a history of cardiac ischemic attacks. As described in the passage, the sequestration model predicts, "Upon injury or infection and consequent release of an antigen from sequestration, a self immune response is triggered." **The credited answer is choice C**; it is known that damage to cardiac tissue (i.e. injury) can expose antigens such as cardiac myosin that are normally sequestered from auto-reactive antibodies. Although this could also be caused by molecular mimicry, the association between exposed cardiac tissue and injury through heart attack is consistent with a sequestration model. **Choice A is not credited** because it is very hard to imagine how circulating red blood cells could be "sequestered," particularly as the circulatory system is linked to the lymphatic system. Autoimmune hyperthyroidism is another name for Grave's disease. The failure to negatively select autoantibodies that are causal for Grave's disease would result in their circulation into the periphery where they would have access to the thyroid stimulating hormone receptor. **Choice B is not credited. Choice D is not credited** because, in this case, the lupus is driven by estrogen, a hormone that is released into the bloodstream.

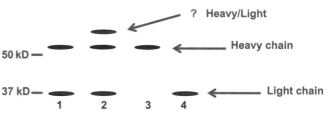

Figure 6. Gel electrophoresis analysis of immunoglobulins yields two bands on extensive treatment with DTT.

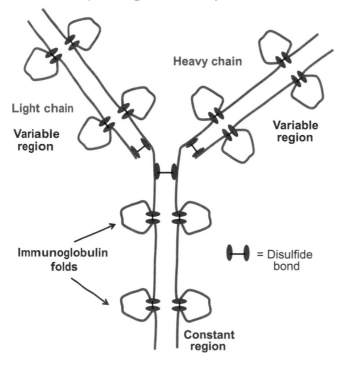

Figure 5. Structure of heterotetrameric immunoglobulin.

PATHWAY

Mucins

The Muc1 gene encodes a large transmembrane glycoprotein and functions to protect cellular surfaces from microbial/immunological attack. Studies in mice suggest that Muc1 must be actively removed from the uterus for implantation, an event occurring four days post-fertilization. How Muc1 expression is regulated is unclear; however, it has been hypothesized that estrogen and progesterone control the levels of Muc1 transcription. To test this, researchers set up three experiments with a Muc1 transcriptional reporter system. Through the placement of a luciferase reporter gene downstream of the Muc1 promoter in a plasmid, Muc1 transcription could then be monitored via a luciferase assay. The data was determined as a fold increase normalized to a negative vehicle control.

Experiment 1: The Muc1 luciferase reporter was transfected into HEC-1A cells along with a plasmid encoding either estrogen receptor, progesterone receptor isoform A (PRA), or progesterone receptor isoform B (PRB). Further, these cells were treated with estrogen, progesterone, or the progesterone antagonist RU486. The PRE-luciferase reporter contains a promoter known to respond to progesterone. The PRA was found to be active in a parallel experiment (not shown).

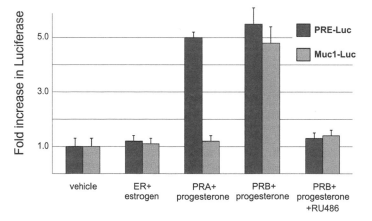

Experiment 2: HEC-1A cells were transfected with the Muc1-Luciferase reporter and a plasmid encoding the PRB. Muc1-Luciferase activity was then tested as a function of increasing doses of progesterone (nM) to the cells.

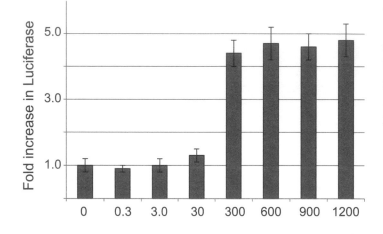

Experiment 3. HEC-1A cells were transfected with the Muc1-Luciferase reporter, altered ratios of plasmids encoding PRB and PRA, and treated with constant levels of progesterone. Data is displayed as fold over vehicle background.

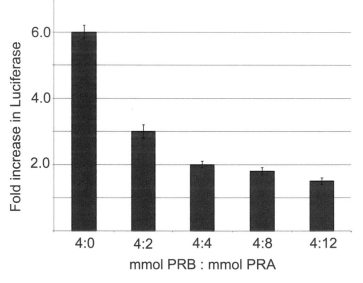

1) If blood levels of progesterone are 40 nM, what must be true for the effects observed in experiment 2 to be physiologically relevant?

A. Progesterone is directly secreted into the uterus.

B. Endometrial progesterone concentrations can be observed to be 10-fold higher than plasma.

C. Endometrial epithelia cells produce progesterone to a concentration of 400 nM.

D. Uterine transcriptional response to progesterone is 10-fold higher than the signal inducing it.

2) Based upon the results in experiment 1, which of the following must be true to conclude that estrogen does not activate Muc1 transcription?

A. The estrogen used in the experiment was produced in the ovary.

B. The estrogen used in the experiment can activate an estrogen-responsive promoter.

C. The estrogen used in the experiment is not biologically active.

D. The HEC-1A cell line expresses endogenous estrogen receptor.

3) Based upon the results of all three experiments, which of the following is true?

     I. PRA inhibits Muc1 transcription.
    II. PRB activates Muc1 transcription.
   III. PRA inhibits PRB function.
   IV. PRB inhibits PRA function.

A. I, III

B. II, III

C. III, IV

D. I, II, IV

4) A mouse with both copies of the Muc1 gene deleted within uterine epithelial cells would have which of the following phenotypes?

A. enhanced fertility

B. reduced fertility

C. no change in fertility

D. cannot be predicted

5) Expression analysis of advanced stage lung tumors determined that Muc1 is overexpressed. How would this be predicted to effect tumorigenicity?

A. Enhance it, because Muc1 is oncogenic.

B. Inhibit it, because Muc1 is a tumor suppressor.

C. Enhance it, because Muc1 is immunoprotective.

D. Inhibit it, because Muc1 is antimicrobial.

6) Based upon the experiments presented in the passage, at what nanomolar concentration range of progesterone would a linear response in Muc1 transcription be expected?

A. 0-30

B. 30-100

C. 300-600

D. 600-1200

7) A pharmaceutical company develops a compound capable of removing Muc1 glycoproteins. Which of the following could be a potential side effect of such a drug?

A. altered progesterone levels

B. altered progesterone receptor levels

C. sensitivity to RU486

D. sensitivity to bacterial infection

Mucins

Annotations.
1) B 2) B 3) B 4) A 5) C 6) B 7) D

	Foundation 2: Cell Physiology-C			Foundation 3: Neurobiology-A Other Systems-B		
	C			**A**	**B**	
Concepts						
Reasoning	5,7				4	
Research	2					
Data				3,6	1	

Big Picture. This passage very likely introduced completely new biology for nearly everyone. The MCAT will expect that you have a basic understanding of the reproductive system and fertilization but not an intimate understanding of Mucins and their role in hormonal regulation during reproduction. In fact, the expectation is that you have never heard of Mucins and that this passage represents the first time that this word has been uttered. Moreover, this passage really tested your ability to assimilate and interpret experimental results based upon Mucin expression as a function of hormones. All three experiments presented key points (one per experiment) and these points generated an overall body of information that was important for using critical reasoning skills to answer questions. Notice also, that this passage integrated multiple concepts. You needed to understand some basic molecular biology as it pertains to transcription and how promoters are specifically activated by hormone receptors. Basic knowledge of the progesterone receptor and estrogen receptor, while generally useful for the MCAT, was not required to answer the questions presented here.

1) **B. Endometrial progesterone concentrations can be observed to be 10-fold higher than plasma.** This question cued you to immediately focus in on experiment 2. This experiment is a classic dose analysis where increasing amounts of progesterone are added in order to find a linear response. Based upon the data presented in the experiment, only doses of 300 nM and higher generate appreciable transcription from the Muc1-driven luciferase reporter. The question then provides you with additional information regarding the blood concentration of progesterone being 40 nM. On first inspection this experiment does not appear to be physiologically relevant. How can you reconcile this data? **Choice A should be eliminated** because all hormones are secreted into the bloodstream. **Choice C is wrong** because uterine epithelial cells do not produce progesterone. This leaves choices B and D, both of which looked reasonable. The **problem with choice D** is that even if uterine cells respond ten-times higher than the signal inducing them, if this signal concentration isn't above the threshold to cause induction then you won't see activity regardless. Therefore, **choice B is correct** where raising local concentrations of progesterone in cells can create a cellular environment with high enough progesterone concentrations to trigger Muc1 transcription.

2) **B. The estrogen used in the experiment can activate an estrogen-responsive promoter.** This is a very important experimental concept: How does one appropriately interpret a negative result? The data presented in Figure 1 suggests that estrogen is incapable of activating the Muc1 promoter because you fail to see any activation when estrogen is added to the media. However, you must consider the fact that you don't know if the estrogen that was added was even active to begin with! For all we know, it could have been left on the counter for weeks by accident. Or it could have been another compound through mislabeling! While these may seem like pedestrian explanations, they cannot be ruled out. However, if you knew from another assay that the estrogen is active, then you would be able to conclude that it indeed does not activate the Muc1 promoter. This would be a positive control in the experiment. This really leaves only **choice B as correct**. Note that **choice A is incorrect** because estrogen can indeed be chemically synthesized. Further, note that **choice C is incorrect** because the use of biologically

inactive hormone for an experiment is simply not logical in this case, and **choice D is incorrect** because experiment 1 clearly indicates that the estrogen receptor is being exogenously expressed in Hec-1A cells.

3) **B. II, III.** Experiment 1 addresses the first two Roman numerals and it can be concluded that the progesterone receptor isoform B activates the Muc1 promoter while the progesterone isoform A does not activate the promoter (**Fig. 1**).

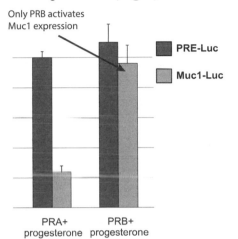

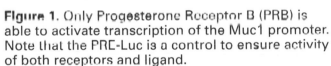

Figure 1. Only Progesterone Receptor B (PRB) is able to activate transcription of the Muc1 promoter. Note that the PRE-Luc is a control to ensure activity of both receptors and ligand.

Additionally, there is a subtle, yet significant, conclusion that experiment 1 allows you to make, which is that progesterone receptor A does not inhibit the Muc1 promoter because the luciferase activity is not reduced below that of vehicle (**Fig. 2**). This rules out Roman numeral I and rules in Roman numeral II, therefore **choices A, C, and D are not correct**.

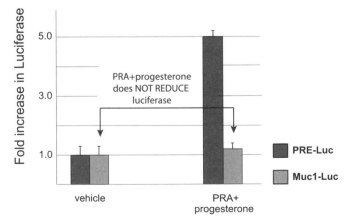

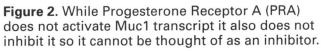

Figure 2. While Progesterone Receptor A (PRA) does not activate Muc1 transcript it also does not inhibit it so it cannot be thought of as an inhibitor.

The results presented from experiment 3 address the other two Roman numerals, although this wasn't necessary to get the answer correct. Experiment 3 demonstrates that if the levels of progesterone receptor isoform B are held constant and then levels of progesterone receptor isoform A are progressively increased there is a decrease in luciferase activity from the Muc1 promoter (**Fig. 3**). The conclusion that is reached is that PRA can inhibit PRB. This makes Roman numeral III true and IV false. Therefore, **choice B is correct**.

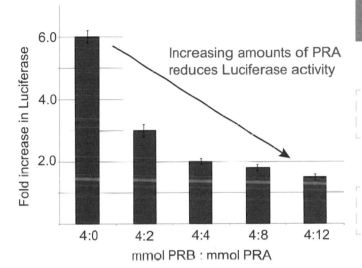

Figure 3. Increasing the amount of PRA causes a loss of responsiveness of PRB to addition of progesterone.

4) **A. enhanced fertility.** This was essentially a reading comprehension problem. The first paragraph of the passage describes the key points about Muc1. These include the fact that it must be removed to allow for implantation to occur (**Fig. 4**). Therefore, the simplest outcome of a Muc1 deletion, specifically in the uterus, would be to increase fertility. Therefore, **choice A is correct**.

Figure 4. Implantation of a fertilized embryo in the uterus is dependent upon the reduced expression of Muc1 in the endometrial cells.

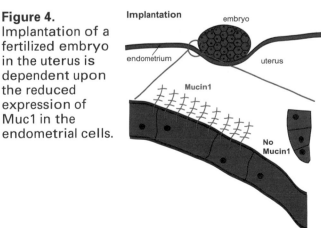

Mucins

5) C. Enhance it, because Muc1 is immunoprotective. First of all, you should employ simple logic. Given that the question stem states that "advanced stage cancer" overexpresses Muc1, it can be deduced that this is most likely to enhance tumorigenicity rather than inhibit it. This effectively **rules out choices B and D**. From this point, you had to apply what you have learned about one system of the body (reproductive) and apply to a diseased state. The passage states that Muc1 is immunoprotective in nature and tumors by nature are supposed to trigger immune responses as this is a primary goal of the cell-mediated arm of the immune system. The expression of Muc1 on the surface of tumors can therefore act to "protect" the tumor from the host's normal defenses (**Fig. 5**). Indeed, many studies have demonstrated this to be the case. Even though Muc1 has been found to aid in tumorigenesis, there is no indication from the passage that it can act as an oncogene which promotes cell growth. Therefore **choice A is incorrect.**

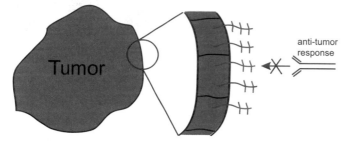

Figure 5. Tumors overexpress Muc1 in order to protect themselves against host immune responses.

6) B. 30-100. Of the experiments presented in the passage, only experiment 2 utilized a dose-response to appropriately answer this question. The data presented in experiment 2 did not generate a classical dose-response, however, as can be seen (**Fig. 6**), there is a large jump in luciferase activity between 30 nM and 300 nM that is not linear. This is also a 10-fold increase in progesterone suggesting that if the experiment included smaller increments of progesterone between these two points, a linear response would have been observed. Based upon this logic, only **choice B is correct.**

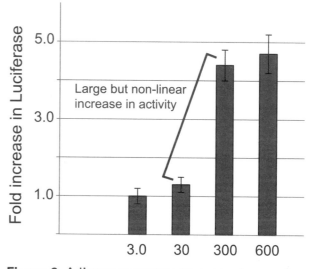

Figure 6. A linear response to progesterone is not observed in the given data. It is possible that a linear response exists between the 30 and 300 datapoints.

7) D. sensitivity to bacterial infection. This was another reasoning question where you really had to gather the true function of Muc1 from the passage. Given its "negative" function towards implantation, a drug to inhibit its expression could in fact improve fertility. However, given the normal function of Muc1 is to protect cells against bacterial infection (and immunological attack), inhibiting its function could cause a risk for infection. The other answer choices are not supported by the passage although they are mentioned in the passage. Be aware that the MCAT tends to have wrong answer choices that seem relevant but in the end, they simply are not correct.

Notes:

2

3

Med-
PATHWAY

Digestion

Both histamine and gastrin stimulate parietal cells to release acid, a process inhibited by somatostatin. As acidic chyme passes into the duodenum, S cells release secretin and this induces the pancreas to release bicarbonate. Both secretin and chyme enhance the release of cholecystokinin (CKK) from I cells. The CKK peptide inhibits the rate of gastric emptying into the duodenum and promotes the release of pancreatic enzymes and bile (**Fig. 1**).

The failure to release sufficient pancreatic enzymes causes nutrient malabsorption, leading to loose, greasy stools, or steatorrhea. Both direct and indirect tests have been used to examine pancreatic function. One oral test uses a reporter molecule consisting of fluorescein conjugated to butyric acid. Normally, pancreatic enzymes will hydrolyze this ester molecule in the duodenum. The products are released into hepatic circulation; after processing in the liver, fluorescein, but not the conjugate, is detected in the urine.

Two patients complaining of abdominal pain were evaluated for pancreatic malfunction, or insufficiency. Both were treated with fluorescein conjugated to butyric acid. They were also given equivalent amounts of free fluorescein ($C_{20}H_{12}O_5$) on separate occasions. The kidneys rapidly cleared the free fluorescein in both patient samples as determined by urine measurements (**Fig. 2**).

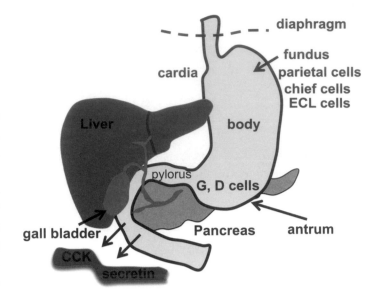

Figure 1. Key elements of the digestive system. Most cells of the stomach are innervated with the vagus nerve through the enteric nervous system.

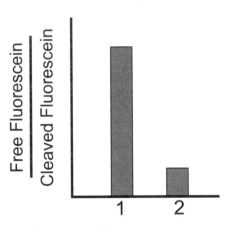

Figure 2. Test for determining pancreatic insufficiency in two patients.

1) **Which patient displays results that are most consistent with pancreatic insufficiency?**

   A. Patient 1 because absorbance of free fluorescein is lower than Patient 2.

   B. Patient 1 because the relative ratio of free/cleaved fluorescein is higher than Patient 2.

   C. Patient 2 because absorbance of free fluorescein is higher than Patient 1.

   D. Patient 2 because the relative ratio of free/cleaved fluorescein is lower than Patient 1.

2) **Which of the following can be concluded from the data?**

   A. Patient 1 has higher levels of pepsinogen than Patient 2.

   B. Patient 2 has higher levels of pepsinogen than Patient 1.

   C. Patient 1 has higher levels of functional chymotrypsin than Patient 2.

   D. Patient 2 has higher levels of functional chymotrypsin than Patient 1.

3) **One clinical assay for detecting pancreatic sufficiency involves monitoring the release of fluorescein ($C_{20}H_{12}O_5$) from its C4 esterified form. After cleavage, the products can be monitored by gas chromatography with a hydrophobic resin. Which of the following is true?**

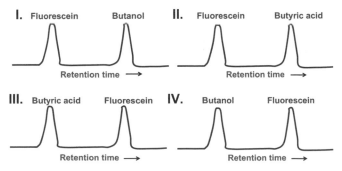

   A. Chromatogram profile I is from Patient 1.

   B. Chromatogram profile II is from Patient 2.

   C. Chromatogram profile III is from Patient 1.

   D. Chromatogram profile IV is from Patient 2.

4) **Stomach ulcers in Zollinger-Ellison syndrome are caused by excessive secretion of acid, or hypergastrinemia. Which of the following agents would be least effective at treating this?**

   A. cholecystokinin receptor antagonist

   B. histamine receptor antagonist

   C. proton pump inhibitors

   D. somatostatin receptor antagonist

5) **A small drug has a single carboxyl group pK_a of 5.9 and was found to cross membranes only when uncharged. Which of the following statements regarding this drug is true?**

   A. Ionized in the stomach; unable to be absorbed.

   B. Neutral in the stomach; able to be absorbed.

   C. Ionized in the duodenum; able to be absorbed.

   D. Neutral in the duodenum, unable to be absorbed.

6) **One assay for pancreatic insufficiency involves oral administration of ^{14}C-triglycerides. Pancreatic enzymes normally convert these into glycerol and fatty acids that are then oxidized to $^{14}CO_2$. Which of the following is true with respect to any detected levels of $^{14}CO_2$?**

   A. Independent of blood oxygen saturation.

   B. Directly released from acetyl CoA during oxidation in the Krebs cycle.

   C. Inversely correlates with the fatty acid levels detected from steatorrhea.

   D. Derived primarily from glycolysis.

7) **Why was free fluorescein separately administered?**

   A. To establish a baseline absorbance value.

   B. To determine renal sufficiency.

   C. To measure pancreatic enzyme activity.

   D. Because fluorescein, not its ester, is detected in urine.

Digestion

	Foundation 3: Neurobiology-A Other Systems-B			Foundation 5: Separation-C		
	A	**B**		**C**		
Concepts	4	5				
Reasoning		6				
Research		7				
Data		1,2		3		

Big Picture. The control of digestion is an important topic and incorporates multiple learning issues from different disciplines. This passage breaks down into two parts: the control of stomach acid secretion and the role of the pancreas in digestion. Accompanying this are some vocabulary terms that every budding physician should know. These terms and others are listed in Table 1.

This passage asks three questions based upon interpretation of what appears to be a very simple experiment in Figure 2. The key to this passage is an understanding of the experiment. Although the patients complained of symptoms consistent with pancreatic insufficiency, the data suggest that only one of them has this. The fluorescein experiments reveal that Patient 1 has pancreatic insufficiency, but Patient 2 appears normal for pancreatic function.

ITEM	FUNCTION
1. Muscarinic receptor	Acetylcholine/G protein coupled receptors
2. Gastrin	Peptide hormone; stimulates H^+ secretion
3. Somatostatin	Inhibits stomach acid secretion
4. Pepsinogen	Stomach protease converted to pepsin
5. Secretin	Stimulates bicarbonate release in duodenum
6. Cholecystokinin	Peptide hormone; ↑ fat/protein digestion
7. α-amylase	Hydrolyzes α bonds of polysaccharides
8. (phospho)lipase	Hydrolyzes (phospho)esters in phospho(lipids)
9. Chymotrypsin	Pancreatic protease targets hydrophobic residues
10. Elastase-1	Pancreatic serine protease
11. Carboxypeptidases	Proteases that target C-terminal residues
12. Enterokinase	Duodenal enzyme converts pancreatic trypsinogen

Table 1. Important items described in passage. Note that the function listed is the one most relevant to the contents of the passage.

1) **B. Patient 1 because the relative ratio of free/cleaved fluorescein is higher than Patient 2.** It is critical to properly interpret the data presented in Figure 2. The passage states that, "The kidneys rapidly cleared the free fluorescein in both patient samples as determined by urine measurements." There is no difference between patients in clearing fluorescein. Interpret this mathematically to mean that the numerator in the ratio of free fluorescein/cleaved fluorescein will be the same in both patients. This **eliminates choices A and C.** Therefore, Patients 1 and 2 differ in their ability to generate fluorescein derived from cleavage by pancreatic enzymes. Lower values of cleaved fluorescein reflect the inability of pancreatic enzymes to hydrolyze the test substrate. These low values are seen with Patient 1 because a lower denominator will generate a larger ratio. The interpretation of the data is that Patient 1 has pancreatic insufficiency and that Patient 2 is normal. **Choice B is correct.**

2) **D. Patient 2 has higher levels of functional chymotrypsin than Patient 1.** Immediately note that pepsinogen is a stomach protease (zymogen) that is converted into pepsin (**Table 1**). As the fluorescein test discussed in the passage examines pancreatic function, **choices A and B are eliminated.** There is no way to tell from the data presented what the status of pepsinogen is in the two patients. In contrast, chymotrypsin is a pancreatic enzyme. As discussed in the Big Picture as well as in question 1, Patient 2 is normal and would be expected to secrete higher levels of functional chymotrypsin than Patient 1 who has pancreatic insufficiency.

3) **D. Chromatogram profile IV is from Patient 2.** In order to arrive at the correct answer, two things must be figured out: the chemical reaction and the gas chromatogram. The passage and stem both discuss that fluorescein is administered in the esterified form. A normal pancreas (pancreatic sufficiency) will supply the enzyme activity necessary to hydrolyze the ester. Recall that the passage states the administered compound is fluorescein conjugated to butyric acid and that this comprises the ester. Get in the habit of deciphering the chemistry without necessarily being able to see the molecular structures as you know that:

ESTER = CARBOXYLIC ACID + ALCOHOL

Therefore, hydrolysis of fluorescein conjugated to butyric acid through an ester linkage should yield butanol and fluorescein (the acid). This eliminates profiles II and III (**choices B and C are wrong**) because there will be no butyric acid detected, only butanol.

Arriving at the correct answer now requires an understanding of gas-liquid chromatography. In this separation technique, the most volatile component will be detected first. This must be butanol, a four-carbon alcohol, as it is much smaller than fluorescein, which has twenty carbons ($C_{20}H_{12}O_5$)! Therefore, **choice A is eliminated**. Also, note that Patient 2 is normal and secretes the pancreatic enzymes that hydrolyze the fluorescein ester. In contrast, Patient 1, who has pancreatic insufficiency, might not be expected to produce the products shown on the gas-liquid chromatography experiment.

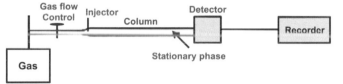

Figure 3. Gas-liquid chromatography.

Recall that like many forms of chromatography, there are two phases: a mobile phase and a solid, stationary phase. In gas-liquid chromatography, the mobile phase is usually an inert gas and the stationary phase is a liquid-gel phase (a hydrophobic resin in this case) that coats the walls of the column.

During a gas chromatography experiment, a sample is injected to the column where it is immediately vaporized with heat. As gas is introduced into the column, the vaporized molecules are carried into the column where they can interact with either the gaseous or liquid phase. The amount of time a molecule interacts with the stationary phase (liquid gel) depends on its volatility. The retention time reflects this; higher retention times signify a stronger interaction with the liquid phase. This would translate into having a higher boiling point (less volatile). As butanol clearly has a lower boiling point than fluorescein, it would have a shorter retention time as shown in profile IV (**choice D is correct**) in the question. This explains why butanol elutes first. .

4) **D. somatostatin receptor antagonist.** Successful treatment of hypergastrinemia would inhibit stomach acid production. As mentioned in the first paragraph of the passage, somatostatin reduces parietal cell release of acid. Therefore, inhibition of somatostatin signaling with a receptor antagonist would promote more, not less, release of H^+ from the stomach. **Choice D is the correct answer** because somatostatin receptor antagonists would be an ineffective therapeutic.

The passage states that CCK inhibits gastric emptying. Therefore, CCK antagonists would promote the precocious release of stomach contents into the duodenum. This would reduce the amount of acid in the stomach. Therefore, this is a viable therapeutic approach, making **choice A wrong**. A histamine receptor antagonist would lower the release of acid from parietal cells, and this too would help the condition (**choice B is incorrect**). Proton pump inhibitors would also reduce stomach lumen acid secretion and this is the most common form of treatment for this disease, making **C a wrong choice**.

5) **B. Neutral in the stomach; able to be absorbed.** As per the passage, the stomach parietal cells secrete acid and the pancreas releases bicarbonate into the duodenum. You should know that the pH of the stomach and duodenum substantially vary. Recall that the pH in the stomach and duodenum are ~2.0 and ~6.0, respectively. For convenience, round the pK_a of 5.9 to 6.0, and then use the Henderson-Hasselbalch equation ($pH = pK_a + \log [A^-]/[HA]$) to solve for the ratio $[A^-]/[HA]$. A^- represents the ionized carboxyl group and HA represents the neutral species. This will determine the net charge of the molecule in each location. In the stomach, $[A^-]/[HA]$ = antilog -4 (you should be able to do this math off the top of your head!). Therefore, $[A^-]/[HA]$ = .0001, meaning that there is one charged molecule for every ten thousand that are neutral! Overall, the molecule is very neutral in the stomach and will be absorbed. **Choice B is correct**. In the duodenum, the Henderson-Hasselbalch equation boils down to $[A^-] = [HA]$, indicating that 50% of the molecules will be charged at this pH. Thus, although half of the molecules are uncharged, half of the material will be absorbed in the duodenum, an amount far less than in the stomach.

3

5

6) **C. Inversely correlates with the fatty acid levels detected from steatorrhea.** The detection of $^{14}CO_2$ in the breath reflects the capacity of the pancreas to produce lipases that can catabolize the ingested and radiolabeled triglycerides into glycerol and fatty acids. With respect to the pancreas, higher detected levels of undigested triglycerides and fat in the stool are consistent with a deficiency in pancreatic function. Therefore, since steatorrhea (pancreatic derived or otherwise) is a condition of reduced triglyceride catabolism, the levels of $^{14}CO_2$ detected would inversely correlate with the fatty acid levels detected in the stool. **Choice C is the correct answer.**

^{14}C-triglycerides will be hydrolyzed by pancreatic lipases in the duodenum. Once distributed to tissue, one fate of the fats is to be broken down into acetyl CoA via β-oxidation. The two carbon equivalents of acetyl CoA are then oxidized via the TCA cycle into $^{14}CO_2$, but you should know that the actual carbons that are released as CO_2 are derived directly from oxaloacetate (OAA), not acetyl CoA (hence the term "equivalents"). **Choice B is wrong**. Since β-oxidation requires oxygen, low oxygen (i.e. anaerobic) saturation could obscure the results, **eliminating choice A**. Because there is no CO_2 derived from glycolysis, **choice D is wrong**. Recall that glycolysis produces ATP and NADH, but since glucose is not completely oxidized until the carbon skeletons arrive in the mitochondrial, no CO_2 is derived from glycolysis.

7) **A. To establish a baseline absorbance value.** The purpose of administering free fluorescein is to generate an individual baseline for absorbance. In principle, a failure to detect fluorescein in the urine could reflect individual abilities to absorb the compound from the stomach and/or small intestine as opposed to a pancreatic defect, or even a defect in renal clearance. This **eliminates choices B and C**. The fact that the fluorescein-ester is not detected in the urine has nothing to do with establishing a baseline for free fluorescein absorption. **Choice D is incorrect**.

3

5

PATHWAY

Periodic Table of Elements

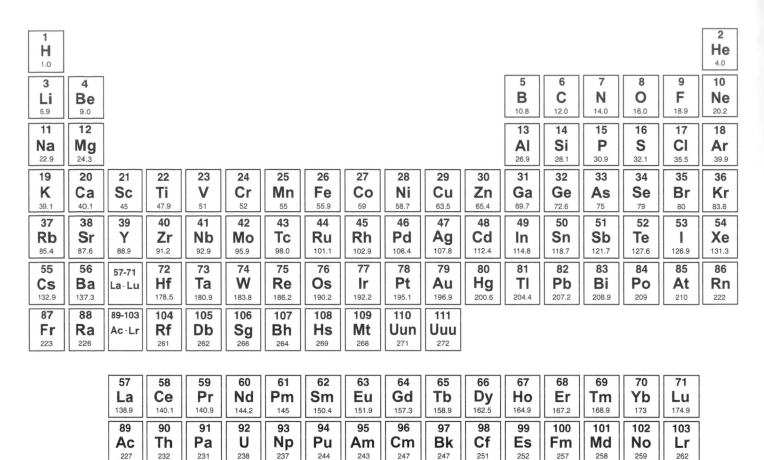

Chemical and Physical Foundations of Biological Systems

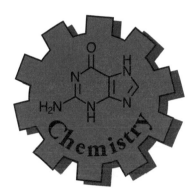

Sarcomere Length-Tension

To investigate the role of cellular factors impacting the length-tension relationship of cardiac myofibers, scientists conducted two experiments. Both experiments used an apparatus where isolated myofibers could be subject to length alterations and the resultant force could be monitored. One end of a 1.8 μm myofiber is secured on a force transducer and the other is attached to a torque motor. The general experimental procedure was as follows:

1) The myofiber was immersed in a "relaxing" solution that contained 10^{-9} M calcium.

2) The myofiber was stretched to 2.3 μm in length.

3) The myofiber was then transferred to an "active" solution that contained high levels of calcium.

4) Force was measured to be 30 kN/m^2.

5) Experiments were repeated where stretch distances were decreased at 0.1 μm intervals. Force measurements were recorded relative to maximum length.

Experiment 1: Researchers conducted the experimental scheme either in the presence of wild-type (wt) cardiac troponin protein (blue boxes) or with a mutant (mt) protein (red circles). The results are presented in Figure 1.

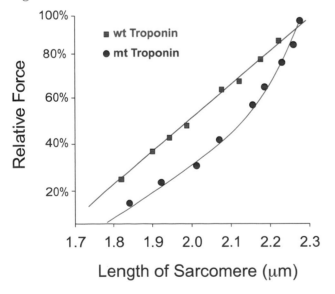

Figure 1. Measurements of relative force generated by sarcomeres that have been stretched in the presence of wild-type or mutant troponin proteins.

Experiment 2: At 2.3 μm, the concentration of calcium in the activating solution was varied for myofibers with either wild-type (blue boxes) or mutant cardiac troponin protein (red circles). The results are presented in Figure 2.

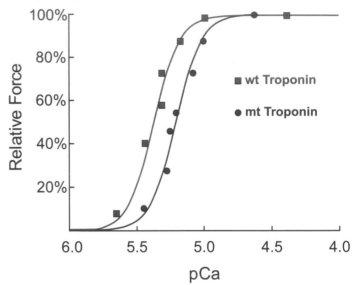

Figure 2. Measurements of relative force generation of sarcomeres in the presence of wild-type or mutant troponin proteins as a function of calcium concentration.

126

1) **Based upon the data in experiment 1, sarcomere behavior approximates which physical law?**

   A. Newton's First law

   B. Newton's Second law

   C. Hooke's law

   D. Stokes' law

2) **Calculate the concentration of calcium when sarcomeres with wild-type troponin reach 50% maximum force?**

   A. 3.0×10^{-6} M

   B. 5.5×10^{-6} M

   C. 3.0×10^{-5} M

   D. 5.5×10^{-5} M

3) **What is the velocity of a sarcomere that is released from its maximum stretch point and contracts back to its resting length in 2.9 ns?**

   A. $5/3 \times 10^{-16}$ m/s

   B. $5/3 \times 10^{-15}$ m/s

   C. $5/3 \times 10^{2}$ m/s

   D. $5/3 \times 10^{3}$ m/s

4) **The mutation in troponin likely causes reduced:**

   A. function in the C subunit.

   B. function in the I subunit.

   C. function in the T subunit.

   D. interaction with tropomyosin.

5) **What best describes the length-tension relationship of a cardiac sarcomere with wt troponin?**

   A. proportional and linear

   B. proportional and sigmoidal

   C. not proportional and linear

   D. not proportional and sigmoidal

6) **How much additional work must the heart perform in order increase the velocity of blood 10-fold?**

   A. $10^{-1/2}$

   B. $10^{1/2}$

   C. 10^{1}

   D. 10^{2}

3

4

Sarcomere Length-Tension

Annotations.
1) C 2) B 3) C 4) A 5) C 6) B

	Foundation 3: Other Systems-B			Foundation 4: Motion-A Fluids-B	
	B			**A**	**B**
Concepts				3	6
Reasoning					
Research				5	
Data	4			1,2	

Big Picture. While not directly referred to, this passage dealt with The Frank-Starling model. This model predicts that increases in diastolic volume leads to concomitant increases in ventricular output. This theory is grounded, in part, in the length-tension relationship in cardiomyocytes. This relationship is based upon both physical and cellular factors. Physically, it involves: (1) the lateral spacing of thick/thin filaments; (2) the total number of active cross-bridges; (3) restoring forces associated with deformations in sarcomere geometry. Cellular factors include: (1) the action potential associated within the cardiomyocytes; (2) changes in intracellular calcium levels; (3) the response of troponin proteins to calcium.

While this passage investigated the molecular basis of this concept, the questions were highly dependent on your understanding of the presented data. In fact, other than question six, all of the questions required a working knowledge of how the two experiments were conducted or specific elements presented in the results. One pitfall was the X-axis of Figure 2. Note that it is given as "pCa," which means the negative $\log_{10}$ of the concentration of calcium. This is analogous to pH, which is the negative $\log_{10}$ of the proton concentration. Because of this, you needed to appreciate that concentration increased as you tracked to the right on the x-axis even though the labeled values diminished.

1) **C. Hooke's law.** Newton's first law states that if the net force on an object is constant, then the velocity of the object will not change. This does not apply to experiment 1 so **choice A is incorrect**. Newton's second law states that the net force applied to an object produces a proportional acceleration. This law also does not apply, making **choice B incorrect**. Stokes' law applies to drag force imposed by viscous fluids, which is clearly not applicable in experiment 1, making **choice D incorrect**. While Hooke's law is normally thought of in terms of springs, it is a principle that approximates the response of an elastic body (in this case the sarcomere) to displacement (stretching) and measurement of the resulting relative force. This is precisely what is going on in experiment 1 making **choice C correct**.

2) **B. 5.5×10^{-6} M.** This question exemplifies the technique of estimation that is vital to succeed on the MCAT. The question asks for the calcium concentration when the wild-type troponin reaches 50% of its maximum force. You should have been able to visualize what is shown below on your own (**Fig. 3**). Identify that the concentration is slightly larger than a pCa of 5.5, it falls between 5.5 and 5.0. Recall that as the pCa values get smaller, concentration increases!! (Think of pCa like pH; smaller pH values mean more protons.)

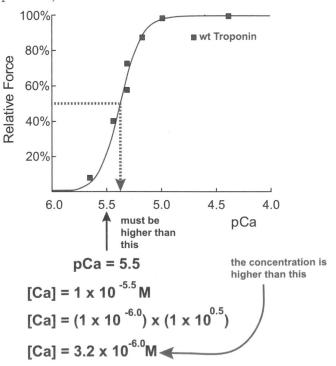

Figure 3. Estimation of Ca^{2+} concentration when sarcomeres with wild-type troponin reach 50% of the maximum force.

At a pCa of 5 the Ca^{2+} concentration would be 1×10^{-5} M and at a pCa of 6 the Ca^{2+} concentration would be 1×10^{-6} M. Given that the calcium concentration falls between 5.5 and 5.0 the concentration must be greater than 1×10^{-6} M. The concentration of calcium when pCa is 5.5 is roughly 3.2×10^{-6} M (**Fig. 3**) but the concentration when 50% activity is reached is slightly higher. This **ruled out choice A**. Importantly, while it is slightly higher, it did not reach a pCa of 5.0, **ruling out choices C and D**.

3) **C. 5/3 x 10^2 m/s.** The passage describes that the resting length of a myofiber is 1.8 μm while it also states in the experimental setup description that it is stretched to a maximum length of 2.3 μm. These points were also apparent in Figure 1. This translates to one end of the sarcomere traveling 0.5 μm in 2.9 ns as stated in the question. Remembering that velocity is distance traveled per time you simply needed to divide 0.5 μm by 2.9 ns as shown below (**Fig. 4**).

$$v = \frac{(0.5 \times 10^{-6}\text{m})}{(3.0 \times 10^{-9}\text{s})}$$

$$v = \frac{(5.0 \times 10^{-7}\text{m})}{(3.0 \times 10^{-9}\text{s})}$$

$$v = \frac{5}{3} \times 10^2 \text{m/s}$$

Figure 4. Calculations to determine the velocity of a recoiling sarcomere.

4) **A. function in the C subunit.** You needed outside knowledge of the three troponin subunits. Troponin T binds tropomyosin to form the troponin-tropomyosin complex. Reduced function in this subunit would predictably lead to cross-bridge formation in the absence of calcium, which is not observed, making **choice C incorrect**. Note that this logic also **eliminated choice D**, as it is an identical answer as choice C. Troponin I binds to actin in an inhibitory way that is relieved upon the addition of calcium. Reduced function of this subunit would also give rise to calcium-independent cross-bridge formation. Therefore, **choice B is incorrect**. Troponin C binds to calcium and is responsible for the calcium responsive behavior of the troponin-tropomyosin complex. Reduced function in this subunit would make the muscle less responsive to calcium, making **choice A correct**.

5) **C. not proportional and linear.** This question wanted to know how the curves were shaped, but didn't explicitly ask which curve you should be looking at. Only experiment 1 compared the relative force produced by stretching sarcomeres to a specific length; therefore, this is the best representative of the length-tension relationship. This immediately **ruled out choices B and D** because there were no sigmoidal curves in experiment 1 (only experiment 2). The sarcomere supplemented with wild-type troponin generated a linear curve, but note that this curve did not intersect the origin, which it must, in order to be classified as proportional, making **choice A incorrect**. Based upon this observation, **choice C is correct**.

6) **B. $10^{1/2}$.** This question did not require any information from the passage and only dealt with the work-energy theorem. Recall that any work done on an object is equal to the amount of energy that the object has attained. In this case, given that the blood is moving faster, you should have used the kinetic energy formula. Rearrange the formula to solve for velocity and then isolate the two variables mentioned in the question: velocity (v) and kinetic energy (KE). As is seen, velocity will change with the square root of the kinetic energy, making **choice B correct** (**Fig. 5**).

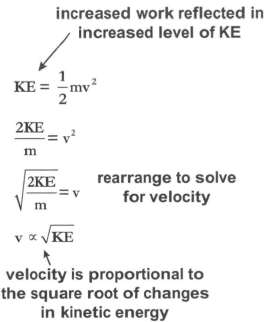

increased work reflected in increased level of KE

$$KE = \frac{1}{2}mv^2$$

$$\frac{2KE}{m} = v^2$$

$$\sqrt{\frac{2KE}{m}} = v \qquad \text{rearrange to solve for velocity}$$

$$v \propto \sqrt{KE}$$

velocity is proportional to the square root of changes in kinetic energy

Figure 5. Calculations to determine how velocity relates to changes in kinetic energy.

Turtle Buoyancy

While the primary function of the pulmonary system is gas exchange, marine organisms utilize these organs to alter buoyancy when diving. Sea turtles have mastered the alteration of buoyancy enabling them to dive to great depths. Boyle's Law complicates diving as it predicts a decrease in lung volume with increasing depth, thus increasing the sea turtle total body density.

Two hypotheses have been put forward to explain how the lungs can be used as buoyancy organs to achieve neutral buoyancy. The first hypothesis is called active depth selection (ADS) and it predicts that the pulmonary air volume is adjusted before diving to achieve a desired depth. The second hypothesis is called passive depth selection (PDS) and it predicts that stationary depth is chosen as a function of air volume in the lungs.

Marine biologists tested which of these two potential mechanisms sea turtles use. They measured dive duration and depth of two female Loggerhead turtles (A and B) in an aquatic tank that was 30 m deep. Each turtle was tested under two distinct experimental conditions: unweighted or weighted. The body masses of the turtles averaged 90 kg (Turtle A) and 120 kg (Turtle B) and the mass of the weights were 1 kg and 1.5 kg, respectively. Dive depth and duration was measured >1000 times and is displayed with depth as a function of dive duration (**Fig. 1**).

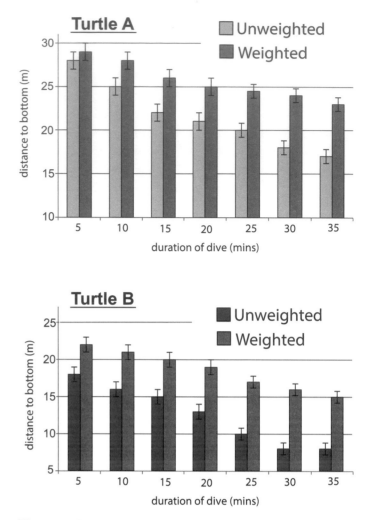

Figure 1. Dive depth and duration of Loggerhead turtles. The results for Turtle A are in the upper panel and Turtle B in the lower panel.

1) **According to Archimedes' Principle, which of the following is true for Loggerhead turtles?**

   A. Greater upward force at deeper depths and greater downward force at shallow depths.

   B. Greater upward force at shallow depths and greater downward force at deeper depths.

   C. Equal forces at all depths due to neutral buoyancy.

   D. Unequal forces at all depths due to neutral buoyancy.

2) **Calculate the gauge pressure exhibited on Turtle A at the maximum depth of her unweighted, 25-minute dive.**

   A. 1×10^4 Pa.

   B. 1×10^5 Pa.

   C. 2×10^4 Pa.

   D. 2×10^5 Pa.

3) **Based upon the data in Figure 1, which type of mechanism do Loggerhead turtles use to achieve neutral buoyancy?**

   A. ADS

   B. ADS when weighted, PDS when unweighted

   C. PDS

   D. PDS when weighted, ADS when unweighted

4) **An object floating in a tank of water is 40% exposed to the air is then moved to a tank with a fluid that has a density of 3.0 g/cm³. What percentage of the object will be submerged in the new fluid?**

   A. 20%

   B. 30%

   C. 40%

   D. 50%

5) **If the experimental conditions were changed such that the specific gravity of the fluid was 2.0, the sea turtle would:**

   A. require more inspired air to achieve the same depth.

   B. require less inspired air to achieve the same depth.

   C. use ADS when weighted and PDS when unweighted.

   D. use PDS when weighted and PDS when unweighted.

6) **In order to achieve neutral buoyancy, which respiratory capacity would turtles likely alter?**

   A. expiratory reserve volume

   B. inspiratory reserve volume

   C. residual volume

   D. tidal volume

7) **A Loggerhead turtle swims (0.8 m/s) directly across a 40 m wide river. If the turtle arrives at the other side 60 m downstream of her starting point, what is the velocity of the current?**

   A. 4/6 m/s

   B. 5/6 m/s

   C. 6/5 m/s

   D. 6/4 m/s

Turtle Buoyancy

	Foundation 3: Other Systems-B			Foundation 4: Motion-A Fluids-B		
	B			**A**	**B**	
Concepts				7	2	
Reasoning	6				1,4	
Research					5	
Data					3	

Big Picture. This passage combined the commonly tested Archimedes' principle with the respiratory system. There was also an important element of reading comprehension, as you had to understand the difference between ADS and PDS and how the experiment was designed to distinguish between ADS and PDS. The passage was not very clear on this issue, which is typical for an MCAT passage. According to the ADS hypothesis, Loggerhead turtles always prefer to dive to a certain depth for specific duration of time and will achieve that depth regardless of whether weight is added to their bodies or not. Alternatively, if the hypothesis predicts that Loggerhead turtles have no specific depth in mind, but rather they prefer to only go to a specific depth where they have achieved neutral buoyancy, then PDS is the mechanism. Therefore, the purpose of analyzing their depths and times, with or without weights, is to determine whether or not they go to different depths. This point was critical to answer question 3 and also related to questions 5 and 6. The passage also required that you bring in the foundational concepts of buoyancy, pressure, and displacement to answer the remainder of the questions.

1) **B. Greater upward force at shallow depths and greater downward force at deeper depths.** This question required that you understood the concepts of Archimedes' Principle and Boyle's Law. You may have had an advantage if you are a diver, but this certainly was not a prerequisite to get the question correct. When learning Archimedes' Principle in undergraduate physics, it is most common to consider only "objects" that are immersed in fluids rather than living organisms, so this question could have easily confused you. The main difference between the two is that the undergraduate physics "objects" usually do not experience changes in their density as a function of depth, but an organism with a lung full of air certainly will. The passage gave you a clue regarding this point with the sentence that describes how lung volume will decrease with increasing depth (due to the rising external gauge pressure), thereby increasing the density of the turtle. As seen below (**Fig. 2**), with increasing depth, the volume of the turtle lungs will decrease thereby increasing its overall density. This increases the downward force **ruling out choice C**. There will be a specific point where the downward force will be precisely equal the buoyant force: the point of neutral buoyancy. Anything above this results in an increased upwards force (buoyant force), and anything below results in an increased downward force (weight). This **makes choice B correct**. Note that **choice D makes no sense** because it disagrees with neutral buoyancy.

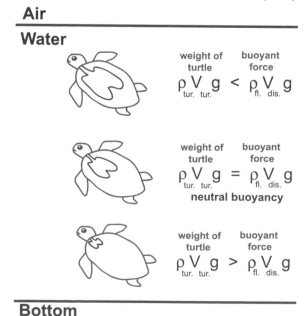

Air

Water

weight of turtle   buoyant force

$$\rho_{tur.} V_{tur.} g < \rho_{fl.} V_{dis.} g$$

weight of turtle   buoyant force

$$\rho_{tur.} V_{tur.} g = \rho_{fl.} V_{dis.} g$$
neutral buoyancy

weight of turtle   buoyant force

$$\rho_{tur.} V_{tur.} g > \rho_{fl.} V_{dis.} g$$

Bottom

Figure 2. Impact of depth on turtle lung volume and buoyancy according to Boyle's Law and Archimedes' Principle.

2) B. 1 x 10⁵ Pa. First, you had to look at the top panel of Figure 1 to retrieve the maximum depth that was for a 25-minute dive duration in the unweighted state. There was a devious trick here, as you had to pay attention to the y-axis as it states "distance to bottom" and NOT depth. So the value of 20 meters, which is what you derived from the graph, is the distance to the bottom at the maximum depth. The passage states that the tank depth is a total of 30 meters making the actual depth (D) of Turtle A at this point 10 meters. This was the value to plug into the gauge pressure formula. Note that you needed to already memorize the density of water (ρ), and you should also utilize the form of "g" that is 10 N/kg to facilitate unit cancellation (**Fig. 3**).

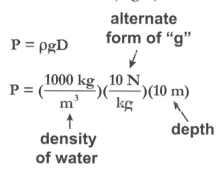

Figure 3. Calculating gauge pressure using the depth of 10 meters for Turtle A.

3) C. PDS. The passage provides definitions for both hypotheses, each of which explains how Loggerhead turtles achieve specific diving depths. The active depth selection (ADS) model predicts that the animal chooses a depth it wants to get to and then adjusts its air intake to achieve neutral buoyancy at that depth. The passive depth selection (PDS) model is simpler and predicts that the organism will choose a stationary depth as soon as neutral buoyancy is achieved, which is based upon the volume of air in the lungs. Once you were able to get a general sense of the difference between these two models, you then had to determine which model the data supports. The ADS model would predict that (weighted or unweighted) if the turtle is under water for 20 minutes, it would always go to the same depth. The data does not show this result. Moreover, if you look at it logically, the ADS model suggests that an animal

has the ability to know its weight ahead of time and to inhale the correct amount of air to achieve neutral buoyancy at a specific depth. This level of self-awareness is not observed in nature, making **choice A incorrect**. Rather, the turtle will dive until it reaches neutral buoyancy, and if it is heavier (due to the weights) it will not dive as far. This makes **choice C correct**. Notice that the trends in the data are the same for weighted and unweighted, suggesting that only one model was active in either case. This allows you to immediately **rule out choices B and D**.

4) A. 20%. This was a free-standing question placed within a passage largely devoted to Archimedes' Principle. While this question only required information presented in the question, it was not straightforward. Immediately identify that if an object is 40% exposed to air, it will be 60% submerged, which is the critical number when working with buoyant force (F_B) (**Fig. 4**). From this point, use the given values to determine the density of the object (ρ_{ob}), keeping in mind that the density of the fluid (ρ_{fl}), which in this case is water, is something that you should already know (1.0 g/cm³). Once you calculate the object density, apply this number to a new Archimedes' equilibrium by plugging in the new fluid density and solving for the volume of fluid that is displaced in terms of the object's volume (**Fig. 4**). While not explicitly pointed out, bear in mind that "g" readily cancelled in both sets of calculations.

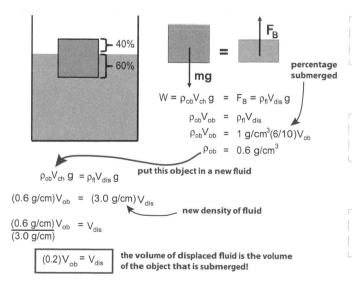

Figure 4. Calculations to determine percentage of an object submerged in a new fluid based upon the volume exposed to air while submerged in water.

5) B. require less inspired air to achieve the same depth. First, you should **eliminate both choices C and D** since the two hypotheses for how turtles choose depth do not make any mention to changes in or reliance on specific gravity of the liquid. From there, realize that this is a very tricky question so taking it step-wise was the way to go. If the specific gravity of the fluid is 2.0, then it will be twice as dense as water. This causes the upward buoyant force to increase, making it more difficult for the turtle to dive down to the same depth. In response to this, the turtle would want to increase its body density in order to raise its weight, thereby counteracting the increase in upward buoyant force with an increased downward force. To increase its body density, the turtle should inspire <u>less</u> air making **choice B correct.**

6) D. tidal volume. You needed to recall the foundational concept of lung volume and apply some reasoning to it. If the Loggerhead turtle wants to adjust how deep it needs to go to achieve neutral buoyancy, it will adjust the amount of air in its lungs. This will create a higher or lower body density, and therefore allow the turtle to toggle its weight to counteract the buoyant force. The most logical way to achieve this is to take in a larger or smaller breath of air, which translates to a change in tidal volume (**Fig. 5**). As is shown in Figure 5, typical ventilation exists within the tidal volume (narrow green oscillations) leaving room for further inhalation if necessary (Inspiratory reserve volume) or further exhalation (Expiratory reserve volume). The vital capacity is defined by the extremes of ventilation and the remaining volume is the residual volume.

7) C. 6/5 m/s. This question required that you recall foundational kinematics formulas and relationships. At first glance, it may have appeared that trigonometry was required but this was indeed not the case. First, determine the amount of time (t) it took for the turtle to cross the river, which is the turtle's displacement (d) (**Fig. 6**). Then take that answer to calculate the velocity (v) of the river current.

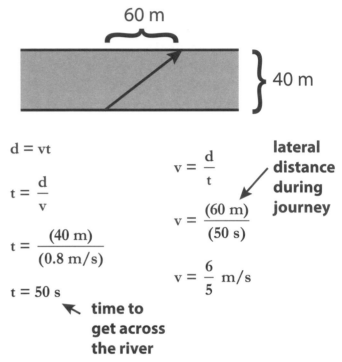

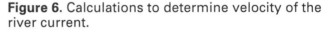

$$d = vt$$

$$t = \frac{d}{v}$$

$$t = \frac{(40 \text{ m})}{(0.8 \text{ m/s})}$$

$$t = 50 \text{ s}$$

↖ **time to get across the river**

$$v = \frac{d}{t}$$

lateral distance during journey

$$v = \frac{(60 \text{ m})}{(50 \text{ s})}$$

$$v = \frac{6}{5} \text{ m/s}$$

Figure 6. Calculations to determine velocity of the river current.

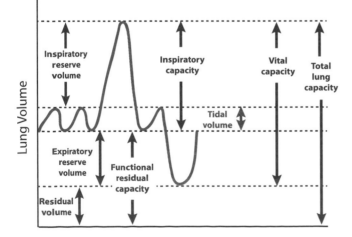

Figure 5. Lung volumes.

Notes:

3

4

PATHWAY

Atherosclerosis

The human circulatory system is considered a closed system where flow rate (Q) simply depends on the pressure gradient divided by total peripheral resistance (R). Poiseuille's law can explain hemodynamic equilibrium through consideration of the length of the artery (L), blood viscosity (η) or resistance to flow, and the radius of the vessel itself (r). In blocked, or stenotic arteries, turbulent flow is achieved at lower flow rates (**Fig. 1**). The velocity when laminar flow is converted to turbulent flow is called the "critical velocity" (V_c) and is dependent not only on blood viscosity and vessel radius, but also on the density of blood (nearly equivalent to water) and the Reynolds number (Re), which is approximately equal to 1000 for blood.

To understand the relationship between arteriole stenosis, blood viscosity, hematocrit (% packed erythrocytes), and smoking, physicians conducted an analysis of blood from three types of individuals. Group A were healthy controls, Group B were light smokers with one coronary artery stenosis, and Group C were heavy smokers with two coronary arteries that had stenosis. Ten subjects were present within each group and blood was isolated and analyzed for: blood viscosity, % packed red blood cell volume (measurement of hematocrit), and plasma viscosity. The results are shown below in Figure 2 (note that no significant difference in plasma viscosity was observed).

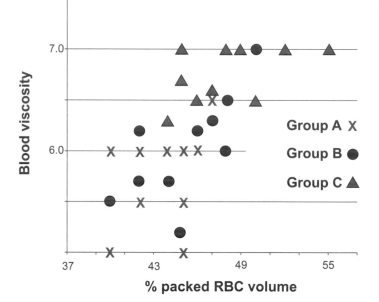

Figure 2. Scatterplot analysis of blood viscosity and packed RBC volume in patients.

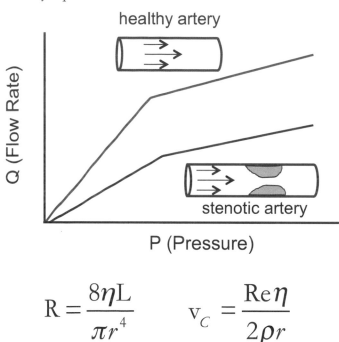

$$R = \frac{8\eta L}{\pi r^4} \qquad v_C = \frac{\mathrm{Re}\,\eta}{2\rho r}$$

Figure 1. Upper. Altered flow rate in an obstructed artery. Lower: formulas for peripheral resistance and critical velocity.

1) **Which of the following can be concluded from the data presented in Figure 1?**

   A. The ΔP required to achieve ΔQ is less in the stenotic artery.

   B. The ΔP required to achieve ΔQ is greater in the stenotic artery.

   C. The ΔQ required to achieve ΔP is less in the stenotic artery.

   D. The ΔQ required to achieve ΔP is greater in the stenotic artery.

2) **What biological change could explain why Group C displayed such different measurements relative to Group A?**

   A. Compensatory decreases in blood pressure due to increased levels of CO in the bloodstream.

   B. Compensatory increases in blood pressure due to decreased levels of CO in the bloodstream.

   C. Compensatory decreases in hematocrit due to decreased levels of CO in bloodstream.

   D. Compensatory increases in hematocrit due to increased levels of CO in bloodstream.

3) **An increase of 20% in the blood viscosity will cause what percentage decrease in blood flow rate?**

   A. 16%

   B. 20%

   C. 80%

   D. 84%

4) **Assuming no other changes, if the flow rate in an artery was reduced 50% due to a plaque, what factor multiplied by the original artery radius would be the new radius at the plaque?**

   A. $(0.5)^{1/4}$

   B. $(2)^{1/4}$

   C. $(0.5)^4$

   D. $(2)^4$

5) **All of the following are outcomes of arterial stenosis except:**

   A. increased turbulent flow near obstruction.

   B. increased velocity near obstruction.

   C. collapse of the artery due to decreased pressure near obstruction.

   D. expansion of the artery due to increased pressure near obstruction.

6) **By how much does flow rate of an artery decrease if the length were doubled and the diameter were decreased by a factor of 2?**

   A. 8-fold

   B. 16-fold

   C. 32 fold

   D. 64-fold

7) **What conclusion is best supported by the results shown in Figure 2?**

   A. Smoking contributes to an increase in hematocrit.

   B. Smoking correlates with an increase in hematocrit.

   C. Smoking contributes to a decrease in blood viscosity.

   D. Smoking correlates with a decrease in blood viscosity.

Atherosclerosis

Annotations.
1) B 2) D 3) A 4) A 5) D 6) C 7) B

	Foundation 3: Other Systems-B			Foundation 4: Fluids-B		
	B			**B**		
Concepts				3,4,6		
Reasoning				5		
Research	2					
Data	7			1		

Big Picture. As is seen in the grid, this passage merged the concepts of blood circulation and fluid dynamics. These two points were wrapped around two display items that presented related ideas, but did so in an unrelated fashion. The plot compared the flow rate as a function of pressure for a healthy versus stenotic artery (**Fig. 1**). You had to use the brief description of the concepts in the passage and your outside knowledge to realize that the inflection points of both graphs represent the transition from laminar to turbulent flow. This is because there is no longer a linear response in flow as a function of pressure. The scatterplot required more time to cull through (**Fig. 2**). You had to identify that Groups B and C had increased blood viscosity and hematocrit and this correlated with increased levels of smoking. The key word is correlated, but you could draw no further conclusion (remember correlation versus causation!).

The questions were generally distributed into two types of categories. The first was reasoning/conceptual where you had to apply formulas to determine mathematical outcomes. The second was to extract useful information from the data and apply that information to either make or justify conclusions.

1) **B. The ΔP required to achieve ΔQ is greater in the stenotic artery.** The passage states the flow rate depends on the pressure gradient but the reverse cannot be true. This **eliminates choices C and D.** From there, you needed to inspect the differential behavior of the two arteries in terms of how they each responded to increases in pressure gradients. Using the dotted lines as a guide (**Fig. 3**), you can determine that the stenotic artery required an additional change in pressure to achieve the same change in flow rate as the healthy artery, making **choice B correct.**

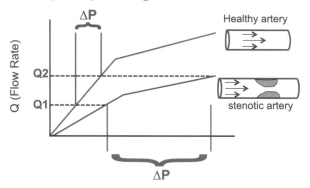

Figure 3. Graphical representation showing how a stenotic artery requires a greater change in pressure to achieve the same change in flow rate as the healthy artery.

2) **D. Compensatory increases in hematocrit due to increased levels of CO in bloodstream.** You should have immediately identified the fact that the data in Figure 2 does not give you enough information to make conclusions about the patients' blood pressure. This effectively **ruled out choices A and B.** You needed to focus on Group A (control) versus Group C (**Fig. 4**). Group C has a higher packed RBC volume (hematocrit) than Group A.

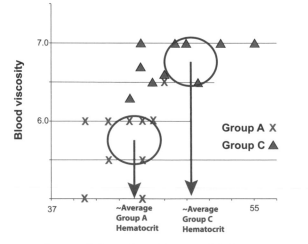

Figure 4. Group C (smokers) have a higher hematocrit than healthy control (Group A) patients.

138

This fact alone demonstrated that **choice D is the correct answer** and that **choice C is incorrect**. Note that it was not important to understand the concept of how CO levels changed in the bloodstream of smokers. As a background point, it is well-documented that due to the amount of CO released by burning cigarettes and the subsequent inhalation of that CO, smokers will indeed have an increase in the level of CO in their blood. This has a counterintuitive impact on hematocrit because the excess amount of CO binds to hemoglobin and competes with oxygen binding. The body will compensate for this reduced pool of functional hemoglobin by making more, thereby increasing the total number of erythrocytes in the blood.

3) **A. 16%.** While the flow rate equation is something that you should have known going into the passage, it was also described in the first paragraph. Recall that Q is the flow rate, ΔP is the pressure change and R is the resistance. Note that a 20% increase in blood viscosity should cause the same increase in overall resistance as seen to the right (**Fig. 5**) that was also provided in Figure 1. At that point, you needed to determine how flow rate would change in response to a 1.2-fold increase (or 20%) in resistance. The math was more deceptive than you probably initially thought and it was beneficial to consider that 1.2-fold increase is equivalent to an increase using a conversion factor of 6/5 (**Fig. 5**). In the equations shown to the right, note that R^o is the initial radius, Q^o is the original flow rate, and Q' is the new flow rate.

4) **A. $(0.5)^{1/4}$.** This question was just flat out challenging. You had to integrate two formulas together to determine how one variable was proportional to another. First, identify that the flow rate formula, which you should already know, (but was given to you in the first paragraph) tells you that flow rate is proportional to the inverse of the resistance (**Fig. 6**). Second, identify from the provided resistance formula that resistance is proportional to one over the radius to the fourth power. Combine those two proportionalities to determine that flow rate is proportional to the radius to the fourth power. Rearrange this to identify that radius is proportional to the fourth power of the flow rate. So, if the flow rate is reduced by two (or multiplied by one-half), the radius will respond by the fourth power of that value, making **choice C correct**. This is worked out to the right (**Fig. 6**).

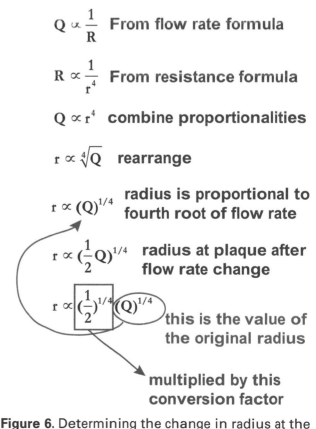

$$Q = \frac{\Delta P}{R} \qquad R = \frac{8\eta L}{\pi r^4}$$

$Q \propto \dfrac{1}{R}$ isolate variables

$Q \propto \dfrac{1}{(1.2)R^o}$ new radius in terms of original radius

$Q' = \dfrac{1}{(1.2)}(Q^o)$ new flow rate in terms of original flow rate

$Q' = \dfrac{1}{(\frac{6}{5})}(Q^o)$ convert 1.2 to a fraction

$Q' = \dfrac{5}{6}(Q^o)$

$Q' = 0.84(Q^o)$ new flow rate is 84% of the old flow rate (16% down)

Figure 5. Calculating the reduction in flow rate after a change in resistance.

$Q \propto \dfrac{1}{R}$ **From flow rate formula**

$R \propto \dfrac{1}{r^4}$ **From resistance formula**

$Q \propto r^4$ **combine proportionalities**

$r \propto \sqrt[4]{Q}$ **rearrange**

$r \propto (Q)^{1/4}$ **radius is proportional to fourth root of flow rate**

$r \propto (\frac{1}{2}Q)^{1/4}$ **radius at plaque after flow rate change**

$r \propto (\frac{1}{2})^{1/4}(Q)^{1/4}$ **this is the value of the original radius**

multiplied by this conversion factor

Figure 6. Determining the change in radius at the plaque given a change in flow rate.

5) D. expansion of the artery due to increased pressure near the obstruction. You needed to inspect Figure 1 again to understand what is physically happening in a stenotic artery. The key point is that narrowing (reduced radius (r)) causes a reduced cross-sectional area (A), and this causes an increase in the velocity (v) of blood flowing through the obstructed area and, therefore, increased turbulence (**Fig. 7**). This point made **choices A and B incorrect** because the statements are true. Recall the Equation of continuity and Bernoulli's equation and you should realize that the increase in velocity (caused by the decreased cross-sectional area) in the stenotic artery should cause a drop in pressure. This reduced pressure inside the artery near the obstruction allows the external pressure on the artery to exceed the internal pressure, causing it to collapse. **Choice C is incorrect** as it is a true statement. By the same token, **choice D is the correct answer** as it is a false statement.

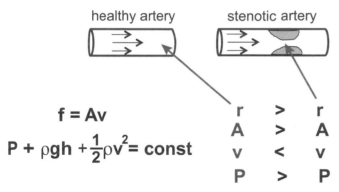

Figure 7. Changes in physical properties of a stenotic artery versus a health artery.

6) C. 32-fold. Here, you had to realize that two variables were being changed (length and diameter/radius) so the resistance would change accordingly. This would be expected to alter the flow rate. The passage provides you with the equation to describe how resistance is dependent on vessel length and radius. If length is doubled, then the new resistance will be twice the original resistance (**Fig. 8**). If the radius is decreased by a factor of two, the new resistance will be 16-fold larger than the original resistance (**Fig. 8**). Taken together, there is a 32-fold increase in overall resistance making the flow rate decrease by that amount. **Choice C is therefore correct**.

$$Q \propto \frac{1}{R}$$

$$R \propto L$$

$$R \propto 2L \quad \textbf{New R=2R}^{o}$$

$$R \propto \frac{1}{r^4}$$

$$R \propto \frac{1}{(\frac{1}{2}r)^4}$$

$$R \propto 16r \quad \textbf{New R=16R}^{o}$$

$$Q \propto \frac{1}{32R}$$

Overall resistance increases 32-fold

Figure 8. Calculating a change in flow given two changes in properties that impact resistance.

7) B. Smoking correlates with an increase in hematocrit. The explanation to this question can be considered by looking again at Figure 4. Group C patients are the heavy smokers and you can identify that they also have an increased blood viscosity and increased packed RBC volume (increased hematocrit). This immediately **ruled out choices C and D** as they cite the wrong direction for viscosity. Both answer choices A and B refer to the correct trend in hematocrit, but **choice A is incorrect** because it describes a classic over-interpretation of results. The data do not demonstrate that smoking causes (or contributes to) an increase in hematocrit, but rather that it is correlated with an increase. This makes **choice B correct**. Even though, ultimately, it is now known that smoking contributes to increases in hematocrit, the data presented in the scatterplot do not support that conclusion.

3

4

PATHWAY

Bile Salts

In non-hepatic tissue, excess cholesterol not delivered back to the liver for excretion is modified with activated fatty acids to form cytoplasmic storage droplets. In addition to controlling membrane fluidity, cholesterol is a precursor to vitamin D, steroids such as estrogen and aldosterone, and bile acids and salts. Ionized bile acids are preferentially incorporated into micelles, and these powerful detergents function in transport and digestion of lipophilic molecules. In addition to bile salts, bile contains phospholipids (lecithin) and cholesterol. Bile is released into the duodenum in response to hormones and is the primary method for eliminating intact cholesterol from the body.

Multiple oxidation events result in the conversion of cholesterol to the primary bile salts: cholate and chenodeoxycholate (**Fig. 1**). These salts are often conjugated with either glycine (glycocholic acid) or taurine (taurocholic acid) prior to being released into the duodenum. Conjugation alters ionization constants and promotes emulsification. Although passive absorption of bile occurs throughout the length of the digestive tract, bile acids are primarily absorbed by the ASBT sodium-dependent transporter in the terminal ileum. Approximately 90% of the bile acids are absorbed and delivered back to the liver via enterohepatic circulation. Any bile salts not absorbed in the ileum are deconjugated by colonic bacteria. This forms the secondary bile acids deoxycholate and lithocholate, some of which are excreted as feces.

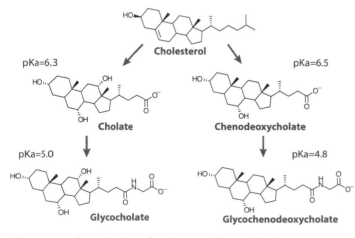

Figure. 1. Synthesis of primary bile acids from cholesterol.

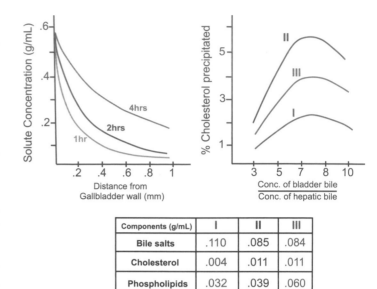

Components (g/mL)	I	II	III
Bile salts	.110	.085	.084
Cholesterol	.004	.011	.011
Phospholipids	.032	.039	.060

Figure 2. Left, bile components (solute) vs distance from wall. Measurements were taken at three different time points. **Right,** % cholesterol precipitated as function of bile concentration (g/ml) using values from the table.

Explanations for the formation of gallstones have included an excess of cholesterol relative to bile acids and phospholipids. Despite this, there appears to be no difference in the concentration of gall bladder bile components from centrifuged samples of healthy individuals vs. patients with gallstones. A second contributing factor to stone formation involves the ability for the gall bladder to concentrate and distribute bile. Indeed, a failure of the gall bladder to contract increases the likelihood of stone formation. To further understand the importance of bile components in the development of gallstones, two experiments were conducted. First, the concentration of bile components as a function of their position within the gall bladder was measured over time (**Fig. 2, left graph**). Due to the diffusion of water out of the gall bladder, the concentration of these species will increase with time. The second experiment investigated cholesterol precipitation as a function of altered bile components (**Fig. 2, right & table**).

1) In non-hepatic tissue the ACAT enzyme acylates cholesterol. This would lead to a(n):

A. increase the K_{sp} of the product.

B. decrease the K_{sp} of the product.

C. increase in bile production.

D. decrease in bile production.

2) According to the data in Figure 2, gallstones are more likely to form:

A. near the radial center of the gall bladder.

B. near the wall of the gall bladder.

C. with increased time.

D. with decreased time.

3) Which of the following hypotheses is most validated after a comparison between conditions II and III?

A. Increased phospholipid concentration leads to decreased cholesterol precipitation.

B. Increased phospholipid concentration leads to increased cholesterol precipitation.

C. Increased cholesterol concentration leads to decreased cholesterol precipitation.

D. Decreased cholesterol concentration leads to increased cholesterol precipitation.

4) Conjugation of cholate with glycine effectively lowers the pK_a by:

A. favoring incorporation into micelles.

B. generating more conjugated product.

C. facilitating formation of secondary bile acids.

D. increasing the formation of gallstones.

5) The conjugated bile acids have lower pK_a values than their precursors due to:

A. resonance stabilization.

B. decreased hydrogen bonding.

C. inductive effects.

D. increased molecular weight.

6) The density of a cholesterol droplet is $1.05 \ g/cm^3$. If a cholesterol droplet is placed into a fluid with a specific gravity of 4.0, how much fold increase of the droplet is protruding from the fluid than is submerged?

A. 2

B. 3

C. 4

D. 5

7) The ASBT symporter preferentially transports charged species across the intestinal lumen. Approximately what percentage of glycochenodeoxycholate will be transported at pH 6.8?

A. 90%

B. 10%

C. 50%

D. 99%

143

Bile Salts

	Foundation 4: Fluids-B			Foundation 5: Water-A Mol. Interactions-B Biomolecules-D		
	B			**A**	**B**	**D**
Concepts				7		
Reasoning	6				4,5	1
Research						
Data					2,3	

Big Picture. The emphasis of this passage was on acid/base chemistry as it relates to solubility as well as the physics concepts of fluids (Archimedes' Principle). Note the heavy emphasis on reasoning and data interpretation. Bile acids and salts are an important topic for the MCAT as their physical properties are derived from fundamental chemical and physical principles. That means a thorough understanding of them necessarily involves a multidisciplinary approach. In particular, this includes acid base chemistry, solubility, as well as fluids and buoyancy. As background knowledge, you should know that the liver makes bile, but the gall bladder secretes it through the common bile duct in order to "emulsify" fats. In other words, bile is required to digest lipids. This passage included a complicated looking chemical synthesis image that tested your ability to realize the effects of chemical modifications on solubility and on pK_a. In addition, this passage had a very tricky set of experiments that measured the concentration of bile solute as a function of proximity to the gall bladder wall (graph on left). You needed to realize that the closer to the wall of the gall bladder, the concentration of solutes is at its highest. This increases the chance of gallstone formation. Moreover, the graph on the right demonstrated how altering the concentration of solute components within the bile itself alters the amount of cholesterol that precipitates out of the bile.

1) **B. decrease the K_{sp} of the product.** The passage states that, "Excess cholesterol not delivered back to the liver for excretion is modified with activated fatty acids to form cytoplasmic droplets." The term "acylation" refers to this modification. Cholesterol is a very hydrophobic molecule and is therefore not very soluble in water. You should be able to deduce from the structure of cholesterol that the lone hydroxyl group participates in an acylation reaction. As can be seen below in Figure 3, modification of cholesterol through acylation by ACAT results in the formation of an ester from an activated fatty acid. (Recall that activated fatty acids are CoA derivatives.) This would generate a more hydrophobic product via the addition of alkyl groups (indicated by the R group which represents an alkyl chain). Therefore, the solubility product, which is a function of the overall molar solubility, would be expected to decrease in the cholesterol ester. **Choice A is wrong**, since it states the opposite. In addition, there is no reason to believe from the passage that acetylated cholesterol alters bile production, making **choices C and D both wrong**.

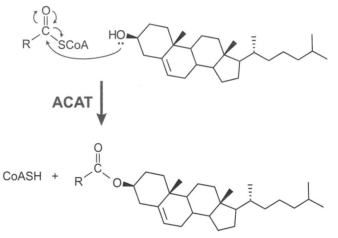

Figure 3. Acetylation of cholesterol.

2) **B. near the wall of the gall bladder.** From the passage, higher concentrations of bile constituents lead to an increased tendency to form stones. Figure 2 (and Figure 4 on the adjacent page) shows that the bile solute concentration is highest near the wall of the bladder. This means that stones are most likely to form here. **Choice A is therefore wrong**, since it states the opposite. Further, Figure 2 shows that, at high solute concentrations near the wall, this is largely independent of time (**Fig. 4**, green circle).

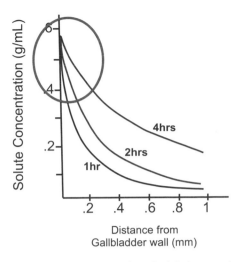

Figure 4. Solute concentration is highest when closest to wall.

3) **A. Increased phospholipid concentration leads to decreased cholesterol precipitation.** The key here is to analyze the data systematically. Isolate the variables between conditions II and III and determine what is being changed. While the bile salts are very slightly reduced, the cholesterol is unchanged making **choices C and D incorrect** but the level of phospholipids is doubled, so this should be what you focus on as the major difference between conditions II and III. By looking at the graph above, you should also realize that condition III results in less precipitation of cholesterol than in condition II, making **choice B incorrect**. The main conclusion that can be made validates a hypothesis that increased levels of phospholipid can decrease cholesterol precipitation.

4) **A. favoring incorporation into micelles.** Lowering the pKa means that more species will exist in the ionized form at physiologic pH. In addition, the passage states that, "Ionized bile acids are preferentially incorporated into micelles…" From this, it can be concluded, without any prior knowledge of micelles, that **choice A is the correct answer**. It can be concluded that **choice B is wrong** because lowering pKa has nothing to do with the amount of conjugated product generated. **Choice C is incorrect** because the formation of secondary bile acids occurs through deconjugation in the ileum as mentioned in the passage. Further, since conjugation of bile acids with glycine or taurine increases the solubility of the compound, gallstones would not be expected to contain glycolated bile salts making **choice D wrong**.

Although the question does not require knowledge of micelles, you should know what they are and Figure 5 describes micelles. Unlike phospholipids which are largely seen in bilayers, fatty acids and bile salts form micelles at a critical micellar concentration (CMC). Below the CMC value, the lipids exist as a solution of monomers. Above the CMC, the lipid forms micelles. The concentration of lipids required to form micelles can be determined through multiple methods including conductivity and absorbance. The concentration of cholesterol, bile salts, and lipids such as phosphatidylcholine are above the CMC in the GI tract, ensuring their micellar formation that facilitates absorption.

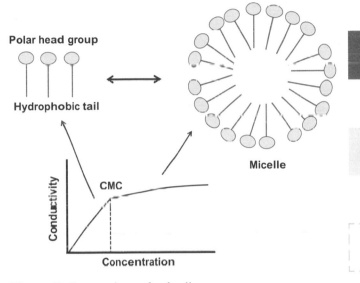

Figure 5. Formation of micelles.

5) **C. inductive effects.** Glycocholate is a stronger acid (lower pKa) than cholate because of the electron withdrawing power of the nitrogen atom in glycocholate (**Fig. 6**). As nitrogen is more electronegative than carbon, it will draw electrons towards itself, making the acidic proton of the carboxylic acid functional group (not shown) easier to dissociate. This effective increase in the acidity of the carboxyl proton of glycocholate lowers the pKa. In cholate, the atom analogous to the nitrogen in glycocholate is a carbon. Because carbon is largely electroneutral, there are minimal inductive effects (indicated by the dashed arrow). Keeping in mind that carbons (or "R groups") tend to donate electrons, electron induction occurs in an opposite manner to glycocholate. Note that induction occurs through sigma bonds, not pi bonds as is the case for resonance stabilization. This is why **A is a wrong answer choice. Choice B is**

wrong because the presence of the nitrogen in glycocholate would increase hydrogen bonding, not decrease it. **Choice D is wrong** because, although the molecular weight of glycocholate > cholate, this has nothing to do with the relative magnitude of the ionization constants of the compounds.

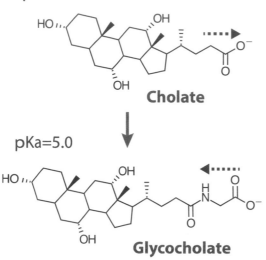

pKa=6.3

Cholate

pKa=5.0

Glycocholate

Figure 6. The lower pK_a of Glycocholate is due to the stronger inductive effects of the electronegative nitrogen. This allows for stabilization of the negative charge on the carboxylate oxygen.

6) **B. 3.** This is a classic Archimedes' Principle question, but it has some misleading numbers that are given. First of all, realize that a fluid with a specific gravity of 4.0 means that it will have a density of 4.0 g/cm^3. This means that the cholesterol droplet is 4 times less dense (ρ_{ch}) than the fluid (ρ_{fl}) and it will be floating. As shown in Figure 7, the weight of the cholesterol droplet will be equal to the buoyant force of the fluid. Note the use of the weight equation that is derived from mg (mass can also equal to density times volume (ρV) using the density equation $\rho = mV$). Following the series of equations in Figure 7, the volume of displaced fluid (V_{dis}) equals one-fourth the volume of the cholesterol droplet (V_{ch}). This translates to ¼ of the droplet being submerged in the fluid. The answer, however, is not four (**choice C is wrong**) because if ¼ is submerged (25%) then ¾

is above the fluid (75%) generating a 3:1 ratio of the amount of cholesterol out of the fluid relative to submerged **making choice B correct**.

7) **D. 99%.** To get to the finish line with this passage, you have to apply the Henderson-Hasselbalch equation, which you will need to know and know how to use for the MCAT, as shown below:

$$pH = pK_a + \log [A^-]/[HA]$$ or if you prefer:

$$pH = pK_a - \log [HA]/[A^-]$$

In this case, A^- represents the ionized conjugate base, glycochenodeoxycholate, and HA stands for glycochenodeoxycholic acid. Solve for the ratio of $[A^-]/[HA]$ given that the pH = 6.8 and the pK_a = 4.8. The difference between the pH and the pK_a is 2.0. Recall that pK_a is on a log scale, so that a difference of one represents a 10 fold change. Or you can plug and chug if you want. By plugging and chugging, you will arrive at $\log [A^-]/[HA] = 2$. The antilog of 2 is 100, meaning that $[A^-]/[HA] = 100/1$, or $[A^-]/[HA] = .01$, hence there is 100 times more ionized form of the molecule than there is of the neutral form of the molecule. When the pH > pK_a, there is a loss of protons at a functional group with the pK_a that is closest to the pH given.

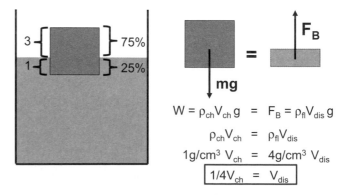

Figure 7. Using Archimedes' Principle to calculate percentage of an object submerged/protruding due to buoyant force.

Notes:

Multiple Sclerosis

Two critical structural properties determining action potential conduction velocity are axonal diameter and myelination. Experiments using squid giant nerve fibers allowed for the derivation of an equation (**Equation 1**) relating conduction velocity to the electrical parameters of the nerve: [d (axon diameter), ρ (resistivity of neuron interior), C (membrane capacitance per area), and R* (unit area resistance of membrane during excitation)].

$$v = \sqrt{\frac{d}{8\rho C^2 R^*}}$$

Equation 1

Myelinated axons exhibit clustering of Na^+ channels, allowing for saltatory conduction required for appropriate neuron function. Typical measurements of human axon characteristics are shown below (**Table 1**).

Table 1. (* denotes a per unit length value)

Physical Property	Myelinated Axon	Demyelinated Axon
Radius of Axon	4×10^{-6} m	4×10^{-6} m
Resistance*	6.4×10^9 Ω/m	6.4×10^9 Ω/m
Capacitance*	9×10^{-10} F/m	4×10^{-7} F/m
Conductivity*	2×10^{-7} Ω⁻¹/m	2×10^{-4} Ω⁻¹/m

Multiple Sclerosis (MS) is a disease where progressive demyelination diminishes neuron function through disrupting saltatory conduction, a process that neurologically sensitizes MS patients to temperature increases. However, interventions that produce a transient reduction in serum calcium ions improve conduction rates in MS patients.

To investigate the impact of temperature on nerve function, conduction velocities of isolated ulnar nerves were measured from three different subject groups of mice. The data were averaged and fitted to a linear regression model (**Fig. 1**). Blocking temperature, denoted as "X," is defined as the temperature where conduction was no longer detected.

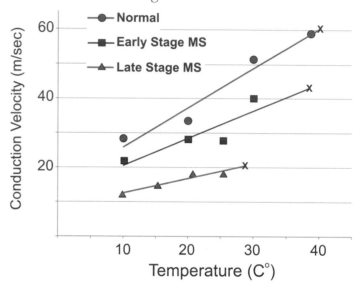

Figure 1. Measurement of conduction velocity as a function of temperature. Control rodents were healthy (Normal) whereas the other two experimental groups exhibited mild (Early stage) or severe (Late stage) MS symptoms.

148

1) Which of the following graphs represents the relationship between myelination and blocking temperature?

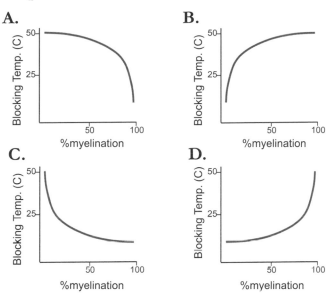

A.

B.

C.

D.

2) Calculate the amount of energy required to recharge a demyelinated axon following depolarization?

A. 2×10^{-9} J/m

B. 2×10^{9} J/m

C. 8×10^{-9} J/m

D. 8×10^{9} J/m

3) All of the following statements comparing myelinated and demyelinated axons are true except:

A. Myelinated axons have higher conduction velocity than demyelinated axons.

B. Demyelinated axons undergo conduction block at a higher temperature than myelinated axons.

C. Ion transport in myelinated axons occurs over a greater temperature range than demyelinated axons.

D. Ion transport in demyelinated axons occurs over a smaller temperature range than myelinated axons.

4) If the axon radius is changed to ¼ its initial amount, the resulting conduction velocity would:

A. increase by 2-fold.

B. decrease by 2-fold.

C. increase by 16-fold.

D. decrease by 16-fold.

5) What is the amount of power required to recharge an axon if energy expended per action potential is 2×10^{-9} J/m and the length of an action potential is 10^{-2} seconds?

A. 5×10^{-11} W/m

B. 2×10^{-9} W/m

C. 2×10^{-7} W/m

D. 5×10^{-7} W/m

6) Which is the most likely outcome if MS patients were treated with a calcitonin antagonist?

A. Decreased conduction velocity

B. Re-myelination of motor neurons

C. Increased conduction velocity

D. Cannot be determined

7) Calculate the number of Na^+ ions that cross a demyelinated axon during a neuronal action potential:

A. 2×10^{-11}/m

B. 4×10^{-8}/m

C. 4×10^{8}/m

D. 2×10^{11}/m

3

4

Multiple Sclerosis

Annotations.
1) B 2) A 3) B 4) B 5) C 6) D 7) D

	Foundation 3: Neurobiology-A			Foundation 4: Motion-A Electrochem.-C	
	A			A	C
Concepts				4	2,5
Reasoning	6				7
Research					
Data	3				1

Big Picture. This passage emphasized the basic foundational concepts of physics including electrical transmission, power/energy, and velocity. These topics were all woven together in the context of Multiple Sclerosis (MS), a prevalent and degenerative neurological disease.

No background knowledge of MS was required and the passage provided you with only limited factual details regarding the disease. However, it was important to note that patients with MS have diminished conduction velocity and sensitivity of conduction to temperature as well as the vague comment about calcium reduction being beneficial. These points were all that you needed to get a grasp of the data that was presented in Figure 1. Notice that the graph was not overly intuitive as it incorporated several points at once. You should have realized that as MS progresses: (1) the overall conduction velocities were reduced; (2) conduction velocities existed over a more limited temperature range; (3) blocking temperatures were lower as a function of disease progression. What was not as obvious was that disease progression also correlates with degree of myelination (i.e. decreased myelination occurs with disease progression).

Finally, you needed to be able to work with both the formula for conduction velocity (which was probably new to you) and the table of values for myelinated versus demyelinated axons.

1) **B.** For this question you had to analyze the data presented in Figure 1 and then apply the findings to the series of graphs that were presented in the question stem. However, the problem was that Figure 1 did not directly give you a relationship between percentage of myelination and blocking temperature, but it did actually provide you with enough information to get an accurate idea of what the relationship between myelination and temperature are. First of all, appreciate from the passage that normal axons should be near 100% myelinated. In contrast, early stage MS patients would have a lower percentage of myelinated axons and later stage patients would exhibit even lower percentages of myelination. Moreover, the "X" on the graphs denoted the blocking temperature so you should have identified that there is a reduction in blocking temperature as the degree of myelination decreased. This **ruled out choices A and C**. Next, you had to realize the difference between answer choices B and D. In choice B, the blocking temperature is reduced with decreasing percentage of myelination but <u>does so gradually at first and then accelerates downward</u>. Answer choice D presents the opposite scenario as there is a significant decrease initially and then it gradually levels off. When inspecting Figure 1 for the trend that the blocking temperature exhibited, you will notice that it is reduced gradually at first and then accelerates downward (**Fig. 2**). This makes **choice B correct**.

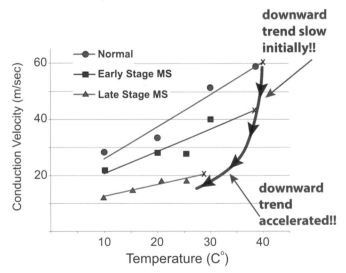

Figure 2. Accelerating downward trend of blocking temperature as an axon becomes progressively demyelinated.

2) A. 2 x 10⁻⁹ J/m. The amount of energy required to recharge a demyelinated axon following depolarization is equal to the amount of potential energy (PE) the axon has in the resting state. In other words, you needed to use one of the electrical potential energy formulas to arrive at the correct answer. The capacitance (C) of a demyelinated axon is provided in the passage but the voltage change (V) during an action potential is not. This should be outside knowledge that you had walking into the exam. Recall that resting membrane potential is -70mV, which then changes to +35mV during an action potential. This gives a voltage change of about 100mV or 1×10^{-1} volts. This was the "missing value" to plug into the equation as shown below (**Fig. 3**).

$$PE = \frac{1}{2}CV^2$$

From table

$$PE = \frac{1}{2}(4 \times 10^{-7} \, \frac{F}{m})(1 \times 10^{-1} V)^2$$

From...your brain

$$PE = (2 \times 10^{-7})(1 \times 10^{-2})\frac{J}{m}$$

$$PE = 2 \times 10^{-9} \frac{J}{m}$$

Figure 3. Calculations to determine the amount of energy required to recharge a demyelinated axon.

3) B. Demyelinated axons undergo conduction block at a higher temperature than myelinated axons. While not directly referenced in the question stem, you needed to inspect the results presented in Table 1 and Figure 1 in order to correctly answer this question. Among the most straightforward results was the fact that normal (myelinated) axons had higher conducting velocities than early/late stage MS axons (demyelinated) making **choice A incorrect** (because it's a supported conclusion). Also, you should have noted that the regression lines presented in Figure 1 represent the temperature range that conduction velocity can be measured. The lines became progressively shorter as the axon became demyelinated. This result supported both **choices C and D so they were also incorrect**. The results in Figure 1 do not support the conclusion that demyelinated axons undergo conduction block at higher temperatures but, in fact, support the opposite conclusion. This makes **choice B correct**.

4) B. decrease by 2-fold. This was a "formula-management" question where you had to handle a novel mathematical relationship and make a conclusion. First, isolate the two variables in the question stem to determine that conduction velocity is proportional to the square root of the axon diameter (**Fig. 4** and **Equation 1**). The same relationship is true for the radius, since changes in diameter and radius are directly proportional to one another. If the diameter decreases, note that the velocity must also decrease ruling out choices A and C. From there, the square root of four is two so **choice B is correct**.

$$v = \sqrt{\frac{d}{8\rho C^2 R^*}}$$ **Formula provided by passage**

$$v \propto \sqrt{d}$$ **velocity is proportional to diameter (therefore radius)**

$$v \propto \sqrt{\frac{d}{4}}$$ **diameter is reduced by 4-fold**

$$v \downarrow 2$$

Figure 4. Relationship between conduction velocity and diameter (i.e. radius).

5) C. 2 x 10⁻⁷ W/m. This question is as straightforward as it looked so don't overthink it. You did not need to get any of the values from Table 1 because the question stem provided you with all that you needed. You were looking to calculate the power per unit distance (P) so the standard equation applied (P = W/t where W = work per unit distance and t = time) and then you just "plugged and chugged" (**Fig. 5**).

$$P = \frac{W}{t} \qquad P = \frac{2 \times 10^{-9} J/m}{10^{-2} secs} \qquad P = 2 \times 10^{-7} \frac{W}{m}$$

Figure 5. Calculations to determine power.

6) D. Cannot be determined. This question was entirely dependent on the phrase, "Interventions that produce a transient reduction in calcium ions improve conduction rates in MS patients." Moreover, you had to understand that if a patient is treated with a calcitonin antagonist, they would experience an increase in serum calcium levels. The natural inclination would be that this should worsen their condition, but be very careful here. A graphical representation of the logic you needed to understand this point is shown below (**Fig. 6**). As you can see, the statement informs you that reductions in calcium improve conduction rates but that statement tells you nothing about increases in calcium levels. Therefore, you cannot anticipate the outcome of increasing calcium levels on conduction rates making **choice D correct**. This type of question gets at the heart of interpreting data and, more specifically, not over-interpreting observations to the point of extrapolating outcomes.

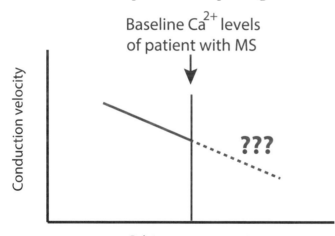

Figure 6. The provided relationship of reduced calcium levels improving conduction velocity does not state that increasing calcium concentration will reduce conduction velocity.

7) D. 2×10^{11}/m. This was a two-part physics problem in that you had to the answer to the first calculation to plug into the second formula. There was some relatedness between this question and question 2 in that you had to "bring to the table" that 0.1V is the change in potential during an action potential. First, determine the amount of charge crossing a membrane, which used a standard formula that related charge (Q) to capacitance (C) and voltage (V) (**Fig. 7**). Notice that the numerical answer to this first equation was **choice B but this is not the correct answer** because the question stem is asking for particle number. You had to plug the charge value into another equation, which relates quantized charge to number of charged particles (n) where each particle has an elementary charge (e) (**Fig. 7**). From there, you could arrive at the correct answer.

$$Q = CV$$

Note that capacitance is per unit length (from Table 1)

$$Q = (4 \times 10^{-7} \frac{F}{m})(0.1V) \leftarrow \text{estimated voltage change during AP}$$

$$Q = 4 \times 10^{-8} \frac{C}{m} \leftarrow \text{charge per unit length of demyelingated axon during AP}$$

$$Q = ne \leftarrow \text{alternative formula to related particle number}$$

$$n = \frac{Q}{e} = \frac{(4 \times 10^{-8} \frac{C}{m})}{(1.6 \times 10^{-19} C/particle)}$$

$$n = 2 \times 10^{11} \text{particles/m} \quad \text{You need to memorize this number!}$$

Figure 7. Calculating the number of particles crossing an axonal membrane during an AP.

Notes:

PATHWAY

Glaucoma

The use of medicinal marijuana has become more common as a remedy for ocular hypertension associated with glaucoma, a group of eye disorders marked by increased intraocular pressure. Its active component, tetrahydrocannabinol (THC), is well known for its low level of aqueous solubility. In an effort to increase the solubility and enhance the effects of the topical delivery of THC to patients with glaucoma, scientists generated two carboxylate derivatives: THC hemisuccinate ester (THC-HS) and THC hemiglutarate ester (THC-HG) (**Fig. 1**).

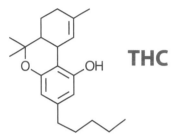

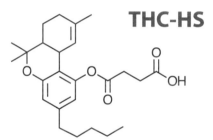

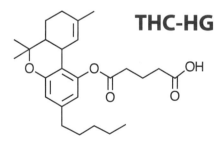

Figure 1. THC and THC derivatives.

Experiment 1. To evaluate the effects on aqueous solubility, THC derivatives were individually tested for solubility in an aqueous solution that was supplemented with arginine as an ion pair (**Fig. 2**).

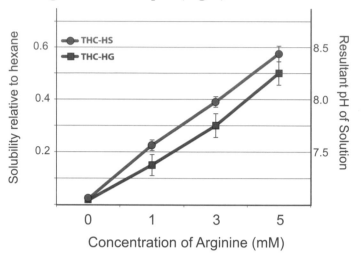

Figure 2. Effect of Arginine on THC derivative solubility.

Experiment 2. To monitor the impact on corneal permeability, an apparatus is used where an isolated rabbit cornea is placed between two fluid-filled chambers. Compounds are added to the donor chamber and flux across the corneal membrane is monitored. The transport for each compound is then measured as a function of pH in the presence or absence of arginine in the donor chamber (**Fig. 3**).

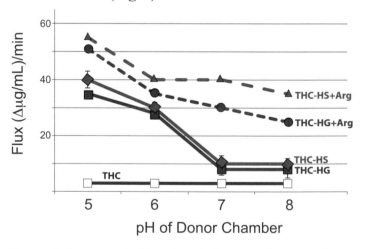

Figure 3. Impact of pH and arginine supplementation on THC derivative flux.

1) Which amino acid would most likely behave similar to arginine in Figure 2?

A. Alanine

B. Aspartate

C. Histidine

D. Leucine

2) At pH = 8, why does the presence of arginine enhance THC derivative transport?

A. Arginine freely diffuses across all membranes.

B. Arginine shields THC carboxylates.

C. Arginine protonates THC carboxylates.

D. Arginine raises the pH of the donor chamber.

3) Which of the following conclusions cannot be made based upon the data in Figures 2 and 3?

A. Arginine-mediated THC solubility causes increased corneal flux.

B. Arginine-induced increases in pH decrease corneal transport.

C. Charged THC derivatives transport less efficiently than uncharged.

D. Ion pairing between THC and arginine causes increased corneal flux.

4) Based upon the chart of refractive indices below, which of the following is true?

Region of eye	n
Cornea	1.34
Lens center	1.41
Aqueous humor	1.33
Lens cover	1.38

A. Light refracts the least through the cornea.

B. Light refracts the least through the lens cover.

C. Light travels slowest through the lens center.

D. Light travels slowest through aqueous humor.

5) Which aqueous solution would be most effective in extracting THC-HS from a mixture of THC-HS and THC dissolved in hexane?

A. 10% hydrogen chloride

B. 10% sodium bicarbonate

C. 10% sodium chloride

D. 10% sodium hydroxide

6) How far in front of a converging lens (focal length = 3 cm) must an object be placed to generate an image whose height is 3 times that of the object?

A. 3 cm

B. -3 cm

C. 4 cm

D. -4 cm

7) Calculate the pH of a solution of THC-HS (pKa = 4.0) where the concentration of the ionized form is 0.4M and the neutral form is 0.004M.

A. 2

B. 3

C. 5

D. 6

8) An eye disorder containing a focal point within the vitreous humor would require what kind of lens to correct it?

A. Diverging lens with negative power.

B. Converging lens with negative power.

C. Diverging lens with positive power.

D. Converging lens with positive power.

Glaucoma

Annotations.

1) C   2) B   3) B   4) C   5) B   6) C   7) D   8) A

	Foundation 4: Light-D			Foundation 5: Water-A Separation-C Biomolecules-D		
	D			**A**	**C**	**D**
Concepts	4,6,8					
Reasoning				7	5	
Research				3		
Data						1,2

Big Picture. This passage featured the physics concept of how light interacts with matter (i.e. optics) as well as some general chemistry concepts that included solubility, acid/base properties, and properties of amino acids. These concepts were all put into a biochemical context involving the use of Tetrahydrocannabinol (THC) as a treatment for glaucoma. The presumed mechanism of action of THC, which is the active ingredient in marijuana, is that it lowers pressure in the eye, thereby alleviating the symptoms of glaucoma. The major property of THC that limits it as a mainstream medicine is its extreme insolubility in aqueous solvents and this passage was based upon that information.

There were two clusters of questions presented here. The first were purely conceptual and required outside fundamental knowledge of optics. The remainder of the questions drew from different areas of biochemistry/general chemistry and required you to understand the data presented in the passage. Keep in mind this passage could have gone in a direction that included more organic chemistry featuring questions on the presented structures, but there were no such direct questions presented.

1) **C. Histidine.** This question is basically asking you which amino acid has similar chemical and physical properties to that of arginine. A question like this does touch upon a greater issue for students as to whether you should invest the time memorizing amino acid side chain structures. A short answer to this would be that it won't hurt you to know them but we do not recommend spending hours with flashcards in order to get to that point. Rather, you should be familiar with a few key amino acid side chains with a particular emphasis on their properties. For example, there are three basic (positively charged) amino acids: arginine, lysine, and histidine. Recalling this straightforward fact was enough in this case to determine that **choice C is correct**. Alanine and leucine, choices A and D, are both hydrophobic and nonpolar amino acids. Aspartate, choice B, is an acidic amino acid.

2) **B. Arginine shields THC carboxylates.** This was a difficult and subtle point to glean from the data presented in Figure 2. The best strategy is to first use process of elimination to thin out the field of answer choices. Extending from the discussion in question 1, arginine is a basic amino acid and is therefore positively charged at pH values below 10. Given that it is charged at all pH values tested in the experiments, it would not freely diffuse across cell membranes **making choice A incorrect**. Answer choice D is one of the hardest to reject as it is a factual statement. The data in Figure 2 clearly demonstrates that the resultant pH after addition of arginine increases, however, this would not be predicted to enhance THC derivative transport. In fact, increasing the pH of the solution would, if anything, act to further increase the number of THC derivatives that are negatively charged thereby reducing their transport. This makes **choice D wrong**. Protonating THC carboxylates would reduce their overall charge and predictably increase their membrane transport. However, arginine is a basic amino acid (not acidic), so it would not be predicted to protonate the carboxylate group of THC making **choice C wrong**. By default, **choice B is correct** but you should also note that the passage made reference to arginine acting as an "ion pair" with the THC derivative. Ion pairing, or ion-association, occurs when ions of opposite charge associate with one another in solution to form a chemically distinct (and in this case neutral) species. So, in essence, the positive R-group of arginine will

interact with the negative charge of the THC-carboxylate thereby shielding both groups to allow better transport across the corneal membrane (**Fig. 4**).

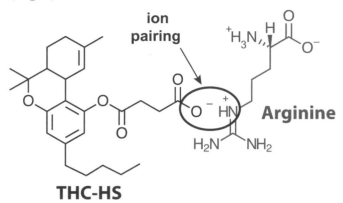

Figure 4. Ion pairing between the carboxylate of THC-HS and the protonated R-group of arginine.

3) **B. Arginine-induced increases in pH decrease corneal transport.** This is one of the most challenging types of MCAT questions that you will encounter. It tests your ability to understand the limitations of an experimental design in terms of what conclusions are justified by the results versus over-interpretations of the results that are not supported by the data. The data presented in Figure 3 demonstrates that when THC derivatives are supplemented with arginine, the level of transport is enhanced at all pH values relative to not adding arginine. Moreover, you should have also observed that as the pH increases the enhancement of THC derivative transport was reduced. Answer choices A and D are directly supported by the results and are explained further in the annotation for question 2. As these conclusions can be made, **choices A and D are incorrect**. The necessity of adding arginine to create an ion pair with the THC derivatives is all based upon the fundamental rule that charged species transport poorly across cell membranes. The data support this well-known rule making **choice C a justified conclusion and therefore incorrect**. The remaining choice B is difficult to exclude because it sure looks as if increasing the pH decreases corneal transport. The problem with choice B is that it isn't specific for THC derivative transport across the corneal membrane but, rather, is a blanket statement to say transport in general is inhibited by increases in pH. If the experiment measured the transport of a variety of substrates as a function of pH and all were observed to have reduced transport at higher pH values, then this

conclusion could be more justified. However, given that only one chemical species is analyzed, the statement is too broad; therefore, **choice B is correct**.

4) **C. Light travels slowest through the lens center.** Use a common test-taking strategy that involves ranking in a question like this. Upon quick inspection of the answer choices, you should note that there are quantitative extremes being associated with each value. These types of extreme answer choices can only be associated with the extremes within the question ranking. In other words, the aqueous humor (n = 1.33) and lens center (1.41) have the lowest and highest index of refraction. This **rules out answer choices A and B**. From this point, you had to recall the foundational meaning of index of refraction. This is a unit-less value that is solved by the equation: $n = c/v$, where n is the index of refraction, c is the speed of light in a vacuum, and v is the velocity of light in a specified medium. While not important to answer this question correctly, commit to memory that the index of refraction can never be less than one as this would assume that the speed of light in a material exceeds that in a vacuum. Importantly, the greater the index of refraction then the greater the degree of refraction of the light and the slower it travels in the medium that is specified, making **choice C correct**.

5) **B. 10% sodium bicarbonate.** In organic extractions, a solution is added to the mixture of the compounds in order to cause one of them to be differentially soluble compared to the other. In other words, you needed to identify the chemical difference between THC and THC-HS. Upon inspection of Figure 1, it is clear that THC has a phenol group (weak organic acid) and the THC-HS has a carboxylic acid group (strong organic acid). Treating either of these compounds with a strong acid such as hydrogen chloride or the relatively inert salt, sodium chloride, will not result in any reaction. Therefore **choices A and C are incorrect**. Either of these compounds can be deprotonated when treated with a strong base (e.g. sodium hydroxide) to create a negative charge, which increases their solubility in aqueous solvents. However, only THC-HS with the stronger carboxylic acid group can be deprotonated by a weaker base (e.g. sodium bicarbonate). Therefore this will be an effective method to specifically extract it **making choice B correct**.

6) C. 4 cm. This question seems easy enough, until you actually start to set it up. Please be advised that you must have the two major optics equations (the lens and magnification equations, shown in Figure 5) committed to memory. Realize that at this point the relatively straightforward variety of lens equation problems gives you two out of three of the variables but this one did not. Use algebra to get one variable in terms of another. Follow the equation worked out below to arrive at the correct answer:

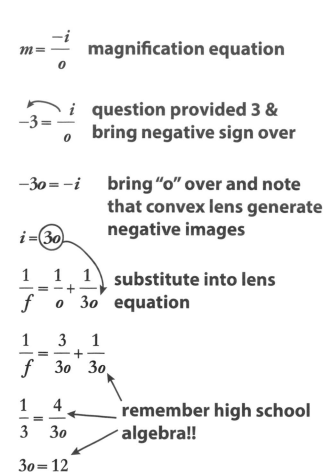

$$\frac{1}{f} = \frac{1}{o} + \frac{1}{i} \quad \textbf{lens equation}$$

$$m = \frac{-i}{o} \quad \textbf{magnification equation}$$

$$-3 = \frac{i}{o} \quad \textbf{question provided 3 \& bring negative sign over}$$

$$-3o = -i \quad \textbf{bring "o" over and note that convex lens generate negative images}$$

$$i = \boxed{3o}$$

$$\frac{1}{f} = \frac{1}{o} + \frac{1}{3o} \quad \textbf{substitute into lens equation}$$

$$\frac{1}{f} = \frac{3}{3o} + \frac{1}{3o}$$

$$\frac{1}{3} = \frac{4}{3o} \quad \textbf{remember high school algebra!!}$$

$$3o = 12$$

$$o = 4\,cm$$

Figure 5. Calculating object distance using the lens and magnification equations. Note: f = focal length, o = object distance, i = image distance, m = degree of magnification.

7) D. 6. This question is a classical use of the Henderson-Hasselbalch equation and the question stem gave you all of the values that you needed to calculate pH. Obviously, if you did not recognize this point, it was difficult to approximate the answer. The steps required to get the answer correct are shown below. Note that the $\log_{10}$ of 100 is two.

$$pH = pKa + \log_{10}\left(\frac{[A^-]}{[HA]}\right)$$

$$pH = 4 + \log_{10}\left(\frac{[0.4]}{[0.004]}\right)$$

$$pH = 4 + \log_{10}(100)$$

$$pH = 4 + 2 = 6$$

Figure 6. Using Henderson-Hasselbalch to calculate pH of a solution.

8) A. Diverging lens with negative power. Recall that all diverging lenses have negative power whereas all converging lens have positive power. This effectively **rules out choices B and C**. The diagram below (**Fig. 7**) depicts what this question is describing where the light entering the eye reaches a focal length well short of the distance back to the retina (in the vitreous humor). This means that the eye lens is "over-converging" the light so if the light were to enter the lens slightly more diverged, through the use of a diverging lens, then the focal length would be placed back onto the retina.

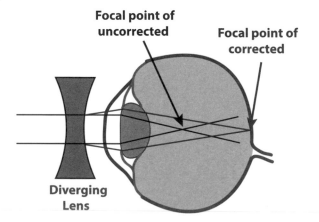

Figure 7. Correctional use of a diverging lens to reposition the focal point in myopia.

PATHWAY

Jaundice

The limited lifespan of erythrocytes necessitates a mechanism for removing heme and recycling iron from circulation. Heme undergoes oxidation and subsequent reduction utilizing NADPH to form a chemical compound known as bilirubin. The solubility of bilirubin is enhanced through the conjugation to UDP-glucuronate, which is converted to urobilinogen and stercobilin by colonic bacteria. This ultimately gives pigment to human feces and urine.

Neonatal jaundice is primarily caused by the lack of expression of UDP-glucuronosyltransferase, which is normally expressed in the liver ~37 weeks into gestation. The buildup of bilirubin in the blood and interstitial fluids leads to the appearance of a yellowish hue to the skin and sclera of the eyes and, if left untreated, can result in neurological damage.

"Phototherapy" has become the standard of care for neonatal jaundice. It is clear that blue light is the most effective in promoting bilirubin clearance in infants. The general model (**Fig. 1**) that has been put forth by scientists is that blue light induces changes in the bilirubin structure, specifically at the 4Z and 15Z bonds, creating a series of geometric isomers. Collectively termed "photobilirubin," these isomers are readily converted back to bilirubin. While these products are more hydrophilic than bilirubin, the primary product called lumirubin is thought to be the main compound cleared through excretion.

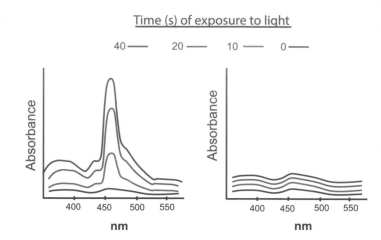

Figure 2. Absorbance spectra of extracted aqueous serum from Groups A (left) or Group B (right). Numbers represent time of excitation in seconds.

To identify bilirubin isomers in response to phototherapy, scientists employed a strategy utilizing a Gunn rat model, which is homozygous deficient for bilirubin UDP-glucuronosyltransferase. These specific rats were then divided into two groups: A and B. Group A rats were shaven, irradiated with blue light for 3.5 hours, while group B rats were neither shaven nor treated with blue light. Both groups were outfitted with catheters into the common bile duct and the femoral vein to remove samples. After group A was treated with light for 3.5 hours and group B was incubated in the dark for same amount of time, serum was isolated and extracted with chloroform followed by a second extraction with ether. Most of the bilirubin is removed through this technique, leaving primarily an aqueous solution. The spectrophotometric analysis of the purified aqueous phase is shown (**Fig. 2**).

Figure 1. Photoconversion of Bilirubin to Lumirubin. Irradiation of Bilirubin generates a group of isomers known as Photorubin, which in turn can convert to Lumirubin.

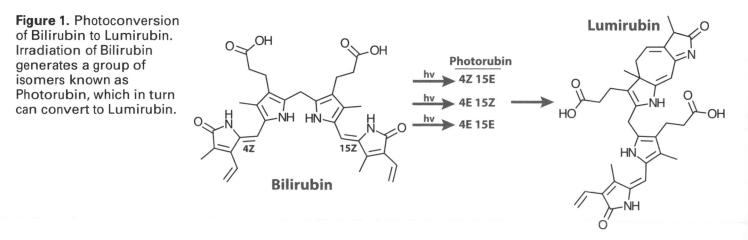

1) **Which is more hydrophilic?**

A. Bilirubin, because of increased intermolecular bonds with the aqueous environment.

B. Bilirubin, because of increased intramolecular bonding with the aqueous environment.

C. Lumirubin because of increased intermolecular bonding with the aqueous environment.

D. Lumirubin because of increased intramolecular bonding with the aqueous environment.

2) **Despite its preferential absorbance for blue light, physicians have observed that bilirubin can also effectively be broken down by green light. Which of the following hypotheses likely explains this observation?**

A. Increased energy associated with green light compensates for its poor absorbance by bilirubin.

B. Increased energy associated with blue light compensates for its poor absorbance by bilirubin.

C. The increased wavelength of green light provides greater depth of penetration through skin.

D. The increased energy of green light causes a greater amount of photobilirubin.

3) **Calculate the light intensity in W/m if a 36 W blue light is exposed to the surface of a baby if placed 1.0 m away? (Assume the light radiates evenly outward.)**

A. 2

B. 3

C. 4

D. 6

4) **The maximum absorbance of bilirubin is at 450 nm, however, when conjugated to albumin, this absorbance increases to 475 nm. Calculate the difference in energy of these two forms of light (h = 6.6 x 10^{-34} m^{2}kg/s).**

A. 7/8 x 10^{-35} J

B. 7/8 x 10^{-17} J

C. 7/8 x 10^{17} J

D. 7/8 x 10^{35} J

5) **Why do the mice in group A have a photoreactive compound present despite the fact that bilirubin is removed to near completion by chloroform?**

A. Phototherapy induced the formation of photorubin.

B. There was an accumulation of lumirubin.

C. There was an accumulation of soluble bilirubin.

D. Oxidation and reduction of bilirubin was stimulated by phototherapy.

6) **The relationship between bilirubin and lumirubin can be best described as:**

A. enantiomers.

B. diastereomers.

C. geometric isomers.

D. constitutional isomers.

Jaundice

Annotations.

1) C 2) C 3) B 4) C 5) B 6) D

	Foundation 4: Light-D			Foundation 5: Mol. Interactions-B		
	D			**B**		
Concepts	3,4			6		
Reasoning				1		
Research	2					
Data				5		

Big Picture. This passage connects the ideas of how light interacts with biomolecules and how this molecular interaction functions in a physiological system. One of the challenges in this passage is the terminology. It is dense and the words are not the type that one uses on a daily basis, unless of course, you are a doctor. Jaundice is a real, common problem making the biochemistry, organic chemistry, and physics that are in play highly relevant to medicine. Once you get to medical school, you will see all of this again. The passage was rich in providing you with process of elimination answer choices, making several questions more workable. One challenge is to not get intimidated by chemical structures such as those shown in the passage. You needed to get the basic point that bilirubin is not easily cleared by the body because of its insolubility in the blood so steps are necessary to get make the molecule more water-soluble. This is normally achieved through the conjugation to UDP-glucuronate, which provides the necessary polar groups present in the hydroxyls of the glucose ring to allow its excretion into the digestive lumen. Moreover, you needed to get the fine details, which describe the chemistry that photobilirubin can undergo but a large portion of it converts back to bilirubin while some of it becomes lumirubin, which is cleared due to its solubility.

1) **C. Lumirubin because of increased intermolecular bonding with the aqueous environment.** A potentially misleading question if you try to take it head on. Use your basic knowledge of solubility and attack the answers as if you were holding a flashcard with the definition of hydrophilic in your hand. For a compound to be hydrophilic (soluble in water) you would want it to undergo bonding with the water, not itself. This logic effectively **rules out choices B and D**. Remember that intramolecular interactions are defined as interactions occurring between different functional groups on the same molecules while intermolecular interactions occur between different functional groups on different molecules. From that point, some context clues in the passage could have guided you to the correct answer. For example, the passage states that the lumirubin is cleared through excretion, which is an indicator of its hydrophilic nature. Moreover, the passage states that bilirubin is less hydrophilic than its photorubin products and that bilirubin is effectively extracted by chloroform, an organic (hydrophobic) solvent. All of these signs point to bilirubin being hydrophobic. If you missed these signs and just prefer to look at the chemical structures, then you would have noticed that many of the atoms capable of making hydrogen bonding-interactions in bilirubin are juxtaposed to each other, promoting intramolecular interactions, whereas in lumirubin they have been moved further away, promoting intermolecular interactions. This is illustrated in Figure 3. Given this arrangement, **choice C is the best answer.**

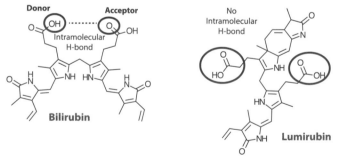

Figure 3. Lumirubin has greater intermolecular hydrogen bonding than Bilirubin.

2) **C. The increased wavelength of green light provides greater depth of penetration through skin.** This question relied on your ability to remember something that you were taught at a very young age: the colors of the rainbow (ROY G BIV). While it isn't critical to remember the wavelength of each specific color, it is important to know either end of

the spectrum. So, you will need to know that red light has a wavelength of 700 nm and violet light has a wavelength of 400 nm. Given that the wavelength decreases as you move toward the violet light, then the frequency increases as you move toward violet light. Following the E = hf (E = energy, h = Planck's constant, f = frequency), then so does the energy. This means that green light has less energy than blue light. This means that **choices A and D are incorrect**. Furthermore, note that **choice B just doesn't answer the question** because it isn't referring to green light. Only **choice C states the only accurate fact** attempting to describe why green light is nearly as effective as blue light despite its lower energy state.

3) **B. 3.** This question challenged your ability to remember geometric formulas, specifically the surface area of a sphere. Recall that light will be emitted from a bulb equally in all directions so that the power (P) of the light is uniform at a given radius distributed through three dimensions (hence area of a sphere (A) and not a circle). The formula I = P/A (I = intensity) was used and the area of a sphere is $4\pi r^2$. This was calculated to be $(4)(3.14)(1)^2 = \sim 12$ m². Thus, $36W/12m^2 = 3$.

4) **C. 7/8 x 10¹⁷ J.** Recall the formula to calculate energy associated with electromagnetic radiation: E = hf, and in this case: E = h(c/λ) where c = speed of light in a vacuum and λ = wavelength. Here you had to substitute in and also realize that the exponents were the only major mathematical concern in that all of the answers had 7/8. Following this expression, we get E = $(6.6 \times 10^{-34})(3 \times 10^8/25 \times 10^{-9})$, and note the correct use of division of exponents (subtracting a negative means adding a positive) so the answer will have 10^{-17}, leaving only **choice C as the correct possibility**.

5) **B. There was an accumulation of lumirubin.** It is important to understand that due to their deficiency in bilirubin glucuronidation, these rats will have an extreme buildup in bilirubin and basically suffer from jaundice their whole lives. This phenotype makes this rat a good model for the disease. The experiment describes using a catheter to isolate serum from the blood. As the passage describes that bilirubin is poorly soluble in blood, we would expect that very little of it is present in the serum of these mice. Moreover, any that is present will be purified away

using chloroform extraction. These statements **rule out choice C** as there would not be any soluble bilirubin created. Moreover, the passage does not describe both oxidation and reduction of bilirubin, **ruling out choice D**. This leaves answer choices A and B left, but **A is not a good choice** as the passage states that photorubin readily converts back to bilirubin. This leaves **B as the correct answer choice** as only lumirubin would accumulate and survive the chloroform extraction because it is water-soluble.

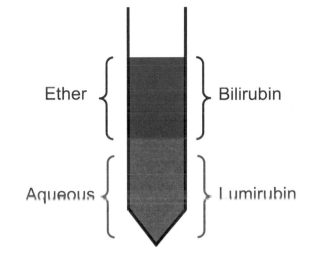

Figure 4. Extraction of Bilirubin from Lumirubin through differential solubility.

6) **D. constitutional isomers.** This question requires you to spend some time looking at the structures. The passage clearly provides you with the information relating to how bilirubin and photorubin are related because the cis/trans status of bonds 4 and 15 are indicated. However, the lumirubin does not indicate where bonds 4 and 15 have gone and, the structure is turned a bit. Gross inspection of both structures should provide you with a "feel" for the two compounds that something is actually quite different (aside from them being rotated). Try counting the number of rings in either structure and you will find that lumirubin has 5 rings while bilirubin has only 4. This should indicate that there is a difference in the overall connectivity, making them constitutional isomers, as the molecular formulas are the same. Remembering that enantiomers are complete mirror images of each other, diastereomers differ in the absolute configuration of groups in at least one but not all of a molecule's chiral centers and geometric isomers differ by the rotation of groups around a double bond or ring structure (these are also referred to as cis-/trans- or E-/Z- isomers).

Grave's Disease

In Grave's disease, circulating autoantibodies stimulate thyroid function from a euthyroid (normal) to a hyperthyroid state. These antibodies mimic thyroid stimulating hormone (TSH), causing an increased production of the iodinated thyroid pro-hormone thyroxine (T4). The excess T4 leads to its increase conversion into either triiodothyronine (T3) or reverse T3 (rT3) (**Fig. 1**). T3 binds to the thyroid nuclear receptor (TR) and regulates transcriptional programs in effector cells.

Physicians treated patients with hyperthyroidism with two doses of ^{131}I, which has a half-life of eight days and undergoes β-decay to destroy thyroid tissue. The initial mass of the thyroid was estimated, the amount of radionuclide present in thyroid 24 hours after treatment was recorded, and the resultant functional state of the thyroid was determined (**Tables 1 and 2**).

Table 1. Low dosage schedule for ^{131}I.

Thyroid mass (g)	μCi in thyroid (24hr)	Outcome
10-25	45	euthyroid
26-50	60	euthyroid
51-75	75	hyperthyroid
76-100	100	hyperthyroid

Table 2. High dosage schedule for ^{131}I.

Thyroid mass (g)	μCi in thyroid (24hr)	Outcome
10-25	80	hypothyroid
26-50	105	hypothyroid
51-75	150	euthyroid
76-100	200	euthyroid

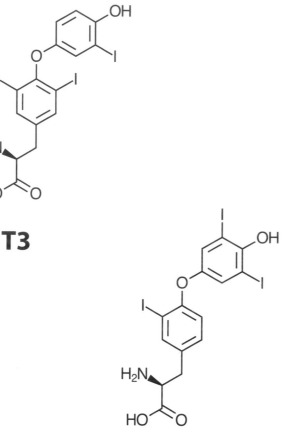

T3

rT3

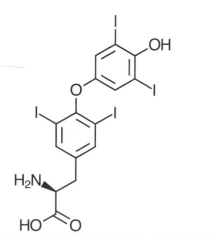

T4

Figure 1. Structures of thyroid hormones.

1) **Iodide is concentrated in thyroid follicles through a basolateral Na⁺ symporter prior to being converted to an iodine intermediate. Which of the following reactions best represents this?**

A. $I^- + H_2O_2 \rightarrow I_2 + H_2O$

B. $I_2 + H_2O \rightarrow I^- + H_2O_2$

C. $I_2 + H_2O_2 \rightarrow I^- + H_2O$

D. $I^- + H_2O \rightarrow I_2 + H_2O_2$

2) **What is the appropriate treatment regimen for Grave's disease based upon Tables 1 & 2?**

A. Low levels for both large and small thyroids.

B. High levels for both large and small thyroids.

C. Low levels for small thyroids and high levels for large thyroids.

D. High levels for small thyroids and low levels for large thyroids.

3) **Which of the following would be least capable of distinguishing between samples of T3 and T4?**

A. UV spectroscopy

B. H-NMR spectroscopy

C. Mass spectroscopy

D. Thin layer chromatography

4) **Which of the following atoms represents the likely stable product of ¹³¹I decay?**

A. $^{130}_{53}Te$

B. $^{131}_{54}Xe$

C. $^{131}_{54}Te$

D. $^{131}_{53}Xe$

5) **Which type of reaction would be most expected to take place during the generation of T4 from T3?**

A. electrophilic substitution

B. electrophilic elimination

C. nucleophilic substitution

D. nucleophilic addition

6) **Women treated with ¹³¹I are cautioned against getting pregnant due to potential birth defects. If a three order of magnitude reduction of administered ¹³¹I is recommended, which of the following expressions represents the time (in days) required to reach this point?**

A. $(8)(\ln 1/1000)$

B. $(8)(\ln 1000/1)$

C. $(\ln 8)(1000/1)$

D. $(\ln 8)(1/1000)$

7) **Which of the following answer choices represents the H-NMR spectra of thyroxine and triiodothyronine?**

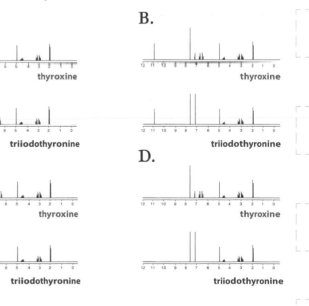

165

Grave's Disease

Annotations.

1) A   2) C   3) A   4) B   5) A   6) B   7) A

	Foundation 4: Electrochem.-C Light-D Atoms-E		Foundation 5: Biomolecules-D		
	C	**D**	**E**	**D**		
Concepts		3	4	5		
Reasoning	1	7	6			
Research						
Data			2			

Big Picture. This passage dealt with an area of biology that may be a soft spot for many students. Accordingly, it was likely that you did not have significant working knowledge of how the thyroid functions, the molecular basis for Grave's disease, and how radioactive iodine can be used to treat this disease. Deficiencies on these points should not have alarmed you as many of the questions dealt with foundational knowledge of general and organic chemistry. These points included radioactive decay, half-life, redox reactions, and spectroscopy.

The biological context for this passage was, as mentioned, the thyroid gland and its production of specific chemicals that regulate gene expression. Below (**Fig. 2**), we expound upon what was mentioned in the passage. Normally, in response to thyroid stimulating hormone (TSH), the thyroid will release T3 and T4, which ultimately control body metabolism by altering gene expression.

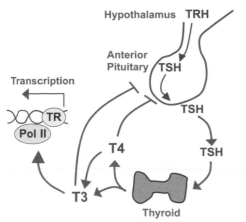

Figure 2. The hypothalamus-pituitary axis regulates the production of thyroid stimulating hormone (TSH).

1) **A. $I^- + H_2O_2 \rightarrow I_2 + H_2O$.** The first clue in this problem was from the question stem stating that a Na^+ symporter was being used. This type of transport mechanism would carry two ions across together and given that sodium is in its cationic state (positively charged), then the other ion would be expected to be in its anionic state (negatively charged). **Choices B and C are incorrect** because the iodine state (I_2) would not be the reactant but rather the product since the atoms here are not negatively charged. This leaves answer choices A or D, which differ in the use of either water or peroxide facilitating the conversion of iodine. Notice that the oxidation state of iodine is going from -1 to zero and thus is an oxidation reaction. Therefore, the other chemical species must be reduced during the reaction. The oxidation state of oxygen in peroxide is -1 whereas in water it is -2. Therefore the desired reaction will have peroxide getting converted to water, **eliminating choice D.**

2) **C. Low levels for small thyroids and high levels for large thyroids.** The goal of ^{131}I therapy is to destroy enough thyroid follicle cells to bring thyroid function back to normal (euthyroid). A balance must be achieved: too strong of a dose can destroy the thyroid (hypothyroid) and patients not receiving enough ^{131}I will still exhibit hyperthyroidism. You had to identify the trends in the data (shown in Figure 3) to determine that **choice C is correct.**

Low dose therapy

Thyroid mass (g)	µCi in thyroid (24hr)	Outcome	
10-25	45	euthyroid	} effective
26-50	60	euthyroid	
51-75	75	hyperthyroid	} ineffective
76-100	100	hyperthyroid	

High dose therapy

Thyroid mass (g)	µCi in thyroid (24hr)	Outcome	
10-25	80	hypothyroid	} too strong
26-50	105	hypothyroid	
51-75	150	euthyroid	} effective
76-100	200	euthyroid	

Figure 3. Comparing dose effects on thyroid function.

3) A. UV spectroscopy. In a question like this, the key point to identify is the difference between the two compounds in question. Thyroxine (T4) has an additional iodine atom in place of a hydrogen atom in T3. This makes the masses of the two compounds different and therefore distinguishable using mass spectroscopy (**choice C is incorrect**). The same rationale would make H-NMR spectroscopy also effective in distinguishing the two compounds, making **choice B incorrect**. Thin layer chromatography (TLC) separates compounds with differential polarities, and so the additional iodide group will alter the overall polarity of T4. This makes this technique also suitable for distinguishing between T3 and T4, making **choice D incorrect**. Recall that UV spectroscopy takes advantage of the differences in absorbance that can occur between two compounds. UV spectroscopy takes advantage of the capacity for Pi (π) electrons to absorb ultraviolet light and excite electrons to higher molecular orbitals. As the number of π electrons are equal in T3 and T4, there is no basis for thinking that UV spectroscopy could effectively distinguish between the two structures, making **choice A correct**.

4) B. $^{131}_{54}$ Xe. All β decay results in the production of daughter nuclides with the same mass as the initial material. This **rules out choice A** because its mass is not the same as ^{131}I. By definition, β-decay involves the conversion of a neutron into a proton and concomitant release of a β particle. A β particle is nearly equivalent to an electron and is a way to counterbalance the acquisition of a new positive charge when the neutron is converted to a proton. Given that there is a net gain in the proton number, the atomic number must increase by one. Iodine has an atomic number of 53, so the element created must be Xenon with an atomic number of 54. Answer **choice B is therefore correct**. Through decay, ^{131}I releases a β particle and undergoes gamma decay that further releases energy (**Fig. 4**). This process leads to the apoptosis of thyroid follicle cells and is the basis of the therapeutic benefit in Grave's disease.

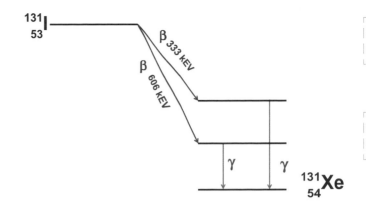

Figure 4. β-decay of ^{131}I.

5) A. electrophilic substitution. This question required that you inspect the two molecules that were given in the passage. The only difference between the two was the substitution of hydrogen for iodine on one of the benzene rings in the molecule. Given that this difference would be derived from an electrophilic reaction, **choices B and D were wrong**. It cannot be nucleophilic since those reactions on a benzene ring would result in an atom or group other that H being replaced. The substitution of iodine into an electron-rich, aromatic ring system like benzene occurs through a process called "electrophilic aromatic halogenation," which is a form of electrophilic aromatic substitution (EAS). This makes **choice A correct.**

167

6) B. (8)(ln1000/1). At first glance, this seems like a pretty standard half-life question, but the answer choices may have made you think twice. Recall the formula to calculate the amount of radioactive material (N) based upon a starting amount of material (N_o), an amount of time that has transpired (t), and a given half-life ($t_{1/2}$), which is 8 days. Recall that three orders of magnitude means 1000. This means that you are looking to get a ratio of N_o/N equal to 1000 in order to achieve a three order of magnitude (3 logs) reduction in radioactive iodine from this initial formula, the calculations are shown (**Fig. 5**). Note that even though there are no calculators used on the MCAT, this style of question is by no means unlikely.

$$N = N_o e^{-(t/t_{1/2})}$$

Divide by N $$\frac{N}{N_o} = e^{-(t/t_{1/2})}$$

$$\frac{N}{N_o} = \frac{1}{e^{(t/t_{1/2})}} \quad \text{negative exp. means 1/x}$$

flip num. & den. $$\frac{N_o}{N} = e^{(t/t_{1/2})}$$

natural log both sides $$(\ln)\frac{N_o}{N} = (\ln)\, e^{(t/t_{1/2})}$$

$$(\ln)\frac{N_o}{N} = \frac{t}{t_{1/2}}$$

$$(t_{1/2})(\ln\frac{N_o}{N}) = t$$

$$(8)(\ln1000) = t$$

Figure 5. Calculations to determine time for a particular radioactive decay level to be reached.

7) A. At first glance, this question seemed like a very hard-core organic chemistry one. However, the MCAT is unlikely to get too sophisticated with H-NMR spectroscopy, so use the same basic points to eliminate answer choices. Recall that protons present in organic acids (e.g. carboxylic acids) are heavily shifted downfield (>10 ppm). Conceptually, this is because they are highly deshielded as they will exist partially as ionized species. Both thyroxine and triiodothyroxine possess such a proton (**Fig. 6**) and this **eliminates choices C and D**. From this point, you should have focused on the fundamental differences between the two structures and the differences between the H-NMR plots shown in choices A and B. The structural differences lie in the upper aromatic ring where thyroxine has one less hydrogen and the other two hydrogens bound to the aromatic ring experience equivalent electronic environments and should therefore give rise to a single tall peak. In contrast, triiodothyroxine possesses three hydrogens bound to its aromatic ring and each of these experience unique electronic environments and should give rise to three peaks. This is diagrammed in Figure 6.

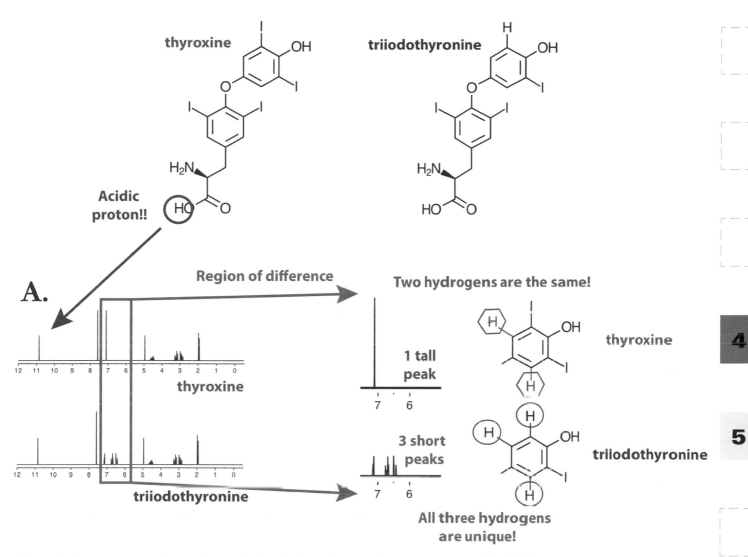

Figure 6. Structures of thyroxine and triiodothyroxine and a comparison of H-NMR spectra.

Biomineralization

Magnetotactic bacteria (MTB) contain a unique membrane-bound organelle called a magnetosome, which contains crystals of iron oxide magnetite (Fe_3O_4) or iron sulfide greigite (Fe_3S_4). MTB creates magnetite in three stages: 1) incorporation of raw materials into the cell, 2) rearrangement of minerals using redox chemistry, 3) growth of precipitated crystals. MTB surfaces have organic ligands (e.g. carboxyl, hydroxyl, and phosphoryl groups) that serve to attract external metals. There are two potential mechanisms used to import iron: (1) a specific ferrous iron transporter that is encoded by the FeoB1 gene; (2) the uptake of the less soluble ferric ion using iron chelators known as siderophores. To investigate how materials are brought into MTB, and its importance, two experiments are performed.

Experiment 1. Transport of either Fe(II) or Fe(III) was monitored in the presence (wt) or absence (mt) of a FeoB1 gene. Various concentrations of extracellular iron were supplied as either ferric ammonium citrate or ferrous chloride. Transport was then monitored. Figure 1 shows the results for experiment 1.

Experiment 2. This was performed to measure the amount of magnetite produced as a function of external pH conditions. MTB were grown under four different pH values and two characteristics were measured: (1) bacterial growth rate; (2) the number of crystals formed per bacterium. Figure 2 shows the results for experiment 2.

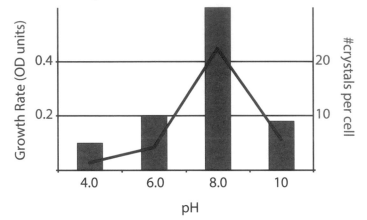

Figure 2. Measurement of MTB growth and crystal formation at different pH levels. The growth rate is indicated by the line and the number of crystals per cell is indicated by the bars on this graph.

Figure 1. Measurement of iron flux into MTB as a function of Fe concentration. mt = mutant; wt = wild-type.

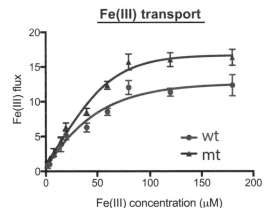

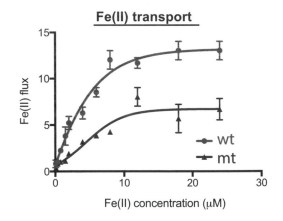

1) An extracellular source of iron is iron(III) hydroxide, which has a $K_{sp} = 5.4 \times 10^{-17}$ M^4 at 25°C. What is the concentration of ferric ions required to reach molar solubility?

A. 3×10^{-6} M

B. 3×10^{-5} M

C. 3×10^{-4} M

D. 3×10^{-3} M

2) Why might slight increases in pH lead to increased magnetite crystal formation?

A. It enhances expression of siderophores.

B. It represses expression of siderophores.

C. Deprotonation of functional groups favors electrostatic attraction to ferric/ferrous ions.

D. Protonation of functional groups favors electrostatic attraction to ferric/ferrous ions.

3) What was the purpose of using ferric ammonium citrate in the experiments?

A. This compound is necessary for transport into MTB.

B. The Fe oxidation state is +3, making it optimal for crystal formation.

C. Increase its solubility to promote import.

D. Decrease its solubility to promote precipitation on the MTB cell wall.

4) Which of the following represents the electron configuration of the ferrous ion?

A. $1s^2 \, 2s^2 \, 2p^6 \, 3s^2 \, 3p^6 \, 3d^6$

B. $1s^2 \, 2s^2 \, 2p^6 \, 3s^2 \, 4s^1 \, 3d^5$

C. $1s^2 \, 2s^2 \, 2p^6 \, 3s^2 \, 4s^2 \, 3d^4$

D. $1s^2 \, 2s^2 \, 2p^6 \, 3s^2 \, 4s^2 \, 3d^6$

5) Researchers have shown that a bacterial nitrite reductase can accelerate the oxidation of the ferrous ion. Which pair of reactions represents this finding?

A. $NO_2^- \rightarrow NO$ / $Fe^{2+} \rightarrow Fe^{3+}$

B. $NO_3^- \rightarrow NO_2^-$ / $Fe^{2+} \rightarrow Fe^{3+}$

C. $NO_2^- \rightarrow NO_3^-$ / $Fe^{2+} \rightarrow Fe^{3+}$

D. $NO_2^- \rightarrow NO_3^-$ / $Fe^{3+} \rightarrow Fe^{2+}$

6) Which of the following hypotheses explains the altered flux in ferric kinetics in the FeoB1 mutant?

A. Increased K_m of ferric antiporters as compensation for reduced ferrous ion import.

B. Decreased K_m of ferric antiporters as compensation for reduced ferrous ion import.

C. Increased expression of ferric antiporters.

D. FeoB1 mutant transporters now conduct ferric ions.

7) If MTB swim antiparallel with a magnetic field toward a south pole. Using the right-hand rule, in which direction will the net magnetic force align?

A. South

B. East

C. West

D. None

8) Which of the following indicators would be appropriate to ensure that the extracellular conditions do not exceed pH = 9 ?

A. bromcresol green ($pK_b = 9.1$)

B. thymol blue ($pK_b = 5.2$)

C. alizarine yellow ($pK_b = 3.5$)

D. indigo carmine ($pK_b = 2.0$)

Biomineralization

Annotations.
1) B 2) C 3) C 4) A 5) A 6) C 7) D 8) B

Foundation 4: Electrochem.-C Atoms-E			Foundation 5: Water-A Biomolecules-D Thermo/Kinetics-E		
C	E		A	D	E
Concepts 7	4		1,5,8		
Reasoning				2	
Research			3		
Data					6

Big Picture. While this passage presented two experiments, the questions were more driven by your understanding of concepts. In particular, this passage was very chemistry-rich and required your knowledge of oxidization states, solubility, indicators, and electron configuration. What made the passage integrative was the inclusion of transport kinetics as the data in Figure 1. Keep in mind that a passage like this one could go in numerous directions. The focus could have easily gone into questions dealing with magnetism from a physics perspective (which there was only one) and could have come at you from a chemistry perspective with an impetus on comparing paramagnetic versus diamagnetic materials. Rather, the content was focused more on issues of electrons. You needed to know the rules of electron configuration (in particular the order by which you remove electrons), have an understanding of solubility and be comfortable calculating molar solubility. Finally, the passage threw in a question regarding magnetic forces. Overall, this level of integration between multiple subject matters increases the overall difficulty of the passage, but the reliance on data interpretation was relatively low.

1) **B. 3×10^{-5} M.** This is a common "K_{sp}" type of question where you need to be able to mathematically determine molar solubility and the concentration of ions. Keep in mind that calculators are not required, and this is what your scratch paper should look like (**Fig. 3**):

$Fe(OH)_3 \rightarrow Fe^{3+} + 3OH^-$ **iron is in the ferric state**

$K_{sp} = [Fe^{3+}][OH^-]^3$ **use the K_{sp} expression**

$K_{sp} = [x][3x]^3$ **substitute in "x" to solve equation**

$5.4 \times 10^{-17} = 27x^4$
move decimal to the right

$54 \times 10^{-18} = 27x^4$
divide by 27

$2 \times 10^{-18} = x^4$
take the fourth root

$1 \times 10^{-4.5} = x$
split exponent

$(1 \times 10^{-5})(1 \times 10^{0.5}) = x$
this is the square root of ten!

$3 \times 10^{-5} = x$

Figure 3. Ksp calculations to determine ferric ion concentration.

It is worth pointing out a few mathematical tricks that were employed here. First, realize that ferric hydroxide will ionize into four ions. This necessitates the value x^4 as shown above. Expect on the MCAT that the K_{sp} will be given in such a way to help simplify the math at some point during your calculations. Also, identify the next challenge that dealt with the fourth root of negative eighteen, which is -4.5. The use of a decimal in an exponent is not something that you are used to and probably looks "ugly." In order to make the exponent "pretty" (i.e. a whole number), you can split the exponent into two values as shown above. After this is done, you arrive at the value of ~3 x 10^{-5}, which is the molar solubility. Note that the question did not ask for molar solubility, but rather it asked for the concentration of ferric ions. In this particular case, "x" also gave you concentration of ferric ions (line 3 above). Therefore, **choice B is correct**. Had the question asked for hydroxide ion concentration at the K_{sp}, then the answer would have been 9 x 10^{-5} ("3x" as per line 3 in **Fig. 3**).

2) **C. Deprotonation of functional groups favors electrostatic attraction to ferric/ferrous ions.** This question directly refers to experiment 2, but no specific information from that figure was required to answer the question – it was a distractor. Additionally, the passage made no reference to how siderophore expression is regulated, so **choices A and B are incorrect.** You must recall from organic chemistry that acidic functional groups (e.g. carboxyl, hydroxyl, and phosphoryl groups) become deprotonated (i.e. negatively charged) at higher pH. This would be expected to favor electrostatic interactions with the positive ferrous and ferric ions. (**Fig. 4**). The increased interaction will attract the positively charged iron ions putting them into an optimal position for transport across the MTB cellular membrane.

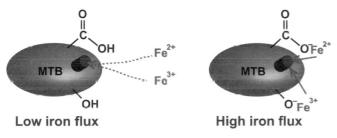

Low iron flux   **High iron flux**

Figure 4. At lower pH, iron flux is low because there are fewer negative charges on the cell surface to attract the positively charged iron ions. At high pH, iron flux is higher as the negative surface charges will attract iron ions.

3) **C. Increase its solubility to promote import.** You should probably just commit this to memory: at physiological pH, ferric ions are considerably less soluble than ferrous ions. The passage also stated that "…the less soluble ferric ion…" if you didn't know this in advance. Also, it is tough to remember which is which. As an aid, remember that if you are out on a date with someone, you would say it is just the "2 of us" (ferrous is +2) but if an annoying third person were to join you then it would make you "sick!!" (ferric, +3). To make the ferric ions more soluble, a soluble counter ion like ammonium citrate is necessary because according to solubility rules, all ammonium salts are soluble. This makes **choice C correct. Choice A is incorrect** because the passage states that there are two methods of iron import and **choice B is wrong** because iron is needed both in the +2 and +3 states in magnetite. **Choice D is incorrect** since the ammonium citrate salts would increase solubility as described above and choice D states that there is a decrease in solubility.

4) **A. $1s^2\,2s^2\,2p^6\,3s^2\,3p^6\,3d^6$.** This is an electron configuration problem, so the Aufbau principle applies to filling orbitals with electrons. Note that Fe is the eighth atom across the periodic table in the fourth row. Therefore, it will have 8 electrons in its 4s and 3d orbitals. The ferrous ion has lost two of its electrons and although the 3d orbitals are filled after the 4s, electrons are removed from the 4s orbital first. This makes **choice A the only viable option.**

5) **A. $NO_2^- \rightarrow NO$ / $Fe^{2+} \rightarrow Fe^{3+}$.** Use some strategy with this question; first realize that the question states that nitrite is getting reduced to accelerate the oxidation of the ferrous ion. This immediately **ruled out choice D** because this shows a reduction in the ferric ion. From there, it came down to your ability to know what the chemical formula for nitrite is. If you remembered that nitrite is NO_2^-, then this **eliminated choice B.** The last point that you had to realize is that if you reduce nitrate then this generates nitric oxide rather than nitrate. This **ruled out choice C.** For now on, remember the differences between nitrate (NO_3^-), nitrite (NO_2^-), and nitric oxide (NO) (don't confuse the last one with nitrous oxide, which is N_2O and is no laughing matter!!).

Biomineralization

6) C. Increased expression of ferric antiporters. The mutation tested in Experiment 1 is in the FeoB1 gene, which encodes the ferrous ion transporter. The effect of the mutation is seen very clearly in the graph in Figure 1 (right panel) where the MTB mutant FeoB1 gene transports the ferrous ion at a lower rate. Closer inspection of the graphs demonstrates that the V_{max} is different under both genetic conditions (or genotypes) (**Fig. 5**). The trick here is that the question is asking about the <u>ferric ion transport</u>, which is depicted in the graph on the left. Unexpectedly, when the FeoB1 gene is mutated, there is a greater amount of ferric ion transported across the membrane.

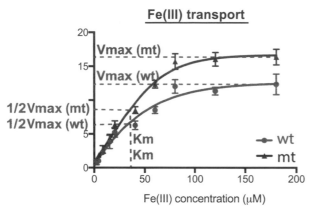

Figure 5. Compensation promotes ferric ion transport when ferrous ion transport is compromised.

Notice that the V_{max} is higher when the FeoB1 gene is mutated without any significant change to the K_m (**choices A and B are eliminated**). The only way to increase V_{max} like this is to have more ferric ion antiporters making **choice C correct. Choice D is not correct** as antiporters have been selected by evolution to be highly specific for their substrates. There would have to be a collection of simultaneous mutations created to alter the antiporters specificity, which is highly unlikely to occur.

7) D. None. This question was very misleading because the right-hand rule was brought up in the question stem. This makes you want to whip out your right hand and start pointing fingers. Well, think first!! If an object is moving in a direction that is parallel (0°) or antiparallel (180°) with the magnetic field, then it will never feel any magnetic force, making **choice D totally correct**.

8) B. thymol blue (pK$_b$ = 5.2). Recall that the choice of indicator should be based upon the pH of interest, in this case 9, being close to the pK_a of the weak acid. Moreover, this weak acid should exist as two distinct colors when it is in the conjugate acid versus conjugate base form. This problem was tricky because it gave the <u>pK$_b$ of each indicator</u>. You will need to remember that $pK_a + pK_b = pK_w$ and that pK_w is equal to 14. So, you needed to subtract the given pK_b values from 14 in order to get the corresponding pK_a. The temptation was to mark answer choice A because it gave 9 as the answer, but this would mean that the pK_a of bromcresol green is 5. This makes **choice B correct** because thymol blue will have a pK_a of ~9. The reason that an indicator must be chosen to have a pK_a near the pH of interest is because it will then change color once that pH has moved either above or below that point.

4

5

Tumor Hypoxia

Increased levels of carbon dioxide and the accumulation of lactic acid in tumors results from increased metabolism resulting in the generation of protons. While this results in a reduced extracellular pH (pH_e), the action of proton pumps maintains the intracellular pH (pH_i) within tumor cells at near normal levels (pH ~7.2). More importantly, this pH gradient alters the ionization states of chemotherapeutic agents (**Table 1**). This impacts the tumor uptake of drugs and, ultimately, the effectiveness of treatment.

Table 1. Relative protonation status of common drugs as a function of pH.

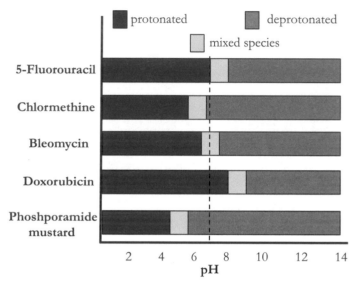

For drugs acting as weak acids that can cross the plasma membrane, the ratio of intracellular drug concentration (Ci) to extracellular drug concentration (Ce) can be calculated by:

$$Ci/Ce = (1+10^{pH_i-pK_a}) / (1+10^{pH_e-pK_a})$$

To test the impact of extracellular pH on drug effectiveness, scientists monitored cell survival of MDA-614 breast cancer cells after treatment with either of two chemotherapeutic drugs: Daunorubicin (**Fig. 1**) and Paclitaxel (**Fig. 2**). The drugs were added at various concentrations under two different pH conditions and the percentage of cells viable relative to cells grown under standard conditions in the absence of supplemented drug. The results of these two experiments are shown below.

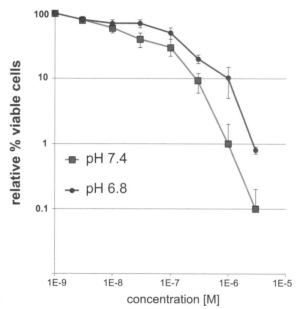

Figure 1. Effects of Daunorubicin on cell survival under two pH conditions. Concentration refers to the amount of supplemented drug.

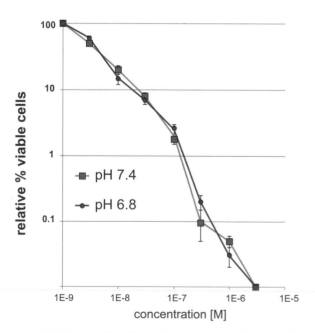

Figure 2. Effects of Paclitaxel on cell survival under two pH conditions. Concentration refers to the amount of supplemented drug.

1) Based upon information presented in the passage, which of the following is true?

    I. Low pH_e enhances cellular uptake of acidic drugs.

    II. Reduced extracelluar proton concentration enhances the cellular uptake of basic drugs.

    III. High pH_e enhances cellular uptake of basic drugs.

A. I

B. I, III

C. II, III

D. I, II, III

2) If Doxorubicin contains a weakly basic functional group, which of the following solutions, when injected near the site of the tumor, would increase its cellular uptake?

A. $NaHCO_3$

B. K_2SO_4

C. NH_4Cl

D. NaI

3) Calculate the concentration of the deprotonated form of 5-Fluorouracil if its overall concentration is 0.4 M and pH = 6.8.

A. 0.0036 M

B. 0.036 M

C. 0.36 M

D. 3.6 M

4) Which control experiments must be performed in order for scientists to conclude that Daunorubicin is more active at higher pH?

    I. Daunorubicin must be shown to reduce viability of another cell line.

    II. MDA-614 viability must be tested under both pH conditions.

    III. Daunorubicin stability must be measured under both pH conditions.

A. I, III

B. II

C. II, III

D. I, II, III

5) What is the C_i/C_e of Chlormethine when the extracellular pH = 6.2?

A. 1/5

B. 1/2

C. 2

D. 5

6) Which of the following statements explains the behavior of Paclitaxel in Figure 2?

A. Paclitaxel is less active than chlormethine.

B. Paclitaxel is a zwitterion.

C. MDA-614 cells are highly sensitive to paclitaxel.

D. Paclitaxel is highly soluble.

7) 5-Fluorouracil acts as a suicide inhibitor of thymidylate reductase. Which of the following best describes this type of inhibitor?

A. Binds reversibly to the active site.

B. Binds irreversibly to the active site.

C. Binds reversible to an allosteric site.

D. Binds irreversibly to an allosteric site.

Tumor Hypoxia

Annotations.
1) D 2) A 3) B 4) C 5) D 6) B 7) B

	Foundation 1: Biochemistry-A			Foundation 5: Water-A Biomolecules-D		
	A			A	D	
Concepts	7			2,3		
Reasoning				1,5		
Research				4		
Data					6	

Big Picture. This passage focuses on pH and dealt almost exclusively with your understanding of pK_a values and how they influence drug efficacy. An underlying theme to this passage, which was adeptly not mentioned, was knowing the Henderson-Hasselbalch equation. Rather than provide you with this familiar relationship, the passage instead presented you with what should have been a completely unfamiliar equation. Moreover, the data presented in Table 1 also was an alternative way to express the Henderson-Hasselbalch relationship as you should have recognized the compounds will lose a proton at pH values above their pK_a and gain a proton at pH values below their pK_a.

The important biological corollary to these relationships is that charged drugs generally do not cross plasma membranes. This is an important feature of any drug used in clinical treatment. Therefore, a consideration of the pK_a of the drug, combined with the pH of the environment where you want the drug delivered, is critical. For example, a simple compound that has a single ionizable group with a pK_a of 5.0 will only have one out of a hundred molecules in the neutral state at pH = 7.0. However, in the stomach, where the pH is closer to 2.0, then nearly all of the drug will be neutral. Thus, more of the drug will be absorbed in the stomach than the small intestine (ignoring surface area effects).

1) **D. I, II, III.** As with any Roman numeral style questions, use what you know about the Roman numeral selections to rule out wrong answers. Specifically, you should have identified that statements II and III were synonymous and therefore could not be individually chosen as an answer. This approach was particularly powerful as it **ruled out choices B and C**. From there you needed to use reasoning and information provided in the first paragraph. As shown in the diagram (**Fig. 3**), an acidic drug will be charged at higher pH (for example at physiological pH in the blood) but will become protonated when in proximity to a tumor due to the reduced pH. The protonation of the acidic group neutralizes the overall charge of the drug enhancing its ability to cross the cell membrane. In contrast, a basic drug will be more neutral at higher pH and will likely become charged when pH is reduced. Once it is charged, it will have a reduced ability to cross the membrane. Based upon these points, all three Roman numerals are true statements and **choice D is correct**.

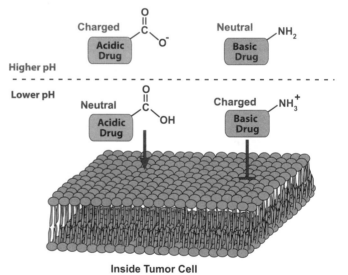

Figure 3. Altered extracellular pH near tumor cell surfaces differentially affects membrane diffusion characteristics of chemotherapeutic drugs. Acidic drugs become protonated and neutral at a lower pH thereby crossing the plasma membrane. Basic drugs become protonated but more charged and have reduced ability to cross the membrane at a lower pH.

2) **A. NaHCO₃.** This question was a reasoning-style question because it required that you put together multiple concepts and make a conclusion based upon how they are related. As mentioned in the passage and elaborated upon further in the annotation for question 1, a basic drug will become more neutral as the pH is increased. This is because protons are titrated off. Therefore, the correct answer in this case would be a basic salt. So, in essence, this question is really asking you to identify which of the following salts in basic. The only basic salt was choice A because bicarbonate is the conjugate based of carbonic acid, which is a weak acid.

K_2SO_4 is a neutral salt because sulfate is the conjugate base of the strong acid, sulfuric acid, so it therefore has no basic properties in water, making **choice B incorrect**. While potassium is a group I cation, it is also neutral. **Choice C is wrong** because NH_4Cl is an acidic salt as ammonium is the conjugate acid of the weak basic ammonia. Finally, NaI is also a neutral salt because iodide is the conjugate base of the strong hydroiodic acid, making **choice D incorrect**.

3) **B. 0.036 M.** While not given to you in the passage, you should have a strong familiarity with the Henderson-Hasselbalch equation. The necessary calculations are shown below (**Fig. 4**).

$$pH = pK_a + \log_{10} \frac{[A^-]}{[HA]}$$

$$6.8 = 7.8 + \log_{10} \frac{[A^-]}{[HA]}$$

$$-1.0 = \log_{10} \frac{[A^-]}{[HA]} \quad \text{means there is 10X more HA than } A^-$$

The value of "-1.0"

[HA] + [A⁻] = 0.4M

10x + x = 0.4M   setup algebraic expression

11x = 0.4M

x = 0.036M

Figure 4. Using the Henderson-Hasselbalch equation to determine the concentration of deprotonated 5FU.

You first had to identify the pK$_a$ of 5FU, which you could attain from Table 1. The pK$_a$ is the midpoint of the gray box (the pH where the deprotonated and protonated forms of 5FU are equal in concentration). The pK$_a$ is ~ 8 and to keep the math simple, you can estimate the pK$_a$ to be 7.8. This leads to a negative one as an answer on the left side of the equation and that value reflects the $\log_{10}$ of the ratio of deprotonated to protonated compound (5FU). This translates to a 10-fold excess of the protonated form relative to the deprotonated form. From there, identify that the total concentration of 5FU is made up of both forms so the algebraic expression was necessary to finish the job here. You did not have to arrive at the exact answer as none of the answer choices required significant precision.

4) **C. II, III.** Here, you needed to understand some basic elements of research design in order to justify any conclusion made from the experimental data. Figure 1 demonstrates that at higher pH, Daunorubicin is more effective at killing MDA-614 breast cancer cells than at lower pH values. This conclusion is the most straightforward to arrive at and is consistent with the results. Having said this, there are several assumptions that are made that needed to be addressed in order for this conclusion to be valid. First of all, if MDA-614 cell viability is on its own effected by pH changes, then the conclusion could be invalid. This makes Roman numeral II an essential control to test, thus **choice D incorrect**. Moreover, as is observed for many other compounds, it is certainly possible that pH impacts the stability of Daunorubicin. Therefore, this should also be tested to validate the conclusion making **choice B incorrect**. Whether or not Daunorubicin impacts cell viability of another cell line is irrelevant to making a conclusion that pH impacts its activity, so Roman numeral I is not a necessary control. Therefore, **choice C is correct**.

5) D. 5. You first needed to look at Table 1 to determine the pK_a of Chlormethine. This should be centered within the gray region of its bar making it around 6.2. The passage stated that the intracellular pH is near 7.2 and the question provided an extracellular pH of 6.2. Taken together, you needed to then substitute these values into the equation provided. The math is shown below (**Fig. 5**).

$$C_i/C_e = (1+10^{pH_i-pK_a})/(1+10^{pH_e-pK_a})$$
↳ Given in passage

$$pH_i=7.2; pH_e=6.2; pK_a=6.2$$
↳ Given in question

$$C_i/C_e = (1+10^{7.2-6.2})/(1+10^{6.2-6.2})$$
↳ substitute in values

$$C_i/C_e = (1+10^1)/(1+10^0)$$

$$C_i/C_e = (11)/(2)$$

$$C_i/C_e = \sim 5$$

Figure 5. Calculations required to determine ratio of intracellular to extracellular drug concentrations.

6) B. Paclitaxel is a zwitterion. This was a deceptively challenging question. First, you had to identify that in Figure 2, the two different pH levels behave in an identical fashion. There are two possibilities that would explain this result. First, paclitaxel has no ionizable proton groups so its overall structure/charge will not be altered at either pH. However, this possibility was not present in any of the answer choices. The second explanation could be that there are two ionizable proton groups where one is acidic (e.g. carboxylate) and the other is basic (e.g. amine). In this scenario, reducing the pH would make the acidic group more neutral but the basic group more charged. Conversely, increasing pH would make the basic group more neutral and the acidic group more charged. In other words, any changes in pH would not alter the effectiveness of paclitaxel because at either pH the molecule would still carry a charge. This would lower the ability of paclitaxel to enter the cell under both conditions tested. **Choice B is consistent with this scenario and is therefore correct**. Note that the other choices, while possibly true, did not explain the pH-independent effects of Paclitaxel.

7) B. Binds irreversibly to the active site. Suicide inhibitors are fairly common in biology and a fundamental biochemical concept. These inhibitors function different from classical competitive or noncompetitive inhibitors as they are not reversible. This fact **ruled out choices A and C**. Importantly, these inhibitors will bind to the active sites of enzymes and form an irreversible covalent bond, thereby permanently inhibiting the enzyme's catalytic ability. This made **choice B correct**.

In the specific case of 5FU (**Fig. 6**), the question states that it is a thymidylate synthetase (TS) suicide inhibitor and this causes a loss in dTMP production, thereby stopping DNA replication. The mechanism of this is shown in Figure 6. Under normal conditions, TS converts dUMP into dTMP using methylene-THF as a methyl donor. Given the high similarity of FdUMP to dUMP, TS utilizes this as a substrate and forms a covalent intermediate that when combined with methylene-THF, forms a product that cannot be released by the enzyme. This terminal product is where the term "suicide" is derived from as there is no pathway to regenerate a catalytic enzyme.

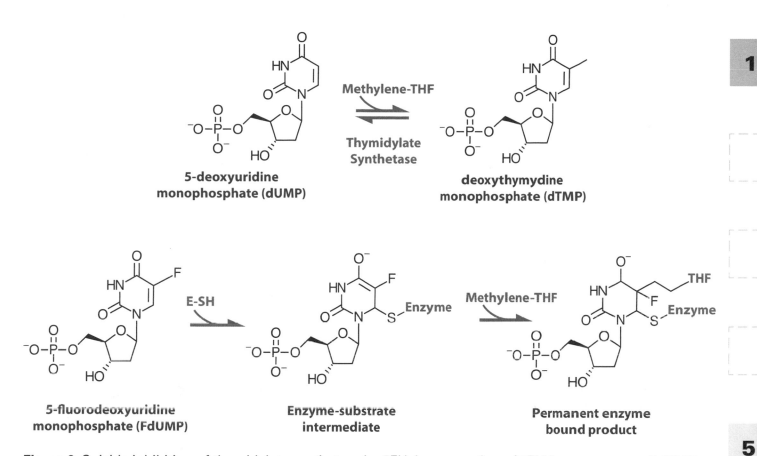

Figure 6. Suicide inhibition of thymidylate synthetase by 5FU. Incorporation of 5FU is necessary as FdUMP cannot cross cellular membranes (since it is highly charged given the phosphate group!). Cells will convert 5FU to FdUMP and then thymidylate synthase will react with it and methylene-THF to form an irreversible enzyme complex incapable of catalyzing any further reactions.

Kidney Glutaminase

Under conditions of chronic acidosis, the kidney will utilize circulating glutamine (GLN) to produce ammonium (**Fig. 1**). This is accomplished through a concerted mechanism first involving the deamination of glutamine by the enzyme glutaminase (GLS) followed by the deamination of glutamate by glutamate dehydrogenase (GDH). The production of ammonium is accompanied by the creation of bicarbonate, which is transferred into the interstitium. Two experiments were performed to investigate glutamine metabolism in the kidney.

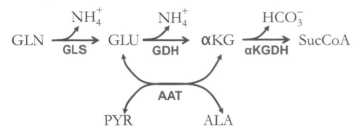

Figure 1. Breakdown of glutamine to form ammonium.

Experiment 1. Scientists incubated renal epithelial cells with increasing amounts of glutamine supplemented into the cell media. The levels of glutamine (**Fig. 2**, <u>dotted lines</u>) and ammonium (**Fig. 2**, <u>solid lines</u>) were then measured using a time course assay.

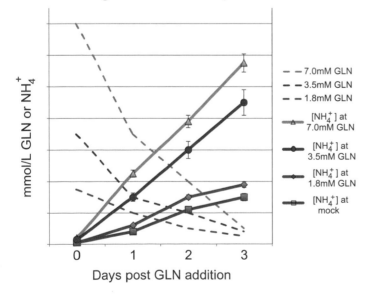

Figure 2. Production of ammonium in renal cells as a function of supplemented glutamine.

Experiment 2. Using a constant level of supplemented glutamine, scientists measured the amount of ammonium produced when cells were grown under a number of distinct pH conditions relative to a standard pH (7.85) (**Fig. 3**). After incubation, cell lysates were prepared and assayed for glutaminase activity. This was assessed by incubating the lysates with supplemented glutamine and the reactions were stopped with 0.7N HCl. The lysates were then added to a buffer containing recombinant GDH, nicotinamide adenine dinucleotide, and adenosine diphosphate. Levels of reduced NAD^+ were monitored using absorbance at 340 nm (**Fig. 3**).

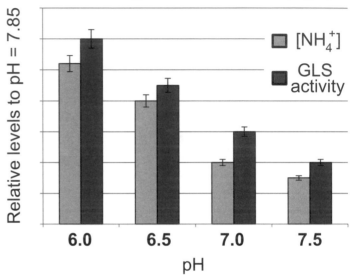

Figure 3. Measurement of ammonium produced by renal cells and their glutaminase activity as various pH levels.

1) **In which of the following condition(s) will the kidney produce ammonium from glutamine?**

     I. High altitude dwelling
     II. Pyruvate dehydrogenase deficiency
     III. Congenital defect in urea cycle

A. I

B. II

C. III

D. II, III

2) **Which of the following is true at pH = 6.0?**

A. pK_b of NH_3 > pK_a of NH_4^+

B. K_b of NH_3 < K_a of NH_4^+

C. pK_b of NH_3 < pK_a of NH_4^+

D. K_b of NH_3 < pK_a of NH_4^+

3) **Which of the following was the likely hypothesis of experiment 2?**

A. The fate of supplemented glutamine is to drive ammonium synthesis.

B. Ammonium generated from glutamine will reduce the pH of the cellular surroundings.

C. Ammonium produced via glutaminolysis will buffer media that cells grow in.

D. The rate of glutaminolysis is increased in response to increased proton concentration.

4) **The molecular geometry of ammonia can best be described as:**

A. tetrahedral.

B. trigonal pyramidal.

C. bent.

D. trigonal bipyrimidal.

5) **In experiment 1, ammonium is produced despite the absence of supplemented glutamine (mock). Which hypothesis likely explains this observation?**

A. Endogenous glutamine is being utilized to generate ammonium.

B. Chemical reduction of glutamine is occurring even in the absence of its supplementation.

C. There is a specific decrease in α-ketoglutarate dehydrogenase activity.

D. There is an increase in bicarbonate production.

6) **Experiment 2 directly monitors the progress of which of the following reactions?**

A. $Glu + NAD^+ \rightarrow \alpha KG + NADH$

B. $Gln + NAD^+ \rightarrow Glu + NADH$

C. $Glu + NADH \rightarrow \alpha KG + NAD^+$

D. $Gln + NADH \rightarrow Glu + NAD^+$

7) **To alter the pH in experiment 2, scientists altered the levels of carbonic acid. Calculate the pH of a 0.3 M solution of carbonic acid ($K_a = 4.3 \times 10^{-7}$).**

A. 3.0

B. 3.5

C. 4.3

D. 5.3

Kidney Glutaminase

Annotations.
1) B 2) C 3) D 4) B 5) A 6) A 7) B

	Foundation 4: Atoms-E			Foundation 5: Water-A Biomolecules-D Thermo/Kinetics-E		
	E			A	D	E
Concepts	4			2,7		
Reasoning					1	
Research						3
Data					5,6	

Big Picture. This passage featured some relatively challenging biochemistry intermingled with general chemistry topics. The presented data was particularly tough to interpret on the fly as it was displayed in a confusing manner. It was important to digest the data from the two experiments as four of the questions directly referred to the two experiments. Figure 2 had both dotted lines to represent glutamine concentration and solid lines of matching color to denote that the concentrations of ammonium measure were at a given level of supplemented glutamine. The other primary figure (**Fig. 3**) was a more standard way to present as it measured the amount of glutaminase activity and ammonium produced at different pH levels. You had to recognize that both of these values increased at lower pH. Finally, there was some technical description of how the glutaminase assay was performed and this was directly addressed in question 6.

The content of this passage represents an area of metabolism that you might not be familiar with, but could certainly learn very quickly. This is why the pathway was displayed in Figure 1. In this situation, you should quickly read through this type of description and move to the experimental description as fast as possible.

1) **B. II.** The passage briefly outlines that ammonium is produced from glutamine under conditions of chronic acidosis. So what this question is really asking you is: under what conditions will the body encounter acidosis? At high altitudes the body compensates for the reduced concentration of oxygen in the atmosphere by increasing the expiration rate. This lowers the amount of carbon dioxide in the blood through increased exhalation, causing a drop in serum carbonic acid levels and a resulting increase in the pH of the blood. This is alkalosis. Therefore, Roman numeral I is incorrect, making **choice A wrong**. A defect in pyruvate dehydrogenase would reduce the flux of carbon into the Krebs cycle as acetyl CoA would not be generated. This would have several predicted effects. First, cells would become more reliant on glycolysis to produce ATP, and the buildup of excess pyruvate would increase the amount of lactate being made to raise levels of NAD^+. Recall that oxidized NAD^+ is generated to drive glycolysis. The increased lactate would cause acidosis making Roman numeral II correct. Therefore **choice C is wrong**. Roman numeral III is wrong because defects in the urea cycle would generate alkalosis, not acidosis. This is because the urea cycle takes free ammonia generated in the liver and incorporates it into a carbamoyl phosphate molecule that is used to generate citrulline through a reaction with ornithine. Defects in the urea cycle would prevent the flux of nitrogen through the cycle and cause a build up of free ammonia. This **eliminates choices C and D**.

2) **C. pK_b of NH_3 < pK_a of NH_4^+.** First, identify the fact that the pH that was given in the question is irrelevant when comparing pK_a values. The pK_a (and K_a for that matter) are equilibrium expressions and therefore only depend on temperature. Knowing this did not necessarily provide any advantage to getting the correct answer but eliminated a distractor that could have bogged you down. From there, the answer choices were tricky to sift through, as there was a high degree of symmetry in how they were arranged. You should be familiar with the pK_a of ammonium (NH_4^+) as it is one of the two ionizable groups in amino acids and has a pK_a around 9.25 (under standard conditions). This means that the K_a of ammonium is ~5.5×10^{-10}. Given these values, which you should commit to memory, you can extrapolate other values. For example, if the pK_a of NH_4^+ is

9.25, then the pK_b of NH_3 is around 4.75 as these two values should add up to 14. This also means that the K_b of NH_3 is ~2 x 10^{-5}. The only other value that you needed to have an estimate of was the pK_a of ammonia. Use logic here as the pK_a value reflects the propensity that a given compound has to release a proton. Low pK_a values reflect a stronger acid and higher K_a. Ammonia is considered a base and will therefore have a relatively small K_a value (and large pK_a). These points are all summarized in the chart below (**Fig. 4**). The only answer that adheres to the values presented in Figure 4 is **choice C, which is the correct answer**.

group	K_a	K_b	pK_a	pK_b
$-NH_3$	small	2×10^{-5}	36	4.7
$-NH_4^+$	5.5×10^{-10}	small	9.3	large

Figure 4. Table of acid/base constants for ammonia and ammonium.

3) D. The rate of glutaminolysis is increased in response to increased proton concentration. This is an experimental design question that required you to work backwards from the results and reason what the hypothesis may have been. A key component of the data gathered from experiment 2 was that glutaminase activity and ammonium production were measured at different pH levels. This meant that the hypothesis had this component intrinsically woven into it. This fact effectively **ruled out choices A and C** because they do not directly address changes in pH. Note that choice A is the likely hypothesis of experiment 1, so be careful to avoid these types of traps. An additional important point to note was the researchers manipulated pH in the experiment and did not measure the change of pH throughout the experiment. This point gets at cause versus effect and **ruled out choice B**. Given the experimental design, a hypothesis that posits glutaminolysis will be more robust under low pH conditions is most plausible. This makes **choice D correct**.

4) B. trigonal pyramidal. This was a conceptual question that required you to recall the basic ideas of valence shell electron pair repulsion (VSEPR) theory, which determines molecular shape. Ammonia is tricky as there is distinction between "molecular

geometry" and "electron pair geometry." The question asks for molecular geometry, which for ammonia is trigonal pyramidal. If the lone pair electron is taken into account, the electron pair geometry is tetrahedral. The difference between these two perspectives is shown (**Fig. 5**).

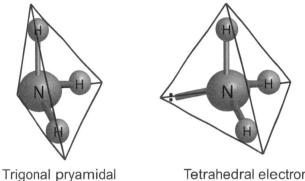

Trigonal pryamidal molecular geometry

Tetrahedral electron pair geometry

Figure 5. The molecular and electron pair geometry for ammonia.

5) A. Endogenous glutamine is being utilized to generate ammonium. The question is specifically referring to the solid red line presented in experiment 1 (**Fig. 6**). In this case, there was no glutamine added to the media, yet there was still a measurable increase in the levels of ammonium over time.

This particular condition was important in this experiment as it assessed the "background" level of ammonium production. There could be several reasons why cells produce ammonium in the absence of supplemented glutamine, but only one of those was presented in the answer choices. This was best identified using process of elimination. **Choice B is incorrect** because the deamination of glutamine is not considered a reduction reaction because there is not a simple electron number/position change. Further, **choice C is wrong** because a decrease in α-ketoglutarate (αKG) dehydrogenase activity would not be expected to result in increased glutamine or

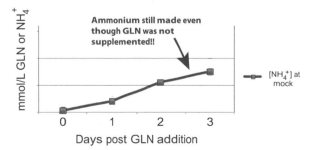

Figure 6. Production of ammonium from cells that did not have supplemented glutamine.

185

subsequent ammonium production. Answer choice D is a true statement because, according to the pathway provided in the passage (**Fig. 1**), ammonium production would result in bicarbonate production, but this fails to explain <u>why</u> there is an increase in ammonium production. Therefore, **choice D is incorrect**. You should realize that cells have endogenous glutamine present independently of its experimental supplementation. Because it can be derived from αKG, glutamine is not normally considered an essential amino acid, thus cells have the ability to synthesize it. In the experiment, this level of endogenous glutamine must be enough to generate and accumulate low levels of ammonium over the course of the experiment. **Choice A is therefore correct**.

6) **A. Glu + NAD⁺ → αKG + NADH.** A key word in the question stem was "directly." This biochemical assay is meant to measure the amount of glutaminase activity present in a cell lysate but it doesn't do so in a direct manner. Instead, the glutamate (GLU) produced by the glutaminase is subsequently converted into αKG as outlined in Figure 1. The passage states "Levels of reduced NAD⁺ were monitored using absorbance at 340 nm" and therefore the correct answer choice must have NADH as a product. This fact **ruled out choices C and D**. Given that recombinant GDH was added to the reaction that was being monitored, conversion of glutamate (GLU) to αKG was being monitored, making **choice A correct**. **Choice B is incorrect** because this would have only been true if the monitored reaction involved the supplementation of GLS.

7) **B. 3.5.** This is a flat out mathematical calculation that you should be familiar with: determining the pH of a given concentration of a weak acid. The required calculations are shown below (**Fig. 7**). It is not necessary to write out all of these steps as this wastes valuable time. Rather, pick up the equation at the position marked with the green asterisk. Based upon the math, only **choice B can be correct**. Be careful converting concentrations to pH using negative log base 10. If the concentration of protons were 1×10^{-4} M, then the pH would naturally be 4.0. In this example, we have a <u>HIGHER</u> concentration of protons, as the math gave us roughly 3.5×10^{-4} M. So the pH will be <u>LOWER</u> than 4 but HIGHER than 3.

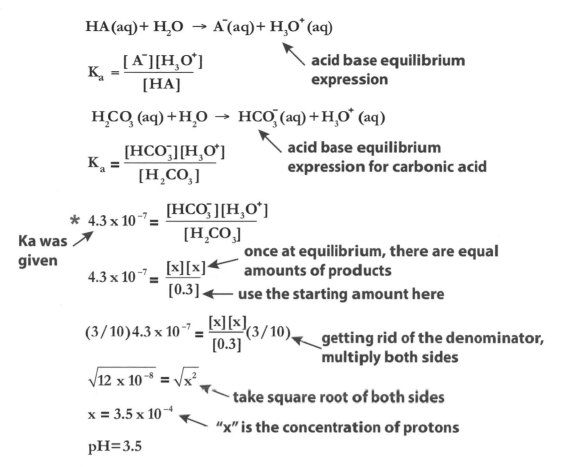

$$HA(aq) + H_2O \rightarrow A^-(aq) + H_3O^+(aq)$$

$$K_a = \frac{[A^-][H_3O^+]}{[HA]}$$ acid base equilibrium expression

$$H_2CO_3(aq) + H_2O \rightarrow HCO_3^-(aq) + H_3O^+(aq)$$

$$K_a = \frac{[HCO_3^-][H_3O^+]}{[H_2CO_3]}$$ acid base equilibrium expression for carbonic acid

Ka was given * $$4.3 \times 10^{-7} = \frac{[HCO_3^-][H_3O^+]}{[H_2CO_3]}$$

$$4.3 \times 10^{-7} = \frac{[x][x]}{[0.3]}$$ once at equilibrium, there are equal amounts of products

use the starting amount here

$$(3/10)\,4.3 \times 10^{-7} = \frac{[x][x]}{[0.3]}(3/10)$$ getting rid of the denominator, multiply both sides

$$\sqrt{12 \times 10^{-8}} = \sqrt{x^2}$$ take square root of both sides

$$x = 3.5 \times 10^{-4}$$ "x" is the concentration of protons

$$pH = 3.5$$

Figure 7. Calculating the pH of a weak acid.

4

5

SILAC

While most peptide bonds favor the trans configuration over the cis, the specific bond of X-Pro (X = any other amino acid) exhibits unfavorable interactions in both forms. Hence, the two states of proline are nearly isoenergetic (**Fig. 1**). The cis-trans interconversion of X-Pro is catalyzed by peptidylprolyl-isomerase (PPIase) enzymes, such as Ess1, which utilize a mechanism that involves the disruption of the partial double bond character present within the peptide bond.

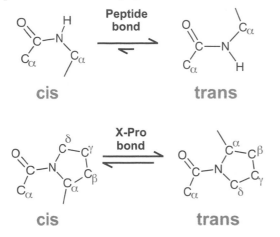

Figure 1. Isomers of peptide bonds and X-Pro peptide bonds.

The protein Rpb1 contains multiple X-Pro motifs that are isomerized by the Ess1 PPIase. To determine the effect of depleting Ess1 on Rpb1 protein interactions, scientists utilized a technique called: **S**table **I**sotope **L**abeling by **A**mino acids in **C**ell culture (SILAC, **Fig. 2**). In this approach, cell lines expressing FLAG-tagged Rpb1 were grown in the presence of ^{12}C–(light) or ^{13}C–(heavy) labeled lysine. Additionally, the cellular levels of Ess1 were depleted in the ^{13}C-labeled cells using an RNA interference protocol that specifically targeted the Ess1 gene. Protein complexes associating with Rpb1 from each sample were purified by affinity chromatography and mixed in a 1:1 ratio before being subjected to SDS-PAGE analysis. Excised protein bands were analyzed by liquid chromatography and mass spectrometry analysis. In this process, proteins are digested and vaporized; this mixture is injected into the mass spectrometer where it is ionized, accelerated, deflected and then quantified as a function of the charge to mass ratio (M/Z).

Figure 2. SILAC workflow. Cells are incubated with either light or heavy amino acids. Nuclear extracts are prepared from both conditions and Rpb1–interacting proteins are purified using FLAG antibodies. Eluates are resolved by SDS–PAGE and subject to liquid chromatography (LC)–mass spectrometry (MS).

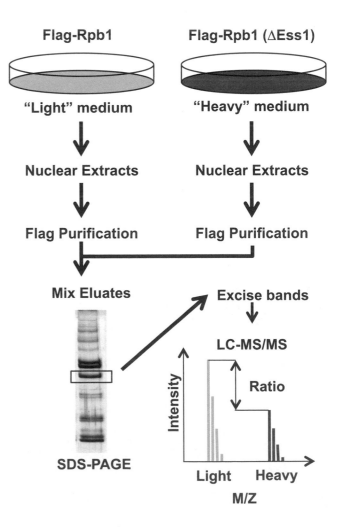

1) An increase in the M/Z ratio of the heavy labeled cell lysates in mass spectrometry would be caused by:

   A. dysfunctional ionization.

   B. poor labeling with the light isotope.

   C. increased deflection of peptides.

   D. decreased deflection of peptides.

2) An alternative SILAC approach employs the use of "heavy and light" arginine. How might the experimental results be affected given the cellular conversion of arginine to proline?

   A. Reduced Rpb1 interactions in the heavy media.

   B. Reduced Rpb1 interactions in the light media.

   C. Underestimation of Rpb1 interactions in the heavy media.

   D. Overestimation of Rpb1 interactions in the light media.

3) Which statement, if true, would likely prevent the SILAC experiment from identifying Ess1-dependent protein interactions?

   A. Failure of labeled lysine to impact Ess1 function.

   B. Ess1 is normally present at low levels.

   C. Multiple cellular Ess1 isozymes.

   D. Ess1 is normally present at high levels.

4) All of the following are examples of acceptable electron quantum number sets for a ^{15}N except:

   A. 2, 0, 1, +1/2

   B. 2, 0, 0, +1/2

   C. 2, 1, -1, +1/2

   D. 2, 1, 1, +1/2

5) Proline hydroxylation is essential for collagen function. All of the following properties of these hydroxylation events would be elevated as a consequence except:

   A. hydrogen bonding.

   B. aqueous solubility.

   C. vapor pressure.

   D. ionic interactions.

6) Which of the following represents a resonance structure at pH = 7 of the trans peptide bond drawn in Figure 1?

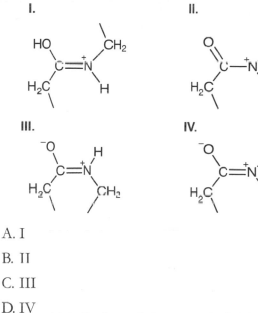

   A. I

   B. II

   C. III

   D. IV

7) Which form of proline would predominate at pH = 5.5?

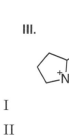

   A. I

   B. II

   C. III

   D. IV

SILAC

Annotations.
1) A 2) C 3) C 4) A 5) C 6) D 7) B

	Foundation 4: Atoms-E			Foundation 5: Water-A Mol. Interactions-B Biomolecules-D		
	E			**A**	**B**	**D**
Concepts	1,4				6	7
Reasoning				5		
Research	2					
Data						3

Big Picture. This passage integrated three general principles together: the chemistry of proline isomerization, the use of SILAC as a tool for mass spectrometry, and atomic theory. These principles were all tested in the context of a biological scenario involving proline isomerases. The assumption here is that you have never heard of these enzymes, nor are you very familiar with SILAC. Bear in mind that mass spectrometry is listed by the AAMC as an area of content knowledge that you must have going into the exam so a question such as the first one is not as obscure as you may have thought. In light of that, the annotation for this question will provide some of the necessary background information that should fill in any of your knowledge gaps.

Reading this passage should have been quick as it does not contain a great deal of information. The first column uses just three sentences to refresh (or introduce) the idea of proline cis/trans configuration compared to other amino acids and how cells alter that configuration enzymatically. All you needed to gather was that proline isomerases exist and that proline can exist in either form (essentially the content in Figure 1). The key pieces of information in the second column were the workflow of SILAC and how this related to the biological question that was posed.

1) **A. dysfunctional ionization.** This was purely a conceptual question that required a basic working knowledge of mass spectrometry (MS). Given this, it is worth discussing how the technique works (**Fig. 3**). Initially, a mixture of proteins is digested by proteases, creating a complex mixture of peptides that are separated by liquid chromatography (LC). These samples are then vaporized and injected into the MS device. In this first step, or ionization, removal of one or more electrons from atoms generates a positive ionic charge within the atoms that make up the peptide fragments. The ionization step establishes the overall mass to charge ratio (M/Z) of the peptides. The positively charged peptide fragments are then accelerated so that they have the same kinetic energy. The next step involves the use of an electromagnet and results in deflection of the peptides as a function of their mass and their overall positive charge. An important feature of this step is the degree of deflection depends on the M/Z ratio but the electromagnet itself does not determine the M/Z ratio. The deflected peptides are deflected and detected, allowing the mass to be calculated based upon the amount of current produced.

The question stem states the M/Z ratio is altered, which can only be caused by dysfunctional ionization, making **choice A correct**. The level of deflection is dependent upon the M/Z ratio but will not alter it, therefore **choices C and D are incorrect**. Finally, the poor labeling by SILAC would act to decrease the mass thereby reducing the M/Z ratio making **choice B incorrect**.

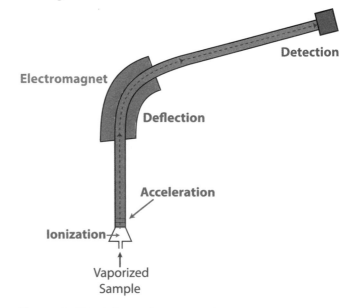

Figure 3. Workflow of mass spectrometer.

2) **C. Underestimation of Rpb1 interactions in the heavy media.** Conceptually, you should immediately **rule out answer choices A and B** because the choice of carbon isotope does not affect the interactions with Rpb1. Recall that isotopes will retain all chemical and physical properties in biological systems. The other "trick" to this problem was identifying the fact that the ^{12}C–(light) labeling really doesn't label anything, as carbon-12 is the most abundant naturally occurring isotope. This didn't immediately rule out answer choice D, but it did make it very unlikely. Labeling with an amino acid that is capable of being converted into something else, even another amino acid, will reduce the number of arginines that are "heavy" in peptides from Rpb1-interacting proteins. Given this point, the key result is a reduction then **choice C is the only correct answer.**

3) **C. Multiple cellular Ess1 isozymes.** The primary goal of the experiment described in the passage is to identify proteins that interact with Rpb1 as a function of proline being in a specific isomeric state. The biological conditions being tested are the presence or the absence of the prolyl isomerase, Ess1. The key assumption was that in the absence of Ess1, there is no compensatory mechanism for lack of cellular Ess1 as this would yield deceptive results. Thus, if there were an Ess1 isozyme present, it would not be targeted by RNA interference (RNAi) because this technique was described in the passage as specifically targeting the Ess1 gene. RNAi is effective in depleting abundant or rare mRNA/proteins so the levels in cells is not an important feature. This ruled out **choices B and D**. Finally, **choice A was incorrect** because the labeling of lysine is neutral for Ess1 function as it is an isotope.

4) **A. 2, 0, 1, +1/2.** Note that the electronic quantum number for ^{15}N will be the same as for ^{14}N. The question then boils down to a purely conceptual one that requires you to remember the rules for electron quantum numbers. The first quantum number or principle quantum number (denoted as "n") refers to the electron shell or energy level. The values of "n" can range from 1 to 6. The second quantum number, or azimuthal quantum number (denoted as "ℓ") describes the subshell and can have values that depend on n based upon the arithmetic relationship: $\ell = 0, 1, 2, \ldots, n\text{-}1$. The third quantum number is called the magnetic quantum number (m_ℓ) and describes the number and orientation of orbitals within a shell. The values of m_ℓ are also arithmetically dependent upon previous values where m_ℓ ranges from $-\ell$ to $+\ell$. Finally, the spin quantum number (m_s) describes the spin of the electron within a given orbital and can only ever equal $+1/2$ or $-1/2$. Taken together, these rules allow for only **answer choice A to be correct**. A summary of the initial quantum numbers for most of the atoms that would be tested on the MCAT is shown below (**Fig. 4**).

Sub Shell	QUANTUM NUMBERS			
	n	ℓ	m_ℓ	m_s
1s	1	0	0	+1/2 -1/2
2s	2	0	0	+1/2 -1/2
2p	2	1	-1, 0, 1	+1/2 -1/2
3s	3	0	0	+1/2 -1/2
3p	3	1	-1, 0, 1	+1/2 -1/2
3d	3	2	-2, -1, 0 -1, 2	+1/2 -1/2
4s	4	0	0	+1/2 -1/2
4p	4	1	-1, 0, 1	+1/2 -1/2
4d	4	2	-2, -1, 0 -1, 2	+1/2 -1/2
4f	4	3	-3, -2, -1 0, 1, 2, 3	+1/2 -1/2

Figure 4. Quantum numbers for the first four subshell electrons on the periodic table.

5) **C. vapor pressure.** The addition of a hydroxyl group to proline will alter several of its chemical and physical properties. Immediately identify that hydroxyproline will possess additional hydrogen bonding capacity; therefore, **choice A is incorrect**. The additional hydrogen bonding will also increase its ionic character and its solubility in aqueous solvents, such as water; therefore **choices B and D are also incorrect**. The basic principles of general chemistry predict that increased hydrogen bonding will also increase boiling point while simultaneously reducing vapor pressure. Based upon this, hydroxyproline would be predicted to have reduced vapor pressure, therefore **choice C is correct.**

Typically, when you think of an amino acid modification, the phosphorylation of either serine or threonine comes to mind. This is because these residues are the most commonly phosphorylated ones. There are actually many other types of posttranslational modifications that are used by cells to alter the properties of proteins. In the case of proline, hydroxylation is possible within its R-group (**Fig. 5**) and this modification is extensive within collagen α-chains.

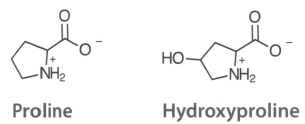

Proline   Hydroxyproline

Figure 5. Structures of Proline and Hydroxyproline.

6) **D. IV.** This was a relatively straightforward question worded in a particularly challenging way. First of all, the question stem asks for a resonance structure of the trans isomer of the peptide bond. This immediately **ruled out choice C** because that structure was in the cis form. The trans isomeric form that was shown in the passage is represented again in the figure (**Fig. 6, upper**). Be careful as **choice B was incorrect** because it just regenerated the trans isomer, but the question stem was asking for the <u>resonance structure</u> of this isomer. This only left answer choices A and D as possibilities and both were potential resonance structures of the trans isomer. The question stem specified that the pH = 7 so this **ruled out choice A** because the carboxyl group would not be protonated at this pH. Note also that a cardinal rule for resonance structures is that they must have the same overall charge as the parental structure; only **choice D fulfilled this requirement.**

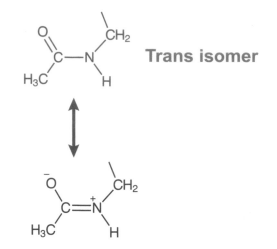

Figure 6. Trans isomer of the peptide bond and its resonance structure at pH = 7.

7) **B. II.** This question may seem unfair at first, as it required that you had committed to memory the pK_a of both the carboxyl and amino groups of proline. The MCAT requires that you know these values as they are fundamental to protein structure and, quite honestly, are nearly the same for all amino acids. So if you have not done so, remember that in amino acids: the pK_a of COOH~2 and the pK_a of NH_3~11. The distinct acidic and basic properties of these two groups determine the relative abundance of the different charged states at various pH values. This is summarized in the chart below for proline (**Fig. 7**). Given the information presented in the table above, at pH = 5.5, the zwitterionic form of proline would predominate making **choice B correct.**

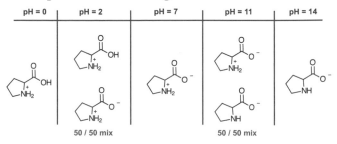

Figure 7. Protonation states of proline as a function of pH.

Notes:

PATHWAY

Lipid Purification

Although most fatty acid oxidation occurs in the mitochondria (**Fig. 1**), peroxisomes initiate the oxidation of very long chain fatty acids (VLCFAs) containing >22 carbons. Defects in VLCFA catabolism cause a number of biological disorders, including the peroxisomal diseases Zellweger syndrome and X-linked adrenoleukodystrophy (X-ALD). Zellweger patients often have defects in dihydroxyacetone phosphate 1-acyltransferase (DHAP-AT) activity.

Scientists hypothesized that the excess levels of non-catabolized fatty acids observed in X-ALD patients could be attributable to two reasons: (1) failure to properly import the fatty acid into the target peroxisomes; (2) failure to catabolize the fat subsequent to transport. To test these two models, extracts from either normal or X-ALD cells were prepared and the crude peroxisomes were isolated by sucrose gradient density purification to remove contaminating mitochondria. Purified peroxisomes were treated with a transport buffer containing either ^{14}C-cerotic acid (C26:0) or ^{14}C-capric acid (C10:0) and incubated. After centrifugation, the amount of radioactive material was counted for both the soluble and peroxisomal fractions. The data for both samples were plotted (**Fig. 2**).

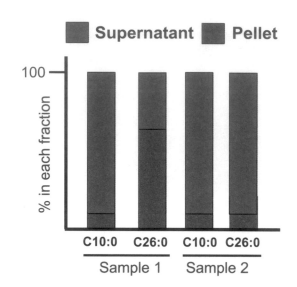

Figure 2. Measurement of radiolabeled fatty acids.

Figure 1. Degradation of palmitic acid.

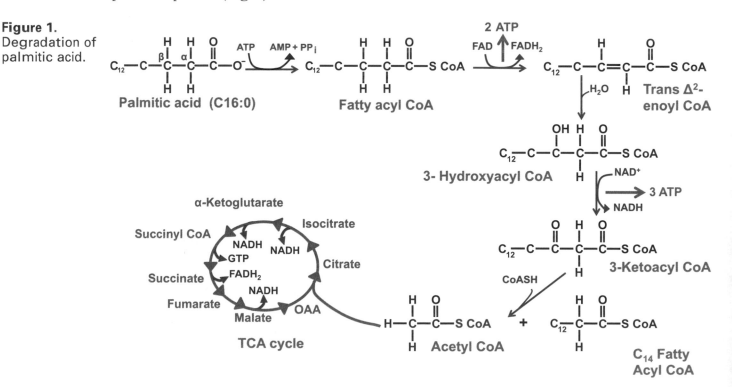

194

1) Activating fatty acids for β oxidation requires two ATP equivalents. Complete oxidation of palmitoleic acid (C16:1) would yield how many net ATP molecules?

A. 125

B. 127

C. 129

D. 131

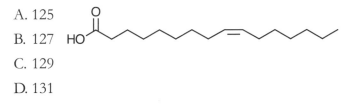

2) Patients with X-ALD have a defect in an ABC transporter. Which of the following represents an X-ALD patient sample?

A. #1 as C26:0 is mostly in the pellet.

B. #1 as C10:0 is mostly in the supernatant.

C. #2 as C26:0 is mostly in the supernatant.

D. #2 as C10:0 is mostly in the pellet.

3) Biochemical extraction experiments were instrumental in discovering that patients with X-ALD had lipid inclusions in various cells. Which of the following would be the least likely solvent to solubilize these inclusions?

A. Acetone

B. Chloroform

C. Diethylether

D. Hexane

4) During the identification of lipids in Zellweger patients, the lipids are isolated using a hydrophobic column. The best conditions for elution from this column would be with:

A. isopropanol.

B. 0.20 M NaCl, pH = 7.4.

C. 1.0 M NaCl, pH = 7.4.

D. toluene.

5) An experiment was performed to examine the relationship between VLCFA chain lengths and their association with lipid bilayers. Which of the following is true?

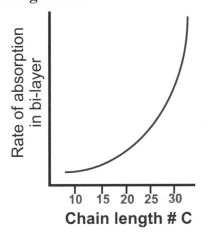

A. Lignoceric acid (C23:0) has a lower rate of desorption than palmitic acid (C16:0).

B. Palmitic acid (C16:0) has a higher rate of absorption than lignoceric acid (C23:0).

C. Cerotic acid (C26:0) has a higher rate of desorption than lignoceric acid (C23:0).

D. Palmitic acid (C16:0) has a lower rate of desorption than cerotic acid (C26:0).

6) Which of the following products is formed by the DHAP-AT enzyme?

A. I

B. II

C. III

D. IV

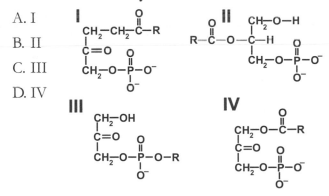

7) Which of the following observations confirms the integrity of the sucrose gradient purification step?

A. The presence of C26:0 in the X-ALD supernatant.

B. The presence of C10:0 in the pellets of both samples.

C. The absence of C10:0 in the X-ALD pellet.

D. The presence of C10:0 in the supernatants of both samples.

Lipid Purification

Annotations.

1) B 2) C 3) A 4) D 5) A 6) D 7) D

	Foundation 1: Metabolism-D			Foundation 5: Separation-C		
	D			**C**		
Concepts						
Reasoning	1			3,4		
Research	2,7					
Data	6			5		

Big Picture. This passage discusses β oxidation of fatty acids and highlights some key points that are likely to appear on the MCAT. Fatty acid metabolism is a giant topic that cannot be corralled into one passage as its intricate biological and chemical details have implications in numerous aspects of cellular physiology.

This passage focused on peroxisomal oxidation of VLCFAs in the context of two genetic diseases. Additional questions covering experimental design and energy obtained from fatty acid catabolism are posed in light of the information provided in the passage. While positioned in a biologically relevant setting, this passage almost exclusively tested organic chemistry, general chemistry, and biochemistry principles. Further, there was a significant emphasis placed upon your ability to digest and interpret details of the experiment described in the passage.

1) B. 127. Counting the number of ATPs generated from the oxidation of fatty acids (or other molecules like glucose) is a common MCAT problem type. Importantly, this passage provided you with enough information to answer this question, but it did require some careful bookkeeping. From Figure 1, you can assign each $FADH_2$ and NADH as generating 2 and 3 ATP molecules from electron transport, respectively. Note that all reducing power generated in Figure 1 is in the mitochondria as that is where β-oxidation (for C16:1) and TCA occur. Other sources may list different values such as 2.5 ATP for NADH and 1.5 ATP for $FADH_2$, but 2 and 3 are more likely what you will encounter on a question such as this.

Regardless, there are some basic rules to follow for these types of problems. Given that palmitic acid has 16 carbons, it will undergo 7 cycles of β-oxidation with an additional acetyl CoA left over at the end that is oxidized in the TCA cycle (**Fig. 3**). Each acetyl CoA will count as 12 ATPs as this is the net gain from TCA (11 ATP from $NADH/FADH_2$ + 1 GTP) and this can be seen in Figure 1. Since each cycle generates one acetyl CoA, there will be a total of 8 acetyl CoA molecules generated from the oxidation of palmitic acid. Therefore, there will be (12)(8) = 96 ATP molecules generated from those acetyl CoA molecules.

What about the NADH and $FADH_2$ molecules made during β-oxidation? Note that in Figure 1 (Step 2), $FADH_2$ is generated from a dehydrogenase that introduces a double bond into the molecule. Since palmitoleic acid <u>already has a double bond</u>, there will be one less $FADH_2$ generated, or 2 less ATP, from complete oxidation. Therefore, from 7 cycles there will be 7 NADH (21 ATP) and 6 $FADH_2$ (12 ATP) generated from each cycle. The total ATP count is now 96 + 21 + 12 = 129 ATP. Is that it? No, remember that the passage stem says it takes 2 ATP equivalents to activate the fatty acid into a fatty acyl CoA. Therefore, the correct answer is 129-2 = 127.

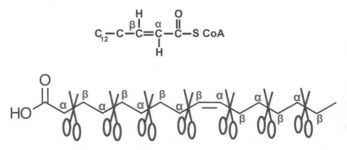

Figure 3. Position of cleavage events and double bond in palmitoleic acid.

2) C. #2 as C26:0 is mostly in the supernatant. The question stem states that patients with X-ALD have a defect in an ABC transporter. From the passage, the relevant fatty acid for transport in X-ALD is cerotic acid (C26:0), a VLCFA. Therefore, failure to transport ^{14}C labeled cerotic acid (C26:0) would leave all of the radiolabel in the supernatant (**Fig. 4**). This is the transport defect in X-ALD, so cells from these patients should not be able to incorporate the label into the peroxisome. Only wild-type cells (sample #1) should have significant radioactivity in their pellet. The experimental data given in Figure 2 demonstrates that sample #1 has C26:0 in the pellet meaning that this fatty acid was successfully transported into the peroxisome while sample #2 has this VLCFA in the supernatant. Based upon these points, **choice C is correct**.

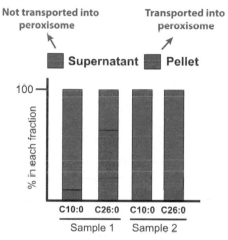

Figure 4. Peroxisomal transport of fatty acids.

3) A. Acetone. The most polar substance is the correct answer. Like dissolves like! That's all that there is to answer this question. Lipid inclusions are very nonpolar due to their long hydrophobic carbon moieties and dissolve in nonpolar solvents. One general method for determining polarity is through the dielectric constant. Any dielectric constant below 15 is typical of a nonpolar molecule. Shown in the figure (**Fig. 5**) is a list of the compounds and their relative dielectric constants. You should be readily familiar with these compounds without any knowledge of the dielectric constant. Diethylether and chloroform are used in organic extractions and you should have already seen them in an organic chemistry lab. They are nonpolar and are wrong choices for this question. The simple structure of hexane also gives away the not so hidden fact that it is very nonpolar. Only acetone is left. As a ketone, it has a dipole moment with the carbonyl group that can participate

in hydrogen bonding with water. Note that there is no need to memorize these numbers, yet you should now have enough of an understanding of them to be able to interpret situations where they might be given.

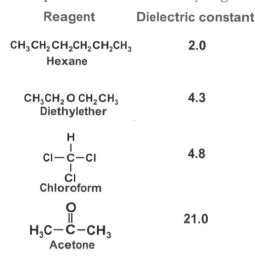

Figure 5. Ranking of polarity of compounds as a function of the dielectric constant listed in order of increasing polarity from top (least polar) to bottom (most polar).

4) D. toluene. The lipids are bound to the column via hydrophobic interactions through their long alkene or alkane chain. Therefore, nonpolar solvents would be best at interfering with complexes formed on the columns through nonpolar interactions. This **eliminates choices B and C**, as both solutions are aqueous, and the salt would not be expected to interfere with the hydrophobic interactions. In fact, salt will strengthen the hydrophobic effect and is therefore a good buffer for binding, but not elution. So what about choices A and D? Toluene has no polar groups (**Fig. 6**), but isopropanol is an alcohol and this is polar, making **choice A incorrect**. Toluene is therefore the most hydrophobic of the four choices, making it the correct answer.

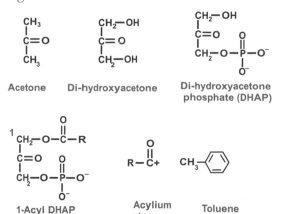

Figure 6. Common structures.

197

Lipid Purification

5) **A. Lignoceric acid (C23:0) has a lower rate of desorption than palmitic acid (C16:0).** The graph clearly shows that the rate of absorption is proportional to the length of the chain. It is also clear from the graph that the rate of absorption for the relative chain lengths of the three discussed fats are cerotic (C26:0) > lignoceric (C23:0) > palmitic (C16:0). The next important thing to recognize is that on the Y-axis, the data is presented as "rate of <u>absorption</u> in bilayer." However, some of the answer choices are presented as the rate of <u>desorption</u>. As absorption is the opposite of desorption, a high rate of absorption translates into a low rate of desorption. **Choice A is correct** because the higher the carbon chain number, the higher the rate of absorption (or the lower the rate of desorption). As lignoceric acid (C23:0) > palmitic acid (C16:0), the rate of lignoceric desorption is lower than palmitic acid.

Applying the same rationale as above will eliminate the other choices. **Choice B is wrong** because palmitic acid (C16:0) has less carbon atoms in the backbone than lignoceric acid (C23:0) and would have a lower absorption rate. Continuing with this approach, **choice C is also wrong**. Cerotic acid (C26:0) is larger than lignoceric (C23:0), and therefore has a higher absorption rate or a <u>lower</u> desorption rate. Lastly, **choice D is wrong** because palmitic acid (C16:0) is smaller than cerotic acid (C26:0), indicating that palmitic acid has a higher rate of desorption than cerotic acid or a lower rate of absorption; this option is really saying the same thing as answer choice B.

6) **D. IV.** As implied in the name of the enzyme, dihydroxyacetone phosphate 1-acyltransferase (DHAP-AT), uses dihydroxyacetone-phosphate (DHAP) as a substrate to transfer acyl groups to the "1" position. The top carbon bound to the functional alcohol group is number 1, by convention in organic molecule drawings such as these (**Fig. 6**). This **eliminates** choices B and C as they add on to the 2 and 3 positions, respectively. Note that an acyl group can be derived from the acylium ion (**Fig. 6**). Therefore, <u>any</u> carbonyl derivative has an acyl group. This includes amides and esters. In the case of DHAP-AT, the "R" group would be a generic designation for a VLCFA. **Choice A is incorrect** since there is an extra C added along with the acyl group onto the 1 position. This additional carbon would suggest that the substrate starting material was not DHAP.

7) **D. The presence of C10:0 in the supernatants of both samples.** Recall that the mitochondria would be expected to contain C10:0 fats, but not C26:0 as this VLCFA is oxidized in the peroxisome. The passage directly states that the purpose of the sucrose gradient is to purify away contaminating mitochondria. This is to ensure that the experimental transport assay is focused on peroxisomes. Immediately identify that **choice B is incorrect** because very little capric acid (C10:0) is detected in the pellets of either sample. Further, understand that cerotic acid is a VLCFA and is the experimental variable. The fact that cerotic acid is observed in the pellet of sample #1 (control) and not in sample #2 (X-ALD) is the point of the experiment and is a result that tests the hypothesis in study 2, but does not address the integrity of the sucrose gradient. This **rules out choices A and C.** The medium length capric acid was used in the experiment to determine the levels of contaminating mitochondria present in the preparation. The fact that the majority of capric acid that was added to either sample did not centrifuge in the pellet (and remained in the supernatant) suggests that there were little contaminating mitochondria. If the levels of contaminating mitochondria were high, then there would be corresponding high levels of labeled C10:0 detected in the pellet. These observations suggest that the integrity of the sucrose gradient was optimal making **choice D correct.**

Notes:

Sialic Acid

Defects in sialic acid (**Fig. 1A**) modification of cell surface proteins cause Salla disease, a neurological disorder. Two methodologies have been recently used to identify sialic acid-containing proteins.

Method I. In the presence of aniline, mild oxidation of cell surface sialic acid primary alcohols into aldehydes will occur (**Fig. 1B**). By introducing aminooxybiotin to sialic acid-containing aldehydes, biotinylated conjugates to sialic acids are generated through aldoxime linkages. After addition of streptavidin-coated agarose beads, sialic acid conjugates are retrieved through the high affinity between streptavidin and biotin (**Fig. 1B**).

Method II. This employs a metabolic labeling protocol with the sialic acid analog (Sia53), a compound that possesses an aldehyde functional group and is readily taken up by cells. Cell surface Sia53 readily reacts with hydroxylamines and can be processed through the biotin-streptavidin protocol.

In a first set of experiments, scientists grew two different cell lines in media that was supplemented with sialic acid (+Sialic acid) or not supplemented with sialic acid (-Sialic acid). Using Method I, they found that cell line #1 contained higher levels of endogenous sialylated proteins than cell line #2 (**Fig. 2A**). In a second set of experiments, Sia53 was added to both cell lines in excess of endogenous sialic levels observed in cell line #1. After 48 hours, cell membranes were collected and treated with aminooxybiotin in preparation for streptavidin isolation and quantification (**Fig. 2B**).

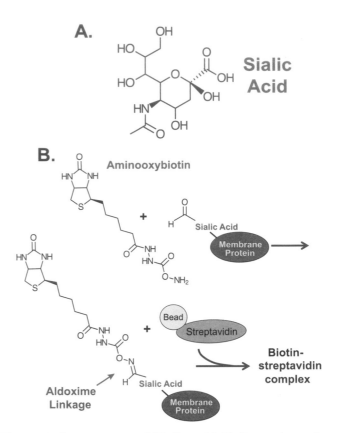

Figure 1. A. structure of Sialic acid. **B.** Detection of sialic acid-containing proteins through a two-step process of chemical modification and use of biotin-streptavidin.

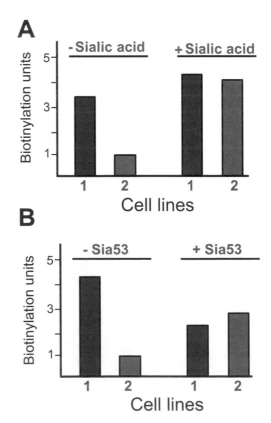

Figure 2. Detection of sialic acid-containing proteins via mild oxidation and the sialic acid analog Sia53.

1) **An aldoxime is an:**

   A. amine.

   B. enamine.

   C. imine.

   D. amide.

2) **Cell line #2 most likely has a defect in:**

   A. membrane localization of sialylated proteins.

   B. Golgi modification.

   C. sialic acid synthesis.

   D. oligosaccharide transfer.

3) **Which of the following is true with respect to Sia53?**

   A. Suppresses synthesis of sialic acid and is a poorer substrate for sialyltransferases than sialic acid.

   B. Suppresses synthesis of sialic acid and is a better substrate for sialyltransferases than sialic acid.

   C. Promotes synthesis of sialic acid and is a poorer substrate for sialyltransferases than sialic acid.

   D. Promotes synthesis of sialic acid and is a better substrate for sialyltransferases than sialic acid.

4) **One concern with cell line #2 is that the mild oxidation creates aldehydes that are not specific for sialic acid. What is the maximal percentage of this background that is not sialic acid-dependent?**

   A. 10%

   B. 25%

   C. 33%

   D. 75%

5) **What effect does the addition of sialic acid have on the optical activity of aminooxybiotin?**

   A. Increases due to the addition of the chiral sialic acid.

   B. Decreases due to the addition of the achiral sialic acid.

   C. Has no effect because the aminooxybiotin chiral centers do not participate in the addition reaction.

   D. Cannot be determined.

6) **A researcher accidentally used KMnO₄ for an extended period of time in an attempt to modify cell surface sialic acid residues. Which of the following functional group(s) would be created from this reaction?**

       I. Aldehyde
       II. Ketone
       III. Carboxylic Acid

   A. I, II

   B. II

   C. II, III

   D. I, III

7) **Sialic acid best described as a(n):**

   A. aldose because it forms an acetal.

   B. ketose because it forms a hemiacetal.

   C. ketose because it forms a hemiketal.

   D. aldose because it forms a ketal.

Sialic Acid

Annotations.
1) C   2) C   3) A   4) B   5) D   6) C   7) C

	Foundation 2: Cell Biology-A			Foundation 5: Mol. Interactions-B Biomolecules-D Thermo/Kinetics-E		
	A			**B**	**D**	**E**
Concepts					1	
Reasoning				5	6,7	
Research						
Data	2				4	3

Big Picture. Sialic acid is required for proper development and cellular physiology. This passage focused on an experimental scheme designed to identify sialylated proteins. Note that both methodologies employed chemical approaches that did not alter any biological process occurring in the host. This is known as bioorthogonal chemistry.

Sialic acid is a name given to any member of a family of 9 carbon sugars, so there are "multiple sialic acids" with N-acetylneuraminic acid being the most common (**Fig. 3**). Although the passage asks experimental questions and requires data interpretation, it also tests some chemistry and has a single cell biological question. MCAT passages commonly put principles into some biological context. This includes nomenclature, functional groups, and the difference between a ketose and aldose. These should be relatively straightforward questions to answer provided that you know this material as background information.

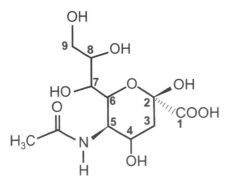

Figure 3. N-acetylneuraminic acid contains 9 carbons.

1) **C. imine.** This question was tricky because the actual aldoxime structure was not explicitly shown to you but, rather, there was reference to an "aldoxime linkage." As defined, aldoximes are a type of oxime, which itself is a type of imine that has a hydroxyl bound to the imine nitrogen. The text stated that the aminooxybiotin groups are attached to the sialic acid modifications via aldoxime linkages and inspection of Figure 2 shows the presence of an imine at that exact junction. This was the key to getting the question correct. Note the other nitrogen-containing structures shown in Figure 4 for your reference.

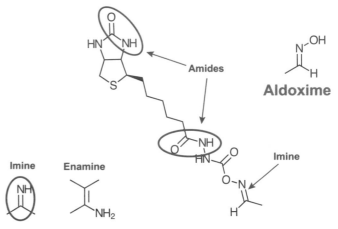

Figure 4. Imines and other functional groups.

2) **C. sialic acid synthesis.** The key to this question is to compare the data in presented in Figure 2A (highlighted in **Fig. 5**). The data shows that when cell line #2 is supplemented with exogenous sialic acid, it becomes as capable at sialylating proteins as cell line #1. This change was detected by the levels of purified biotinylation units, which are nearly equal to those for cell line #1 without sialic acid. This means that cell line #2 is proficient in taking up exogenous sialic acid and incorporating it into membrane proteins. This **eliminates choices A, B, and D**.

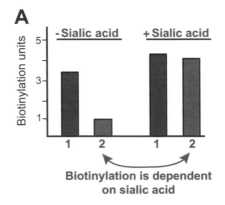

Figure 5. Sialic acid induced biotinylation shows that cell line #2 is proficient in processing sialic acid.

3) A. Suppresses synthesis of sialic acid and is a poorer substrate for sialyltransferases than sialic acid. Note that the addition of sialic acid to cell line #1 <u>increases</u> biotinylation, but the addition of Sia53 <u>decreases</u> biotinylation derived from cell line #1 as shown in Figure 2B in the passage and expanded on in Figure 6 below. This is consistent with Sia53 inhibiting sialic acid synthesis rather than promoting it, thereby **eliminating choices C and D**.

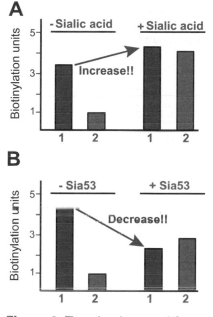

Figure 6. Trends observed from experiment.

From this point, you needed to determine if Sia53 is a better or worse substrate for sialyltransferases than sialic acid (Note that chemical analogs do not necessarily behave in a predictable manner, so inspecting the data is essential). As shown, addition of either sialic acid or Sia53 increases recovered biotinylation units for cell line #2 (**Fig. 7**). The extent of increase is more (steeper slope) for sialic acid, meaning that Sia53 is less efficiently incorporated into proteins making **choice A correct**.

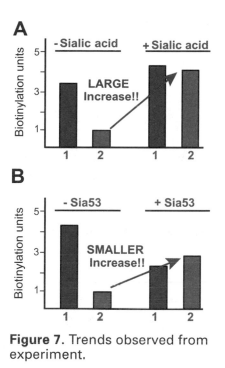

Figure 7. Trends observed from experiment.

4) B. 25%. In the absence of supplemented sialic acid, there is 1.0 unit of biotinylation for cell line #2. However, upon addition of sialic acid, there is an increase to 4.0 units (as seen in **Fig. 7**). This increase is dependent on sialic acid, but the initial biotinylation detected from cell line #2 may or may not be dependent on <u>endogenous</u> sialic acid. If all of this "baseline" biotinylation were due to nonspecific oxidation, then the entire 1.0 unit of biotinylation recovered would be due to this background. Therefore, the maximum amount of non-sialylated biotinylated product is 1.0 unit/4.0 units = 0.25 = 25%.

5) D. Cannot be determined. This is a common MCAT trick when it comes to stereochemistry. Recall that optical activity is the ability of most chiral compounds to rotate plane-polarized light. It is an empirical property only determined through experimentation. The key to this question was realizing that the addition of bonds to aminooxybiotin through the addition of sialic acid creates a completely new structure. When this happens, the new product's optical activity has no relationship to the reactants. Thus, it cannot be determined.

6) **C. II, III.** Following the description of method I in the passage and the labeled structure in Figure 4 (a labeled version of Figure 1A), the only primary alcohol (on carbon 9) in sialic acid would be oxidized to an aldehyde. In the presence of a strong oxidizing agent, such as $KMnO_4$, the aldehyde can be further oxidized into a carboxylic acid (**statement III is correct**). The secondary alcohol groups (carbons 4, 7, and 8) would be oxidized to ketones (**statement II is correct**).

7) **C. ketose because it forms a hemiketal.** Use the cyclical structure and work "backwards" or recognize that carbon 2 is in a hemiketal linkage (**Fig. 8**). The hydroxyl group at carbon 6 of sialic acid attacks the keto of carbon 2, the anomeric carbon, and forms a hemiketal. Therefore, sialic acid is a ketose and hemiketals are formed from ketones and alcohols. A hemiacetal can only be formed from an aldehyde reacting with an alcohol. An acetal is only formed from a carbonyl reacting with two alcohols and a ketal is the acetal formed after a ketone reactions with two alcohols.

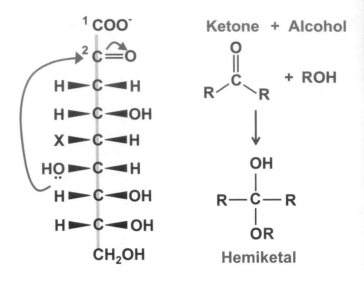

X = H₃COCHN

Figure 8. Sialic acid forms a hemiketal.

Notes:

2

5

PATHWAY

Chymotrypsin

The active site of chymotrypsin contains three amino acids that are involved in catalysis. Serine residue 195 was initially identified as particularly important through labeling experiments using Diisopropyl phosphofluoridate (DIPF).

In order to investigate chymotrypsin activity, an artificial substrate, p-nitrophenyl 2-benzyl propanoate (PN2BP), was incubated with the enzyme at its optimum pH of 7.5. A rapid "burst" of product was formed followed by its gradual accumulation. This burst was not observed when an amide test substrate was used (**Fig. 1**). In both cases, the levels of artificial substrates were in excess due to the high K_m of chymotrypsin for these molecules. These studies, in conjunction with X-ray crystallography, led to the elucidation of the mechanism of chymotrypsin (**Fig. 2**), which has been conserved throughout evolution by a multitude of species.

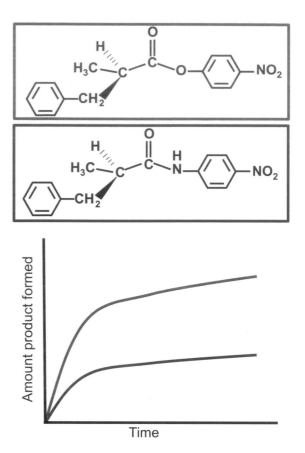

Figure 1. Timecourse of hydrolysis of carbonyl compounds by purified chymotrypsin.

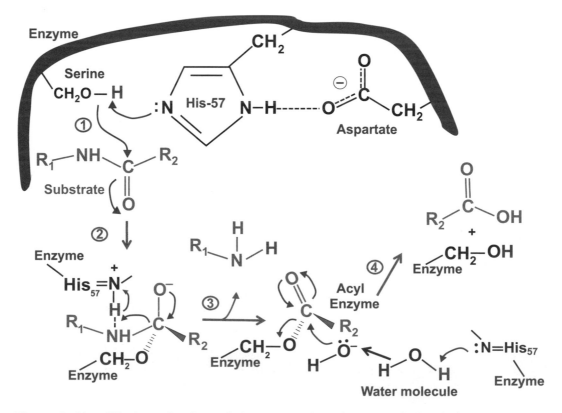

Figure 2. Simplified mechanism of chymotrypsin using a catalytic triad.
1. Serine attacks peptide carbonyl. 2. Formation of tetrahedral intermediate.
3. Generation of acyl intermediate and amine. 4. Generation of carboxylic acid.

1) **Which of the following is true regarding the role of histidine in the mechanism of chymotrypsin?**

A. Acts as both a general acid and a general base.

B. Acts as a general base only.

C. Acts as a general acid only.

D. Acts as neither a general acid nor a general base.

2) **Rank the four nucleophiles listed below in the order of decreasing strength.**

A. $OH^- > H_2O > NH_2^- > NH_3$

B. $NH_2^- > OH^- > NH_3 > H_2O$

C. $OH^- > NH_2^- > H_2O > NH_3$

D. $NH_2^- > OH^- > H_2O > NH_3$

3) **Based upon the test substrates used with chymotrypsin, which of the following statements is most accurate?**

A. The acyl intermediate forms faster from esters because they are more reactive than amides.

B. The acyl intermediate forms faster from amides because they are more reactive than esters.

C. The hydrolysis of the acyl intermediate is slower when derived from amides because they are less reactive than esters.

D. The hydrolysis of the acyl intermediate is faster when derived from amides because they are more reactive than esters.

4) **After using PN2BP as a substrate with chymotrypsin, which of the following structures most correctly represents the product formed after reaction of the acyl enzyme intermediate?**

A. 1

B. 2

C. 3

D. 4

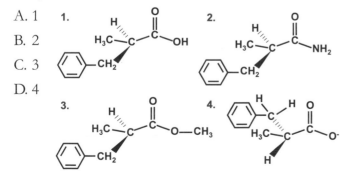

5) **Various forms of chymotrypsin exist. Which would be the best chromatographic method to purify and enrich enzyme form 2 from total cell lysates with no contaminating enzyme form 1 at pH = 7.0?**

Form	Amino acids	Isolelectric point	optimum pH	K_m
1	247	5.1	7.8	.063 mM
2	259	8.2	7.4	.071 mM

A. Gel filtration

B. Thin Layer Chromatography

C. Anion exchange

D. Cation exchange

6) **All of the following are functions water molecules present at the chymotrypsin active site except:**

A. regenerating the enzyme.

B. releasing the substrate.

C. undergoing electrophilic attack.

D. acting as an acid.

7) **Which of the following graphs represents the effect of pH on the velocity of step 3 in the chymotrypsin reaction?**

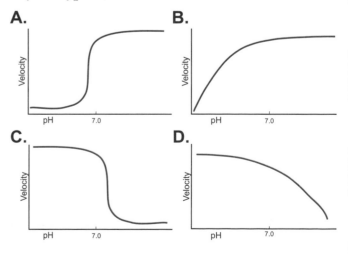

Chymotrypsin

	Foundation 1: Biochemistry-A			Foundation 5: Water-A Separation-C Biomolecules-D		
	A			**A**	**C**	**D**
Concepts	1				5	
Reasoning						
Research				7		
Data				6		2,3,4

Big Picture. This passage covers topics ranging from organic chemistry to kinetics. The passage was relatively short and should have been read in less than two minutes. Three of the questions dealt with the data presented in Figure 1 while the last two questions tested the mechanism of Figure 2. This passage is a typical MCAT physics/chemistry section passage as it emphasizes knowledge of chemistry in a biological context.

The elucidation of the mechanism of chymotrypsin was a major advance in biochemistry for several reasons. Notably, it was the first enzyme for which a covalent intermediate that inactivated the enzyme was discovered. Only when water reacts with this intermediate to release the final product does the enzyme return to its pre-catalytic, active state. From this, you should appreciate the fact that the chymotrypsin mechanism occurs in two steps. The bi-phasic nature of the reaction can be seen in Figure 1.

While not directly mentioned in the passage, proteases such as chymotrypsin are used in the human body to hydrolyze peptide bonds present in proteins to produce new carboxylic acid and amine ends associated with shorter protein or peptide products. Although the free energy of hydrolysis of a peptide bond is energetically favorable, the peptide bond is kinetically stable due to its planar resonance structure. Consequently, the carbonyl carbon in a peptide bond is less electrophilic than those found in other carbonyl carbons, including ester linkages.

1) A. Acts as both a general acid and a general base. Recall that the definition of "general" acid catalysis is when an acid protonates a species during the rate-determining step. The opposite term is "specific" acid catalysis where the acid protonates a species prior to the rate-determining step. The distinction for the two types of base catalysis follows analogous logic.

General acid and base chemistry is an important tool used by enzymes. In the case of chymotrypsin, we can see that histidine–57 uses both general acid and base catalysis to generate the acyl intermediate (shown below in **Fig. 3**). In the first step of the reaction, the imidazole nitrogen of histidine–57 abstracts a proton from serine–195, generating a strong, negatively charged nucleophile, which attacks the electrophilic carbonyl carbon in the peptide bond. In this first step histidine–57 acts as a base by removing the acidic proton. Histidine–57 also protonates the nitrogen present within the peptide bond presumably when the tetrahedral intermediate forms; in this step histidine–57 is using a general acid catalysis mechanism. Importantly, this mode of catalysis generates the leaving group: $R_1–NH_2$, which is a better leaving group than $R_1–NH^-$. Why? This is because the weakest base is always the best leaving group. The bond between the carbon and the weak base leaving group is weaker than it is between a carbon and a stronger base leaving group meaning that the bond is easier to break.

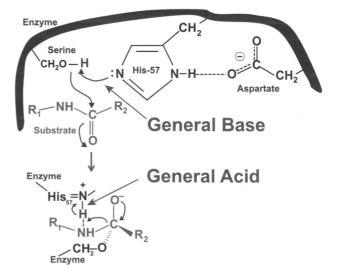

Figure 3. Histidine acts in both general acid and base catalysis.

2) **B. NH$_2^-$ > OH$^-$ > NH$_3$ > H$_2$O.** Nucleophiles contain electron density and, as a result, attack electrophilic centers. In general, nucleophilic strength increases as the negative charge on the molecule increases. This means that OH$^-$ is a stronger nucleophile than H$_2$O and that NH$_2^-$ is a stronger nucleophile than NH$_3$. All answer choices conform to this. What about OH$^-$ vs. NH$_2^-$? Nucleophilicity decreases with increasing electronegativity, meaning that NH$_2^-$ is more nucleophilic than OH$^-$. Why? As nitrogen is less electronegative than oxygen, it cannot support a negative charge as well as oxygen. Thus, the nitrogen atom is more nucleophilic (reactive) than oxygen because it is less stable in its negatively charged state. This logic effectively **eliminates choices A and C**. What about H$_2$O vs. NH$_3$? An analogous argument follows: nitrogen is less electronegative than oxygen and because of this, it is a stronger base. A stronger base makes a better nucleophile, making that atom more likely to share electrons with the electrophile. This **eliminates choice D**.

3) **A. The acyl intermediate forms faster from esters because they are more reactive than amides.** The mechanism of the chymotrypsin reaction occurs in two distinct kinetic steps as seen in Figure 4. The bi-phasic mechanism consists of: A) formation of the acyl intermediate; and B) hydrolysis of the acyl intermediate to form the final product.

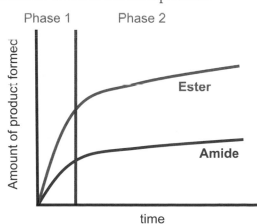

Figure 4. Bi-phasic mechanism of chymotrypsin and comparison of reaction rates between an ester and amide substrate.

Esters are more reactive than amides. Why? Think about the leaving group again. The leaving group in an ester is an alcohol and the leaving group in an amide is an amine, namely NH$_2^-$. NH$_2^-$ is a strong base and, notably, a stronger base than the RO$^-$ that leaves resulting from ester hydrolysis. Since the weakest base is the best leaving group, the amide is less reactive than the ester. Amides are the most-stable carbonyl compounds and this property makes them less reactive than esters. This **eliminates choices B and D. Choice C is wrong** because the slopes of the second phase for each substrate are similar so they have similar rates. This means that a reaction step prior to hydrolysis of the acyl intermediate is responsible for the different initial rates of product formation. The only prior catalytic steps are the formation of the tetrahedral intermediate and the formation of the acyl intermediate. Given the relative reactivity of nitrogen versus oxygen as the leaving group discussed above, it is the formation of the acyl intermediate which is the discriminating step.

4) **D. 4.** Take note that PN2BP is an ester and therefore the hydrolysis of its acyl intermediate will generate a carboxylic acid, **eliminating choices B and C**. So what about choices A and D? They are both acids, but one is ionized and one is not. As the passage describes the assay as occurring at pH = 7.5 (well above the pK$_a$ of carboxylic acid, which you recall is ~2-3.0), the acid will certainly be ionized, meaning that **choice A is incorrect**. Note that another difference between A and D is rotation around single bonds. The stereochemistry has not changed. This was an important distractor because if you chose to focus on stereochemistry first, you would have wasted time. However, if you realized the correct ionization state (as described above), then attempting to differentiate stereochemistry was not necessary to get the question correct.

5) **D. Cation exchange.** This question required that you had a fundamental understanding of various types of chromatography. Recall that gel filtration separates species based on their sizes. Because the two proteins described in the question have similar amino acid numbers, their sizes are expected to be similar, to the point that they will not be resolved using gel filtration. Therefore, **choice A is eliminated**. Thin layer chromatography (TLC) separates

Chymotrypsin

species based upon polarity and is not suitable for proteins, making **choice B incorrect**. Further supporting answer choice B as being incorrect is the fact that we are given no information regarding the polar nature of the proteins. The only significant difference between the two proteins that was provided in the table is their isolelectric points, the pH at which each protein has a net charge of zero. This is the key thing to focus on and should tell you that the best way to purify form 2 is through ion exchange, but which type of ion exchange?

As a general rule, you should know that if the pI > pH, then the protein will have a net positive charge when all of the charges from the side groups are considered. Likewise, if pI < pH, the protein will have a total net negative charge. This means that a cation exchange column can be readily used (the matrix has negatively charged species on them) to bind form 2 (**Fig. 5**). Form 1, and most other proteins present in cell lysates, would not be expected to bind to this column under these conditions as it has a pI of 5.1. Since 5.1 < 7.4, the overall charge of this protein would be negative, meaning that it would "flow through" the column. Only form 2 should stick (in addition to a small number of other cellular proteins with a similar pI). After binding, the pH can be changed such that pH > pI. This would change the overall charge of form 2 to negative and would elute the protein from the column.

An anion exchange column would also be effective to separate form 2 from enzyme form 1 because only form 1 would stick to the column. This would mean that form 2 would flow through the column. This would not as effectively enrich form 2, as many cellular proteins would also flow through. Additionally, the ability to wash the column following binding is lost in this approach making **choice C incorrect**.

6) **C. undergoing electrophilic attack.** This question requires you to focus on step 4 of the mechanism shown in Figure 2 (re-displayed in **Fig. 6**). Notice that the water molecule plays a critical role and is involved in multiple forms of chemistry. Process of elimination should have been used to arrive at the correct answer. First, the water molecule acts as an acid as it is deprotonated by histidine–57, therefore **choice D is incorrect**. The ultimate function of the water molecule, which follows the preceding two steps, is to cause release of the newly formed C-terminal end of the protein substrate through hydrolysis. This regenerates the enzyme making **choices A and B incorrect**. Following this deprotonatation, the oxygen is now capable of acting as a nucleophile where it can attack the carbonyl on the C-terminal end of the original protein substrate. This makes **choice C correct**.

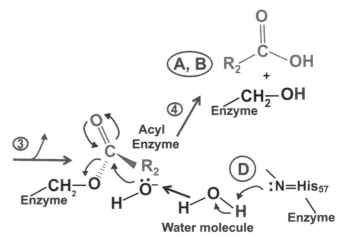

Figure 6. Role of water in the mechanism of chymotrypsin proteolysis.

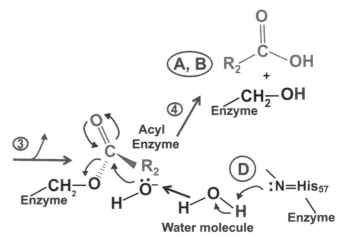

Figure 5. Cation exchange can be used to separate the two forms of an enzyme.

7) C. This problem focuses on a specific step in the chymotrypsin mechanism. Shown (**Fig. 7**) is the function of histidine–57 in the third step of the reaction mechanism. Recall that histidine is unique in that its pK_a (~6.0) is near physiological pH (7.4). Focus on the fact that histidine is acting as a general acid by protonating the substrate in this step, thereby creating a better leaving group. Therefore, this reaction will occur most robustly when histidine is protonated, which will occur under low pH **ruling out choices A and B**. From there, you had to remember that histidine will undergo a rapid change in protonation status at its pK_a (as opposed to a gradual change) and will lose activity very rapidly, once pH > pK_a. This **rules out choice D** since at pH 7.0 there is still a gradual change in the reaction. This point makes **choice C correct**.

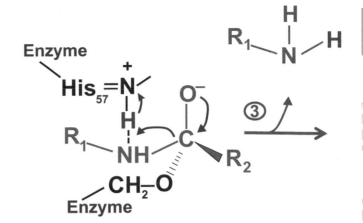

Figure 7. Histidine–57 is a general acid.

Phenylketonuria

The gene for phenylalanine hydroxylase (PAH) lies on chromosome 12 and encodes a monooxygenase enzyme. PAH uses its active site to bind biopterin, a cofactor that exists in both the tetrahydro (BH_4) and dihydro (BH_2) forms. Deficiencies in PAH are causal for the disease phenylketonuria (PKU). Like PAH, tyrosine hydroxylase also uses biopterin as a redox cofactor and is required for the synthesis of catecholamines such as dopamine (**Fig. 1**). Steady-state levels of dopamine are further maintained by its catabolic enzyme catechol-O-methyl transferase (COMT). In addition to reduced tyrosine synthesis, mutations in PAH also result in the accumulation of phenylalanine. This drives the synthesis of its transaminated product that acts as a neurotoxin, causing many of the symptoms of PKU.

In most cases, long-term treatment for PKU involves significant dietary restrictions to prevent the accumulation of phenylalanine metabolites. To further study the role of different protein sources as therapy for PKU patients, doctors used four diets composed of proteins of varying amino acid composition, but identical levels and types of fats and carbohydrates. Postprandial serum levels of insulin, glucagon, and blood urea nitrogen (BUN), a product of the urea cycle, were measured to assess the efficacy of dietary management of PKU (**Fig. 2**).

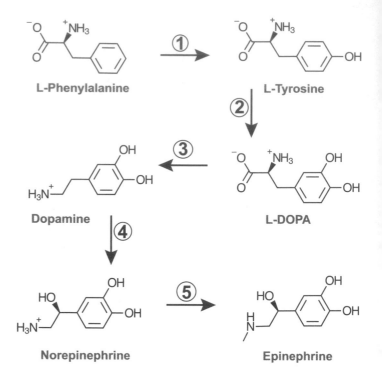

Figure 1. Phenylalanine is a precursor to dopamine and norepinephrine. PAH catalyzes step 1.

Mutation	Diet	Insulin / Glucagon	BUN
Catalytic	1	High	Low
Regulatory	2	Low	High
Oligomerization	3	High	High
Catalytic	4	Low	Low

Figure 2. PKU patients with defined mutations in PAH domains were placed on specific diets prior to measuring key metabolic values to determine efficacy of treatment.

1) **Administering biopterin derivatives to some patients with mutations in PAH has been shown to alleviate symptoms of PKU. A patient having a mutation in which domain of PAH would most likely respond to this therapy?**

   A. catalytic

   B. oligomerization

   C. regulatory

   D. catalytic or regulatory

2) **The BH_4 chiral carbons outside of the ring structure are numbered as shown. What is the absolute configuration at carbons 1 and 2?**

   A. 1S, 2S

   B. 1R, 2S

   C. 1S, 2R

   D. 1R, 2R

   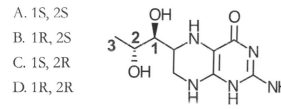

3) **Which pair of half reactions correctly depicts the reaction performed by PAH?**

   A. $H_2O \rightarrow O_2$; $BH_2 \rightarrow BH_4$

   B. $O_2 \rightarrow H_2O$; $BH_4 \rightarrow BH_2$

   C. $H_2O \rightarrow O_2$; $BH_4 \rightarrow BH_2$

   D. $O_2 \rightarrow H_2O$; $BH_2 \rightarrow BH_4$

4) **Which diet best manages the symptoms of PKU?**

   A. 1

   B. 2

   C. 3

   D. 4

5) **Which of the following metabolites is toxic in PKU?**

   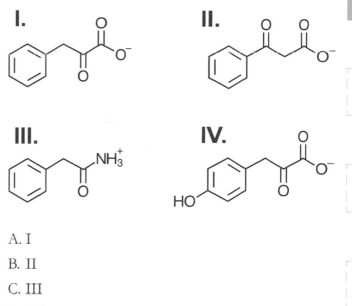

   A. I

   B. II

   C. III

   D. IV

6) **Parkinson's disease patients display motor symptoms that result from the death of dopamine generating cells in the brain. All of the following would be beneficial treatments of this disease except:**

   A. increased levels of L-DOPA.

   B. dopamine receptor agonists.

   C. dihydrobiopterin (BH_2).

   D. catechol-O-methyl transferase (COMT) inhibitors.

7) **Which of the following statements, if true, would prevent any conclusions from being made regarding the effects of the four diets?**

   A. The PKU patients were not the same sex.

   B. Individual expressivity varied widely.

   C. The PKU mutations were equally penetrant.

   D. The initial BUN levels were not low.

Phenylketonuria

Annotations.
1) A   2) C   3) B   4) A   5) A   6) C   7) B

	Foundation 1: Biochemistry-A Metabolism-D		Foundation 5: Mol. Interactions-B Biomolecules-D		
	A	**D**	**B**	**D**	
Concepts			2		
Reasoning	1	3		5,6	
Research		7			
Data	4				

Big Picture. This passage focuses on the metabolism of phenylalanine and its role in the disease PKU. Recall that phenylalanine is an essential amino acid and has multiple fates (**Fig. 3**) that are regulated by hormones such as insulin. Phenylalanine is incorporated into protein under anabolic conditions (i.e. high insulin), converted into the amino acid tyrosine, or transaminated for catabolism. In a transamination reaction, the amino group is transferred to α-ketoglutarate to generate glutamate and the cognate α-ketoacid. In the case of phenylalanine, this generates the toxic compound phenylpyruvate. As free ammonia is toxic, glutamate carries excess nitrogen and delivers it for processing in the urea cycle (**Fig. 3**).

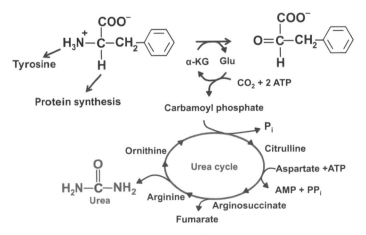

Figure 3. Three fates of phenylalanine.

1) **A. catalytic.** Mutations in the catalytic domain of PAH would be expected to reduce the binding affinity of the enzyme for BH4. Therefore, a higher concentration of BH4 would be needed to bind to the mutant site and drive the reaction forward via Le Chatelier's principle. Because BH4 binds to the catalytic site, those PAH mutations in this region would be expected to be most responsive to this form of treatment. Mutations in the other domains of PAH would mean that the enzyme's ability to bind BH4 is unaffected and adding BH4 would not impact oligomerization or regulation.

2) **C. 1S, 2R.** Remember that chiral carbons are sp^3 hybridized and have four different substituents attached to them. Now use the Cahn-Ingold-Prelog rules to determine the absolute configuration at each carbon. Assign priorities 1-4 where the highest priority is given to the atom with the highest atomic number attached to the chiral center. If the smallest priority (the 4th priority) is pointed "in the back" with a hatched line, then draw an arrow from 1-3: if this arrow rotates in a clockwise direction then the absolute configuration is "R" and if this arrow rotates in a counter-clockwise direction then the absolute configuration is "S." If the 4th priority is pointing "in the front" (as indicated by being attached to the solid wedge) then the absolute configuration is opposite from the configuration that you see.

This structure poses an additional level of complexity as in both cases the chiral carbons are each attached to constituents of the same atomic number, namely carbon. This means that you have to go out at least one more bond to look for differences in order to determine the higher priority between the two carbons.

In the case of BH4, you had to first determine the configuration for carbon 1. As depicted in Figure 4, the first priority is assigned to the oxygen atom in the hydroxyl group as it has the highest atomic number. The last or 4th priority is not directly shown to you but is implied since the carbon atom is uncharged it must have 4 bonds and the one missing bond is to a H atom and that bond must be "in the back" since all other bonding directions for an sp^3 hybridized carbon atom are shown. The other two substituents are both carbon. To determine the priority of the other two carbons, you needed to examine the atomic number of the groups attached to each carbon (N, C,

H) vs (O, C, H), remember to move out only one bond at a time in the direction going away from the chiral center. Because the atomic number of N < O, the carbon linked to oxygen has a higher priority and is assigned a priority of "2." Now that the priorities are assigned form 1-4, after an arrow is drawn from 1 to 3, it is apparent that the direction is counter-clockwise, or the configuration is S.

For the case of chiral carbon 2, you will notice an analogous scenario with attachments of a single oxygen, a single hydrogen and two carbon atoms. The same approach should be used to calculate priority assignments as shown (**Fig. 4**). After the assignment of priorities, the arrow is drawn from 1-3. This arrow is in a counter-clockwise direction suggesting the S configuration. However, the smallest group (H) is in the front, the opposite orientation from where you need it to be so, the absolute configuration is the opposite from what you see. Thus, the absolute configuration for chiral center 2 is S.

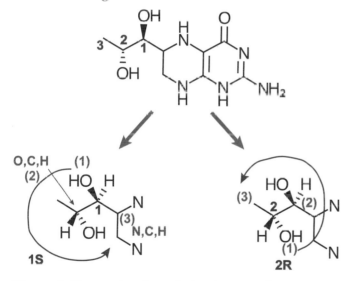

Figure 4. Determination of absolute configuration around chiral carbons in tetrahydrobiopterin. The numbers in blue text and parenthesis indicate the priority assignments and the red numbers show the chiral center that is being analyzed.

3) B. $O_2 \rightarrow H_2O$; $BH_4 \rightarrow BH_2$. As inferred from the passage, a monooxygenase such as PAH splits O_2 and places one oxygen atom on phenylalanine to make tyrosine as the other is reduced to water (**Fig. 5A**). Therefore **choices A and C are incorrect.**

From this point, you had to identify that tetrahydrobiopterin supply the 2 needed hydrogen atoms for this reaction (**Fig. 5A**). This passage-based logic effectively **eliminates choices A and D**.

4) A. 1. An optimal dietary treatment plan for PKU allows for the incorporation of phenylalanine into proteins. This would reduce or even prevent the conversion of phenylalanine into phenylpyruvate, the toxic, and transaminated phenylketone product. As phenylalanine would be shunted away from its conversion into tyrosine, the requirement for tyrosine in PKU patients is therefore met through dietary sources. Based upon this reasoning, food sources that stimulate insulin release would promote the conversion of dietary phenylalanine into protein and would minimize its catabolism via transamination.

Recall that insulin is anabolic and promotes the synthesis of proteins (as well as glycogen and fat). Glucagon is the opposite of insulin and the release of glucagon is inhibited by insulin. Thus, an optimal diet should increase the insulin/glucagon ratio (low glucagon), **eliminating choices B and D**. What about urea? High levels of urea are the result of transamination of phenylalanine (and other amino acids; **Fig. 3**), a scenario that would yield the toxic, transaminated product. Thus, low blood urea nitrogen (BUN) levels are consistent with reduced catabolism of phenylalanine, **eliminating choice C**. Note that the nature of the mutation is irrelevant for this question as all patients display symptoms of PKU.

A.

B.

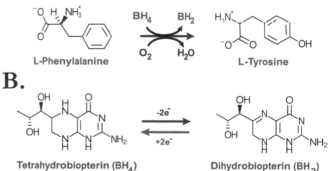

Figure 5. Phenylalanine hydroxylase is a monooxygenase that reduces tetrahydrobiopterin (BH_4) to dihydrobiopterin (BH_2). This reaction is coupled to the hydroxylation of phenylalanine.

Phenylketonuria

5) A   I. Phenylalanine transaminase uses pyridoxal phosphate (Vitamin B_6) as a co-factor in the transamination of phenylalanine to phenylpyruvate. The amino group from phenylalanine is concomitantly added to α–ketoglutarate to generate glutamate (**Fig. 6**). As most amino acids use α–ketoglutarate as a substrate in transamination, glutamate is the carrier of the ammonium group during amino acid metabolism. (Alanine is also a carrier and is transaminated into pyruvate).

Excessive amino acids are transaminated in reactions driven by mass action (Le Chatelier's principle). In PKU, excessive phenylalanine is transaminated into phenylpyruvate. As discussed, transamination reactions swap an amino group from a donor and change it into a keto group, generating the cognate α–keto acid (**Fig. 6**). For phenylalanine this is phenylpyruvate and is represented by structure I. **Choice A is correct**. Note that **choice D is incorrect** as it has an additional hydroxyl moiety on the phenyl group. Structure II has the keto group in the wrong position (**choice B is wrong**) and structure III has an amino group (**choice C is wrong**).

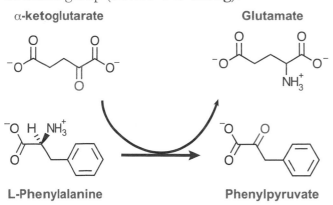

Figure 6. Transamination of phenylalanine.

6) C. dihydrobiopterin (BH₂). Since Parkinson's disease is marked by the failure to produce dopamine (in a section of the midbrain known as the substantia nigra), a common therapeutic avenue is to increase the levels of dopamine. Increased levels of BH_2 would favor the conversion of L-DOPA into tyrosine (**Fig. 7**, reverse reaction), making **choice C the correct answer** (as it would not increase dopamine). L-DOPA and inhibitors of Catechol-O-methyl transferase (COMT) would both favor an increase in dopamine levels (**choices A and D are wrong**) through providing either substrate (choice A) or preventing the breakdown of dopamine (choice D). Dopamine receptor agonists would mimic dopamine action and are therefore valuable in treatment of Parkinson's. Thus, **choice B is wrong**.

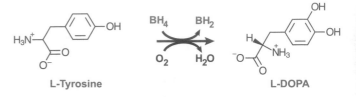

Figure 7. Tyrosine hydroxylase uses BH_4 to generate L-DOPA in a manner analogous to phenylalanine hydroxylase.

7) B. Individual expressivity varied widely. This question challenged your ability to understand how a study is properly designed. There were four PKU patients depicted in Figure 2 and each was given a different diet. There is no reason to believe that the sex of the participant was an important factor to consider because the genetic defect in PKU, the perturbation of the PAH gene, resides on chromosome 12 (as mentioned in the first sentence), an autosome. PKU is not a sex-linked disease, making **choice A incorrect**.

The study description was provided both in the passage and in the legend of Figure 2 where it was stated that each of the study participants had PKU. This indicates two important facts: 1) By definition, the patients have equal penetrance as they each had the disease. Recall that the genetic term "penetrance" refers to the likelihood of a gene mutation generating an associated phenotype (in this case, a disease). 2) By virtue of suffering from PKU, the blood urea nitrogen (BUN) levels will be initially high as phenylpyruvate is being made in amounts that are deleterious (**Fig. 3**). Both of these two points effectively **ruled out choices C and D**. By process of elimination, **choice B is correct**. To expound further, however, recall that the genetic term "expressivity" refers to <u>variations</u> in a phenotype among individuals that carry a particular genotype. In other words, expressivity refers to the degree of penetrance. In order for the conclusions to be valid in this study, it should be assumed that there will be little to no variation in expressivity and that each of the patients suffers from PKU in comparable manners.

PATHWAY

Cox Inhibitors

Signal transduction pathways that activate phospholipase A2 release fatty acids from the C-2 carbon of the glycerol backbone. This generates arachidonic acid ($C20:4\Delta^{5, 8, 11, 14}$), a signaling molecule that is converted into various mediators by the action of two cyclooxygenase (COX) enzymes, COX1 and COX2. These enzymes are similar in structure and function, but have different modes of expression. COX enzymes are inhibited by aspirin and other nonsteroidal anti-inflammatory drugs (NSAIDs). COX1 is constitutively expressed, but COX2 is inducible in response to various signals, including those that activate inflammatory pathways such as tumor necrosis factor (TNF).

COX1 and COX2 generate the prostanoids, including prostaglandins, prostacyclin, and leukotrienes. In platelets, only COX1 is present and it generates thromboxane A2, a mediator of platelet aggregation and blood clotting. In addition, COX enzymes regulate angiogenesis, production of the mucus lining, and blood pressure in renal arterioles. Because of their pivotal role in these critical physiological processes, inhibition of COX enzymes is a highly active area of study.

In order to generate specific COX2 inhibitors that prevent stomach bleeding, scientists modified aspirin with various chemical groups to generate three new compounds. Each of these derivatives was tested for its ability to interact with the COX2 enzyme by determining the rate constants of association (k_1) and dissociation (k_{-1}) of the inhibitor at equilibrium. Formation of the EI* complex represents a nearly irreversible event that effectively eliminates enzyme function (**Table 1**).

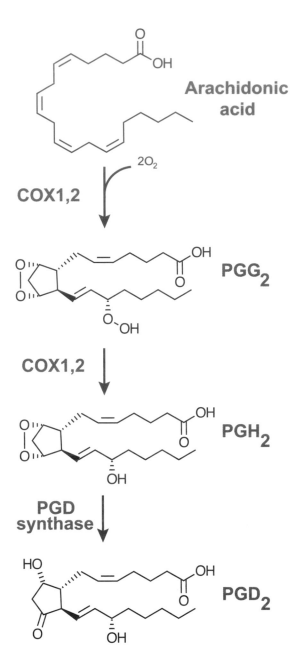

Figure 1. Mechanism of cyclooxygenases in the production of prostaglandins. PGG2 (Prostaglandin G2), PGH2 (Prostaglandin H2), PGD2 (Prostaglandin D2).

Drug	k_1	k_{-1}	k_2
1	4×10^7	2×10^{-2}	6×10^5
2	4×10^5	2×10^{-2}	7×10^7
3	3×10^7	5×10^{-3}	6×10^4

Table 1. Determination of rate constant values for three cyclooxygenase drug inhibitors. Units of k_1: $M^{-1}s^{-1}$, k_{-1} and k_2: s^{-1}

1) At equilibrium, the dissociation constant K_D can be used to determine the strength of binding of a COX enzyme inhibitor. Which of the following is true with respect to K_D values?

   A. K_D Drug #1 = 5 x 10^{-10} M^{-1}

   B. K_D Drug #1 = 5 x 10^{-10} M

   C. K_D Drug #2 = 2 x 10^{-3} M

   D. K_D Drug #2 = 5 x 10^{-3} M^{-1}

2) The conversion of PGG_2 into PGH_2 is coupled to which of the following reactions?

   A. $O_2 \rightarrow H_2O$

   B. 2 GSH → G-S-S-G

   C. OAA → Malate

   D. Pyruvate → Lactate

3) Which of the following statements is true regarding the affinity for various drugs and COX2?

   A. Drug #1 has the lowest affinity for COX2.

   B. Drug #1 has the highest affinity for COX2.

   C. Drug #3 has the lowest affinity for COX2.

   D. Drug #3 has the highest affinity for COX2.

4) Which of the following statements is true?

   A. Both reaction rates and rate constants are dependent on concentrations.

   B. Only reaction rates are dependent on concentration.

   C. Neither reaction rates nor rate constants are dependent on concentration.

   D. Only rate constants are dependent on concentration.

5) Which of the following drugs would provide the most effective inhibition for COX2?

   A. #1

   B. #2

   C. #3

   D. Cannot be determined

6) Scientists added TNF to cells to examine the induction of prostaglandin synthesis from arachidonic acid. Which experimental control is the most useful to be conducted in parallel?

   A. Addition of COX2 inhibitors in the presence of TNF.

   B. Addition of COX1 inhibitors in the absence of TNF.

   C. Addition of phospholipase A2 inhibitors in the presence of TNF.

   D. Addition of a TNF inhibitor in the absence of TNF.

7) Which of the following enzymes would be most capable of catalyzing the conversion of PGE_2 to $PGF2\alpha$ as shown?

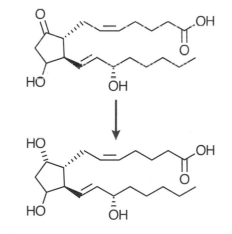

   A. 9-aldo reductase

   B. 12-aldo reductase

   C. 9-keto reductase

   D. 12-keto reductase

Cox Inhibitors

Annotations.

1) B   2) B   3) D   4) B   5) B   6) A   7) C

	Foundation 2: Cell Physiology-C			Foundation 5: Biomolecules-D Thermo/Kinetics-E		
	C			D	E	
Concepts				7	4	
Reasoning					2	
Research	6					
Data					1,3,5	

Big Picture. This passage discusses the biological importance and chemical activities of cyclooxygenase (COX) enzymes. The action of these enzymes is critical to a vast array of physiological systems. Both COX enzymes are bi-functional enzymes catalyzing the first two steps in the conversion of arachidonic acid into prostaglandin G2 (PGG2). These two steps involve the formation of a cyclooxygen ring as well as a peroxide linkage. The product, PGG2, can then be converted into several distinct signaling chemicals that play roles in: renal homeostasis, sleep-awake cycles, inflammation, and thrombosis. While the passage discussed both COX1 and COX2, the questions did not test on specific differences between the two enzymes.

Within this biological context, the passage was focused on enzymology and heavily weighted towards the concepts of rate constants, affinity constants, and dissociations constants. Three of the questions dealt directly with these topics and used the data presented in Table 1 (questions 1, 3, and 5), while question 4 was purely conceptual dealing with reaction rates/rate constants. Two of the other questions (2 and 7) tested your ability to identify the nature of chemical reactions in pathways that you are not likely familiar with.

1) **B. K_D Drug #1 = 5×10^{-10} M.** This question was entirely dependent on your ability to recall the mathematical definition of the dissociation constant (K_D) as it related to both on and off-rates. In the relationship diagramed below (**Fig. 2**), the dissociation constant is equal to the off-rate (k_{-1}) divided by the on-rate (k_1). At equilibrium, the concentration of all species does not change and the dissociation constant can be measured.

$$E + I \underset{k_{-1}}{\overset{k_1}{\rightleftharpoons}} EI \qquad \begin{aligned} k_1 &= k_{on} \\ k_{-1} &= k_{off} \end{aligned}$$

$$K_D = \frac{k_{off}}{k_{on}} = \frac{k_{-1}}{k_1}$$

rate of forward reaction: $[E][I]k_1$

rate of reverse reaction: $[EI]k_{-1}$

At Equilibrium

$$[E][I]k_1 = [EI]k_{-1}$$

$$\frac{k_{-1}}{k_1} = \frac{[E][I]}{[EI]}$$

$$K_D = \frac{[E][I]}{[EI]}$$

Figure 2. Calculation of dissociation constant using forward and reverse rate constants.

Given this relationship and plugging in the values from Table 1, the **correct answer is choice B.** Furthermore, the relationship shown in Figure 2 also demonstrates that the units of K_D are [M]. Even if you did not recall the dissociation constant formula from Figure 2 you could eliminated two answers if you remembered that the units of K_D are M.

2) B. 2 GSH → G-S-S-G. The question directly refers to one of the steps shown in Figure 1. Specifically, you needed to identify that when PGG2 is converted to PGH2, the peroxy acid group is reduced to a secondary alcohol group (**Fig. 3**, upper panel). Therefore, this reaction should be coupled to an oxidation reaction and this is what you needed to identify in the answer choices. **Choice A is incorrect** because the formation of water from oxygen is a reduction reaction. In fact, this is where the phrase "oxygen is the final electron acceptor" in the electron transport chain is derived from. The formation of OAA from malate is also reduction as is the formation of lactate from pyruvate (making **choices C and D wrong**). The latter reaction is the basis of fermentation, which occurs to oxidize more NADH. Further, you should recognize from the order of the oxidative TCA cycle that OAA being converted into malate is a reduction reaction. It is the reverse of the reaction that occurs in the TCA cycle. The molecule "GSH" is reduced glutathione and this molecule is commonly used as a source of reducing equivalents and is oxidized in the process with the formation of a disulfide bond. Even if you were not familiar with glutathione and its nomenclature, you should have drawn an analogy between reduced and oxidized cysteine (i.e. disulfide bridges). This makes **choice B correct.**

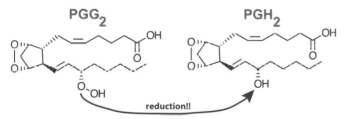

Need oxidation:

A. $O_2 \rightarrow H_2O$ **Reduction**

B. 2 GSH → G-S-S-G **Oxidation**

C. OAA → Malate **Reduction**

D. Pyruvate → Lactate **Reduction**

Figure 3. Correct Redox pairing. Conversion of PGG2 to PGH2 is a reduction reaction and choice B is the only oxidation reaction.

3) D. Drug #3 has the highest affinity for COX2. Based upon the data presented in Table 1, you should have derived two additional columns using the data presented and relatively simple arithmetic (**Fig. 4**). As discussed in the annotation of question 1, the K_D of a reaction can be determined through the ratio of the k_{off} (k_{-1}) to k_{on} (k_1). This can be used to generate a column of dissociation constants and this column agrees with the answer for question 1 since a lower dissociation constant is consistent with a higher affinity. An additional column could have been generated that provides the inverse of the dissociation constant. This is called the binding constant or the association constant (or K_A). Large K_A values represent higher affinities between enzyme and substrate. Based upon this, drug #3 will have the highest affinity to COX2 whereas drug #2 will have the lowest affinity, making **choice D correct.**

Drug	k_1	k_{-1}	k_2	$K_A = \frac{k_1}{k_{-1}}$	$K_D = \frac{k_{-1}}{k_1}$
1	4×10^7	2×10^{-2}	6×10^5	2×10^9	5×10^{-10}
2	4×10^5	2×10^{-2}	7×10^7	2×10^7	5×10^{-8}
3	3×10^1	5×10^3	6×10^4	6×10^9	1.7×10^{-10}

Figure 4. Table demonstrating both binding constants and dissociation constants.

4) B. Only reaction rates are dependent on concentration. This is a purely conceptual problem that tested your ability to recall the fundamental differences between rates and rate constants. The rate of a reaction depends on the rate constant as well as the concentration of reactants that are present in the rate-limiting step (**Fig. 5**). This fact made **choices C and D incorrect**. On the contrary, the rate constant does not depend on concentrations of any species. In fact, the rate constant is only dependent on the activation energy (E_a), the Arrhenius factor (A), temperature (t), and the ideal gas constant (R). These points make **choice B correct.**

$$\text{rate} = k \, [\text{reactant \#1}] \, [\text{reactant \#2}]$$

$$k = Ae^{\frac{-E_a}{RT}}$$

Figure 5. The rate and rate constant equations.

5) B. #2. The last sentence of the passage states that the formation of the EI* complex represents a nearly irreversible event effectively eliminating enzyme function. Therefore, the drug that creates this product at the highest rate would be the most effective inhibitor of COX2 function. This reaction step is governed by the rate constant k_2, therefore the drug with the highest k_2 would be the most effective (**Fig. 6**). This makes **choice B the correct answer**.

Drug	k_1	k_{-1}	k_2	$K_A = \frac{k_1}{k_{-1}}$	$K_D = \frac{k_{-1}}{k_1}$
1	4×10^7	2×10^{-2}	6×10^5	2×10^9	5×10^{-10}
2	4×10^5	2×10^{-2}	7×10^7	2×10^7	5×10^{-8}
3	3×10^7	5×10^{-3}	6×10^4	6×10^9	1.7×10^{-10}

Figure 6. Table highlighting the rate of formation (k_2) of the stable inhibited product.

6) A. Addition of COX2 inhibitors in the presence of TNF. The passage states that COX2 expression is induced by TNF; this experiment is therefore expected to measure the level of this induction event. Of course, this is an <u>indirect</u> measurement of COX2 expression levels as the measurement will determine the amount of prostaglandin synthesis as a function of TNF addition. One critical experimental control that should be included in the study design is to be certain that any induced prostaglandin synthesis detected as a function of TNF is derived from COX expression and not from a secondary source. In light of this, the best parallel experiment to conduct would be to inhibit the activity of COX2 using an inhibitor following treatment with TNF. This would allow for the assessment of what level of background prostaglandin synthesis is occurring following TNF treatment that is not due to COX2. This makes **choice A the best and correct answer**. Choices B, C, and D do not help you measure the influence of COX2 on prostaglandin production.

7) C. 9-keto reductase. In addition to the fact that the reaction presented in the question is not depicted in Figure 1, there were two key elements to get this correct: nomenclature of the two compounds and the type of reaction that was taking place (**Fig. 7**). First, recognize that IUPAC nomenclature rules state that once the longest carbon chain has been determined, the first carbon is identified to place the highest priority functional groups on the lowest number carbon. In other words, the carboxylic acid should be placed at carbon #1. Given this, the reaction is taking place at carbon #9 thereby **eliminating choices B and D**. Further recognize that the carbonyl present at carbon #9 is a ketone, which is reduced to a hydroxyl. Since the reactant functional group is a ketone (keto) and not an aldehyde (aldo), **choice A is incorrect** and this makes **choice C correct**.

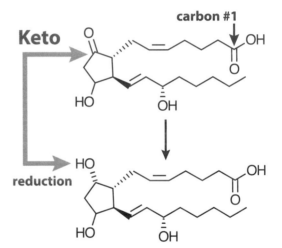

Figure 7. Nomenclature and reaction of converting PGE$_2$ to PGF2α.

Notes:

Psychological, Social, and Biological Foundations of Behavior

Psychophysics

Psychophysics is the study of the relationship between an external stimulus and its perception and representation across the range of human sensory detection. One of the most important relationships in psychophysics is known as Weber's law, which states that the detectable difference between two stimuli (often called the "just noticeable difference," or JND) is directly proportional to stimulus magnitude; formally:

$$k = \Delta i / i$$

where the function k depends on: Δ = a difference value (JND), and i = stimulus intensity level (i.e. loudness). The value of Δ (the threshold for detection) is directly proportional to the stimulus intensity. If Δ (JND) for loudness at 10 db = 1 db, the perceiver will detect a difference between auditory stimuli of 10 db and 11 db (but not < 11 db). An extension of Weber's law postulates a consistent logarithmic relationship between stimulus intensity and sensation magnitude.

Stevens determined empirically the following modified relationship between stimulus intensity level and stimulus perception, formally:

$$\text{Subjective Intensity (SI)} = ki^{a}$$

where k = a constant, i = stimulus intensity level, and a = an exponent that varies widely based on the sensory modality and the individual stimulus. Stevens observed the relationships depicted in Figure 1 involving brightness, line length, and pain (electric shock).

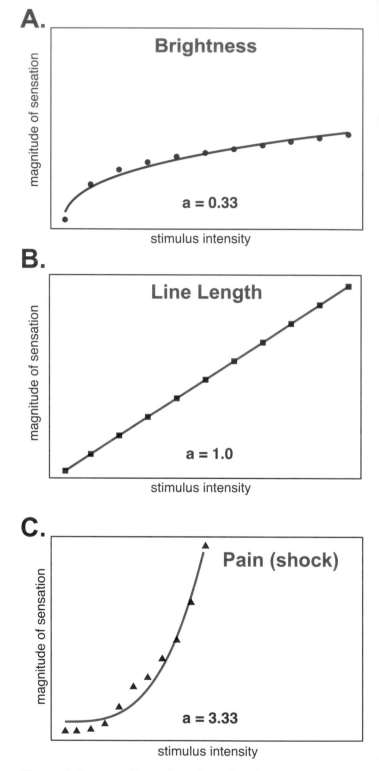

Figure 1. Stevens' Law functions for three sensory modalities.

226

1) An experiment is conducted in which individuals are asked to judge the saltiness of several foods. Which of the statements best characterizes the following data?

Sodium content (mg)	Related "saltiness"
0	1
100	10
200	19
300	25
400	32
600	36

A. The data support Weber's law; the JND is a linear constant.

B. The data support Stevens' law; the psychophysical relationship is an exponential function.

C. Both Weber's law and Stevens' law have equal utility because both accurately depict the data.

D. Neither law holds; psychophysics focuses primarily on stimuli at the limits of human perception.

2) At a concert you notice that the third movement was played louder than the second movement, which was played louder than the first. This phenomenon most closely aligns with which psychophysical theory?

A. Weber's law because you are detecting the difference (JND) in loudness rather than the absolute magnitude.

B. Weber's law because the JND is a relative constant between the loudness in the music.

C. Stevens' law because you can quantify the relative difference in loudness.

D. Stevens' law because the relationship between the movements is non-linear.

3) Stevens used a technique in which the individual was asked to assign an intensity value to each stimulus. Weber simply had people judge two stimuli as same/different. Which of the following statements best describes the relationships between Weber's and Stevens' law?

A. Stevens findings invalidate Weber because the two equations make opposite predictions about the relationships between stimuli and perception.

B. Stevens' law is more general than Weber's law; it more accurately describes psychophysical relationships across a broader range of sensory phenomena.

C. Stevens' and Weber's measurement techniques are sufficiently different to prevent direct comparison.

D. Both laws are equally accurate; human sensory and judgment systems operate differently depending on the manner in which the stimuli are presented.

4) What is the most important distinction between $k = \Delta i / i$ and $SI = ki^a$?

A. The interpretation of i is different, which renders the formulae incomparable.

B. Stevens' law is a power function, which characterizes non-linear relationships between stimulus intensity and subjective perception.

C. Stevens' law is limited; it cannot account for JNDs.

D. Weber's law better characterizes psychophysical relationships at low intensity (dim lights, light weights); Stevens' law better characterizes psychophysical relationships at high intensities.

5) Weber's law suggests the following:

A. Individuals become systematically less sensitive to changes in stimulus intensity as the intensity increases.

B. Detection thresholds change exponentially with stimulus intensity.

C. Both A and B.

D. None of the above.

Psychophysics

Annotations.
1) B 2) A 3) B 4) B 5) A

	Foundation 6: Psychophys.-A		Foundation 7: Individual Diffs.-A		
	A		A		
Concepts	3		5		
Reasoning	4				
Research	2				
Data	1				

Big Picture. Sensation and perception, or how humans perceive and assimilate their external environment, is a fundamental domain in the behavioral sciences. This will likely be a featured topic on the MCAT. Historically, it was the first area in which psychologists attempted to create systems for quantifying subjective experience (termed psychophysics). Content in this area may include data (tables or figures) in which one factor (F1) is a physical stimulus varied along some dimension (e.g. brightness, loudness, length), and the other factor (F2) is an individual's (or group average) subjective perception of that stimulus. Psychophysics is about as quantitative as the behavioral sciences get, and passage questions may include equations describing the relationship between F1 and F2. While you were given equations in this passage, they did not require complex mathematical derivations beyond linear or simple non-linear functions with a single free parameter. This passage focused on understanding and contrasting two leading quantitative theories in psychophysics. Mastery of the questions requires recognizing the shape of functions based on tabular data, knowing what each theory predicts, and understanding the limitations of each.

1) B. The data support Stevens' law; the psychophysical relationship is an exponential function. The table provides information that allows you to visualize, or quickly graph, the relationship between salt content and subjective perception of saltiness. At lower sodium levels the relationship appears linear, but begins to decelerate (flatten) as the sodium content increases. This is a classic power (exponential) function. In the passage, recall the following equation:

$$\text{Subjective Intensity (SI)} = ki^a$$

This is a power function (the exponent is a dead giveaway). Therefore, **choice B is the credited answer.** Choice C is tempting but still incorrect. It is indeed accurate that both Weber's law and Steven's law predict subjective intensity increases with stimulus intensity. However, **choice C is not the credited answer** because the two theories do not have equal utility in describing the data in the Table. Steven's law fits the data better than Weber's law, which would predict a linear relationship. **Choice A is not the credited answer** because the data do not describe a linear function, which you should quickly deduce from the table or by plotting the data. (It may be useful to graph data by hand from tables or equations to help visualize functions and relationships. While you do not have the ability to create a computer-based graph, you should consider a scratch paper version as shown in Figure 2 below).

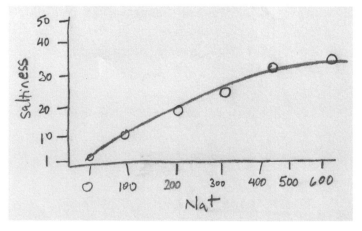

Figure 2. Sketched figure of the Table 1 data.

Choice D should be eliminated quickly. The definition provided in the passage states that psychophysics examines a range of stimulus intensities and modalities, not just the limits of human perception.

2) **A. Weber's law because you are detecting the difference (JND) in loudness rather than absolute magnitude. Choice A is credited** because the question provides no quantitative information about the magnitude of the stimulus intensity, only that each successive movement is louder. **Choices B, C, and D are not credited** because they all require information about the absolute value of the signal (loudness). Therefore, for choices B, C, and D, you do not have enough information to justify these answers. Choices B, C, and D could only be (potentially) credited if you were given actual stimulus values.

3) **B. Stevens' law is more general than Weber's law; it more accurately describes psychophysical relationships across a broader range of sensory phenomena.** The last sentence of the passage and Figure 1 both indicate that Steven's law is robust in depicting perception across a range of sensory modalities (pain, brightness, length). This provides sufficient information to conclude that **choice B is the credited answer**. From the passage and the other questions, it is clear that both Stevens and Weber make similar predictions — only the form of the psychophysical functions differ. The difference between Weber's linear predictions and Stevens' power function can be subtle, depending on the sensory modalities and the stimulus properties. Indeed, in the middle panel of Figure 1, the exponent in Stevens' equation = 1 and the Weber's and Stevens' make identical predictions. As a result, both **choices A and C are not credited answers**. Unlike choices A and C, choice D asks you to make more subtle distinctions. The first part of the question provides adequate information to **eliminate choice D** because the last paragraph of the passage and question 1 both suggest that Stevens' law is accurate across a broader range of situations.

4) **B. Stevens' law is a power function, which characterizes non-linear relationships between stimulus intensity and subjective perception.** The second paragraph of the passage, Figure 1, and question 1 all indicate that Stevens' law is a power function. This is important because the exponent can vary depending on the sensory modality and the stimulus being perceived (i.e. Figure 1). By comparison, fitting a straight line through the data in all 3 panels of the figure will produce a less accurate account of the data. Therefore, the non-linear power function is better, making **choice B the credited answer**. The term *i* represents stimulus intensity in both equations, making **choice A incorrect**. Choice C is the most straightforward to eliminate based on the last sentence of the passage and Figure 1. Stevens' law is more robust, not more limited; thus **choice C is not credited**. There is no information in the passage regarding the manner in which Weber's law characterizes stimuli at low intensities. Because it predicts a linear relationship, the intensity of the stimulus is not important. Additionally, Figure 1 provides no suggestion that Stevens' Law fits the data better at the high end of the spectrum relative to the low end. For these reasons, **choice D is not credited**.

5) **A. Individuals become systematically less sensitive to changes in stimulus intensity as the intensity increases.** The key to identifying that the **correct choice is A** is to recognize that it describes the fundamental component of the JND. For example, if the JND is 10% for loudness then:

10 db = 1 db

20 db = 2 db, and …

100 db = 10 db.

As the absolute value of the stimulus becomes louder, one becomes less sensitive to changes in that stimulus. In other words, if your music volume is at level 1, you will detect a change of +1 to level 2, but will be unlikely to detect a change of +1 if the volume moves from level 9 to level 10. Because Weber's law predicts a linear function, it is not compatible with the prediction that thresholds change exponentially (that is Stevens' law), so **choice B is not credited**, and it follows logically that **choices C and D are also not credited**.

6

7

Cochlear Implants

A common cause of hearing deficit is sensori-neural dysfunction. Especially prevalent is the loss or absence of transducer hair cells located in the outer ear at birth, which results in irreversible hearing loss and the subsequent absence of language acquisition. Cochlear implant devices, when introduced during childhood, are able to facilitate functional hearing and improve receptive/expressive language development. The device includes an external antenna and microphone, and an internal receiver and receiver-stimulator (electrode array). The internal stimulator extends into the cochlea, circumventing the transducer/hair cells and activating auditory nerve fibers.

Considerable research has been conducted on the optimal patient age of cochlear device implantation and its subsequent impact on children's receptive and expressive language. Experts commonly analyze multiple studies, either through comprehensive review or a process called "meta-analysis," when sufficient data have been gathered on that device. Figure 1 outlines a review of outcomes from multiple cochlear-implant studies focusing on receptive and expressive language skills as a function of age of implant. A second review of multiple studies tracked language development trajectories in children who received cochlear implants at different age levels. The results of this review are summarized in Figure 2.

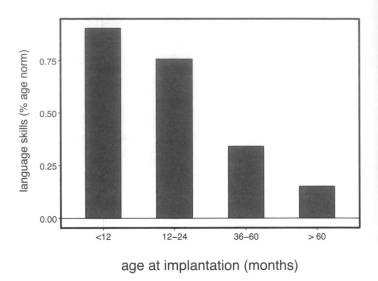

Figure 1. Combined measure of receptive and expressive language skills (expressed as a proportion of normed age standards) based on four age groups of cochlear implantation.

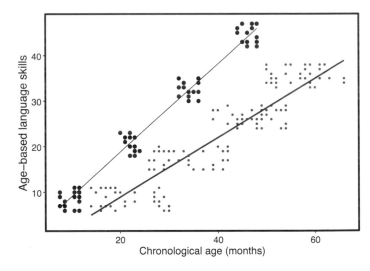

Figure 2. Growth rate of language skills for children receiving cochlear implants before 12 months (black circles) and later than 12 months (blue circles). Data were obtained at baseline and then annually.

1) **Based on both figures, which of the following statements is most accurate?**

   A. Cochlear implant devices are ineffective in patients older than 12 months.

   B. There is a critical period for auditory and language development that peaks before 12 months and declines rapidly near 36-60 months.

   C. The rate of acquisition of language and hearing skills is roughly equivalent for children implanted before and after the age of 12 months.

   D. For children implanted after 12 months, the proportion that acquired age-equivalent language skills was < 0.25.

2) **Which factor is most likely responsible for the age-related success of cochlear implants?**

   A. Greater duration and volume of language training.

   B. Increased exposure to spoken language by parents and trained professionals.

   C. Neural plasticity in the auditory cortex of the developing brain.

   D. Decreased risk for device rejection with increased age.

3) **Under which condition is cochlear implantation least likely to improve hearing and language development?**

   A. A developmental disorder such as autism.

   B. Deformities in the outer ear canal.

   C. Structural pathology in the occipital lobe.

   D. Structural pathology in the temporal lobe.

4) **Bilateral implantation typically produces superior outcomes relative to unilateral implantation because it:**

   A. enables critical hearing features such as source location and separation of speech sounds from background noise.

   B. produces better hemispheric symmetry in the structure of the frontal cortex.

   C. creates abnormal development of neural language centers because language is largely processed in the right hemisphere.

   D. facilitates the transfer of information across the corpus callosum, producing more normalized cortical volumes.

5) **Cochlear implants work because they:**

   A. stimulate the function of the remaining cochlear hair cells.

   B. amplify sound in the tympanic membrane and outer ear.

   C. promote the growth and development of all the major components of the auditory system.

   D. renew stimulation of the auditory nerve, enabling transmission to the auditory cortex.

6) **Which factors would most likely compromise the results shown in the figures?**

       I. Family socioeconomic status
       II. Pre-implant hearing ability
       III. Child birth weight
       IV. Gender

   A. I, III

   B. II, IV

   C. I, II

   D. III, IV

6

7

Cochlear Implants

Annotations.
1) B   2) C   3) D   4) A   5) D   6) C

	Foundation 6: Psychophys.-A Cognition-B			Foundation 7: Individual Diffs.-A		
	A	**B**		**A**		
Concepts	5			3		
Reasoning	4			2		
Research		6				
Data		1				

Big Picture. This passage reflects common areas of emphasis on the MCAT. One is the application of fundamental biological knowledge to the understanding of disease processes. Another is the comprehension of data-based figures and tables. The first paragraph of the passage explains the biomechanics of cochlear implants. A good strategy here would have been to highlight several key terms (e.g. loss of transducer hair cells in outer ear). Underscoring the importance of paragraph 1, some of the questions required that you understand the cochlear implant system. The second paragraph presents data from review studies (i.e. articles that summarize results from multiple studies), and requires you to interpret the data presented in the figures. The most challenging questions in this passage are those that require you to integrate details of the device function (first paragraph) with the implications of the data patterns in the Figures 1 and 2. This level of mastery is a critical skill not just for success on the MCAT, but success in medical school and beyond. Therefore, we as well as the AAMC would like to see aspiring medical students perform well on these types of questions. The three most critical concepts in this passage are: (1) cochlear implants bypass missing transducer hairs and directly stimulate the auditory nerve; (2) implantation is most successful in children < 12 months old; and (3) language development and processing is centered in the auditory cortex of the temporal lobe.

1) **B. There is a critical period for auditory and language development that peaks before 12 months and declines rapidly near 36-60 months.** Figure 1 shows the group differences based on age of implantation. In addition, figure 2 shows differences in the rates of change in language skills for individuals over time (y-axis) as a function of implant ages (x-axis). You can deduce from both figures (as shown below in **Fig. 3**) that hearing and language outcomes are best when the cochlear implant surgery is performed by 12 months of age, and far less effective after 36 months. Thus, **choice B is the correct answer**. The positive slopes in Figure 2 reveal that <u>all</u> children benefit from cochlear implants, albeit at different rates. Therefore, **choice A is not correct**. Moreover, notice the slopes in Figure 2 are different, indicating that rates of improvement are unequal based upon age of implantation. This effectively **eliminates choice C**. By carefully examining Figure 1, you should note that age-related skills are > 0.25 for all groups except those implanted after 36 (but not 12) months. However, answer choice D states: "…<u>for children implanted after 12 months</u>…" which includes the two middle groups (both > 0.25) – making **choice D incorrect**.

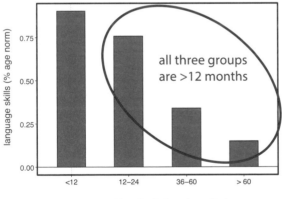

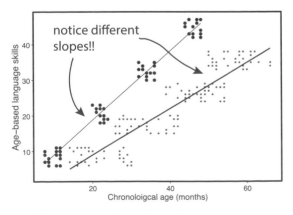

Figure 3. Interpretation of graphs.

2) **C. Neural plasticity in the auditory cortex of the developing brain.** This question requires reasoning skills and a strong background in developmental neurobiology. Choice C may therefore not be immediately recognizable as the best choice. However, Figure 2 reveals that even after equivalent time periods have elapsed (i.e. 12-month time intervals), children implanted by 12 months of age have better language skills at each time interval. Accordingly, you can **eliminate choice A** because the same amount of time has passed and thus equal durations of language training could have occurred in both groups. By the same reasoning, choice B is also not credited, as the amount of post-implant spoken-language exposure would be equivalent between the earlier-implant and later-implant children. There is no information in the passage regarding implant rejection rates, so there is **no basis for selecting choice D**. Recall from previous biology and neuroscience training that the brain goes through the greatest period of neuronal growth in the first year of life. It necessarily follows that a younger brain will be more adaptive (i.e. plasticity) than an older brain. The validity of this information, combined with the elimination of choices A, B, and D, support **choice C as the credited answer**.

3) **D. Structural pathology in the temporal lobe.** To attain credit for question 3 you were required to understand two key points: (1) that cochlear implants enable hearing and language development via bypassing the transducer hair cells and stimulating the auditory nerve in the middle ear; and (2) that language processing is centered in the auditory cortex located in the temporal lobe. **Choice D is the credited answer** because structural pathology within the temporal lobe would likely affect the auditory cortex, thereby directly impacting processing of not just language but all sound. Developmental disorders like autism do feature altered brain and language development, but such disorders are not necessarily specific to the temporal lobe or auditory cortex (most people with autism have normal hearing). The cochlear implant should in principle improve hearing and language in those with autism by the same <u>relative</u> amount as a non-autistic child. This mechanism of action on the auditory nerve and subsequent development of language centers in the temporal lobe should still transpire. For this reason **choice A**

is not the credited answer. As described in the first paragraph, the internal stimulator of the cochlear implant circumvents the sound wave transduction in the <u>outer ear</u>. Since the outer ear is bypassed via the device function, **choice B is not the credited answer**. Finally, the occipital cortex – located in the posterior region of your skull – primarily subserves the processing of visual rather than auditory information. Therefore, **choice C is not the credited answer**.

4) **A. enables critical hearing features such as source location and separation of speech sounds from background noise.** The answer choices in this question contain quite a bit of technical jargon related to brain structure and function. However, you do not need to understand all of the jargon to identify the credited answer. Instead, you could examine the passage content and use deductive reasoning. Human auditory and visual systems rely on processing of multiple information sources to create a "map" of the auditory or visual input. This allows us to "see" the world in three dimensions and locate the source of individual stimuli (like the sound of your friend's voice in a noisy, crowded room). People who only have vision in one eye or hearing in one ear have visual or auditory deficiencies. Utilizing auditory input from both ears enables normal hearing and language, making **choice A the credited answer**.

You may not know if hemispheric symmetry is important in language and hearing, but you should recognize that the auditory cortex is in the temporal (not frontal) lobe. Additionally, there is nothing in the passage to suggest hemispheric symmetry plays a key role. For these reasons, **choice B is not the credited answer**. No information is provided to suggest that unilateral implantation would lead to abnormal development. Perhaps more straight-forward, the language center in the auditory lobe is situated in the left (not right) hemisphere. For these reasons, **choice C is wrong**. As an aside, children with damage to the language center in the left hemisphere often compensate by shifting this function to the temporal lobe in the right hemisphere. This phenomenon is exemplary of primate neural plasticity. **Choice D is not credited** because nothing in the passage indicates that brain volumes and information transfer across the corpus callosum are important to hearing or language processing.

6

7

5) D. renew stimulation of the auditory nerve, enabling transmission to the auditory cortex. This question is the most straightforward to answer correctly because the necessary information was housed in the first paragraph. It describes the cochlear implant device, highlighting the fact that it bypasses the damaged transducer hair cells of the outer ear and stimulates the auditory nerve located the middle ear. Therefore, **choice D is the correct answer**. Since the other three answer choices all refer to the outer ear – either directly in the case of choices A and B or indirectly in the case of choice C – **choices A, B, and C are all incorrect**.

6) C. I, II. Various factors can compromise research outcomes when they affect the dependent variable (i.e. language skills in Figures 1 and 2). Often, these are factors that co-vary with the independent variable of interest. The independent variable of interest in Figures 1 and 2 is age of cochlear implant. **The first item you should eliminate is gender (IV)**, which should not interact with age of implantation or have any effect on language development. If you eliminate gender, you can **eliminate choices B and D**. From there, utilize a process of elimination test-taking strategy and inspect the remaining two choices. Notice that Statement I is common to both answer choices therefore you do not need to determine its validity to receive credit. Rather, you needed to focus on whether statement II or III is accurate. It should be apparent that hearing ability before implant will be related to hearing ability (and language skills) after the implant. Thus, statement II is accurate making **choice C the credited answer**. While not essential to finding the credited answer, you may also deduce that parents from a higher socioeconomic class will have more available resources to devote to their child's language training and hearing therapy than those from a lower socioeconomic class. Even though from a test-taking strategy standpoint you didn't need to know this; you can also **identify statement I as a valid choice**.

6

7

PATHWAY

Taste Perception

Taste is processed in the gustatory cortex, which synapses with sensory axons running through the chora tympanii and cranial nerves VII-X. The majority of peripheral taste cells (called fungiform papillae) are found on the anterior surface of the tongue. Individual differences in taste perception, particularly the sensation of bitterness, are linked to the genes TASR1 and TAS2R38, both located on chromosome 7. Based on familial studies, it was concluded that allelic differences characterize individuals classified as being a "taster," "non-taster," or "super-taster." Two experiments were conducted to examine taste sensitivity in the population.

Experiment 1. Scientists used a test compound (PROP), which has a range of taste perceptions from bitter to tasteless, to measure taste sensitivity in individuals. Following the experiment, individuals were genotyped for their allelic distribution for TASR1 (**Fig. 1**).

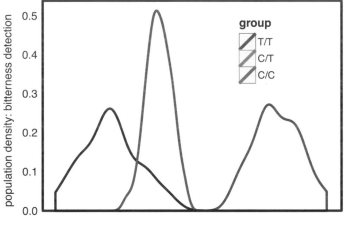

Figure 1. Relative frequency in the population of ratings of bitterness (y-axis) across a broad range PROP concentrations (.0032 - .32 nM, moving low to high on the x-axis), separated into 3 groups based on genotype. Group designations in the legend refer to allelic variations.

Experiment 2. Scientists tested three groups of individuals separated based on differential expression of the TAS2R38 gene. The experiment used two levels of PROP (low versus high) as well as NaCl and caffeine to assess differences in taste perception (**Table 1**).

Table 1. Percentage of people within each group that could taste the compound.

	NaCl	PROP-L	PROP-H	Caffeine
Group 1	17	5	45	50
Group 2	25	50	90	60
Group 3	7	0	0	40

1) Which of the following would likely be observed in supertasters?

A. The largest number of fungiform papillae.

B. The greatest density of sensory nerve fibers in the chorda tympanii.

C. The largest volume in the gustatory cortex.

D. All of the above.

2) In Table 1, why might scientists choose to include NaCl in the measurement ratings?

A. As a control or standard to scale the bitterness of PROP relative to perceived sweetness across individuals with different subjective ratings.

B. As a control or standard to scale the bitterness of PROP relative to perceived saltiness across individuals with different subjective ratings.

C. In order to discriminate tasters from supertasters, using the ratio of NaCl·PROP ratings.

D. Both A and C.

3) What is the most likely pairing of taste group (Grp) in Table 1 and allele group in Figure 1?

A. Grp 1 and C/T; Grp 2 and T/T; Grp 3 and C/C

B. Grp 1 and C/C; Grp 2 and T/T; Grp 3 and C/T

C. Grp 1 and T/T; Grp 2 and C/T; Grp 3 and C/C

D. Grp 1 and T/T; Grp 2 and C/C; Grp 3 and C/T

4) What conclusion can be made based upon the data in Figure 1?

A. PROP thresholds are predictive in classifying individuals who are homozygous or heterozygous for the dominant taste allele.

B. PROP tasting results from both functional and non-functional polymorphisms on chromosome 7.

C. PROP tasting is an incompletely dominant trait.

D. PROP tasting is a co-dominant trait.

5) Based on the data in Figure 1 and Table 1, which group and allelic trait is most likely the supertasters?

A. Group 1, C/T

B. Group 2, T/T

C. Group 3, C/C

D. None of these combinations

6) Supertasters not only have the most intense taste sensations, they also perceive more intense oral pain to aversive stimuli such as capsaicin derived from chili peppers. What is the most likely reason for this phenomenon?

A. An acquired sensitivity to oral/gustatory stimuli.

B. Greater density of taste receptors and sensory nerves in the mouth and tongue.

C. An association between the genes that mediate taste perception and pain perception.

D. A heightened sensitivity to the perception of stimuli across all sensory modalities in supertasters.

6

7

Taste Perception

Annotations.
1) D 2) B 3) A 4) C 5) B 6) B

	Foundation 6: Psychophys.-A			Foundation 7: Individual Diffs.-A		
	A			**A**		
Concepts				4		
Reasoning	1,6					
Research	2					
Data	3			5		

Big Picture. This passage covers material from Foundation 6A, psychophysics. Specifically, it is focused on the sensation and perception of taste. It also covers content in Foundation 7, individual differences, in the context of behavioral genetics. Success on this passage will require the following skills: content knowledge about psychophysics; basic principles in genetics; interpretation of graphs and tables; and reasoning based on the data presented in the figure and table. Figure 1 presents a relative frequency distribution in a population (in this case the human species). No matter how they are presented (lines, bars, etc.), relative frequency graphs will always total to 1.0 (100% of the sampled or total population). Understanding distributional graphs, e.g. histograms and frequency plots (sometimes called 'density plots'), is important in both the behavioral sciences and genetics. While not in the present set of questions, characteristics of normal (e.g. "bell-shaped" or "Gaussian") distributions should be a part of your preparation for the behavioral sciences section. This includes the percentages and standard deviation units of the population that fall along given points in a normal distribution.

1) **D. All of the above.** The first two sentences of the passage indicate that taste (e.g. processing of gustatory stimuli) is facilitated by fungiform papillae (choice A), sensory nerve fibers in the chorda tympanii (choice B), and the gustatory cortex (choice C). Since the choices all refer to having <u>more</u> anatomical resources for taste processing (e.g. number, density, volume), it can be concluded via deductive reasoning that **choices A, B, and C are all correct**.

2) **B. As a control or standard to scale the bitterness of PROP relative to perceived saltiness across individuals with different subjective ratings.** The most efficient way to arrive at the correct answer to this question is through the process of elimination. The first step requires recognition that NaCl is common table salt. While, it might be experimentally advantageous to pair PROP (bitter) with sugar (sweet) because they are on opposite ends of the taste spectrum, this pairing of bitter to sweet in these answer choices was included as a distractor. Because PROP is bitter and NaCl is salty (not sweet), **choices A and D can be quickly eliminated**. Next, notice in Table 1 that trends for taste detection move in the same direction for both NaCl and PROP. In other words, supertasters are more sensitive to <u>both</u> PROP and NaCl, thus the ratio of NaCl to PROP offers no measurement advantage (and indeed the ratio of 7:0 would cause measurement problems). Accordingly, **choice C can be eliminated**. Once A, D, and C have been eliminated, by default the **correct answer is choice B**.

3) **A. Grp 1 and C/T; Grp 2 and T/T; Grp 3 and C/C.** From Table 1, it is clear that Group 2 is the most sensitive to PROP, which – per the passage – makes that group likely to be the supertasters. Logically, then, Group 3 are the "non-tasters" (0 bitterness rating to PROP). To correctly match the groups to the correct alleles subsequently requires understanding distributions along the x-axis in Figure 1. The lowest concentration of PROP is on the leftmost part of the x-axis (this is noted in the figure caption, and most scientific graphs are scaled from low to high on the x-axis). Therefore, the T/T allele group (red), clustered toward the left portion of the x-axis indicating sensitivity to the smallest PROP concentration, is likely to include the "supertasters," matching the T/T allele to Group 2. This makes

choices **C and D incorrect**, because T/T is not matched to Group 2. Since the C/C allele group clusters on the opposite end of the scale, they are the least sensitive and most likely to include the "non-tasters," matching the C/C allele to Group 3. It is only necessary to match T/T to Group 2 and C/C to Group 3 to then identify **choice A as the correct answer**.

4) **C. PROP tasting is an incomplete dominant.** The passage does not describe the exact nature of which allele of TASR1 is dominant or recessive. However, this was not required to determine the answer; the data in Figure 1 was sufficient. If the T and C alleles are dominant and recessive in the classical Mendelian sense, you would predict only two possible phenotypes: super-taster or non-taster. If this were indeed true, then the heterozygous genotype (i.e. T/C) would look identical to the homozygous dominant phenotype (i.e. T/T). Graphically this would look like Figure 2.

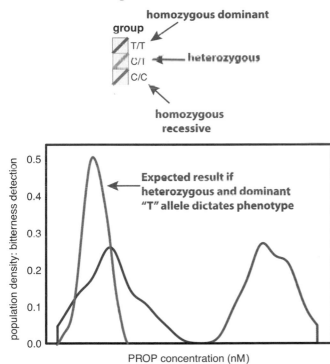

Figure 2. Predicted results in alleles are classically dominant and recessive.

As the results shown in Figure 2 are not in agreement with those in Figure 1, there must be an additional genetic caveat in play. Recall from Mendelian genetics that incomplete dominance is an intermediate form where one allele (for a given trait) is not completely dominant over another allele. The

result is a mixed phenotype that is a combination of the dominant and recessive phenotypes. This makes **choice C the correct answer**, because of the overlap in taste perception phenotypes between the T/T and C/T alleles. **Choice A is incorrect** for the same reason: PROP thresholds are not predictive for classifying alleles as there is significant overlap in T/T and C/T. **Choice B is incorrect** because, while the passage notes that genes for taste perception are located on chromosome 7, no information is provided about functional and non-functional polymorphisms. **Choice D is incorrect** because co-dominance is not consistent with the distributions shown in Figure 1. In co-dominance, both alleles are expressed completely and contribute equally to the phenotype (e.g. being AB blood type). It would not be possible to express a phenotype that is both highly sensitive and non-sensitive to PROP (i.e. for someone to be both a "supertaster" and a "non-taster").

5) **B. Group 2, T/T.** Similar to question 3, you can deduce that **choice B is correct** because Group 2 is most sensitive to PROP given the high ratings, and the T/T allele group is most sensitive to PROP given the frequency distribution clustered at the lowest PROP concentrations. This immediately **eliminates choice D**. Table 2 shows that Group 3 has bitterness ratings of 0 ("non-tasters"), making **choice C incorrect**. Because Group 1 has lower ratings than Group 2 and the C/T allele is shifted rightward relative to T/T, **choice A is incorrect**.

6) **B. Greater density of taste receptors and sensory nerves in the mouth and tongue.** This question is potentially difficult because each of the answer choices offers a plausible explanation, so it is not easy to immediately dismiss one or two answer choices. **Choice A is not credited** and is the least convincing because it suggests an acquired/learned phenomenon, despite most of the passage being focused on genetically-controlled differences in taste perception. **Choice B is the credited answer** because it directly follows from information in the passage's first paragraph, related to physiological factors that control taste perception. **Choices C and D are not the credited answer**; while they offer reasonable (testable) hypotheses, neither is discussed in the passage. Therefore, there is not sufficient information to justify answer choices C or D.

Antisaccades and Schizophrenia

The visual system is a highly sensitive marker of CNS diseases in neurology and psychiatry. A fundamental process of the visual system is the saccade, a rapid movement of the eyes from one point to another. An antisaccade, in contrast, requires an individual to look away from, rather than toward, a stimulus (e.g. if the stimulus is on the left, then look right). The antisaccade requires cognitive control over the reflex to look at something when it when it enters the field of view. Saccades are controlled by interconnected neural circuits, including the frontal and supplementary eye fields, prefrontal cortex, superior colliculus, anterior cingulate, and striatum. A successful antisaccade requires inhibiting neural activation in the frontal eye fields and superior colliculus. Inhibiting these regions is enabled by activating the supplementary eye fields and prefrontal cortex.

Patients with schizophrenia have difficulty performing antisaccades. Figure 1 summarizes collective results from three experiments that used functional magnetic resonance imaging (fMRI) to examine the neural correlates of antisaccade performance in schizophrenia. Red and yellow highlighted areas show regions in which schizophrenic patients had different patterns of blood-oxygen level dependent (BOLD) activation compared to controls. The fMRI analyses contrasted trials entailing antisaccade errors with trials entailing successful antisaccades.

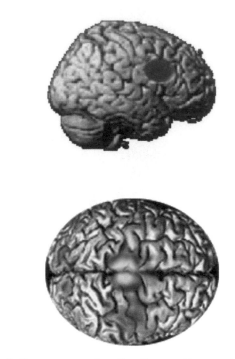

Figure 1. Summary of activation patterns showing BOLD activation differences between schizophrenic and control subjects during antisaccade testing. Top: sagittal view. Bottom: axial view.

1) **Which conclusion is supported by the data shown in Figure 1?**

   A. There were few differences in the brains of schizophrenic patients and controls during saccadic movements.

   B. Differences in activation in prefrontal cortex and supplemental eye fields are consistent with neuroscientific evidence on antisaccades.

   C. Difference in activation in occipital cortex and superior colliculus are consistent with neuro-scientific evidence on antisaccades.

   D. Differences in activation in posterior cingulate and temporal cortex are inconsistent with neuro-scientific evidence on antisaccades.

2) **Suppose, based on Figure 1, scientists claim to have discovered a biological diagnosis for schizophrenia based on neural activity during antisaccade performance. Which of the following statements best represents the validity of this claim?**

   A. The claim is valid. Many studies found similar results in schizophrenic patients.

   B. The claim is valid. Biologically-based diagnoses are, *prima facie,* superior to clinical, symptom-based diagnoses.

   C. The claim is not valid. Data from three experiments is not sufficient evidence upon to which to base a medical diagnosis.

   D. The claim is not valid. The areas of neural activation are inconsistent with evidence on brain regions controlling the visual system, making a claim of a biological diagnosis implausible.

3) **Which of the following statements most accurately describes the results in Figure 1?**

   A. Less BOLD activation suggests less neuronal firing in these areas, because neurons recruit oxygenated blood required to generate action potentials.

   B. Less BOLD activation suggests abnormal brain structure in schizophrenia, because neuronal activation patterns were different than control subjects.

   C. Less BOLD activation is more difficult to interpret than greater BOLD activation, because less activation suggests a larger ratio of deoxygenated blood in the key brain regions.

   D. Less BOLD activation introduces measurement problems; since oxygenated blood is paramagnetic, less regional BOLD activation could be a result of low hemoglobin.

4) **Similar antisaccade deficits have been observed in patients with Alzheimer's disease, Parkinson's disease, and traumatic brain injury. Based on this link, which of the following conclusion(s) have experts most likely drawn?**

   A. Antisaccade deficits point to a common genetic liability for CNS disease.

   B. Antisaccade deficits point to a common biological marker of deficient cortical control over more reflexive action processes.

   C. Both A and B.

   D. None of the above.

5) **Which of the following poses the greatest threat to the scientific validity of the results in Figure 1?**

   A. Use of different methods to measure antisac-cades across the three experiments.

   B. Use of different fMRI techniques to measure brain activation across the three experiments.

   C. Significant differences in age between the schizo-phrenic and control subjects.

   D. All of the above.

Antisaccades and Schizophrenia

Annotations.
1) B   2) C   3) A   4) B   5) D

	Foundation 6: Psychophys.-A Cognition-B			Foundation 7: Individual Diffs.-A		
	A	**B**		**A**		
Concepts				3		
Reasoning		2		4		
Research				5		
Data	1					

Big Picture. Neuroscience will be an important component of the behavioral sciences section of the MCAT. You should be able to distinguish different brain regions and their respective functions. Further, you should have an understanding of the techniques used to measure brain functions; such as functional magnetic resonance imaging (fMRI). Many students encounter fMRI in basic neuroscience or cognitive psychology. In this passage, you were provided information about the circuitry that governs saccadic movements, and were required to integrate that information with the fMRI data in Figure 1 to answer questions about brain locations and functions.

Additional questions probed (1) understanding of research design, and (2) reasoning about the implications of brain function as it relates to psychiatric and neurological disease. The behavioral sciences section is likely to cover the major psychiatric diseases; you should be familiar with schizophrenia, mood disorders, anxiety, etc. Question 5 focused on factors that can undermine experimental validity in the behavioral sciences such as non-matching experimental groups and differences in techniques across experiments. The passage covers Foundations 6A, 6B and 7A in a manner that links brain function and cognition. You should study those domains, as MCAT questions may require their integration.

1) B. Differences in activation in prefrontal cortex and supplemental eye fields are consistent with neuroscientific evidence on antisaccades. This question has two key features: (1) Information in the passage that antisaccades are facilitated through activation of prefrontal cortex and supplemental eye fields. This information is located in the last sentence of the first paragraph. (2) Location of key brain regions from the fMRI images provided in Figure 1, which highlights prefrontal cortex (top image) and supplemental eye fields (bottom image). Figure 2 (below) provides specifics regarding these brain regions. **Choice B is correct** because it includes the prefrontal cortex and supplemental eye fields. In theory, you could identify the correct answer by examining either the information in the passage or Figure 1. However, to be certain, it is important to both draw from the information provided in the passage and verify it based on the locations of activation in Figure 1. You might be tempted to select choice C, because it mentions occipital cortex (which facilitates processing of visual information as it enters the brain via the optical nerves) and the superior colliculus (which facilitate saccades). However, **choice C is**

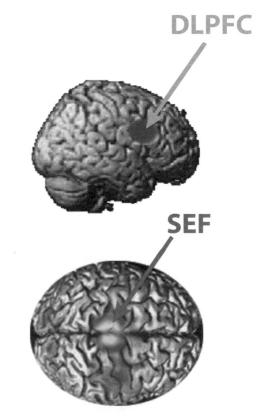

Figure 2. Specification of the locations of the dorsolateral prefrontal cortex (DLPFC, top) and supplementary eye fields (SEF, bottom) shown in Figure 1.

incorrect because the occipital cortex is in the posterior (e.g. back) lobe of the brain, and the superior colliculus is located deep in the mid-brain. Similarly, **choice D is incorrect** because the temporal cortex (temporal lobe) and posterior cingulate not are located in the areas of activation highlighted in Figure 1. The temporal cortex is located toward the back of the brain, just anterior to the occipital cortex. The anterior cingulate is part of the limbic lobe, a deeper brain structure than the prefrontal cortex or supplementary eye fields. **Choice A is incorrect**, as it is simply inconsistent with the content of the passage and the fMRI data in Figure 1.

2) **C. The claim is not valid. Data from three experiments is not sufficient evidence upon to which to base a medical diagnosis.** This question assesses the ability to reason about research findings and conclusions that can be drawn from the data. For a disease as complex as schizophrenia – for which biological etiologies and diagnoses have long been sought – three experiments does not constitute a valid database from which to conclude a biological diagnosis can be made. It follows that **choice C is the correct answer**. Once you have discerned that it would not only be rash, but medically unethical, to base a diagnosis on three studies, you can eliminate **choices A and B as incorrect**. Regarding choice B, it may be valid in principle to conclude that biological diagnoses are more accurate and useful than symptom-based diagnoses (particularly since many diseases have similar symptom presentation). However, this holds only when biologically-based diagnoses provide increased diagnostic and treatment accuracy. In the behavioral sciences, biological etiologies are mostly incomplete, and only symptom-based diagnoses are currently considered valid in psychiatry. For many behavioral scientists, biological diagnoses of mental disorders are a major goal. **Choice D is incorrect**: returning to the passage and Figure 1, the areas of neural activation are indeed perfectly consistent with evidence on brain regions controlling the visual system, and antisaccades in particular.

3) **A. Less BOLD activation suggests less neuronal firing in these areas, because neurons recruit oxygenated blood required for energy needed to generate action potentials.** To answer this question, it is necessary to understand the basic concepts behind functional magnetic resonance imaging (fMRI), including blood-oxygen-level-dependent (BOLD) contrast analyses. Unlike other cells, neurons do not utilize energy from internal stores of glucose and oxygen. To generate an action potential, energy must be recruited quickly into the neuron. Oxygenated blood releases oxygen to active neurons via the hemodynamic response; and does so at a greater rate than inactive neurons. Oxygenated blood has a greater concentration of iron than deoxygenated blood (thus the root "hemo" from the metallic "hemoproteins"). This causes a difference in magnetic susceptibility between oxygenated and deoxygenated blood. This difference is exploited to interpret brain activity in fMRI using a high strength magnet. It follows that less BOLD activation in a given region means relatively less recruitment of oxygen to that brain region. **Choice A is correct** because it is the most consistent with the above information. **Choice B is incorrect** because it refers to "abnormal brain structure," and fMRI provides information about BOLD activation, not brain structure. **Choice C is incorrect** because fMRI provides information about the relative contrast of BOLD activity, thus lesser activation and greater activation are equally measurable. **Choice D is incorrect** because less BOLD activation is not a measurement problem, per se. While low hemoglobin can introduce measurement problems in fMRI, recall that the BOLD measurement is a relative contrast in recruitment of oxygenated blood to specific regions. Low hemoglobin would not necessarily produce less activation in a specific region during performance on an fMRI task such as an antisaccade. More likely, it would create problems in the signal to noise ratio across the whole brain due to low magnetism of the blood.

6

7

4) **B. Antisaccade deficits point to a common biological marker of deficient cortical control over more reflexive action processes.** In this reasoning-based question, you can use test-taking strategy to eliminate answer choices. Simply because antisaccades are a common biological marker across diseases, it does not follow that they share a common genetic liability. For example, traumatic brain injury results from an external force to the head (e.g. head to the windshield during a car crash) sufficient to damage the underlying tissues; this is not a genetic liability. Consequently, **choices A and C can be eliminated**. Because antisaccade deficits have been observed in all these patient groups, and the passage notes that successful antisaccades require cortical control, **choice B is the correct answer**, and **choice D is incorrect**.

5) **D. All of the above.** A, B, and C are all correct. **Choice A is correct** because any time different methods are used, direct comparisons between experiments is compromised. **Choice B is correct** because using different fMRI techniques (and, more generally, any different scientific measurement techniques) can produce different results, making comparisons across studies invalid. **Choice C is correct** because brain function, including antisaccade error rates, and visual information processing, changes across the lifespan. Thus, age differences between groups can confound brain-imaging studies.

Notes:

6

7

PATHWAY

Executive Functioning

Childhood psychiatric disorders include the Disruptive Behavior Disorders (DBD), which are based on behaviors comprising the core symptoms of the disorders (e.g. defiance and aggression). These DBDs frequently co-occur with Attention-Deficit Hyperactivity Disorder (ADHD). Mental health professionals often struggle to make accurate differential diagnoses between ADHD and the DBDs.

Various theories have been proposed to distinguish the etiologies of ADHD and the DBDs. One leading theory is that the observable symptoms of DBDs represent learned behaviors, while ADHD results from deficits in executive cognitive functioning (EF) due to brain abnormalities. To test this, researchers administered a series of EF measures to children ages 12-17 diagnosed with ADHD (Group 1), a DBD (Group 2), or both (Group 3). Three measures of EF were obtained:

(1) <u>Continuous performance task (CPT)</u>: a measure of sustained and selective attention and impulsivity. Total number of errors of omission and commission were reported.

(2) <u>Stroop test</u>: a measure of cognitive flexibility and processing speed. Total task completion time for each participant was compared to expected time, based on a normative comparison group.

(3) <u>Working memory</u>: average scores were reported, normalized with a mean = 100 and a standard deviation = 15.

Mean scores for tests were subjected to a one-way Analysis of Variance (ANOVA). The results are presented in Table 1.

Table 1: Results of one-way ANOVA

Subtest	Group 1	Group 2	Group 3	F-value
CPT				
omissions	5	4	6	2.65
commissions	12	6	13	38.25**
Stroop task	-1.23	-0.81	-1.21	3.81*
Working Mem.	85	93	87	5.39**

$* \ p \leq .05, ** \ p \leq .01$

Following test administration, subjects were told a short story. One week later, each subject was asked to repeat the story verbatim; responses were scored based on accuracy. During this follow-up test, subjects in Groups 1 and 3 demonstrated significantly lower accuracy compared with Group 2.

1) **Which of the following statements is best supported by the results in Table 1?**

   A. Group 2 performed statistically significantly better than at least one of the other groups on working memory.

   B. Group 2 did not demonstrate significant deficits in executive functioning.

   C. Omission errors were significantly different between Groups 2 and 3.

   D. There were no statistically significant differences between Group 1 and Group 3 on any of the tests administered.

2) **Which of the following represents the greatest weakness in the study design?**

   A. The lack of a non-disordered (healthy) control group.

   B. The lack of random assignment to groups.

   C. The use of children as subjects.

   D. The use of multiple measures of executive functioning.

3) **If researchers wanted to replicate this study using functional magnetic resonance imaging (fMRI), what area of the brain should the researchers target?**

   A. The occipital lobes.

   B. The brain stem.

   C. The parietal lobes.

   D. The frontal lobes.

4) **The most direct test of working memory is when subjects are:**

   A. read a list of unrelated words and then instructed to repeat the list 90 minutes later.

   B. given one minute to name as many different fruits as possible.

   C. read a series of numbers, and then immediately asked to restate the numbers in reverse order.

   D. shown a complex geometric design, then immediately asked to redraw the design from memory.

5) **What specific memory ability was being assessed when subjects were asked to recall the details of the short story?**

   A. Sensory memory.

   B. Declarative memory.

   C. Procedural memory.

   D. Short-term memory.

6

7

Executive Functioning

Annotations.
1) A   2) A   3) D   4) C   5) B

	Foundation 6: Cognition-B			Foundation 7: Individual Diffs.-A		
	B			**A**		
Concepts				3		
Reasoning	5					
Research	4			2		
Data	1					

Big Picture. This passage covers material from cognition (e.g. executive functioning, brain functions, and types of memory), individual differences (e.g. childhood psychiatric disorders), and interpretation of statistical data. Table 1 presents results from an ANOVA, which is a test that allows comparison of differences among multiple groups. The F-value (the primary metric reported for ANOVA) is significant, indicating that among all possible two-group comparisons (1 vs. 2, 1 vs. 3, and 2 vs. 3), at least one of those comparisons contains a statistically significant difference. Note that the absolute value of F is relative to the sample size, and therefore the absolute value of F does not necessarily indicate statistical significance. Rather, the p-value is the estimated probability of rejecting the null (alternative) hypothesis, when that hypothesis is true. In other words, if the experiment were repeated 100 times, results similar to those obtained would be expected at least 95 times. The scientifically accepted convention for a "significant" result is $p < .05$. Therefore, lower p-values provide more confidence in the obtained results.

1) **A. Group 2 performed statistically significantly better than at least one of the other groups on working memory.** As described in the Big Picture, a p-value $< .05$ from an ANOVA result indicates that, among all possible two-group comparisons, at least one of the comparisons across the three groups contains a statistically significant difference. **Choice A is correct** because it is the only option consistent with this description. **Choice B is incorrect** because "significant deficits in executive functioning" is not clearly defined (relative to what?); and is therefore not an objective conclusion that can be drawn from the Table or the statistical results. **Choice C is incorrect** owing to the absence of a statistically significant effect. Note that in contrast to the other measurements in the Table, there is not a listed p-value (i.e. no asterisk next to the F score). In scientific reports, this indicates the p-value was $> .05$ and therefore not significant. **Choice D is incorrect** because Table 1 provides insufficient information to conclude whether or not Group 1 was significantly different than Group 3 on any of the tests. While a significant F score on ANOVA indicates that at least two groups were significantly different, it does not indicate which groups (e.g. 1 vs. 2, 1 vs. 3, 2 vs. 3). That information is obtained from further (follow-up, or "contrast") tests that typically follow an ANOVA.

2) **A. The lack of a non-disordered (healthy) control group.** The passage does not describe the experimental design in depth. However, it is important to recognize fundamental principles in experimental design. When evaluating the answer choices, focus on those that: (1) accurately describe the experiment and (2) identify any potential limitations. One fundamental rule in experimental design is a control condition (in this case a group of typically developing children) that provides a standard of comparison. This is equivalent to a placebo condition in a study examining drug effects. **Choice A is correct** as it offers a "non-disordered (healthy) control group." **Choice B is incorrect** because, while random assignment is a useful design principle, it is

248

impossible in certain experiments such as this one. We cannot randomly assign a child to have ADHD or a DBD. It is equivalent to conducting a study on gender differences and randomly assigning subjects into a male or female group. **Choice C is incorrect** because children are enrolled as participants in research all the time. Furthermore, it is unethical to exclude children with diseases from research. **Choice D is incorrect**. As long as subjects are not exhausted or bored, having multiple measures of a variable of interest is typically an asset, in that it provides greater measurement sensitivity.

3) **D. The frontal lobes.** This question requires knowledge of the types of brain functions being measured. Importantly, you do not need to know the details of fMRI to address the question (however, in general you should be familiar with fMRI for the MCAT). Rather, the introduction of fMRI serves as a distractor within the question stem. The passage focuses on "executive cognitive functioning," (EF) which refers to higher-level processes such as impulse control, planning, and organizing. EF is largely subserved by the frontal lobes, making **choice D correct**. This is therefore a content knowledge question. The frontal lobes are important in childhood psychiatric disorders. The frontal lobes are present at birth, but remain underdeveloped until adulthood (ergo, relative to adults, children and adolescents are poor at executive tasks). The occipital lobes are primarily associated with processing of visual stimuli, making **choice A incorrect**. You would expect the occipital lobes to be active during tasks involving visual stimuli, but the activation would not reflect differences between groups in executive functioning. **Choice B is incorrect** as the midbrain, pons and medulla, comprise the brain stem, which is largely responsible for vital life functions (e.g. breathing, heartbeat). **Choice C is incorrect** because the parietal lobes process tactile information and integrate other sensory input, and are not primary constituents of EF.

4) **C. read a series of numbers, and then immediately asked to restate the numbers in reverse order.** Working memory refers to our ability to hold information for short time periods, and then not only recall, but also manipulate the information in some way. For this question, it is therefore necessary evaluate the answer choices based on two criteria: the test must require both the short-term storage and manipulation of information. Short-term memory is quite short, on the order of tens of seconds. It follows that **choice C is the correct answer**: the list of numbers only needs to be retained for a few seconds, and the subjects have to manipulate the numbers (i.e. reverse the order) before restating them. A retention duration of 90 minutes is a test of long-term memory, making **choice A is incorrect**. By asking subjects to recall previously learned material, **choice B is also incorrect**, as it is also reflects long-term memory processes. Choice B is actually tests "recall fluency," or how quickly one can access specific long-term memories. **Choice D is not correct** because, although it describes a test of short-term memory, it does not require the subjects to manipulate the data and is thus does not entail working memory.

5) **B. Declarative memory.** As with the previous question, this question assesses knowledge of the different types of memory. The subjects were asked to read a story and then repeat it one week later. The one-week duration indicates that long-term memory is needed for recall of the story. Because subjects were asked to recall simple details of the story, the test was assessing declarative memory, making **choice B correct**. Both declarative memory and procedural memory describe aspects of long-term memory. Declarative memory refers to consciously recalled facts, while procedural memory refers to memory for skills that require voluntary actions (e.g. tying a shoe or riding a bike). **Choice C is incorrect** because the story recall does not require procedural memory. **Choice D is incorrect** because it refers to short-term memory. Sensory memory is also a short-term memory process (the shortest) and refers to the brain's ability to retain sensory input in the absence of a stimulus. Accordingly, **choice A is incorrect**.

Language Formation

Psycholinguistics is the study of the psychological and neurobiological structures that enable humans to learn, use, and understand language. Ethnolinguistics is primarily concerned with how culture affects language acquisition, and in turn, a person's perception of the world.

Culture affects the historical development of a language system. For example, in English-speaking nuclear family cultures, there are sex-specific terms for parents (i.e. "mother" and "father") and separate terms delineating relative generations (i.e. "grand," "great," "great-great," etc.). In contrast, Asian cultures traditionally have multigenerational families living together, and they semantically differentiate between paternal and maternal grandfathers with different words.

Language theorists have hypothesized that language acquisition has a direct and causal effect on cognitive development. It follows that the depth and breadth of vocabulary usage about a given concept is directly related to the complexity of the native language regarding that concept.

In a key experiment, English-speaking subjects, who have 11 basic color names, were compared with subjects from Papua New Guinea whose language (Berinmo) limits their description of color. Participants from both groups were shown identical palettes with an array of colors. They were initially asked to name each color and then later recall the name. The results are shown below (**Fig. 1**).

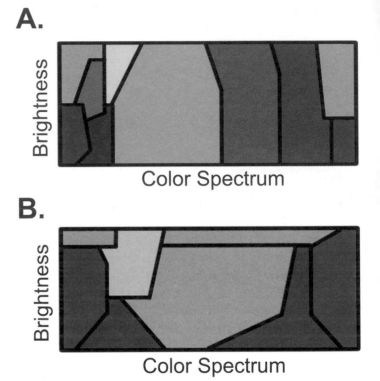

Figure 1. Unique color names given by (A) English-speaking; (B) Berinmo.

1) Which of the following best states the probable hypothesis being tested in the "color naming, color recall" study (Fig. 1)?

A. Participants from different cultures will have different ways of describing a variety of colors.

B. Cultural differences in the overall size of vocabulary affect the complexity of cognition in that culture.

C. The theories of the Psycholinguistic school of language acquisition bear merit and warrant further investigation.

D. Compared to the Berinmo, English-speaking participants will perceive and describe a wider variety of colors.

2. The statement, "The depth and breadth of cognitions experienced by any given person are in direct relation to the depth and breadth of the vocabulary available to that person" best supports which of the following?

A. Individuals will not understand a concept that does not exist in their language system.

B. The greater the variety of vocabulary a language system has, the harder it will be to succinctly express ideas.

C. Individuals who speak languages with few words are not as intelligent as those who speak languages with many words.

D. Polylingual individuals are more intelligent than monolingual individuals.

3) Which of the following represents the best grounds for criticizing the use of "vocabulary size" as a sole measure of intelligence?

A. Lack of test-retest reliability

B. Lack of inter-rater reliability

C. Lack of norm group

D. Lack of content validity

4) If fMRI were used to assess the participants' ability to perceive color variety, which area of the brain would be the focus of the analysis?

A. Frontal lobe

B. Parietal lobe

C. Occipital lobe

D. Temporal lobe

5) Which of the following statements is most consistent with the Behaviorist school of language acquisition?

A. Humans develop language as a result of early childhood interactions with adults, who shape infant linguistic approximations through praise.

B. A brain based Language Acquisition Device makes it possible for children to learn a behavioral vocabulary.

C. Language abilities are instinctual, with certain rules of grammar native to the brain at birth.

D. Children develop language within a system of rules for grammar and vocabulary, which are modeled and reinforced in a social context.

6) Which of the following variables is the most important subject characteristic to control in the study described in the passage?

A. Number of languages spoken

B. Occupation of subject

C. Need for corrective lenses

D. Level of education

6

7

Language Formation

Annotations.
1) D   2) A   3) D   4) C   5) A   6) A

	Foundation 6: Psychophys.-A Cognition-B		Foundation 7: Individual Diffs.-A Learning-C		
	A	**B**	**A**	**C**	
Concepts	4		3	5	
Reasoning		2			
Research			6		
Data	1				

Big Picture. The MCAT science questions may require several different forms of data interpretation. They may not always come in the form of traditional graphs you are accustomed to seeing. Figure 1 is a good example of a unique data presentation, which requires thinking "outside the box" to interpret the data. The focus here is not necessarily on noting data trends, but instead focusing on big picture ideas. This will test your critical reading skills as much as your scientific reasoning skills. While reading, try not to get too bogged down in understanding every word presented, as every word is probably not important. Try to get the general sense of what the author is conveying. This passage boils down to the following: culture affects language development; there are various schools of thought regarding language acquisition; and here is a study testing one of those schools of thought.

1) **D. Compared to the Berinmo, English-speaking participants will perceive and describe a wider variety of colors.** Usually, a good answer to an MCAT critical reading question (which this question parallels) is going to be broad and noncommittal. A good scientific hypothesis, however, is very specific and makes predictions about the key factors being tested by the study. **Choices A and B are not correct** as they are too broad to be research hypotheses. **Choice C is also incorrect.** While it likely describes why the researchers are interested in this topic, it is not a hypothesis. **Choice D is the correct answer.** This might have tricked you because it contradicts the study's conclusion. Remember, though, that hypotheses are not always supported by the experimental data.

2) **A. Individuals will not understand a concept that does not exist in their language system.** This question is a test of your logical reasoning skills, which mirrors the requirements to succeed in the critical reasoning section of the MCAT. When you need to employ logic to test a statement, or its possible corollaries, ask yourself the following questions: (1) With which elements are you dealing? In this case, "depth/breadth of cognition" and "depth/breadth of vocabulary" are the elements. (2) How do these elements functionally relate to each other (e.g. directly).

Following this logic, you can eliminate answer choices that introduce elements not included in the question stem statement: **choices C and D are therefore not correct** because they mention "intelligence" (never mind that both choices are derogatory, which makes them generally inferior MCAT answer choices). **Choice B is incorrect** because the question stem statement was not about succinctness of expression. The **correct response – choice A –** reflects the direct correlation between cognitive awareness of a concept and existence of a word for that concept.

3) D. Lack of content validity. This question is about test construction with regard to accepted models of intelligence. Since the publication of the first intelligence test in 1905, the field of psychology has largely conceptualized intelligence as a complex construct that cannot be reduced to, or reflected in, a single mental skill. A test that uses "vocabulary size" as its only measure of intelligence would be just as inappropriate as one that relied solely on "math computation speed." Content validity is a non-statistical estimate of whether a test measures all aspects of a particular construct based on the questions it includes (e.g. its content). Having a test based only on vocabulary size would have limited content validity, making **choice D the best answer**.

This question requires an understanding of the concepts of reliability vs. validity. Simply, the term "reliable" translates to "consistent," while "valid" means "accurate." A test with good reliability does not necessarily have good validity (and vice versa). In fact, the test described in this question would likely have great reliability. A test taker with a poor vocabulary would end up with a low IQ the first, second, and third time he takes the test (test-retest reliability), making **choice A incorrect**. In addition, the results would likely be the same across multiple examiners (inter-rater reliability), making **choice B incorrect**. While "norm group" is a concept in test construction, the question does not provide sufficient information about norms or standardization, making **choice C incorrect**.

4) C. Occipital lobe. Color perception, like many cognitive functions, is a complex process involving multiple brain circuits. However, visual processing is largely accomplished in the occipital cortex, making **choice C correct**. Indeed, optic nerve fibers project to the occipital cortex. The primary function of each of the four lobes is listed below.

- Frontal lobe – higher executive functions, including attention, memory, decision-making and motivation.
- Occipital lobe – visual processing
- Parietal lobes – sensory processing, subserves processing of tactile information
- Temporal lobes – auditory processing

5) A. Humans develop language as a result of early childhood interactions with adults, who shape infant linguistic approximations through praise. Language acquisition can be divided into three schools of thought.

(1) The Behaviorist school, derived from the work of B. F. Skinner, posits that language comes from operant conditioning processes – reinforcing certain behaviors, i.e. sounds, which makes them more probable. For example, when a baby coos and babbles, its caregivers reward that behavior with affection, and so the baby coos and babbles more. The first time the babbling approximates "mama," the mother squeals with delight and lavishes the infant with praise, increasing the likelihood that "mama" will become a more frequent behavior. **Choice A is the correct answer** as it describes this process.

(2) The Nativist school, developed by Noam Chomsky, stands in contrast to the Behaviorist school. According to nativism, humans are born with innate (i.e. "native") neurological structures that are hard-wired for language. A strict nativist would argue that a child is born with a Language Acquisition Device (LAD) that comes hard-wired with a set of common grammatical rules. **Choices B and C are not correct** because both describe the Nativist theory. While choice C is a pretty good summary of nativism, choice B uses the term "behavioral vocabulary," which might be confusing because of the word "behavioral." However, the thrust of choice B clearly suggests that the language is innate and hard-wired rather than developed through reinforcement.

(3) The Social Interactionist school, originated by Vygotsky, holds that language is learned within a social context. Experienced language users model correct usage to language learners (e.g. babies), and then reinforce language usage in those users. There is significant overlap between the Behaviorist and Interactionist models; however, social interactionism is not a strict stimulus-response process (as promoted by the Behaviorist school). Remember that Social Interactionism emphasizes the overall social context more than the influence of rewards and punishments. **Choice D is not the correct answer** because it more strongly reflects Social Interactionism than the Behaviorist theory.

6

7

Language Formation

6) **A. Number of languages spoken.** When you are asked a question about control conditions (which also might be termed "confounding variables"), the focus is on the experimental design. Good experiments account for variables that could bias the results and lead to inaccurate conclusions. For example, if a cancer scientist examined white blood cell count in patients as a dependent measure, but failed to account for the presence of infection, the results would be invalid. **Choice A is correct** because the passage clearly emphasizes that range of vocabulary on a given concept is related to the native language complexity about that concept. Since someone who speaks multiple languages is likely to have greater range of language complexity, failure to account for this variable could clearly bias the results. Clearly, one's occupation should have no impact on the perception and naming of colors (which should have developed long before an occupation was selected), making **choice B incorrect**. Likewise, the level of education is not relevant; the ability to recognize and name basic colors is consistent across all people (without disabilities) even in the most uneducated individuals. It follows that **choice D is incorrect**. The need for corrective lenses serves as a distractor, but even with impaired vision, color perception and naming should not vary across individuals. Therefore, **choice C is incorrect**. Additionally, notice that the question does not imply that those individuals were not allowed to wear their corrective lenses – leaving you with insufficient information to conclude that this would be a suitable answer choice.

Notes:

6

7

Med–
PATHWAY

255

Sleep and Stress Hormones

Sleep deprivation activates stress systems, which leads to neuroendocrine release and disruptions in sleep architecture. Physiologically, biological stress (e.g. pain) or psychological stress activates two neurobiological systems: the hypothalamic-pituitary-adrenal (HPA) axis and the adrenal-medulla axis. The HPA axis regulates the release of the well-established hormone cascade: CRH > ACTH > cortisol from the adrenal gland. The adrenal-medulla axis regulates the release of adrenaline peripherally. ACHT, cortisol, and adrenaline are all biomarkers of stress, and they alter the sleep architecture in unique ways. For example, sleep onset coincides with a decrease in ACTH and cortisol levels.

Normal sleep follows a predictable sequence, characterized by rapid eye movement (REM) sleep and non-REM sleep. Non-REM sleep has three stages. Stage 1 is lighter sleep in which the brain produces high amplitude but slow temporal (θ) brain waves. In stage 2, the brain produces rapid bouts of variable-amplitude brain waves as the individual moves into deeper sleep.

In stage 3, the individual moves into deep sleep and the brain produces pronounced slow brain waves (Δ). During stage 3, the body strengthens the immune system, potentially buffering the damaging effects caused by chronic stress. Because these circadian processes are regulated in the hypothalamus, activation of stress systems in the HPA axis disrupts not only sleep onset and duration, but also the progression through each stage.

A research team conducts an experiment to study 100 police officers with a history of on-duty trauma. At 9:00 PM, 50 officers view pictures of nature scenes and 50 view pictures of violent assaults. At 9:45 PM, all officers provide saliva samples and then stay overnight in a sleep laboratory while being monitored by EEG (brain electrical activity). The table below shows summary data of the experimental results.

Table 1. Means from all dependent variables in the two groups of police officers

Group	Cortisol level (µg/dL)	ACTH level (pg/mL)	θ activity (min)	Δ activity (min)
1	30	60	117	121
2	18	40	93	197

1) **Based on the data, which was the most likely experimental arrangement?**

   A. Group 1 viewed nature scenes, Group 2 viewed violent scenes.

   B. Group 2 viewed nature scenes, Group 1 viewed violent scenes.

   C. Group 2 was the target of the sleep manipulation.

   D. The groups cannot be determined.

2) **If functional MRI was used to examine neural activation during the viewing of the pictures, in what brain region would the differences between groups be the greatest?**

   A. Limbic system

   B. Occipital cortex

   C. Adrenal medulla

   D. Corpus callosum

3) **Which is the most appropriate statistical technique to analyze the presented data?**

   A. Correlation

   B. ANOVA

   C. Survival curves

   D. Z scores

4) **Which statement best characterizes the relationship between HIV+ status and sleep?**

   A. The virus kills cells in the hypothalamus resulting in circadian rhythm abnormalities.

   B. Compromised immune function leads to chronic fatigue, which decreases cortisol production and sleep patterns during nighttime.

   C. Compromised immune function increases HPA axis activity, which interferes with both stage 3 sleep and immune function.

   D. There is no clear relationship between the virus and mechanisms involved in sleep.

5) **What is the best way for researchers to examine the direct relationship between stress and sleep?**

   A. T-tests on θ and Δ activity

   B. ANOVA on saliva sample markers

   C. Linear regression between cortisol and θ/Δ activity

   D. Z score analysis of cortisol and θ/Δ activity

6) **Diphenhydramine is a common sleep aid that, in the CNS, antagonizes histamine receptors. Based on this information, which statement most accurately describes one important mechanism of the neural action of histamine?**

   A. It promotes active firing in the hypothalamus during waking and diminishes firing rates during slow wave sleep.

   B. It promotes the release of stress hormones in the adrenal-medulla axis.

   C. It promotes active firing in the hypothalamus during slow wave sleep and diminishes firing rates during waking.

   D. It inhibits the release of stress hormones in the adrenal-medulla axis.

7) **People with anxiety disorders typically have difficulty sleeping. Which of the following are most accurate in characterizing interactions between anxiety and sleep?**

   I. Nicotine is helpful in promoting sleep in those with anxiety

   II. Benzodiazepines are helpful in promoting sleep in those with anxiety

   III. Individuals with anxiety have blunted ACTH levels

   IV. Individuals with anxiety have heightened ACTH levels

   A. I and III

   B. II and IV

   C. II and III

   D. I and IV

Sleep and Stress Hormones

Annotations.
1) B   2) A   3) B   4) C   5) C   6) A   7) B

	Foundation 6: Emotion/Stress-C			Foundation 7: Individual Diffs.-A		
	C			A		
Concepts				2,6		
Reasoning				4,7		
Research	5					
Data	1,3					

Big Picture. A common theme in the behavioral sciences passages is the focus on understanding the connections between psychological processes (in this case, stress) and basic neurobehavioral processes such as hormone regulation, transmitter systems, and sleep. Making these connections requires (a) thinking about how systems interact, and (b) a solid understanding of central nervous system structure and function. In addition, this passage requires that you have a basic understanding of biostatistics. Nearly all experiments in neuroscience and the behavioral sciences rely on statistical testing to confirm the reliability of findings. The majority of statistical testing is based on the general linear model and the assumption that the data follow a normal (Gaussian, or bell-shaped) distribution. The first paragraph has a considerable amount of jargon and technical detail, only some of which is needed to answer the questions correctly. You should be able to refer back to first paragraph if needed, but avoid getting lost in the minutia.

1) **B. Group 2 viewed nature scenes, Group 1 viewed violent scenes.** Answering this question correctly requires integrating the second paragraph of the passage with Table 1. First, you must predict how the data from the experiment will turn out (paragraph 3) based on the information provided on sleep and the primary neurochemicals related to stress. Basically, when the officers are exposed to violent material (Group 1), it should activate stress systems and subsequently disrupt sleep architecture. Second, you should be able to confirm this prediction by reading Table I, which reveals increased cortisol and ACTH levels and higher stage 1 levels (light sleep) and lower stage 3 levels (deep sleep) in Group 1. It follows that Group 1 viewed the violent scenes, making **choice B the correct answer.** Answer choice A makes the opposite conclusion, so **choice A is incorrect.** Since the data predict that Group 2 viewed the nature scenes and Group 1 viewed the violent scenes, the experimenters were trying to manipulate stress and sleep systems in Group 1, making **choice C incorrect.** Both the passage and Table I provide sufficient information to determine the group assignment in the experiment. Therefore **choice D should be the quickest to eliminate as incorrect.**

2) **A. Limbic system.** To answer this question correctly, it is necessary to know that the hypothalamus (a primary component of the HPA axis) is located in the limbic system. **Choice A is correct**, because it is consistent with this information. **Choice B is incorrect** because the occipital cortex is part of the cerebral cortex located in the posterior region of the brain, while the limbic system is a midbrain structure. **Choice C is incorrect** because the adrenal medulla is not in the CNS (this information is provided in the passage). The corpus callosum is a bundle of white matter (association) brain cells. Standard functional MRI techniques do not measure activity in white matter fibers in this region, making **choice D an incorrect choice.** Two useful neuroscience content areas to study for the behavioral science section of the MCAT are: (1) a basic understanding of the major brain regions: the four lobes; the major structures of the cerebral cortex, midbrain, and lower brain; and (2) the basic brain imaging techniques, including magnetic resonance imaging (MRI) and positron emission tomography (PET).

3) B. ANOVA. This question requires a solid understanding of statistics. One of the first principles critical to understanding statistical analysis is being able to match the experimental design to the appropriate statistical test. You should be familiar with ANOVA (Analysis of Variance), correlation, and Z-scores if you have had a statistics course. If you have had a course in epidemiology (common in Public Health sciences) or in medical statistics, then you may be familiar with survival curves. If you are unfamiliar with most of these tests, it will be useful to brush up on stats by taking a course or getting an intermediate level textbook. This experiment used a between-group design that focused on comparing group differences resulting from the independent variable (i.e. viewing nature or violent scenes). This design is most commonly analyzed via ANOVA, making **choice B the correct answer.** Correlation cannot provide an answer about differences between two groups, it examines the relationship between two variables (e.g. height and weight). Therefore, **choice A is incorrect.** Survival curves examine the change in one or more variables over time (e.g. survival rates of groups of cancer patients over 36 months after receiving different chemotherapies). Because the experiment does not focus on group differences over multiple time points, **choice C is also incorrect.** Note, however, that if the experiment had been designed differently and Table 1 had presented multiple time points, a survival curve could in theory be used. However, such analyses are very rare for a laboratory experiment in the behavioral sciences, which primary use ANOVA models to examine the data. A Z score (sometimes called a standardized score) is simply a transformation of the individual data points to represent their distance above or below the mean. **Choice D is incorrect** because a Z score is not a statistical analysis; it is a data transformation.

4) C. Compromised immune function increases HPA axis activity, which interferes with both stage 3 sleep and immune function. To correctly identify this answer, you must connect knowledge of HIV with and stress and sleep functions. The information related to stress and sleep is provided in the passage. **Choice C is the credited answer:** stressing the immune system activates HPA-axis reactivity. You can deduce from the passage that increased HPA axis activity disrupts stage 3 sleep. **Choice B is not the credited answer,** but is a close distractor based on similarity to choice C. However, the key is to recognize that while chronic fatigue is a well-documented symptom of HIV, there is no evidence that chronic fatigue in HIV decreases cortisol levels. It is also important to recognize, based on the passage, that increased cortisol production (not decreased) is associated with disruption of the sleep cycle. **Choice A is not the credited answer.** While toxicity to hypothalamic and medulla cells may produce circadian abnormalities, there is no information in the passage or the literature that HIV positive status is related to neurotoxicity. One important distinction to make in examining this question is the difference between HIV status and acquired immunodeficiency syndrome (AIDS). While there is CNS and other organ compromise associated with later-stage AIDS, similar compromise is not prevalent in HIV+ status, and not all individuals convert from HIV+ status to AIDS. **Choice D is not the credited answer.** Even if you do not have a working knowledge of the health consequences of HIV and AIDS, you should be able to deduce that living with this virus is related to fatigue and activation of stress symptoms. You know from the passage that stress and sleep are linked, and thus can eliminate choice D.

5) C. Linear regression between cortisol and θ/Δ activity. Like question 3, this question tests your knowledge of statistics. The key words are "direct relationship." Direct relationships are typically assessed by regression techniques. In the case of linear regression, the stress variable (cortisol) can be plotted on one axis and the sleep variable (θ/Δ activity) plotted on the other axis. Using the simple linear equation $y = bx + a$, the relationship can be assessed by examining how well the data are described by a straight line through the data. **Choice A is not the best answer** because t-tests are typically used to evaluate the difference between two data distributions (e.g. the minutes of slow wave sleep between the two groups). Similarly, **choice C is not the best answer** because (a) ANOVA is used to evaluate differences in two (or usually more) distributions (typically between groups), and (b) because the question asked about comparing stress and sleep whereas the saliva data measure stress hormones, not sleep patterns. As in question 3, **choice D is incorrect** because a Z score is a type of data transformation, not a statistical test.

6) A. It promotes active firing in the hypothalamus during waking and diminishes firing rates during slow wave sleep. To determine that **choice A is the correct answer**, you must identify and integrate several key pieces of information. First, you should recognize that the hypothalamus regulates circadian (sleep) cycles. This information is in the passage. Second, you must understand the fundamental role of agonists and antagonists in neurotransmission. Agonists occupy receptor sites on neurons and promote electrochemical transmission in the neurons they occupy. Antagonists also occupy receptor sites on neurons, but they have the opposite function of inhibiting firing. If you have ever taken diphenhydramine for allergies, you will be familiar with the groggy feeling and sleepiness that results. You can conclude that (1) modulating activity in the hypothalamus can effect sleep/wake cycles, and (2) that one mechanism of action of histamine receptors is to promote wakefulness. By antagonizing this process (decreasing firing at receptors in hypothalamus) diphenhydramine reduces wakefulness and promotes sleep. **Choices B and D are incorrect** because the adrenal-medulla axis is in the peripheral system, not the CNS, which is the focal point of this question. Additionally, in the case of choice B, the release of stress hormones disrupts rather than promotes sleep. This information is in the passage. **Choice C is incorrect** as it describes the opposite effect – neurotransmission (firing) of histamine receptors in the hypothalamus will promote wakefulness rather than slow wave sleep.

7) B. II and IV. To evaluate this question, it is necessary to break down statements I through IV individually. In statement I, recognize that nicotine is a relatively powerful stimulant. As a stimulant, it is likely to keep people awake rather than promote sleep, and likely to make people with anxiety more stressed. Therefore, **choices A and D can be eliminated**. Statement II suggests that benzodiazepines can help reduce anxiety and promote sleep, which is correct. While you may not have been exposed to basic pharmacology in your pre-med training, most neuroscience courses cover the major drug classes. Benzodiazepines are a major class of drugs prescribed primarily to treat anxiety disorders, and secondarily to help with insomnia. Therefore, both choices B and C are partly correct. However, **choice B is the credited answer** because ACTH is a stress hormone released by the HPA axis. Clearly, stress and anxiety are closely linked. It follows that people with anxiety disorders will have higher ACTH levels. **Choice C is not the credited answer** because it suggests the opposite, blunted ACTH levels in people with anxiety disorders.

6

7

PATHWAY

Biological Models of Anxiety

The biomedical model of human health primarily considers physiological factors when attempting to understand illness. When applied to mental disorders, this model assumes that such disorders can be conceptualized as diseases and typically treated by psychopharmacology. Alternatively, the biopsychosocial model considers environmental and psychological factors in addition to biological factors when determining mental health.

Presented with these two models, a group of researchers posited that the biopsychosocial model provides a better basis for the treatment of mental disorders. The researchers randomly assigned subjects diagnosed with Generalized Anxiety Disorder (GAD) into one of three treatment groups: Medication-only, Therapy-only, and Multimodal. Subjects in the Medication-only group received daily treatment with a benzodiazepine (i.e. clonazepam). Subjects in the Therapy-only group received weekly Cognitive Behavioral Therapy (CBT) sessions. Subjects in the Multimodal group received both treatment modalities. At three time periods during the study (pre-treatment, four weeks, eight weeks), subjects were asked to rate their average daily level of anxiety on a ten-point scale (1 = "no anxiety" to 10 = "paralyzing fear"). Figure 1 shows the results of this study.

At the end of eight weeks, researchers discontinued treatment for all study subjects. Subjects were then asked to return four weeks later for a follow-up meeting, at which time they repeated the subjective anxiety ratings shown in Figure 2.

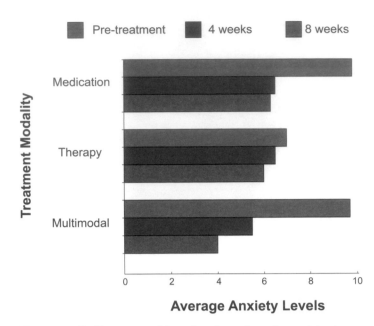

Figure 1. Self-reported levels of anxiety for subject groups at 0, 4, and 8 weeks.

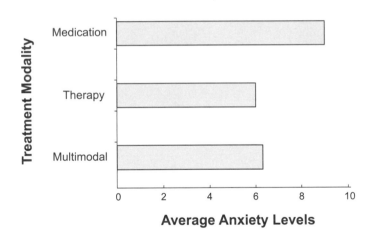

Figure 2. Self-reported levels of anxiety at follow-up.

1) Assume that, within each group, the differences between pre-treatment and 8-week anxiety levels are statistically significant for the Medication-only and the Multimodal groups. Which of the following conclusions is best supported?

A. The biomedical model shows the most promise; subjects in the Therapy-only group did not experience significant symptom reduction.

B. The biopsychosocial model is supported; subjects in the Multimodal group experienced the greatest symptom reduction.

C. Results are inconclusive; the significance of the between-group differences at the 8-week period was not reported.

D. Any successful treatment modality must include medication; the Therapy-only group did not demonstrate significant symptom reduction.

2) Based on the results of this study, the researchers hypothesize that clonazepam is a uniquely effective medication for relieving symptoms of GAD. Which experiment best tests this hypothesis?

A. Repeat the study with the addition of a placebo-control group, including clonazepam.

B. Repeat the study with the addition of a no-treatment control group and clonazepam.

C. Repeat the study using multiple Medication-only groups with different anti-anxiety medications, including clonazepam.

D. Repeat the study adding clonazepam to the other (non-medication) group in the original study.

3) Which of the following best explains changes in anxiety across the entire study, including follow-up?

A. Clonazepam acutely reduced anxiety, whereas CBT promoted sustained improvement.

B. The Multimodal group experienced no benefits from medication.

C. The Therapy-only and Multimodal groups continued treatment after the study.

D. CBT was a more effective treatment than medication for reducing symptoms of anxiety.

4) What confounding element of this study prevents ruling out the possibility that symptoms simply change over time independent of treatment?

A. Failure to account for personal differences between subjects.

B. Failure to include a no-treatment control group.

C. Failure to consider the possible genetic etiology of anxiety.

D. Only including one medication and one therapy model in the study.

5) "Avoidance" of a feared stimulus is a defining characteristic symptom of GAD. Avoidance behavior reduces anxiety symptoms in the short-term, but results in chronic anxiety symptoms. This is an example of what kind of sociopsychological process?

A. Modeling.

B. Observational learning.

C. Classical conditioning.

D. Operant conditioning.

6

7

Biological Models of Anxiety

Annotations.
1) B   2) C   3) A   4) B   5) D

	Foundation 6: Emotion/Stress-C			Foundation 7: Individual Diffs.-A Learning-C		
	C			A	C	
Concepts					5	
Reasoning	3					
Research				2,4		
Data				1		

Big Picture. This passage describes a fairly standard mental health treatment experiment, in which multiple treatment methods are compared at different time points during treatment. While the data from this experiment are presented in two charts, the use of two charts is unnecessary. The data from Figure 2 could just as easily have been represented as a fourth time point in Figure 1. Splitting the data into two charts adds complexity to the passage, as it adds an extra step to the task of interpretation. You should recognize this as a common MCAT technique designed to slow you down, as it camouflages testable points that would be more obvious if they were presented as a single figure. This approach allows the MCAT to differentiate efficient from non-efficient test-taking methods. When you are presented with multiple charts, note how the charts overlap – in this case, entirely – and what obvious data trends exist, but don't get bogged down in possibly irrelevant details.

1) **B. The biopsychosocial model is supported; subjects in the Multimodal group experienced the greatest symptom reduction.** The key to this question is to know what can – and cannot – be inferred from statistically "significant" results. When a scientific article states that the results are statistically significant, it implies a given probability that the results were not due to chance. In the experiment described in this passage, the researcher applied three treatments – therapy, medication, and multi-modal – and tested the resulting changes in anxiety symptoms. Since the Medication-only and Multimodal groups experienced significant symptom reduction, those are the two treatment models that have statistical support for being effective. That does not mean that the Therapy-only treatment did not work, rather that the statistical test on that group's data did not indicate a significant outcome. In fact, we can see from Figure 1 that the Therapy-only group did experience symptom reduction, but the change was not as great and not statistically significant.

Question 1 requires you to determine the greatest change in anxiety levels from pre-treatment to week 8. To do this, you can calculate the approximate difference for each treatment: Medication = 4 (10-6); Therapy = 1 (7-6); and Multimodal = 6 (10-4). It follows that **choice B is correct** because the Multimodal treatment produced that greatest reduction in symptoms.

Choice A is temping because the Medication-only group showed greater symptom reduction than the Therapy-only group. However **choice A is not correct** because we cannot say that it is the most promising, since the Multimodal shows an even greater change. **Choice D is incorrect** and attempts to confuse you by juxtaposing "significant" with "successful" (they are not synonymous). Note that there is no context to establish what "successful" means in the passage or question. Furthermore, there was a decrease in anxiety in every condition. **Choice C is incorrect** because it addresses the concept of between-group differences – a comparison of one group to another at each time point (e.g. the difference between each therapy group at week 8). However, the question stem focuses on within-group differences, or changes in data within a group over time.

2) C. Repeat the study using multiple Medication-only groups with different anti-anxiety medications, including clonazepam. In this question stem, the researchers think that clonazepam is a "uniquely effective medication" for treating anxiety. In order to demonstrate this, the researchers would need to compare the effects of clonazepam <u>to those of other medications</u>. **Choice C is correct**, as it describes an experiment testing the effectiveness of clonazepam versus other drugs. **Choices A and B are both incorrect** because they do not describe experiments that test clonazepam relative to other medications. In general, controls groups are important, but in this case it would not provide any information about relative differences among drugs. **Choice D is incorrect.** We cannot draw conclusions about clonazepam versus other drugs unless we directly compare it to other drugs. Since clonazepam was added to every condition, no comparison can be drawn regarding its effectiveness.

3) A. Clonazepam acutely reduced anxiety, whereas CBT promoted sustained improvement. First eliminate choice C; there is no information provided about <u>treatment</u> after week 8.

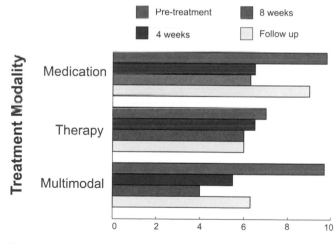

Figure 3. Changes in anxiety throughout the entire course of the experiment. X axis = average anxiety levels.

Figure 3 is a composite of Figures 1 and 2. It shows the following: 1) Anxiety levels in the Medicatin-only group first decreased from 10 to about 6 (at week 8), then increased to 9 at follow-up. Anxiety levels in the Therapy group decreased from about 7 to 6 (at week 8), and were sustained at 6

during follow-up. 3) Anxiety levels in the Multimodal group decreased from 10 to about 4 (at week 8), then rose back to 6 at follow-up. It is unclear why the anxiety levels rebounded for the Medication-only and Multimodal groups; however, the variable those two groups have in common is clonazepam, which was removed after week 8. Therefore, clonazepam acutely reduced anxiety in two groups. In the Therapy-only group, anxiety levels decreased, albeit it slightly, from 7 to 6 (in week 8), but remained nearly the same at follow-up. The small amount of improvement was sustainable as seen by anxiety levels at follow-up (**Fig. 3**). Therefore, **choice A is correct** because conditions that included clonazepam (Medication and Multimodal) produced decreases over the first eight weeks and increases at follow-up, while Therapy produced small changes that were sustained at follow-up. **Choice B is incorrect** because the phrase "no benefits from medication" is inaccurate – all groups had decreased levels of anxiety at some point in the study; they did receive <u>some</u> benefit. **Choice D is not credited** because the phrasing "more effective" is ambiguous; there is no clarity regarding acute (i.e. short-term) changes versus sustained improvement (i.e. follow-up). Therefore, "more effective" is ambiguous with regard to the question.

4) B. Failure to include a no-treatment control group. A study confound is a flaw in the experimental design. This study did not account for the possibility that patients' anxiety symptoms may spontaneously get better over time – without any intervention. The only way to scientifically control for this possibility is to include a no-treatment control group. **Choice B is therefore the best answer.** The other three answer choices do not address experimental design with regard to change over time and are therefore not good answers.

5) D. Operant conditioning. This question does not require interpretation of the experiment described in the passage. Avoidance is when a person evades an unpleasant or feared situation because of the anxiety symptoms that the situation produces. Avoidance fits the definition of operant conditioning in the following way: a person is presented with a stimulus that produces anxiety, they respond with a volitional behavior (i.e. avoidance), the behavior is reinforced with symptom reduction (because the anxiety-producing stimulus is not present), and this increases the future occurrence of the avoiding behavior. The above situation is precisely what is described by operant conditioning, making **choice D correct**. "Modeling" and "observational learning" (choices A and B, respectively) both refer to social learning theory, but they do not apply to avoidance. Therefore, **choices A and B are incorrect**. Classical conditioning (e.g. Pavlov's dogs) is described in choice C. Classical conditioning encompasses reflexive (not volitional) responding to a stimulus, making **choice C incorrect**.

PATHWAY

Community Health, a small medical clinic that provides primary care services, has a psychiatrist, a geriatrician, and a psychologist who provides family and cognitive-behavioral therapy. Today's patient load at Community Health included the following:

Patient 1 is a talkative, 63-year-old, right-handed male who has been coming to the clinic for the past five years for regular check-ups and hypertension (HTN) medication management. Today, while checking in at the front desk, he had difficulty responding to simple questions and spoke in a broken, stilted fashion. His first words to the receptionist were, "Doctor… car Wednesday… John… ah, sometimes store… ten o'clock." When the receptionist asked follow-up questions, he appeared to understand, but was not able to respond fluently. Attempting to write his responses did not result in noticeable improvement.

Patient 2 is a 49-year-old male who was diagnosed with schizophrenia at age 23. Initially, his symptoms were successfully controlled with an atypical antipsychotic, clozapine, and he was able to live semi-independently. In his mid-30s, patient 2's positive symptoms relapsed and his medication was changed to the first-generation antipsychotic, haloperidol. Patient 2 now receives monthly appointments for medication management. During today's visit, his medical team observed symptoms of Parkinson's disease, as he has begun to demonstrate tremors and odd facial tics.

Patient 3 is a 17-year-old female high school student. She has always been a high achiever: good grades, active in her church youth group, and a starter on her school's basketball team. Patient 3 visited the clinic today complaining of chronic headaches and general achiness. During an interview with the physician, she reported losing her appetite, difficulty sleeping at night, and trouble concentrating in class. Her mother reported that she has been unmotivated, irritable and argumentative.

Patient 4 is a 38-year-old female, who recently moved back in with her elderly parents after her second divorce. Because of her history of unstable relationships, her parents requested that she see a counselor. Since beginning counseling, Patient 4 has switched therapists three times, and is on her fourth therapist in ten months. This morning she showed up seven hours early for her appointment, and stated to the receptionist that it was a "matter of life and death" that she see the psychologist now. The receptionist informed her that the psychologist was not on the premises, but would be available at the scheduled time. The receptionist then offered to call 911. At that point, Patient 4 grabbed the pen out of the receptionist's hand and threatened to stab herself in the arm.

1) **The physician at the clinic suspects that Patient 1 has suffered a stroke, and orders a brain scan. If Patient 1 had a stroke, what area of the brain is most likely to show damage?**

   A. Right Parietal Lobe

   B. Left Frontal Lobe

   C. Brain Stem

   D. Corpus Callosum

2) **Based on information in the passage, which symptoms were most likely responsible for the decision to change to the antipsychotic haloperidol?**

   A. Increasing social withdrawal

   B. Emotional withdrawal

   C. Severe memory deficit

   D. Auditory hallucinations

3) **Patient 2's psychiatrist increased the dosage of the antipsychotic haloperidol and made a referral to a neurologist. Was the change in haloperidol dosage the right decision?**

   A. Yes, Parkinson's disease can be treated with haloperidol.

   B. Yes, Parkinson's-like tics in schizophrenia are best treated with antipsychotics.

   C. No, antipsychotic medications like haloperidol are known to produce Parkinson's-like tics.

   D. No, because haloperidol causes symptoms of Alzheimer's disease, not Parkinson's.

4) **The psychiatrist suspects that Patient 3 has a mood disorder, but is unsure of the specific type. Which of the following questions would be least helpful in making an accurate diagnosis?**

   A. "Have you had thoughts of harming yourself in the past month?"

   B. "Have you experienced periods of racing thoughts and an elevated mood?"

   C. "How long have your symptoms persisted?"

   D. "What is your history with drug and alcohol use?"

5) **The psychiatrist determines that Patient 4 has a personality disorder. Which of the following personality disorders is most likely?**

   A. Borderline

   B. Schizoid

   C. Avoidant

   D. Paranoid

6) **The physician treating Patient 1 is participating in a clinical trial comparing the sensitivity of biological markers for diagnosing schizophrenia and Huntington's disease. Which of the following markers would be most critical to include?**

   A. fMRI brain abnormalities

   B. inflammatory kinases in blood

   C. DNA sequencing for mutations

   D. response to L-Dopa therapy

6

7

Case Studies / Brain Disorders

Annotations.
1) B 2) D 3) C 4) D 5) A 6) C

	Foundation 6: Cognition-B			Foundation 7: Individual Diffs.-A		
	B			**A**		
Concepts	1			2,5		
Reasoning	3			4		
Research	6					
Data						

Big Picture. Passages of this type are not common, they contain no data, figures or tables. Unlike the critical reasoning (verbal) section, which also contains no data, figures or tables, outside content knowledge was required to successfully answer the questions. In this passage, this includes a number of psychiatric and neurological disorders (e.g. schizophrenia, mood disorders, Parkinson's disease, and Huntington's disease). This case study format is featured in medical reports that you are likely to encounter in your medical career. Note that due to the case study format, the grid shows no coverage in data. However, the questions are still challenging as they require a broad range of content and strong reasoning skills.

1) **B. Left Frontal Lobe.** Patient 1 demonstrates a behavior pattern that is very common in aphasia: a receptive or expressive language disorder caused by dysfunction in a localized region of the brain. The most common causes of acute aphasia are head injury and stroke. There are various types of aphasias; each defined by the region of the brain affected. The two most common aphasias are Broca's and Wernicke's. Broca's aphasia impairs the ability to translate thought into speech (i.e. expressive aphasia). It results from damage to Broca's area, located in the lower portion of the left frontal lobe. Therefore, **choice B is correct**. Choice B is congruent with "Broca's area" (located in the left frontal lobe), and Broca's aphasia is consistent with patient 1's symptoms. **Choices A, C, and D are all incorrect** because these brain regions are not associated with the forms of language processing discussed in the passage. Broca's aphasia does not affect the ability to understand speech. Wernicke's aphasia impairs the ability to comprehend spoken or written language (i.e. receptive aphasia). Speech production is not impaired, however, understanding even one's own speech can be disrupted. Wernicke's area is located in the left temporal lobe. Note: For questions about language, it is important to know that it is processed primarily in the left hemisphere.

2) **D. Auditory hallucinations.** Schizophrenia is a severe form of mental illness that creates an enormous burden on individuals, families, and the health care system. The symptoms of schizophrenia can be grouped into three categories: positive, negative, and cognitive. The positive symptoms describe abnormal perception and expression (e.g. hallucinations, delusions, disorganized speech, or disorganized behavior). **Choice D is therefore the correct answer choice.** The negative symptoms represent a loss of social interaction and emotional expression (e.g. loss of motivation, no emotion, poor hygiene, and social withdrawal). **Choices A and B are incorrect** because social and emotional withdrawal are negative symptoms. Cognitive symptoms involve dysfunctional executive processes (e.g. problems with attention, memory, and reasoning). **Choice C is incorrect** because a memory deficit is a cognitive symptom. We know from the passage that Patient 2

changed medication due to a relapse of positive symptoms (hallucinations), so the key in this question was to identify the positive symptom.

3) **C. No, antipsychotic medications like haloperidol are known to produce Parkinson's-like tics.** While the causes of schizophrenia are still not clear, it is known that the disease is associated with an overexpression of the neurotransmitter dopamine. Many of the most common antipsychotics are dopamine antagonists, meaning they inhibit dopamine transmission. While these medications can be quite effective at reducing symptoms, they are associated with long term side effects, including weight gain, anxiety, and narcolepsy. Reducing dopamine levels over a period of years can actually lead to Parkinson's-like body movements (tics) called extra-pyramidal syndrome. It follows that **choice C is the correct answer choice** based on the Parkinson's-like side effects. Indeed, Parkinson's is treated with L-Dopa, a dopamine agonist that exerts the opposite effect of haloperidol. **Choices A and B are incorrect.** Haloperidol and most antipsychotics would be contraindicated medications for patients with Parkinson's. Some of the first approved antipsychotics – including haloperidol – are notorious for their unpleasant side effects and their use has to be closely monitored. Some side effects may become permanent; persisting even after the medication is terminated. The physician should not have increased the dose of haloperidol. The referral to the neurologist was indicated, as the tics are common neurological symptoms. However, they are not common symptoms in Alzheimer's disease, making **choice D an incorrect answer choice.**

4) **D. "What is your history with drug and alcohol use?"** While there are a number of separate "mood disorders" defined by the DSM-5, they can all be broadly grouped into two categories, differentiated by whether the patient has ever experienced a <u>manic</u> episode. Simply, mania is the opposite of depression and describes a state of extreme mood elevation, often occurring in conjunction with extremely disinhibited and risky behaviors. Mood disorders with manic episodes include: (1) <u>Bipolar disorder</u>: Manic episodes with or without intermittent depressive episodes. (2) <u>Cyclothymia</u>: Periods of mania alternating with periods of mild depression. Mood disorders without manic episodes include, <u>Major depressive disorder (MDD)</u>, which involves acute periods of severe mood depression. <u>Dysthymia</u> presents as chronic depressed mood that is less severe than MDD.

The symptoms of Patient 3 are all indicative of depression or dysthymia. The question stem asks for the <u>least</u> helpful question for a diagnosis. Drugs like cocaine and alcohol can induce a mood disorder or symptoms that mimic mania and depression; they would confuse the diagnosis rather than be helpful. Hence, **choice D is the credited answer** because it is the least helpful.

The question in **choice B is not credited** because it addresses a symptom of mania, which <u>would</u> be helpful in categorizing the mood disorder. **Choice C is also not the credited answer** because it helps distinguish between dysthymia and MDD. **Choice A is not the credited answer** because thoughts of self-harm, including suicidal ideas, are hallmark symptoms of depression. Therefore, this question would be very helpful. To correctly answer a question with content of this nature, you will need to be familiar with the basic categories of mental illness in psychiatry.

5) **A. Borderline.** This question requires a basic understanding of the personality disorders (PDs). Patient 4 presents with volatile emotions, threats of self-harm, poor interpersonal boundaries, and a history of multiple unstable relationships. These are the core symptoms of borderline PD, making **choice A correct.** Other PDs listed in the questions include schizoid, avoidant, and paranoid. People with schizoid PD do not care about social relationships and often do not have them. People with avoidant PD are timid and shun social relationships. People with paranoid PD are characterized by chronic mistrust and suspicion. Because schizoid, avoidant, and paranoid PD do not feature the key borderline symptoms **choices B, C, and D are all incorrect.**

6) **C. DNA sequencing for mutations.** This question centers on knowledge of research methods and of the etiology of Huntington's disease. By asking you to identify the critical markers for the diseases, the question probes your understanding of assays that would be useful in diagnosing schizophrenia and Huntington's. Recall that Huntington's – unlike schizophrenia – is among the diseases caused by a single genetic mutation (expansion of a cytosine-adenine-guanine, or CAG, triplet repeat). Clearly, DNA sequencing can readily identify Huntington's disease from schizophrenia, making **C the best answer choice**. While fMRI (brain) and hematology (blood) both potentially provide information about these diseases, they do not offer the specificity of DNA sequencing. Accordingly, **choices A and B are not credited**. L-Dopa is a drug used to treat Parkinson's disease, and is not relevant to the question. Therefore, **choice D is incorrect**.

6

7

Med-PATHWAY

Obedience to Authority

In *Obedience to Authority*, Milgram described experiments in which subjects were instructed to potentially administer harm to another person. In the original setup, a researcher in a white lab coat informed the subjects that they would serve as a teacher and test word association with a (fictitious) learner, or confederate. The researcher instructed subjects that they must administer an electric shock to the learner for incorrect answers. Shock intensity was increased following each incorrect answer, up to a maximum value. The goal of the experiments was to determine obedience to authority. The original results, when first presented to the public, surprised even experienced psychologists. Milgram subsequently conducted multiple variations of this experiment. The results of some of these variations are described in Table 1.

Milgram's findings have had several important implications. First is how these results applied to historical tragedies such as the 20th century Jewish Holocaust. For example, during the Nuremberg trials, many accused Nazi war criminals pleaded, "I was just following orders," as their sole defense. Second is whether or not these experiments were ethically defensible. This latter point is exemplified by the following contradiction: Milgram's subjects were advised during the experiment that no actual "tissue damage" would result from the electric shocks; however, subjects were exposed to feigned screams of pain and pleas to stop from the confederate learners. These seminal findings have laid the foundations for modern research ethics guidelines.

Table 1.

Variable	% subjects delivering max shock
original setup	66
teacher/learner diff. gender	35
researcher orders by phone	23
off-campus	47
teacher chooses shock level	3
teacher dresses informally	20

1) When Milgram replicated his initial experiment with female subjects, he found no significant differences between the rates at which men and women would administer the highest level of shock. Which of the following is best supported by this statement?

A. Women and men reacted the same to researcher requests to administer the highest shock level.

B. Women and men complied at identical rates to the researcher requests to administer the highest shock level.

C. Small differences between male and female rates of compliance may have existed.

D. All participants, male and female, ultimately administered the highest shock level.

2) Relative to the original setup, what happened to the average participant compliance rates regarding informal attire of the researcher? They:

A. varied based on cultural attitude.

B. decreased.

C. did not change.

D. increased.

3) A research assistant is surprised to see the first subject administer a "harmful" dose of electricity and begins to draw conclusions about the subject. Which of the following best illustrates a fundamental attribution error?

A. "Clearly the subject is being unduly influenced by the experimental attributes."

B. "I may have done the same thing, under the circumstances."

C. "This man is either weak willed, or a sadist."

D. "If the majority of subjects behave this way, we will need to reconsider the nature of morality."

4) The Milgram experiment took place prior to the establishment of standardized ethical guidelines for human research. If this experiment took place today, which of the following would not constitute a breach of the current accepted ethical guidelines?

A. The researcher used a confederate posing as another test subject to aid in deception.

B. The researcher did not explain the true nature of the study to subjects following the experiments.

C. The researcher did not make clear the voluntary nature of participation.

D. The use of deception denied the subjects their right to provide informed consent.

5) Although Milgram's original experiment included only male subjects, later variations recruited female subjects. Which of the following was most likely observed following the addition of female participants?

A. They were more apt to comply with researcher requests to apply the highest level of shock.

B. They were more likely than males to be traumatized as a result of participation in this experiment.

C. They were more likely than their male counterparts to vocalize their emotional reactions to the experiment.

D. They were angrier than male subjects at having been deceived by researchers.

6) Do Milgram's findings substantiate the "just following orders" defense provided at the Nuremberg trials?

A. Yes, because Milgram's subjects did not bear ill will toward the learners.

B. No, because Milgram's subjects did bear ill will toward the learners.

C. Yes, because Milgram's subjects believed that they were not inflicting permanent harm.

D. No, because Milgram's subjects believed that they were not inflicting permanent harm.

7

8

Obedience to Authority

Annotations.
1) C 2) B 3) C 4) A 5) C 6) D

	Foundation 7: Social Psych.-B			Foundation 8: Attributions-B Social Interaction-C	
	B			B	C
Concepts				3	
Reasoning	2,6				
Research	4				5
Data	1				

Big Picture. This passage focused on the field of social psychology, which is Foundation 7B. The Milgram work on obedience to authority, as described in the passage, represented a landmark set of studies in the field of social psychology. Given its importance to the field, it could be expected to be a content area on the MCAT, with questions regarding attribution theory, gender differences in emotional expression, identity formation, and ethics. Thus, you were also tested across Foundation 8.

While this passage focused on only a few iterations of Milgram's work, he actually performed nineteen variations examining unique factors such as gender, context, and appearance of the researcher. This work was considered seminal because it challenged our preconceived notions about obedience and attributions about peoples' behavior. Nobody, not even Milgram, anticipated that humans in general, who pride themselves on individualism and free-thinking, would comply at such high rates. Notably, the questionable ethics associated with the study led to improved ethical regulations for studies involving human subjects.

1) **C. Small differences between male and female rates of compliance may have existed.** Although you will not have to know any statistical formulas in the behavioral sciences section, you do need to have a general understanding of fundamental statistical concepts. "No significant difference" does not mean "no difference." For example, if you are comparing the height of a man who is 6'0" with that of one who is 6'1", that one inch difference might not mean much, statistically. There is a difference – it's just not significant. **Choice C is correct** because (1) it focuses on compliance and (2) it best reflects the phrasing "no significant differences" in the question stem. If we know that there was no statistical difference between male compliance and female compliance, we suspect that the two numbers were at least close. However, we don't know how close, so **choice B is incorrect** because it is too restrictive. Choice A uses the term "reacted," which has various interpretations and is not specific – thus **choice A is not correct**. We don't know how women "reacted," we only have information about their compliance rates relative to the original experiment (see Table 1). There could have been emotional or physical reactions that were unrelated to whether or not they complied with the researcher's request. In fact, the reactions by many of the participants were videotaped, and show a broad range of physical and emotional discomfort even in those who continued to deliver shocks. **Choice D is incorrect** because Table 1 clearly shows that not all participants administered the highest shock level.

2) **B. decreased.** You could answer this question correctly by examining Table 1. By doing so, you can identify a decrease from 66% to 20% making **choice B correct**. We know that symbols of authority (e.g. badges, uniforms, etc.) elicit generally greater compliance. If we remove the experimenter's symbols of authority – the lab coat and the clipboard – then compliance rates should (and did) go down, **making choices C and D incorrect**. Because there is no information regarding cultural attitude, **choice A is wrong**.

3) **C. "This man is either weak willed, or a sadist."** A fundamental attribution error refers to our natural tendency to attribute the behavior of others to dispositional factors (i.e. character traits) rather than situational or contextual factors. For example, when

you are driving down the highway and a recklessly speeding driver cuts you off, you are more likely to think, "That guy is a jerk!" as opposed to, "That poor man must be having some sort of an emergency." In this question, the correct answer choice should describe this subject's behavior in terms of a character trait rather than a situational context. **Choice C is correct** because it best parallels the "recklessly speeding jerk" example. **Choice A is the opposite**, relying on contextual factors to explain the behavior (it also uses "attribute" in an unrelated fashion as a lure). With this particular attribution bias, we are not concerned with explaining our own behavior, so **choice B is incorrect**. Finally, **choice D is incorrect** because it describes the thoughts of many people who read about this experiment, but does not explicitly illustrate a fundamental attribution error.

4) **A. The researcher used a confederate posing as another test subject to aid in deception.** Public reaction to the controversial nature of Milgram's experiments helped to prompt the establishment of Institutional Review Boards (IRBs) that are now responsible for approving research that uses human or animal subjects. IRBs are tasked with upholding ethical guidelines established by state licensing boards and professional organizations. Most of these ethical guidelines are common sense and support the guiding principle, "do no harm." Some of the ethical guidelines that are pertinent to this question include:

- Participants must be fully informed of the risks and benefits of the study prior to providing their voluntary consent.
- Consent to participate remains voluntary throughout the experiment and subjects may withdraw at any time.
- Deception is to be avoided, unless it is necessary in order to reach meaningful results and only if deceiving the participants would not cause undue harm.
- If deception is to be used, participants must be informed of the true nature of the study as soon as it is feasible to do so.

    Choices B and C are incorrect because they violate these guidelines directly. Because choice A allows for deception, it might appear to be a breach of ethical guidelines. However **choice A is correct** because the use of confederates would be "necessary in order to reach meaningful results." **Choice D is incorrect** because it acknowledges that participants

did not know they would be exposed to a potentially traumatizing experience and therefore they could not provide informed consent.

5) **C. They were more likely than their male counterparts to vocalize their emotional reactions to the experiment.** This question is about gender differences in experienced and expressed emotions, an area in which "common knowledge" is unfortunately skewed by unfounded stereotypes. Research demonstrates that females are more emotionally expressive than males; in other words, they are more prone to say what they are feeling. The prevailing theory underlying this behavior is called socialization, e.g. males learn from an early age that expressing one's emotions is not a masculine quality. There is no support for the notion that emotional expression equates to emotional fragility. These data support **choice C as the best answer**. Because they embody a misguided stereotype, **choices A and B are not credited**. There is no reason to believe that females would have been more emotionally traumatized by the experience, or more compliant than their male counterparts. **Choice D is not credited** because it implies a specific emotion that female participants felt in reaction to being deceived, which is not discussed in the passage.

6) **D. No, because Milgram's subjects believed that they were not inflicting permanent harm.** There were two challenges to this question: (1) the reciprocal structure of the answer choices, and (2) applying the results of Milgram's study to the defense of the soldiers. While both the subjects in Milgram's study and the Nazi soldiers were obedient to authority (thus suggesting that Milgram's results substantiate the defense) there are some key differences between the two groups. First, it is posited that the many of the soldiers harbored ill will toward their victims – presumably motivated by racial hatred. Given the fact that Milgram's subjects had no prior relationship with the confederate learners, there was unlikely to be racial hatred. The second difference lies in the fact that Milgram informed his subjects that no permanent bodily harm would come to the learners. Clearly, the soldiers were aware of the bodily harm that would come to their victims. The combination of these two differences disallows Milgram's findings from substantiating the defense put forth by the soldiers and therefore **choice D is credited**.

7

8

Behavioral Tolerance

Tolerance refers to an attenuation of the effect of a drug such that an increase in dose is required to produce the original effect. Figure 1 compares the effects of various drug doses on response rate after the initial acute exposure (red circles), and after receiving drug chronically over time (green squares). In the top example, the effect of drug is to systematically decrease response rate with increasing dose. In the bottom example, the curve is bi-tonic: the drug first increases and then decreases response rate. When behavioral (non-physiological) factors influence the development of tolerance to a drug, it is referred to as behavioral tolerance.

One important behavioral factor that can influence the development of tolerance is reinforcement loss. For example, a food-deprived rat is trained to lever press for food reinforcement. If the initial effect of drug decreases response rate and causes a loss of reinforcement, then the "reinforcement-loss" hypothesis predicts that tolerance will develop to the disruptive effects of drug on lever-pressing (e.g. loss of food) – an adaptive mechanism. However, if there is no reinforcement loss, then the theory predicts that tolerance will not develop.

One caveat to the reinforcement-loss hypothesis relates to other possible sources of reinforcement in the environment. For example, a subject is exposed to two alternating reinforcement schedules (options), where one has a high rate of reinforcement relative to the other. A drug is introduced that disrupts responding in both schedules and results in reinforcement loss. After chronic drug administration, tolerance develops only in the component that was associated with the high rates of reinforcement (i.e. more food). This occurs despite reinforcement loss in both schedules. When the reinforcement level influences tolerance development, it is described as the reinforcement-density hypothesis.

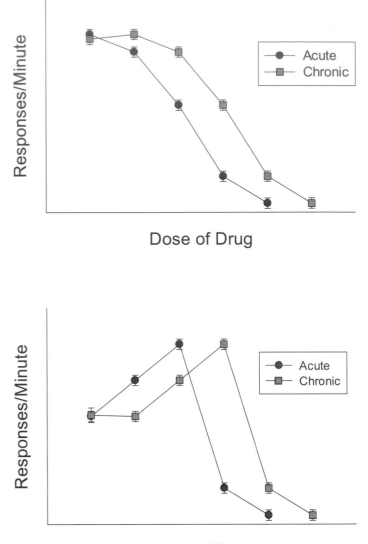

Figure 1. Top panel: Negative sigmoidal dose response curves for acute and chronic drug dosing, with tolerance demonstrated by a rightward shift in the chronic dosing condition. **Bottom panel:** Bi-tonic dose response curves for acute and chronic drug dosing, with tolerance demonstrated by a rightward shift in the chronic dosing condition. Note that confirmation of tolerance requires consideration of the entire dose-response function.

1) A researcher gives animals acute and chronic administrations of a single drug dose (e.g. 10 mg). Acute administration initially decreases rates of behavior, which then return to baseline levels following chronic administration. Can the researcher conclude that tolerance was observed and why?

A. Yes, behavior returned to baseline levels following chronic administration.

B. Yes, the same dose was administered, enhancing the likelihood of learning.

C. No, chronic administration resulted in the opposite effect of acute administration.

D. No, the dose-effect curve may be bi-tonic.

2) A new drug decreases response rate. Which reinforcement schedule combination would be the most likely to produce tolerance under one schedule but not the other?

A. Fixed-interval 1 min, Variable-interval 1 min

B. Variable-ratio 30, Fixed-ratio 30

C. Fixed-interval 10 s, Variable-ratio 5

D. Fixed-ratio 1, Fixed-interval 30 s

3) Which of the following examples is least like the others?

A. Decreased locomotor activity in mice drinking from a bowl of milk following chronic cocaine.

B. An experienced heroin addict uses heroin for the first time at a friend's house and overdoses.

C. A college student that was impaired after 2 beers now needs 6 beers to get the same effect.

D. A cigarette smoker switches to using e-cigarettes and experiences no withdrawal.

4) An individual is stopped by the police for suspected DUI. The person shows no signs of impairment in speech or motor coordination, but the breathalyzer indicates an alcohol level well above the legal limit. The most likely explanation for this discrepancy is:

A. situational tolerance.

B. physiological tolerance.

C. behavioral tolerance.

D. none of the above.

5) Based on Figure 1, which of the following is the least important for identifying tolerance?

A. Duration of chronic dosing regiment

B. Range of doses assessed

C. Exceeding the ED_{50} of the drug

D. Type of drug used

6) Which drug would most likely result in a bi-tonic dose-effect curve on cognitive performance?

A. Caffeine

B. Morphine

C. Alcohol

D. LSD

6

7

Behavioral Tolerance

	Foundation 6: Cognition-B			Foundation 7: Individual Diffs.-A Learning-C		
	B			**A**	**C**	
Concepts					2	
Reasoning				3	4	
Research	6					
Data	5				1	

Big Picture. Recall that tolerance is an attenuation of a drug effect. This means more drug (e.g. a higher dose) is required to produce the initial effect, which is evident graphically in a right-ward shift in the dose-response curve. For example, focusing on the circled data point in Figure 2 below, notice how the same dose has less effect on response rates, highlighted by the upward arrow. Chronic administration resulted in tolerance (a right-ward shift in the dose-effect curve), and a dose that previously decrease responding by approximately 50% now exerts less effect. Likewise, a higher dose is now required to recapture the initial effect, highlighted by the right-ward arrow. Note that you

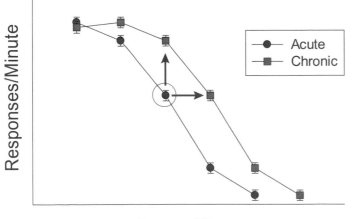

Figure 2. Comparison of acute and chronic effects of drug. Following chronic dosing, the initial acute effects of a dose have been attenuated as highlighted by the up arrow, and a higher dose is required to recapture the same effect as shown by the right arrow.

cannot tell whether tolerance has occurred without examining the full range of the dose-effect curve. For example, in a bi-tonic dose-response curve, chronic administration may result in a left-ward shift in that curve (see Figure 3 upward arrow). If only a single dose had been examined, it may appear that tolerance had occurred when it did not (in fact, the opposite transpired).

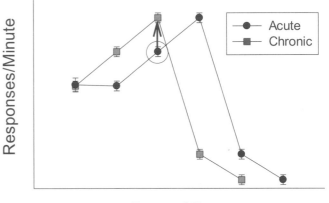

Figure 3. Based only on the circled dose, one may erroneously conclude that tolerance to the rate-decreasing effects of the drug has occurred. However, characterization of the entire dose-effect curve clearly shows sensitization.

Success in this passage will require recognition of basic schedules of reinforcement. Four common schedules of reinforcement are:

1. **Fixed-ratio**: reinforcement is delivered once a set number of N responses is made.
2. **Variable-ratio**: reinforcement is delivered once on average, N responses are made. The actual number of responses varies within a predefined range.
3. **Fixed-interval**: reinforcement is delivered for the first response made after N time has passed.
4. **Variable-interval**: reinforcement is delivered for the first response once on average, N time has elapsed. The actual time interval varies within a predefined range.

One important characteristic of these schedules of reinforcement is that response rate is closely tied with reinforcer rate for both types of ratio schedules. For interval schedules, the rate of reinforcement will reach a maximum value due to the time requirement.

1) **D. No, the dose-effect curve may be bi-tonic.** A central point of the current passage is that you cannot assume that tolerance has occurred by only observing drug effects at a single dose. As shown in the bottom of Figure 1, this is because a bi-tonic curve can produce different results depending on the following: 1) where a given dose lies on the dose-response curve; and 2) which direction the curve shifts following chronic dosing. All other answers focus on what is happening at a single dose; **choices A, B, and C are all incorrect** for this reason. It follows that the **correct answer is choice D.**

2) **D. Fixed-ratio 1, Fixed-interval 30 s.** The primary focus for this question is to determine which response option presents the greatest discrepancy in reinforcement rates? Recall from the reinforcement density hypothesis that the contrast between two reinforcement schedules can engender tolerance. The difference between making 1 response per reward and waiting and 30 s for each reward is the largest discrepancy, making **choice D the correct answer.** A difference in 5 responses and 10 s is less discrepant than choice D, thus **choice C is incorrect.** It is reasonable to quickly **eliminate choices A and B** because they provide similar rates of reinforcement.

3) **B. An experienced heroin addict uses heroin for the first time at a friend's house and overdoses.** All of the examples except for answer choice B are examples of tolerance. Because it describes increased sensitivity to a drug's effect (not tolerance), **choice B is correct.** Only example B does not describe tolerance. Cocaine is a psychomotor stimulant, which increases locomotor activity. **Choice A is incorrect** and unlike choice B because decreased locomotor activity following chronic cocaine is an example of behavioral tolerance. In answer choice C, recall the passage states that tolerance is the "attenuation of the effect of a drug such that an increase in dose is required to produce the original effect," making **choice C incorrect**, as it is unlike choice B. Finally, **choice D is incorrect** and unlike choice B. Rather, it is an example of maintaining tolerance as the active ingredient (nicotine) is the same in both cigarettes and e-cigarettes.

4) **C. behavioral tolerance.** This question requires content knowledge and reasoning based on the passage. The passage notes that behavioral tolerance is a process that relates to non-physiological factors. It follows that **choice C is the correct answer** because this question stem describes behavioral tolerance, i.e. lack of impairment in speech and motor coordination. (Presumably this is due in part to more than one previous experience carrying out these actions while intoxicated with a high BAL – indicative of an alcohol use disorder). Since the driver's BAL was well above the legal limit, **choice B is incorrect**; it can be assumed that physiological tolerance was not responsible for the lack of impairment in speech or motor coordination. **Choice A is incorrect**; situational tolerance is not described in the passage.

5) **D. Type of drug used.** A key concept in this passage is that characterizing a full dose-response function is important for assessing tolerance. As long as the dose response function is fully characterized (i.e. a range of doses is tested), the specific drug class is not critical for assessing whether or not tolerance has occurred, making **choice D correct.** As depicted in Figure 1, some duration of chronic drug administration is necessary in order to observe tolerance, thus **choice A is incorrect.** A range of doses is necessary to determine the shape of a full dose-response function, making **choice B incorrect.** The ED_{50} is the effective dose at which the half-maximum effect of the drug is observed, and differences in ED_{50} do serve as an important marker for tolerance; therefore **choice C is incorrect.**

6) **A. Caffeine.** Regarding drugs and cognitive performance, a common finding is an inverted U-shaped function between stimulants (e.g. caffeine, cocaine, amphetamine, methylphenidate, etc.) and cognitive performance. Specifically, low- to medium-doses enhance performance, and higher doses degrade performance. Accordingly, **choice A is the correct answer.** In contrast, there is no evidence that traditional depressants (e.g. alcohol, morphine) improve cognitive performance, making **choices B and C incorrect.** Likewise, hallucinogens like LSD certainly do not improve cognitive performance, making **choice D incorrect.**

6

7

Contingency Management

Cigarette smoking is a significant public health concern. While many try to quit, most relapse within a week. This is unfortunate, as early abstinence is a significant predictor of longer-term abstinence. Contingency management (CM) is a treatment that provides incentives for meeting a target behavior, such as abstinence from smoking. CM has potential efficacy because it provides additional, relatively immediate incentives for remaining abstinent. For example, many of the possible consequences of continuing to smoke (e.g. cancer, death, emphysema) are likely to be delayed for years or may not even occur.

Figure 1 (top panel) shows results from a study testing CM as a treatment for smoking. Half of the treatment-seeking smokers were randomized to receive CM-treatment during the first two weeks of a quit attempt. The other half was designated as the control group. Smokers visited the clinic three times a week and presented a breath carbon monoxide (CO) sample. The half-life of breath CO is approximately 2 to 5 hrs. A breath CO ≤ 4 ppm indicates recent abstinence, ≥ 10 ppm indicates recent smoking, and ≥ 18 ppm indicates heavy smoking. Participants in the treatment group received cash payments for breath CO samples ≤ 4 ppm at each study visit. A follow-up visit to assess longer-term abstinence was scheduled for 6-months after the end of the study.

Figure 1 (top panel) shows the proportion of individuals that were abstinent in the CM group (red) vs. the control group (orange) during the first two weeks of the quit attempt, and at a 6-month follow-up visit. Based on these results, a second group of researchers attempted a systematic replication and obtained the results shown in Figure 1 (bottom panel).

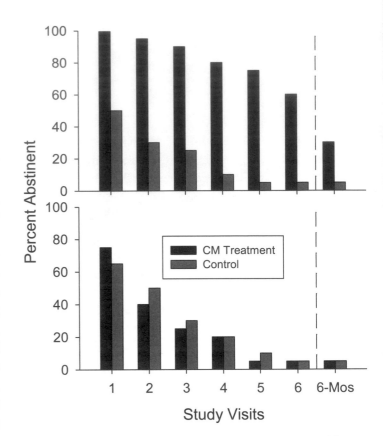

Figure 1. Percent of individuals found to be smoking abstinent in the 1st study (top) and the replication (bottom) across study visits.

1) Which statistical test is the most appropriate for assessing the efficacy of CM for the data shown in Figure 1?

A. t-tests

B. Chi-Square

C. Pearson correlation

D. Analysis of Variance (ANOVA)

2) Assuming that all recipients received $100 at the initiation of the study and then had to pay $5 each time they had a CO > 10, on what behavioral principle would this treatment be based?

A. Positive reinforcement

B. Negative reinforcement

C. Positive punishment

D. Negative punishment

3) If all recipients were paid $10,000 to quit smoking, would this study be ethical?

A. Yes, because compensation is a standard ethical component of human research.

B. No, because the amount is so high it could be construed as coercive.

C. Yes, because the study outcome could save the lives of the participants.

D. No, because compensation is not a standard ethical component of human research.

4) In the study presented in the passage, one of the groups is labeled as "control." What would be the most appropriate control group?

A. A group receiving no treatment.

B. A paid non-smoker group.

C. A group paid regardless of smoking status.

D. A group of smokers not seeking treatment.

5) Which of the following are possible reasons that study 2 failed to replicate the results of study 1?

    I. Differences in baseline smoking frequencies between study 1 and 2.
    II. Study 2 did not pay recipients until visit 6.
    III. Study 2 participants were lighter smokers than study 1.

A. I, III

B. I, II

C. I, II, III

D. I

6) Serum cotinine levels are a more sensitive measurement for the presence of nicotine relative to breath CO due to greater half-life. How might the data have changed if cotinine measures were used?

A. Less false abstinence

B. More false positives

C. More false abstinence

D. Less false positives

7) What is the biggest experimental weakness of study 1?

A. Focusing on the first two weeks of the quit attempt.

B. Giving cash that could be used to buy cigarettes.

C. Not accounting for the use of other drugs (e.g. alcohol) in both groups.

D. Having three study visits per week.

6

7

Annotations.
1) D 2) D 3) B 4) C 5) B 6) A 7) D

Big Picture. Success in this passage requires breaking down and isolating the primary features of the experiment (a behavioral treatment) and judging its strengths and weaknesses. Astute readers will immediately notice that many of the experimental details are purposefully left vague. Overall, a behavioral treatment is being tested among treatment-seeking smokers. Results from the first study indicate that individuals receiving CM treatment were more likely to be abstinent (as measured by breath CO). However, the second study failed to replicate these findings. It is noteworthy that if a subject population is treatment seeking, ethics dictate that some type of established treatment must be made available to both groups. Also, as there is a discrepancy in the findings between the first and second study, you should focus on which aspects of the experimental design might explain these differences. Finally, notice that the half-life of breath CO (stated in the passage) leaves a window open for smoking that may not be detected using thrice-weekly visits and CO tests.

1) **D. Analysis of Variance (ANOVA).** This question is tricky as it asks you to visualize the results based on breath CO as opposed to percent abstinent. First, recall situations that are appropriate for ANOVA. ANOVA is used to compare two or more means divided by their pooled standard deviation. Additionally, ANOVA can account for repeated measures. None of the other statistical tests listed in the answer choices are capable of measuring repeated observations. Accordingly, **choice D is the correct answer**. Chi square measures differences in expected proportions, which in this case would be inappropriate because it would obscure the experimental design, making **choice B incorrect**. T-test is typically used to compare two groups at a single time point. Since subjects were measured at multiple time points, **choice A is incorrect**. Pearson correlation is a variation of regression analysis, which tests the relationship between two variables, but does not test differences between groups, making **choice C incorrect**.

2) **D. Negative punishment.** This question presents a frequently misunderstood (and misused) concept in behavioral psychology. Basically, people associate terms such as punishment and negative as being "bad," and reinforcement and positive as being "good." These are inaccurate distinctions in the reinforcement/punishment matrix. You may be asked questions that require you to distinguish among these behavioral processes. Table 1 shows how to properly break down the relationship between these four types of consequences.

Table 1

What happens to the behavior	What is happening in the environment	
	Something is added	Something is taken away
Increases	Positive Reinforcement	Negative Reinforcement
Decreases	Positive Punishment	Negative Reinforcement

You only need to make two determinations. First, what is happening in the environment? If something is being added, like receiving money or receiving a shock, then it is <u>positive</u>. If something is being taken away, such as losing money or removal of shock, then it is <u>negative</u>. Second, what happens to the behavior? If the behavior increases, then it's <u>reinforcement</u>. If the behavior decreases, it's <u>punishment</u>. In question two, money is being taken away (negative) and the goal is to reduce smoking (punishment), so the **correct answer is choice D** – negative punishment. **Choices A and B are incorrect** because they refer to a consequence in which some thing is being added (positive). **Choice C is incorrect** because it describes reinforcement, which would have the putative effect of increasing smoking.

3) **B. No, because the amount is so high it could be construed as coercive.** In order to answer this question, it is necessary to know basic principles regarding ethics in clinical research. Compensation should generally be commensurate to the time and effort that a participant puts into the study. It follows that $10,000 for a 2-week study is too high, and would be considered coercive, making **choice B the correct answer**. Accordingly, you can quickly **eliminate choices A and C**. By process of elimination, **choice D can also be eliminated** – many research studies involve some type of compensation.

4) **C. A group paid regardless of smoking status.** Optimally, a control condition is the same as the experimental condition except that one aspect is changed (e.g. the treatment being tested). Additionally, the passage explicitly states that <u>all participants were treatment seekers</u>. **Choice C is the correct answer**; it represents an optimal control group utilizing the same population as the experimental group and matching monetary compensation. The only difference between the two groups is whether or not money is being provided based on smoking (CO level), which is the focus of the contingency management treatment. If the goal of the experiment is to examine treatment effectiveness, **choices B (non-smokers) and D (non-treatment seekers) can be eliminated**. Answer choice A could represent a viable control group, but **choice A is not the correct answer** because a no-treatment group would introduce a large number of uncontrolled between-group differences. This would make it difficult to draw defensible conclusions from the results.

5) **B. I, II.** First, from a strategic test-taking perspective, it is not necessary to spend time considering option I because all answer choices contain it (it provides no information on which to make a choice). A key to understanding this question is awareness of the factors that affect reinforcement efficacy. Three primary factors are: 1) the magnitude of reinforcement; 2) the immediacy of reinforcement; and 3) the response effort required to receive reinforcement. In the question, holding payment back to until visit 6 is likely to reduce the utility of the monetary incentive to promote abstinence, thereby making **Option II (choice B) the correct answer**. In contrast, **Option III is incorrect (choices A and C)** because lighter smokers should have less difficulty achieving abstinence, but subjects in study 2 had more difficulty remaining abstinent.

6) **A. Less false abstinence.** This question required an understanding of two key points: 1) the difference between CO and cotinine to monitor smoking; 2) the difference between false positives/negatives. The advantage of cotinine over CO is that is it is eliminated from the body more slowly. This provides better protection against false negatives (e.g. falsely indicating abstinence even though recent smoking occurred); therefore **choice A is correct** (less chance of false negatives) and **choice C is incorrect** (more chance of false negatives). False positives do not apply in this case, making **choices B and D incorrect**, but could include a flawed test for smoking that erroneously indicated recent smoking when none has occurred.

On a broader note, understanding the logistics of false positives/negatives is important to your success on the MCAT (and subsequently as a physician). This area can be confusing. Table 2 organizes this information and defines the important terms.

Table 2

Test Outcome	Condition Outcome	
	Positive	Negative
Positive	**A** True Positive	**B** False Positive (Type I Error)
Negative	**C** False Negative (Type II Error)	**D** True Negative

Contingency Management

<u>Important terms (refer to Table cells for A-D)</u>:

Sensitivity $= A/(A+C)$. Sensitivity describes a test's ability to identify a condition correctly, or the probability of obtaining a positive test result when the condition is positive (e.g. test says there is cancer and the patient has cancer).

Specificity $= D/(D+B)$. This is the flip side of sensitivity, and describes a test's ability to correctly identify if a condition is not present (e.g. test says no cancer and the patient does not have cancer).

Accuracy $= (A+D)/(A+B+C+D)$. The proportion of true results (e.g. true positives and true negatives) in the entire sample is described by the term accuracy (e.g. accurately identify if cancer is there or not).

Precision $= A/(A+B)$. Precision describes the proportion of true results out of all positive test outcomes (e.g. how often the test is correct when the test outcome identifies cancer).

7) **D. Having three study visits per week.** A different way to think about <u>experimental weakness</u> is to ask: What other variables could affect the validity of the results and conclusions? Given the relatively short half-life of breath CO and the thrice-weekly study sessions, the biggest weakness is high likelihood of false negatives. Thus, **choice D is credited**: participants could time their smoking to evade detection via CO monitoring. This problem could be mitigated through more frequent measurement or cotinine measurement. **Choice A is not credited**; the passage states that most people relapse in the first two weeks, so it is an important feature of the study. Answer choices B and C are potential weaknesses, but the question asks for the greatest weakness, and these are less severe weaknesses. Thus, **choices B and C are not credited**.

6

7

PATHWAY

Impulsivity

Impulsivity is associated with behaviors that may be harmful to one's self or others, and which are inappropriate to a given context. Three common measures of impulsivity are trait impulsivity, response inhibition, and delay discounting. Trait impulsivity covers a range of persistent behavior patterns, including hasty decisions and actions without consideration for consequences. Response inhibition encompasses rapid action without the ability to withhold that action when necessary. Response inhibition can be measured by having individuals make a response in the presence of one stimulus (Go) and then to stop or inhibit that response when a second (Stop) stimulus is introduced. Delay discounting describes how a reward loses value as a function of increasing delay to its receipt. Experimental assessment of discounting involves presenting people with choices between a smaller, immediate vs. a larger, delayed reward. The value of the immediate reward is adjusted until a point of subjective equality (or "indifference point") is obtained. By obtaining indifference points at different delays, a delay discounting function can be assessed.

$$V = A/(1 + kD) \qquad \text{(Equation 1)}$$

Equation 1 represents a hyperbolic model of delay discounting that describes how a reward of some amount (A) changes in value (V) as a function of delay (D). The free-parameter k describes the rate of delay discounting, with greater delay discounting (higher k value) indicating higher levels of impulsivity. Note that an important feature of this hyperbolic function is that discounting occurs more rapidly at shorter delays relative to longer delays. Figure 1 depicts median indifference points obtained for a group of individuals with substance use disorders and a group of control subjects. Curved lines represent the best-fit curves to Equation 1 for group A (blue) and group B (red).

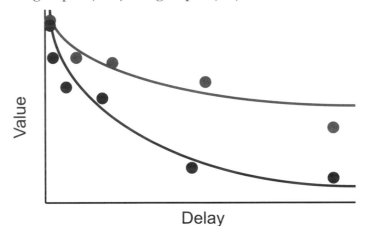

Figure 1. Hyperbolic delay discounting function for groups A and B.

1) Which of the following is the best example of an impulsive behavior?

   A. Riding a roller coaster

   B. Playing video games

   C. Cigarette smoking

   D. Eating savory food

2) Which of the following would not be an example of impulsivity that is related to delay discounting?

   A. Setting your alarm the night before and then pressing the snooze in the morning.

   B. Overspending while shopping for clothes.

   C. Waiting until the night before the test to study.

   D. Seeing cocaine and then immediately using it without consideration.

3) Which of the following represents the delay at which the reward's subjective value is decreased by 50% according to the hyperbolic model??

   A. $1/k$

   B. $k/2$

   C. k^2

   D. k^{-2}

4) A person trying to lose weight eats a donut. What type of impulsivity best describes this example?

   A. Trait impulsivity

   B. Response inhibition

   C. Hyperbolic delay discounting

   D. Exponential delay discounting

5) In Figure 1, which curve likely represents the control group, and which curve depicts greater impulsivity?

   A. A, A

   B. A, B

   C. B, A

   D. B, B

6) An assessment querying behavior patterns over the past year would most likely be measuring which type of impulsivity?

   A. Trait impulsivity

   B. Response inhibition

   C. Delay discounting

   D. Exponential impulsivity

7

8

Impulsivity

Annotations.
1) C   2) D   3) A   4) C   5) B   6) A

	Foundation 7: Individual Diffs.-A Learning-C			Foundation 8: Self-identity-A		
	A	C		A		
Concepts	1	4				
Reasoning	2	3				
Research				6		
Data				5		

Big Picture. This passage is focused on impulsivity, an important but complex concept in the behavioral sciences. This topic is challenging because people tend to think of impulsivity as a single type of behavior or action. However, decades of research have shown that impulsivity is actually multi-faceted. Different aspects of impulsivity have different properties, and they do not necessarily co-vary. For example, a person may be impulsive according to the delay discounting assessment, but have normal levels of response inhibition. The most common measures of impulsivity are presented in the passage (e.g. trait impulsivity, response inhibition, and delay discounting). Success on the questions requires understanding the different types of impulsivity as described in the passage text, and comprehension of curve fitting and non-linear (hyperbolic) equations.

1) **C. Cigarette smoking.** In the appropriate context, each of the answers could potentially be an example of impulsivity. The key to this question is in the first sentence of the passage, "Impulsivity is associated with behaviors that may be harmful to one's self or others." Because smoking is the example that is most clearly harmful, **choice C is credited**. While options A, B, and D are potentially dangerous or harmful, none of them causes obvious harm. Additionally, smoking is a well-established example of choosing an immediate reward (the pharmacological effects of nicotine) over a more delayed reward of greater value (one's health). Thus **choices A, B, and D are not credited** because they are less suitable examples compared to choice B.

2) **D. Seeing cocaine and then immediately using it without consideration.** Recall that delay discounting involves making "choices between a smaller, more immediate reward vs. a larger, more delayed one." **Choice D is correct** because it most closely matches the description of response inhibition, or acting without thinking about the consequences. Notice that all options except D can be framed as engaging in choices between immediately available options (e.g. pressing snooze, spending money, not study) vs. delayed options (e.g. getting to work on time, saving money, doing well on the test). Because they are all examples of delay discounting, **choices A, B, and C are incorrect**.

3) **A. $1/k$.** This question requires you to manipulate Equation 1 to derive the delay at which a reward's subjective value is decreased by half.

$$V = A/(1 + kD) \qquad (1)$$

The parameter V (subjective value) that you are solving for is ½ of A (initial amount). Therefore, you can replace V in the equation above with ½A.

$$\tfrac{1}{2}A = A/(1 + kD)$$

Cancel A from each side.

$$\tfrac{1}{2} = 1/(1 + kD)$$

Cross multiply and solve for D.

$$1 + kD = 2$$
$$kD = 1$$
$$\mathbf{D = 1/k}$$

4) C. Hyperbolic delay discounting. The question introduces a situation requiring a choice between two events with different time windows (e.g. losing weight over time vs. eating a donut now). This means it is a form of delay discounting. **Choice C is correct**, as it is consistent with hyperbolic discounting as described in the passage and Figure 1. The passage and Figure 1 do not discuss exponential discounting. Further, the choice to eat a donut while dieting is not consistent with an exponential model. Therefore, **choice D is incorrect**. One key to understanding hyperbolic discounting is it "…occurs more rapidly at shorter delays relative to longer delays." This is important as preference shifts are predicted in a hyperbolic model, whereas preferences would remain consistent in an exponential model of discounting. Figure 2 below illustrates why this is the case.

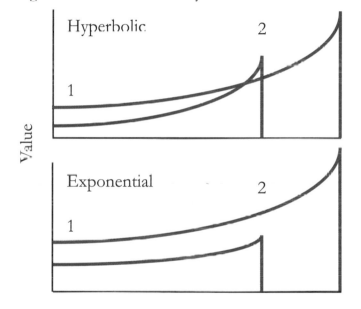

Figure 2. Hypothetical discounting curves predicted by hyperbolic and exponential discounting models.

The x-axis represents the time it would take until a reward is obtained and the y-axis represents the subjective value of each reward. The value of losing weight is represented by the red curve (e.g. higher value, temporally farther away), whereas eating a donut is represented by the green curve (e.g. smaller value, immediately available). Therefore, at time point 1, when both options are temporally far away, the value of losing weight is > eating a donut for both hyperbolic and exponential discounting. However, at time point 2, when the donut is immediately available and at its maximum value, preference (value) shifts in the hyperbolic model but not the exponential model. **Choices A and B are incorrect** because they do not describe delay discounting processes, and their definitions are inconsistent with the question stem.

5) B. A, B. Recall from the passage, the "<u>free-parameter *k* describes the rate of delay discounting, with greater delay discounting indicating higher levels of impulsivity</u>." Therefore, higher impulsivity is associated with a higher rate of delay discounting. Since delay discounting describes how the subjective value of a reward decreases with delay, then greater delay discounting (i.e. greater impulsivity) is indicated by more rapid decreases in the subjective value of a reward over time. In Figure 1, this is indicated by the steeper, shallower curve B – which is consistent with the more impulsive group of subjects. Additionally, you should be able to deduce that the group with a substance use disorder will be more impulsive. Thus, **choice B is correct**. It follows that **choices A and C can be eliminated** because they depict less impulsivity. **Choice D can be eliminated** because group B (control) is <u>less</u> impulsive compared to group A.

6) A. Trait impulsivity. The key to this passage is the phrase "<u>patterns over the past year</u>" in the question stem. It is consonant with the phrase "<u>persistent behavior patterns</u>," used in the passage to describe trait impulsivity – making **choice A the credited answer**. Conceptually and experimentally, both response inhibition and delay discounting focus on state-like (i.e. current) behavior patterns rather than stable trait-like (i.e. long-term) behavior patterns. Accordingly, **choices B and C are not credited**. Recall that the three types of impulsivity discussed in the passage are trait, response inhibition, and delay discounting. As the term "exponential impulsivity" is not used in the passage, **choice D is not credited**.

7

8

Identity Formation

Research has focused on how stereotypic images presented in video games affect the attitudes and self-images of players. In one study, a group of researchers investigated whether the gender of the game player impacts how a stereotypical image is perceived. Young adults (average age = 19) were initially divided into two groups based on gender and given a survey that assessed a variety of topics, including general demographics (**Table 1**) as well as personal video game use (**Table 2**). Next, participants were asked to play three different video games, each one was defined by how it presented a specific gender stereotype. (1) **Gender-neutral**: a sports-themed game in which male and female characters were dressed modestly. (2) **Negative male**: an "action shooter" game where the male protagonist is aggressive and violent. (3) **Negative female**: a football game in which the female cheerleaders are scantily clad and frequently display sexually provocative poses. After 10 minutes of gameplay, the subjects were asked whether or not they believed the games presented a negative gender stereotype. The results are shown in Figure 1.

Table 1.

Question	Male	Female
# of games owned?		
0-4	22	37
5-10	26	19
>10	11	3
Hours/week played?		
<2	17	30
2-8	21	21
>8	19	8
Age started playing?		
Before age 5	10	4
Ages 5-10	29	19
After age 10	7	19
Never (I don't play)	11	17

Table 2.

Factor	n	%
Gender		
Male	57	49
Female	59	51
Age		
<18	23	20
18-20	59	51
21-22	29	25
>22	5	4
Family Income		
<50k	25	22
50k-75k	41	35
75k-100k	29	25
>100k	21	18

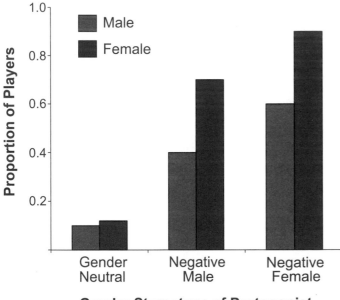

Figure 1. Proportion of participants who believed game presented negative gender stereotype.

1) Which of the following general conclusions is best supported by the results of this study?

A. Across gender, the more individuals play violent video games the less likely they are to recognize negative stereotypes in those games.

B. Children who start playing video games at a younger age are more likely to play more hours per week.

C. Children who are from higher income homes are more likely to own and play video games.

D. Across gender, people are less likely to identify "violent" as a negative male stereotype than they are to identify "hypersexual" as a negative female stereotype.

2) If the study instructions included the phrase, "The study aim is to assess changes in fine motor skills in response to difficulty level." Which of the following best assesses the ethical permissibility of this deception?

A. Unethical. Researchers are ethically obligated to reveal the true purpose of a study to participants before informed consent.

B. Unethical. It is never ethically permissible for a researcher to use deception in the course of a study involving minors.

C. Ethical. Minor deceptions are ethically permissible when non-deceptive alternatives are not feasible.

D. Ethical. Standard research guidelines do not address the use of deception with study participants.

3) Which statistical outcome is least likely depicted in Figure 1?

A. A significant main effect of gender.

B. A significant main effect of stereotype.

C. A significant interaction of gender by stereotype.

D. A significant interaction of gender by age started playing.

4) During follow-up, participants were asked if it was "OK" for kids to play video games with a rating of "M" ("Mature"). Nineteen percent of the participants endorsed the response, "Yes, if most of their friends also play those games." According to Kohlberg's theory of moral development, this response best represents which level of moral reasoning?

A. Level 1: Preconventional Morality

B. Level 2: Conventional Morality

C. Level 3: Postconventional Morality

D. Level 4: Transcendent Morality

5) Which of the following statements is most consistent with how cognitive dissonance theory might apply to this study?

A. Participants who identified with the game's protagonist were less likely to endorse that game as an example of a negative stereotype.

B. Participants who identified with the game's protagonist were more likely to endorse that game as an example of a negative stereotype.

C. Participants who did not identify with the game's protagonist were less likely to endorse that game as an example of a negative stereotype.

D. Participants who did not identify with the game's protagonist were more likely to endorse that game as an example of a negative stereotype.

6) The statement: "Negative stereotypes persist because it behooves the current power structure for them to persist," is an example of which of the following schools of thought regarding the development of social structure?

A. Social constructionism

B. Symbolic interactionism

C. Functionalism

D. Conflict theory

8

9

Identity Formation

Annotations.
1) D 2) C 3) C 4) B 5) A 6) D

	Foundation 8: Self-identity-A Attributions-B		Foundation 9: Social Structure-A	
	A	**B**	**A**	
Concepts	4		6	
Reasoning		5		
Research	3	2		
Data	1			

Big Picture. This passage is about identity formation and how gender and media influence self-identity and perception of stereotypes. Importantly, males are less inclined than females to recognize either stereotype as negative. Figure 2 is a reproduction of the data in the passage and shows that males are consistently less likely than females to recognize gender stereotypes (i.e. blue bars lower than red bars).

Figure 2.
Reproduction of Figure 1 from the passage.

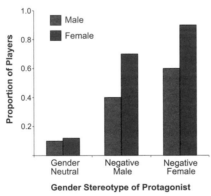

The figure and two tables in the passage present a considerable amount of information, which is consistent with those typically presented in social science research (e.g. several tables filled with a lot of data). While such tables can potentially contain important information, these tables are extraneous in the current passage. MCAT passages may be presented in this manner, and it is important to scan the passage and questions to determine which data, tables, and figures are needed to answer the questions and which are superfluous. In this particular passage, only Figure 1 is needed to answer the data-based questions (numbers 1, 4, and 6).

1) **D. Across gender, people are less likely to identify "violent" as a negative male stereotype than they are to identify "hypersexual" as a negative female stereotype.** This question requires determining which answer choices can be addressed in the data and which cannot. The goal of the study was to determine the effect of video games on gender stereotypes. While Tables 1 and 2 presented an array of demographic data, the experiment itself focused on gender stereotypes as the independent variable. Recall from the passage that, "researchers investigated whether the gender of the player impacts how a stereotypical image is perceived." This effectively **rules out choices A, B, and C** because they all refer to data in Tables 1 and 2, which do not address gender stereotypes. **Choice D is correct** because it summarizes the trend displayed in Figure 1, in which both males and females (red and blue bars) are higher for negative female stereotypes than for negative male stereotypes.

2) **C. Ethical. Minor deceptions are ethically permissible when non-deceptive alternatives are not feasible.** This question tests knowledge regarding the ethical principles that applies to research with human subjects. The American Psychological Association's (APA) ethical standards (Deception in Research) states that although it is not typical to employ deception with human subjects, it is ethically permissible under certain circumstances: (1) telling the subjects the truth would inappropriately skew the results of valuable research; (2) the study is not expected to result in emotional or physical pain for the subject(s); and (3) researchers debrief the study participants once it is feasible. Since deception under certain conditions is allowed, **choice A is not credited**. This specific principal does not address deception with minors (parents/guardians still have to give consent), so **choice B is not credited**. Because standard guidelines of research do emphasize deception, **choice D is incorrect**. You could arrive at **correct answer choice C** by process of elimination. Priming, a way of biasing the subject toward the goals of the study, might have been a factor in this experiment without deception. If participants knew the study was about negative stereotypes, they might be primed to look for them in the video game, which could bias the results.

3) **C. A significant interaction of gender by stereotype.** In this passage, you are asked to make an estimate of the statistical outcomes based on the data patterns shown in Figure 1. You must read the question carefully, as it asked for the <u>least likely</u> outcome. When a factor like gender (i.e. the red and blue bars) is higher in every condition, the statistical outcome will very likely be a "main effect" for that factor. In Figure 1, the red bars (female) are higher than the blue bars (male) in each condition, suggesting a main effect of gender (note the bracketed differences across the bars below in Figure 3). Since the question is asking for the <u>least likely</u> outcome, **choice A is not credited**. The overall proportion of players (Y-axis) increases across stereotype condition (X-axis) depicted by the increasing trend for both bars across Neutral, Negative Male, and Negative Female conditions (note the trend depicted by the dashed arrow in Figure 3). Thus, similar to choice A, **choice B is not credited** because there is likely a main effect of the factor of gender stereotype.

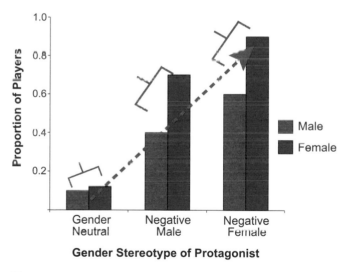

Figure 3.

A statistically significant interaction is evident in a figure when bars (or data lines) move in different directions across conditions. For example, if the red bars were higher than the blue bars in the Negative Male condition and vice versa in the Negative Female condition, an interaction would be likely. Since the bars all trend in the same direction across all three conditions, there is clearly no interaction, making **choice C the credited answer**. Answer choice D also suggests an interaction. More importantly, age is not represented in Figure 1; therefore you do not have sufficient information to determine if there was a statistically significant interaction between gender and age started playing. Therefore, **choice D is not the credited answer**.

4) **B. Level 2: Conventional Morality.** This question covers the model of moral reasoning proposed by Kohlberg. The model has <u>three</u> levels: (1) <u>Preconventional</u> Morality (focus on self); (2) <u>Conventional</u> Morality (social relationships and rules); (3) <u>Postconventional</u> Morality (abstract relationships between right and wrong). The respondents who answered, "Yes, if most of their friends also play those games" were concerned about fitting in with a social group. This is most consistent with the stage of Conventional Morality, making **choice C correct, and choices A and B incorrect**. Because there is no Transcendent Morality in Kohlberg's theory, **choice D is incorrect**.

Psychology is replete with stage theories about personality development. Each theory contributes a unique perspective to the field. In preparing for the MCAT exam, you should be familiar with the key terms and concepts for the following stage theorists:
- Freud (id, ego, superego)
- Piaget (cognitive/reasoning)
- Vygotsky (bio-social)
- Erikson (identity formation)
- Kohlberg (moral reasoning)

5) **A. Participants who identified with the game's protagonist were less likely to endorse that game as an example of a negative stereotype.** The theory of cognitive dissonance states that people experience discomfort when they hold two opposing beliefs or intentions at the same time. People can decrease discomfort by changing/modifying their conflicting beliefs or actions, and minimizing the importance of the conflicting belief.

In this study, a player identifying with the stereotyped protagonists may experience dissonance by labeling the stereotype "negative." Those participants might relieve their dissonance by rationalizing the stereotypical video game character as more neutral or positive. This is precisely what is described in the **correct choice A**. Answer choice B is the opposite of A, making **choice B incorrect**. Finally, **choices C and D** are incorrect because neither one describes a situation where an individual would simultaneously hold two opposing beliefs, e.g. they would not be examples of cognitive dissonance.

8

9

6) **D. Conflict theory.** There are four theoretical approaches to understanding social structures that are important for the behavioral sciences section:

1. **Social constructionism** speaks to the notion that social constructs (e.g. morals, culture, laws, etc.) are constantly evolving and develop out of social interactions, rather than from necessity of nature.

2. **Symbolic interactionism** states that reality itself is largely formed and understood by humans on an interactive level. How we conceptualize our reality is based on how we interact with the things and people around us. This theory is unique among the four in that it is the only "microsociological" theory– focusing on interactions between people and their environment, as opposed to the structure of society, as a whole.

3. **Functionalism** (or structural functionalism) views society as having arisen from an evolutionary process, with its current systems working together to promote ongoing stability and growth.

4. **Conflict theory** stands in opposition to structural functionalism, noting that, in societies, there always exist power differentials, and the social constructs that we experience are put in to place by those in power in order to maintain power.

Choice D is correct because the statement "…behooves the current power structure…" is most consistent with conflict theory.

8

9

PATHWAY

Information Processing

Hick's Law describes a relationship between reaction time to identify and respond to a target and the number of potential targets (e.g. stimuli). Hick's Law can be expressed as a+b(log$_2$n), where *n* is the number of targets, *b* is the slope and *a* is the intercept. The function is often expressed as a+b(BITS), where BITS represents units of information. For example, 1, 2, 4, 8, and 16 targets would be expressed as 0, 1, 2, 3, and 4 BITS (log$_2$(1)=0, log$_2$(2)=1, and so on). The slope of the equation is postulated to represent the amount of information (BITS) that must be stored and processed in the brain.

Hick's law has been considered as an index of intelligence. If intelligence is conceptualized as the speed and efficiency of information processing, described as "rate of gain of information," one potential measure of IQ is the slope of the Hick's function. This relationship is characterized in Figure 1. This "rate of gain" theory of intelligence and reaction time assumes there are excitatory brain nodes (neural networks) that process and transmit information about visual stimuli and goal-directed action. More efficient neural networks are less perturbed by increased information (targets), as measured by reaction time changes, providing an index of intelligence.

In an experiment testing the "rate of gain" model of intelligence, researchers trained both pigeons and college students on reaction time tasks resembling those commonly used to test Hick's law. They obtained results represented in Figure 2. While intercepts differ, slopes between pigeon and college student groups did not differ appreciably.

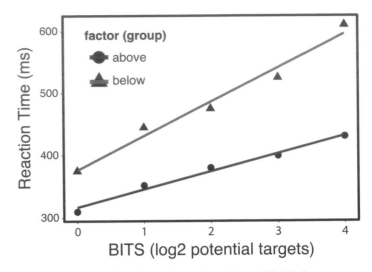

Figure 1. Reaction time functions fit to Hick's Law, expressed as a+b(BITS), for two groups of high school students of above average (red line) and below average (blue line) intelligence.

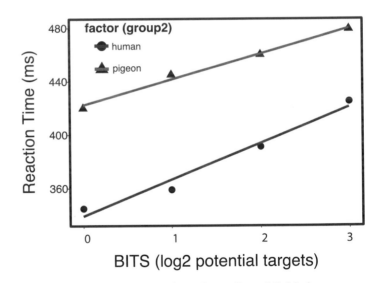

Figure 2. Reaction time functions fit to Hick's Law, expressed as a+b(BITS), for a group of college students (red) and a group of pigeons (blue).

298

1) Based on studies of reaction time and cognitive ability, including the data represented in Figure 1, which statement most likely describes the "rate of gain" view of the neuroscience of intelligence?

A. Density of nerve fibers is related to information processing efficiency and cognitive ability.

B. Larger cortical volume engenders information processing efficiency and resulting cognitive ability.

C. The speed of neural transmission sets limits on information processing, restrictions on memory retrieval, and ultimately level of cognitive ability.

D. The organized networks that subserve attention and constrain information processing speed can be measured precisely via choice reaction time.

2) Suppose neonatologists studied the connection between birth weight and information processing speed at 2 years of age and obtained the results shown in Table 1. What is the most valid conclusion based on the table?

Birth weight	b parameter, Hick's Law
3-5 pounds	67.5
5-6 pounds	55.1
6-7 pounds	46.6
> 8 pounds	45.3

A. Birth weight is negatively related to IQ.

B. There is a linear relationship between birth weight and information processing speed.

C. Lower birth weight is related to higher intercept of the reaction time function.

D. Lower birth weight is related to greater slope of the reaction time function.

3) What factors other than intelligence and information processing speed might account for the data shown in Figure 1?

A. Experience playing video games.

B. Motivation of the test taker.

C. Visual acuity.

D. All of the above.

4) What is the most reasonable conclusion that can be drawn from Figure 2 with regard to the comparison of human and pigeon performance?

A. The data undermine theories that postulate complex reaction time (e.g. information processing) speed is a measure of intelligence.

B. Based on the slope of their reaction time functions, pigeons are about as intelligent as humans.

C. There exist different forms of "intelligences" (e.g. abilities like reaction time) across species that have developed due to natural selection.

D. Hick's law is only valid in describing the reaction time patterns of humans and cannot be applied to other species.

5) Standard measures of intelligence (i.e. IQ tests) are based on comparisons of standard deviation units from an estimated population mean. What is the primary advantage of utilizing this type of measurement system?

A. It allows for precise estimation of individual scores relative to a normative range, ranked by percentile along a normal curve.

B. It allows for direct comparison of any two individuals taking the same test.

C. Because intelligence is heritable, it allows for estimation of intelligence between parents and offspring.

D. Because intelligence is an imprecise measurement concept, it provides a culture, gender, and bias-free estimate to compare different groups.

6

8

Information Processing

Annotations.
1) C 2) D 3) D 4) C 5) A

	Foundation 6: Cognition-B			Foundation 8: Attributions-B		
	B			**B**		
Concepts				5		
Reasoning	1					
Research				3		
Data	2,4					

Big Picture. The focus of this passage is on a theory developed to understand intelligence as a form of information processing speed. It is based on reaction time differences, which have limitations. However, Hick's Law produces robust data well described by a simple linear function. Similar to other behavioral science passages, you are required to understand the basic principles of linear functions, including the interpretation of slopes and intercepts. A key to questions 2 and 4 is the understanding that steeper slopes indicate less efficient information processing. Questions 3 and 5 require reasoning about valid conclusions that can be drawn from experimental (question 3) and standardized (question 5) tests, including the influence of factors that can invalidate and bias data. Additionally, question 5 requires basic understanding of population mean and standard deviation based on normal distributions (also referred to as bell-shaped or Gaussian distributions).

1) **C. The speed of neural transmission sets limits on information processing, restrictions on memory retrieval, and ultimately level of cognitive ability.** The rate of gain theory is basically an inference from reaction times about how rapidly information from the environment is processed, providing an index of cognitive efficiency. Efficiency is in turn hypothesized to be an indicator of intelligence, making **choice C the correct answer.** Figure 1 supports this interpretation, as reaction times increase less rapidly as a function of BITS of information in the more intelligent group. While it may appear accurate upon first reading, **choice D is incorrect** because, while these networks are believed to modulate attention and processing speed, reaction time does not precisely index (a) how these the neural networks are organized, or (b) if the subjects are paying attention. Slow reaction could be due to lack of attention, but reaction does not precisely measure this (we would need to know where the subject's eyes were fixated when stimuli were presented). **Choice A is incorrect** because the rate of gain theory makes no hypotheses regarding nerve fiber density, only speed/efficiency of neural transmission. (Greater fiber density is not an *a priori* indicator of speed). By analogous reasoning, **choice B is incorrect** because the rate of gain theory makes no hypotheses about cortical volume.

2) **D. Lower birth weight is related to greater slope of the reaction time function.** The primary skill needed to answer this question is the ability to interpret the data in Table 1. You should recognize from the passage that the *b* parameter refers to the slope of a linear equation, and that the slope generally increases as birthweight decreases. Therefore, **choice D is the correct answer.** Because the table provides no information about the intercept (the *a* parameter), there is no basis for a decision about the accuracy of choice C, making **choice C incorrect.** To determine that **choice B is incorrect**, you must recognize that fitting a linear function to a dataset does make the data linear. Rather, the R-squared value (an indicator of how well an equation fits, or predicts, the obtained data) would be reduced, as the slope-birthweight relationship shown in the Table is not linear at higher birthweights. Indeed, it appears to asymptote after birthweight reaches 6 pounds. **Choice A is**

incorrect because, while the rate of gain theory posits that lower slopes (e.g. greater processing speed) are an indicator of intelligence, IQ is a measure based on psychometric tests. The Table does not provided any data based on IQ measurements. While slope (b parameter) is likely related to IQ, it is not a direct measure of IQ.

3) **D. All of the above.** This question requires knowledge of scientific research; specifically, the recognition of factors that can influence data beyond those intended by the experimenter. Experience with video games can increase target detection, finger dexterity and reaction time (most video games require all these elements). Thus, **choice A is correct.** The motivation of the test taker will always have a substantial impact on performance in an experimental setting. Accordingly, motivation is often a concern in human experimental research, and **choice B is also correct.** Because visual acuity could modify the ability to detect the target (e.g. light stimulus), someone with a visual impairment, i.e. not wearing needed corrective lenses, may have compromised reaction time due to the visual constraint. Therefore, **choice C is correct.**

4) **C. There exist different forms of "intelligences" (e.g. abilities like reaction time) across species that have developed due to natural selection.** This question requires interpretation of, and reasoning about, the data. **Choice B can be readily eliminated** based on simple logic. Answer choice A is not as easily dismissed. If humans and pigeons do not have substantially different slopes in their respective reaction times, and reaction time is a measure of processing speed (a putative index of intelligence) it would seem that the theory is flawed. However, **choice A is not the credited answer** because it is not the best answer choice among the four options. The **credited choice is C**, as it provides a more scientifically accurate explanation. Through natural selection, some species have evolved different skills and complex behaviors that are adaptive to their survival. Pigeons need to recognize and react to (eat) food quickly to compete for limited resources with other birds. Honey bees "waggle dance" to provide information about food locations to other bees, and dolphins echolocate to detect food, predators, and

other dolphins. All of these behaviors are "adaptive" skills in that they enhance competitive fitness and survival. **Choice D is not credited** because the data in Figure 2 reveal that Hick's law <u>does</u> describe the behavior of pigeons quite well. Pigeon performance conforms to the same constraints as human performance.

5) **A. It allows for precise estimation of individual scores relative to a normative range, ranked by percentile along a normal curve.** Correctly answering this question requires understanding the basic assumptions behind standardized testing, particularly normal distributions, means and standard deviation (SD) units. As shown in Figure 3, a normal curve has 50% of the sample below the 50th percentile and 50% above. If the standard deviation is 15, then ≈84% of the scores (34.1+34.1+13.6+2.1) will fall below one standard deviation unit (e.g. below 115), and ≈98% will fall below two standard deviation units (e.g. below 130).

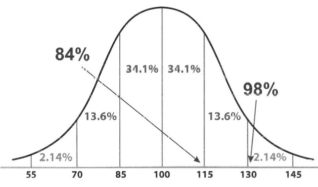

Figure 3. Normal curve with a mean = 100 and standard deviation = 15. Scores are shown on the X-axis, and percent of the population falling within each standard deviation unit is shown in each space above the score.

Therefore, a test sample with a normal distribution and standardized scoring units (SD) provides the means to precisely estimate where on the curve any given score falls (by percentile) compared to the population on which it is normed. MCAT, GRE, and SAT tests all use this normed, standardized approach to evaluate performance. It follows that **choice A is the correct answer.** It is not necessary to have a normed, standardized test to compare any two scores, just pick the higher/lower score of the two. Therefore **choice B is not correct.** While it is true that intelligence is partly heritable, standardized scores do necessarily enable the estimation of intelligence between parents and offspring. As long as the test and scoring system are the same between parent and child, the scores need not be normed and standardized to estimate how heritable (e.g. correlated) the scores of parents and children are. Using standardized tests would be advantageous, but not necessary. Therefore, **choice C is not correct**. It is well established that intelligence tests may have modest biases when it comes to gender and cultural groups. Some aptitude tests are even biased based on level of education attained (if taken as an adult). Additionally, it does not follow that an imprecise measurement system is bias-free (in fact the opposite in more likely to be true). Thus, the question itself is logically inconsistent and **choice D is incorrect**.

6

8

PATHWAY

Cycle of Violence

Individuals who are abused or neglected as children are more likely as adolescents and adults to be involved in delinquency, violent crime, and child abuse. This pattern is known as the "cycle of violence." Psychiatrists who interviewed violent prisoners provided initial data through descriptive case reports. Subsequently, public health research by social psychologists and criminologists provided more comprehensive data linking child abuse/neglect to violence later in life.

A study on the cycle of violence examined two sources of information: (1) court records of individuals convicted of violent crimes as adults; and (2) matching data records on abuse from county and state offices of child protective services. Data were obtained for four categories of abuse: physical abuse, neglect, sexual abuse, and both physical and sexual abuse. Table 1 presents the data from this study.

Subsequent research using a longitudinal design examined criminal behavior in individuals identified by the courts as having been abused or neglected as children. Severity (type, frequency, and duration of abuse) was estimated based on court records. Individual subject records were examined in 6-year intervals beginning at age 12 and continuing to age 30. The data are presented in Table 2.

Table 1. Arrest records for violent offenses broken down by type of abuse.

Group	N	% Arrest for violent offense
Physical abuse	187	16.8 *
Neglect	611	11.5
Sexual abuse	235	6.2
Physical and sexual abuse	151	15.5 **

* $p < .01$, greater than sexual abuse
** $p < .05$, greater than sexual abuse

Table 2. Estimated rates of violent criminal behavior across three age periods in 250 individuals abused/neglected as children and 200 non-abused controls. Severity of abuse is grouped into three categories: 1 = none; 2 = low-moderate; 3 = severe.

Age Period	Group	Mean offenses
13-18	1	1.8
	2	2.4
	3	4.7
	--	
19-24	1	0.8
	2	2.1
	3	3.3
	--	
25-30	1	0.9
	2	1.9
	3	3.1

1) **Between Table 1 and Table 2, which data set provides a stronger case for the "cycle of violence" theory; why?**

   A. Table 1; it provides a more detailed description of the different types of abuse.

   B. Table 1; it provides a larger sample size and greater generalization to the population.

   C. Table 2; it follows the same individuals over time and includes a control group.

   D. Table 2; it follows trends in criminal behavior over a decade.

2) **Which learning theory is most consistent with the "cycle of violence" data?**

   A. Modeling

   B. Operant conditioning

   C. Classical conditioning

   D. Conformity

3) **Which of the following statements is not supported by the data in Table 1?**

   A. Violent offending is less likely in victims of neglect than physical abuse.

   B. Children who are both physically and sexually abused are at increased risk for violent crime compared to sexual abuse alone.

   C. Children who are abused and neglected are at increased risk for violent crime compared to those who are not abused.

   D. If the data represent a random unbiased sample, neglect is more prevalent than abuse.

4) **The sociological theory of family violence that posits low-income groups use family violence as a more acceptable form of settling disputes is called:**

   A. societal structure theory.

   B. subculture of violence theory.

   C. resource theory.

   D. exchange/social control theory.

5) **The data in Table 2 are consistent with which of the following conclusions?**

   A. Juvenile delinquents are more likely than non-delinquents to be criminals as adults.

   B. Violence is a heritable trait in families.

   C. Child abuse/neglect is a primary cause of criminal violence during adulthood.

   D. Rates of violent crime are relative stable across individuals during early adulthood.

8

9

Cycle of Violence

	Foundation 8: Social Interaction-C			Foundation 9: Social Structure-A		
	C			**A**		
Concepts	2			4		
Reasoning	1			5		
Research						
Data	3					

Big Picture. This passage covers material from Foundations 8C and 9A; both foundations are focused on social behavior. Here, social interactions are presented in the context of violence, including both violent crime and family violence. Questions 1, 3 and 5 require reasoning and interpretation about the data presented in Tables 1 and 2. Similar to other behavioral foundations passages, question 1 requires that you integrate information across the two datasets (Table 1 and Table 2). Question 1 also requires that you utilize the information in the tables to make inferences about strengths and weaknesses in experimental design. Question 2 requires content knowledge regarding psychological learning theory. Question 4 requires content knowledge regarding sociological theories of family violence.

1) **C. Table 2; it follows the same individuals over time and includes a control group.** Research that seeks to understand the association between variables over long time periods (e.g. years) can be complicated by numerous factors. These alternative factors – variables not examined by the researcher, called "confounding" variables – may be responsible for the relationships that are uncovered in the statistical analysis. For example, in this passage numerous factors could affect relationships between childhood abuse and adult criminal violence (e.g. divorce, adolescent peer relations, drug use). Therefore, using a subject as his/her own control by examining relationships in the same individuals over time (termed a "longitudinal" design) helps to minimize variability due to uncontrolled factors. Additionally, the need for a control group is important in studies of this type to properly analyze the specific influence of the variable of interest (abuse). For example, if involvement in gangs were a strong predictor of violent crime, a control group of children who were <u>not</u> abused/neglected but were involved in gang activity would be important, in order to measure the influence of gangs relative to abuse/neglect. In the absence of a proper control group (which is the case in Table 1), the researchers might conclude that abuse was a predictor of violence when in fact abuse was confounded with gang activity. For these reasons – following the same subjects over time and using a control group – **choice C is the correct answer.** Choice B is a challenging lure. It mentions two important factors in behavioral science – sample size and generalizability. Typically, as sample size increases the data more accurately represent the population of interest, and thus allow for better generalization of the study results to the entire population (assuming sampling without bias). This is particularly true for observational and public health studies, like those described in the passage, because such studies do not manipulate variables under controlled conditions. However, **choice B is not the credited answer** because the study described in Table 1 does not include a control group. Therefore, while certain types of abuse predict later criminal violence, it is unknown if these rates are higher than those in nonabused persons. This distinction is important to confirm the cycle of violence hypothesis, because – as noted above – other variables could explain the

relationship. **Choice A is not the credited answer** because, while analyzing different types of abuse helps specify nuances in the cycle of violence hypothesis, it does not test the cycle of violence hypothesis per se, e.g. it does not provide proper controls over alternative (confounding) factors such as a control group comparison. **Choice D is not the credited answer**. While it is ambitious and desirable to follow individuals over a decade, the length of time examined does not translate to the integrity of the experimental design, the quality of the data collected, or the statistical results. Therefore, following trends for 10 years (versus, say, 5 years) does not directly provide a stronger case for the hypothesis.

2) **A. Modeling.** Modeling, also known as social learning theory, is a theory associated with the psychologist Albert Bandura. It posits that people learn from one another by observation and imitation of other people's behavior, attitudes, and the outcomes of social interactions. Much of social learning during development involves children modeling the behavior of their parents. **Choice A is the correct answer** because the cycle of violence theory is most consistent with modeling/social learning theory. Operant conditioning is associated with the psychologist B.F. Skinner. It posits that learning is the result of "shaping" (small modifications in behavior) based on the antecedents (cues) and consequences (e.g. reinforcement and punishment) of behavior. **Choice B is not the correct answer** because the cycle of violence theory is not entirely consistent with operant conditioning. There is not as clear a rationale as to why an abused child would necessarily be reinforced (by parents or peers) for being violent. Classical conditioning is a learning theory associated with Ivan Pavlov. It posits that automatic ("reflexive") actions elicited by stimuli (smell of food → salivation) become paired with other previously neutral stimuli (ringing bell → smell of food) and the previous neutral stimuli become conditioned to elicit the same response (ringing bell → salivation). **Choice C is incorrect** because there is no clear connection between classical conditioning theory and the cycle of violence theory. **Choice D is incorrect** because conformity is not a learning theory. Conformity is a concept from social psychology that refers to a change a person's in belief or action in order to fit in with a group,

in response to actual or imagined social norms or group pressure. Rather than being consistent with the cycle of violence theory, conformity might explain violent crime in adolescence as a result of gang involvement.

3) **C. Children who are abused and neglected are at increased risk for violent crime compared to those who are not abused.** Close inspection of Table 1 reveals that only abused children were included in the analyses (non-abused children were excluded), making it difficult to conclude that abuse increases risk for violence above a base rate. Therefore **choice C is correct** because the question asks which statement is _not_ supported by the data. **Choice A is incorrect** because it is supported by the Table 1 data: violent offending is less likely in victims of neglect. **Choice B is incorrect** because it is supported by the Table 1 data: physical plus sexual abuse confers greater likelihood for future violence than sexual abuse alone. **Choice D is incorrect** because, if the sampling was truly unbiased and representative of actual rates in the US population, neglect is more prevalent (611) than physical and/or sexual abuse (187, 235, 151).

4) **B. subculture of violence theory.** This question requires content knowledge regarding sociological theories of family violence. The subculture of violence theory suggests that in lower-SES groups, violence among family members is a more common and acceptable means of social interaction and resolving conflicts. It follows that **choice B is the correct answer** as it is most consistent with the question stem. Societal structure theory holds that family violence is due to an imbalance in the family power structure, largely constructed around male dominance via physical and economic control. **Choice A is incorrect** because it is not consistent with the question stem. Resource theory holds that decision making and behavioral authority within the family is based on the resources that each person has in the relationship, e.g. financial, social, organizational (usually male dominated). It is also directed more toward explanations of spousal abuse than child abuse. Accordingly, **choice C is incorrect**. Exchange/social control theory of aggression and family violence is related to the balance of costs and

Cycle of Violence

rewards. Violence and abuse are used when the rewards are greater than the costs. Because (a) social controls are diminished in the private nature of the home (vs. workplace), (b) the reluctance of social institutions to intervene, and (c) and the low risk of detection, the costs of abuse and violence are reduced relative to rewards (e.g. power, control). Like resource theory, this theory is commonly applied to spousal abuse. **Choice D is incorrect** because it is inconsistent with the question stem

5) **D. Rates of violent crime are relative stable across individuals during early adulthood.** This question requires accurate determination of the data trends presented in Table 2. Defining early adulthood as the period from 18 to 30 (the 2nd and 3rd age periods in Table 2), it can be seen that within each group there is little change between period 2 (age 19-24) and period 3 (age 25-30). The mean difference is 0.1 or 0.2 for all groups. This supports the claim that violent crime rates are stable across this time period, making **choice D the correct answer**. Answer choice A suggests a comparison between delinquents and non-delinquents. However, examining the age period 13-18, all groups have criminal offenses. Therefore, all the groups have a documented history of juvenile delinquency (and you are not presented with individual data on those who did and did not have violent offenses). It follows that it is not possible, based on Table 2, to compare delinquents to non-delinquents, making **choice A incorrect**. Because there is no information about parental arrest records, **choice B should be readily eliminated**, as the Table does not provide any information about heritability. While child abuse may be a predictor of adult criminal violence, the word "cause" should be a red flag. Table 2 provides correlational data drawn from court records. Recall the scientific edict that "correlation does not equal causation." Additionally, this kind of non-experimental study design – using existing records rather than manipulated, experimentally controlled variables – is generally not appropriate for addressing questions of causation. Therefore, **answer choice C is incorrect**.

PATHWAY

Health Care Disparities

In America, the disparity experienced in mental and physical well being between white and minority populations has been well-documented. Early attempts to describe this "health gap" were based on (biased) beliefs that whites were physically healthier due to superior genetics. Modern research has demonstrated that mental health and physical health are influenced by other non-genetic variables, such as socioeconomic status (SES), education, and institutional discrimination.

Studies have shown that race and SES are associated; lower SES populations have a more diverse racial and ethnic makeup. These groups have reduced access to routine medical care, pharmaceuticals, and high quality nutrition, all of which contribute to poorer health outcomes. Recently, researchers examined how stress – long known to be associated with increased health risks – interacts with SES and race to affect long-term health outcomes.

Data were collected during a 25-year longitudinal study about the influence of social, psychological, and behavioral factors on health. Table 1 reports selected demographic information of study participants. Table 2 (below) presents correlations between particular demographic variables and how functionally limited a participant felt due to health concerns. Table 3 presents the relationship between stress variables, education outcomes and income.

	Severity of Limitation
Gender	.024
(0=male, 1=female)	
Age (in years)	.24***
Education (in years)	-.14**
Income (in US$)	-.18***

*$p<.05$, **$p<.01$, ***$p<.001$

Table 2. Correlation between demographic variable and functional health based on self-report on a 10 point scale (0 = no limitation, 10 = completely limited).

Demographic Variables	% of Participants
Age in years	
25-44	52.2
45-64	28.3
65+	19.5
Race	
Nonblack	89.0
Black	11.0
Education in years	
0-11	25.6
12-15	54.7
16+	19.7
Annual household income in dollars	
< 10,000	19.2
10,000 - 29,000	40.5
30,000+	40.3

Note: n = 3,617

Table 1. Selected demographic information.

	Education (in years)			Income (in dollars)		
Stress Variable	<12	12-15	>15	<10k	10k-29k	30k+
% widowed	2.5	1.3	.8	5.3	1.0	.5
% divorced	31.6	28.4	13.3	25.0	28.5	22.1
% had child die	11.3	5.0	1.4	6.1	5.6	4.2
% assaulted	31.1	18.8	17.1	25.0	22.0	17.0

Table 3. Percent of participants who experienced indicated "Stress Experience" by education and income.

1) Based on Table 2, which of the following is the best conclusion about the relationship between a participant's income and his/her self-reported functional health?

   A. Those with higher income were more likely than those with lower income to report extreme limitations to functional health.

   B. Those with higher income were less likely than those with lower income to report extreme limitations to functional health.

   C. As income increased, the severity of reported functional limitations due to health concerns tended to decrease.

   D. As income decreased, the severity of reported functional limitations due to health concerns tended to decrease.

2) A follow-up study assessed hormone levels in those participants with the highest self-reported stress levels. Which of the following is the least likely finding of this study?

   A. Cortisol, epinephrine, and norepinephrine levels were higher than in the general population.

   B. Participants in this follow-up study were more likely to report higher severity of limitation in health in the initial study.

   C. Cortisol levels were higher compared to the general population, but norepinephrine and epinephrine levels were slightly lower.

   D. Participants in this follow-up study had lower family incomes and education levels than those not chosen for the follow-up study.

3) In the 25-year longitudinal study, which of the following variables, if not accounted for, could have effects that directly bias the results?

   A. Number of children in the household.

   B. Average temperature in state of residence.

   C. Respondent's number of siblings.

   D. Number of colleges in the city of residence.

4) Which is the most accurate interpretation of selected data reported in Table 3?

   A. Individuals with less than 12 years of education who also earned less than $10,000 per year had a greater than 50% chance of having been assaulted.

   B. Earning a higher income causes increased protection from high-stress life events.

   C. Higher education results in increased income.

   D. Participants earning greater than $30,000 per year, or with greater than 15 years of education, were the least likely participants to report a high-stress life event.

5) Which of the following choices illustrates an example of institutional discrimination that may contribute to poor health outcomes?

   A. A medical clinic system located in a large, urban hub shifts from a third-party (e.g. Medicaid) to a private pay system.

   B. A state psychiatry licensing board deems it unethical to attempt to "cure" homosexuality.

   C. A physician systematically meets with Caucasian patients for twice as long as he meets with minority patients.

   D. A Caucasian physician secretly believes that minority mothers are too lenient with male children.

6) Current US demographic trends show increasing populations in large cities. Which change would most likely limit access to health care for the greatest percentage of the population?

   A. Provide training and economic incentives for health care providers to become bilingual.

   B. Shift funding for subsidized health care clinics from urban to rural areas.

   C. Increase opportunities for naturalized immigrants to access work opportunities.

   D. Increase minimum age of retirement before a citizen can access Medicare.

9

10

Health Care Disparities

	Foundation 9: Demographics-B			Foundation 10: Social Equality-A		
	B			**A**		
Concepts				2		
Reasoning	6			5		
Research	3					
Data				1,4		

Big Picture. This passage covers complex inter-actions among multiple variables, and correlations with long-term health outcomes. There are a number of tables with different formats, including percentages, correlations, and significance levels. With this level of data density, it would be wise to first read and inspect the tables, then go to the questions to determine which information is going to be relevant. For example, note that Table 1 is not needed to answer any of the questions. This is a common approach on the MCAT.

One conclusion that can be drawn from the passage is that both income and education are positively associated with better health. Minority populations often experience more health-related limitations in several domains of their life. These are largely a result of non-racial factors (e.g. SES). Another variable affecting long-term health outcomes is stress. Acute stressors (e.g. the death of a loved one) can have an immediate impact on mental and physical well being and can carry long-lasting ramifications for general health (e.g. loss of a job). Chronic stressors, like living in a high-crime environment, can have a profound impact on long-term physical and mental health.

1) **C. As income increased, the severity of reported functional limitations due to health concerns tended to decrease.** Table 2 presents correlations between certain demographic variables and "Severity of Limitation." According to the legend, the severity of limitation is based on a 10-point self-report scale, indicating that higher numbers predict lower functional health. Three variables result in significant correlations: "Age" is positively correlated (0.24), while both "Education" (-0.14) and "Income" (-0.18) are negatively correlated. Simply stated – as age increases so do self-reported limitations in health (positive correlation). Furthermore, as education and income increase, health-related limitations decrease (negative correlation). **Choice C is correct** because it correctly describes the negative correlation between increased income and decreased health concerns. It also bears repeating, correlation does not equal causation. The MCAT is likely to test you on this often-confused issue.

Choice A is incorrect because it is in the wrong direction; higher income is associated with better health. **Choice B is incorrect** because the term "extreme" cannot be discerned from the data presented in Table 2. This answer choice is a potential distractor, in that it describes an association that is in the correct direction. **Choice D is incorrect** because it describes a correlation that is the opposite of choice C.

2) **C. Cortisol levels were higher compared to the general population, but norepinephrine and epinephrine levels were slightly lower.** Regarding the physiology of stress, three important biochemicals are epinephrine (i.e. adrenaline), norepinephrine, and cortisol. All three are released in response to psychological stressors and increase physiological arousal (i.e. "fight or flight"). Typically, these biochemicals are released in response to short-term threats, and once the threats have passed, they are attenuated. When one is faced with long-term stressors, however – for example, if one is chronically worried about being out of work and being able to support a family – these hormones can be released continuously, which can have profoundly negative health results. Persistently elevated cortisol, for example, can lead to a depressed immune system, chronic fatigue, obesity, and increased risk for heart attack.

The question states that subjects had high stress levels. As a result, an increase in each of the three major stress hormones is anticipated. Therefore, answer choices consistent with such increases should be eliminated – as the question asks for the least likely choice. **Choice C is correct** because, while it correctly predicts increased cortisol, reduced levels of epinephrine and norepinephrine are not expected. **Choice A is incorrect** because it is an expected finding (all biochemical levels elevated). The scientific literature (and logic) suggests that increased stress is associated with poorer health, so **choice B is incorrect** as it describes another expected finding. The data in the passage (Table 3) indicate that lower income and education are associated with higher levels of chronic stress, which makes **choice D incorrect**, as it is also a likely finding.

3) **A. Number of children in the household.** This research design question requires the identification of confounding factors that can interfere with study results. To arrive at the correct answer, you must recognize which of the listed variables is most likely to induce long-term stress (recall the study lasted 25 years). Raising multiple children is a well documented stressor on parents; generally, more children equates to more stress. Because of the relationship between children in the household and stress, **choice A is the credited answer**. While temperature may relate to weather conditions (which could plausibly relate to stress), there is no direct relationship between temperature per se and long-term stress, therefore **choice B is not credited**. Choice C refers to the number of siblings of the respondent, not the number in the household. This subtle distinction makes choice C tempting. However, since the respondents are adults, sibling relationships are not necessarily stressful, and number of siblings is not a direct stressor. Therefore, **choice C is not credited**. Because, it is not clear how the number of colleges could plausibly increase stress levels, **choice D can be readily eliminated**.

4) **D. Participants earning greater than $30,000 per year, or with greater than 15 years of education, were the least likely participants to report a high-stress life event.** Table 3 provides the percent of individuals in specific demographic categories that reported experiencing significant life stressors. It is important to note that this table presents an association and makes no attempt to draw causal conclusions. Indeed, this kind of experiment is not able to determine cause-effect relationships. **Choice B and choice C are not credited responses** because they describe causal relationships ("results in" = "causes"). It is also noteworthy that, based on Table 3, it is not possible to determine how education and income interact. Those variables are presented distinctly from each other. **Choice A is not credited** because it discusses the relationships among education, income, and assault, which are not provided by the table. **Choice D is the credited answer**. It is an accurate description of what is presented in the table. Participants in those two categories (> $30,000; > 15 years) were the least likely to have reported a major life stressor.

5) **A. A medical clinic system located in a large, urban hub shifts from a third-party to a private pay system.** While this passage indirectly addresses institutional discrimination, it does not explicitly define it. "Institutional discrimination" refers to policies and/or practices of an institution that systematically result in poorer outcomes for one group as a result of that group's race, gender, sexual orientation, age, nationality, etc. The **credited response is choice A**. It describes a practice that could discriminate against racial minorities and contribute to poor health outcomes. In the US, racial minority groups are disproportionately represented in urban areas and rely more heavily on social service health care payment systems (e.g. Medicaid) to access medical treatment. When a medical provider does not accept insurance in lieu of private pay (i.e. cash), it may ostracize individuals who cannot afford to shoulder a heavy bill. **Choice C is incorrect** as it confuses "institutional" with "individual." This physician may be liable on charges of racial discrimination, but not necessarily as a result of a system-wide policy or practice. **Choice D is incorrect** because it confuses "discrimination" with "prejudice." "Discrimination" refers to behaviors, while "prejudice" refers to beliefs. **Choice B is incorrect**; while it describes an institutional policy, that policy it is intended to reduce discrimination.

6) B. Shift funding for subsidized health care clinics from urban to rural areas. The demographic makeup of the US is projected to change dramatically by the year 2050, with major implications for the country's workforce and health care systems. Statistics show an expected change in the following racial/ethnic demographics: (1) Roughly 20% of the US population will be comprised of immigrants and will constitute the largest percentage of US population growth. (2) The US Latino population will triple in size. (3) White, Non-Hispanics will become a minority. (4) The US will continue to experience increased urbanization, as more of the population moves out of rural areas and into the cities.

This question contains the type of convoluted language that you may encounter on the MCAT (e.g. "…would most likely limit access…"). What this essentially means is: "Which of the following would be detrimental to the most people in terms health care?" So, you should be looking for the answer choice that stands in contrast to projected demographic changes. **Choice B is the credited answer** because it advocates for increasing access in rural communities to the detriment of the urban population. Due to expected increase in urbanization, this would likely hurt more than it would help, in terms of the number of individuals receiving health care. **Choice A is not credited** because it acknowledges the growth in immigrant populations and provides an option (i.e. bilingual health care providers) for immigrants to receive increased access. **Choice C is not credited**. It is an arguable economic point, but would likely increase access to health care for two reasons: (1) more employed citizens increases the tax-paying workforce, which could increase access to health care for non-working elderly; and (2) employed citizens typically have greater access to health care through employer group insurance. Choice D speaks to a politically and socially complex topic – whether or not to increase the retirement age in America, the implications of which are somewhat unclear. It is possible that raising the retirement age would increase taxpayers in the workforce, thereby increasing the availability of taxpayer funded social services (e.g. Medicare). However, it is also possible that raising the retirement age would reduce access to social services for those elderly who would then have to wait to qualify. Because the implications of this answer are ambiguous, **choice D is not credited**.

PATHWAY

Med-

9

10

Critical Analysis and Reasoning Skills

On October 29, 1929, the US stock market crashed on Black Tuesday, an event that has been cited as the primary driver behind the Great Depression. This resulted in large reductions in industrial production and wholesale prices. Most scholars support the notion that multiple factors caused the depression, but they have debated to which extent the crisis was caused by a failure of the free market or a failure of the US government to properly regulate the supply of money. To address the crisis, Congress enacted important legislation to radically change the nature of banking in the US. The Banking Act of 1933, commonly referred to as the Glass-Steagall Act, was a key aspect of this legislation and severely limited financial institutions from acquiring commercial securities with individual account holders' deposits. During President Clinton's term, the Gramm-Leach-Bliley Act was signed, which repealed the key provisions of the Glass-Steagall Act.

In the late 2000s, another financial crisis involving large losses in the stock market, called the Great Recession of 2008, occurred. Many believe this economic crisis was caused by multiple factors, with particular emphasis on the collapse of the sub-prime mortgage industry in the US. With the famous collapse of Lehman Brothers in 2008, additional economic flaws were exposed, spreading chaos throughout global markets.

During the many discussions regarding pre-recession factors that exposed the economy to the crisis of 2008, the most prominent factor was the "housing bubble," i.e. the over-inflation of housing prices that started around 2001. At this time, the US was coming out of a recession created by the "dot.com bubble," an over-inflation of the value of the technological business sector. To address this, the Federal Reserve lowered interest rates, providing easily accessible credit for businesses and individuals. This was enabled by laxer lending standards synthesized from new regulations established by the federal government.

The increase in available credit coupled with reduced monitoring regulations led to a system of banking pejoratively called "shadow banking." This term was coined by Paul McCulley and is defined as institutions and markets that perform in the banking industry, but do so without the regulatory systems that govern traditional depository institutions. In essence, the lending companies "made their own rules" about mortgages. A key example of this was the introduction of a derivative known as a credit default swap (CDS). This financial instrument was used as insurance against a default on a mortgage loan or bond and was, unfortunately, not regulated by Congress or by existing banking laws. In a CDS, a buyer pays a fee and in return receives payment in the event of a default. This enticed speculators to buy mortgage securities from banks in order to position themselves to profit upon default. This eventually led to mass defaults by lending institutions in the mortgage securities markets because CDS vendors were unable to pay back investors after default. As a result, Congress bailed out many financial institutions which cost taxpayers hundreds of billions of dollars.

The steep rise in mortgage defaults during this period is widely attributed to the heavy use of "sub-prime" lending, a practice where banks loaned money with unfavorable interest rates (e.g. adjustable mortgages) to borrowers with risky credit histories. As a result, home foreclosures dramatically increased, and credit became more difficult to obtain, forcing many individuals to declare personal bankruptcy. In fact, at the height of the recession, the average personal debt of an American was 127% of their annual disposable income.

1) **The author would least agree with which of the following statements?**

   A. Additional regulation should have been enacted to regulate traditional banks.

   B. The failure to properly regulate the money supply contributed to the Great Depression.

   C. Derivatives should have government regulation.

   D. Over-inflated housing prices led to the 2008 crisis.

2) **If the federal government had raised interest rates on lending in the early 2000s, which of the following would the author most agree with?**

   A. Financial institutions would not have been able to avoid bankruptcy.

   B. The burden from individual debt would have been decreased.

   C. The shadow banking system would have been easier to develop.

   D. There would have been more government regulation.

3) **All the following resulted from the repeal of the Glass-Steagall Act, except:**

   A. the unregulated shadow banking system flourished.

   B. it became easier for individuals and businesses to qualify for loans.

   C. homes were more affordable because favorable mortgages, like adjustable rate mortgages, were available.

   D. derivatives like the credit default swap derivative became available to investors.

4) **Which of the following is least likely the result of the creation of the shadow banking system?**

   A. A crash in the stock market and real estate prices.

   B. Successful passage of the Gramm-Leach-Bliley Act.

   C. Circumvention of traditional banking regulations.

   D. Obtaining lower interest credit on easier terms.

5) **According to the author, if there were tighter government regulations on credit default swap derivatives, which of the following could have been avoided?**

   A. Creation of the shadow banking system.

   B. Tax breaks for corporations.

   C. Institutional reliance on the government bailout.

   D. Reduced levels of mortgage default.

6) **Which of the following would be the most direct effect from the "dot.com bubble" on the Great Recession?**

   A. Reduction in a government employee's benefits.

   B. Changes in the corporate tax code.

   C. Lobbying against the passage of a bill by Congress.

   D. Individual obtaining a loan to purchase a new car.

Annotations.

1) A   2) B   3) C   4) B   5) C   6) D

	Foundation 1: Comprehension	Foundation 2: Integration of multiple concepts	Foundation 3: Reasoning beyond text
Concepts	3		
Inference	1		
Integration		4,6	
Application			2
Assessment			5

Big Picture. This passage was written from a perspective of an individual who believes that events that led up to the Great Depression were in many ways parallel to those that led to the Great Recession. Both the Great Depression of the 1930s and the Great Recession of 2008 caused widespread economic chaos in the US and around the world. As a consequence of the Great Depression, the US Congress passed various forms of legislation, like the Glass-Steagall Act, that were designed to address the problem and prevent further calamity. This law was repealed by the Gramm-Leach-Bliley Act, an event that many consider to be a watershed moment that put the US on the path to the 2008 Great Recession. The author of the passage used these facts and others to try and sell her/his viewpoint that some of the laws passed to prevent another Great Depression were slowly repealed over the years, which may have contributed to the cause of the Great Recession. Various causes of the Great Recession are detailed, as well as how these issues were allowed to develop and the resulting problems faced by the populous. There is an overall negative theme regarding the scenario that led to the Great Recession and the author is very specific about the economic examples used to describe how it started. The author is most likely an academic in the field of economics writing this passage as a warning to prevent a repeat of past mistakes.

1) **A. Additional regulation should have been enacted to regulate traditional banks.** For this question, you are looking for the answer not supported by the passage. **Choice A is the credited answer** because the answer discusses the regulation of traditional banks. The critical word in this answer choice that made it incorrect was "traditional." The passage describes how non-traditional lending institutions, which lacked government regulation, established the shadow banking system. **Choice B is incorrect** because the author states in the first paragraph that the inability of the federal government to properly regulate the money supply was a contributing factor to the Great Depression. **Choice C is incorrect** because the passage states derivatives like credit default swaps were not regulated by Congress. The author's use of the word "unfortunately" to describe this lack of regulation leads one to believe the author feels they should be regulated. **Choice D can be eliminated** because, in the third paragraph, the author states that the over-inflation of housing prices was a prominent factor in the 2008 crisis.

2) **B. The burden from individual debt would have been decreased. Choice B is the credited answer** because the passage discusses how lower interest rates made credit more available. Higher interest rates would have had the opposite effect, reducing available credit, meaning individuals would not have been able to secure as many loans, reducing the amount of individual debt. **Choice A is incorrect** because there is no information available in the passage to determine the effect of corporate bankruptcy from a change in interest rates. **Choice C is eliminated** because the passage states that increased available credit was one factor contributing to the creation of the shadow banking system. Higher interest rates would have reduced available credit, making it more difficult for the shadow banking system to develop. **Choice D can be ruled out** because the passage provides no correlation between government regulations and higher interest rates. An important economic point to consider is that while an increase in interest rates could dissuade individuals from borrowing (thereby reducing their individual debt), it could also increase their individual debt

because obligatory purchases such as a home or car would have enormously high rates. In the early 1980s, mortgage interest rates were >10%, which increased personal debt. Having said this, it is an important critical reasoning skill to realize that the question asked for the statement that the author would most likely agree with, not the clearest predictive economic outcome; this is beyond the scope of what was discussed in the passage.

3) **C. homes were more affordable because favorable mortgages, like adjustable rate mortgages, were available. Choice C is the credited answer** because the last paragraph of the passage states that adjustable rate mortgages are unfavorable, not favorable for the individual. The key point to gather from the content of the passage was that borrowers had an easier time qualifying for loans, but not that these loans were more affordable or favorable. **Choice A can be eliminated** because the first paragraph discusses how the repealing of the Glass-Steagall Act reduced the amount of regulation, which is favorable for the shadow banking system. This latter point was recapitulated again in the beginning of paragraph four. **Choice B is incorrect** because, again, elimination of regulations allowed lenders to reduce lending qualifications, making it easier to borrow money. **Choice D is ruled out** because the credit default swap was used as an example of a new derivative offered because of the absence of regulation. The passage explicitly referred to these latter two points.

4) **B. Successful passage the Gramm-Leach-Bliley Act. Choice B is the credited answer** because the first paragraph states that the Gramm-Leach-Bliley Act repealed regulations from the Glass-Steagall Act. Thus, this act help create the shadow banking system; it was not a result of it. **Choice A is ruled out** because the passage discusses how unregulated lending within the shadow banking system lead to a large number of mortgage defaults. **Choice C is eliminated** because the shadow banking system was defined by the passage as a system of lending that circumvents traditional bank lending. **Choice D is incorrect** because the passage specifically discusses how the shadow banking system made credit more available and easier to obtain.

5) **C. Institutional reliance on the government bailout. Choice C is the credited answer** because the passage states that institutions needed government bailouts after they were unable to pay back debts in the mortgage securities markets. If tighter regulations had prevented or limited the number of derivatives sold, institutions would have had an easier time paying the derivatives and reducing their reliance on government bailouts. Keep in mind that this is the predicted outcome according to the logic presented by the author in paragraph four. **Choice A is incorrect** because tight regulations would have predictably limited the availability of such derivatives. **Choice B can be ruled out** because the passage does not provide a link between tighter regulations and corporate taxes. **Choice D is eliminated** because the amount of mortgage defaults was not described by the passage as specifically dependent on the regulation of the credit default swap derivative. The passage only states that mortgage defaults occurred because individuals were provided mortgages they couldn't afford.

6) **D. Individual obtaining a loan to purchase a new car.** The one result from the "dot.com bubble" discussed in the passage was the lowering of interest rates. **Choice D is the credited answer** because lower interest rates would make it easier for an individual to obtain a loan. The passage does not make a correlation between the topics described in answer choices A, B or C and the "dot.com bubble," so you cannot speculate how they could affect one another. This eliminates these three choices

Church Heresy

During the transition from paganism to Christianity, the initial organization and development of the Catholic Church faced numerous obstacles. There was competition with other belief systems, including Gnosticism whose followers shunned the material world through their belief in divine spirits. In addition, some scholars have suggested that the early church was fragmented, leading to multiple, discredited interpretations of the story of Christ by different creeds. Despite the fact that it was illegal to practice Christianity in Rome until the Edict of Milan, signed by Constantine in 313, Christianity experienced a rapid growth in the number of followers during the first few centuries. As a result, a diverse number of creeds arose with differing opinions on the life and relationship between Jesus Christ and God. There were a large number of diverse church doctrines that were acknowledged; for example, Western European churches accepted the Book of Revelation, which was rejected by Eastern European churches.

A serious threat to church orthodoxy lay within the contention of core doctrines of faith, such as the relationship between Jesus Christ and God. Heresies of this type included one from Marcion of Scope. In his treatise *Antithesis,* Marcion contrasted the views of God from the New Testament and the Old Testament, claiming that the teachings of Jesus were incompatible with the Old Testament. Marcion also taught that Jesus' body was an imitation of a material body, a theory at odds with the description of the Incarnation of Christ by the church, which states Jesus was born, died and resurrected.

Pelagius rejected the church doctrine that all men are born with sin and that human perfection and salvation can only be attained through the grace of God. Pelagianism, which was condemned by the Council of Carthage, advocated that original sin failed to taint human nature and that man, not God, was in charge of his own salvation. Contrary to widespread belief, man chooses to do good or evil without the aid of the Divine. This posed a problem for the church and was eventually reconciled by St. Augustine who defined "prevenient grace" as the power invested in man by God to perform good acts that could lead to salvation.

Another serious heresy occurred during the reign of Constantine. Arius, a priest from Alexandria, taught his followers that Christ could not be one with the Creator because the Son of God is born from the Father. Instead, Christ was the first and highest of all created beings: the Logos. This caused Bishop Alexander to order Arius defrocked, but not before Arius had influenced a wide number of clergy. Constantine then wrote to both Alexander and Arius:

"I had proposed to lead back to a single form the ideas which all people conceive of the Deity; for I feel strongly that if I could induce men to unite on that subject, the conduct of public affairs would be considerably eased. But alas! I hear that there are more disputes among you recently in Africa."

To address Arius' position, Constantine organized an ecumenical council, known as the Council of Nicea, which was designed to generate orthodoxy amongst nearly 300 bishops gathered from the vast reaches of the Roman Empire. Virtually all in attendance adopted the Nicean Creed to counteract the challenge created by Arius' heresy. The Nicean Creed established the Holy Trinity as a single entity that included the Holy Spirit, God and Jesus Christ and decided upon a universal date for Easter to celebrate the resurrection of Jesus Christ. This solved the problem Arius raised within church doctrine and became a major cornerstone of the Christian fate.

1) **Opposition to Pelagianism was theologically necessary because it:**

   A. denied that God has omnipotent power.

   B. was illegal to practice Christianity.

   C. promoted Old Testament teachings of God.

   D. absolved people of responsible choices.

2) **Marcion's beliefs about the Incarnate are most consistent with the beliefs of:**

   A. Pelagius

   B. Constantine

   C. Arius

   D. Gnosticism

3) **Which of the following conclusions was made at the Council of Nicea?**

   A. Man has free will.

   B. Christ and God are co-eternal.

   C. Easter signifies the resurrection of Christ.

   D. Christ was a created being.

4) **According to the passage, which of the following would be an example of heresy?**

   A. Believing in the Holy Trinity before the Nicean Creed was created.

   B. Thinking it was man's responsibility to prove one's worth to receive salvation.

   C. Practicing Christianity before the Edict of Milan.

   D. Belief that God gave us the ability to seek salvation.

5) **If Christianity had a consensus doctrine from the beginning, all the following problems could have been avoided except:**

   A. multiple creeds being taught to spread the will of God.

   B. differing interpretations of the relationship between Jesus Christ and God.

   C. the original, illegal practice of Christianity within the Roman Empire.

   D. perceived contradictions between the Old and New Testaments.

6) **According to the passage, which of the following statements is not true?**

   A. Arius believed that Jesus Christ was not one with the Creator and not a real being.

   B. Various heretical beliefs forced Christian leadership to hold councils to restore orthodoxy.

   C. Constantine imprisoned Christians for practicing their faith.

   D. Christianity competed against other religions and itself to gain followers.

Church Heresy

Annotations.
1) A 2) D 3) B 4) B 5) C 6) A

	Foundation 1: Comprehension	Foundation 2: Integration of multiple concepts	Foundation 3: Reasoning beyond text
Concepts	2		
Inference	3		
Integration		1,6	
Application			5
Assessment			4

Big Picture. Overall, this passage discusses the beginning of Christianity and the difficulties it faced upon its growth. The first few centuries after the birth and death of Jesus Christ saw an enormous rise in the popularity of Christianity. A corresponding decrease in paganism ensued, but during these early times, Christianity had alternative interpretations. The rapid rise of Christianity resulted in fragmented interpretations of the key principles of the faith. This included the relationship between Jesus Christ and God, as well as man's role in his own salvation. Such intense discourse generated an orthodox church positioned to thrive after the fall of the Roman Empire, but heresy due to no fundamental dogma still plagued the church. The passage presents the early history of Christianity's rise in popularity without much commentary or opinion, suggesting the author was likely a historian.

1) **A. denied that God has omnipotent power. Choice A is the credited answer** because Pelagianism states that man can control his path to salvation by making good choices in the eyes of God. The passage describes how the traditional doctrine had held that God determines man's salvation, making God all-powerful. **Choice B is incorrect** because, although it was stated that Christianity was illegal to practice in the Roman Empire prior to the Edict of Milan, this has nothing to do with a theological argument. **Choice C can be ruled out** because there was no connection made in the passage between Pelagianism and the Old Testament. Pelagius taught that man's choices could lead to salvation, meaning that people are responsible for their choices and not absolved from them. This **eliminates choice D**.

2) **D. Gnosticism.** As described in the passage, Marcion taught that Jesus' body was an imitation of a material body, a theory at odds with the Incarnation of Christ that states Jesus was born, died and then resurrected. **Choice D is the credited answer** because Gnosticism did not believe in the birth of Jesus Christ, but rather believed in divine spirits. **Choices A and C are incorrect** because both Pelagius and Arius believed in the birth of Jesus Christ. Constantine supported and organized the Council of Nicea, which developed a unified doctrine for Christianity, a unified doctrine of Christianity that preached the concept of the Incarnation of Christ, **eliminating choice B.**

3) **B. Christ and God are co-eternal.** The Council of Nicea addressed the heresy of Arius regarding the relationship between Christ and God. **Choice B is the credited answer** because it established the Holy Trinity to include God, Christ and the Holy Spirit and defined them as a single entity making them all eternal. **Choices A and D were not addressed** by the Council of Nicea making them incorrect. While **choice C is tempting, it is incorrect** because the council only assigned a date to the resurrection. The council of Nicea did not define the event of Easter.

4) **B. Thinking it was man's responsibility to prove one's worth to receive salvation. Choice B is the credited answer** because this was defined as a heretical belief held by Pelagius: that man, not a divine power, was responsible for one's salvation. **Choice A is incorrect** because the Holy Trinity was established by the Council of Nicea to stop heretical beliefs. **Choice C is ruled out** because this statement deals with the Roman law that made Christianity legal, not heresy. **Choice D is eliminated** because it is defined throughout the passage that Church orthodoxy believes that divine power grants followers salvation.

5) **C. the original, illegal practice of Christianity within the Roman Empire.** The question stem provides you with new information that fundamentally changes the topic of the passage and asks you interpret the consequence. **Choice C is the credited answer** because the legality of Christianity within the ruling government has nothing to do with an internal, unified doctrine for Christianity. **Choices A, B and D are all incorrect** because they are all issues of heresy, and a singular orthodoxy agreed upon by religious leaders would have eliminated individual interpretations that contradicted one another, leading to all the problems of heresy.

6) **A. Arius believed that Jesus Christ was not one with the Creator and not a real being.** Exhibit care with the wording of this question stem as you are looking for the false answer. **Choice A is the credited answer** because while Arius believed Jesus Christ was not one with the Creator, he did believe Jesus was a real being. **Choice B is incorrect** because the passage discussed multiple councils such as the Council of Carthage and the Council of Nicea, each of which addressed the problem of heresy. **Choice C is eliminated** because as emperor, Constantine enforced the laws that imprisoned Christians before the Edict of Milan. **Choice D is incorrect** because the first paragraph of the passage discussed both the problems within Christianity and conflicts with other beliefs to gain new followers.

Paleolithic Diet

Differences in the diets between our Stone Age ancestors and modern humans residing in industrialized nations are believed to have important ramifications on contemporary health. While modern day hunter and gatherer societies are scarce, dozens have been studied over the last 30 years, and the majority of them are noted to consume greater than 50% of their calories from meat; however, there is significant variation in the levels of meat consumption in these societies. For example, The Inuit of Greenland eat large amounts of fish, a food that begins to appear in the diet of Stone Age people around 100,000 years ago. However, the Gwi people of Africa consume approximately 25% meat. One important conclusion drawn from these studies on modern hunter-gatherers is that conditions such as type 2 diabetes and cardiovascular diseases appear virtually absent, and they are not believed to have plagued Stone Age humans either. Further, life expectancy alone cannot explain the rapid rise in nutritional diseases such as diabetes over the last century, since some members of modern hunter-gatherer societies live well into their fifties.

Initially introduced by Eaton and Konner in 1985, the Paleolithic diet emulates Stone Age diets that relied on naturally available sources of plants and animals, while modern sources of food, such as grains and dairy products, were not available. However, as the Paleolithic period began approximately two million years ago and ended with the Neolithic Revolution, Stone Age diets were not uniform. The Neolithic period began ~10,000 years ago and was the era in which humans began to cultivate land and domesticate animals for food. This transition from a nomadic lifestyle into an agrarian lifestyle occurred in multiple places around the globe, within a small time frame, and is highlighted by cattle domestication and the cultivation of grains and legumes. Although farming introduced new diseases (e.g. animal parasites) into newly formed agrarian societies, the Neolithic Revolution is said to have allowed childbirth to occur on average once every 2.5 years, as opposed to once every 3.5 years in the Paleolithic period.

Although early hominids in the Paleolithic period relied primarily on fruits, evidence suggests hominids living later in this period consumed larger quantities of meat. The transition to eating larger quantities of meat is believed to have had important anatomical implications for hominids. Calorie-rich meat, as opposed to the lower caloric plant diets enjoyed by apes, is believed to have provided the fuel necessary to grow larger in size and strength. However, meat derived from livestock and purchased in markets is notably different than the meat consumed by our Paleolithic ancestors because farm raised meat has higher fat content.

One significant rationale for the current meat-rich Paleolithic diet concerns the "evolutionary discordance hypothesis" of Eaton and Konner. This states that the current epidemic of obesity, cardiovascular disease and diabetes in the Western world is a consequence of a "mismatch" between the genes of our Stone Age ancestors and current lifestyles that rely on starchy, processed foods and other forms of nutrition unavailable in the past. In short, modern day humans have a genetic makeup similar to their Stone Age ancestors, but live in a fast food world.

1) **Which of the following is the least likely consequence of the Neolithic Revolution?**

A. Increase of starch in human diet.

B. Increase in irrigation.

C. Increase in population size.

D. Increase in less sedentary society.

2) **What is the main goal of the author?**

A. To bring awareness to how diet can affect health and longevity.

B. To promote a calorie rich diet for human evolution.

C. To promote the Paleolithic diet as the healthiest diet for humans.

D. To discuss the positive results of the Neolithic Revolution.

3) **Which of the following statements would contradict the evolutionary discordance hypothesis?**

A. The presence of starch granules in fossilized teeth of Neolithic samples.

B. The recent ability of adult humans to metabolize the lactose commonly found in milk.

C. The reliance of early hominid diets on fruits.

D. Calorie-rich meat diets allowed humans to grow larger in size and strength.

4) **Which piece of information would argue against the author's premise that diet has a link to disease?**

A. Evidence of a pre-Neolithic tribe that ate a high fat diet.

B. Pre-Neolithic fossil samples showing a genetic predisposition for individuals to have breast cancer.

C. Finding a modern day hunter-gatherer society with multiple occurrences of heart attacks.

D. A significant rise in dental caries observed in the Neolithic period.

5) **According to the passage, which of the following statements is true?**

A. Due to evolution, our genes are no longer compatible with a Paleolithic diet.

B. The Inuit diet resembles a Paleolithic diet compared to the Gwi peoples' diet.

C. The Neolithic Revolution introduced new factors that threatened human health.

D. High protein diets lead to diabetes and cardio-vascular disease.

Paleolithic Diet

Annotations.
1) D 2) A 3) B 4) C 5) C

	Foundation 1: Comprehension	Foundation 2: Integration of multiple concepts	Foundation 3: Reasoning beyond text
Concepts	1		
Inference	5		
Integration		2,3	
Application			
Assessment			4

Big Picture. The overall theme of this passage discusses the impact of human diet on our health. It compares the diets of our ancestors to common modern day diets and discusses the impacts of these differences. The main comparison made is between the diet of hominids in the Paleolithic Era and current human diets. The passage also explores the possible relationship between the change in diet and the rise in numerous diseases currently plaguing modern society. The author talks about the transition that occurred in hominid diets to help explain how our current diet evolved. This is mostly a fact-based passage, but the author does seem concerned with finding a reason for the rise in diseases we currently face. The author probably works in the health care industry, more specifically with nutrition, and wants to identify reasons for the rise in diseases like diabetes, so they can be combated.

1) **D. Increase in less sedentary society.** From the passage, we know the Neolithic Revolution was the beginning of the switch from a nomadic to an agrarian lifestyle for humans. **Choice D is the credited answer** because humans are no longer constantly moving, so their lifestyle would become more sedentary, not less. **Choice A is eliminated** because the passage states human diet consisted of grains and legumes which would increase the amount of starch in human diet. **Choice B is incorrect** because irrigation would be used to provide water to farmland. **Choice C is eliminated** because the last sentence of the second paragraph tells you the birth rate increased during the Neolithic Revolution.

2) **A. To bring awareness to how diet can affect health and longevity.** For this question, you must anticipate the overall reason why the author wrote the passage. While the author provides historical facts about humans' diet, it is all related back to human health and the current rise in diseases that were not a problem for humans in the past. **Choice A is the credited answer** because it is broad enough to encompass the theme of the author. **Choice B is incorrect** because, while the author states that a calorie-rich diet caused humans to evolve to be larger and stronger, it is just one fact given, making it too narrow. **Choice C is eliminated** because the author never provides an opinion about which type of diet is best for humans. **Choice D is incorrect** because discussing the Neolithic Revolution was only part of the passage, again making it too narrow of a topic to represent an overall perspective.

3) **B. The recent ability of adult humans to metabolize the lactose commonly found in milk.** To answer this question, you need to know that the "evolutionary discordance hypothesis" states that modern day humans share the same genetic makeup as their Stone Age ancestors; however, we eat starchy, processed foods and dairy rather than naturally available sources of plants and animals. **Choice B is the credited answer** because being able to process dairy would be a new ability since Paleolithic societies did not consume dairy products. **Choice A is incorrect** because, according to the second paragraph, Neolithic societies started to eat grains. **Choice C is eliminated** because the passage states that fruit was a staple of the Paleolithic diet. **Choice D is incorrect** because, while this was a fact given in the passage, no relationship was made between the evolutionary discordance hypothesis and this fact.

4) **C. Finding a modern day hunter-gatherer society with multiple occurrences of heart attacks.** **Choice C is the credited answer** because recorded heart attacks would suggest cardiovascular disease, which the author describes as not being an issue for Paleolithic cultures because of their hunter-gatherer diet. **Choice A is eliminated** because evidence of a high fat diet is not evidence of increased disease. No information is provided about disease. **Choice B is incorrect** because the author makes no link between diet and cancer. **Choice D is eliminated** because a rise in dental caries during the Neolithic period would support the premise that diet is linked to disease. Recall that during the Neolithic period, the farming of plants and animals was introduced. Such a change has been attributed to the development of various medical conditions (e.g. dental caries) that were absent during the Paleolithic period.

5) **C. The Neolithic Revolution introduced new factors that threatened human health. Choice C is the credited answer** because the second paragraph states that humans faced new diseases from living in close proximity to domesticated animals. The passage provides no facts to support the idea that our genes are currently incompatible with the Paleolithic diet, so **choice A can be eliminated**. If anything, the passage supports the idea that our genes are not compatible with our current diet. **Choice B is incorrect** because the first paragraph states Inuits have a higher protein content in their diet compared to the Gwi. Therefore, the Gwi diet would more resemble a Paleolithic diet. **Choice D is eliminated** because the passage implies our current diet could be, at least, partly responsible for the increases in diseases we face now but never specifically claims or supports the idea that high protein diets alone are responsible.

Ebola Epidemic

The Ebola virus primarily targets mononuclear phagocytes and hepatocytes and causes symptoms in patients a short time after infection (nausea, vomiting, internal bleeding and organ failure), with a high mortality rate. Ebola is likely contracted from bats, birds or primates, such as crab-eating macaques, and can be spread through both blood and bodily fluids.

First identified in Zaire and Sudan, the Ebola virus has caused several major outbreaks in Sub-Saharan African populations of both humans and primates. The 2014 West African outbreak is the most severe epidemic to date in the brief history of the virus. As there is no known cure for Ebola, the World Health Organization (WHO) has called for the use of experimental drugs that have yet to be clinically tested and approved by the US Food and Drug Administration (FDA). Although Ebola was first identified in 1976, relatively few research dollars have been invested in the disease compared to HIV and other maladies, such as malaria, due to lack of profitability. Some have argued that the for-profit pharmaceutical model, where stock value is the greatest concern, does not encourage investing in diseases like Ebola.

Experimental treatments for Ebola have shown promise in non-human primate models, including vaccines derived from viruses such as adenovirus and vesicular stomatitis Indiana virus (VSIV). In some cases, recombinant VSIV virions expressing Ebola viral proteins on their surface are used as antigens during immunization, a process that can take up to 6 months. Two new therapeutics targeting Ebola have received widespread attention. The first is a cocktail of Ebola antibodies (MB-003) that recognizes the outer membrane glycoprotein of the Ebola virus. This promising approach has prevented infection in monkeys. MB-003 antibodies are produced in tobacco plants and have been dubbed "plantibodies." A second drug, developed by a Canadian firm which has been funded in part by grants from the US Department of Defense (DOD) to fight bioterrorism. TKM-Ebola is a lipid nanoparticle that harbors "small interfering" RNA molecules designed to specifically disrupt viral gene expression. While a promising approach, the variable reduction in viral gene expression has raised concerns about the efficacy of RNA interference. Prior to the West African outbreak, the nanoparticle drug was placed on hold from the FDA due to safety concerns, but since the outbreak, the FDA has relaxed its position and allowed for limited testing in Ebola patients. Despite promising results from the experimental treatments, limited supply of drugs has been problematic during the current Ebola epidemic.

Recently, two American relief workers and a Spanish priest received experimental treatments for Ebola. One of them, Dr. Kent Bradly, received a blood transfusion from a patient who had previously survived the disease, while the other two patients received laboratory-derived therapeutics. Although the Spanish priest died, the other two patients survived, lifting hopes for an effective Ebola treatment. However, the company that provided the drug specified that it only be used on aid workers, sparking a controversy about who should receive the limited supply of therapeutics. Since the vast majority of infected patients are African, it has been argued that Western aid workers are receiving preferential treatment by receiving the experimental medicines first. Others have responded saying this is an unfair and biased criticism of Ebola treatment in Africa asking: What would they say if the experiment had failed? Currently, the limited availability of drugs ensures unequal access to treatment, but the next generation of anti-viral therapies for the Ebola virus are being mobilized to treat the outbreak in Guinea and to help prevent future epidemics.

1) According to the passage, what is most likely to fail in an Ebola patient?

A. Aorta

B. Liver

C. Lymphatic system

D. Bone marrow

2) Which organization was least concerned about the detrimental side effects of experimental Ebola treatments?

A. WHO

B. FDA

C. Relief workers

D. DOD

3) Research into Ebola vaccines was most likely motivated by which of the following?

A. Its role in primate evolution.

B. Humanitarian concerns.

C. Its role in the immune system.

D. Its role in bioterrorism.

4) If a biotech firm developing an experimental Ebola therapy experienced a large stock price increase, this could be due to:

A. public demand for a treatment.

B. confidence in the technique of "plantibodies."

C. confidence in the drug's profitability.

D. a large pharmaceutical company acquiring the biotech firm.

5) If experimental Ebola treatments had initially been used on West African patients with an unsuccessful outcome, headlines from someone critical of providing aid first to Westerners might read:

A. drug companies fail to tame Ebola virus.

B. FDA regulations hinder progress against Ebola.

C. Ebola ravages Africa, doctors helpless.

D. African patients used as guinea pigs to find Ebola cure.

6) Which of the following statements is false?

A. Limited numbers of treatments raise an ethical question about priority of individuals treated.

B. The current Ebola outbreak confirms global concern about an Ebola pandemic.

C. A capitalistic economy leaves a population susceptible to emerging diseases.

D. Government and health agencies need coordinated responses to disease outbreaks.

Ebola Epidemic

	Foundation 1: Comprehension	Foundation 2: Integration of multiple concepts	Foundation 3: Reasoning beyond text
Concepts	2		
Inference	1		
Integration		3,6	
Application			5
Assessment			4

Big Picture. The passage discusses the Ebola outbreak in Africa and provides a general history about the Ebola virus. The author discusses symptoms and possible sources of infection, but you should walk away from the introduction recognizing how little is known about Ebola. Next, the development of different types of experimental treatments is discussed, as well as the agencies responsible. Finally, the author explores the response to the current epidemic and covers both the moral and ethical arguments stemming from the current treatment procedures. Overall, this is a fact-based article that provides general information to inform the reader of the seriousness of an Ebola outbreak and gives an unbiased explanation of concerns from all agencies and individuals involved in the situation.

1) **B. Liver.** In the first paragraph of the passage, you are given a list of symptoms from Ebola. They were: nausea, vomiting, internal bleeding and organ failure. **Choice B is the credited answer** because liver would be covered under organ failure. The passage also states that Ebola targets hepatocytes, which further supports liver as the credited answer. **Choices A, C and D are incorrect** as they would not fall under any of the symptoms you were given.

2) **A. WHO. Choice A is the credited answer** because the passage discusses how the WHO called for the use of experimental treatments that had not been clinically tested. In fact, it was the FDA who was reluctant to allow the use of experimental treatments and later reversed its position to allow these treatments to be used **making choice B incorrect**. The passage does not discuss the stance of the DOD or relief workers on the treatment of infected patients, **eliminating choices C and D**.

3) **D. Its role in bioterrorism.** For this question, you must remember to make your decision based solely on the information provided by the passage. Therefore, **choice B is eliminated** because the passage states that few treatments are being developed because they aren't profitable, which is not consistent with humanitarian concerns. **Choices A and C are incorrect** because the passage does not discuss Ebola's role in either primate evolution or the immune system. **Choice D is the credited answer** because the passage states the DOD was a main funding source for one of the experimental treatments. The DOD routinely funds disease research to develop cures for soldiers to be used if they are ever exposed to a biological agent.

4) **C. confidence in the drug's profitability.** The passage states that few companies are developing Ebola treatments because it is not a profitable market. **Choice C is the credited answer** because when a company's profits increase, so does its stock price. So if the treatment is deemed profitable, the company's stock will likely rise. **Choice A is incorrect** because demand for a treatment does not correlate to the number of people who may actually need to purchase the treatment, thus making it profitable. **Choice B is incorrect** because confidence in a technique does not ensure success of a treatment or profitability. **Choice D is incorrect** because it is beyond the scope of the passage. You are provided no information about the results of one company purchasing another.

5) **D. African patients used as guinea pigs to find Ebola cure.** The passage describes how the critics are upset that Western relief workers were being treated first and feel that African patients were being marginalized. **Choice D is the credited answer** because if the treatment didn't work, then they would claim the patients are being mistreated as per the author's question in the last paragraph. **Choices A, B and C are eliminated** because these are sensationalist headlines and could be applied regardless of whether Western aid workers or African patients are treated first

6) **B. The current Ebola outbreak confirms global concern about an Ebola pandemic. Choice B is the credited answer** because the passage provides no supporting data regarding the capacity for Ebola to become a pandemic, or that there's reason for global concern regarding this. **Choice A is incorrect** because the issue of who should be treated first, relief workers or patients, is raised in the last paragraph. **Choice C can be ruled out** because the passage informs the reader that some diseases are not well studied because treatment is not regarded as profitable. A capitalist economy is based on a business for profit model and would react to emerging diseases only after the market became profitable, thereby leaving the population susceptible. The passage discussed how both the WHO and FDA disagreed on treatment procedures but eventually agree upon a singular course of action allowing untested treatments to be use on human patients, which **eliminates choice D**.

Mongols

Born in 1162, Temujin united numerous tribes on the central Asian plateau north of China in the early 1200s. Afterwards, he assumed the name Genghis Khan. These tribes, including the Jin, Merkits, Tatars, Naimans and Tanguts, were all in conflict with one another prior to the arrival of Genghis Khan, and his arrival led to the newly formed Mongolian empire which stretched for over a million square miles at its peak. As a result, Genghis Khan would become one of the most feared rulers in history before his death in 1227. The dominance of the Mongols under the rule of Genghis Khan, his sons and grandson Khubla Khan, was the result of highly innovative strategies, such as the expansion of warfare to include the use of a naval fleet and the development of explosive bombs thrown from the hands.

Khan lived by the military rule of law known as Yassa, which means "to set in order." Although no known written record of Yassa exists, historians have gained insight into its inner workings and codes from secondhand sources. Using this code Khan seamlessly integrated a myriad of conquered tribes into his realm despite the religious diversity of his new subjects. One practice that helped Genghis Khan accomplish this was to promise both civilians and soldiers a portion of the wealth from conquered territories. In addition, promotion within the military, with the exception of Khan's family members, was based upon merit rather than family, religion or race. Genghis Khan was also said to have given his enemies sufficient opportunity to surrender and become vassals to avoid war. At the end of his life, Genghis Khan attempted to create a civil state under the code of Yassa that would have established legal equality for all citizens of the empire, including women, but no record of its implementation has been found.

Genghis Khan formed a courier system known as the "Yam," which doubled as security for foreign dignitaries like Marco Polo, who described his adventures into Mongolia through the Silk Road in 1269. Genghis Khan used the Yam as spies, sending them to various parts of Europe and Asia to monitor a region for political and military weakness, spanning periods of time as long as 10 years. Despite his political and economic success, Genghis Khan is noted as one of the most ruthless leaders in history. After the Shah of the Khwarezmid tribe in historical Persia executed a Mongolian emissary and violated an agreement to trade goods along the Silk Road, Genghis Khan invaded and decimated the population. The resulting war with the Khwarezmids is regarded as was one of the bloodiest battles in history, with the Mongols killing up to 75% of the entire population.

The legacy of Genghis Khan is expansive, with his organizational and bookkeeping methods still studied at universities; and his image and name appear on various commercial products throughout modern day Mongolia. He also heavily contributed to the genealogy of the Mongolian race. Using DNA sequencing technology, the lineage of the Mongols has been traced back to a Y chromosomal signature sequence that originated in Mongolia approximately 1,000 years ago, and which is credited to Genghis Khan. This "Genghis Khan Y chromosome" has been found in more than a dozen large populations from the Pacific Ocean to the Caspian Sea, and it has been estimated that approximately 0.5% of the world's population carries this signature chromosome.

1) **According to the passage, which statement is true?**

   A. Historical text claims Genghis Khan used the code of Yassa to integrate tribes he conquered.

   B. Historians use the "Genghis Y chromosome" to define the borders of the Mongolian empire.

   C. Khan engendered the favor of his subjects by distributing plunder after military campaigns.

   D. The Shah of Khwarezmid betrayed Khan's friendship resulting in the slaughter of Shah's tribe.

2) **According to the passage, which type of school might have materials relating to Genghis Khan's rule?**

   A. Military school

   B. Accounting school

   C. Law school

   D. Medical school

3) **If Genghis Khan had not used the Yassa code to build the Mongolian empire, which of the following statements would be false?**

   A. Genghis Khan would not be known as one of the most ruthless leaders in history.

   B. Genghis Khan's family members would receive military promotion based on familial ties.

   C. Genghis Khan would have established the Yam.

   D. The Mongolian Empire would have had a more difficult time assimilating rival tribes.

4) **Marco Polo is said to have visited Mongolia. He most likely met:**

   A. Genghis Khan

   B. Khubla Khan

   C. Shah of the Khwarezmids

   D. Temujin

5) **Which of the following is least likely to be true about Genghis Khan?**

   A. His most trusted generals were former enemies.

   B. Preferred peaceful surrender to war.

   C. Created a Mongol race from bonded nomadic tribes.

   D. Forgave business partners after failed dealings.

6) **Genghis Khan created the Yam for all the following reasons, except to:**

   A. escort foreign emissaries through the Mongolian empire.

   B. provide information to help build battle plans against adversaries.

   C. eliminate the leaders of rival tribes.

   D. determine the leadership qualities of rulers from other countries.

Mongols

Annotations.
1) C 2) B 3) A 4) B 5) D 6) C

	Foundation 1: Comprehension	Foundation 2: Integration of multiple concepts	Foundation 3: Reasoning beyond text
Concepts	4		
Inference	6		
Integration		1,5	
Application			2
Assessment			3

Big Picture. This passage gives a historical account of the life of Genghis Khan, his accomplishments and how they still affect us today. The author starts with the establishment of the Mongolian empire and provides facts throughout Khan's life. The author provides examples of how both the military and civilian populations were affected and ruled during the peak of the Mongolian Empire and how Khan's influences are still felt today. Recent genetic studies further prove his influence with the discovery of a chromosome traced back to his lineage, which is possessed by a significant number of people today. This passage is largely composed of facts regarding the life of Genghis Khan, indicating that the write is likely a historian.

1) **C. Khan engendered the favor of his subjects by distributing plunder after military campaigns. Choice C is the credited answer** because the second paragraph describes how offering to divide up the wealth accumulated from new territories was used to integrate conquered tribes. **Choice A is incorrect** because the passage states there is no written record of the Yassa code so there is no historical text to confirm this statement. **Choice B is incorrect** because the passage never describes how the "Genghis Y chromosome" was used to define the borders of the Mongolian empire, only that a genetic study has found a large number of people possess the chromosome. **Choice D is eliminated** because the passage states the Shah violated a trade agreement, not Khan's friendship.

2) **B. Accounting school. Choice B is the credited answer** because the last paragraph states Genghis Khan's organizational and bookkeeping methods are still studied today, which best correlates to accounting school. **Choice A is incorrect** because the passage never mentions Khan's military tactics being studied, only that they were innovative at the time. **Choice C can be eliminated** because the passage states there is no written record of the Yassa code, which is the system of law Khan used to rule his subjects, and that only historians have tried to discover the specifics of the Yassa code. **Choice D is eliminated** because the passage never discusses any medical advancement attributable to the Mongolian empire.

3) A. Genghis Khan would not be known as one of the most ruthless leaders in history. Choice A is the credited answer because the discussion about Genghis Khan being known as a ruthless leader was not done within the context of how Genghis Khan implemented the Yassa code within his empire. Therefore, the use of the Yassa code would be irrelevant to Genghis Khan's reputation as a ruthless leader. **Choice B is ruled out** because the passage states that promotion of Genghis Khan's family within the military was an exception to the Yassa code; therefore, it still would have occurred if the Yassa code was not used. **Choice C is incorrect** because the creation and use of the Yam by Genghis Khan was discussed outside the context of the Yassa code. **Choice D is eliminated** because the passage states the use of the Yassa code helped Genghis Khan "…seamlessly integrated a myriad of conquered tribes into his realm despite the religious diversity of his new subjects."

4) B. Khubla Khan. The passage states that Marco Polo visited Mongolia in 1269. **Choice A is incorrect** because you are told Genghis Khan died in 1227 so they could not have met one another. Temujin and Genghis Khan are the same person, so **choice D can be eliminated**. Genghis Khan killed the Shah of the Khwarezmids, so again, the timing is impossible and **choice C can be ruled out**. Khubla Khan is the only person who could have been alive when Marco Polo traveled to the Far East, so **choice B is the credited answer**.

5) D. Forgave business partners after failed dealings. Choice D is the credited answer because Genghis Khan killed the Shah of the Khwarezmids and his people after he broke a trade agreement, so it appears Khan is not forgiving of his business partners. **Choice A is incorrect** because the second paragraph discusses how successful Khan was at integrating conquered tribes into his kingdom, partially because one could advance within the military solely on merit regardless of race or religion. **Choice B is eliminated** because the passage states how Khan gave his enemies ample time to choose surrender over battle. The first paragraph discusses how Khan was successful at uniting numerous tribes into the Mongol empire, **ruling out choice C**.

6) C. eliminate the leaders of rival tribes. Choice C is the credited answer because the passage never mentions Khan using the Yam to assassinate leaders from other countries. **Choice A is eliminated** because the passage states Khan created the Yam to double as security for foreign dignitaries. **Choice B can be ruled out** because the passage states the Yam looked for any military weaknesses in foreign countries, which would be critical information for building any battle plan against an enemy. **Choice D is incorrect** because the passage tells you the Yam looked for political weaknesses in a region, which would bring the quality of leadership into question.

E-cigarettes

Cigarette smoking is the single most preventable cause of death and morbidity in the United States and is directly responsible for one out of five annual deaths in the US. This is more than all deaths caused by HIV, illicit drugs, alcohol, murder, suicide and motor vehicle accidents combined. This has caused the popularity of electronic (E)-cigarettes to increase dramatically in the last few years. Currently, the prototypical E-cigarette consists of three elements: nicotine housed in either a propylene glycol or glycerin solution, a heating element that transforms the nicotine source into inhalable vapor, and a battery that powers the heating source. The nicotine source is also often garnished with various flavors.

While early studies suggested that nicotine administration from an E-cigarette was either very low or non-existent, subsequent analyses have demonstrated that individuals can achieve nicotine blood plasma levels comparable to cigarettes. This has resulted in an increased use of E-cigarettes and generated a heated debate among researchers and clinicians. The FDA has intervened, warning the manufacturers of E-cigarettes about the lack of consistency in nicotine delivery, the presence of toxic chemicals from combustion, and companies' undocumented claims regarding the efficacy of E-cigarettes. Currently, the FDA regulates E-cigarettes in a manner similar to tobacco products. However, provided that E-cigarettes continue to not be directly marketed as a cessation device, E-cigarettes will not fall under FDA regulations that other nicotine-replacement products do, such as nicotine gums, patches, lozenges, and inhalers.

Regardless of how E-cigarettes are marketed, some view them as a healthy alternative to conventional cigarettes that could potentially supplant their use among society. The most detrimental aspect of cigarette smoking is derived from combustion. Combustion is largely responsible for tissue damage and the development of various cancers, particularly lung cancer, which is the leading cause of cancer deaths. Traditional cigarettes also have hundreds of additives like acetaldehyde, toluene, hexamine and arsenic that are designed to enhance nicotine delivery and absorption, while E-cigarettes do not contain comparable quantities of these toxic chemicals.

A recent study of E-cigarettes published in Lancet used a randomized trial of 657 people split into three groups: group A used nicotine E-cigarettes, group B used nicotine patches, and group C used placebo E-cigarettes. After six months, 7.0% of group A achieved smoking abstinence while 6.0% of group B achieved abstinence and 4.0% of group C achieved abstinence. The sample size was considered too small to determine if the E-cigarettes were more effective than patches at helping individuals to achieve smoking abstinence.

There are still many that point out the potential detriments of E-cigarettes. Manufacturers have produced E-cigarettes with a variety of exotic flavors, which many argue will increase the use among adolescents and young adults, ushering in a new generation of nicotine-dependent youth. E-cigarette manufacturers are also using popular television and movie stars as spokespeople, as well as allowing individuals to personalize their E-cigarettes to increase their "sexiness." Another potential detriment of E-cigarettes is their potential dual-use, which means smokers would use E-cigarettes under situations where they can't smoke regular cigarettes but would continue to smoke regular cigarettes when able. It is possible that if E-cigarettes become widely accepted and visible in contexts where smoking has been either banned or greatly reduced (e.g. theatres, restaurants, bars, etc.), the result would be desensitization to smoking in general.

1) **What is the main purpose of the passage?**

   A. To explore the methods used by manufacturers to sell E-cigarettes.

   B. To discuss what type of product E-cigarettes should be classified as.

   C. To compare E-cigarettes to cigarettes and discuss the positives and negatives of E-cigarettes.

   D. To show how E-cigarettes are less hazardous to one's health than regular cigarettes.

2) **Compared to traditional cigarettes, which is a true statement about E-cigarettes?**

   A. E-cigarettes are the most popular alternative to cigarettes.

   B. E-cigarettes are a smoking cessation device.

   C. E-cigarettes are more effective than nicotine patches.

   D. Nicotine is absorbed more slowly from E-cigarettes.

3) **The inclusion of some additives into cigarettes is analogous to:**

   A. high sugar content in soda.

   B. decreased trans-fat concentration in cookies.

   C. high cholesterol in shellfish.

   D. personalized appearance of E-cigarettes.

4) **According to the author, what is a reason why people believe E-cigarettes will increase the level of nicotine use per person?**

   A. Inclusion of fewer additives.

   B. Safer source of nicotine than cigarettes.

   C. Increased opportunity to self-administer nicotine throughout the day.

   D. Easier delivery of nicotine.

5) **If data supported the conclusion that E-cigarettes were an effective cessation device, which of the following statements would be true?**

   A. More famous people would seek to endorse E-cigarettes.

   B. The FDA would impose tighter regulations on E-cigarettes.

   C. E-cigarettes would be more widely accepted in places like theatres, restaurants, and bars.

   D. There would be a dramatic drop in lung cancer in the general population.

6) **Which of the following is a false statement?**

   A. E-cigarette manufacturers are trying to market their product as trendy.

   B. The percentages determined in the E-cigarette study were too close to draw a conclusion.

   C. E-cigarettes' effectiveness as a cessation device is still unproven.

   D. Lack of regulations on E-cigarettes has caused concerns from the FDA.

E-cigarettes

	Foundation 1: Comprehension	Foundation 2: Integration of multiple concepts	Foundation 3: Reasoning beyond text
Concepts	2		
Inference	4		
Integration		1,6	
Application			3
Assessment			5

Big Picture. This passage discusses E-cigarettes and how they fit into the overall cigarette market. A background is provided about the dangers of smoking and how that has fueled the development and interest in E-cigarettes. You are then provided information about how regular cigarettes and E-cigarettes differ, both in government regulation and functional delivery of nicotine to the body. The author also explains how there is still a lack of scientifically valid studies to support any possible benefits of E-cigarettes. Finally, the potential social drawbacks of E-cigarettes are examined in terms of increased acceptance of smoking rather than helping users break the habit of smoking. Overall, this is an informative and fair discussion about the positive potential of E-cigarettes balanced with potential problems. The author is most likely a health care professional whose primary concern is patient well-being and is hopeful about E-cigarettes potential use as a cessation device, but is also cognizant of its potential downfalls.

1) **C. To compare E-cigarettes to cigarettes and discuss the positives and negatives of E-cigarettes.** Following the discussion in the Big Picture, this passage seeks to inform you about the positive and negative attributes of E-cigarettes in a critical but seemingly unbiased fashion. **Choices A, B and D can be eliminated** because they don't encompass all the topics covered within the passage. While each answer choice brings up an issue discussed in the passage, they are all covered by a single paragraph making it too narrow to cover the purpose of the entire passage. **Choice C is the credited answer** because it is the most general statement that encompasses all the topics discussed by the author throughout the passage.

2) **D. Nicotine is absorbed more slowly from E-cigarettes.** This question requires that you have full command of the details presented in the passage and that you are able to eliminate answer choices based upon whether they agree or disagree with those details. **Choice D is the credited answer** because the passage discusses the additives in cigarettes that help the body absorb nicotine faster and notes these are not significantly present in E-cigarettes. The passage never discusses the popularity of E-cigarettes, **eliminating choice A**. The passage also states that E-cigarettes are not a cessation device, **eliminating choice B**. The passage discusses a study done to answer this question but you were told it that the sample size was not large enough to support any conclusion making **choice C incorrect**.

3) **A. high sugar content in soda.** For this analogy question, the key is recognizing that the artificial additives are what you are using as a comparative. **Choice A is the credited answer** because sugar is an artificial additive in soda. **Choice B is incorrect** because you are removing a component from the product. **Choice C can be eliminated** because high cholesterol in shellfish is not an artificial additive. **Choice D is incorrect** because personalized appearance of E-cigarettes is a marketing tool, not an additive.

4) **C. Increased opportunity to self-administer nicotine throughout the day. Choice C is the credited answer** because the author describes how detractors make the argument that E-cigarettes can be a dual use tool that allows people to smoke in more locations. **Choice A is incorrect** because it contradicts statements in the passage in that fewer additives would predictably make it harder to absorb nicotine into the bloodstream reducing general nicotine use. The passage discusses how there is no data to support the notion that E-cigarettes are safer, so **choice B cannot be correct**. The passage states it is easier to absorb nicotine from cigarettes than E-cigarettes, **eliminating choice D**.

5) **B. The FDA would impose tighter regulations on E-cigarettes.** In this question, you are given a new piece of information and asked to determine how this information would change the discussion in the passage. **Choice B is the credited answer** because the passage states that E-cigarettes have looser government regulations due to the fact that they are not classified as a cessation device. Thus, if they were, the FDA would be able to impose tighter regulations on E-cigarettes. **Choices A and D can be eliminated** because these are assumptions that cannot be made from the information you are given in the passage. **Choice C is incorrect** because the passage states that E-cigarettes are already used in these locations.

6) **B. The percentages determined in the E-cigarette study were too close to draw a conclusion. Choice B is the credited answer** because the passage states that the study did not have a statistically significant sample size so the percentages in the results are meaningless. If there was a statistically significant sample size you could draw a conclusion regardless of how close the percentages are. **Choice A is incorrect** because the passage talks about how manufacturers are using famous people to advertise and allowing people to customize the look of their E-cigarettes. The passage mentions that E-cigarettes are unproven as a cessation device making **choice C incorrect**. The passage states the FDA has warned E-cigarettes manufacturers about their claims, **eliminating choice D**.

Geothermal Energy

Geothermal energy is a sustainable and renewable energy source within the grasp of humanity. The heat derived from geothermal energy within the Earth originated from two sources: the initial formation of the planet, combined with the radioactive decay of elements at the Earth's core. The temperature difference between the core and surface creates a geothermal gradient that supplies continuous conduction of geothermal energy in the form of heat. This heat is transferred from the core to the mantle to the crust, causing some of the thinner portions of the crust to rise to as much as 700° F. The core annually produces over 44 terawatts of energy, which is approximately twice the global consumption of energy.

The production of electricity and direct heating are two major examples of how geothermal energy has been harnessed. For example, Iceland's unique geographic location situated over a thin portion of the Earth's crust makes the island volcanically active. Iceland has taken advantage of this geothermal energy to fulfill its heating requirements and has five major geothermal power plants satisfying over a quarter of the country's electrical needs. Geothermal heating also provides hot water to over 80% of the country's buildings. Although there are 24 countries currently operating geothermal plants, evidence for the use of geothermal energy dates back to ancient times. For example, a 3rd century hot spring tub has been discovered in China. In fact, the Romans pioneered the commercialization of geothermal energy by using hot springs in public baths as well as for under floor heating. More contemporary advancements of geothermal energy use include geysers and volcanic mud to reduce costs in the production of industrial chemicals. In addition, geothermal energy has spurred innovation, including the creation of the heat pump and new building materials that serve as more efficient conduits for energy transfer. Today, both steam and hot water from geysers are used for heating various types of buildings across the globe. Despite the fact that commercial power plants were not widely used in the Western hemisphere until the early 20th century, the United States is currently the world's leader in geothermal energy production.

Unfortunately, areas where geothermal energy can be harnessed are limited by the boundaries between tectonic plates, which are not uniformly accessible to all countries. While it is has been cost effective in specific regions where geothermal energy is readily accessible, less accessible energy has required expensive and dangerous deep drilling procedures. Further, the combination of a high failure rate and the high costs of exploration have disincentivized the widespread use of geothermal energy. However, there are clear advantages: geothermal energy does not require fossil fuels, and it is therefore independent of energy price fluctuations, and it requires minimal land and water resources. Currently, energy markets are recalcitrant to energy produced from these sources as it translates to an increase in cost that the consumer is unwilling to accept. Continuing technological advancements in the industry have reduced costs by 25% over the last two decades. While geothermal energy production does release greenhouse gases like carbon dioxide, hydrogen sulfide, and methane, it is a fraction of the amount produced by fossil fuels.

1) **Which of the following is not an example of the origins of geothermal energy?**

   A. Decay of uranium-235.

   B. Coalescence of dust and gases to form planet Earth.

   C. Decay of uranium-238.

   D. Conduction of energy from core to mantle to crust.

2) **The geographical location of Iceland provides an advantage for geothermal energy production. Which of the following examples would represent a similar advantage for a region?**

   A. Technological advances resulting in extraction of oil from shale deposits in Alberta.

   B. Formation of the Rocky Mountains, shaping the Great Plains into a successful agricultural industry.

   C. Mediterranean Sea separating Europe from Africa.

   D. Tax incentives in Texas to energy companies to use renewable wind resources.

3) **Which of the following was not provided by the passage as an advancement developed by the geothermal energy industry?**

   A. Stronger PVC pipes for building infrastructures.

   B. Reduced costs for sulfuric acid production.

   C. More efficient heat pumps for new homes.

   D. Better insulation for heating buildings.

4) **The author would agree with all of the following statements except:**

   A. Geothermal energy can be a long term, renewable energy source.

   B. Geothermal energy is an expensive and dangerous energy source to develop.

   C. Humanity has exploited geothermal energy since the 3rd century.

   D. Replacing coal burning energy plants with geothermal plants will reduce production of greenhouse gases.

5) **According to the passage, which of the following would allow geothermal energy to become more widely utilized?**

   A. Energy sectors tolerating a 5% increase in costs.

   B. An increase in energy exploration.

   C. Reducing the amount of greenhouse gases produced during geothermal energy production.

   D. An overall reduction in the energy needs of humanity.

6) **With which statement would the author most likely agree with?**

   A. A 25% reduction in the cost of geothermal energy would make greenhouse gas production irrelevant.

   B. Iceland's culture has evolved around their development of geothermal energy.

   C. Production of greenhouse gases by geothermal energy is an acceptable consequence when compared to pollution from coal-based energy production.

   D. Greenhouse gases are a justifiable consequence because they reduce price fluctuations.

Geothermal Energy

Annotations.
1) D 2) B 3) D 4) C 5) A 6) C

	Foundation 1: Comprehension	Foundation 2: Integration of multiple concepts	Foundation 3: Reasoning beyond text
Concepts	3		
Inference	1		
Integration		4,6	
Application			5
Assessment			2

Big Picture. This passage discusses the potential of geothermal energy as an alternative energy source for humanity. The author is highly versed in this topic and cites many of its specific details and historical context. The author is likely someone who is in the energy industry and is perhaps an engineer or an energy consultant. When you encounter passages such as this, keep in mind that they are likely to include substance that can be guided by opinion, so try to be cognizant of what the opinion of the author is, as you may have questions that are asking you to anticipate this opinion. In this passage, the author is in favor of geothermal energy as an alternative energy source, but at the same time, the author is also very knowledgeable about its history and its limitations. Further, the author appears to be aware of both sides of the argument as to whether geothermal energy is the way to go, but she/he falls short of giving any political perspective that she/he may have (e.g. liberal versus conservative). Overall, the author seems intent on providing a descriptive perspective on the history of geothermal energy and appears more intent on the reader appreciating its history and geographical limitations. In other words, this is probably not an opinion piece written in the New York Times, but rather, a descriptive column that might appear in National Geographic.

1) **D. Conduction of energy from core to mantle to crust.** This question requires that you sift through the wording present in the first paragraph. Moreover, you must identify that the question stem requires you to find the example that is not true. **Choice D is the credited answer** because it deals with the transfer of energy, not the generation of energy. **Choice B** is incorrect because the passage states that 20% of all geothermal energy was generated during the planets formation. **Choices A and C** are incorrect because the passage states that 80% of geothermal energy is generated by the radioactive decay of minerals, and both of these forms of uranium are radioactive.

2) **B. Formation of the Rocky Mountains, shaping the Great Plains into a successful agricultural industry.** Here, you must identify the type of relationship and then draw an appropriate analogy. The stem states that a geographical advantage is in place that gives Iceland access to geothermal energy. Therefore, you must identify an analogous situation where a geographical status provides an advantage to a society. Given this, **choices A and D are ruled out** because they deal with technical and economical advantages rather than geographical ones. The distractor in both of these cases is the reference to energy production, potentially fulfilling half of the analogy construction. **Choice C is incorrect** because it describes a geographical advantage but fails to demonstrate how this benefits the nearby society. **Choice B is the credited answer** because it discusses a strictly geological advantage that has a positive economic impact on society.

3) **D. Better insulation for heating buildings.** This question asks for an advancement that is not linked to geothermal energy in the passage. **Choice D is the credited answer** because the author does not mention anything about building insulation. Creation of new building materials for more efficient pipes is mentioned making **choice A incorrect**. Further, there is a direct reference to the use of volcanic mud in chemical production making **choice B incorrect**. Finally, the passage directly mentions advancements in heat pumps making **choice D incorrect**.

4) **C. Humanity has exploited geothermal energy since the 3rd century.** This is a typical MCAT style question in that it requires you to understand what the author is thinking. The statements that are consistent with the author's viewpoint can all be found in the passage. Therefore, you need only to find the statements in the passage, and then rule them out. **Choice A** is mentioned at the beginning of the first paragraph, while **choice B** is discussed at the beginning of the third paragraph. **Choice D** is discussed in the last sentence of the passage. **Choice C is the credited answer** because while it's mentioned that geothermal energy was used in the 3rd century, there is never an opinion regarding exploitation given by the author. It was used as a factual example. Note: These types of questions can get one notch harder if they provide you with statements not present in the passage, thereby requiring you to understand how they each relate to the collective viewpoint of the author.

5) **A. Energy sectors tolerating a 5% increase in costs.** There was one reference in the passage to the recalcitrance of energy markets to geothermal energy because of the increased cost to the consumer. Given this, **choice A is the credited answer** because the passage implies that it would directly alleviate this concern. According to the passage, if an increase was tolerated, then it would allow greater utilization of geothermal energy. **Choice B is incorrect** because increased exploration would not reduce the cost. Likewise, **choices C and D are wrong** because they would do nothing to decrease the cost of geothermal energy allowing it to be a more widely used energy source.

6) **C. Production of greenhouse gases by geothermal energy is an acceptable consequence when compared to pollution from coal-based energy production.** This is a more challenging "what is the author thinking question" because many of the answer choices deal with issues raised in the passage. Despite this fact, notice that choices A and B are not directly mentioned in the passage, nor can they be inferred. **Choice C is the credited answer** because the author makes this statement at the very end of the passage. **Choice D is incorrect** because the amount of greenhouse gases produced is not linked to cost of energy production.

Cluny Monks

In 910, Duke William of Aquitaine issued a land grant for the formation of a new monastery, which became one of the most influential and wealthy monastic orders of the Middle Ages: the Cluny order. Duke William chose Berno, an abbot from a Benedictine monastery, to decide on the location of this new order, and Berno picked the Duke's isolated hunting lodge at Cluniacum in France for the location of the Cluny order. Berno was the first Abbot of Cluny, who, as the head of the order, governed all monasteries throughout Europe. The formation of the Cluny order, however, was not an altruistic act, since the church at the time often sold "salvation" to wealthy nobles near the ends of their lives.

Duke William insisted upon one condition with the creation of the order, which turned out to be instrumental in the rise of the Cluny monks. When the charter was written, Duke William ensured that the order was only answerable to the papacy in Rome. This made the order unobligated to outside influences that commonly plagued churches, and allowed the monastery to avoid problems like simony, nepotism, pressure from special interests, and even influence from the founder or his family. Several additional aspects of the organization of the Cluny order were unique for its time. For example, existing members voted in all newly accepted monks, a practice unheard of at the time. Another distinguishing feature of the order was that its endowed wealth alleviated the burden of monks performing manual labor to support the monastery. This allowed a stronger devotion to education as well as political and economic reforms.

The great influence of the Cluny order was also due to a weak papacy in Rome that was hindered by the politics of the nobles. As the order was able to act in its own interests, it became a respected mediator and advisor to the nobility through the counseling of popes, the kings of Spain and France, and even William the Conqueror of England. Having such influence allowed the order to accumulate wealth and to convince influential individuals to accept the teachings of the Church.

At the height of the Cluny prominence, a decision was made to exert their influence in a military capacity. A Moslem army had swept through and conquered the Iberian Peninsula in the 8th century and established it as an Islamic state. At this time, Christians adopted the concept of jihad, or "holy war," to retake the conquered lands of the Iberian Peninsula. This "crusade," was signified through the donning of a red cross on their armor. By 1017, the abbots of Cluny fully supported the idea of retaking the regions of the Iberian Peninsula held by the Moslems and funded over 20 military campaigns. The Cluny Monks created strong and lucrative connections with Spain as a result of their involvement in the expulsion of Moslem armies from Iberia. Compostela was one of the towns liberated and quickly became a popular pilgrimage site, and by the 11th century, it had numerous annual visitors. The Cluny monks profited from this by establishing additional churches as rest points for travelers along the roads throughout France and Spain. This also increased the monks' influence by allowing them to spread their teaching to travelers, increasing the number of church patrons.

1) **None of the following actions could have happened within the Cluny order except:**

   A. having the relatives of Duke William request religious favors from the monks.

   B. assigning a position to a Lord that purchased his title in the monastery.

   C. an existing monk trying to give his position in the order to a nephew.

   D. an individual being assigned a position and title by monks of the order.

2) **Assuming that the papacy was strong during the height of the Cluny order, which of the following statements would the author most agree with?**

   A. The Cluny monks would have sold positions in the monastery to nobles.

   B. The monks would have had to resort to farming to provide food for the order.

   C. Fewer noblemen would have sought advice from the Abbot of Cluny.

   D. Duke William would have created a less restrictive charter to protect the Order.

3) **Which of the following is least likely to have resulted from the liberation of Compostela?**

   A. The Cluny monks gained greater influence with the King of France.

   B. The monks were able to spread their teachings.

   C. The Cluny monks gained greater influence with the King of Spain.

   D. The Cluny monks gained more lands in both France and Spain.

4) **Assuming that the Cluny monks had failed to acquire wealth, all the following statements could be true except:**

   A. The monks would have had less time for prayer and study.

   B. The Abbot of Cluny would have been advisor to fewer kings and popes.

   C. The monks would have maintained the structures of their churches themselves.

   D. Over 20 crusades would not have been launched to retake Northern Spain.

5) **Which of the following statements would the author most disagree with?**

   A. Cluny monks spread their religion to both the common man and nobles.

   B. Cluny monks advanced their agenda through wealth and influence.

   C. The Cluny order benefited from poor church leadership.

   D. The creation of the Cluny order was a selfless act.

6) **Which of the following arguments would least likely be used by a cynical opponent of the crusades in order to reduce justification for Cluny monk's support?**

   A. It is unjust for Cluny monks to reclaim a territory that was established as an Islamic state.

   B. The Cluny monks only were interested in reclaiming the Iberian Peninsula to establish a lucrative relationship with Spain.

   C. Increasing the number of patrons was the primary impetus for the Cluny monks to support the crusades.

   D. The expansion of Cluny monk-supported churches was in the best interest of the Cluny order.

Cluny Monks

	Foundation 1: Comprehension	Foundation 2: Integration of multiple concepts	Foundation 3: Reasoning beyond text
Concepts	1		
Inference	3		
Integration		5,6	
Application			2
Assessment			4

Big Picture. This passage gives a historical account of the Cluny monks, which was one of the most powerful orders of its time. The passage begins by explaining how the order was originally founded and the unusual stipulations that provided the Cluny monks protection against the common problems monasteries faced at the time, and how this helped them to gain wealth and influence. Also discussed is how the order used its wealth and influence to support multiple crusades into Spain against the Islamic state in control of the region at the time and the benefits the order received from funding these crusades.

Several of the questions were worded in misleading ways that required higher-level reasoning. For example, questions 2 and 4 both required that you imagine an opposite scenario to be true than what was described in the passage and then ascertain the predicted outcome. Moreover, question 1 required you to identify an exception while question 5 required you to determine which statement the author would disagree with the most. In addition to the challenging question structures, many of them required that you determine the opinion of the author based upon primarily a factual article without any commentary or opinion about the actions of the monks. This is particularly challenging as the author is most likely a historian thus her/his opinions are mostly grounded in facts and typically hidden from view.

1) **D. an individual being assigned a position and title by monks of the order. Choice A can be eliminated** because the passaged stated that the original charter for the order specifically stipulated that relatives of Duke William could not interfere with the working of the monastery. **Choices B and C are also incorrect** because the second paragraph described how the original charter prevented Lords from purchasing positions within the church and prohibited nepotism. **Choice D is the credited answer** because the second paragraph describes how new monks were voted into the order by the existing members of the church.

2) **C. Fewer noblemen would have sought advice from the Abbot of Cluny.** This question was challenging because it required you to assume that the papacy was strong during the height of the Cluny order, which is in contradiction to what the passage described as historical fact. Therefore, you needed to identify the consequences of a weak papacy described in the passage and then determine which of the answer choices were most consistent with the opposite of those consequences. Given this approach, **choice C is the credited answer** because the passage directly discusses how a weak papacy allowed the monks to gain a great deal of influence and become trusted council for numerous nobles. The flaw with **choices A, B and C** is that there is no link provided by the passage between the papacy and any of these issues. It would be an unsubstantiated guess to conclude that any of these events would have happened with a strong papacy, in the absence of any evidence to support the claim.

3) A. The Cluny monks gained greater influence with the King of France. An effective way to approach this question is to eliminate answer choices supported by the passage as the question stem requires the least likely answer choice. The specific content germane to this question was located within the last paragraph of the passage where the pilgrimages to Compostela was discussed. **Choice B can be ruled out** because the end of the passage states the monks were able to increase their patronage by aiding travelers on the way to Compostela. Further, **choice C is incorrect** because the last paragraph discusses how the crusade strengthened their relations with Spain, making it logical to assume they will have more influence with the King of Spain. **Choice D is eliminated** because the passage says the monks built new churches as rest areas along the roads for both Spanish and French travelers, meaning they would need new lands to do so. **Choice A is the credited answer** because the passage does not discuss the monks' relationship with the King of France in relation to the liberation of Compostela.

4) B. The Abbot of Cluny would have been advisor to fewer kings and popes. Similar to question 2, this question required you to first assume an opposite scenario described in the passage. Essentially, this question is looking for the answer choice that was not a result of the monks' wealth. **Choice B is the credited answer** because the passage tells us the Cluny monks gained their influence and became advisors to many nobles because of a weak papacy in Rome, not as a result of their wealth. **Choice A is incorrect** because the second paragraph states that the monks' wealth freed them from the normal manual labor needed to support the monastery, giving them more time for prayer and education. **Choice C can be ruled out** since the monks' wealth also would have freed them from manual labor such as maintaining church structures. **Choice D can also be eliminated** because the last paragraph tells us the Cluny monks funded the campaigns to retake the Iberian Peninsula, therefore they would not have taken place without the wealth of the Cluny monks.

5) D. The creation of the Cluny order was a selfless act. Choice D is the credited answer because the first paragraph states the creation of the order was not an altruistic act by Duke William, but rather a way to buy salvation. **Choice A is ruled out** because the passage discusses the monks' influence with nobles and also discusses how they increased the number of church patrons by providing rest points for travelers in France and Spain. **Choice B is incorrect** because the passage provides a specific example, the crusades in Spain, where the monks were advancing their agenda through wealth and influence. **Choice C can be ruled out** because the third paragraph tells us the Cluny monks were able to gain much of their influence due to a weak papacy.

6) A. It is unjust for Cluny monks to reclaim a territory that was established as an Islamic state. To reduce justification for Cluny monk support for the crusades, a cynical opponent would highlight outcomes of the crusades that benefited Cluny monks and claim that these were factors in the Cluny monks' support. These counterarguments would put a negative light on the Cluny monks' decision to support the crusades thereby making their role unjustified. The last paragraph describes several of the outcomes of the crusades that were beneficial to the Cluny monks. A cynical opponent would attempt to manipulate these benefits to suit their argument against the Cluny monks. **Choices B, C, and D** were all described in the passage as fortuitous outcomes of the crusades that worked in the favor of the Cluny monks. Therefore, opponents would use a cynical version of these facts to support their counterargument making these choices incorrect. **Choice A is correct** as there is no statement made in the passage about the Cluny monks' position regarding the justness of the Islamic state.

Black Plague

In the late 1340s, one of the greatest pandemics in history swept across the known world. Commonly referred to as "The Black Death," the Black Plague killed up to an estimated 50% of the entire population of Western Europe with thousands of dead bodies visibly piling up in large cities. Three forms of the Black Plague, all of which rapidly killed their hosts within a few weeks, were described in medieval Europe. The bubonic strain caused swelling of the lymph nodes, while the pneumonic form infected the lungs, and the third and least common type, the septicemic form, infected and poisoned the blood. In the final stages of the disease, victims' skin would turn black from sub-epidermal hemorrhaging.

The epic amount of death that occurred during an intense three-year outbreak of the Black Plague had drastic ramifications for all aspects of society. The Italian author Boccaccio wrote the contemporary masterpiece *The Decameron* about life during the height of the Black Plague in medieval Florence. His descriptions portrayed contemporary life so accurately, it has been said that it could have depicted any city in Europe. The economy was not only affected by a reduced labor force, but port officials regularly turned away ships from the East fearing that they were infested with the Black Plague. This caused acrimony and occurred despite the fact that the origins of the Black Plague were still mysterious in medieval Europe. The general anxiety over the Black Plague fostered armed conflicts, some of which resulted in the first documented examples of biological warfare where both attackers and defenders catapulted plague-ravaged corpses into enemy camps. During a battle in 1347 at Caffa in Crimea, the Mongol army catapulted diseased corpses over city walls and infected the Genoese traders defending the city. The traders eventually travelled home to Italy, and this has been credited by some as the first time the Black Plague was introduced to Europe.

Multiple factors contributed to the spread of the Black Plague. Compared to today's standards, living conditions in medieval Europe were highly unsanitary. Clean water was considered valuable, so people rarely bathed. The feces and urine collected in chamber pots was commonly thrown out of windows into the streets and people lived in close proximity to animals. Health care professionals exacerbated the situation as barbers and doctors regularly bled their patients and disposed of the blood in the streets.

During the Middle Ages, various theories were offered to explain the Black Plague, which was first called the Black Plague in the 17th century in reference to the dreadful, gloomy period. The King of France put forth the most widely circulating theory that blamed the disease on a conjunction of three planets that caused a "great pestilence in the air." As people were scared, they were also quick to blame those they were told were at fault, leading to the persecution of various ethnic groups and even individuals with skin disorders. Doctors were unable to remedy the plague, and people turned to religious groups that offered their followers reassurances that focused on the will of God and redemption.

The origins of the "Great Plague" have been traced to Yersinia pestis, a bacterium discovered in 1894 by Alexandre Yersin. Paul-Louis Simond determined the mechanisms of transmission of the plague through the realization that the bacterium obstructed the guts of fleas and caused them to regurgitate Y. pestis into their hosts, often black Asian rats, during foraging. Recent DNA analysis of skeletons residing at known plague burial sites has identified two clades of Y. pestis in separate mass graves from disparate parts of Europe that appear antecedent to the two modern strains of Y. pestis.

1) **The Great Plague was referred to as the "Black" Plague because:**

   A. black Asian rats propagated the disease.

   B. sub-epidermal hemorrhaging of the victims.

   C. hopelessness of the times.

   D. description in Boccaccio's *The Decameron*.

2) **The Black Plague most likely caused all of the following to occur in Western Europe except:**

   A. labor shortages.

   B. loss of confidence in medicine.

   C. increased interest in religion.

   D. advancements in warfare technology.

3) **According to the passage, which of the following would have helped to diminish the spread of the Black Plague?**

   A. Regular garbage pickup.

   B. Indoor plumbing.

   C. Better trained nurses.

   D. More hospitals.

4) **Although physicians had no explanation for the plague outbreak, religious groups provided the public with answers. Which of the following statements is the author least likely to agree with?**

   A. People wanted reassurances more than they wanted facts.

   B. Physicians lacked the equipment and training to properly investigate the cause of the Black Plague.

   C. Religious leaders exploited the fears of the common man to gain wealth and influence.

   D. Certain ethic groups were wrongly persecuted.

5) **The Great Plague is widely believed to have originated in the Far East. From the passage, which of the following is most likely true with respect to its widespread transmission into Europe?**

   A. At least two waves of infection were responsible for the European outbreak in the 1340s.

   B. The Mongol army is responsible for the introduction of the plague into Europe.

   C. The plague was caused by the conjunction of the planets.

   D. Lack of sanitary conditions caused the transmission of the plague into Europe.

6) **Which of the following facts would least support the notion that the author's use of the term, 'the known world,' is not the result of Eurocentrism?**

   A. The author is of Asian ancestry.

   B. The author is aware of many examples of non-European plague victims.

   C. The author cites primary sources from multiple continents.

   D. The author's publication was read by students all over the world.

Black Plague

Annotations.

1) C 2) D 3) B 4) C 5) A 6) D

	Foundation 1: Comprehension	Foundation 2: Integration of multiple concepts	Foundation 3: Reasoning beyond text
Concepts	2		
Inference	4		
Integration		1,3	
Application			5
Assessment			6

Big Picture. This passage was nearly devoid of any opinion of the author and is mostly a general description of the Black Plague. The author is pointing out that history's account of the Black Plague of Europe is an important lesson, especially as every aspect of society was affected. Indeed man's economic models and beliefs in various institutions, including medicine and religion, were altered. The Black Plague of the mid 1340s is notable as it wiped out nearly one half of Western Europe. Although epidemiological data and other records can be erroneous, or even absent, for this area, the three years of terror are well documented and a whopping 200,000,000 people are believed to have been killed. Boccaccio's *The Decameron* gives account of a group of people trying to escape the plague ravaging through medieval Florence. Further, European economies were decimated because trading ships were barred from docking at ports and the large number of mortalities created huge labor shortages. The passage discusses the disease, its effects on society, and then the beliefs of its origin in both medieval and modern times. This includes recent DNA sequence analysis from mass burial sites known to be associated with medieval plague deaths. The author is likely a historian with a specialty towards medieval Europe.

1) **C. hopelessness of the times.** The passage associates the color black with the Black Plague at multiple points, making this question tricky. Only one of those references was phrased in a way that could connect it as being causative for naming of the pandemic. **Choice C is the credited answer** because the fourth paragraph tells us the term was first used in the 17th century to describe a dreadful, gloomy period. **Choice A is incorrect** because while Asian black rats were believed to carry the fleas that were host to the bacteria, it is not suggested as the origin of the term "black." **Choice B can be eliminated** because sub-epidermal hemorrhaging was a symptom of the disease, not the origin of the term "black." **Choice D is ruled out** because the passage makes no reference between Boccaccio's *The Decameron* and the origin of the disease's name.

2) **D. advancements in warfare technology. Choice D is the credited answer** because while the passage references the first cases of biological warfare, it does not discuss any technical advances in equipment used in warfare at the time. The passage directly describes how the massive amount of mortality during the Black Plague created vast labor shortages making **choice A incorrect**. As the Black Plague affected all aspects of society **choices B and C can be eliminated** because the passage reads, "Doctors were unable to remedy the plague, and people turned to religious groups," demonstrating that people lost confidence in doctors and then turned to religion for answers.

3) **B. Indoor plumbing.** Realize that the question stem specifically asks for a reason that was contained in the passage. The passage discusses both lack of bathing and the disposal of human waste on the streets as reasons for the spread of the disease. Indoor plumbing would have alleviated both of these problems, making **choice B the credited answer**. While picking up garbage might have aided in reducing the spread of the plague, garbage as a source of the plague is not directly discussed in the passage, making **choice A incorrect**. Likewise, better trained nurses or more hospitals were not addressed in the passage as ways to help control the spread of the plague, **ruling out choices C and D**.

4) C. Religious leaders exploited the fears of the common man to gain wealth and influence. The question stem requires you to identify a statement that the author will not agree with. **Choice C is the credited answer** because the author did not express an opinion about the intent behind the religious leaders' actions, but rather only provided a factual account of what happened. Another aspect to recognize is the use of the word "exploited," which has a very strong and prolific negative connotation. Such language is avoided for more neutral stances, so answer choices containing such language are typically wrong, which for this question stem, makes it the credited answer. The other answer choices are statements that draw support from the passage. **Choice A can be eliminated** because the passage explains how people sought religion after medicine failed, suggesting they were seeking reassurances. **Choice B is incorrect** because physicians were unable to properly investigate the cause of the Black Plague. Note that it was in the late 1800s, some 500+ years after the Great Plague of the mid 1300s, that the causative agent was discovered. **Choice D can be ruled out** because the passage states that various ethnic groups, as well as people with skin disorders, were blamed for the onset of the plague.

5) A. At least two waves of infection were responsible for the European outbreak in the 1340s. The passage states that two clades (i.e. genetic branches) of Y. pestis have been found in various mass graves known to contain victims of the Black Plague. This is consistent with two separate waves of transmission of the plague into Europe making **choice A the credited answer.** Had you not known the definition of the word "clade," it would not have been immediately apparent why choice A was correct making you rely on process of elimination. The passage did provide relatively straightforward reasons to eliminate the other answer choices. Although the Mongol army could have accounted for the initial transmission of the plague into Europe, they are only credited with this single case, not two distinct strains, so **choice B is incorrect**. This is especially true as the separate strains of Y. pestis were found in disparate gravesites throughout Europe, suggesting multiple points of entry into Europe. **Choice C can be ruled out** because this was a prevailing medieval explanation for the cause of the plague that was championed by the King of France. Lack of sanitary conditions in Europe would have enhanced the spreading of the disease once in Europe. The question stem asks for a reason for its transmission into Europe, **eliminating choice D**.

6) D. The author's publication was read by students all over the world. The suggestion that the author is Eurocentric means that the article is written by someone with only European culture in mind. Thus, the point of view and the details of the passage would be heavily slanted toward Europe. This question is tricky because it is asking for an answer that supports a double negative because of the use of the "…least…not…" in the sentence. Therefore, you are looking for an answer that suggests the author is Eurocentric. **Choices A, B and C can all be eliminated** as each one suggests that the author has research and perspective from other parts of the world. In other words, the author is not Eurocentric thereby eliminating all three as possible answers. Therefore, **choice D is the credited answer** because the background of the individuals that read the article does not provide any information about the author, giving no support to whether or not the author is Eurocentric.

Crimea

The 1917 Bolshevik Revolution paved the way for the formation of the Soviet Republic, a vast region composed of multiple ethnicities and cultures. Upon its break up in 1991, multiple regions split up and declared autonomy from the newly formed Russian Federation. Multiple Baltic countries including Estonia, Lithuania, Latvia as well as Ukraine all declared autonomy, and all but Ukraine joined NATO, a military alliance with the US and parts of Europe. One key facet of the NATO charter is a principle of mutual defense between members. Consistent with its abstention, Ukraine housed a Russian military base in the Crimean region of the country. Large numbers of Russian nationals reside in the former Soviet states, but in some parts of the Eastern Ukraine and Crimea, at least 60% of the residents are Russian nationals.

Crimea first became part of Russia in 1945, when Joseph Stalin took over the region. The majority of its population was ethnic Russian with minority groups of ethnic Ukrainian and Crimean Tartars, the latter of which were deported by Stalin and waited decades to return to their homeland. In 1954, Nikita Khrushchev made Crimea part of the Ukrainian Republic, which was part of the Soviet Union until it dissolved; Ukraine formed an autonomous country in 1991. Ukraine maintained close ties to Russia, both economically and militarily, by signing long-term energy deals with Russia, while Russia bought billions of dollars of Ukrainian bonds and signed a long-term lease for a military base in Crimea to support its Black Sea fleet. The recent political infighting in the Ukraine is a microchasm of the philosophical divide between Russia and the West, and encapsulates the challenges to the existing cultural traditions.

A less contemporary example of this growing rift can be seen with the Orange Revolution of 2004-5. This event was highlighted by acts of civil disobedience carried out in protest of election results in the Ukraine between Viktor Yushchenko and Viktor Yanukovych. The two candidates, alike in name, were opposed in their policies towards Russia; Yanukovych was pro-Russian and Yushchenko promoted entry into the European Union (EU). The Supreme Court of Ukraine ordered a run-off election to resolve the dispute. Yushchenko won a second run-off election and Yanukovych served as prime minister from 2006-7 under President Yushchenko. In 2010, Yanukovych won the presidency. As Ukraine was in heavy debt, Yanukovych sought outside assistance. Instead of ratifying a pending economic alliance agreement with the European Union, Yanukovych instead accepted a bank loan bailout from Russia, establishing closer economic ties with Russia. This apparent turn of events was met with riots and deadly clashes in Ukraine. As a consequence, Yanukovych was removed from office by Parliament, a move that Russia claimed was orchestrated by US influence, and Russian authorities declared that Ukraine was in violation of its constitution. The president's removal, coupled with the riots throughout Ukraine, led Russia, under Vladimir Putin, to invade Crimea and annex the territory. Moscow claimed this was a measure to protect the large number of Russian nationals living in Ukraine.

In March 2014, while gunmen occupied a government building, the Crimean Parliament dissolved its government and declared independence from Ukraine. The next day, Parliament requested Crimea be annexed by Russia which led the two parties to sign a treaty allowing Russia to annex Crimea, a move unrecognized by the US and Europe, providing another reason to increase tension between East and West. A hasty referendum vote was conducted, and it was reported that 83% of the population voted, with over 95% voting to become part of Russia.

1) **Which of the following Russian leaders can best be described as acting outside of the interests of Russia?**

   A. Khrushchev

   B. Yushchenko

   C. Putin

   D. Yanukovych

2) **Which of the following statements best describes the author's purpose for writing the passage?**

   A. Revealing that the US has interfered with elections in Ukraine.

   B. Demonstrating the limits of political partnership between the US and Russia.

   C. Describing the events that led to the conflict between Ukraine and Russia.

   D. Claiming that Russia has interfered in the autonomy of Ukraine.

3) **Which of the following statements would the author least agree with?**

   A. The US would be obligated to defend Estonia in the event of a Russian invasion.

   B. Yushchenko should have signed an economic treaty with Russia.

   C. The Crimean people democratically decided their fate with Russia.

   D. The removal of Yanukovych from power was criticized by Russia.

4) **The Ukrainian conflict has been provided as evidence that the "Cold War" between East and West is still ongoing. Which of the following examples would least support this idea?**

   A. The European Union issuing economic sanctions on Russia for the crisis in Crimea.

   B. The Russians conducting military exercises near the border with Ukraine.

   C. The Russian annexation of Crimea.

   D. The signing of gas contracts between Russia and China.

5) **Which statement best describes the initial response of the Russian government after the dismissal of President Viktor Yanukovych?**

   A. Make Ukraine pay its overdue bank loans.

   B. Claim Russia's national right to annex Crimea.

   C. Claim Crimea was mistakenly given to Ukraine.

   D. Claim Ukraine violated its constitution.

6) **If Nikita Khrushchev never declared Crimea part of the Ukrainian Republic, which the follow events could have been avoided?**

   A. Ukrainian impeachment of President Yanukovych.

   B. Displacement of the Crimean Tartars.

   C. Russian expense to lease a naval base for its Black Sea fleet.

   D. Tension filled relations between Russia and the United States.

Crimea

Annotations.

1) A 2) C 3) B 4) D 5) D 6) C

	Foundation 1: Comprehension	Foundation 2: Integration of multiple concepts	Foundation 3: Reasoning beyond text
Concepts	5		
Inference	1		
Integration		2,3	
Application			4
Assessment			6

Big Picture. The author provides a brief summary of a very rich and elaborate topic: Crimean history, particularly its relationship with Russia. The first section of the passage describes the Bolshevik revolution of 1917 and the formation of the USSR, followed by reference to Joseph Stalin's role in expelling the native Tartars, as well as the fact that Khrushchev made Crimea part of the Ukrainian Republic. The central event at the core of the passage was when Ukraine became autonomous in 1991, after the fall of the Soviet Union, retaining Crimea as part of its territory. A broad discussion of Ukrainian politics over the last decade is provided to set the stage for the events that lead to Russia's annexation of Crimea. This article provides more of a historical perspective of events surrounding and leading up to Russia's annexation of Crimea and offers no direct commentary or opinions on the actions of the parties involved. Nevertheless, the impression that the author gives, judging by the tone, is that she/he is not Russian as no justification for Russian policy is provided, leading one to question Russian decision making on Ukraine throughout the article. It is possible that this article could appear in a magazine like National Geographic but it could be disguised in a mainstream article as a "non-biased" factual account.

1) **A. Khrushchev.** This was a reading comprehension problem that required you pay attention to the question stem and then look for clues in the passage. **Choices B and D can be eliminated** because both Yushchenko and Yanukovych were political leaders in Ukraine, not Russia. The passage states that Putin acted on behalf of Russian nationals: "Moscow claimed that this [Crimean annexation] was a measure to protect the large number of Russian nationals living in Ukraine." This supports the notion that Putin acted in the defense of Russian interests so **choice C can be ruled out**. In contrast, the passage describes how Khrushchev gave away land from the USSR to an autonomous Ukrainian Republic (although Ukraine was part of the USSR!). Effectively however, in the end, Khrushchev gave away Crimea, territory that was part of Russia, claimed by Stalin for Russia, so this can easily be interpreted as acting outside of the interests of Russia. This makes **choice A the best answer**.

2) **C. Describing the events that led to the conflict between the Ukraine and Russia.** For this style of question, you must make a judgment about the overall message the author hoped to convey to the reader. This passage can best be described as a short description of the relationship between Ukraine and Russia, particularly with respect to Crimea, making **choice C the credited answer**. The passage reveals no information regarding any possible interference in Ukrainian elections by the US, so **choice A can be eliminated**. The passage does not discuss political partnerships between the US and Russia where limitations could be tested, thus making **choice B incorrect**. The passage fails to provide any facts to support the claim that Russia has interfered with the autonomy of Ukraine, **ruling out choice D**. Be careful with choice D; although many people believe this to be true, there is nothing in the passage to validate this opinion.

3) B. Yushchenko should have signed an economic treaty with Russia. This question tests a key critical reasoning skill, which is to determine how an author feels about something even though no opinion about the choices is provided. You need to identify facts described by the author that are presented in the passage to determine if statements are congruent with those facts. **Choice A can be eliminated** because, as stated in the passage, Estonia joined NATO, and in the charter agreement between members, mutual protection is promised. The author therefore agrees, at least passively, that the US would have to defend Estonia in the event of a Russian invasion. **Choice C is incorrect** because the passage states that the people in Crimea voted to be annexed by Russia. Further, the passage states that 83% of the people voted, implying that the people of Crimea democratically decided their fate. **Choice D is ruled out** because the passage states that, upon removal of Yanukovych from power, Russia claimed that this move was orchestrated by US influence, criticizing their involvement. **Choice B is the credited answer** because the author states no opinion nor provides any facts as to whether Yushchenko should have signed a treaty with Russia, but simply states that a treaty was signed.

4) D. The signing of gas contracts between Russia and China. Here you are required to find the example that least supports the thesis provided in the question stem. **Choice D is the credited answer** because a gas contract between Russia and China is the least relevant to the tension in relations between Russia and the West. **Choices A, B, and C can all be eliminated** because they represent retaliatory measures that both the US/Europe and Russia can take upon one another in response to the situation in Crimea. While the passage discusses no details regarding the "Cold War," a period of Russian-US tensions marked by large military escalations and minimal diplomatic ties, the passage does discuss NATO, an institution derived from the Cold War. As the recent role of Russia in Ukraine has been criticized by the US and Europe, one can interpret these events to be reminiscent of the Cold War.

5) D. Claim Ukraine violated its constitution. The passage describes how the dismissal of President Viktor Yanukovych by the Ukrainian Parliament destabilized Ukraine, resulting in riots and violence. The immediate Russian response was to declare that Ukraine had violated its constitution, making **choice D the credited answer**. While the passage discusses loans between Ukraine and Russia, no information is provided about the payment terms of these agreements, **eliminating choice A**. The passage states that after Russia's claims of Western interference and proclamations that the Ukrainian Parliament violated its constitution, the Russian response was the invasion and annexation of Crimea under the declared policy of the right to protect Russian nationals residing in Crimea. This makes **choice B incorrect**. The passage states how Khrushchev made Crimea part of the Ukrainian Republic decades before these events started to unfold and is irrelevant to the reactions of all parties involved, so **choice C can be ruled out**.

6) C. Russian expense to lease a naval base for its Black Sea fleet. This is a challenging question as you must take the events that followed the declaration of Crimea as part of Ukraine and flip them over. **Choice A can be ruled out** because President Yanukovych was impeached for political reasons, not a dispute over ownership of Crimea. **Choice B is incorrect** because Stalin displaced the Tartars in the 1940s after taking control of the region following World War II, well before Khrushchev made his decision. **Choice D can be eliminated** because the last paragraph describes how the dispute over Crimea was just another issue in a long list of problems creating tension between Russia and the United States. **Choice C is the credited answer** because the passage illustrates that Russia signed the lease for the Crimean naval base, after Ukraine became a sovereign nation, so that Russia would still have access to the Black Sea. This would not have been necessary if Crimea was still part of Russia as it was when Stalin took control of the region.

Hominid Origins

The relationship between anatomically modern humans and Neanderthals, our closest ancestors, has been debated for years. How and why Homo neanderthalensis died off and gave rise to modern humans has been the subject of many studies. Whether humans co-existed with Neanderthals has been a mystery since the discovery of Neanderthals in Germany nearly 200 years ago. One major theory is that Homo sapiens outcompeted Neanderthals, or possibly conquered them in warfare. Scientists generally agree that Neanderthals spread out from Europe and Asia approximately 180,000 years ago and died off about 40,000 years ago. Some reports have claimed that pockets of Neanderthals survived longer and lived on the Iberian Peninsula approximately 30,000 years ago.

Researchers have long used radiocarbon dating to help determine the relationship between Homo sapiens and other hominid species, such as Homo neanderthalensis. However, the accuracy of radiocarbon dating has been contested, with continuing debate. During the life of an organism, both ^{12}C and the isotope ^{14}C are taken up and incorporated into tissue such as bone. At death, no new carbon is incorporated into bone, and the radioactive decay of ^{14}C can be used to determine its age. However, contaminating ^{12}C deposited in bone can make this analysis ambiguous. Such ambiguity in radiocarbon dating has hindered the determination of the relationship between modern Homo sapiens and Homo neanderthalensis. Further complicating comparative studies between humans and Neanderthals is the fact that not all known Neanderthal sites have skeletal remains. Instead, researchers have been able to study various artifacts and stone tools that have been associated with hominid species such as Neanderthals.

Data from fossils suggests that anatomically modern humans (AMHs) originated approximately 200,000 years ago in Africa and then spread out to Europe and Asia. Commonly proposed theories have held that the Neanderthals became extinct through climate change or conflict with modern day humans. Both humans and Neanderthals are believed to have diverged from Homo heidlebergensis, an African ancestor who lived around 700,000 years ago. Around 45,000 years ago, Europe was dominated by Neanderthals, with modern humans living in isolated pockets, like in Italy, as evidenced by the Uluzzian stone-tools. Recent improvements in dating techniques suggest that over the next five millennia, the Neanderthal population became extinct.

The Denisova cave in Siberia has contributed much to our understanding of hominid species. Both Neanderthals and modern humans have been found here. Furthermore, another homo genus called Denisovans, has been recently discovered in the cave where two teeth and a finger bone were recovered. Using procedures that drastically cut down on contaminating ^{12}C combined with improved radiocarbon dating techniques, scientists have discovered much about Denisovans and their relationship to other hominid species. The DNA sequence of one tooth displayed a high degree of similarity to the finger bone but still had some differences. The DNA sequences obtained from the second tooth showed surprisingly high levels of DNA sequence variation from the other two samples with more similarities to Homo heidlebergensis than anticipated.

Scientists have now mapped the genomic DNA sequences of chimpanzees, Homo sapiens, Denisovans and Neanderthals from both mitochondrial and nuclear sources. Modern day Homo sapiens contain up to 4% Neanderthal sequence. Denisovan DNA has been found in modern Southeast Asian cultures where they make up to 5% of Aboriginal Australian DNA, compared to over 15% Denisovan DNA similarity in Neanderthals.

1) **Which of the following is true?**

   A. Human interaction with Neanderthals remains a mystery since the discovery of Neanderthals on the Iberian Peninsula 200 years ago.

   B. Homo heidlebergensis and anatomically modern humans share a common ancestor.

   C. As our nearest ancestors, Neanderthals were extinct in Europe before the arrival of humans.

   D. Radiocarbon dating is a useful tool for researchers and continues to become more accurate.

2) **The main goal of the passage is to:**

   A. determine if humans and Neanderthals co-existed.

   B. examine the genealogy between humans and other hominid species.

   C. discuss scientific techniques used to date artifacts.

   D. discuss the difficulties around determining hominid species interaction.

3) **Which of the following discoveries would shed light on human and Neanderthal interaction?**

   A. Finding a common ancestor for humans and Neanderthals that lived 400,000 years ago.

   B. Improved radiocarbon dating to an accuracy within 100 years.

   C. Discovering a field with numerous stone weapons and fossils from both humans and Neanderthals.

   D. Discovering a fully preserved Neanderthal in a glacier.

4) **If a report stating that data supporting the existence of Neanderthals on the Iberian Peninsula 30,000 years ago was inaccurate, then this would most likely be due to:**

   A. the discovery of Uluzzian tools in Iberia.

   B. ^{12}C contamination.

   C. co-habitation of multiple hominid species.

   D. discovery of high levels of DNA sequence variation in samples from Denisova cave.

5) **According to the passage, what has the Denisova cave provided?**

   A. DNA samples used to examine genetic similarities between hominid species.

   B. Proof that multiple hominid species co-habituated.

   C. Development of a more accurate carbon dating technique.

   D. Discovery of Uluzzian stone-tools.

Hominid Origins

	Foundation 1: Comprehension	Foundation 2: Integration of multiple concepts	Foundation 3: Reasoning beyond text
Concepts			
Inference	5		
Integration		1,2	
Application			3
Assessment			4

Big Picture. This passage takes an anthropological look at modern humans' relationship to other hominid species, specifically their coexistence with Neanderthals. The controversy over when and how Neanderthals became extinct is mentioned as a lead-in and the text transitions to presenting current research being done on the topic. The author discusses the main scientific tool researchers use and the limitations of radiocarbon dating. Finally, a specific excavation site is discussed, which contained the fossilized remains of multiple hominid species. This site provided tissue samples for DNA sequencing, allowing genetic comparisons between species. This is a technically written passage, providing information about scientific tools and findings regarding multiple hominid species. The author is most likely a researcher in the field of anthropology.

1) **D. Radiocarbon dating is a useful tool for researchers and continues to become more accurate. Choice D is the credited answer** because the passage states that radiocarbon dating is a technique long used by researchers and that new advances have made it a more accurate dating system. **Choice A is incorrect** because the first paragraph states that Neanderthals were discovered in Germany 200 years ago, not the Iberian Peninsula. **Choice B is wrong** because Homo heidlebergensis is the common ancestor for humans and Neanderthals, therefore, Homo heidlebergensis cannot have a common ancestor with humans. The passage discusses the mystery surrounding human and Neanderthal coexistence, so Neanderthals could not have been extinct before modern humans evolved, **eliminating choice C.**

2) **D. discuss the difficulties around determining hominid species interaction.** To answer the "main purpose" style of question, you want to look for the answer choice that best encompasses all of the topics discussed by the passage. **Choices A, B and C are incorrect** because they are all singular topics discussed within the passage; they do not represent the main theme throughout the entire passage. Choice A is tempting, but it is too narrow in scope because two additional hominid species are discussed along with humans and Neanderthals. **Choice D is the credited answer** because it uses broad enough terms (i.e. hominid species) to encompass the discussion throughout the passage.

3) C. Discovering a field with numerous stone weapons and fossils from both humans and Neanderthals. This question stem is asking for an additional piece of information that, when taken in context with the rest of the passage, would help answer a question that the facts presented in the passage did not. **Choice A is incorrect** because finding an additional common ancestor between humans and Neanderthals would provide no more information about how they interacted. There is no instance presented in the passage where highly accurate radio-carbon dating would shed light on the co-existence of humans and Neanderthals, **eliminating choice B**. While finding a fully preserved Neanderthal would be exciting, it would not give addition information about how humans and Neanderthals interacted, **ruling out choice D**. The passage did discuss a theory that humans eliminated Neanderthals through warfare. Therefore, finding a field with stone weapons and fossils of both species together would suggest it was a battlefield, helping to corroborate this theory and providing evidence about how humans and Neanderthals interacted. This makes **choice C the credited answer**.

4) B. ^{12}C contamination. The key piece of information in the question stem is the specific time frame for the existence of Neanderthals. **Choice D is the credited answer** because the passage discusses how ^{12}C contamination can make radiocarbon dating inaccurate, bringing into question the claim that Neanderthals were living 30,000 years ago. **Choice A is incorrect** because Uluzzian tools are only mentioned as evidence for the presence of modern humans. **Choice C is wrong** because co-habitation of multiple hominid species has no bearing on the time frame of when the Neanderthals lived. **Choice D can be eliminated** because, again, DNA sequencing cannot be used to determine a specific time frame of when Neanderthals may have lived on the Iberian Peninsula.

5) A. DNA samples used to examine genetic similarities between hominid species. **Choice A is the credited answer** because the last two paragraphs discuss how researchers were surprised by the amount of genetic differences found in fossil samples taken from the Denisova cave. **Choice B is incorrect** because no specific information about the radiocarbon dating of the fossils was provided. Just because the fossils were found in the same location, this does not mean they all lived there during the same time frame. The passage states researchers were using previously developed radiocarbon dating techniques, not developing new ones, **ruling out choice C**. The passage does not mention Uluzzian tools in relation to the Denisova cave, so **choice D can be eliminated**.

Drug Advertising

The direct-to-consumer advertising (DTCA) of prescription pharmaceuticals is currently legal in two industrialized countries: the US and New Zealand. In a recent study, only automobile advertising exceeded that of pharmaceutical advertising in the US. In fact, on average, Americans spend more time watching drug advertisements on television than they do seeing their doctor in a given year. The frequency of DTCA jumped after the FDA relaxed its rules on risk information in 1997. There are three major forms of DTCA: 1) full product ads which give full product name and must list all adverse health effects; 2) reminder ads that mention the name of the product, but fail to make health claims; 3) disease awareness ads that mention a specific condition, but fail to mention the name of the drug.

Often touted by advertisers as benefiting public health through mechanisms such as awareness and education, adherence to treatment, and stimulating discussions between doctors and patients, DTCA has a ubiquitous presence in the US. The statement, "Ask your doctor about…" is now one of the most heard phrases on television and radio, and emotive messages often trump science, as ads spend most of their time associating drugs with happiness. One pharmaceutical company has averaged almost $250 million per year promoting the proton pump inhibitor Nexium, while the overall advertising dollars spent on DTCA has escalated to twice the budget of the entire FDA. In 2005, drug sales exceeded $4.5 billion, providing conclusive evidence that DTCA promotes consumer demand, and in 2009, the top ten selling drugs accounted for 36% of spending on DTCA. A study of nearly 50 drugs advertised during a five-year period reported a median return of over $2 in sales for every $1 invested in DTCA, with the top brand reaching $6.50 in sales.

Although advertisers commonly promote new drugs as breakthrough medicine, typically they are not. Of the approximately 900 drugs approved in France over a 10-year period, 10% were deemed as therapeutic advances with the vast majority being classified as providing no additional benefit. In addition, multiple safety concerns have been raised regarding some products heavily marketed through DTCA. The most noteworthy case is that of the Cox-2 inhibitor Vioxx, a heavily advertised drug found to be inappropriate for prescription use due to known cardiovascular risks unreported to the FDA. Vioxx was amongst the most heavily prescribed drugs from the time of its approval by the FDA in the late 1990s until its global withdrawal in 2004. However, because of the effectiveness of DTCA, patients still requested Vioxx after its removal from the market-place, despite conclusive data showing it caused an increased risk of heart attack. In fact, over 100,000 heart attacks have been attributed to Vioxx in the tens of millions of patients who used the drug. DTCA has also generated confusion regarding the boundaries between true psychological conditions and normal fluctuations in human emotion in the case of anti-depression medications. DTCA has been shown to discourage healthy lifestyle changes by consistently claiming, "…There is no need to change your diet or exercise regimen…."

Consumers desire more information on drug therapeutics, and this has been one of the justifications used by advertisers to promote DTCA. However, as advertisements expand markets by encouraging patients to seek care, in contrast to physician-oriented advocacy, it is difficult to separate the apparent conflict of interest between selling drugs and providing unbiased information. Frosh and colleagues described DTCA as a "large and expensive uncontrolled experiment in population health."

1) **What is most likely to occur if DTCA were legal in an industrialized nation?**

   A. Better educated patients.

   B. An improvement in cost effective treatment.

   C. A shift in prescribing practices.

   D. An improvement in treatment quality.

2) **One way to circumvent restrictions on DTCA is to:**

   A. encourage physicians to prescribe a drug through door-to-door sales.

   B. promote a "disease awareness" campaign.

   C. provide free drug samples to doctors for patient distribution.

   D. encourage lawmakers to pass non-restrictive legislation.

3) **Pharmaceutical advertisers would argue that DTCA:**

   A. improves patient compliance to follow treatment protocol.

   B. provides better replacement treatment.

   C. reduces the burden of emergency room visits.

   D. makes the public aware of safe, new drugs with FDA approval.

4) **The author would disagree with all the following statements except:**

   A. All drugs advertised by DTCA are profitable.

   B. DTCA is successful because patients want information about drugs.

   C. Proton pump inhibitors are the most successful DTCA products.

   D. Rapid stimulation of new, FDA approved drugs is beneficial.

5) **In general, the author would agree with which statement about product advertising?**

   A. Firearms advertisements would lead to more deaths.

   B. Increased product placement for hard liquor would lead to increased alcoholism.

   C. More drug commercials will to lead to more effective patient treatments.

   D. Additional automotive ads would lead to increased car sales.

6) **The Vioxx case exposed all the following problems with DTCA except:**

   A. patients can become confused about drug effectiveness.

   B. the FDA's drug approval process has flaws.

   C. DTCA can make patients feel they don't need to change unhealthy habits.

   D. extensive marketing with DTCA can cause patients to request drug treatments even after proven dangerous.

Drug Advertising

	Foundation 1: Comprehension	Foundation 2: Integration of multiple concepts	Foundation 3: Reasoning beyond text
Concepts	5,6		
Inference			
Integration		3,4	
Application			2
Assessment			1

Big Picture. This passage discusses a specific type of advertising called direct-to-consumer advertising (DTCA) used by pharmaceutical companies to promote their drugs. The author starts by explaining what DTCA is and provides facts about how powerful this advertising style is at selling drugs to consumers. The author is knowledgeable about this topic, using specific drugs as examples and detailed economic data to support her/his claims. Next, the author discusses the potential hazards this type of advertising presents to the public and cites a specific example where harm came to patients. This is where you can start to make a judgment on the opinion of the author. In the second half of the passage, the author primarily provides negative examples of DTCAs and leaves the reader with the impression that she/he doesn't support DTCA. This should lead the reader to believe the author most likely works with patients for a profession, as opposed to a pharmaceutical company.

1) **C. A shift in prescribing practices. Choice C is the credited answer** because the beginning of the passage discussed how DTCA can influence patients to request certain drugs, causing a shift in their prescription. The example of Vioxx shows that DTCA does not always educate patients or improve treatment quality **eliminating choices A and D**. The passage never establishes a link between DTCA and more cost effective treatments, making **choice B incorrect**.

2) **B. promote a "disease awareness" campaign.** For this question you want to remember DTCA stands for direct-to-consumer advertising. **Choices A and C are incorrect** because these are marketing tools used to encourage doctors to prescribe a drug. **Choice D can be ruled out** because this is an effort to change current restrictions, not a method to circumvent them. The passage discusses "disease awareness" ads as a type of DTCA. The key to these ads is that they do not mention any specific drug, only symptoms, avoiding any restrictions there might be about directly marketing a specific drug to consumers. Therefore, **choice B is the credited answer**.

3) A. improves patient compliance to follow treatment protocol. The second paragraph of the passage discusses pharmaceutical companies' defense of DTCA: adherence to treatment. This makes **choice A the credited answer.** Both treatment replacement and reduction in emergency room visits are not discussed and are beyond the scope of the passage, **eliminating choices B and C.** The author presents the example of Vioxx to demonstrate that FDA approval does not always guarantee a drug to be safe, making **choice D incorrect.**

4) B. DTCA is successful because patients want information about drugs. This is a common style of question that would be seen on the MCAT. In this case, the correct answer is the one the author would agree with, allowing you to eliminate false statements. The author discusses how profitable DTCAs can be, but does not state that it works for every drug sold. Be careful of answer choices using terms like "all or none." Rarely does an answer choice deal in totality, so **choice A is eliminated.** The example of Nexium, the proton pump inhibitor, was used to show how much a company can spend on DTCAs. The passage does not discuss the success of Nexium and certainly does not say it was the most successful drug. Again, be careful of wording in answer choices that make absolute statements; **choice C is incorrect.** The example of Vioxx was not safe despite FDA approval, so **choice D can be ruled out.** The final paragraph of the passage starts by pointing out patients' desire for more information about drugs, making **choice B the credited answer.**

5) D. Additional automotive ads would leads to increased car sales. For this analogy question you need to extrapolate the author's beliefs about DTCAs to advertising in general. **Choice D is the credited answer** because the author discusses at length how DTCAs increase the sale of drugs, which is analogous to additional car ads leading to increased car sales. **None of the other answer choices** makes a link between additional advertising and increased sales. They are all assumptions beyond the scope of the passage.

6) C. DTCA can make patients feel they don't need to change unhealthy habits. For this question, you are looking for the one answer choice that was not mentioned in connection to the Vioxx example. **Choice C is the credited answer** because the author mentions this as an overall problem created by DTCAs, not as a direct result of the Vioxx case. The Vioxx case does expose problems with the FDA approval process since it was later discovered that Vioxx was harmful, despite FDA approval. This **eliminates choice B.** The author discusses how patients still requested Vioxx even after it was removed from the market and even after data was released to the public showing its dangerous side effects displaying confusion by the patients. This **rules out choice A.** The passage further states, patient requests for Vioxx after removal from the market was the result of the heavy marketing campaign for Vioxx through DTCA, making **choice D incorrect.**

Economic Theory

Mercantilism was the dominant economic system during the Renaissance and emphasized money-based exchange. By establishing high tariffs on imports, plus other restrictions, mercantilism encouraged the domestic production of goods. A robust labor force was required to keep up with production and export, resulting in industrious countries becoming wealthy through trade imbalances. The mercantile system meant the state acted under a national economic policy to increase its wealth through a trade surplus. At the time, France was one of the most successful examples of mercantilism, becoming the most powerful country in Europe. France used this wealth to strengthen its military assets and increase colonial expansion in the Americas, which fostered conflict with rival European countries.

One criticism of mercantilism is that the state's intervention in economic affairs fails to promote the welfare of its populous. The Physiocrats, founded by Quesnay as the first school of economic thinkers, concluded that a mercantilist economy would lead to shortages in resources and emphasized a productive work force as the source of a nation's wealth. This led to the promotion of the idea that individual laborers should be free to act on their own accordance by choosing their own occupation without any help or hindrance from the state. This notion of "laissez faire" economics appealed to Adam Smith, the founder of modern economic thought. Smith had met Quesnay in London and their interactions contributed to the ideas presented in 1776 by Smith in *Wealth of Nations,* one of the most successful documents on the political and economic thoughts of capitalism.

Smith agreed that the wealth of a nation is derived from the production of goods by its labor force and resources, believing that increased production could be accomplished through division of labor and the introduction of machinery. Smith reasoned that people will not be inclined to produce things if they are not deemed worthwhile. Smith championed the thought that only through an individual's self interest could the best outcome for society be achieved.

This is illustrated in Smith's famous quote:

> "It is not from the benevolence of the butcher, brewer, or baker that we can expect our dinner, but from their regard to their own self interest."

Key to Smith's thoughts was the notion that an "Invisible Hand" maintained an order between production and the value of goods. Smith advocated that personal gain promotes societal gain, driven through our own self-interests and competition rather than any intrinsic desire for man to barter.

The German economist Karl Marx criticized Smith and felt that the economic value of commodities should be linked to the labor expended in producing them. He assumed that labor is socially necessary, or in demand, and money is therefore just the intermediate step between the consumer and the producer. Marx asserts that the capitalist largely buys articles for resale and devalues the contribution of the laborer in the final valued price of the goods. For example, a furniture company sells their product for more money than it cost for the labor and supplies, and this difference, called the surplus value, belongs to the capitalist and not the laborer who performed the work. However, if a capital improvement was made by the company through the acquisition of a machine which produces double the amount of furniture per unit time, then the laborers would not be entitled to receive twice the wages. Marx believed industrialization of the production of goods encourages overproduction, which reduces demand, making capitalism intrinsically unfair to the worker.

1) **A mercantile economic system resulted in new laws and regulations. Which would contribute the least to a successful mercantile economy?**

   A. Reduced freight taxes on products leaving the country.

   B. Increased immigration bolstering the labor pool.

   C. Nationals taking jobs in foreign countries.

   D. Increased tariffs on imports.

2) **The "Invisible Hand" most likely represents:**

   A. unregulated markets in the absence of government intervention.

   B. market regulation balancing supply and demand.

   C. government intervention through tariffs on imports and exports.

   D. market regulation driven by increased surplus value.

3) **Which statement would be most consistent with the thoughts of Karl Marx?**

   A. Improved production efficiencies result in higher wages.

   B. Overproduction results in unsold goods.

   C. Economic value is hindered by the labor expended to produce them.

   D. Overproduction results in lower wages for laborers.

4) **Profit sharing occurs when employees receive bonus wages for achieving defined sales marks. Such practices might be interpreted to ameliorate the "flaw" in which system?**

   A. Marxism

   B. Physiocratism

   C. Mercantilism

   D. Capitalism

5) **Which of the following statements is true?**

   A. Marxism will drain resources from a nation through internal consumption.

   B. Surplus value in capitalism is shared by laborers.

   C. Laissez faire economics promotes national wealth through the labor force.

   D. Socially necessary labor refers to minimum wages.

6) **Which of the following statements is the author least likely to agree with?**

   A. Smith promoted capitalism driven by government regulation protecting a nation's self-interest.

   B. Quesnay felt the trade imbalance generated in Mercantilism would deplete a nation's raw materials.

   C. Mercantilism is based off the concept of exporting more than you import.

   D. Marx believed a worker's value is sacrificed for profit in capitalism.

Economic Theory

	Foundation 1: Comprehension	Foundation 2: Integration of multiple concepts	Foundation 3: Reasoning beyond text
Concepts	2		
Inference	3		
Integration		5,6	
Application			4
Assessment			1

Big Picture. This passage discusses multiple economic systems throughout history. Mercantilism is the first system to be introduced and the author provides the theory behind how it works. Next, competing economic systems are introduced with explanations provided about how they are designed to work. The author spends the majority of the time discussing how each system affects the well being of the labor force. At no point in the passage does the author express any opinion regarding the positives or negatives of the different economic systems. The author merely compares and contrasts the different aspects and philosophies behind each economic system. The author is most likely an academic with a historical background providing nothing more than factual information.

1) **C. Nationals taking jobs in foreign countries.** As described in the passage, mercantilism is based on the concept of exporting large amounts of goods, which requires a large work force to produce. **Choice C is the credited answer** because nationals leaving to take jobs in other countries will deplete the work force, reducing the amount of goods produced. **Choice A can be ruled out** because reducing the taxes on a product will cause the price to be lower, making it more affordable and easier to sell. Increased immigration would strengthen the work force and benefit mercantilism, making **choice B incorrect**. Increasing taxes on imports functions to create a trade imbalance favoring the country increasing tariffs, which is one key to a strong mercantile system; this **eliminates choice D**.

2) **B. market regulation balancing supply and demand.** Adam Smith's definition of the "Invisible Hand" is the key piece of information needed to answer this question. It was defined as the force that regulated the price of goods produced, which is determined by a person's self-interest. **Choice B the credited answer** because if a person will profit by supplying more product, they will do so, and they will likewise produce less when there is less demand or profit. **Choice A can be eliminated** because it is not an unregulated market; it is regulated, in this case by the "Invisible Hand." **Choice C is incorrect** because the government is regulating the market, not personal self-interest. **Choice D is ruled out** because again, the market is being regulated by something other than personal self-interest.

3) **B. Overproduction results in unsold goods. Choice B is the credited answer** because the last sentence of the passage discusses how overproduction will decrease demand, which means the goods produced are not being sold. **Choice A is ruled out** because Marx states industrialization encourages overproduction, reducing demand. He claims that this is unfair to the worker as wages would not be increased. **Choice C can be eliminated** because Marx argues that capitalism is unfair to the worker and says nothing negative about the worker. While Marx says overproduction is unfair to the worker, he never specifically ties that issue to wages. Therefore, **choice D is incorrect**, because an assumption about wages can not be made.

4) **D. Capitalism.** The key to this question is to realize the term "flaw" refers to a practice that is unfair to the worker. **Choice D is the credited answer** because bonuses help correct the flaw Marx points out in capitalism, which he defines as surplus value, where the business takes profit away from the worker. Bonuses would help give that profit back to the worker. **Choice A is incorrect** because Marxism is a system that favors the worker. **Choice B is ruled out** because Physiocrats promoted the freedom of choice for workers, allowing them to pursue any avenue that is most profitable for them. This favored the worker. **Choice C is eliminated** because mercantilism promotes profit through export, so workers would profit from the sales of goods.

5) **C. Laissez faire economics promotes national wealth through the labor force.** In the second paragraph, laissez faire economics states that the wealth of a nation is its work force, making **choice C the credited answer**. Marx never discusses how a nation's resources fit into his economic theory so **choice A can be eliminated**. The last paragraph defines surplus value as a way workers lose value for their work, making **choice B incorrect**. The passage never discusses the topic of minimum wages so this answer choice is beyond the scope of the passage, **ruling out choice D**.

6) **A. Smith promoted capitalism driven by government regulation protecting a nation's self-interest.** Remember for this question type, the statement that is false will be the correct answer. **Choice A is the credited answer** because Smith believed the market was regulated but the "Invisible Hand," not by the government. **Choice B is incorrect** because in the second paragraph, Quesnay claims mercantilism will lead to shortages in resources. **Choice C is eliminated** because the first paragraph states that the mercantile system increases its wealth through a trade surplus. **Choice D is eliminated** because in the last paragraph Marx provides multiple examples of how capitalism devalues the worker through concepts like surplus value and overproduction.

Water Fluoridation

In the early 1900s, dental surgeons probed the cause of "mottled enamel," or fluorosis, a brown-stained tooth condition that arises through impairment in tooth enamel development. They concluded that the occurrence of fluorosis inversely correlated with the prevalence of natural fluoride in water supplies.

It is now widely believed that fluoride is not normally required for human health. Despite this, humans have significant and alarming exposure to fluoride; it is abundant in multiple forms, found in food and used in multiple industrial applications including plastics, ceramics, and pesticides.

A 1937 study on fluorosis published by Dean and colleagues concluded that water supplemented with an optimum dose of 1.0 part per million (ppm) of fluoride could prevent fluorosis as well as cavities (i.e. dental caries). Subsequent studies also reported positive health effects from water fluoridation. Although further evaluation of these data has raised a number of concerns regarding its accuracy, municipalities in the US and other countries have adopted a public policy of artificially supplementing public drinking water with fluoride.

Multiple public health agencies, including the World Health Organization (WHO), US Center for Disease Control, and the American Dental Association have all endorsed the treatment of public drinking water with fluoride. They claim it has significantly reduced tooth decay for all receiving it and is especially important in poor areas. The WHO has even declared fluoride as an essential nutrient although no fluorine-deficient disease has ever been identified. Although originally declared to reduce dental caries by as much as 60%, the WHO and others now claim that fluoridation of public drinking water reduces tooth decay by approximately 15%. Notably, fluoride treatment is believed to reduce the prevalence of dental cavities, which are commonly caused by acid-secreting bacteria that erode the enamel layer. The major positive effect of fluoride on teeth concerns its ability to generate fluorapatite, a mineral in both bone and tooth enamel. Along with calcium and magnesium, fluorapatite is believed to render teeth less susceptible to acid-based erosion.

Publicly fluoridated water supplies have been controversial since their introduction in the 1950s, and fluoridation has even been described as a Communist plot to control American health. Yet, others have claimed that it violates medical consent laws. One scientific criticism concerns the method of how fluoridation is delivered through drinking water. As the impact of fluoride on tooth enamel is most effective when applied in a topical fashion, delivering fluoride through public water supplies should be discouraged. This is further underscored by the fact that the formation of fluorapatite is dependent on calcium and magnesium. Importantly, artificial fluoride water treatment is usually monitored for consistent fluoride levels near 1.0 ppm, but it is difficult to control consumption on an individual basis. As such, when combined with non-aqueous sources, artificially fluoridated water consumption fails to normalize for the dose delivery. Interestingly, since the 1980s, in the US, a rise in dental fluorosis positively correlates with fluoridated water programs. Skeletal fluorosis and fluoride toxicity would be expected to increase, as excess fluoride competes with iodide for incorporation into thyroid hormones. One study with subjects from New Delhi who received high fluoride levels in water showed that nearly one half of participants had hypothyroidism. Excess fluoride has also been linked to cognitive impairment and cancer. Despite public backlash derived from these flaws and the documented negative consequences of exposure to high fluoride levels, many policy makers continue to advocate for fluoride water treatment programs.

1) **Those against fluoridation of public water on ethical grounds would most likely be opposed to:**

   A. putting fluoride in a brand of toothpaste.

   B. public water purification programs.

   C. using fluorohydrocarbons as refrigerants.

   D. required vaccination for school enrollment.

2) **According to the author, fluoride would most accurately be classified as a:**

   A. pollutant.

   B. medicine.

   C. nutrient.

   D. supplement.

3) **Assume that fluoride has been implemented as a therapeutic. For which of the following medical applications would fluoride be most suitable?**

   A. skeletal fluorosis

   B. hyperthyroidism

   C. cognitive impairment

   D. cancer

4) **The author would most likely support:**

   A. improved daily allowable fluid consumption for fluoride.

   B. standardization of fluoride levels in water.

   C. increased regulation of industrial fluoride discharge.

   D. individualized consent for fluoride water consumption.

5) **To determine the role of fluoride in tooth decay, a study examined subjects prior to and following termination of a fluoride water treatment program. Which of the following would be most critical for making an appropriate comparison in this study?**

   A. Bottled water consumption patterns.

   B. Number of fluoride-deficient subjects.

   C. Fluoride levels in treated water after termination.

   D. Determination of optimal fluoride dosing.

6) **Those currently in favor of treating public drinking water with fluoride would argue that it most significantly:**

   A. promotes individual freedom.

   B. promotes overall health.

   C. prevents fluorosis.

   D. reduces health care inequality.

7) **The author argues that current health care policy regarding the use of fluoride in public water supplies is flawed because it:**

   A. fails to consider fluorosis.

   B. relies on ingestion.

   C. promotes dental caries.

   D. uses evidence-based policy.

Water Fluoridation

Annotations.

1) D 2) A 3) B 4) C 5) C 6) D 7) B

	Foundation 1: Comprehension	Foundation 2: Integration of multiple concepts	Foundation 3: Reasoning beyond text
Concepts	2		
Inference	7		
Integration		4,6	
Application			3,5
Assessment			1

Big Picture. This passage examines the history and health impacts of the practice of public water fluoridation. The discussion starts with a historical look at the reasons why fluoride started to be added to public water supplies. The author is obviously knowledgeable about the subject, presenting numerous facts about fluoride. There is an emphasis on the negative health risks of fluoride, and the passage presents the general opinion that adding fluoride to public water should be discontinued, as the risks outweigh the benefits. Additionally, the author discusses the difference in efficacy between oral ingestion and topical application of fluoride and the futility of the current delivery system. This opinion would lead one to believe that the author works in the health industry and is an advocate for public safety.

1) **D. required vaccination for school enrollment.** The passage describes how critics argue that it should be a person's choice if they use fluoride as a supplement. **Choice D is the credited answer** because a required vaccination would preclude such a choice. **Choice A is incorrect** because a person could choose not to use that type of toothpaste. Water purification programs and the use of fluorohydrocarbons as a refrigerant aren't programs that affect public health as was described for an additive like fluoride, **eliminating choices B and C**.

2) **A. pollutant.** To answer this question you must recognize that the author possesses a negative opinion of the use of fluoride. **Choice A is the credited answer** because the author discusses fluoride toxicity and how fluoride is not required for normal physiology. **Choice B is incorrect** because the author does not describe any role for fluoride as a medicine. Fluoride is not a nutrient, according to the passage, thereby **eliminating choice C**. In fact, the author states: "It is now widely believed that fluorine is not normally required for human health." **Choice D can be removed** because it is stated that excess fluoride causes fluorosis and is physiologically unnecessary, so there is no reason to believe that fluoride is a "supplement."

3) **B. hyperthyroidism.** The passage cites a study from New Delhi where excess fluoride levels caused hypothyroidism. **Choice B is the credited answer** because fluoride treatment for hyperthyroidism would be a logical solution. **Choice A is incorrect** because the passage states that fluoride treatments are responsible for skeletal fluorosis. The passage also describes how fluoride treatments have been linked to both cancer and cognitive impairment **removing choices C and D** as possible answers.

4) C. increased regulation of industrial fluoride discharge. Choice C is the credited answer because the author's tone throughout the passage is that fluoride in the water is unhealthy so additional regulation in the form of controlling industrial fluoride release would help reduce fluoride exposure to the public. **Choices A and B can be eliminated** because the author believes that fluoride treatment of public water is largely harmful making it unlikely that she/he would approve any daily allowable consumption values for fluoride. The author is against any amount of fluoridation and consent from the public would unlikely change this belief, **removing choice D**.

5) C. Fluoride levels in drinking water after treatment. This question is challenging because it requires you to apply what you learned in the passage to a new situation. Thus, you must reason beyond the text. For the study described in the question stem, it is important to determine that the fluoride levels actually dropped during the second part of the experiment, making **choice C the credited answer**. This gives the researchers the ability to measure before and after levels and compare them with outcomes. **Choice A is incorrect** because a subject's bottled water consumption is not critical for the final analysis of the experiment (only tap water is fluoridated). The author states there has never been a description of a fluoride-deficient person, making **choice B irrelevant**. Optimal fluoride dosage is not required despite the fact that the researchers should know the levels of fluoride being put into the water. This **eliminates choice D**. The passage discusses how it is difficult to determine an optimal dose because the amount of fluoride consumed varies on an individual basis.

6) D. reduces health care inequality. The passage states that advocates of water fluoridation claim it has significantly reduced tooth decay, especially in poor areas, making **choice D the credited answer**. **Choice A is incorrect** because the passage describes how fluoridation of public water often comes without any choice, not freedom of choice. **Choice B is eliminated** because the author cites multiple deleterious links between fluoridation and diseases: fluorosis, cognitive impairment, thyroid disorder, and cancer. **Choice C is incorrect** because it's stated that excess fluoride promotes fluorosis.

7) B. relies on ingestion. Choice B is the credited answer because the author discussed how fluoridation has been shown to be most effective when topically applied to teeth. Therefore, a mode of treatment relying on ingestion would be flawed in the author's opinion. **Choice A can be removed** because the public fluoride treatment program was started to combat fluorosis. **Choice C is incorrect** because the WHO estimates that water fluoridation reduces dental caries by approximately 15%. The passage cites a study claiming the benefits of fluoride as the reason for the initiation of the public fluoride treatment program, **eliminating choice D**.

Boethius Chaucer

Boethius was a famous philosopher and senator in the Holy Roman Empire during the 6th century. His views upset the Emperor and this led to the incarceration of Boethius. During this time, he wrote the *The Consolation of Philosophy,* a philosophical treatise on the position of man in the world. Boethius' query was: Why do good people suffer despite their virtuous behavior? To this end, he engages in discussion with Lady Philosophy over free will and destiny. Boethius' chief concern was that the life of man is naturally chaotic, so there is no reward for virtuous living. He asserts that Lady Fortune's wheel is fickle and in a world controlled by the Prime Mover, man holds a tenuous position over the outcome of his life.

Lady Philosophy tells Boethius that although he can see cause and effect in the world, man's perception is limited due to his temporal view of events throughout his life. This is not divine, as Divinity sees the past, present, and future as one event. Fundamentally, Lady Fortune is mutable through chance and so is the life of man since the objects of man's desires embodied by Lady Fortune, such as fame and riches, are transient. Lady Philosophy convinces Boethius these things are "false happiness," capricious and subject to the actions of the Prime Mover who institutes change in the world through Saturn, a dark and unpredictable force. Other Gods affected by the Prime Mover include Jupiter, who is rational, Mars, the God of war, and Venus, the Goddess of love. In this ordered scheme, life on Earth experiences the most variability.

Boethius' ideas became popular during medieval times and greatly influenced Geoffrey Chaucer, who translated *The Consolation of Philosophy* into Middle English in the 14th century. Chaucer also wrote *The Knight's Tale,* a book thought to be an adaption of *The Consolation of Philosophy* that describes a romantic story between Emelye, the sister of the Queen, and two cousins, Palamon and Arcite. The cousins are captured as prisoners of war and locked away in a tower in Athens, during which time, they see Emelye through their barred windows; they both fall in love with her. Arcite is granted his freedom from prison while Palamon has to escape. They both leave Athens but decide to secretly return to pursue Emelye. By chance, Palamon and Arcite encounter one another, and a fight ensues. Theseus, the Duke of Athens, stops the fight and arranges for a formal, civilized duel to take place, with Emeyle's hand in marriage as the reward.

Prior to the duel, Palamon, Arcite, and Emelye each pray to an Oracle. Palamon prays to Venus to console his pain with love. Arcite asks Mars for victory in battle. The Gods promise both cousins that they will each receive what they desire. Emelye has never met or spent time with either cousin, so she prays to Diana the Goddess of chastity. She asks to remain a virgin unless this is incompatible with her fate, in which case, she wishes to marry the man who loves her most. Palamon is wounded during the fight and Arcite is declared the winner. However, immediately after the victory Arcite is killed when an earthquake throws him from his horse, leaving Palamon to marry Emelye. During the chaotic scene after Arcite's death, Theseus makes an impassioned speech to help calm the masses and explains what has just transpired, saying "…to make virtue of necessity."

1) According to Boethius, the character Theseus from *The Knight's Tale,* would most resemble which God?

   A. Saturn

   B. Jupiter

   C. Mars

   D. Venus

2) According to the passage, all the following statements are true except:

   A. While Boethius was popular with the Romans, his views angered the Emperor.

   B. The theological hierarchy that Romans believed in dictated that man was at the whim of fate.

   C. The message in Geoffrey Chaucer's *The Knight's Tale* followed the teachings of Boethius.

   D. Man can only understand and react to the world around him and doesn't understand time as a whole.

3) If Lady Fortune was not responsible for man's fate, all the following statements would be true except:

   A. Boethius' would have lived a more honorable life.

   B. Riches and fame are fleeting desires embodied by Lady Fortune.

   C. A thief should only expect bad things to happen to her/him.

   D. Man is in control of his own destiny.

4) Which example does not agree with Boethius' view that life is chaotic and there is no reward for virtuous living?

   A. Being injured in a car accident on the way home from volunteering for charity.

   B. Doctors' inability to cure a cancer patient.

   C. Testifying against a murderer and then falling down a flight of stairs leaving the courthouse.

   D. Rescuing a person from a burning building and being hospitalized for smoke inhalation.

5) Lady Philosophy would agree with all the following statements except:

   A. Man would rather have 15 minutes of fame than be provided a stable job.

   B. Man understands he should not steal because he would be imprisoned.

   C. Man has free will and would choose those things that would bring him happiness.

   D. Man can make choices for himself but does not know the result of those choices.

Boethius Chaucer

Annotations.
1) B 2) A 3) D 4) B 5) C

	Foundation 1: Comprehension	Foundation 2: Integration of multiple concepts	Foundation 3: Reasoning beyond text
Concepts	2		
Inference	1		
Integration		5	
Application			3
Assessment			4

Big Picture. Free will and destiny has been a mainstay of philosophical discussion through the ages. This passage introduces the Roman Senator Boethius' views on free will and destiny from his work *The Consolation of Philosophy*. The basic philosophy is that man is not in control of his destiny and how one lives is irrelevant to the events that occurs to him. Next, the passage explores Boethius' influence on Chaucer's *The Knight's Tale*, written in the 14th century. It is well established that Chaucer translated *The Consolation of Philosophy* into Middle English and at the same time Chaucer wrote *The Knight's Tale*. Many believe Chaucer's work was influenced by Boethius' teaching and explores how man's actions can't change one's fate. This passage is strictly factual, most likely written by a historian who expresses no opinion on the subject's philosophy.

1) **B. Jupiter. Choice B is the credited answer** because Theseus is portrayed as logical, bringing order to a chaotic situation. He stops Palamon and Arcite from fighting and organizes a formal, civilized duel. Theseus also tries to calm the masses and restore order after the shock of Arcite's death. These points are all consistent with the passage's description of Jupiter. **Choice A is incorrect** because, as stated in the passage, Saturn institutes change in the world through unpredictable force, which does not describe Theseus' actions. **Choices C and D are incorrect** because Mars and Venus represent the Gods of war and love, respectively, which are not consistent with the description of Theseus.

2) **A. While Boethius was popular with the Romans, his views angered the Emperor.** This is a typical MCAT style of question where it asks for the statement that is "not true." Therefore, you can eliminate any answer supported by the passage. **Choice B is incorrect** because the last half of the second paragraph supports it where it is stated that the Prime Mover influences all events. **Choice C is ruled out** because at the beginning of the third paragraph it is stated that Boetheus' teachings influenced Chaucer's *The Knight's Tale*. Lady Philosophy states that man understands cause and effect in the world around him, but not time as it is one singular event, **eliminating choice D**. While it is stated that Boethius was popular in the 14th century, no mention was made of his popularity with Roman subjects during the Roman Empire, making **choice A the credited answer**.

3) D. Man is in control of his own destiny. Similar to what was required to receive credit for question 2, you are looking for the one false statement. According to the passage, Lady Fortune is responsible for the random events that happen to a person and is the main reason why Boethius doesn't believe in a virtuous life. Therefore, if man's life was not controlled by random events, then one should live a virtuous life to expect positive things to happen. Therefore, **choices A and C are incorrect**. The passage states that Lady Fortune represents fame and fortune, and no information is provided stating this would change if she were not in control of man's fate. Therefore, **choice B is eliminated**. The last sentence of the first paragraph states that the Prime Mover is in control of man's destiny, not Lady Fortune, so man would not be in control of his destiny. This makes **choice D the credited answer**.

4) B. Doctors' inability to cure a cancer patient. The first and second paragraphs discuss Boethius' belief that life is chaotic and there is no point to being virtuous because it is random whether good or bad things happen to you. So for this question, you can eliminate answers where somebody is living a good or virtuous life but still experiences a negative, random event. **Choices A, C and D are eliminated** because these are all examples of a person performing virtuous acts, yet still experiences negative consequences as a result. **Choice B is the credited answer** because you don't know if the patient has lived a good or virtuous life because the patient bears the consequence of this negative event.

5) C. Man has free will and would choose those things that would bring him happiness. For this question, the correct answer will be the statement that Lady Philosophy would least likely to agree with. **Choice C is the credited answer** because Lady Philosophy states that man's desires and choices will ultimately not bring happiness. **Choice A is incorrect** because fame is one of the things stated that would not bring happiness. The passage discusses that man understands cause and effect in the world. Prison is the effect of stealing. Therefore, **choice B can be eliminated**. Lady Philosophy tells Boethius that man does have free will to choose what he does, but that fate controls the results of those actions. This **rules out choice D**.

Charlemagne

Charlemagne reunited Europe for the first time in centuries by expanding his Frankish state to create the Carolingian Empire. He executed dozens of military campaigns to expand the empire to encompass from what is now France to Germany and down into parts of Italy, rivaling the breadth of the Byzantine Empire in the East.

The Holy Roman Church crowned Charlemagne emperor, the first since the collapse of the Western Roman Empire three centuries earlier. This put Charlemagne in conflict with the Byzantine Empire, since its ruler also claimed to be emperor. The crowning of Charlemagne as Roman emperor on Christmas Day in the year 800 was done under unusual circumstances. Einhard, Charlemagne's biographer, wrote that Charlemagne had no prior knowledge that he would receive the crowning by the Pope. This has prompted some historians to claim that Pope Leo III went forward with the coronation without Charlemagne's knowledge as a method to engineer conflict with the Byzantines, particularly as there was tension with Empress Irena of Constantinople. This set up centuries of conflict between Western and Eastern empires over imperial authority. In 799, the Pope had fled Rome and sought protection from Charlemagne, who then restored the Pope to power in Rome. Charlemagne's family had a history of supporting the church; his father assisted the papacy against threats of the Lombards, who occupied Northern Italy.

Despite living the majority of his life at war, Charlemagne installed many social, political and economic reforms, establishing important norms that can still be seen today. This was called the Carolingian Renaissance and is considered the first of three medieval renaissances. Unlike the Italian Renaissance, however, the major changes were limited to the clergy. During this time, the regional Latin language spoken in the Western Roman Empire was being fragmented into dialects that would ultimately formulate the romance languages that we know today. The growing level of illiteracy in Latin created shortages of scribes and made it difficult to recruit preachers to the clergy, as they could not read the Bible in Latin to churchgoers. Charlemagne was passionate about learning, and he addressed this problem by instituting educational programs that taught Latin and emulated those of the Christian Roman Empire. In fact, a wide amount of the art, architecture, and music created during the Carolingian Renaissance mirrored that of the Roman Empire.

Charlemagne also implemented various economic reforms. One of the more important was instituting a common monetary standard. At the time, the currency was based on a gold standard, but gold was a rare commodity and primarily mined from politically unstable Africa. Thus, gold shortages made this standard untenable. Charlemagne's solution was to change the monetary system to a silver standard, an abundant metal, where one pound of silver was used to create 20 sous, a unit in accounting, and derived from the sous was the denier, the main currency used in trade. The modern example of this system can be seen with the British pound, where a sous translates to a shilling and denier to a penny. Charlemagne also created the first money lending system that charged interest rates, but this was disfavored by the church who declared charging interest on loans illegal; the system was abolished. Another change in the monetary system enacted by Charlemagne was the establishment of fundamental accounting practices to monitor spending within his kingdom. Through the course of adopting these new practices, increased attention to jurisprudence occurred. This led to the development of a system where conflicts were resolved through the judgment of individuals of equal social standing to those in disagreement.

1) **According to the passage, which of the following justified Charlemagne's decision to make a fundamental change to the monetary system?**

A. Charlemagne's armed conflicts with African nations created a shortage of gold.

B. It was a way to circumvent the church declaring that money lending was illegal.

C. Silver was a readily available material on which to base the monetary system.

D. An accounting system based on the sous and denier was more efficient.

2) **Which of the following nicknames would the author most likely advocate for Charlemagne?**

A. Father of Europe

B. King of Rome

C. Conqueror of the Byzantine Empire

D. Savior of Pope Leo III

3) **Which of the following best describes why Pope Leo III crowned Charlemagne emperor?**

    I. As a reward for defending against the Lombards.

    II. To undermine the authority of Irena.

    III. To help the church regain control of Italy.

A. I

B. I, II

C. III

D. II, III

4) **According to the passage, which of the following is most accurate?**

A. The crowning of Charlemagne by Pope Adrian I was done for political reasons.

B. History recognizes Charlemagne as both a general and administrator.

C. Charlemagne's education reforms helped combat illiteracy throughout the population.

D. The Carolingian Renaissance marked a significant divergence from the Christian Roman Empire.

5) **Which of the following would most likely have resulted if the political instability in Africa had failed to halt the gold trade during the Carolingian Renaissance?**

A. New methods of accounting would not have developed.

B. An increase in hostilities between Charlemagne and the Byzantine Empire.

C. Modern British currency would not be based on the pound.

D. The scope of educational reforms could have been expanded.

6) **The notion of conflicts being heard by individuals of equal standing is analogous to what current practice in the US legal system?**

A. Defendants not being required to "take the stand" and be cross-examined by a lawyer.

B. Defendants are presumed innocent until proven guilty.

C. Cases are heard by a grand jury before deciding if the case will go to trial.

D. A defendant will be judged by a trial of their peers.

Charlemagne

Annotations.
1) C 2) A 3) D 4) B 5) C 6) D

	Foundation 1: Comprehension	Foundation 2: Integration of multiple concepts	Foundation 3: Reasoning beyond text
Concepts	1		
Inference	3		
Integration		2,4	
Application			5
Assessment			6

Big Picture. This passage provides an historical account of some of the exploits of Charlemagne. He is widely considered an important historical figure because of his unification of Europe during the creation of the Carolingian empire. Historians note that the crowning of Charlemagne came as a surprise, and this has raised a number of questions regarding his ascension to emperor. In any event, the coronation of Charlemagne is an event that shaped the foundations of Europe, as we know it today, through conflicts with the Byzantine Empire. Although mostly known for his military accomplishments, Charlemagne is also known for instituting progressive policies that benefited education as well as the monetary and judicial systems. While the author begins by providing historically driven facts about Charlemagne as a military ruler, a significant amount of time is spent discussing specific social and economic reforms he instituted. The author's perspective is that of a historian, but it should be noted, the author seems to want to provide a broader view of Charlemagne's impact on the European population, other than that of just conqueror. Moreover, there is a sense of admiration for Charlemagne that the author provides as detected by the generally positive tone used throughout the passage.

1) **C. Silver was a readily available material on which to base the monetary system.** This is a deceptively challenging question because, if you are not careful, you can choose the wrong answer without giving it much thought. The most tempting answer is **choice A, but this is not correct** because the passage never states Charlemagne was at war with any African nations. The reason given for the gold shortages was political instability. **Choice C is the credited answer** because the passage states that Charlemagne's solution to the gold shortage was to base the monetary system on silver, which was abundant. **Choice B is incorrect** because the passage does not describe how Charlemagne tried to maintain his lending system. Rather, there is only a reference that lending was ended after the church declared money-lending illegal. **Choice D is ruled out** because the passage provides no information about the how the sous or denier made accounting easier.

2) **A. Father of Europe.** This question requires that you consider all of the description of Charlemagne provided by the author and then anticipate how she/he feels about him. Process of elimination is effective in this case. **Choice B is eliminated** because Charlemagne was crowned the Emperor of Rome, not the King. **Choice C is incorrect** because there is nothing in the passage that describes Charlemagne as a conqueror of the Byzantine Empire. **Choice D is ruled out** because Charlemagne was not the savior of Pope Leo III, rather the Pope fled from Rome to Charlemagne to request his assistance in returning to power. **Choice A is the credited answer** because the passage describes how Charlemagne united Western Europe through the creation of the Carolingian Empire. Given that the other answer choices are incorrect and the passage description of how Charlemagne ruled all of Europe, Father of Europe is the best answer.

3) D. II, III. As with any Roman numeral question, gravitate towards the Roman numerals that you have clear criteria for ruling in or out and use that to eliminate answer choices. The passage states that some believe Pope Leo III crowned Charlemagne the emperor of Rome in order to undermine the Byzantine Empire, which was governed by the Empress Irena at the time. This makes **II correct**. The passage also states that Charlemagne helped restore Pope Leo III to power, making **III correct**. Charlemagne's father, not Charlemagne defended the Papacy against the Lombards, making **I incorrect**. Therefore, **choice D is correct** since statements **II and III are true**.

4) B. History recognizes Charlemagne as both a general and administrator. Choice B is the credited answer because this represents the main theme of the entire passage. The first half of the passage acknowledges his accomplishments as a military leader, creating the Carolingian Empire, while the second half discusses all his accomplishments as an administrator of his empire. **Choice A is ruled out** because Pope Adrian I did not crown Charlemagne the emperor; it was Pope Leo III who crowned Charlemagne. **Choice C can be eliminated** because the passage states Charlemagne's educational reforms benefited the clergy rather than the population as a whole. The passage describes how Charlemagne emulated the Christian Roman Empire, borrowing many aspect of Roman Society including architecture and school administration. If anything, this represented a convergence to the Christian Roman Empire rather than a divergence, making **choice D incorrect**.

5) C. Modern British currency would not be based on the pound. The last paragraph of the passage contains the logic flow required to answer this question. **Choice C is the credited answer** because the passage discusses how changing to a silver-based monetary system formulated the basis for modern British currency. **Choice A is incorrect** as it is an assumption outside the scope of the passage. **Choice B can be ruled out** because the passage does not link any conflict between Charlemagne and the Byzantine Empire due to the trade of gold. **Choice D is eliminated** because the passage does not discuss any relationship between the scope of educational reforms and the type of currency in use.

6) D. A defendant will be judged by a trial of their peers. The passage states that "…a system where conflicts were resolved through the judgment of individuals of equal social standing to those in disagreement" was developed. Given this, the strongest analogous situation would be a "trial of your peers" making **choice D correct**. **Choices A and C are eliminated** because these answers are procedural aspects of a trial, not an ideal of how a conflict should be resolved. **Choice B can be eliminated** because this is the ideal behind the right of a defendant, not how to resolve the disagreement.

Medicare

Health care in the US is more expensive to deliver than health care in other developed countries and has steadily risen faster than inflation. The majority of developed countries, excluding the US, have adopted a less expensive, single payer system. Currently, the topic of who should pay for rising health care costs is a subject of intense Congressional debate. This is an important policy issue, particularly since health care costs due to Medicare are now a major impetus for rising national debt in the US. According to the article, "A Bitter Pill" published in Time Magazine, the amount of money reportedly spent in the US on health care was approximately $3.0 trillion, which is 27% more than the average spent in other developed countries. It further states roughly $850 billion is expended on Medicare and, despite this high degree of spending on Medicare, the quality of health care delivered in the US is beginning to lag behind other developed nations as measured by variables regarding health and mortality.

Medicare was designed to improve the quality of health care for American seniors (65 and older), paid for by payroll deduction taken during an individual's employment, then distributed by the agency to pay the medical bills of the elderly. Before Medicare was passed, approximately 33% of people aged 65 or older had no health insurance, but now the solvency of Medicare is being challenged by skyrocketing costs that were not anticipated. For example, in 1965, the cost of Medicare was forecasted to be $12 billion in 1990, but was well over $100 billion that year. Additionally, critics of Medicare claim that it discourages self-reliance and puts the burdens of some people's health on the pocketbook of others.

In "The Bitter Pill," author Steven Brill examines some of the causes underlying the large increases in Medicare payments. For example, Congress has passed rigid rules on Medicare reimbursements for medical bills, such as the law mandating the amount paid for all prescription drugs will be determined by the manufacturer's average price plus a premium of 6.0%. However, unlike the regulations in other developed countries, there are no price controls for medicine in the US. The consequence of this policy is particularly evident in examples of life-saving therapeutics made by only one company. Under these conditions, a great deal of pressure is placed on an upward pricing model that does not follow the typical supply and demand rules to set a price. The traditional justification for this pricing policy lies within the high cost of research and development, a number that is usually below the profit margin and advertising budget used to market existing drugs.

In addition to lacking price controls, Medicare has been prohibited by Congress from purchasing drugs in bulk, which if allowed to do, would result in price breaks enjoyed by private insurance companies that could be passed on to US taxpayers. Although a major buyer of pharmaceuticals, Medicare is strangely prohibited by Congress from engaging in comparative effectiveness (CE), a process used to determine which of two clinically equivalent drugs is better to purchase when they differ in price. Although Medicare cannot participate in CE, it is ironic that medical research journals commonly publish the results of CE from studies that are funded by Federal sources as well as pharmaceutical firms. Admirably, a group of doctors at Sloan Kettering Cancer Center recently stopped dispensing a drug because a suitable alternative was found to be far less expensive. This resulted in the manufacturer significantly reducing the price of the therapeutic.

1) **According to the passage, the author would be most concerned with:**

A. how to reduce insurance rates for health care.

B. who should pay the costs of increased health care.

C. how mandates contribute to health care costs.

D. examining the relationship between drug profits and R&D costs.

2) **The type of senior health care advocated by the author would most likely be a:**

A. single payer system without CE.

B. single payer system with CE.

C. multi-payer system without CE.

D. multi-payer system with CE.

3) **If Congress passed regulations to control the price of medicine, which statement could be true?**

A. Cost of unique treatments would be regulated by normal pricing determinants.

B. The cost of drug treatments would go down because they would be purchased in bulk.

C. It would help lower the high cost of research and development.

D. Medicare reimbursement would become simpler.

4) **The biggest contributor to the erroneous forecast of Medicare costs in 1965 can most likely be attributed to:**

A. mismanagement of Medicare.

B. the unregulated costs of purchasing drugs.

C. a decreased ratio of enrollee/workers.

D. increased costs of drug R&D.

5) **Congress prohibiting Medicare from purchasing bulk prescription drugs is analogous to which of the following?**

A. Buying airplane tickets from different airlines for arrival and return legs of a vacation.

B. Buying one $1 lottery ticket, rather than ten $1 lottery tickets.

C. Going to the emergency room for treatment rather than your doctor.

D. Purchasing a 2-pack of batteries for $2 rather than a 12-pack for $10.

6) **According to Steven Brill, which statement is false?**

A. The large amount of money spent on Medicare correlates to the high degree of care provided.

B. Regulations regarding the reimbursement process are responsible for increased costs of Medicare.

C. Lack of price control regulations on drug treatments has driven up the cost of health care.

D. The US spends over a quarter more per year in health care dollars than other developed countries.

Medicare

Annotations.

1) C   2) B   3) A   4) D   5) D   6) A

	Foundation 1: Comprehension	Foundation 2: Integration of multiple concepts	Foundation 3: Reasoning beyond text
Concepts	2		
Inference	4		
Integration		1,6	
Application			5
Assessment			3

Big Picture. This passage discusses health care in the US. A brief overview is given about how health care is set up in the US compared to other countries, before the focus shifts to Medicare specifically. The author also references a previous article discussing the US health care system. This means you know have to keep in mind there are opinions of two authors that must be kept separate. The author explains why Medicare was created, then takes a closer look at how it is run and regulated by the government. You can start to determine the author's opinion of Medicare regulations since the examples presented are in a negative light. They point out the inefficacy of how Medicare is run while providing possible changes that can be made to improve the system. Overall, the author's tone is negative concerning the US' health care system. The author is most likely an administrator in the health care industry, and her/his major concern deals with cost and budgeting.

1) **C. how mandates contribute to health care costs. Choice C is the credited answer** because the author describes multiple examples of how government regulation negatively affects how much Medicare costs. **Choice A can be eliminated** because the author never debates the topic of how to reduce insurance rates for the health care industry. **Choice B is incorrect** because, again, the subject of who should pay for increased health care costs is never addressed in the passage. The author never discussed the relationship between drug profits and R&D costs. They are both discussed independently of one another, so **choice D is ruled out**.

2) **B. single payer system with CE.** This question can be broken down into two parts. First, does the author support a single payer or a multi-payer system? The beginning of the passage states US health care is more expensive than other countries which use a single payer system. This suggests the author supports a single payer system, considering the negative tone throughout the passage about the current US health care system. Second, does the author support comparative effectiveness (CE)? In the last paragraph the author discusses how CE would help reduce the cost of prescription drugs and should be adopted by Medicare. Therefore **choice B is the credited answer** because the author's tone supports a single payer system with CE.

3) **A. Cost of unique treatments would be regulated by normal pricing determinants.** The answer to this question is described in the third paragraph where the author discussed the lack of pricing controls on medicine in the US. **Choice A is the credited answer** because a specific example is provided where if a single company produces a treatment, then pricing is not determined by supply and demand but is at the discretion of the company because there are no regulations in place to limit the price. Therefore, regulations could allow for supply and demand to set the price of a treatment. **Choice B can be ruled out** because no correlation is provided between price control regulations or the ability of a purchaser to buy in bulk. **Choice C is incorrect** because the passage establishes no direct link between pricing controls and the cost of research and development, so this assumption cannot be made. **Choice D is eliminated** because the author discusses Medicare reimbursement and price controls for treatments as separate issues so there is no correlation that can be made between the two of them.

4) **D. increased costs of drug R&D.** At the end of the third paragraph the author states that the traditional justification for the large price increases of therapies is the high cost of research and development. **Choice D is the credited answer** because the costs of new technologies could not have been anticipated in 1965. **Choice A is incorrect** because mismanagement of the Medicare system would not have relevance on the cost for a treatment or drug. Pricing is set by the company that owns the treatment. **Choice B can be ruled out** because the passage discusses the regulations Congress placed on purchasing drugs so there are no unregulated drug purchases. If there was a decrease in the ratio of enrollees to workers, this would mean there would be less money collected but would have no relationship to incorrectly forecasting the future costs of health care, **eliminating choice C.**

5) **D. Purchasing a 2-pack of batteries for $2 rather than a 12-pack for $10.** For this analogy question you want to make sure you know what point the author was trying to make when discussing the issue of purchasing bulk prescription drugs. The author uses it as another example of overpaying for health care services. Your analogy should be an example where you are paying more for an item in one instance, while it is possible to pay less for the same item in bulk. **Choice D is the credited answer** because, doing the math, buying a 12-pack costs $10 but buying six 2-packs will cost you $12, making it cheaper to buy in a larger volume. **Choice B is incorrect** because the cost of the item never changes, regardless of how much you buy. **Choices A and C are eliminated** because you don't know the price point for services to make an analogous comparison.

6) **A. The large amount of money spent on Medicare correlates to the high degree of care provided.** To answer this question you must first recognize that Steven Brill is the writer of the Time magazine article "The Bitter Pill" which the author references. Therefore, you must compare the answer choices to only the information presented from the article rather than the whole of what the author discusses in the passage. **Choice A is the credited answer** because in the first paragraph it is stated that even though the US spends more than any other country, the US quality of care is lagging behind other developed countries, not correlating to a high degree of care. **Choice B is incorrect** because the third paragraph makes this exact statement regarding the current Medicare reimbursement system. **Choice C is eliminated** because the third paragraph cites a specific example of how a lack of price control regulations on drug treatments has driven up the cost of health care. **Choice D is eliminated** because the first paragraph states the US spends 27% more on health care than other developed countries equating to over a quarter more per year.

Scientific Misconduct

Scientific misconduct is defined as the fabrication of research results through any of a variety of methods, including altered gel images or other forms of data manipulation. Additionally, researchers can portray previously published data as new material for publication. Recently, multiple occurrences of paper retractions have received widespread attention, including celebrated findings regarding stem cell research from the Riken Center. In these retracted publications, the authors were found guilty of plagiarism, misidentifying images, and misreported data. This mirrored an earlier falsified report in the field of stem cell research from South Korean scientist Dr. Hwang Woo-suk, which was retracted from the journal Science. Dr. Woo-suk evaded jail time and returned to research where he has published dozens of articles since being embroiled in the stem cell incident.

The increased number of scientific papers retracted is monitored and analyzed using resources like Pubmed, a biomedical library comprised of more than 24 million publications. Currently, the time from publication to retraction has been significantly expedited from approximately 50 months before 2002 (N = 714) to 22 months after 2002 (N = 1,333). In 2011, the scientific journal Nature reported that the number of formal scientific retractions had increased by a factor of 10 in the last decade, while the number of published papers has only increased 40%. According to *Thomson Reuters Web of Science,* there were over 500 retractions reported in 2013, with the majority for error correction; however, there was a significant increase in misconduct cases as well. To reduce the stigma of retracting erroneous information, many scientists would like to see retractions formally divided into two classes: 1) cases of deliberate misconduct and 2) those derived from honest mistakes.

In some cases, papers are retracted from journals with little or no description of the reasons behind the decision. This lack of transparency has been debated by online resources like Retraction Watch, while Pubpeer hosts a forum for scientists to discuss recently published papers. This type of a post-review evaluation of publications has led to numerous cases of formal retraction of published data and represents a new form of scrutiny over scientific accuracy.

What has led to the increase in the numbers of retracted papers? Scientific misconduct is certainly not new, as there is evidence that Gregor Mendel used selective data. In today's competitive research environment, there is a large premium placed on being first to publish new and exciting facts regarding important biological topics such as stem cells. As research is dependent on capital investment for infrastructure and labor, the lifeblood of a research laboratory is research grant funding. Fundamentally, scientific experimentation requires replication for accuracy, providing part of the rationale that research is "self-correcting"; however, the current research environment has been described as one that discourages the replication and verification of published data. This has been traditionally deemed as non-innovative and unworthy of funding by granting agencies. In the new climate of increased research specialization, peer review is not always sufficient to ensure accuracy, evidenced by publication of papers without resolving conflicting reviews. In fact, one retracted paper from Riken had a reviewer question an image later identified as fabricated by the author. Nevertheless, intense pressure to compete for limited funds encourages some to cut corners, resulting in accuracy sacrificed for expediency. In competitive areas such as embryonic stem cells, the desire to be first to discover must be tempered with careful analysis of the quality and accuracy of the data.

1) **Increased retraction of publications is best attributed to:**

A. scientific misconduct in stem cell research.

B. improperly awarded research grants.

C. enhanced scrutiny of publications.

D. improper research design and execution.

2) **The main purpose of this passage is to:**

A. call for a new system of review and verification to ensure the validity of published scientific data.

B. establish a defined system to classify scientific misconduct.

C. increase scrutiny of information published and viewed by the public.

D. inform the public about scientific misconduct occurring in stem cell research.

3) **Experiments described with stem cells have been controversial because they are:**

A. difficult to perform.

B. expensive to conduct.

C. contain speculative results.

D. generated out of competition.

4) **The passage supports the conclusion that:**

A. there will be continued exponential growth of scientific misconduct.

B. post publication review reduces the percentage of retractions.

C. increased research funding will reduce the rates of retraction.

D. publishing first is more likely to lead to paper retraction.

5) **If organizations like Retraction Watch bring more transparency to publication retractions, what is the most likely result?**

A. There will be an immediate drop in the number of scientific misconduct cases.

B. There will be increased scrutiny of published data.

C. There will be clarity to reasons why the retraction occurred.

D. There will be less pressure on scientists to publish data first.

6) **According to the passage, what change would have the greatest impact on reducing retractions?**

A. Increase the number of reviewers.

B. Greater importance placed on data replication of published papers.

C. Strong penalties for scientific misconduct.

D. Better defined classification system for retractions.

Scientific Misconduct

Annotations.

1) D 2) A 3) D 4) D 5) C 6) B

	Foundation 1: Comprehension	Foundation 2: Integration of multiple concepts	Foundation 3: Reasoning beyond text
Concepts	1		
Inference	3		
Integration		2,4	
Application			5
Assessment			6

Big Picture. This passage discusses the topic of scientific misconduct in research and presents scientific misconduct as a growing problem. Specific examples of high profile data falsification are referenced to emphasize this point, and data is presented to show the problem has been increasing over time. The rest of the passage talks about specific problems that have caused this increase and some of the solutions proposed to help combat scientific misconduct. The author is clearly concerned about this issue, meaning she/he is most likely a scientific researcher. The passage was most likely written to inform and spur change to the system in order to help prevent scientific misconduct.

1) **D. improper research design and execution. Choice D is the credited answer** because the last paragraph discusses how the pressure to publishing data first, to secure grant money makes scientific research no longer "self-correcting." This rush has increased both genuine errors due to poor research design and deliberate misconduct, which has increased the number of retractions. **Choice A is ruled out** because stem cell research was only brought as an example not a reason for increased retractions. **Choice B can be eliminated** because the author doesn't discuss the issue of improperly awarded research grants, making this topic beyond the scope of the passage. The enhanced scrutiny of publications is mentioned as a reaction to the increase in retractions, not a reason for increased retractions, making **choice C incorrect.**

2) **A. call for a new system of review and verification to ensure the validity of published data.** When you have a "main purpose" question you want to make sure your answer is broad enough to encompass the main theme of the passage but not so broad that it includes topics not discussed by the author. **Choices B and D are incorrect** because while both are individual topics mentioned in the passage, they are too narrow in focus and do not capture the overall idea the author was trying to convey. **Choice A is the credited answer** because the author discusses the failings of the current scientific review method throughout the passage and discusses some things that are starting to be done to help improve the system. **Choice C is eliminated** because it is too broad. The author is not concerned about all information published, just scientific data.

3) D. generated out of competition. Choice D is the credited answer because at the end of the passage the author discusses how competitive the field of stem cell research is, which has resulted in multiple examples of scientific misconduct. **Choices A, B and C can all be eliminated** because the author never mentions the topics of difficulty, cost or data interpretation in the context of stem cell research, making all these answer choices assumptions.

4) D. publishing first is more likely to lead to paper retraction. Choice D is the credited answer because the author specifically mentions the rush to be the first to publish data as a reason for the increase in scientific misconduct, supporting this idea as a conclusion. **Choice A is incorrect** because the author never speculates on the amount of scientific misconduct there will be in the future. **Choice B can be eliminated** because the passage states that post publication review has increased the number of retractions, not decreased them. While the author discusses funding as a pressure on researchers, no evidence is provided to support the conclusion that more funding will reduce scientific misconduct, **ruling out choice C**.

5) C. There will be clarity to reasons why the retraction occurred. The last sentence of the second paragraph mentions how researchers dislike that reasons are rarely given for retractions and would prefer an established system to classify them. **Choice C is the credited answer** because the passage discusses how the organization Retraction Watch is specifically working to inform researchers about the reasons behind a retraction. **Choice A is ruled out** because there is no evidence supporting the idea that there will be less scientific misconduct if the reason for a retraction is provided. **Choice B can be eliminated** because the amount of review a paper receives is a separate issue to the reason for a retraction. Again, the pressure to publish is a discrete problem from why a paper is retracted, making **choice D incorrect**.

6) B. Greater importance placed on data replication of published papers. Choice B is the credited answer because in the final paragraph, the author discusses how the system no longer places importance on replication of data, increasing the likelihood of mistakes to occur and leading to retractions. So, according to the author, increased importance on data replication would be predicted to alleviate this problem. **Choice A can be eliminated** because the last paragraph discusses the flaws in the peer review system and that papers are published without resolving reviewers' questions about the data. Adding more reviewers would not solve this problem. **Choice C is incorrect** because no evidence is provided to support the idea that harsher penalties will reduce scientific misconduct. While researchers would like a better defined classification system for retractions, there is no correlation established in the passage suggesting this would lead to a reduction in the number of retractions, **ruling out choice D.**

Phoenicians

Situated on the Mediterranean coast in the Middle East, Lebanon has been the source of migrating peoples from various parts of the world for centuries. However, in Lebanon, the concept of a common ancestry has often been met with skepticism. In fact, it is a crime in current day Lebanon to describe your ancestry as "non-Arab." Despite this, Lebanon's Christian roots date back to Jesus and the Apostles Peter and Paul in the first century. In ancient times, (approximately 1 BCE) the people that occupied current Lebanon were known as the Phoenicians. Today, many people, such as the Maronites in Lebanon, claim to have Phoenician ancestry, a distinction that separates them from settlers from the Arabian Peninsula. This has led to the controversial notion of "Phoenicianism" in Lebanon, a claim associated with ancestral purity and the true heritage of Lebanon.

As agile seafarers and traders, the Phoenicians were known by the Greeks and Romans as the "traders in purple," a reference to the dye found in the mulex snail of what is now primarily coastal Lebanon, their historical birthplace. This purple dye was used to generate desirable cloths and formed the basis of purple being used as a royal color. The Phoenicians were at their peak in the first century before Christ and were ultimately overpowered by the Romans in the Punic Wars that spanned from 260-146 BCE. Very few Phoenician writings have survived, but their history has been discovered through writings of contemporary rivals and trading partners.

Multiple theories about the origins of Phoenicians have been put forward. Some believe they originated from Canaanites, while others believe they originated from a poorly understood group of people known as "Sea People," who have also been hypothesized to predate the Phoenicians. Some believe the Sea People taught the Phoenicians how to master the water after their arrival in modern day Lebanon around 1200 BCE. Phoenician culture was also influenced by proximity to the Babylonians and the Assyrians, whose cultures were propagated by the people residing in the Aegean (i.e. Crete). This assisted in the rise of the Greek Golden Age. Growing threats from neighbors like the Assyrians are believed to have prompted the Phoenicians to settle outside of Tyre and Byblos in Lebanon to places such as Carthage (Tunisia in North Africa), Cadiz (in Spain west of Gibraltar), and Tangier (Morocco).

To address the origins of the Phoenicians and how they are related to the current people of Lebanon, blood samples were collected from inhabitants of Tyre and Byblos as well as the Tunisian city of Carthage. By analyzing certain DNA sequence patterns from male donors and comparing to samples from known, early Phoenician burial sites, such as Bir Massouda, an explanation for the history of Lebanese people and human migration has been put forth. By analyzing the rate of change of the Y chromosomal sequences, scientists generated a comprehensive picture of the origin of modern day Lebanese people and how they relate to their ancestors. They also were able to analyze the impact of Phoenician culture on other parts of the world. Dr. Pierre Zalloua has used such genetic analysis to study the anthropological origins of modern day Lebanese people. One major conclusion from the study is that about 30% of people in Lebanon today are "Phoenician," while the majority of DNA samples isolated from donors in Carthage showed a DNA pattern termed M96, a DNA sequence known to have originated in North Africa.

1) **Which of the following study results would support the Maronites' ancestral claims?**

   A. DNA sequencing shows they descended from modern day Turkey.

   B. DNA sequencing shows they descended from the Arabian Peninsula.

   C. DNA sequencing shows that they descended from Canaanites.

   D. DNA sequencing shows that they are of Hebrew origin.

2) **According to the genetic study presented, which of the following statements is true?**

   A. Comparison of X and Y chromosomes proved 30% of Lebanese are of Phoenician descent.

   B. Dr. Zalloua proved most Carthaginians originated from North Africa.

   C. There are enough genetic samples from burial sites to validate the linage claims of Lebanese.

   D. The M96 DNA pattern proved 30% of Lebanese originated from North Africa.

3) **All the following ancestral claims were made except:**

   A. Phoenicians originated from the Sea People.

   B. Phoenicians originated from the Canaanites.

   C. 30% of Lebanese originated from Phoenicians.

   D. Carthaginians originated from the Arabian Peninsula.

4) **Which of the following historical events is most analogous to the fate of the Phoenicians?**

   A. The decline of the Roman Empire.

   B. Civil war resulting in the dissolution of Yugoslavia into multiple states.

   C. Displacement of American Indians by European settlers.

   D. The defeat of the Axis powers in World War II.

5) **Which of the following statements is the author least likely to agree with?**

   A. Phoenicians' reputation was built from the export of commerce.

   B. Genetic studies have defined Phoenicians' ancestry.

   C. Claims of ancestral purity have caused debate for the Lebanese people.

   D. Genetic studies have helped define ancestral lineage.

6) **Which of the following is true regarding our historical knowledge of the Phoenicians?**

   A. It likely represents a biased perspective.

   B. It is based on careful recording from trading partners.

   C. It largely comes from Biblical scripture.

   D. It largely derives from the Maronite people.

Phoenicians

Annotations.
1) C   2) B   3) D   4) C   5) B   6) A

	Foundation 1: Comprehension	Foundation 2: Integration of multiple concepts	Foundation 3: Reasoning beyond text
Concepts	2		
Inference	3		
Integration		5,6	
Application			1
Assessment			4

Big Picture. This passage discusses the origins of Lebanese people and the identity of their modern day ancestors. A brief history of the Phoenician people is provided and related to the controversy over which race(s) of peoples descended from them. A short discussion of the Phoenician accomplishments and civilization is also presented, as well as the mystery behind the origin of the Phoenicians. The author discusses the decline of the Phoenicians and some of their possible fates, but the author acknowledges that historians possess few written records to determine an accurate end. Finally, the author discusses genetic studies taking place to determine which modern societies' lineage can be traced back to the Phoenicians. The passage is a fact-based article with no commentary or opinions presented by the author. The author is most likely a historian.

1) **C. DNA sequencing shows that they descended from Canaanites. Choice C is the credited answer** because the passage states the Phoenicians are believed to be descendants of the Canaanites, so if Maronites were descendants of Canaanites, that would reinforce the Maronites' claim of being of Phoenician descent. **Choices A and D can be eliminated** because there is no link provided in the text between the Phoenicians and Turkey or the Hebrew people. **Choice B is incorrect** because the first paragraph makes a clear distinction between the Phoenicians and settlers for the Arabian Peninsula. Findings suggesting Maronites are descendants of settlers of the Arabian Peninsula would weaken their claim of being from Phoenician descent.

2) **B. Dr. Zalloua proved most Carthaginians originated from North Africa. Choice B is the credited answer** because the last sentence of the passage describes how the majority of DNA samples from Carthage had the M96 DNA pattern characteristic of North Africa. **Choice A is incorrect** because the last paragraph describes how they only used the Y chromosome for genetic testing and not the X chromosome. **Choice C is eliminated** because the last paragraph provides final results from the genetic study. The author states the study showed 30% of Lebanese were Phoenician, not North African, so **choice D can be ruled out.**

3) **D. Carthaginians originated from the Arabian Peninsula.** This question is tricky because it asks for <u>claims</u> made in the passage, not <u>claims supported by scientific fact</u>. In the beginning of the second paragraph, you are given the hypothesis that the Phoenicians could have originated from the Canaanites or the Sea People, making them true statements, **eliminating answer choices A and B.** The last paragraph details how genetic studies conducted proved that 30% of Lebanese were of Phoenician decent, making **choice C incorrect**. The first paragraph states that ancestry from the Phoenicians or settlers from the Arabian Peninsula is distinct. The third paragraph discusses the belief that Phoenicians settled as far away as Carthage, therefore would not have ancestral links to the settlers from the Arabian Peninsula, making **choice D the credited answer.**

4) **C. Displacement of American Indians by European settlers.** The third paragraph describes how neighbors of the Phoenicians (i.e Assyrians) forced the Phoenicians to relocate, displacing them. This is most analogous to the displacement of American Indians by European settlers, making **choice C the credited answer.** The Roman Empire declined in power and eventually dissolved; its people did not relocate geographically, **ruling out choice A.** The same argument can be made about the Axis powers in World War II, so **choice D can be eliminated.** The breaking up of Yugoslavia into multiple states rewrote territorial lines; this was not a result of an outside invader, so **choice B is incorrect.**

5) **B. Genetic studies have defined Phoenicians' ancestry.** Remember, for this question you are looking for the one incorrect answer. **Choice B is the credited answer** because no genetic studies where done to find the Phoenicians' ancestry. The genetic studies determined current day peoples' ancestry. **Choice A can be eliminated** because the first sentence of the second paragraphs states that the Phoenicians were agile seafarers and traders. **Choice C is incorrect** because the first paragraph explains all the controversial claims made by different groups about Phoenician ancestry. **Choice D can be ruled out** because the last paragraph explains the results of the genetic studies done and defines the ancestral lineage of two different groups.

6) **A. It likely represents a biased perspective.** **Choice A is the credited answer** because the second paragraph explains how few Phoenicians writings survived and that their history is based on the writings of contemporary rivals, which would be biased to the perspective of the rivals. **Choice B is incorrect** because the passage states that no Phoenician writings survived and information was pieced together from different sources. This suggests that anything but careful records were kept regarding Phoenician history. **Choice C can be ruled out** because the passage makes no reference to biblical scripture so this would be an assumption. While the Maronite people claim to be descendants of the Phoenicians, there is no connection made in the passage between Maronites and Phoenician history, so **choice D is eliminated.**

Baseball

During American baseball games of the early twentieth century, pitchers dominated the game and this resulted in lower scores. A contributing rule change in 1901 counted foul balls as strikes making it easier for pitchers to strike out batters, thus preventing scoring. However, higher scoring games were more desirable to fans of the time period. This "dead ball era" was characterized by a noticeable scarcity of home runs and lower attendance. From 1900 to 1920, the average number of home runs for home run leaders was less than ten per season, significantly lower than the current average of approximately fifty. To mitigate these concerns, several rule changes were enacted. These included the outlawing of the "spit-ball" pitch, the removal of a scuffed ball from play, and an alteration of the ball to a cork center that traveled further in newly-built baseball stadiums.

During the dead ball era, pitchers often pitched entire games. In 1904, for example, pitchers completed over 87% of games started, compared to 2013 where starting pitchers completed only 2% of games pitched. This trend makes it unlikely that any modern day pitcher can break Cy Young's record of 749 completed games. There are several factors that could have contributed to the reduction of games completed by pitchers over the years. One possible reason is the use of multiple pitchers per game due to the specialization of their pitching duties. For example, a starting pitcher may pitch the first third of the game followed by a middle reliever and then a closer to finish the game.

The introduction of the pitch count reduced the number of pitches thrown by a single player. This count typically limits the number of pitches to 100 and is designed to minimize arm soreness and injury risk. Once 100 pitches have been thrown, a pitcher is removed from the game regardless of score or game portion played. Analogous pitching quotas have been adopted for pitchers in youth leagues. Paradoxically, injuries to baseball pitchers have increased despite the use of pitching quotas, prompting some to claim a higher pitch count is required to develop strong pitching arms and reduce injury.

One of the most common ailments amongst pitchers is a tear in the ulnar collateral ligament. The treatment for this injury, known as Tommy John surgery, which is named after the first player to receive this procedure in 1974, is highly successful. A well known young pitcher, José Fernández, recently underwent this surgery. His early career success has been attributed to his ability to balance fastballs with slower pitches like the curveball. The successful recovery from Tommy John surgery has led some to suggest the contentious point that pitchers actually perform better after the surgery. This has prompted requests for the procedure even in the absence of injury. A competing explanation for improved performance after surgery is from the regimented conditioning that occurs following surgery. Dr. George Paletta, a former team doctor for the St. Louis Cardinals has performed more than 500 Tommy John surgeries. Dr. Paletta was asked about the large increase in surgery numbers since 1974 and responded by saying, "This generation of pitchers is paying the price of sports specialization."

1) **Which of the following changes, if added to baseball, would make Cy Young's record more susceptible to being broken?**

   A. Increasing the size of ball parks.

   B. Increasing the pitch count.

   C. Making foul balls not count as strikes.

   D. Hitting more home runs per game.

2) **Which of the following would most likely reduce the number of Tommy John surgeries?**

   A. Increase in the number of curveballs pitched and decrease in the number of fastballs.

   B. Decreased percentage of youth playing football and basketball and increasing the number playing baseball.

   C. Institute pitch counts for pitchers at all levels of competition.

   D. Increased percentage of youth playing football and soccer and decreasing the number playing baseball.

3) **According to the passage, the institution of a pitch count has:**

   A. reduced the number of Tommy John surgeries.

   B. generated more complete games.

   C. increased injured ulnar collateral ligaments.

   D. increased the number of home runs.

4) **Which of the following least contributed to the end of the dead ball era?**

   A. Increasing the size of ball parks.

   B. Using technology to engineer new types of baseballs.

   C. Eliminating the use of scuffed balls.

   D. Prohibiting certain types of pitches.

5) **If a high school pitcher wishes to reduce his risk of injury, what is his best course of action?**

   A. Reduced pitch counts.

   B. Balance fastballs with curveballs.

   C. Increased pitch count.

   D. Tommy John surgery.

6) **Which of the following statements is the author least likely to agree with?**

   A. The baseball governing body needs to create rules to help protect pitchers from injury.

   B. The rule changes enacted by baseball increased the popularity of the game.

   C. The idea of a pitch count is a controversial topic for the game of baseball.

   D. Currently only theories exist to explain the increased need for Tommy John surgery.

Baseball

Annotations.

1) B 2) D 3) C 4) A 5) C 6) A

	Foundation 1: Comprehension	Foundation 2: Integration of multiple concepts	Foundation 3: Reasoning beyond text
Concepts	3		
Inference	6		
Integration		2,4	
Application			5
Assessment			1

Big Picture. The passage begins with a general introduction to the history of baseball and discusses a specific era of baseball called the "dead ball era" where baseball's popularity waned. Greater detail is provided about the dead ball era linking it to advantages pitchers had while playing the game and introduced measures to take away these advantages. The passage then transitions into a discussion about pitchers in general and the difference in production and injury risk for pitchers as time has progressed. It goes on to discuss in-game management of pitchers and then introduces a specific type of injury pitchers face that has increased in recent years. The end of the passage deals with the treatment, recovery and controversy surrounding this specific type of injury. Overall, the author seems most concerned about the increased incident of injuries and treatment of players. The author most likely works in the health care industry and is more concern about player welfare than the game of baseball.

1) **B. Increasing the pitch count.** For this question you first must remember that the passage mentions Cy Young holding the record for the most complete games pitched. So you want the change that will make it easier for current pitchers to pitch an entire game. **Choices A and D have nothing to do** with how many pitches a pitcher may throw. **Choice C is eliminated** because if foul balls no longer counted as strikes it would likely increase the number of pitches it would take to pitch an entire game because it would be more difficult to get a strike. **Choice B is the credited answer** because additional pitches would give a pitcher more time to finish a game.

2) **D. Increased percentage of youth playing football and soccer and decreasing the number playing baseball.** Here, you must apply logic to the opinions raised by the author throughout the passage. The **credited answer for this question is choice D** because it means there are fewer individuals playing baseball. While there is no change in the percentage of individuals playing baseball that need surgery, a decrease in the number of surgeries will occur because the pool of individuals that could need the surgery has decreased. **Choice B would have the opposite effect** and would increase the possible number of players needing surgery. **Choices A can be eliminated** because the passage does not provide a link between pitch type and the risk of injury. **Choice C is ruled out** because the third paragraph discusses how, paradoxically, injuries to baseball pitchers have increased despite the use of pitch counts.

3) C. increased injured ulnar collateral ligaments. The passage discusses how there has been an increase in Tommy John surgeries since the institution of the pitch count, **eliminating choice A** as a possibility. The passage describes how diagnosis of a torn ulnar collateral ligament means you need Tommy John surgery, therefore, **choice C is the credited answer**. The passage discusses how the institution of pitch counts has further limited the amount of time a pitcher plays making it even more difficult to complete a full game, **ruling out choice B**. The passage provides no relationship between the number of home runs hit and the institution of a pitch count so **choice D is incorrect**.

4) A. Increasing the size of ball parks. The dead ball era is discussed in the first paragraph of the passage. **Choice A is the credited answer** because the size of a ball park is not discussed in relation to a pitcher's performance. **Choice B is incorrect** because the passage states the material at the inner core of baseballs was changed to increase flight distance. **Choices C and D are incorrect** because these changes were listed in the first paragraph, to specifically end the dead ball era.

5) C. Increased pitch count. At the beginning of the fourth paragraph, it is discussed that higher pitch counts will help build a stronger arm and reducing the chance for needing surgery, making **choice C the credited answer**. According to the passage, **choice A would increase** the risk of injury. The passage provides no correlation between types of pitches and probability of injury, and this makes **choice B incorrect**. You are told that pitchers come back stronger from Tommy John surgery but nothing is mentioned about a decrease in chance of re-injury after the surgery, making **choice D incorrect**.

6) A. The baseball governing body needs to create rules to help protect pitchers from injury. A good way to approach a question like this is to eliminate answer choices that are supported by the passage. **Choice B is supported** in the first paragraph. **Choice C represents a main theme** of the passage as the author discusses reasons for and against a pitch count. While Tommy John surgery is discussed at length, no actual data is presented to explain the increase in surgeries. Only opinions are presented, making **choice D a statement the author would agree with**. That leaves **choice A as the credited answer**. At no point does the author discuss the need for new rules to reduce the chance of injuries for pitchers.

References

Actor JK (2014) Introductory Immunology (Academic Press).

Adams DJ (2005) The impact of tumor physiology on camptothecin-based drug development. Curr Med Chem Anticancer Agents 5(1):1-13.

Adams DJ & Morgan LR (2011) Tumor physiology and charge dynamics of anticancer drugs: implications for camptothecin-based drug development. Curr Med Chem 18(9):1367-1372.

Allen DG & Kentish JC (1985) The cellular basis of the length-tension relation in cardiac muscle. J Mol Cell Cardiol 17(9):821-840.

Allen JB, Walberg MW, Edwards MC, & Elledge SJ (1995) Finding prospective partners in the library: the two-hybrid system and phage display find a match. Trends Biochem Sci 20(12):511-516.

Anaya-Bergman C, He J, Jones K, Miyazaki H, Yeudall A, & Lewis JP (2010) Porphyromonas gingivalis ferrous iron transporter FeoB1 influences sensitivity to oxidative stress. Infection and immunity 78(2):688-696.

Anderson WI & Mitchell SM (2007) Phenylketonuria. Clinical Studies in Medical Biochemistry, Glew, R.H.

Arber W, Hattman S, & Dussoix D (1963) On the Host-Controlled Modification of Bacteriophage Lambda. Virology 21:30-35.

Bar-Sagi D (2001) A Ras by any other name. Mol Cell Biol 21(5):1441-1443.

Bartoshuk LM (2000) Comparing sensory experiences across individuals: recent psychophysical advances illuminate genetic variation in taste perception. Chem Senses 25(4):447-460.

Bartoshuk LM (2000) Psychophysical advances aid the study of genetic variation in taste. Appetite 34(1):105.

Bazylinski DA & Frankel RB (2004) Magnetosome formation in prokaryotes. Nat Rev Microbiol 2(3):217-230.

Bendall SC, Hughes C, Stewart MH, Doble B, Bhatia M, & Lajoie GA (2008) Prevention of amino acid conversion in SILAC experiments with embryonic stem cells. Mol Cell Proteomics 7(9):1587-1597.

Bender J, Tark KJ, Reuter B, Kathmann N, & Curtis CE (2013) Differential roles of the frontal and parietal cortices in the control of saccades. Brain Cogn 83(1):1-9.

Berg J, Tymoczko JL, & Stryer L (2002) Biochemistry (W.H. freeman and Company, New York).

Bergreen L (2011) Columbus : the four voyages (Viking, New York) pp xvii, 423 p., 448.

Bertani G & Weigle JJ (1953) Host controlled variation in bacterial viruses. Journal of bacteriology 65(2):113-121.

Blobaum AL & Marnett LJ (2007) Structural and functional basis of cyclooxygenase inhibition. J Med Chem 50(7):1425-1441.

Bomgaars L, Berg SL, & Blaney SM (2001) The development of camptothecin analogs in childhood cancers. The oncologist 6(6):506-516.

Boron WF & Boulpaep EL (Medical physiology : a cellular and molecular approach Updated second edition. Ed pp xiii, 1337 pages.

Bos JL (1989) ras oncogenes in human cancer: a review. Cancer research 49(17):4682-4689.

Brenick A, Henning A, Kellen M, O'Conner A, & Collins M (2007) Social evaluations of stereotypic images in video games: Unfair, legitimate, or "just entertainment"? Youth & Society 38:395-419

Brill S (2013) The Bitter Pill. in Time Magazine.

Bruice PY (2011) Organic chemistry. Prentice Hall.

Buckley TM & Schatzberg AF (2005) On the interactions of the hypothalamic-pituitary-adrenal (HPA) axis and sleep: normal HPA axis activity and circadian rhythm, exemplary sleep disorders. The Journal of clinical endocrinology and metabolism 90(5):3106-3114.

Campbell NA (1993) Biology (Benjamin/Cummings Publishing Company, Inc.).

Cao ZS, Pantazis P, Mendoza J, Early J, Kozielski A, Harris N, & Giovanella B (2003) Structure-activity relationship of alkyl 9-nitrocamptothecin esters. Acta pharmacologica Sinica 24(2):109-119.

Champness W & Snyder L (2008) Molecular Genetics of Bacteria (ASM Press) 3rd Ed.

Christlieb AR (1976) Renin-angiotensin-aldosterone system in diabetes mellitus. Diabetes 25:820-825.

Cinar Y, Senyol AM, & Duman K (2001) Blood viscosity and blood pressure: role of temperature and hyperglycemia. Am J Hypertens 14(5 Pt 1):433-438.

Clark C, Prior M, & Kinsella GJ (2000) Do executive function deficits differentiate between adolescents with ADHD and oppositional defiant/conduct disorder? A neuropsychological study using the Six Elements Test and Hayling Sentence Completion Test. J Abnorm Child Psychol 28(5):403-414.

Coico R (2009) Immunology A Short Course (Wiley-Blackwell).

Coico R, Sunshine G, & Benjamini E (2003) Immunology: A Short Course (Wiley-Liss) 5th Ed.

Cussler EL, Evans DF, & DePalma RG (1970) A model for gallbladder function and cholesterol gallstone formation. Proceedings of the National Academy of Sciences of the United States of America 67(1):400-407.

Dekker J (2006) The three 'C' s of chromosome conformation capture: controls, controls, controls. Nat Methods 3(1):17-21.

Dekker J, Rippe K, Dekker M, & Kleckner N (2002) Capturing chromosome conformation. Science 295(5558):1306-1311.

Dettman SJ, Pinder D, Briggs RJ, Dowell RC, & Leigh JR (2007) Communication development in children who receive the cochlear implant younger than 12 months: risks versus benefits. Ear Hear 28(2 Suppl):11S-18S.

Dolence JM & Poulter CD (1995) A mechanism for posttranslational modifications of proteins by yeast protein farnesyltransferase. Proceedings of the National Academy of Sciences of the United States of America 92(11):5008-5011.

Dolensek J, Skelin M, & Rupnik MS (2011) Calcium dependencies of regulated exocytosis in different endocrine cells. Physiol Res 60 Suppl 1:S29-38.

Durant W (1980) Caesar and Christ (The Story of Civilization III) (Simon & Schuster).

Dyckman KA, Lee AK, Agam Y, Vangel M, Goff DC, Barton JJ, & Manoach DS (2011) Abnormally persistent fMRI activation during antisaccades in schizophrenia: a neural correlate of perseveration? Schizophr Res 132(1):62-68.

E. A (2011) The Trials of Christians in the Middle Ages (AL LAVALLIS ENTERPRISES LLC).

Eaton SB & Konner M (1985) Paleolithic nutrition. A consideration of its nature and current implications. The New England journal of medicine 312(5):283-289.

Fagan JFI (2000) A theory of intelligence as processing: Implication for society. Psychology, Public Policy, and Law 6:168-179.

Fang FC & Casadevall A (2011) Retracted science and the retraction index. Infection and immunity 79(10):3855-3859.

Farmer H, McCabe N, Lord CJ, Tutt AN, Johnson DA, Richardson TB, Santarosa M, Dillon KJ, Hickson I, Knights C, Martin NM, Jackson SP, Smith GC, & Ashworth A (2005) Targeting the DNA repair defect in BRCA mutant cells as a therapeutic strategy. Nature 434(7035):917-921.

Fernandez-Medarde A & Santos E (2011) Ras in cancer and developmental diseases. Genes Cancer 2(3):344-358.

Forsburg SL & Nurse P (1991) Cell cycle regulation in the yeasts Saccharomyces cerevisiae and Schizosaccharomyces pombe. Annu Rev Cell Biol 7:227-256.

Fossette S, Gleiss AC, Myers AE, Garner S, Liebsch N, Whitney NM, Hays GC, Wilson RP, & Lutcavage ME (2010) Behaviour and buoyancy regulation in the deepest-diving reptile: the leatherback turtle. J Exp Biol 213(Pt 23):4074-4083.

Frosch DL, Grande D, Tarn DM, & Kravitz RL (2010) A decade of controversy: balancing policy with evidence in the regulation of prescription drug advertising. American journal of public health 100(1):24-32.

Fukumoto-Motoshita M, Matsuura M, Ohkubo T, Ohkubo H, Kanaka N, Matsushima E, Taira M, Kojima T, & Matsuda T (2009) Hyperfrontality in patients with schizophrenia during saccade and antisaccade tasks: a study with fMRI. Psychiatry Clin Neurosci 63(2):209-217.

George SA, Khan S, Briggs H, & Abelson JL (2010) CRH-stimulated cortisol release and food intake in healthy, non-obese adults. Psychoneuroendocrinology 35(4):607-612.

Gescheider G (1997) Psychophysics: The fundamentals (Psychology Press/Lawrence Erlbaum Associates, New Jersey).

References

Giurgea I, Bellanne-Chantelot C, Ribeiro M, Hubert L, Sempoux C, Robert JJ, Blankenstein O, Hussain K, Brunelle F, Nihoul-Fekete C, Rahier J, Jaubert F, & de Lonlay P (2006) Molecular mechanisms of neonatal hyperinsulinism. Horm Res 66(6):289-296.

Glew RH & Rosenthal MD (2006) Clinical Studies in Medical Biochemistry (Oxford University Press) 3rd Ed.

Gore R (2004) Who were the Phoenicians? in National Geographic, pp 34-49.

Gstraunthaler G, Holcomb T, Feifel E, Liu W, Spitaler N, & Curthoys NP (2000) Differential expression and acid-base regulation of glutaminase mRNAs in gluconeogenic LLC-PK(1)-FBPase(+) cells. Am J Physiol Renal Physiol 278(2):F227-237.

Gstraunthaler G, Landauer F, & Pfaller W (1992) Ammoniagenesis in LLC-PK1 cultures: role of transamination. Am J Physiol 263(1 Pt 1):C47-54.

Hanft LM, Biesiadecki BJ, & McDonald KS (2013) Length dependence of striated muscle force generation is controlled by phosphorylation of cTnI at serines 23/24. J Physiol 591(Pt 18):4535-4547.

Harris CM, Derdowski AM, & Poulter CD (2002) Modulation of the zinc(II) center in protein farnesyltransferase by mutagenesis of the zinc(II) ligands. Biochemistry 41(33):10554-10562.

Hartley BS & Kilby BA (1950) Inhibition of chymotrypsin by diethyl p-nitrophenyl phosphate. Nature 166(4227):784-785.

Hartley BS & Kilby BA (1952) The inhibition of chymotrypsin by diethyl p-nitrophenyl phosphate. Biochem J 50(5):672-678.

Hartley BS & Kilby BA (1954) The reaction of p-nitrophenyl esters with chymotrypsin and insulin. Biochem J 56(2):288-297.

Hartwell LH, Culotti J, Pringle JR, & Reid BJ (1974) Genetic control of the cell division cycle in yeast. Science 183(4120):46-51.

Haussinger D & Sies H (1984) Effect of phenylephrine on glutamate and glutamine metabolism in isolated perfused rat liver. Biochem J 221(3):651-658.

Hibino H, Inanobe A, Furutani K, Murakami S, Findlay I, & Kurachi Y (2010) Inwardly rectifying potassium channels: their structure, function, and physiological roles. Physiol Rev 90(1):291-366.

Higgins ST, Silverman S, & Heil SH (2008) Contingency Management in Substance Abuse Treatment (The Guilford Press, New York, NY).

Hingorani T, Gul W, Elsohly M, Repka MA, & Majumdar S (2012) Effect of ion pairing on in vitro transcorneal permeability of a Delta(9) -tetrahydrocannabinol prodrug: potential in glaucoma therapy. Journal of pharmaceutical sciences 101(2):616-626.

Ho JK, Moser H, Kishimoto Y, & Hamilton JA (1995) Interactions of a very long chain fatty acid with model membranes and serum albumin. Implications for the pathogenesis of adrenoleukodystrophy. J Clin Invest 96(3):1455-1463.

Houten SM, Herrema H, Te Brinke H, Denis S, Ruiter JP, van Dijk TH, Argmann CA, Ottenhoff R, Muller M, Groen AK, Kuipers F, Reijngoud DJ, & Wanders RJ (2013) Impaired amino acid metabolism contributes to fasting-induced hypoglycemia in fatty acid oxidation defects. Human molecular genetics 22(25):5249-5261.

Howard MT, Carlson BA, Anderson CB, & Hatfield DL (2013) Translational redefinition of UGA codons is regulated by selenium availability. J Biol Chem 288(27):19401-19413.

Hummel J, Segu S, Li Y, Irgang S, Jueppner J, & Giavalisco P (2011) Ultra performance liquid chromatography and high resolution mass spectrometry for the analysis of plant lipids. Front Plant Sci 2:54.

Hutton SB & Ettinger U (2006) The antisaccade task as a research tool in psychopathology: a critical review. Psychophysiology 43(3):302-313.

Ingolia NT, Ghaemmaghami S, Newman JR, & Weissman JS (2009) Genome-wide analysis in vivo of translation with nucleotide resolution using ribosome profiling. Science 324(5924):218-223.

Iversen IH & Lattal KA (1991) Experimental analysis of behavior (Elsevier; NY, U.S.A.).

Jensen AR (1998) The suppressed relationship between IQ and the reaction time slope parameter of the Hick function. Intelligence 26:43-52.

Kaji R (2003) Physiology of conduction block in multi-focal motor neuropathy and other demyelinating neuropathies. Muscle Nerve 27(3):285-296.

Kalgutkar AS, Crews BC, Rowlinson SW, Garner C, & Marnett LJ (1999) Discovery of a new class of selective cyclooxygenase-2 (COX-2) inhibitor that covalently modifies the isozyme. Adv Exp Med Biol 469:139-143.

Karlsson FA, Dahlberg PA, & Ritzen EM (1984) Thyroid blocking antibodies in thyroiditis. Acta medica Scandinavica 215(5):461-466.

Klee GG (2000) Cobalamin and folate evaluation: measurement of methylmalonic acid and homocysteine vs vitamin B(12) and folate. Clin Chem 46(8 Pt 2): 1277-1283.

Komeili A (2012) Molecular mechanisms of compartmentalization and biomineralization in magnetotactic bacteria. FEMS Microbiol Rev 36(1):232-255.

Kondo H, Shirakawa R, Higashi T, Kawato M, Fukuda M, Kita T, & Horiuchi H (2006) Constitutive GDP/GTP exchange and secretion-dependent GTP hydrolysis activity for Rab27 in platelets. J Biol Chem 281(39):28657-28665.

Layer P & Keller J (2007) Pancreatic Insufficiency Secondary to Chronic Pancreatitis. Clinical Studies in Medical Biochemistry, (Oxford University Press), 3rd Ed, pp 278-289.

Li Y, Katzmann E, Borg S, & Schuler D (2012) The periplasmic nitrate reductase nap is required for anaerobic growth and involved in redox control of magnetite biomineralization in Magnetospirillum gryphiswaldense. Journal of bacteriology 194(18):4847-4856.

Madden GJ & Bickel WK eds (2010) Impulsivity: The Behavioral and Neurological Science of Discounting (American Psychological Association, Washington, DC).

Marnett LJ, Rowlinson SW, Goodwin DC, Kalgutkar AS, & Lanzo CA (1999) Arachidonic acid oxygenation by COX-1 and COX-2. Mechanisms of catalysis and inhibition. J Biol Chem 274(33):22903-22906.

Maroon H (2013) A geneticist with a unifying message. Nature Middle East.

Masaki A, Fukamizo T, Otakara A, Torikata T, Hayashi K, & Imoto T (1981) Estimation of rate constants in lysozyme-catalyzed reaction of chitooligosaccharides. J Biochem 90(4):1167-1175.

Masui Y (2001) From oocyte maturation to the in vitro cell cycle: the history of discoveries of Maturation-Promoting Factor (MPF) and Cytostatic Factor (CSF). Differentiation 69(1):1-17.

McDonagh AF, Palma LA, & Lightner DA (1980) Blue light and bilirubin excretion. Science 208(4440):145-151.

Milgram S (1974) Obedience to authority: an experimental view (Harper & Row).

Milligan B, Curtin N, & Bone Q (1997) Contractile properties of obliquely striated muscle from the mantle of squid (Alloteuthis subulata) and cuttlefish (Sepia officinalis). J Exp Biol 200(Pt 18):2425-2436.

Minamikawa S, Naito Y, Sato K, Matsuzawa Y, Bando T, & Sakamoto W (2000) Maintenance of neutral buoyancy by depth selection in the loggerhead turtle Caretta caretta. J Exp Biol 203:2967-2975.

Mintzes B (2012) Advertising of prescription-only medicines to the public: does evidence of benefit counterbalance harm? Annual review of public health 33:259-277.

Modrich P & Zabel D (1976) EcoRI endonuclease. Physical and catalytic properties of the homogenous enzyme. J Biol Chem 251(19):5866-5874.

Morgan MA, Ganser A, & Reuter CW (2003) Therapeutic efficacy of prenylation inhibitors in the treatment of myeloid leukemia. Leukemia 17(8):1482-1498.

Mumtaz M, Lin LS, Hui KC, & Mohd Khir AS (2009) Radioiodine I-131 for the therapy of graves' disease. Malays J Med Sci 16(1):25-33.

Nadkarni R, Barkley S, & Fradin C (2013) A comparison of methods to measure the magnetic moment of magnetotactic bacteria through analysis of their trajectories in external magnetic fields. PloS one 8(12):e82064.

References

Nagai Y, Yonemitsu S, Erion DM, Iwasaki T, Stark R, Weismann D, Dong J, Zhang D, Jurczak MJ, Loffler MG, Cresswell J, Yu XX, Murray SF, Bhanot S, Monia BP, Bogan JS, Samuel V, & Shulman GI (2009) The role of peroxisome proliferator-activated receptor gamma coactivator-1 beta in the pathogenesis of fructose-induced insulin resistance. Cell Metab 9(3):252-264.

Ofman R, Dijkstra IM, van Roermund CW, Burger N, Turkenburg M, van Cruchten A, van Engen CE, Wanders RJ, & Kemp S (2010) The role of ELOVL1 in very long-chain fatty acid homeostasis and X-linked adrenoleukodystrophy. EMBO Mol Med 2(3):90-97.

Okano Y, Eisensmith RC, Guttler F, Lichter-Konecki U, Konecki DS, Trefz FK, Dasovich M, Wang T, Henriksen K, Lou H, & et al. (1991) Molecular basis of phenotypic heterogeneity in phenylketonuria. The New England journal of medicine 324(18):1232-1238.

Passel JS & Coh D (2008) U.S. Population Projections: 2005-2050. (Pew Research Center).

Paul AV, van Boom JH, Filippov D, & Wimmer E (1998) Protein-primed RNA synthesis by purified poliovirus RNA polymerase. Nature 393(6682):280-284.

Pearsall DA (1992) The life of Geoffrey Chaucer: a critical biography (Blackwell, Oxford, UK ; Cambridge, Mass.) pp xii, 365.

Peckham S & Awofeso N (2014) Water fluoridation: a critical review of the physiological effects of ingested fluoride as a public health intervention. The Scientific World Journal 2014:293019.

Pennisi E (2013) Human evolution. More genomes from Denisova Cave show mixing of early human groups. Science 340(6134):799.

Perry JL & Carroll ME (2008) The role of impulsive behavior in drug abuse. Psychopharmacology 200(1):1-26.

Peterson NR, Pisoni DB, & Miyamoto RT (2010) Cochlear implants and spoken language processing abilities: review and assessment of the literature. Restor Neurol Neurosci 28(2):237-250.

Platt FM, Boland B, & van der Spoel AC (2012) The cell biology of disease: lysosomal storage disorders: the cellular impact of lysosomal dysfunction. J Cell Biol 199(5):723-734.

Priest SH (2010) Encyclopedia of Science and Technology Communication (SAGE Publications).

Rahn-Lee L & Komeili A (2013) The magnetosome model: insights into the mechanisms of bacterial biomineralization. Front Microbiol 4:352.

Resh MD (2012) Targeting protein lipidation in disease. Trends Mol Med 18(4):206-214.

Rigler R, Pramanik A, Jonasson P, Kratz G, Jansson OT, Nygren P, Stahl S, Ekberg K, Johansson B, Uhlen S, Uhlen M, Jornvall H, & Wahren J (1999) Specific binding of proinsulin C-peptide to human cell membranes. Proceedings of the National Academy of Sciences of the United States of America 96(23):13318-13323.

Rothberg PG, Harris TJ, Nomoto A, & Wimmer E (1978) O4-(5'-uridylyl)tyrosine is the bond between the genome-linked protein and the RNA of poliovirus. Proceedings of the National Academy of Sciences of the United States of America 75(10):4868-4872.

Rowlinson SW, Crews BC, Lanzo CA, & Marnett LJ (1999) The binding of arachidonic acid in the cyclooxygenase active site of mouse prostaglandin endoperoxide synthase-2 (COX-2). A putative L-shaped binding conformation utilizing the top channel region. J Biol Chem 274(33):23305-23310.

Russel M, Lowman HB, & Clackson T (2004) Introduction to phage biology and phage display. Phage Display: A Practical Approach, eds Clackson T & Lowman HB (Oxford University Press), pp 1-26.

Salzinger S, Rosario M, & Feldman RS (2007) Physical child abuse and adolescent violent delinquency: the mediating and moderating roles of personal relationships. Child Maltreat 12(3):208-219.

Samsel A & Seneff S (2013) Glyphosate, pathways to modern diseases II: Celiac sprue and gluten intolerance. Interdisciplinary toxicology 6(4):159-184.

Schauf CL & Davis FA (1974) Impulse conduction in multiple sclerosis: a theoretical basis for modification by temperature and pharmacological agents. J Neurol Neurosurg Psychiatry 37(2):152-161.

Schmidt A, Rauh NR, Nigg EA, & Mayer TU (2006) Cytostatic factor: an activity that puts the cell cycle on hold. J Cell Sci 119(Pt 7):1213-1218.

SenGupta DJ, Zhang B, Kraemer B, Pochart P, Fields S, & Wickens M (1996) A three-hybrid system to detect RNA-protein interactions in vivo. Proceedings of the National Academy of Sciences of the United States of America 93(16):8496-8501.

Seyer A, Cantiello M, Bertrand-Michel J, Roques V, Nauze M, Bezirard V, Collet X, Touboul D, Brunelle A, & Comera C (2013) Lipidomic and spatio-temporal imaging of fat by mass spectrometry in mice duodenum during lipid digestion. PloS one 8(4):e58224.

Singh I, Lazo O, Dhaunsi GS, & Contreras M (1992) Transport of fatty acids into human and rat peroxisomes. Differential transport of palmitic and lignoceric acids and its implication to X-adrenoleukodystrophy. J Biol Chem 267(19):13306-13313.

Soderberg T (2012) Organic Chemistry with a Biological Emphasis.

Soumillion P, Jespers L, Bouchet M, Marchand-Brynaert J, Winter G, & Fastrez J (1994) Selection of beta-lactamase on filamentous bacteriophage by catalytic activity. J Mol Biol 237(4):415-422.

Steen RG, Casadevall A, & Fang FC (2013) Why has the number of scientific retractions increased? PloS one 8(7):e68397.

Stevens S (1986) Psychophysics: Introduction to its perceptual, neural, and social prospects (Transition Books, New Brunswick).

Suzuki DT, Griffiths AJF, Miller JH, & Lewontin RC (1981) An Introduction to Genetic Analysis (W.H. Freeman, San Francisco) erd Ed.

Taubes G (2009) Insulin resistance. Prosperity's plague. Science 325(5938):256-260.

Tepper BJ, White EA, Koelliker Y, Lanzara C, d'Adamo P, & Gasparini P (2009) Genetic variation in taste sensitivity to 6-n-propylthiouracil and its relationship to taste perception and food selection. Ann N Y Acad Sci 1170:126-139.

Toor EW, Evans DF, & Cussler EL (1978) Cholesterol monohydrate growth in model bile solutions. Proceedings of the National Academy of Sciences of the United States of America 75(12):6230-6234.

Trahey M, Milley RJ, Cole GE, Innis M, Paterson H, Marshall CJ, Hall A, & McCormick F (1987) Biochemical and biological properties of the human N-ras p21 protein. Mol Cell Biol 7(1):541-544.

United Healthcare (2013) Cochlear implants: Medical policy. United HealthCare Services, INC.

Usher M, Olami Z, & McClelland JL (2002) hick's law in a stochastic race model with speed-accuracy tradeoff. Journal of Mathematical Psychology 46:704-715

Van Reeth O, Weibel L, Spiegel K, Leproult R, Dugovic C, & Maccari S (2000) Physiological of sleep (review) - Interactions between stress and sleep: From basic research to clinical situations. Sleep Medicine Reviews 4:201-219

Vickrey C & Neuringer A (2000) Pigeon reaction time, Hick's law, and intelligence. Psychon Bull Rev 7(2):284-291.

Wanders RJ, Komen J, & Kemp S (2011) Fatty acid omega-oxidation as a rescue pathway for fatty acid oxidation disorders in humans. FEBS J 278(2):182-194.

Wang Z & Thurmond DC (2009) Mechanisms of biphasic insulin-granule exocytosis - roles of the cytoskeleton, small GTPases and SNARE proteins. J Cell Sci 122(Pt 7):893-903.

Waxman SG (2006) Axonal conduction and injury in multiple sclerosis: the role of sodium channels. Nat Rev Neurosci 7(12):932-941.

Wedemeyer WJ, Welker E, & Scheraga HA (2002) Proline cis-trans isomerization and protein folding. Biochemistry 41(50):14637-14644.

Weiwad WK, Linke WA, & Wussling MH (2000) Sarcomere length-tension relationship of rat cardiac myocytes at lengths greater than optimum. J Mol Cell Cardiol 32(2):247-259.

Widom CS (1989) Does violence beget violence? A critical examination of the literature. Psychol Bull 106(1):3-28.

Widom CS (1989) The cycle of violence. Science 244(4901):160-166.

References

Wilson GN, Holmes RG, Custer J, Lipkowitz JL, Stover J, Datta N, & Hajra A (1986) Zellweger syndrome: diagnostic assays, syndrome delineation, and potential therapy. Am J Med Genet 24(1):69-82.

Yazulla S (2008) Endocannabinoids in the retina: from marijuana to neuroprotection. Prog Retin Eye Res 27(5):501-526.

Yoon JH, Higgins ST, Bradstreet MP, Badger GJ, & Thomas CS (2009) Changes in the relative reinforcing effects of cigarette smoking as a function of initial abstinence. Psychopharmacology (Berl) 205(2):305-318.

Zeng C, Aleshin AE, Hardie JB, Harrison RW, & Fromm HJ (1996) ATP-binding site of human brain hexokinase as studied by molecular modeling and site-directed mutagenesis. Biochemistry 35(40):13157-13164.

Zeng Y, Ramya TN, Dirksen A, Dawson PE, & Paulson JC (2009) High-efficiency labeling of sialylated glycoproteins on living cells. Nat Methods 6(3):207-209.

Zerjal T, Xue Y, Bertorelle G, Wells RS, Bao W, Zhu S, Qamar R, Ayub Q, Mohyuddin A, Fu S, Li P, Yuldasheva N, Ruzibakiev R, Xu J, Shu Q, Du R, Yang H, Hurles ME, Robinson E, Gerelsaikhan T, Dashnyam B, Mehdi SQ, & Tyler-Smith C (2003) The genetic legacy of the Mongols. American journal of human genetics 72(3):717-721.

Zipser D (1970) The Lactose Operon (CSHL Press).